Kingston Libraries

This item can be returned
or renewed at a Kingston
Borough Library on or
before the latest date
stamped below. If the item
is not reserved by another
reader it may be renewed
by telephone up to a
maximum of three times by
quoting your membership
number. Only items issued
for the standard three-week
loan period are renewable.

www.kingston.gov.uk/libraries

Royal
Kingston

11. DEC 04	11. SEP 09	23. JAN 16
249	29. DEC 09	09/02/18
	08. 01. 10	25/6/19
RECALL SUBJECT TO	20. MAY 10	
11 APR 2005		
EXTEND		
20. DEC 07	03. JAN 18	
	18/Jan/18	
12. MAR 09	U 1 MAR 2018	
25. JUN 08	INVESTOR IN PEOPLE	

Letter from America

ALISTAIR COOKE

Letter from America

1946–2004

ALLEN LANE
an imprint of
PENGUIN BOOKS

ALLEN LANE

Published by the Penguin Group
Penguin Books Ltd, 80 Strand, London WC2R ORL, England
Penguin Group (USA) Inc., 375 Hudson Street, New York, New York 10014, USA
Penguin Books Australia Ltd, 250 Camberwell Road, Camberwell, Victoria 3124, Australia
Penguin Books Canada Ltd, 10 Alcorn Avenue, Toronto, Ontario, Canada M4V 3B2
Penguin Books India (P) Ltd, 11 Community Centre, Panchsheel Park, New Delhi – 110 017, India
Penguin Group (NZ), cnr Airborne and Rosedale Roads, Albany, Auckland 1310, New Zealand
Penguin Books (South Africa) (Pty) Ltd, 24 Sturdee Avenue, Rosebank 2196, South Africa

Penguin Books Ltd, Registered Offices: 80 Strand, London WC2R ORL, England

www.penguin.com

This collection first published 2004
1

Set in 9.75/13 pt PostScript Linotype Sabon
Typeset by Rowland Phototypesetting Ltd, Bury St Edmunds, Suffolk
Printed in England by Clays Ltd, St Ives plc

A CIP catalogue record for this book is available from the British Library

ISBN 0-713-99834-2

Contents

The 1960s

The 1970s

The 1980s

The 1990s

List of Illustrations

Introduction

Alistair Cooke was the classic Anglo-American. He embodied the cultural and political bond that linked Britain and the United States during the long half century from the Second World War into the twenty-first century. In the great game of current affairs, he was an observer, not a player. But like the best observers, he helped define the game.

My parents were ardent Americanophiles. As a result they would sit each week listening to *Letter from America*, like wartime refugees glued to a message from a land afar. Cooke kept them in touch with Strong America in the 1950s, Rich America in the 1960s, Questioning America in the 1970s and Uncertain America in the 1980s and 1990s. He never preached. He was accused of ignoring the dark side of American life, but his bias throughout was that of an East Coast liberal conservative. It was the bias of most of his British listeners.

Alistair Cooke's writing was extraordinary. He wrote in conversation and he spoke in prose. In fifty-eight years of *Letter from America* he perfected the journalism of personal witness, adapting it brilliantly to the medium of radio. His mellifluous mid-Atlantic voice treated Britain and America as if they were two armchairs talking to each other, with 'the Pond' as coffee table. Above all, he knew his craft. He never wrote a dull sentence. He never lost touch with narrative, with the commentator as storyteller, learned from his love of theatre and movies. He understood that listeners wanted more than the old standbys of anecdote and opinion. They craved context and history. As his years lengthened into decades, Cooke's journalism acquired a depth inaccessible to younger practitioners.

Here was a man who could recall Hoover and Roosevelt. He could compare Churchill and Truman as orators, for he had heard them both.

He could remember the arrival of air conditioning, the building of freeways, the exploding of the atom bomb and Bobby Jones making the green in one. His letters from America brought the New World into the drawing rooms of the Old, not as a series of sensational events but as a rounded culture. His journalism published and broadcast in the United States returned the compliment. It brought British culture to American attention. In periods when the two countries seemed at risk of tearing apart from each other, he linked hands and held them tight.

Cooke's work and outlook were rooted in his past. He was born with the name of Alfred in 1908 in Salford, Lancashire. His father was a metalworker, Methodist lay preacher and teetotaller. His early theatrical and writing talent was noticed by his teachers, who encouraged him to a Cambridge scholarship. The upwardly mobile Cooke changed his Christian name to Alistair and applied himself furiously to acting, producing and writing. He founded The Mummers and edited *Granta*. By the age of twenty-two he was suggesting himself to the *Manchester Guardian* and the BBC as a contributor on theatre, poetry and literature. In 1932 he struck gold. He won a Harkness Fellowship to Yale and Harvard. The curtain opened on what seemed an even more glittering stage. For the drama of theatre he exchanged the drama of America.

Cooke's early ambition was to become a leading theatre director. This ambition was cursed by his success in transatlantic journalism and the people he met thereby. He was taken up by another British refugee, Charlie Chaplin, and wrote scripts for him. Cooke married an American model, Ruth Emerson (a relative of Ralph Waldo), and moved back and forth between London and America in search of work, becoming the film critic for the BBC in 1934. He wrote a *Letter from London* for NBC, allegedly clocking up 40,000 words for American outlets at the time of the Abdication in 1936. Back in America, he suggested a similar venture in reverse, for the BBC. With the outbreak of war he risked his reputation on both sides of the Atlantic by taking out American citizenship, granted in 1941.

Cooke's career in America was initially that of a normal foreign correspondent. In the 1940s he worked variously for *The Times*, the *Daily Sketch* and the *Daily Herald*. In 1940 he also began regular broadcasts for the BBC, titled *American Letter* (they became *Letter from America* in 1950). Early records show the producers remarking on 'a tendency to be allusive and glib'. Yet throughout the war Cooke built up an audience approaching six million. In 1945 he was asked to cover the opening of the United Nations for the *Manchester Guardian*. Three years later he became that paper's chief American correspondent at the then huge salary of $14,000 a year, a happy homecoming for a son of Salford. He retained this post for a quarter-century.

Working for the *Guardian* in the 1950s and 1960s allowed Cooke to cover the emergence of the new global superpower. He was never a normal news hound. Most correspondents in America were, and still are, 'Beltway fanatics'. They paced the corridors and smoke-filled rooms of Congress and the White House, and saw little else. Washington at the time was still a town with a single industry, that of politics. This was not the sort of town likely to appeal to a man with Cooke's wider interests.

He duly covered America from New York, a fact crucial to the content and style of *Letter from America*. This was controversial. The *Manchester Guardian*'s Washington correspondents at the time were Max Freedman and Richard Scott. The fact that the paper's 'Chief Correspondent' was resident in New York was the source of much bickering. It gave Cooke a reputation among journalists as problematic, indeed 'a nuisance'. He was rarely at the scene of events. His witnessing of the murdered Bobby Kennedy – 'like the stone face of a child lying on a cathedral tomb' – was exceptional. He called it 'a casual chance in a thousand'.

Washington reporting, like British 'lobby journalism', was that of politics and the gossip of the political street. Such coverage is necessary, but never sufficient in depicting a country. Cooke's view of America was different. His America was rich in politics, but politics seen as ordinary Americans saw it, including from television. It was from television that he wrote his celebrated Letters after the death of JFK. To Cooke, the most important event of the week rarely happened in Washington. He travelled to every state, missing only Alaska. America was 'happening' in Little Rock or Dallas or Los Angeles or Chicago. It was Ali versus Frazier, or the death of Dorothy Parker. It was a movie or a ball game or the changing leaves of a New England fall.

*

His presence in New York was also crucial for Cooke's work beyond journalism. Most Americans knew him as a writer and television presenter. He hosted a weekly arts programme, *Omnibus*, for CBS. In 1972 he produced *Alistair Cooke's America*, a television series screened in thirty countries. Recordings are in every public library in America, and the resulting book sold two million copies. He had stopped working for the *Guardian* to produce the series. This in turn led to *Masterpiece Theatre* for the PBS network. In this role millions of Americans came to associate Cooke with the canon of English literature, mostly through the medium of BBC costume dramas. This tweedy, amiable intellectual seemed the perfect custodian of the temple of English drama, from Shakespeare to *Upstairs, Downstairs*. He was to receive four Emmys for his work.

Cooke's lifestyle was that of an East Coast aesthete. His hobbies were American and fanatical: jazz, movies and golf. His first marriage failed, leaving a son, and in 1946 he married an artist, Jane White Hawkes. She came with two children by a former husband and together they had a daughter. The couple moved between a comfortable (rent-controlled) apartment on Fifth Avenue overlooking Central Park and Jane's weekend house on Long Island. The Cookes would 'season' in San Francisco and visit Britain twice a year to see their British family – such visits usually coinciding with Wimbledon and the major golf tournaments.

Letter from America formed a most remarkable sequence of sustained commentary. Its original remit from the BBC was to record 'the passions, manners and flavour of another nation's way of life'. The mission was hardly innovative – witness Cooke's own heroes Mark Twain and H. L. Mencken – but Cooke put it on radio. The result was not a 'column'. Nor does it merit the pompous style of essay. Though the Letters make much use of the first person singular, they have none of the cloying self-regard of modern 'I-journalism'. Cooke is the observer of events, not a participant. I would apply to the Letters the honourable journalistic term of stories. They tell a tale, sometimes two or three. They are one man's take on the world 'as I saw it'.

Cooke accepted the retort that this made him seem ambivalent, a fence-sitter, 'a moral coward for refusing to take a stand'. He was criticized as pussy-footing on Vietnam, and his biographer, Nick

Clarke, records the *Guardian*'s view that 'he had a blind spot about the civil rights movement'. As the years rolled by he moved progressively to the right. His early adoration of Adlai Stevenson was later settled on Ronald Reagan. At the end of his life he accepted the Pentagon line on Iraq. But to every critic he cheerfully replied that 'once every four years . . . I vote'. Beyond that was only 'the discovery that in life the range of irreconcilable points of view, characters, flaws, idiosyncrasies and virtues is astounding'.

The style of the Letters was influential and much imitated in both print and broadcasting. It has come near to parody in its BBC offspring, *From Our Own Correspondent*, anecdotal, herbivorous and mildly self-indulgent. Cooke's version was in a class of its own. Though written and rehearsed for speaking, the Letters remain 'writings', owing a debt to Cooke's tutor, Arthur Quiller-Couch, a champion of simplicity and clarity. They have the laconic touch of Cooke's hero, the Baltimore columnist H. L. Mencken, and display Mencken's hatred of cant and love of plain-speaking. But the mastery of cadence and colour which made *Letter from America* so fluent on the ear was, in my view, born of Cooke's love of theatre. There is no better training for any writer than to listen to the cry of the actor and feel the lash of the newsroom. Cooke benefited from both.

The shared Anglo-American culture is rooted not in politics but in history. *Letter from America* was never a 'home thought from abroad'. It showed no Browning nostalgia for 'the chaffinch on the orchard bough' from a land of the 'gaudy melon-flower'. Nor was Cooke a post-imperial Kipling. His Fifth Avenue apartment bore little comparison with 'an old Moulmein Pagoda looking lazy at the sea'. The surprise of Cooke's America was its familiarity. It was written for and heard by those who knew America from the cinema, music and newsreels.

Britons still look to America before they look anywhere else. They visit America, they absorb American culture, they enjoy American exports, they marry American spouses. More Britons could name the Mayor of New York City or the Governor of California than the leader of any English provincial city. The metropolises of New York and London are Siamese twins, two districts of one city, two venues of one culture. They have more in common with each other than with their respective hinterlands. Hardly an American magazine or newspaper is without a British byline. Hardly a British radio programme is without an American voice. Business, academia, music, art and architecture operate by mid-Atlantic values from mid-Atlantic institutions.

At the end of the Cold War it was asserted that Britain would now 'choose' Europe. Within a decade, in the so-called war on terror and in Iraq, it was emphatically choosing America. The burst of anti-Americanism which accompanied the war was an aberration, not a norm. Indeed, much of the protest over the Iraq war was itself Anglo-American in origin. At the time of Cooke's death the Atlantic bond seemed as tight as ever and the gulf with the rest of the world as wide.

Former Secretary of State Henry Kissinger, with his long experience of office, called the bonds between America and Britain 'matter-of-factly intimate', to a degree 'probably never practised before between sovereign states'. He was echoing de Gaulle's view that Britain 'neither thinks nor acts like a continental nation'. The most recent custodian of the special relationship, Tony Blair, would tell his staff that not to be by America's side through any crisis or travail was 'simply unthinkable'.

Cooke's lifework was to be Boswell to that relationship. *Letter from America* was his diary and his testament. There may be no one America, single and true. But Cooke's America is the truest we have.

Simon Jenkins
July 2004

Editor's Note

The last collection of Alistair Cooke's *Letter from America* was published in 1979 (*The Americans*) and, along with two earlier collections (*Letters from America*, 1951, *Talk About America*, 1968), has been long out of print. Alistair had always intended to complete a fourth collection of letters taken from the 1980s and 1990s – a collection that he liked to refer to as 'The Last Post' – but as time moved on his energies became exclusively dedicated to the writing of his weekly broadcast letter. He maintained this focus of attention right up until the last letter, number 2869, broadcast on 20 February 2004, just six weeks before he died. When he appointed me as his literary executor he also assigned me the task of preparing this volume selected from the entire period of his broadcast letters, 1946–2004. As his book editor and last British publisher of his two collections of essays (*Fun and Games*, 1994, and *Memories of the Great and the Good*, 1999), Alistair knew that I understood his requirements and fortunately he left clear guidelines for this collection.

In his first published volume Alistair wrote in the Preface: 'A good many of the letters I have had from listeners to the series were from people who can hardly put pen to paper. Their taste seemed to coincide with my own: they got pleasure from talks which I felt had managed to convey some human experience in a language most people can understand. These successes average about one in five, but they are not necessarily the ones that look best in print. But by the time the series had run to two hundred there appeared to be a good handful that would survive the translation into black and white. Accordingly, the pieces that follow were selected by this test. They were chosen on no other principle.' With this in mind, for the years 1946–1980, there was no need to go further than to select those letters that I consider to be the best taken from the earlier books. In this process I was much helped by the writer and editor George Perry, who proved, as always, a sound adviser.

The selections made from 1980 to 2004 required more detailed review. Several folders of manuscript letters marked on the outside in Alistair's handwriting as 'The Chosen' were found and then typed up 'squeaky clean', as he had requested, by Patti Yasek, his redoubtable assistant. I have been supported in making the final selection not only by Patti but also by Alistair's daughter Susan Cooke Kittredge. They have both provided huge encouragement and I was relieved that this final selection agreed with so many of Susan's own choices. In addition Stuart Proffitt, Publishing Director at Penguin, has contributed many recommendations and has provided valuable advice in relation to the overall selection. With such wealth of material it has been difficult to achieve a perfect balance for each decade and I have decided to give more emphasis to the second part of Alistair's career where none of the letters has, until now, been published in volume form.

As on his earlier collections I have tried my best to apply Alistair's principle, in choosing those letters that work best in print. I have also provided a wide range of contents, and indeed tried to include some surprises that might correspond on the page to the experience of tuning in on a Friday evening or Sunday morning to hear the often unexpected topic that Alistair was addressing that day. As with the earlier collections the letters 'except for a little trimming and polishing, appear here as they were broadcast'.

There is no better preface that can apply to this collection than Alistair's original opening to the first collection published in 1951 which included the following passage:

Some months after the war was over the BBC asked me to go to London and discuss the sort of broadcasting I might do in what was then called the peace. I had been talking about America to Britain since 1934 and from America to Britain since three years after that. My one-man band met the same fate as everybody else's in the autumn of 1939. And through the war years I doubled in brass and learned to play the solemn trombone of a political commentator. Politics will undoubtedly bedevil us all till the day we die, but when General

MacArthur stood on the deck of the *Missouri* and said in his resounding baritone, 'These proceedings are closed,' I took him at his word and, like most other people, yearned to get back to the important things in life. Even the prospect of early annihilation should not keep us from making the most of our days on this unhappy planet. In the best of times, our days are numbered, anyway. And it would be a crime against Nature for any generation to take the world crisis so solemnly that it put off enjoying those things for which we were presumably designed in the first place, and which the gravest statesmen and the hoarsest politicians hope to make available to all men in the end: I mean the opportunity to do good work, to fall in love, to enjoy friends, to sit under trees, to read, to hit a ball and bounce the baby.

The suspicion that these things are what most men and women everywhere want led me to suggest, in London in 1946, that Britons might be more honestly enticed into an interest in America and Americans by hearing about their way of life and their tastes in these fundamental things than by suffering instruction in the procedures of the American Senate and the subtleties of the corn-hog ratio. Mr Lindsay Wellington, then director of the Home Service, responded so promptly to this that he suggested I forget politics altogether and accept an assignment to talk about anything and everything in America that interested me. To do this for a large and very mixed audience, ranging from shrewd bishops to honest carpenters, was a challenge to explain in the simplest and most vivid terms the passions, the manners, the flavour of another nation's way of life. It was a formidable assignment, for though a man might make sense of his travels in his own way for his own friends, broadcasting demands of him, if he respects the medium at all, that, as the old Greek had it, he 'think like a wise man and talk in the language of the people'. I don't know whether this has ever been done, except at various times by minstrels, the greatest religious teachers and comedians of genius.

But out of this bold ambition grew a series of weekly talks to Britain which I called Letter from America. They were commissioned in March 1946 for a tentative run of thirteen weeks; and by the grace of the BBC, the receptiveness of the British listener, and the stubborn endurance of the pound sterling, they still at this writing go on. After a year or two the number of listeners asking for copies of scripts began to strain the mimeographing resources of the BBC's New York office. Some people took so kindly to them that they urged me to put them out as a book. This has the same effect on a broadcaster as a nomination for the Presidency of the United States on a first-class cement manufacturer. The thing is patently absurd except to his cronies, but the idea first flatters, then haunts him, and he ends by feeling he must accept a sacred duty to save the Republic.

Most of these pieces were written at the end of a week's work without my knowing, as I faced the typewriter, what I was going to talk about. But they were all written in freedom and in pleasure.

Alistair Cooke's *Letter from America* was an astonishing and unique achievement that reached a listening audience of some twenty-two million worldwide. It would have been his hope that these letters will be read, as he wrote them, 'in freedom and in pleasure' throughout the world.

Colin Webb
July 2004

The 1940s

The Immigrant Strain

6 May 1946

An item came over the news-tape the other day about somebody who wanted to organize a National Hobby Club. There is nothing earthshaking in this, but it opens up a field of speculation about Britons and Americans that I should like to graze around in. I saw this item and thought at once about an Englishman I know here, an old, old friend who – to be cold-blooded about it – has a value in this country over and above his value as a character and a good friend. I am, after all, a professional student of a rare species of goldfish – the goldfish being, you will guess, the American people. If you are a goldfish, or if you swim with them long enough, it is impossible to say what are the characteristics of goldfish. But if somebody drops a mackerel into the goldfish bowl, you can see at once all sorts of things that goldfish have and the other things they lack. That is why I am grateful to this English friend, just for being himself and for being around. He forms a stimulating point of comparison. He is a British government official in New York, and though I knew him for many years before he was sent here, I have lately learned many things about him I never knew and about Americans – the race he is at present moving among. For instance, when he comes into a room, one thought always strikes me, and I can say it two ways. I can say, 'Goodness, how short his coat is' or 'Goodness, how long everybody else's is'.

Now, in character – never mind his politics – he is conservative. He is an able and conscientious government official. He likes people and he likes to get through the day and attack in the evening his beloved hobbies, of which he has several. This characteristic alone would make him, in England, a typical civil servant. Here it makes him an oddity. He is a lepidopterist, an expert on moths. And when he was stationed in the Middle East he threw off what I believe to be an authoritative paper on the moths of Iran. Americans meeting him see his black

3

Homburg and his tight coat and his rumply collar, and hear his voice; and they know his type at once. They think they do. But they don't know it at all. If you feel baffled and alarmed at the prospect of differentiating one American type from another, you can take heart. You have more hope of success than Americans, who shuffle through every stereotype of every foreign culture as confidently as they handle the family's pack of cards. Americans are not particularly good at sensing the real elements of another people's culture. It helps them to approach foreigners with carefree warmth and an animated lack of misgiving. It also makes them, on the whole, poor administrators on foreign soil. They find it almost impossible to believe that poorer peoples, far from the Statue of Liberty, should not want in their heart of hearts to become Americans. If it should happen that America, in its new period of world power, comes to do what every other world power has done: if Americans should have to govern large numbers of foreigners, you must expect that Americans will be well hated before they are admired for themselves.

So Americans when they meet this Englishman for the first time at once file away the reflection that though he seems amiable enough, he is rigid, unimaginative, a little pompous, a regular Somerset Maugham colonial type. Then the telephone rings – as it did one night – and it turns out that someone wants to know who sang the vocal in that early Red Nichols record of 'Lazy River'. The Americans present were appalled and relieved to hear my friend give out reams of information on these matters. 'No,' he said to another query, 'I think you'll find that record is a blue label, and it's backed by "Beale Street Blues", with Goodman and Teagarden . . . What? no, no, the cornet is Jack's brother, Charlie – that's right, Charlie Teagarden. Not at all, so long.'

He is also, you gather, a jazz fan. And according to the late great Otis Ferguson he knew more about the history of recorded American jazz than most Americans alive, and wrote knowingly about it when he was in college, years before American intellectuals began to write jazz reviews in the mid-1930s. I doubt if the Foreign Office know about this. I doubt if they care, because he is an Englishman, and eccentricity is therefore the most normal thing about him. By merely being around he makes you notice how comparatively rare with Americans is an orderly set of hobbies; and how even rarer is the quality from which hobbies spring – namely, eccentricity. Active Americans do many things. And in different parts of the country they do routinely things that other parts of the country have never heard about. But by and large they do what other people, what their neighbours, do. There is a good reason for this, and you will be glad to hear we don't have to go back to the Indians for it.

Hobbies, I suggest, are essentially a tribal habit and appear most in a homogeneous nation. English boys in school sit beside other boys who are called Adams and Smith and Rendall and Barnes and Gibbs. They do not have to use up much of their competitive energy showing who is more English than another. A nation which says, 'It isn't done', is much more settled as a community than one which says, 'It's un-American'. Only thirty years ago Theodore Roosevelt made a campaign of urging immigrant Americans to forget their roots, to cease being 'hyphenated Americans'. But there are still in America two generations, the sons and grandsons of immigrants, who are trying to outlive the oddity of their family's ways. For it is a stigma for an American to talk with a foreign accent rather than with an American accent. This is snobbery, of course, but the people who instantly recognize it as such are enviably free from the problem. If it is snobbery, even in this land, it is a real humiliation: it is not the urge of insecure people to be different from others; it is the more pressing urge to be the same, and it is acutely felt among people who are insecure just because they *are* different. In very many American cities where there are large populations of immigrants, this is what happens. The son is, let us say, an Italian. As a boy he is brought up with a mixture of American and Italian habits. He plays baseball, but the big meal of the week is ravioli, and he is allowed little gulps of red wine. (If he is a Pole, he is dolled up once a year and marched in the parade on Pulaski Day.) Then he goes to school. There he mixes with boys called Taylor and Smith and also with other boys called Schenck and Costello and O'Dwyer and Koshuski. He begins to find in time that ravioli is a mild joke at school.

Of course, there are millions of Americans who eat ravioli who are not Italian-Americans, but they are untouched by the kind of problem I am discussing. Ravioli is an American dish by now. And that is another thing. The boy notices that just so much as his own habits and speech were instilled by his parents, by so much does he tend not to fit in. By so much he runs the risk of being a joke; which is no joke to a child. And then, at about the age of 12, an awful thing happens. It is happening all over America all the time, and produces recrimination and heartbreak to the folks still left who came originally from the old country – from Poland or Italy or Czechoslovakia or Russia or Germany or wherever – and who will never master the American language. The boy notices that they speak with an accent. He never knew this before. But now it crowds in on him. Now he starts his own rebellion. And that is serious enough to many fine parents so that in scores, perhaps hundreds, of American cities the schools run night classes for parents, in the English language, to help them keep the affection and respect of their sons and daughters, or grandsons and granddaughters. It is a great theme in American life, and it cannot be dismissed by superficial horror or irritated appeals to decent feeling. In time, of course, masses of such sons and daughters outlive the threat of seeming different. And then, but only then, can they begin to cherish some of their oddity, especially in the way of food and festivals. Their strangeness becomes a grace note to the solid tune of their Americanism. But by that time they are sure of themselves and so able to look on their parents again – God help them – with affection.

So you see how sure of your standing with your companions you have to be to start, in boyhood, cooking up interests that will set you apart from your fellows. It will be no surprise now, I think, to hear from my Englishman that nearly all the members of his natural history club in New York were older men with Anglo-Saxon names – families that have been here for a hundred years or more, that have never felt anything but American. They start with the great advantage of being already something that the Poles and the Germans and the Czechs and the Italians have to get to be the hard way.

You may wonder how an Englishman, and an English accent, fit into all this. Well, Englishmen who live here, no matter how long – first-generation Englishmen – are a special case. They may hope to be mistaken for Bostonians (but not by Bostonians). Yet if they affect any more Americanism than that which has grown into their characters, they do themselves much hurt, and both the country they came from and the country they adopted. There are Irish-Americans and Czech-

Americans and Polish-Americans and German-Americans and Swedish-Americans and Italian-Americans and Greek-Americans. But there are only 'Englishmen in America'. They are always apart and always at once more foreign and more familiar.

And an English accent is by now just another foreign sound. There was a time when an English accent would take an Englishman into homes on the East Coast socially more elevated than the home he left behind him. Such Englishmen were secretly delighted to discover this while believing they were only being taken at their true worth. But the hosts knew better. This social observation was a favourite theme of American writers, New Englanders especially, in the early nineteenth century. Washington Irving once boiled over about a certain kind of British traveller: 'While Englishmen of philosophical spirit and cultivated minds have been sent from England to penetrate the deserts and to study the manners and customs of barbarous nations, it has been left to the broken-down tradesman, the scheming adventurer, the wandering mechanic, the Manchester and Birmingham agent, to be her oracles respecting America.' You can still run into the type. Or you could say more accurately that this attitude is one part of most Englishmen's character that is aroused by a visit to America. But the day is long past when Americans imitated English habits in order to be fashionable. There is, however, one peculiar hangover from that period. It is the convention of speaking English on the American stage. Unlike the British and the Germans, the Americans seem never to have worked out a type of stage speech true to the reality of the life around them. Except in comedies. In most historical American plays, and plays of polite life, the characters talk a form of British English. If you chide Americans about this and say, correctly, that these people in real life would not talk at all like that, they say: 'Well, of course not; they're actors, aren't they?' I always feel in London that no matter how trivial the play, the characters being played would talk more or less that way in life. In this country it is understood as a convention, having nothing to do with social honesty, that actors should adopt an unreal mid-Atlantic lingo known, with a straight face, as Stage Standard. You may have noticed that even in American movies most American historical characters and members of Congress talk a form of British, while what are called 'character parts' talk American.

Englishmen can hardly be blamed if they assume that Americans share their sneaking belief that no American can be distinguished and yet sound American at the same time. It has given some otherwise shrewd English dramatic critics the idea that really educated Americans talk like Englishmen. The fact is that educated Southerners, New Yorkers, Chicagoans or New Englanders could never be mistaken for Britons. And there is something wrong if they could be mistaken for each other. It is a fairly safe rule that if in life you meet an American who sounds English, he is either a transplanted Englishman, or one of those homeless Americans forlornly bearing up under the 'advantages' of an education in Europe. Or he is a phoney. The American dramatic critic, Mr George Jean Nathan, was not intending to be facetious, but merely expressing a perennial American puzzle, when he wrote: 'After thirty years of theatregoing, I still can't make up my mind whether actors talk and behave like Englishmen or whether Englishmen talk and behave like actors.'

Damon Runyon's America

27 December 1946

When Damon Runyon died the papers were black with columns of sentimental farewell from all the New York sports-writers who possess an expanding waistline and a yearning to break with the daily grind of football and the horses and begin to write some profitable short stories on the Runyon model. He is already becoming sweetened into a legend, and it sometimes does take the death of a man who summed up an era or a fashion to make you feel how dead and done with that era is. But Runyon has a peculiar transatlantic interest, because the people who read him in London were not the people who read and admired him here. His English reputation, among highbrows especially, was one of those puzzles that are politely accepted as insoluble by the Americans who run into them. It produced the same sort of shock to cross the Channel and hear intense French intellectuals sneering at the talents of Jean Gabin and Louis Jouvet and wishing the serious French *cinéma* could achieve the *vitalisme* of Jimmy Cagney or 'this tenderness, cynical yet profound' of Humphrey Bogart.

Maybe you are both right. But let us for once go beyond politeness and look into the life and style of a man who, by some trick of understanding or misunderstanding, seemed to a whole generation of Britons to be the most typical American writer of his day: tricky, racy, pungent, slick, amoral. I'd better say at once that I never met an American, unless he was a Broadway nightclub owner, or a racing tout, who took that view of Runyon. And the only intriguing thing about him to many literate Americans was his great reputation in Britain.

Like so many other people who later become identified with the spirit of the place they write about, Runyon was not born there. In fact he was 27 before he ever hit New York. He was born, by a funny coincidence, in Manhattan, but Manhattan, Kansas, which in 1884 must have had a population of several hundreds. Runyon's father was an itinerant printer in the Midwest and West. Runyon followed his father, and it took him through a pioneer's trail of Kansas towns, from Manhattan to Clay Center to Wellington, and finally to Pueblo, Colorado, a small town, not much more than a rundown Indian village, just near what is now the Mesa Verde National Park, where you can see the towns built in the sides of cliffs by Indians whose high civilization crumbled about nine centuries ago. It seems to this day a very unlikely place to set the imagination agog with the 'dolls' and 'characters' of Runyon's imagination.

Young Runyon at 14 ran away to enlist in the Spanish–American war. He was in and out of guerrilla warfare for two years in the Philippines, and came back to Colorado full of tall stories, a tobacco breath, and a trick or two with a poker deck that qualified him at once for the profession of newspaperman. By now his interests were settling into the groove that was to pay off very profitably in later life. He started baseball clubs, ran boxing matches on the side, and rode horses on small tracks in southern Colorado. It would be tempting to add that here he obviously picked up the authentic lingo of baseball and stables, and of the petty gangster and shill and the like. Maybe he did, but again like other writers who have been acclaimed outside their own country for their accurate ways with the spoken language, Runyon was not then or ever later a particularly good writer of American idiom as she is spoke and writ. I would say, and it's not an eccentric opinion, that he could not begin to hold a candle to Westbrook Pegler, or John O'Hara, or the late Otis Ferguson, or the living Red Smith, Jimmy Cannon, John Crosby or Robert Ruark. Some of you may be waiting for the name of Ernest Hemingway. But he would come into this discussion only because he too writes an American idiom that no American has ever spoken. It is the American vernacular heard through a very personal ear-trumpet. The Americans in Hemingway talk more like Hemingway than Americans, but somehow they couldn't be anything else but Americans and Hemingway characters. He tightens their speech and their emotions, like a man over-tuning a six-string guitar, so that the low notes have a sharper twang than they ought and the high notes sound as if they were struck on an icicle.

Damon Runyon, even back in Colorado, must have had some trick of mind and hearing much as a man with terrific astigmatism sees distant objects, in a queer way that makes the vertical lines jarring, but also more exciting than they are when he puts his glasses on. I speak with feeling about this because I am a four-star veteran of the battle with astigmatism. I remember how, at my first dances as a boy, when I didn't know there was anything wrong with my eyes, I'd look across the ballroom floor and see a whole crop of misty, tender wallflowers swooning on the vine. I would slink madly round the edge of the dancers to grab one of these houris for my very own. However, when I came within three feet of the charmer I had singled out to tread on, I saw at once why she was a wallflower, instead of being, say, Ava Gardner, out there on the floor moving like a snowflake, or – to be frank – doing the charleston. When I got close she was rarely a beauty, though she looked human enough and surely had character; but that is unfortunately not what a 15-year-old is looking for in girls. I used to take a quick, mild dislike to these girls, however, because they seemed to have pulled a Jekyll-and-Hyde trick. I discovered from some patient clinical testing later that this is the characteristic deceit of astigmatism. Almost any attractive woman at thirty yards looks to me like a beauty, because the astigmatic gaze softens the hard vertical lines, irons out all the wrinkles, and turns any deep-set pair of eyes into pits of tenderness. In general, the great gift of astigmatism is to rob a face of its peculiar lapses from the ideal and leave you with the Platonic copy of the girl that is laid up in heaven.

That's the way I think it was with Damon Runyon. He first saw New York from afar, and heard about it from the lips of gamblers and soldiers and racetrack touts who had made a haul there, or gone on an immortal bust, or captured some fabulous 'doll'. He swam into New York through the romantic haze of his astigmatism, put his glasses on, liked the Colorado myth a good deal better, and kept his glasses off. He didn't care to put them on again, because he did very nicely selling America and Europe a romantic commodity easy to recognize at a distance. He didn't need, either, to listen for Broadway's slang. The private circus in his mind's eye had a lingo all its own, and he made it up as he went along.

A character in a movie Runyon once wrote called somebody a 'mooley'. The censors wouldn't pass the movie till they'd checked with Runyon. 'What's a mooley?' they asked him nervously. 'A mooley?' he said. 'Why, I don't know, I made it up.' That's the way with nearly all his slang. Most American slang was never made up by writers. It derives from a long American experience of work or play – from the collision of Dutch and French and German with English, or from the Spanish days of the Southwest, or from pioneering, mule-driving, railroading, baseball, poker, the cattle kingdom, mining. A newspaper-man famous for his exposures of corruption in labour politics said to me the other night that he thought he might soon turn his attention to the rackets that go on in the insurance business. Reflectively he said, 'I think I'll sink a pick in it. Might be some pay-dirt there.' That is authentic and natural. There is no such slang phrase current as 'to sink a pick'. But I guess it was a common working expression seventy years ago. It recalls at once the Western miners, who looked at a likely mountain range, spat on their hands and sank their picks in, and came up, some of them, with a fortune in silver.

On the contrary, Damon Runyon's slang is as contrived and roman-tic as Dickens, as synthetic as Broadway. Perhaps that's why it fits, even though Broadway doesn't talk it. If Broadway characters had a vein of crazy property, they might talk that way.

Runyon as a writer never goes as deep as Ring Lardner, and his irony was superficial enough not to sadden him with the knowledge of human meanness and vulgarity, as it did Lardner. Runyon accepted it and was fond of it, which might make him a healthier man and not so good a writer as Lardner. He saw, as a stranger, one very small and flashy section of New York life. He made it over into a puppet world of his own, where gangsters are lovable bums, and greed and vulgarity are fun and hurt nobody – for long. He was able to do this because he preserved and exploited his original innocence, like a certain kind of confidence-man. The British view of Runyon is as confident and odd as Runyon's view of New York, not so much because distance, like astigmatism, lends enchantment, but because Runyon distils and steril-izes for a foreigner the swarming colour and frightening behaviour of the animals known as New Yorkers. All the most popular comic writers deal with some recognizable place, and then flatter your foreignness by letting you in on the secret, the confidential, the positively gen-u-ine low life of the place. So Damon Runyon saves you the expense of the voyage, the very real puzzles of the real thing. He puts you in the know, and the knowledge is a cure in itself because it gets you away from the daily grind and the recognizable life of Leeds or Glasgow or London – or, I ought to add, New York.

You do not have to be a stranger to describe or enjoy this pleasurable and simplified view of the country or a town. I know a wealthy tycoon who now lives in New York. But he started life out West, as a timekeeper with a railroad gang. He has acquired without pain, in later life, a romantic Eastern view of the West, thus throwing into reverse the imaginative mechanism of Damon Runyon. This man is always asking me to come and visit him at his winter home in Arizona. Great country, he says, great people, great life. I mumble something about having work to do. At my age, he too had work to do. But now he goes off before the January snows and comes back in April, when the trees are blossoming. He has taken on a stranger's view of the West that is large, enraptured and sentimental. I thought of his father, who had no view of the West, but just broke it and made it liveable.

I have meant not to answer but only to ask the big question: can anybody ever know what is typical of another country? Is Lawrence's Arabia really Arabia, or only what Lawrence's gallant and secret imagination wanted it to be? Would Byron's poems on Greece have made a Greek laugh, as the English editions of Runyon make Americans laugh, with their glossaries of what the English editor thinks is American slang? We are up against a great and humbling question. And the only consolation I can offer is that the answer is open to anybody, the field is free. I have noticed that insight into American ways has nothing much to do with intellect or education. Most people find in a foreign country what they want to find. And when it comes to handing out the laurels to another nation's writers, the native critics are only the muscle-bound trainers of the day. They have been wrong before. If you go back into the last two centuries and look over their selections of the living immortals, you will be given faith in your own fumbling hunches. And even though we on this side may shudder at the notion that you think we go around talking like Damon Runyon's characters, maybe you are right about his permanent fame. After all, you have been right before, notably about Mark Twain, when all the best people in America, and the most respected critics, considered him something as low and fleeting as a comic strip. Maybe Damon Runyon *has* created a legend more enduring and endurable than the reality, because it is neater and funnier and more exotic and sympathetic – that is to say, more artistic – than crummy, sluttish old Broadway could ever be.

Roughing It

15 October 1948

A hundred years ago the first ship sailed out of New York bound for San Francisco and the American River, where, according to the reports that had drifted East, you lowered a pan into a sluggish stream, shook it several times and sifted out a fortune in gold. By ship round the Horn was only one way, the most tedious and the safest. You could go by way of Panama and Nicaragua and run the risk of malaria or yellow fever. You could sail down to Mexico and face a shorter journey across its width through almost trackless desert and the chance of epidemics and slaughter by bandits.

Most people in the East who for one reason or another felt the urge to Go West decided to go the overland way. Today it is impossible to experience the human ordeal of that great migration, one of the last epics of purely human function before the Industrial Revolution transformed our lives. These people, in New England, and New York and Maryland and Ohio, sat down and planned to walk nearly two thousand miles from St Joseph, Missouri, or Independence, where the locomotive and the steamboat ended and the Middle Ages began. Independence was a more thriving place a century ago than it is today, because it was the outfitting centre for the Forty-Niners. From there you were on your own. You went by mule and drove your wagons and cattle along with you for the remaining eighteen hundred miles. You used a route map drawn by somebody who had once made it and survived. You depended very much, too much, on the hearsay of these people to know where the water-holes were and where you could take a short cut through the mountains.

There was no archetype of the Forty-Niner. They were of every human kind. But early on they learned that they had better travel in packs and most of them elected what they called a captain and two lieutenants. A quartermaster was chosen to look after the provisions. They may sound very martial in a noticeably non-military nation. But they knew, the later companies at any rate, that there were certain unavoidable hazards: flash floods, the rotting of their food, Indians, disease, and the constant challenge to their discipline and courage of reducing the weight of their pack – their implements, even their food supply – when the route was too much for their animals, who set the pace. They figured correctly that no group of human beings, however individually noble, would be likely to stay noble in the desperation of thirst, or spontaneously organize themselves in the event of attack. By the time they started the long journey from Missouri, most of them had formed themselves into companies and agreed on written or unwritten laws. Many of them spent weeks in the East before they left, drawing up written constitutions. Some of these were abided by all the way to California. Others were torn up in anger, stuffed down the captain's throat, or buried with a dead cow.

Most of them through the late spring of 1849 took far too many provisions. It was said that the summer companies had the routes laid out for them by trails of abandoned stoves, pillows, beds, pots and kettles, crowbars, drills, ploughs, harness, trunks, bellows and dish-pans. These, they found, were luxuries to a pioneer. And the word got across the continent that what you needed was one wagon to carry the supplies for every five persons, a mule apiece, rifles and shotguns, a rubber knapsack, an oilcloth cap, two pairs of boots, eight shirts, an overcoat, one pair of drawers, three blankets, a hundred and fifty pounds of flour, twenty-five pounds of bacon, fifteen pounds of coffee, twenty-five of sugar, some baking powder, salt and pepper.

That's as far as I want to go in describing the famous journeys across the plains. But I suspect that any American who started out today, fitted out just this way, and got to California, even if he stuck to the countless concrete highways that slam across hundreds of thousands of miles north and south and east and west – such a man would become some sort of national hero or crank. He would be paced by the newsreel boys, met at intervals by the advertising salesmen of whoever's flour and bacon he was carrying, he would be greeted by the Mayor of San Francisco, he would in the end be flown to Washington and shown in all the papers shaking the President's hand in the White House.

Nothing persists more in the fancy of Europeans, and in the superstitious pride of Americans themselves, than the conviction that Americans are tough and rough and ready, scornful of the European niceties and primmer ways of travel. The last thirty years have turned this belief into unmitigated legend.

One of the most precious books to American book collectors is a copy of Baedeker's *United States* for, I believe, 1906. In the conscientious Baedeker way, it warns the comparatively domesticated European of the coarse pleasures and inconveniences he will have to settle for if he decides to take a holiday in the United States. It is always Baedeker's consolation, however, to the intending tourist that no matter how constant the public spitting, how hard the beds, how ankle-deep the roads and primitive the hotels away from the big cities, the traveller who has any pioneering spirit in him will never regret his courageous visit to the United States because nowhere else will he see the singing colour of the New England fall, the blossom of the South in spring, the grandeur of the Yosemite, the Yellowstone, etc., etc. This guidebook is greatly sought after precisely because today it reads like such a gorgeous joke. If you changed the place-names and made them European, an American could read it with a straight face, since it would record most of his grouches about travelling in Europe today. The application of American technical genius to the mechanics of living has not merely turned the tables on Baedeker, it has turned the American, however reckless or self-reliant his individual character, into the world's most urbanized, most petted traveller.

Mr Richard Neuberger, who lives in the Far West, in Portland, Oregon, has taken up this theme in a magazine piece. He was in Alaska during the war having, as he puts it, 'the sort of experience we had read about eagerly as boys, in the tales of James Fenimore Cooper, Jack London, and Zane Grey'. And, he adds, 'we hated it . . . we talked nostalgically of percale sheets and fluffy towels, or breakfast in bed and tiled bathrooms'. They complained – in Alaska, this is – about 'draughty privies and the lack of dry-cleaning facilities'. Mr Neuberger concludes that 'with a few bold exceptions, we Americans have come to regard the steam-heated hotel and the internal combustion engine as indispensable to any foray in the open'. Nowadays, more millions than ever before (the latest published count was 29,608,318) visit the American National Parks. But according to the Department of the Interior fewer and fewer people each year attempt the two-day hikes, or even drive up the highest peaks, or, having looked at the Grand Canyon, will undertake the day-long mule journey down to the overnight camp at the bottom. It is very hard to say how Americans would compare with other peoples in this newfound lassitude. Driving around most of the National Parks is pretty strenuous in itself. If you could put Yosemite and Yellowstone together, you would have something about the area of Wales whose geography is a combination of Switzerland, Persia and the Day of Judgement. But even so, these parks were lovingly created two generations ago by men who chopped through thousands of feet of lumber, who rode into them on a horse, who discovered the sublime with an axe, a botanist's kit, a piece of bacon, a tent and a stout heart. Now through all of them, even over the hair-raising pass into Tuolumne Meadows on top of the Yosemite, American engineers have built incomparable cement highways, blasted through prehistoric rock, encircling mountains where no other race would dream of cutting out a dirt road.

This suggests a cheerful contradiction. That even if the traveller is a sissy sitting over an internal combustion engine, the heroes who on his behalf comb cement to the smoothness of toothpaste under the desert sun, and build his highways through the Rockies and Sierras: they are Americans too. And this leads us into a famous cliché. I hope I can then lead us out of it. (I have nothing against clichés. Most of them are true, though you have to live through the denial of them to know it.) It is the assumption that the Americans have grown soft and unable to fend for themselves, that their enslaving gadgets, through which they flip their way so expertly, are crutches or props to living, essential to a people sinking contentedly into a decadence that out-Romans the Romans.

I'm sorry to report that the Americans' devotion to urban comfort, their ingenuity with gadgets, even their reliance on them, proves no such thing. In my own experience, the Americans who are most devoted to convertible automobiles and glass-enclosed showers made no complaint on this score when they ripped up Japanese jungles for airfields or waded ashore at Okinawa. The women I know who can whip up a delicious meal in ten minutes with the skilled aid of pressure cookers, bean slicers, electric beaters and deep-frozen vegetables are also the ones who can make the best meal the slow way with none of these things. And the most skilful fisherman I know is a man who can charm a trout with his fingernail, but prefers to have a compact tackle-box along, which contains exquisite scales the size of your thumb and a leader cutter which is a little circle of plastic moulds that exudes fine wire and cuts it in one motion.

Most Americans, even rich ones, were brought up in a culture that never expected somebody else to do the rough work. Most boys in college who can afford good cars can also take them apart and put them together again. This may all be changing. Still, I doubt that a devotion to gadgets is a reflection in the American character of a terrified dependence on them. They are loved for themselves, for the humorous felicity with which they dispose of elementary labour. A

Texan I know, whom I would never like to meet in anger whether the choice of weapons was a jet-propelled torpedo or the back of the raw hand, put it neatly once when he said to me, 'I'll ride fifty miles on a horse for the fun of it, but out of necessity I drive.' One of the irritating troubles about Americans, in violation of the best advice of the best English divines, is that they just don't believe that whatever is uncomfortable is good for the character.

Joe Louis

18 March 1949

The day Joe Louis retired must have brought a moment's pause and a sigh from many people who don't care for sport, the sense of a promised date that would never be kept such as non-musical people felt when Caruso or Paderewski died. On 1 March 1949 it came home to some of us that we should very likely never again see him shuffle with great grace up to some wheezing hulk of a man, bait him with a long left before he brought up the shattering, awful thunderbolt of his right, and then toddle considerately away and wait for the referee to call the roll on yet another ruined reputation.

There are some idols you acquire too early, who later turn into walking parodies of themselves, like a favourite uncle who gets to be a vaudeville bore. There are others – the artists of popularity – who stay just far enough away from the hungry crowd and never glut the appetite they tease. Joe Louis was one of these. I doubt I should ever have seen him, or cared to, if he had not at one time connected with a private occasion. I went down to Baltimore the first day of summer in 1937 to stay with an old friend, a doctor at the Johns Hopkins hospital, who promised himself next day an afternoon off from his messy labours with stomach-aches and corpses. We drove out into the blossoming Worthington and Green Spring valleys. The purple twilight fell. It had been a perfect day, of the kind that makes you grateful for your friendships and stirs the memory of how they first started. I had met this man years before on such an evening when he stopped by my room in college to admire a battered record I had carried across the Atlantic. It was Fats Waller singing the 'Dallas Blues'. Driving back into Baltimore he remembered that Fats was on tap in person just then. 'How about,' he said, 'we go down to darktown and catch him?' There was a little vaudeville house deep in the coloured section of town, and that's where we went. We packed ourselves in with several hundred Negroes too many. They clapped and stomped in time and sweated like the plebs at a Roman circus. It was possibly 95 degrees outdoors and 110 inside. Nobody seemed to care. In the middle of one number, though, something happened outside that rode above the rhythm of the band and the hallelujahs of the audience. Far off from somewhere came a high roar like a tidal wave. The band looked uneasy but played on. It came on nearer, a great sighing and cheering. Suddenly there was a noise of doors splintering and cops barking and women screaming and men going down grabbing their toes and snarling obscenities. The band stopped and the lights went up. The black faces all around us bobbed and flashed. Women threw their heads back and shrieked at the roof. Some people embraced each other and a little girl in pigtails cried. Other people cuffed and swung at each other. We managed to get out whole. Outside, in the villainously lit streets – they still have gaslight in darktown Baltimore – it was like Christmas Eve in darkest Africa. This, it turned out, was the night that Joe Louis won the heavyweight championship, and for one night, in all the lurid dark-towns of America, the black man was king.

The memory of that night has terrified and exhilarated me ever since. The phrase, 'Arise, you have nothing to lose but your chains', must have a terrible appeal to the Negro. Most Southerners know it, and it is why in some places they watch fearfully for every Negro flexing his muscles and wonder if he is somehow connected with the Communists. That immediate fear was not besetting America then as it is now. But the lesson was plain: one Negro had outboxed all the living contenders, no matter how white (and Braddock was whiter when he came out of the ring than when he went in), and he was a racial god.

It took several years, and a run of inevitable victories, and wide familiarity with Joe in the ring and on the newsreels, for Americans to learn a special respect for this quiet, beautiful, mannerly youth, who never thought of himself as anybody's god, who never played his colour up or down, kept his mind on his work, stepped scrupulously aside when an opponent stumbled; and who, when it was all over, said such embarrassing things over the radio that they had to whisk the mike away from him to the loser, who could usually be depended on to say the clichés that were expected of him. They pushed the microphone up to Joe in December 1947, when he had been fought into a dazed parody of his younger self by another old Joe – Jersey Joe Walcott. A sharp little announcer chattered, 'Did he ever have you worried, Joe – at any time?' This is a question expecting the answer, 'No, I felt fine all the time, never better.' Joe said, 'I was worried all the way through. Yes, sir, I ain't 23 any more.'

I know it is hard, perhaps impossible, for any white man to appraise the character of any Negro. If you have lived all your life around Negroes, you inherit certain attitudes towards them. If you are a stranger to them, there is the danger of making them out to be quite the nicest people in America. In a way, nice Negroes have to be; for though Negroes are as good and bad as anybody else, they have one thing in common: they have had, most of them, a worse deal than the white man. A variation of this condescension is to think so poorly of the Negro in general that when he does anything as well as a white man, you have to make him out to be unique. You hear a coloured band and shout that nobody can play a trumpet like a black man (it depends, of course, which black man is being compared with which white). Then you run into Louis Armstrong, who tells you of the first time he heard a white boy – a very pasty-faced boy from Davenport, Iowa – play the cornet. And Armstrong broke into tears. 'Man!' he said, 'might as well lay you down and die, nigger.'

When you come to look at the life and career of Joe Louis, there is the special dilemma that he is a black man, and that even when you have done your best to judge him as other men, there's no way of denying that if he is not the best boxer that ever lived, he is as near to it as we are ever likely to know. He was born in 1914 on a sharecropper's cotton patch in Alabama and was as country-poor as it is possible to be. In theory the farm was – it had been rented as – a cotton and vegetable farm. But the vegetables did not feed the family, not by the time Joe, the seventh child, came along. His father broke, as sharecroppers do, from the daily strain of not making enough in crops either to feed his children or put shoes on them. They had no money to send him to a hospital. So he was carried off to a state institution where he died. A widower came to help out and soon married Joe's mother. And his five children moved in with the eight Louises. Joe got a little more food and went to a one-room school. Then the family moved to Detroit, where the stepfather worked in an automobile factory. Joe went on to trade school and worked in the evenings doing the rounds with an ice-wagon. Then came the Depression, and the family went on relief. This, said Joe, made his mother feel very bad. Years later Joe wrote out a careful cheque for $269, which was the amount of the relief cheques they had had from the government. That, said Joe, made Mrs Brooks, as she now was, feel better.

Whatever a big city means to the poor, Detroit meant to Joe. But it means something else to a hefty Negro lad short of cash. It means gymnasiums and the prospect of a quick take of two or three dollars in improvised fights. When Joe was 18 he came home very late one night and found his stepfather blocking the door. 'Where you been, Joe?' he asked.

'Over to the gym,' said Joe, 'working out.'

'I thought so,' said Mr Brooks, and lectured him about the fate of no-goods getting punch-drunk in gymnasiums. 'You go on foolin' around with boxing, you're never gonna amount to nothin'.'

He says this had him really worried. He asked his mother about it. She said it was all right to be a boxer if that's what you wanted to do most. And that was, in a way, the end of Joe's wayward life. The rest was practice, and workouts, and learning, learning, being knocked to pulp, and learning some more and coming again with a new trick or two.

There is a biography of Joe Louis, there may be several, that makes him talk the way sentimental writers always think simple men talk. It is a fairly nauseating work. But just before Joe retired two first-rate newspapermen, Meyer Berger and Barney Negler, got hold of him for many long sessions and, presumably with one hand in their pockets, transcribed exactly how he talked and what he said, without paying any more attention than Joe Louis does to grammar, simplicity or morals. From a few sentences of this report, I think you can get closer to the sort of man Louis is than from reams of official biographies. Take the bit about his being born with a catlike tread. 'When I got up in fighting,' he says, 'newspaper writers put a lot of words in my mouth. They wrote I was born with movements like a panther, and how I was a born killer. I never said it was wrong before, but the real truth is I was born kind of clumsy-footed. My mother says I liked to stumble a lot when I was a baby ... That footwork the writers say was cat-sense was something Chappie Blackburn drilled into me. That was learned, it wasn't a born thing. He saw I couldn't follow my left hook with a right cross without gettin' my right foot off the floor. It takes a lot of learnin' before you can do it without thinkin'.' Or his explanation of why he never says much. 'When I got to be champion, the writers made a lot of noise about how hard it was to get me to talk. My mother said I was no different when I was a kid. When I went to school the teacher made me say words over and over and by-and-by I got stubborn, I guess, and wouldn't say them at all.'

After he lost a fight in early 1934, before his professional career was technically on the books, his manager told him to stop staying out late with the gang. 'He treated me real good,' says Joe. 'I got to wear some of his clothes made over.' The night he became champion, the night it seemed the whole population of darktown Baltimore poured into that vaudeville theatre, Joe summed up his feelings in an immortal sentence or two:

'He fell in a face-down dive. That made me heavy-weight champion. People figure that was my biggest thrill. But I don't remember no special feelin', I just felt good ... maybe it was because I figured I wouldn't feel a real champ until I got that Schmeling. That's what I fixed on.' (Schmeling it was who rang the only jarring note on Joe's professional record. At the end, it read: 61 bouts, 15 knockouts, 9 decisions, knocked out once. That was in 1936. And exactly one year to the night after he became champion, Joe had his revenge. He did what he 'fixed on'.)

Maybe you will get from this the idea that Joe Louis is a simple soul with quiet manners, a good boy who never had a crafty thought. Of course, he doesn't talk about his respect for his opponents, or his decency and casualness with the crowd, because these are fundamental, the characteristics that a man hardly knows about, or, if he does, keeps quiet about. But there is one remark he makes about his pride in money that should round out the picture. 'People ask me,' he says, '"Joe, what will you do when the big money from fightin' stops comin' in? Won't you have to cut down?" I tell 'em, I'm gonna live good, retired or not retired. I got investments and I got ideas. I'll keep on livin' good. It's them who lived off me who won't be livin' so good.'

Well, there he is, the Brown Bomber no more, a memory of incredible speed, a slow shuffle, a solemn face, a gentleness, a shy acceptance of his greatness. All things considered, a credit to his race. So long as you add Jimmy Cannon's necessary afterthought – the human race, that is.

Washington, DC

9 September 1949

In the Library of Congress in Washington, in the catacombs devoted to the Fine Arts, there is a wonderful piece of nonsense – a painting done by a British artist with the forthright title, *The Burning of Washington by the British in 1814*. It is a boy's re-creation of what was certainly a lurid but also a workmanlike and almost casual piece of destruction. The Americans, who were then in the downy youth of their nationalism, being only twenty-seven years old, had an itch to flex their muscles and get into a fight with the Champ – Great Britain, need I say. They had neither the army, the navy nor the money to fight anybody, and the British regulars landing in Maryland joined up with the British Marines stationed in Chesapeake Bay, who broke their snooze, yawned slightly and walked forty miles to Washington. There they calmly burned down the Capitol, the White House – then known as the President's Palace – and the rest of the new public buildings that in those days were all that distinguished Washington from a fishing town on a marsh. It must have been a very humiliating event, for the President and his wife had to lodge in a boarding-house, and Congress was forced to meet in the Post Office, which had (in the general boredom of the undertaking) been overlooked.

Anyway, the British artist who painted this picture made of it the sort of three-colour advertisement that nations conscious of their strength insist on in their official art, the sort of thing which is now reproduced on breakfast-food containers, under some such title as American Victories, First Series. The picture shows the banks of the Potomac River ringed with cannon. Across the river come the British marines, either standing astride small sailboats, or pointing swords with one knee crooked in the approved position of my Lord Nelson, or sitting placidly rowing and admiring the view. And what a view! Nothing seems to be actually burning, because this would rob the spectator of the careful drawing of proud little buildings that are *about* to be burned. But from every bridge and tower and roof to the horizon puffs what looks like a swarm of barrage balloons, or those wavy circles that enclose the dialogue in comic strips. It is fire and flame. And even the harmless American ships on the opposite shore are writhing in great bags of smoke as impressive as medical illustrations of ulcerated intestines.

The contrast must be obvious between these valiant redcoats waving swords, and the British Treasury experts periodically sitting down in that same city showing their account books to the Americans who can have little fear that the White House will shortly go up in flames. But the contrast I want to go into is not so much about our sadly reversed status as between Washington then and now. Washington exists in everybody's eye as a newsreel image of a dome, a huge statue of Lincoln, a parade of some sort, and Mr Truman on the White House lawn, receiving a model fire-hydrant from the fire chief of Oskawassa, Arkansas. Washington is so much a source and factory of the daily news that we rarely pause in our sleuthing to see what sort of a town it is and who are the people who live there.

Well, it is a town made in the triangular join of two rivers. When I say a town 'made', I mean made. For it is the legitimate boast of Americans that theirs is, like Canberra, one of the few national capitals which was chosen as a plot of naked land and designed as a centre of government and built up brick by brick, instead of – like most other world capitals – having the honour of 'capital' imposed at some late date on a city already mushrooming into importance.

In 1787 the Continental Congress made a nation, made its constitution, and looked around for a place to call its capital. The Southern states almost seceded in a row over the location, and for a time there never seemed to be a possible chance of the choice falling on what its enemies called 'that Indian place in the wilderness'. However, there was a certain dinner-party given by Jefferson, and a few bottles of smooth Madeira persuaded Alexander Hamilton (in exchange for the support of a bill he was sponsoring) to promise to deliver enough Northern votes to clinch the choice of this area on the Potomac, which was cut out of Maryland and Virginia; which General Washington personally inspected and approved of; and which was chosen and called 'the city of Washington in the district of Columbia'. Washington hired a man called L'Enfant to design a federal city. Now L'Enfant was a Frenchman and an eighteenth-century man. He was hipped on the subject of 'vistas' and the idea, which he lovingly copied from Versailles, of having great diagonal avenues cross a gridiron or rectangular network of long streets. The idea was that everywhere the diagonals crossed a vertical and a horizontal street you would have a three-way vista. You could see poachers in all directions. You could put cannon there as a point of tactics. What's more, you'd be able to see the great buildings, when they got built, for miles. It all sounded very elegant and modern. But the real-estate men liked it because it offered an endless series of money-making intersections. This obsessed Frenchman shocked them greatly when he showed up with his plans. For of the six thousand acres set aside for the city, over three thousand were for highways, preposterously wide avenues, anything from a hundred and sixty feet to four hundred feet wide. President Washington stuck by him, and he got his great diagonal avenues. Which is a blessed thing, because it's about all that's recognizable of L'Enfant's plan and still gives to Washington whatever it has of splendour and spaciousness.

The Congress, then, after wandering from Philadelphia to Princeton, to Annapolis, to Trenton and New York, set up shop in Washington in 1800. But the city had a hard time getting itself built, getting lighting and paving and sewers and water. Nobody wanted to finance it. The Congress showed a healthy instinct in the early days, which it has since unhappily suppressed, of wondering why it should put up money to prolong anybody's stay in a mess of shacks on a plain that rises only forty feet above the noxious Potomac. For I should tell you that, from that day to this, Washington lies securely in what the guidebooks call an amphitheatre and what you and I call a swamp. And it has a damp, wheezy, Dickensian sort of winter hardly equalled by London, and a steaming tropical summer not surpassed by the basin of the Nile, or those outposts on the Persian gulf where bad vice-consuls are sent to rot.

For half the nineteenth century, L'Enfant's immense avenues were the joke of all visiting Europeans. To get on to them, you left some-body's house and then, like poor Miss Martineau, had to hoist your skirts, climb a stile or two, slush through a bog on to the highway, and cross a field and a sliver of street to get to another human habitation. Along these Versailles avenues that fell like ornamental swords across a rubbish-heap went big-bellied Congressmen in cutaway coats, hun-ters in coonskin caps, judges lugging their law books with them, acid New England ladies, Indian chiefs (there were the remnants of thirty tribes there when the so-called Father of His Country moved in to take possession). Dickens said in the 1840s that Washington was a place 'of spacious avenues that begin in nothing and lead nowhere; streets a mile long that only want houses, roads, and inhabitants; public build-ings that need but a public to be complete'.

The 1840s were a bustling time, what with railways getting to be taken for granted, and the telegraph, and canals being dug everywhere. To the good businessmen who roamed around Washington hoping for industry and finding none, the capital city was a flop. The towns south of the Potomac managed to get all their land given back to Virginia. Georgetown, to the north, wanted to go back to Maryland but never succeeded. But during the Civil War, Washington was the base of the Northern armies, and into it swarmed everybody who had a favour to sell, a bridge to mend, a new kind of gun, any sort of influence which might help or threaten the Union. It was in those years, and in the lush and corrupt days of the Reconstruction, that Washington became what it has ever since remained – the headquarters not only of the government but also of pressure groups and lobbyists, of manufacturers and pimps and fixers who conceived of a capital as a city dedicated to the manufacture of wealth by intimidating the government. The District itself was in wretched need of money. Its citizens were Americans without a vote (they still are) or a city government to call their own. It had a debt of about $4 million, which in 1874 was increased to $22 million. The federal government had to guarantee this debt and it wasn't paid off until 1922.

In the late 1870s it was decided that somebody would have to try and govern the city, and a municipal corporation was formed with three commissioners chosen by the President.

In this period there was a man called Shepherd, a builder, who gave to Washington its second blessing: a wealth of fine trees. He also got the city clean water and workable sewers, but most of all he started planting trees at a furious rate against a howl of protest from people who thought it was a shameless way to waste public money. He lined L'Enfant's great avenues with English elms, thus for ever defeating the original idea of long, uninterrupted vistas. But he made of a marsh the most shady and leafy town in the United States. Today the streets and squares tower with American elms, with sycamores, with all the glorious variety of American oaks, with lindens and willows, with trees from all over the Union and from many foreign places. The little square right opposite the White House, for instance, has a hundred varieties, with spruce, redwood, magnolia, cherry, holly, basswood, and I don't know what else. And springing up in the unlikeliest places is the Oriental gingko, the Chinese pagoda, and ringing the tidal basin those embarrassing Japanese cherry trees, which when we were at war with Japan had to be called something else, but are always the same, and always perfect.

The best guidebooks seem to be incapable of describing the physical look of Washington from any place but the air. That may be because the commanding avenues seen from the earth look like deserted parade-grounds. From the air, of course, they look like landing-strips, a misconception that several pilots from the hinterland acted on, until the city built a few years ago a big modern airport well outside the town. The man from Mars might well assume that Washington was, indeed, another name for Athens taken over by the American Air Force. For arising at majestic intervals from great avenues are what to the pilot look like more Greek wedding cakes than you'd see at a French chef's golden wedding. When you get nearer to those sleek forbidding piles of white stone, cement and plaster of Paris, you might think them more Roman than Greek, and some more vaguely Italian. I doubt, however, whether you could see in Athens or in Rome such an imposing stack of porticoes and rows of Ionic columns and saucer-domes and inset-arches. They are, you would be right in guessing, government buildings – the Capitol, the Supreme Court building, the Treasury – which is almost an Acropolis in itself. Washington started to build in the 1790s in the inrushing fashion of the Greek Revival (a style in which Americans did delicate and beautiful things when they domesticated it in wood, in the South and New England, as the proper frame for houses and little churches). But whatever was good about the earliest Washington buildings is now to be seen only in the White House and the noble federal houses of Georgetown. For the Greek Revival style was soon succeeded by others, by red-brick Georgian of a humble kind, then by Romanesque, then by all the monstrous colonnades and curlicues of the mid-nineteenth century. At the end of that century there was a World's Fair in Chicago, showing the grandiose plaster-of-Paris façades of the Beaux-Arts exhibition in Paris. Ever since then Washington has lusted after these Roman monsters like a Girl Guide after Mark Antony. Washington would be about as intimate as Nuremberg used to be, if this was all. But happily it has a magnificent park, the finest scenery inside a city's environs, said Lord Bryce, of any city he knew. And it crawls through this graveyard like Virginia creeper over a tombstone. The city is also nibbled at on all sides by suburbs – which city isn't? Some of them are old red-brick Georgian and some we'd better just say are suburban. Indeed, if you went to live in Washington and by some strength of character managed not to be a government employee, you might live in many parts of town and say that rows of nineteenth-century boarding-houses were more typical of Washington than rows of Greek columns. It's true; the two shapes most characteristic of Washington are the Italian palace, where the wage-slaves work, and the bow-windows, where they live.

You'll see that it's impossible to talk about Washington without getting preoccupied with the government and its buildings. But that's because there's practically nothing else. Washington is not a capital like London, which is a government capital but also a capital of banking, of music, of theatre, of eating, of writing and reading, of public sports, of shipping. All those things other than government are centred in New York, which Washingtonians contemptuously think of as Babylon-on-the-Hudson. Washington has no permanent theatres – it is wary of opening them to Negroes, and Washington is embarrassed by Negroes for exactly the same reason that Alabama is: nearly a third of its population is coloured.

Washington has little music that can begin to compare with the great orchestras of New York, Boston, Minneapolis, San Francisco or even Philadelphia. It has indifferent public food. It is as close as Baltimore to the huge Chesapeake Bay, but whereas the tables of Baltimore swill with terrapin stew and snapper-turtle soup and groan with expiring lobsters of a fatness that has to be seen to be believed, Washington for some reason makes no decent use of the gorgeous fish that come gasping up at the end of its streets. The answer may be that Washington stays home. It is not a night-owl town. The Congressmen don't like to be seen in their cups in public. And I doubt if either Sodom or Gomorrah was ever kept going by a population of respectable clerks.

This is another – in fact, the major – by-product of Washington's being nothing but a government city. It is the only town I know which has bred its own species of employee – the 126 clerks who came here in 1800 were neat and sober and have neatly and soberly reproduced their kind, to the tune of 300,000 government clerks. You do not see here the clashing variety of human shape and style and colouring that makes American cities such a challenge to the pleasant senses and some others. In other national capitals it is on the streets that you see mankind's variety. It is indoors – inside the courts and the parliament – that you see a mass of officials, who look as if they'd been run off on an assembly line. Not so in Washington. Here all the types in America, and all the accents, are drawn from the plains and mountains and deserts into the House and Senate Chambers. And on the streets – a population of quiet, slim, self-effacing people in glasses. Indoors, the human jungle, outdoors – the clerks. For it is the Congress and its hangers-on that ride the roost and set the tone of high life. You do not walk down the Strand side-stepping MPs at every turn or cluster around a church to catch Mr Aneurin Bevan at his devotions. In London the Members of Parliament enjoy their true glory only when they are inside the House of Commons. Once outside, they dissolve into the formidable and dominant race known as the Cockneys. But in Washington the politicians, the puffing gauleiters from the provinces, are the rulers. It is this status which gives to the natives of Washington a meek, subterranean life, like that of Parisians during the occupation. They are resigned to it, as a Blackpool landlady is resigned to the profitable uproar of August Bank Holiday.

So, to continue what Mr Churchill would call 'this true account', we have a government capital obsessed and absorbed with governing, and all the feuds and deals and crises that go with it. We have a city with poor food, a nightmare of a climate, dignified by great avenues and by the cascading foliage of magnificent trees. But how, you must be saying, how about the high life, the air of great events, the intrigue?

It is usual to say that Washington is a nest of intrigue. And so it is. And undoubtedly there are more luxurious and louder parties held there than most of the ancient capitals can any longer afford. In this country you would expect the social arbiter to be a woman. And so she is. But ever since Mrs Perle Mesta got made the Minister to Luxembourg there has been a fine rivalry going on, and much well-bred miaowing in well-kept gardens, about who is to succeed Mrs Mesta as the town's leading hostess. I should add here that though not many Washington wives can aspire to toss a battalion of pressed duck at a thousand guests, Washington wives are another breed all to themselves. I never yet met a wife of a man anywhere near the government who didn't bear up splendidly under the intimate knowledge that her husband really swung the election and gave the word for the date of the invasion of Europe. This all, surely, implies a very harem of intrigue.

But intrigue in a capital city suggests the splended briberies of a Talleyrand, the sort of masked ball at which the Secretary of State forgets to dance with the wife of the Turkish ambassador and boom! – another crusade is on the march. Washington is indeed choking with intrigue and gossip. But its intrigue is less like that of the court of Louis XIV and more like that of a vast church bazaar, in which hot-eyed matrons wink and whisper in the hope that Mrs X's pickles will be rejected as too tart and Farmer Y's Poland Farceurs will come in a poor third.

You have heard the word 'pork-barrel' – the President's pork-barrel – and must have wondered what a pork-barrel was doing in so elegant a place as the White House. It is, alas, a permanent though invisible fixture. To be more accurate, it is two fixtures. For there's one pork-barrel for the President and one for the Congress. Like many another American institution, they were created by self-denial and ended by giving a licence to self-indulgence.

Jefferson and his excellent Secretary of the Treasury followed the English custom of using the national income as they thought fit, disbursing lump sums to each department and accounting for the money when the money was spent. But at the first complaint from Congress they decided to adopt the more chivalrous method of asking the Congress to specify its wants and name a price for each of them. The result is the Congressional pork-barrel, which persuades some Congressmen to postpone for ever their interest in what is best for the nation and sends them circulating through back-rooms, offices and parties, ogling an old friend here and charming a stranger there, in the hope of swiping for their constituency an army camp, or getting a new post office built or an old river drained.

The President's private pork-barrel was left him by the Constitution as a consolation prize for having to get the Senate's consent to his appointment of all the big federal jobs, like Cabinet officers and ambassadors. He was allowed to keep certain 'inferior offices', which his party has ever since been eager to help him fill. He it is who appoints a postmaster in Santa Claus, Arizona, a food inspector in New Orleans, a tax collector in Red Cent, Utah. If this seems a harmless vanity, it should be remembered that there are many thousands of these 'inferior offices' scattered across the land and that every one of them represents a Congressman appeased or a Congressman flouted. They tot up to a nice balance of favours and insults that registers with painful accuracy when some bill the President is dying to have passed comes to the vote in the Congress. On a dark day of the Civil War, Lincoln confessed he looked more ashen than usual not from any concern about his armies but because he was worried over a postmastership in Brownsville, Ohio.

Washington was accordingly long ago described as 'a huge hog-wallow where every man's snout is at the pork-barrel'. It is an uncouth image, no doubt, but it is a truer symbol of Washington intrigue than any boudoir gallivanting ever recorded in the White House. Washington tries to perfume this reality with a lot of scented legend about George Washington's eye for a pretty ankle, and how Martha Washington was a fragrant thing in her day. But even this myth doesn't hold up. In our day she has given her name to a wholesome candy. Imagine 'Josephine Buonaparte Cough Drops'!

You have seen that I have done my best to give you a vivid and unprejudiced account of this great capital city where now the ancient empires bow to the dollar. I should like to take you around some more of its glories, but, like Mr Fitzpatrick in the travelogues, we must say a reluctant farewell to the federal city on the Potomac. And so as the sun sinks into the Tidal Basin . . . excuse me, I have just time to make the fast train up to Babylon-on-the-Hudson.

The Fall of New England

21 October 1949

There are times of the year when anybody with an itch for travel must think of those parts of the earth that God favoured above all others when He handed out the seasons. There are two of these that I have enjoyed many times but I still find myself goggling and marvelling every time they come around. One is the English spring and the other is New England in the fall.

The best of English poets have celebrated the rich, sombre English autumn, but an American fall bears little resemblance to that 'season of mists and mellow fruitfulness'. Many famous Britons have put on record their astonishment at the youthful, trumpeting quality of the fall, at the hot days and the Mediterranean blue skies encircling a landscape of blinding scarlet and gold. Lord Bryce, not a reticent man about American vices, couldn't trust his English reserve to speak properly about its virtues. Lloyd George confessed after his only trip to America that no matter how inconclusive his political mission had been he would at least go home remembering the overwhelming experience of the fall. A hundred years ago, Mrs Trollope, who liked very little about these United States, broke down and wrote that at this season of the year 'the whole country goes to glory'.

The fall ranges throughout the whole hardwood or deciduous region of the country, from the north woods of Maine clear across the Midwest as far as the Dakotas and way down South to the foothills of the Rockies in Texas. Since no American can bear to believe that he or his parents chose a second-rate place to be born in, there is no agreement about where the fall is at its best. The residents of the Great Lakes say that no sumacs flame like their sumacs. And the pride of a man from Arkansas in his blazing hawthorn trees is a wild grab at plucking a virtue out of necessity. A native of another land can simply report that the fall of New England is as a four-alarm fire to a lighted match. There is no way to describe it or talk about it, except in the language of Milton and Shakespeare, who never saw it.

But it is possible to say why it's so. Everybody enthuses about the fall but nobody explains it. It is due to a happy accident of climate, a steady brilliance of October sun going to work on the great variety of American hardwoods and the fairly arid soil they stand in. The superiority of New England's fall – of that in Vermont, New Hampshire and Massachusetts especially – is due to their latitude. These states are far enough north to get an early cold spell to quicken the sap before the prolonged sunshine of October brings it out as colour in the leaves. They are far enough south to escape a continuous and withering frost, which is what nips the Canadian fall before it can come to its prime. Farther south – in Pennsylvania, Maryland, Virginia and the Carolinas – they get no cold, except at high altitudes, and by the time the sap is forced up and ready for showing off, the leaves are crumbling and falling.

33

In most temperate countries the strong pigments that have been hidden from view in the greens of summer never do come out, because the autumn brings in rain and mists and threatening grey skies. The whole trick of the New England fall is nothing more complicated than that of a photographic negative handled by a superior developer. In the autumn, the countrymen tell us, the sap is blocked from the leaf by a new growth of hard cells at the base of the twig. So the greens fade. Now all you need is an October of brilliant light and warmth to develop out the yellows and the reds. The only other qualification is a lack of rain. On rich and rainy soils like those of England the leaves stay green too late till the frost kills them. New England, on the contrary, has many causes to lament its rather poor soils. But it never regrets them in the fall, for their very lack of nitrogen stimulates a great range of yellows and golds. And the acid in the leaves is what burns them scarlet. The fall, then, is nothing more than the thorough burning out of what is poor in the soil and what is bitter in the leaf. 'It is,' says Donald Culcross Peattie, 'essentially death that causes all the brave show.' But it is a fierce and productive death.

I once went north from New York City at the very beginning of the fall to meet the peak of it wherever it might be between Maine and southern Connecticut. The first signal of the glory to come is a bare tree, which is never bare until the fall is ready to ripen. It is the butternut tree, and it sheds everything just as the bushes and berries are beginning to trickle out their purple. By the green edge of the parkway on which I was driving, little piles of brown leaves, already dead, lay at the foot of hickory trees. The ferns were dry. The bracken and blueberry bushes were wine-dark, the sumac a throbbing vermilion. Everywhere there was the smell of burning wood, letting off violet wisps of smoke to smear the cloudless sky – like trickles of milk on window panes.

At this point I wanted to take off my glasses, which a notation on my driving licence forbids. This is another thing about the fall. The sparkling clarity of the light gives to short-sighted people the constant sense that their eyesight has marvellously improved and that they are seeing fences, barns, steeples and billboards in the sharp outline they probably have for other people all the time.

I drove up and over the hills across from New York State into

Connecticut, past roadside stands piled high with jugs of cider and pyramids of pumpkins. And then I started to follow a river whose banks were black with stands of evergreen. By now a green field was just another daub on the crowded palette of the landscape. We were still far from the fall's peak. It was still the small, treeless things that were trying to be splendid. The briar and bushes and vines were sparkling. I do not know them well enough to single out their separate charms, but it is an annual joy to see brush which most of the time is a mesh of old wire suddenly disclose a jewel of a flower. Pokeweed, and pitchpine cone, and unpretentious things like partridge berry and jack-in-the-pulpit. All of them have a special shining berry, a bursting husk, a momentary bloom.

I got out of the car and wallowed in the silence and the singing colour and the balmy heat. At the rim of my tyre I noticed that the smooth white cement of the highway had cracked under the tension of a cranberry vine. And through this crack, and edging into the highway, wild cranberries grew. I looked ahead at the engineered boulevard of the highway, pouring like two ribbons of toothpaste to the horizon, quite heedless of its defeat by the concentrated violence of a tiny and delicate vine. That just about put industrial know-how in its proper place. And I climbed back and went on, warming to the excitement of what was to come.

And now the trees took over. After another twenty miles, the evergreens came in thick and fast. Even a pine looked like a new invention seen in its inkiness against a flaming maple. Now I was surrounded by two other properties that make the New England fall unique. First and above all the maple, with its bursting sugar which blazes into scarlet. And then the oaks. An Englishman is surprised to wonder about many slender trees and hear them called oaks. The fat old oak tree of England, with his legs planted solidly on lush damp ground, is a rare sight. But New England has a teeming variety of oaks, and their value as a spectacle is that in the fall they entirely revise your ideas about the infinite fine range of colour between gold and lemon. And beside this perpetual shower of scarlet and lemon and gold, the white birches slid by like slivers of mercury. And rising from the foam of every valley, slim as thermometers, were the white spires of colonial churches, keeping count of the general fever. I had hit the peak, and the state of our language being what it is, in my hands at least, there is no more point in going on about it in prose. Some great composer might convey the majesty of it. Only a child in ecstasy could hit off the youth and hilarity of it. For children are natural impressionists, taking the adjectives of music and knifing them close against the nouns of sight and touch. Every child knows that colour sings and trees walk. But puberty is the end. They acquire the logic that is death to the spirit and life to what is called maturity, and like the rest of us repress the wild energy of their instinctive knowledge. And so we can only guess at the form of art in which perhaps some hundreds of years from now the New England fall will come to be represented. I would take a bet that, by our present resources, Cézanne and Handel together might give a fair account of it. For the present I can only tell you that the fall is wonderful in life and awful in painting.

In this setting you can find an American life, proud but not prosperous, that also seems doomed to die in the industrial democracy that surrounds it. Don't imagine that the small village I am taking you into, in the south of Vermont, is typical of New England today. It is typical of nowhere else, but New England is many things besides small memorials to the declining eighteenth century. The New England puritan of English stock has not been the typical New Englander for two generations. Sixty per cent of the people in the six states of New England have at least one parent foreign born, against only 5 per cent in the Southern states. Today the Connecticut Yankee has only one chance in three of being, like the first settlers, a Protestant with an English name. It's two to one that he's an Italian or a Pole, and a wise newspaper editor once warned me to take for granted that any stranger I met on the streets of New England was a Catholic. To make certain that what I am going to talk about, though once radical and typical in New England, is now conservative and odd, I should also warn you that the typical Yankee is no longer a farmer. In 1790, ninety-seven New Englanders in every hundred lived on the land, and three in towns. In 1870, it was still only twenty-one townsfolk against seventy-nine countrymen. Today in the United States, 56 per cent of the people live in cities. In New England, 77 per cent of the entire population lives in cities, only 23 per cent in the country. So New England is the most industrialized of all American regions. If this shocks you, it would shock most Americans more, for they stubbornly think back to New England as the source and replenisher of all their canniest and most down-to-earth virtues.

Bearing in mind, then, that we are looking at a tiny green spot in the upper-right-hand corner of the turbulent industrial landscape of the northeastern states, let's take a look at the sort of place that bred New England. It is a small valley six miles long and two miles wide. You might say that it was bound by mountains, but to a Westerner they would be low, well-wooded hills, for the hills that enclose this valley are nowhere higher than a thousand feet. Yet the valley is more fertile than most places in Vermont, with grass for summer pasture and winter hay. It grows corn and perhaps a crop of oats. And the farmer's cash in the bank comes from the one cow a year he sells. To a stranger it would look like good sheep country, and so it would be if there weren't out West the vast hills of Montana and Wyoming and Colorado to make it hardly worth while for a Vermonter to breed them. Then, there's so much rock and boulder in the hills of Vermont that by now the oldest Vermont joke tells how the sheep have their noses sharpened so they can get at the grass (God anticipated the plight of Vermont by making sheep with cleft lips).

If you were to motor along this valley, and your car had some sort of trouble, a quiet, hard-bitten Vermonter would in time – his time – appear and tinker awhile and in the end put it right. He wouldn't say a word. And you'd have to be an outlander to try and pay him in any way. For Vermonters, settled long ago on a poor soil, and used to winters that hold more snow than the Arctic, don't expect a smiling face from Nature and don't reflect it in themselves. An Englishman coming here and going straight to Vermont and expecting to meet casual, backslapping people would be in for a ghastly surprise. A man is a stranger there up to the third and fourth generation. And the only reliable way they have of placing a face or a name is to ask who his mother was. (His father simply served his mother's turn.) It's been said that Vermonters look on life as a necessary struggle against evil, a struggle you must make and expect to lose. It's also the only state in the United States where you will hear the word 'thrift' used all the time. They never throw anything away. In a little booklet about this valley I am talking about, written by a couple of natives, you will read this sentence: 'The people are friendly and always willing to help a neighbor. This means more to us who live here than material wealth, which none of us possess.' To walk into the centre of this village of Newfane, you would never believe it. It is a handsome common with a couple of shops, an inn and a quite magnificent courthouse. The town was settled in 1776, but the county courthouse didn't go up until fifty years later, and we can be thankful for that. For in the interval Americans conceived a passion for everything Greek. Believing that they had just successfully established the first genuine democracy since the Greeks and the grandest Republic since Rome, they took to naming their town with classical names. Hence Philadelphia, Annapolis, Laconia, Athens, Sparta, Seneca, Cicero, Troy. Thomas Jefferson built a home with a columned portico. And soon country courts, and inns, and farmhouses were doing the same. It may sound like a dubious fad, but Americans stuck to their preference for wooden houses, and today New England is glorified with hundreds of churches, houses, court-houses, the wood painted white, with pillared porticoes and graceful spires. In this small village in Vermont, the county courthouse is an exquisite symbol of what Americans did in wood with Greek forms.

Opposite the courthouse is the inn, which is also the jail. Newfane has kept up its habit of feeding its prisoners from the inn, and since the inn serves the best food around here, it's sometimes hard to get the inmates out of jail. Theodore Roosevelt said he would like to retire here, commit some 'mild crime' and eat his way through a cheerful old age.

If you went along the valley you would be walking without knowing it through another town called Brookline, for Brookline is simply the scattered houses of the valley. It has less than a hundred people, mostly farmers, and they are their own rulers. Its first town meeting was held in 1795 and the last one was held last week. The names at the first meeting are still there: Moore and Waters, and Ebenezer Wellman and Cyrus Whitecomb, and Christopher Osgood (there has always been a Christopher on the Osgood farm). Walking along the road you might run into the tractor of a Mr Hoyt. He is to all intents a farmer. And so he is. He is also the road commissioner of the valley. His wife, Minnie Hoyt, is the town clerk, a justice of the peace, and when she isn't doing the farming chores she's busy signing fishing licences, or marrying a visiting couple, or telling the comfortable city-people who have made a summer home here that by a decision made at the last town meeting their taxes will be twice as much next year. What is striking to an Englishman here is that the few fairly well-to-do people are all what they call 'summer folks', people who made a farm over as a summer retreat from New York or Boston. But the summer folks are strangers and underlings. The valley has heard many delicate sounds through the years. But it has never heard the advice of a squire or the accent of *noblesse oblige*. The farmers are ruled and rulers. The wealthy stranger goes cap in hand and pays his rates according to Minnie Hoyt and does what Mr Hoyt says to keep his part of the highway safe and sound.

Our pilgrimage ends with an odd little building, a round school-house. It was put up in the 1820s and is shaped like a silo, just one room with five windows equally spaced in a circle around it. It was so built, they say, because at that time the valley lived in fear of a highwayman called 'Thunderbolt', whom no one had ever seen. The schoolmaster, a Scot from Muirkirk, one Dr Wilson, had his desk facing the door and could see through all the windows the first approach of any robber, or of the dreaded Thunderbolt. Thunderbolt's presence seemed to have haunted the valley for a couple of decades, but one gets a reassuring picture of Yankee vigilance in the dour figure of Dr Wilson, spelling out his lessons to the valley children and in the twilight letting his fingers play on the barrel of his shotgun as his protective eye rolled around the five windows.

I leave you with this comforting image of the rude forefathers of today's New Englanders. Having led you so far into a mystery, though, it occurs to me you may wonder if they ever caught Thunderbolt. Yes, they did.

When the good Dr Wilson died they took off the high scarf he always wore and on his neck they saw scars and the marks of chains. Sure enough, *he* was Thunderbolt.

Letter to an Intending Immigrant

16 December 1949

I was going downtown in the subway and was flattened up against the door reading the morning paper of a man breathing into my ear. If anybody in this train had had room to ram his elbow into my lungs, chances are I wouldn't have noticed it. That would have been just an occupational hazard of travelling in New York during the Christmas shopping season. But what I became aware of after a mile or so was a gentle nudge somewhere down there in the direction of my floating rib. This was such a friendly gesture that I tried to swivel my eyeballs in the direction it was coming from. I saw the upturned face of a man who might have been about five feet three or, then again, might have been a six-footer simply frozen at that altitude. He grinned and asked me if my name was Cooke. I said it was and he said his name was Schofield and he'd been in school with me in England twenty . . . well, several years ago. Before we lurched to a stop, his stop, he had time to tell me that he was working in a big department store downtown and had been over here for just about two years. I asked him if he was here for good. He gave a little laugh and said he certainly was. 'I just upped and left,' he said, and the train stopped and he vanished into the gasping school of New Yorkers peering at us through the aquarium windows.

This whole episode didn't last longer than thirty seconds, but it made me glad for him and set me contrasting his obvious good spirits with the fate and the faces of other English people I've run into in the past few years who also 'upped and left'. There was, for instance, an English girl who decided when the war was over that instead of having her children come back home to her from Canada, she would join them over here and start a new life in a new land. Her boy, it turned out, developed one of those boy soprano voices of remarkable purity. She began to fret – in the little Canadian town she'd settled in – and think back longingly to the church schools in England where this voice might be trained. Of course, she was homesick for more things than an English boys' choir. It was a useful and sensible excuse to give to friends on this side. She is back in London now, very contented in austerity, and her boy is proudly singing his head off.

I think also of a young man in his middle twenties who came here, hit on a good job and quickly acquired the usual admirations: the bright tension of New York, the vigour and irony of its people, the autumn weather, the food, the women, the motor parkways, the theatre. For a time he didn't seem to notice that this was costing him twice or more what these good things would have cost him at home if he'd been able to get them. He didn't need to notice, because he was a bachelor and such things as insurance and social security seemed like an old man's babble. This young and strapping Englishman was undoubtedly by now uprooted. His enthusiasm for many American customs was really a surprised contempt for his own previous ignorance of them. This is not a good basis for permanent admiration and he began to lose some of them, as he came to take them for granted. His job didn't pan out, and he found in the short and ruthless space of one month that New York is a bad town, and America a bad country maybe, to be poor in. With what he had left he went to Jamaica. Restlessness of course is a personal thing, but there was a conflict in it that I've noticed in other Britons who've sailed in here with shining eyes and left after a time in a mixed mood that is not pleasant to admit, for it is a mixture of disappointment and defeat. There is surely nothing to be ashamed of in disappointment. But many of these intending settlers can hardly fail to feel that American life is a far more severe challenge than they had figured on, and it has beaten them.

A century ago the whole adventure was, I think, materially harder on the people who made it, but psychologically not so tough. They knew before they ever left home that they were coming to a land with many less material comforts than Europe had to offer. They knew that the essential qualifications were physical hardihood, self-reliance, cheerfulness in the face of the adversity that was bound to come sometime, an indifference to social niceties, and a shrugging acceptance of dirt, bad luck, violence and bankruptcy. The visitors who didn't prepare themselves for these hazards had nowhere to turn for sympathy. Their criticisms sounded niggling and effeminate. Thus in 1820, Washington Irving described such Englishmen: 'They miss some of the snug conveniences and petty comforts which belong to an old, highly-finished and over-populous state of society; where the ranks of useful labour are crowded, and many earn a painful and servile subsistence by studying the very caprices of appetite and self-indulgence. These minor comforts, however, are all-important in the estimation of narrow minds.'

It sounds just like a British criticism of the travelling American today. Only the other day a young American film star (who was born on a small farm) caused a commotion in an 'old, highly-finished' hotel in Paris by demanding an air-conditioned room.

Nowadays an Englishman's complaints would not be likely to turn on such things. Now the material scales are weighted in America's favour. Today you can cross the three thousand miles of the American continent and never want for a private bathroom, a cement highway, a night baseball game, an airplane connection, a pair of nylon stockings or a gallon of ice cream in six different flavours.

But the catch is that America is no more willing than it has ever been to give these things away for free. They are not in this country the luxuries that a secure upper class once exacted from a swarming and servile lower class. They are the minimum demands of comfort made by a population as fertile as its resources, in a country where comfort has accordingly turned into big business. A share of that comfort, a bigger share of satisfying and ingenious comfort than any nation has ever known, can be bought by any worker with a steady wage. But the measure of that steady wage is the energy he can maintain. Visiting teams of British factory managers have remarked on the tenacity with which American workers compete through incentive schemes. You have only to lean out of any midtown window in New York, or in a score of other cities, to notice the furious concentration and energy of construction workers while they are on the job. At 5 o'clock they will quit like an exploding light bulb, but up to that moment they haul and hammer and drill and bulldoze with fearful zest.

A little time ago I left my office, as I usually do, about seven in the evening (not having the instinctive zest of the natives) and saw that the whole lobby of the skyscraper office building – which spans something like the floor-space of Piccadilly Circus – was covered with tarpaulin from which arose a network of ladders and scaffolding, a whole series of wooden platforms running about seven or eight feet from the ceiling. This scaffolding alone looked as if it might take a day or two to put up. But none of it was there at 5 o'clock when the offices of this building disgorged their three or four thousand employees. However, this was only the preparation for the job in hand. The job in hand was the painting of the whole of this great ceiling, which is about thirty feet from the ground. Sixteen men at various intervals were already up on the platforms and beginning to wave a kind of big flat brush, which from my angle looked about as wide as the tail of a whale. I had to come back that night to my office to catch the midnight news. There was not a man in sight, nor a paintbrush, nor any tarpaulin or scaffolding. The night cleaners were already busy with their monster vacuum cleaners. And the ceiling was gleaming with its new paint.

This kind of shock greets the stranger wherever he goes. You have your house painted, or a wall knocked down, or new lighting sockets put in. And I should warn any incurable English perfectionist that half the time you will get a finished job something less than what would satisfy a first-rate craftsman. But this is neither their aim nor their interest. They do what they contract to do with remarkable speed and skill. Then they clean up your disordered home in a final cheerful burst and are on their way back to their wives, their shower-bath, their steak and television sets. These men get paid better than any working-men have ever been paid, allowing for the exchange, the higher cost of living, and all that. The painters I just told you about were earning a $130 a week – £46 10s. – which will take care of quite a lot of high cost of living. (I ought to add, though, that they pay just about the same, £46 10s., one week's wages, for the monthly rent of a small house.) If they work this way, they will keep their job. If they don't, they won't: that is the simple, brutal rule of life in America in prosperous times.

You can see how hard it is to start from scratch in this country, which already has a labour force of over sixty millions, and the fiercest kind of competition at all levels, from the labourer to the managing director. It sounds like a nightmare, and it may well be so to gentle, sensitive people who have no sympathy with the fight for life and merely want to earn enough money to give them leisure in their evenings, some fields to walk across, a little light and air. In the big cities of America these things too come at a high price. I sometimes feel that the house agents and real-estate men in all the big cities have measured every building and gauged exactly how many cubic inches of every little room are touched by sunlight for a few hours of the day. That room, once the estate agents discover its secret, will have its rent doubled. Several million middle-class families in the cities of England have a little back garden which they could reproduce in New York for a mere £5,000.

It is hard for the romantic Englishman or woman to talk to Americans about these anxieties. Apart from seeming a chronic complainer, you will also tend to sound to Americans like a kind of immigrant they were long ago warned about. Washington Irving was on to this type too and wrote of them: 'they may have pictured America to themselves an El Dorado, where gold and silver abounded, and the natives were lacking in sagacity; and where they were to become strangely and suddenly rich in some unforeseen, but easy manner'.

Well, that sort of character will be around for quite a time yet, but he grows increasingly peevish. It may be that present-day America, or rather the movie and magazine myths about it, attracts a semi-playboy type that is too soft to take the known risks of a hundred years ago. Unfortunately, the austerity and anxiety of Europe produce, too, many unassuming and honest people who are looking for nothing more than a competence and a little peace and quiet. To the newcomer there is no easy guarantee of it. Sons of wealth can have it without any effort, for this country now has the biggest class of hereditary rich of any nation on earth. But for the newcomer there will be little concern about how he lived or what he was used to, or the kind of people he moved among. If he wants the same society in America, he must buy his way into it. Not what you seem to be, but what you prove you can do: that is still, for the stranger, the persistent pioneer requirement. You have been warned.

The 1950s

The Summer Bachelor

16 June 1950

An American telephoned me the other day to ask me what was meant by 'flannelled fools'. I had to explain to him that in Britain the summer game is played in flannels. He jumped, wrongly, to the conclusion that boxing was the British summer pastime and that everybody got fitted out for it in long skiing underwear. I introduced him gently to some of the mysteries of cricket, not the least of which is why grown men stand around for most of the day doing nothing at all in temperatures of 50 degrees. I tried to keep my exposition to simple words, but when you are talking about transatlantic weather the simplest words are the most deceiving. I remember once picking up the Paris edition of the New York *Herald Tribune* and looking up to the left-hand corner of the front page to see how the people were faring in the Manhattan midsummer. It prints the weather report of London, Paris and New York, and the newspaper naturally has to take on trust the language of the weather bureau of origin. It said, 'London, fair, 71 degrees, continued hot; Paris, 78, warm; New York, clear, high 83, seasonably cool.'

This could serve as a text for the British export drive, which falters always on the presumption that an American means the same thing as an Englishman when he talks of a 'light suit'. In Britain, it appears to mean light in colour. Here it means light-weight. If this is understood, the golden rule for the textile exporter will then be clear: it is to coax the American buyer into purchasing large quantities of the raw material in Britain – as sheep, if you like – and then let him use it and cut it according to his habits and his needs. For British clothes in America will make a man feel uncomfortable outdoors in summer and indoors in winter. It is possible for a North European to feel at home here any time up to Christmas. He could keep his old habits and his regular suits and feel he was still in a temperate climate. The New Year

47

transports him to the pole, and in a temperature of one above (above zero, that is) the word 'cold' will take on a sharper meaning for a Londoner, say, who has never in his or his forebears' lifetime known anything colder than 9 degrees. Summer here is, however, the bigger problem for the Briton. He is rightly aware that New York is named after old York but he goes on to the fatal assumption that the trip from one to the other involves a direct east-to-west passage of three thousand miles. What he rarely knows is that he has also gone eight hundred miles south, that old York is located on a level with the tundra of Labrador, whereas New York is at the precise latitude of Corfu.

This clash between the romantic legend of our sameness and the facts of life is what sparks the Englishman's shock. He discovers that the changeover from winter to summer life is brutally abrupt, and that to adjust to the violent swing of the thermometer he has to acquire habits more suited to a fieldhand in a banana republic than to the gentle vagaries of a London heatwave. (I recall another London headline: '75 Again Today! No Relief in Sight.') He will discover that New York is more of a summer furnace than a summer festival. He will learn that it has created unfamiliar local institutions. He will soon hear about the summer bachelor, the forgotten man of American folklore.

To appreciate the pathos and charm of the summer bachelor, you have to learn the stages by which a normally jogging and contented husband becomes one. Last week, then, the family took off for our summer house at the end of Long Island. (This is a custom not restricted to what used to be called the upper-middle class. The continental mainland of the United States sweats abominably from May to October and any humane husband who is not fettered to the marriage bed will rent a shack anywhere in the mountains, by a lake or a seashore, as far as possible from Chicago, St Louis, Pittsburgh or a score of other infernos.) The induction into summer bachelorhood is almost as violent as the season that causes it. One day you are living in a normal house or apartment, with carpets, grocery deliveries, timed meals, friends and everything; and the next you'd think the Russians were coming. Your wife is out of bed like a rocket. She beats around the house like a beaver. 'Excuse me,' she says, as I am in the middle of a shrewd sentence on the typewriter, and up comes the carpet. Up come all the carpets. At 10 a.m. the kitchen doorbell buzzes and a huge man in an apron clomps in and, with the aid of three helpers, lugs the carpets away to be stored.

There is a clatter of china in the kitchen. All the civilized eating utensils are going into boxes and cocoons of tissue paper. My wife breaks in again and lifts a warning finger. She indicates one shelf and one drawer. 'There you are,' she says. For the next three months or more I am to use two cracked kitchen plates, a chipped saucer, drink my coffee out of a premature Coronation mug (Edward VIII) and stir it with a spoon bought fifty years ago by her mother, a relentless Southerner. It looks like a petrified alligator, and that is what it's meant to look like. It says on it, 'A present from Jacksonville, Florida'.

Now there is a noise not unlike the furious exhaust that sets in at the tenser moments of science-horror movies ('The radio-isotope, Fleming, throw the safety rod, man!'). It is a team of vacuum cleaners. I stumble into the living room, for it is in darkness. The curtains have come down and four shades have gone up, two white ones on the outside, two green ones inside. The nifty satin upholstery on the sofa is obscured by a dingy slipcover. So are all the upholstered chairs. The lamps are swathed in bedsheets, giving them the appearance of Arab sentinels. A screen is being pulled across the open entrance to the living room, and my wife gives the annual order: 'Stay out of here, remember!' (I have no theories about American wives. They are, so far as I'm concerned, wives.) A mountain of laundry is piling up in the hall. There is a tearing sound coming from the clothes closets – the winter clothes are being entombed in plastic hangers and all the clothes give off a characteristic smell. It used to be mothballs. You used to hear them rattle around in the night. Now they tinkle, for they roll up and down small perforated tins with hooks on them that hang on the racks. The closets are squirted with some noxious chemical, and the ones that contain the winter suits are dynamited with bombs of DDT. This may all sound very drastic. Alas, our insidious summer enemy is a beast unknown to a true temperate climate – the buffalo moth – and if you ignore him, you are apt to confront an interesting wardrobe in the fall, of garments that might have served as targets on a rifle range.

So now, the blankets are entombed, the sheets changed, rooms closed off, refrigerator defrosted and denuded of food (it looks neater that way, to my wife at least, when she returns in October). I am permitted to run the refrigerator sometime later and it will soon contain tins of beer, a mouldy tomato, a box of crackers, and some limes and lemons. Just before the family leaves, she issues the battle orders for the summer campaign: 'Always put the garbage out before you go to bed, never start on a new bottle of milk before you've finished the old one. Never go out and leave the windows open. Keep the shades drawn in the living room. Right?' Very good, General, and goodbye.

The winter cycle is completed the summers that the children go to camp. There is a special fuss to be made with duffel bags and blankets and swimming shorts and two blankets and name tapes. And you all go off to Grand Central Station and align your brood with one of the many regiments of children lined up and waiting for the call to their track and their train. And again you hear one of the most powerful folk songs of America. A stationmaster stands by a large board and he looks at a card in his hand that lists all the names of the camps and the platforms of their outgoing trains. Nine-thirty strikes. And he warms up his baritone and chants: 'Indian Summer – track nineteen. Shining Mountain – seventeen. Pine Grove – twenty-one. Camp Wawokeewe – nine. High Wind – fifteen. Meadow Lark – eighteen. Thunderbolt – twenty-nine.'

It is over. They are gone. You leap to a telephone and locate another displaced person. You bathe and shave and hear yourself singing forgotten songs of liberation. This first evening is unusually high-spirited. The drinks flow free and so does the coarse interchange of remarks about family life. You decide that your companion is a fine man you have tended to underestimate. Then you go home and recall with a start that you are on your own again. You hear your shoes crackle on the dust of the desert that is the long, dark hall. You peek into the living room and switch on a light. The standing lamp by the switch is a dim figure indeed. Its shade has been wrapped around with a fez of crinkly white paper, and it stands there like Lawrence of Arabia in ambush. You duck out and into the bedroom. The silence is chilling. You get a beer and read a little, or stay up and watch the late show, and then the late late show. At three you turn in, and at eight you feel terrible. Each weekend, you suffer the troop trains of the New Haven or Long Island Railroad and limp raggedly into the bosom of your family. On Monday it starts again.

At this point a suspicion will have crossed your mind that has certainly crossed the mind of the summer bachelor. Indeed, George Axelrod made a play about it and called it *The Seven Year Itch*. The title itself suggests a clinical thesis and we will leave it with its author. For most men it does not take seven years to recall that New York contains, among its martyred and lonely millions, an old girlfriend, or some agreeable but impeccable social worker, or some other honest female whose devotion to her work denies her the blissful exile your wife is now embarked on. Peter Arno captured and immortalized this suspicion – of yours – in a cartoon that showed a portly gent, one of those waggish Blimps with the spotted bow tie, marching smartly down Park Avenue with a very trig young woman on his arm. Coming up the avenue, and just level with him, is a majestic matron of about his age. 'Why, George Fitzgerald,' she cries, 'what*ever* keeps you in town?'

I will not blemish a family programme with any other comment than the thought that one of the most profound of all American idioms is that priceless old catchphrase: 'I love my wife but oh you kid.' I bring up this touchy subject because an accident of technology is, I think, about to produce a sociological revolution in the United States. And I know that you expect me to keep you up with sociological revolutions. The cause of this one is the air conditioner. In the old summer days, the summer bachelor went at weekends from the oven of his apartment to undressed days and what he thought of as cool nights. Now he leaves the ice-cool paradise of his apartment for the hot days and the dank nights and the midges and bugs of the country.

Two days ago, a Wednesday, I pressed the elevator button of my apartment house and as the door slid back it revealed the capacious frame of a neighbour of mine from the twelfth floor. He is a retired old gentleman, a notable fisherman and a solid but saucy character. I asked him what kept *him* in town in mid-week. 'Are you kidding?' he said. 'It's like the basin of the Ganges out there. I retreated to this wonderful apartment. And you know what? My wife showed up this morning. God damn!'

'If this goes on,' I said, 'it's going to play the devil with fishing.'

'Fishing nothing,' he said. 'It's going to play hell with marriage.'

It's a Democracy, Isn't It?

15 June 1951

I was standing on the corner of Lexington Avenue on a Sunday in May waiting for a bus. It was a gorgeous day, hot and golden, and there were not many people around. Sunday is more than a bearable day in New York because for one thing there are about a million less cars than usual. No trucks. Suburbanites in for the day pointing up and down and walking with their feet out. A couple of cabs parked outside a lunch-room, the drivers gone for a beer. A family or two hand in hand, taking the children off to the park. A well-dressed upper-crust couple coming across from Park Avenue also hand in hand – a very common sight in New York, for Americans are not much concerned in such matters with what looks proper or what the neighbours will think. A good day – the sort of day when, for all the panicky newspaper headlines, your faith in people, and their needs and inclinations, is restored.

Suddenly, I heard a ghost. It was a familiar ghost, an invisible man somewhere in mid-air saying in a brisk monotone – 'Strike. The count is two and two. Runners on first and third.' This lingo, or the language of which this is a snatch, is something you would hear in a hundred places – homes, cafés, saloons, cars – from then till the end of the first week in October. It is a radio sports announcer covering a ball game – a ball game being, as you probably know, a baseball game.

The voice was coming from nowhere. A young Negro couple, arm in arm, was ambling towards me. But the man's free arm carried a little box. Of course, it was a portable radio. They went down the subway steps, and as they pattered down into the darkness the voice went on floating up, more excited now: 'A base hit to left field. Fuselli's in, Rodgers coming into third.' Nobody else on the street seemed to notice or to care. But if you had cared, and wanted for one day to get away from radio, I don't know where you could have gone. Out at

Coney Island, thousands of bodies would be lying in close proximity not only to thousands of other bodies but to hundreds of other little boxes, tuned high. And the air would be so full of 'He's out' and 'The bases are loaded' and 'Full count', that you'd have had quite a time knowing what the wild waves were saying.

This little picture is meant to produce a shudder in you. If it doesn't, then Britons are not what they used to be, and their passion for privacy, and what's more for respecting the next man's privacy, is dead and gone. Don't misunderstand me. I approve myself very strongly of this feeling. I share it. But it makes me all the less of an American. Only a week ago, I heard a plonking sound, allied to music, quite faint, coming up through the living room floor. It was a neighbour in our apartment house who is either 6 years of age and a promising pianist or 40 years of age and a dope . . . because she – why do I say 'she', I wonder? – has been stuck on that same piece for a month or two now. I grumbled about the sameness of her repertory, and my 12-year-old daughter, idling over a book, said, 'Relax, Pop, you don't have to hear it if you don't want to.'

By this simple remark my daughter didn't mean that I could get up and go downstairs and start a riot, or that I could call the police or take out an injunction. She simply meant I should shut my mind to the sound. I made sure this is what she meant, because when I played aloud with the idea of strangling our tinkling neighbour, she said, 'I don't think that's very nice. She paid *her* rent too, you know.'

Now, I should like to say that I am proud of my daughter and usually turn to her for a response that is commonsensical and unshocked (by, so far as I can make out, anything in life). But I wasn't aware she had acquired so young a fundamental mood or attitude of what Americans call democracy. In Britain, one of the minor duties of good citizenship is not to disturb the private life of other citizens. In this country, it's the other way around – not to disturb other citizens who are enjoying their private life in public. That, as you see, is a heavily loaded interpretation of an attitude that is universal among Americans. And there are limits. Just the same, the decision of a Washington court of appeal not to let advertisers broadcast in public buses only shows how far you can go in America without being stopped.

Americans regard most of us born in Britain as dull, decent, amiable people but given to being rather testy about our rights. So 'Relax, Pop,' says my daughter and goes back to reading her book with one third of her mind, listening to the pianist downstairs with another lobe, and at the same time dreaming on all cylinders about some absent male of the species. Quite aside from the principle involved, this attitude entails a considerable physical feat. It is the ability not to hear what you don't want to hear, what the most famous radio critic in America calls 'selective deafness'. He says it is a faculty essential to an enjoyment of American radio, and it is a faculty that most visiting Britons would rather not develop. Because they soon learn, as Mr Crosby – John, not Bing – remarks, that the advertising people are aware of this conditioned reflex and so from year to year, like drug addicts, they increase the dose of the sales talk they cut into the programmes. Still, nobody hearing his favourite comedian or forum discussion or symphony concert bothers to turn off the 'plug'. He lets it chatter on about some soap that 'atomizes dirt' or a toothpaste that is 'kind to gums but murder on film'. And then, the ecstatic announcer stops, and so back to Bob Hope or 'Whither Europe?' or the Second Symphony of Beethoven.

To watch an American on a beach, or crowding into a subway, or buying a theatre ticket, or sitting at home with his radio on, tells you something about one aspect of the American character: the capacity to withstand a great deal of outside interference, so to speak; a willing acceptance of frenzy which, though it's never self-conscious, amounts to a willingness to let other people have and assert their own lively, and even offensive, character. They are a tough race in this. You are expected – far beyond what other peoples would say were the restraints of manners – to assume that one man's opinion is as good as another's. The expert is an American idol, but only in certain understood fields. He is safe from contradiction if his expertness is in a science – in medicine, technology, industrial research, or in making something with his hands (better, if he uses somebody else's hands, because that shows he has mastered a process which can be left to drones): such things as an automobile, a waterproof watch or a non-riding girdle. But when it comes to ideas about life and love and religion and education and architecture and painting and music, indeed all forms of pleasure, there is a national conviction that an expert is a phoney, or 'wants to be different', and that what matters is you should know what you like and – this is a democracy, isn't it? – speak up and say your piece. It may well be born from generations of living close to many races and many prejudices and temperaments and having to strike a liveable compromise that may not be as smooth as some other societies; but at least it is a society, a going concern, which had to be built not out of a theory but out of the urgent practical need to get along at all.

At any rate, if you want to live here in any spiritual comfort you have to allow for a wide variety of temperament in your friends and neighbours and approve a sharp clash of tastes. An insistence on privacy in such a society looks, as it would not look in Britain, like a form of conceit or neurosis, a refusal to admit the status quo by which you all live. So if the issue ever came up in argument, I think most Americans would say that it is merely elementary good manners and good citizenship to look on yourself as only one member of the community, whether that community is a town, a party, or a family.

It may be what makes Americans so easygoing about their children. I don't know if anyone has ever taken a statistical count, and there may be just as many nagging parents here as anywhere else, but my impression is that if you are what they used to call a severe disciplinarian with children, you get known to the neighbours as a crank. There is a sort of cheerful, unstated assumption that children will grow up and be polite soon enough and that there's no sense for the first fifteen years or so in pretending they are anything but inhabitants of the jungle. (There is a certain family pride in seeing your child become king or queen of the jungle.) The children themselves are of course not aware of being particularly bad or violent or ill-mannered. They have no other system to compare themselves with, and like all children don't even know that any other system exists. Remembering this, you can appreciate that if a 6- or a 10- or a 15-year-old passes you on the street, looks up and says, 'Hi!' he is paying you far more the respect of genuine liking than if he said, 'Good morning, sir' – which would be a very alien, not to say sarcastic, sound in these parts.

The same sort of tolerance explains too, I think, such a seemingly irrelevant thing as the variety of men's clothes in a big city. There is not among Americans anything remotely resembling the uniform of the English city businessman. They dress for themselves, with their own tastes in ties, shirts, shoes; and this gives to an American street a colour, often a garishness, and it makes it pretty impossible for a foreigner to guess at the occupation of the other men around. With women, it is even more difficult. A flock of girls comes into a restaurant and you can't tell the debutante from the shop girl. I remember a Swedish girl on a skiing party watching the swirl of people in the snow and saying, 'Which are the nice people? Who are my kind? Give me a sign.' There are signs. But they are small and subtle and would take her years to learn. And if she stayed here long, she would insensibly shed the signs she sought.

I was taking an Englishman the other night up to my apartment, and as we approached the entrance of the apartment house, I saw a man who lives in the building polishing the radiator of his car. I hissed to call my friend's attention to him as we came close. 'Tell me quick,' I said, 'what sort of an American is this – I mean is he a banker, a real-estate agent, a baseball player or what? – look him over.' My friend leered politely at him sideways. He was a middle-aged dark man, with a black moustache and big eyes. He was hatless. He had on a blue sports coat, slacks of a different colour, a button-down collar and a bright tie. He was polishing away and coughing smoke all over the radiator. Then he bent down to start on the wheels. Standing genially over him was the janitor, saying the utterly meaningless sentence, as we came on it: 'No, sir, not for my money . . . but some guys are that crazy, I reckon.' When we got inside I looked at my friend.

'Oh, I don't know,' he said, 'I should say an advertising man or perhaps the owner of a chain of drugstores.'

'That,' I said, as we went into the lift, 'is a dethroned Archduke.'

He was dethroned by the bullet that shot his great-uncle and started the First World War.

The European's America

23 October 1952

It is the fall. The fall of the year, an American institution now so well known, and even respected, in Europe that you no doubt expect me to take off, as I annually do, about the scarlet maples pouring like a fire through New England, the brilliant light everywhere, the thin milky trails of woodsmoke that rise into a bottomless blue sky. Well, once you've created a stereotype it is time to demolish it. The fall has refinements, even perils, that the autumn in other countries does not share. Once you've learned the big clichés of a country, which are true and which are not, it is the off-beat clichés that really fix the place in your mind, and make it like no other, and may even endear it to you, years later in another country far away. Let me illustrate.

The other morning, just after breakfast, a lady by the name of Miss Frieda Sims was going her rounds on the twenty-seventh floor of a New York hotel. Miss Sims is a floor supervisor and she was looking to see which rooms were vacant, which ones the maids could get into to clean up, which rooms needed to have the breakfast tables removed. She unlocked room number 2752, peeked in and saw the happy disorder of breakfast dishes. She went in to wheel the table out, but she came out in a hurry with no table, and she was screaming.

This sounds like the beginning of one of those classic American crimes, like Miss Lizzie Borden going into the kitchen on a very hot morning to get a cup of coffee. And it goes on promisingly enough, because the next incident involves the hotel's security force, which came running and verified Miss Sims's report. She had stopped screaming by now and she was able to stammer out that there was somebody in there. It wasn't a guest, not like any guest she had ever seen. It was an owl, just a common or garden American barn owl (*Strix flammea* to the initiated), which looks rather like an African wood carving or the top of a totem pole. It seems the owl was just cruising by the hotel at a twenty-seven-storey altitude (there's the New York touch), saw the open window, glanced in at the breakfast dishes and decided to make a landing on the remains of a melon and a couple of shirred eggs. The commissars of the security force (what, before the iron curtain, we just used to call house dicks) evidently made the bird secure. They threw a blanket over it. Then they telephoned the SPCA, which seems a contradictory thing to do, since they were busy smothering the owl. However, a Mr Norton soon came up from the Society with his equipment, a pair of thick gloves; for you should know that the American barn owl has a four-foot wingspread, a curved beak, and what the New York *Herald Tribune* (which gets its reporters into the damnedest places) described with relish as 'razor-sharp talons'.

Mr Norton put his gloves on, embraced the owl with professional tenderness, took it off into the park and set it free. This fugitive from the world of freedom got tangled up in twentieth-century civilization, but within half an hour a man put his hand in the air and the bird flew away in one swoop back to the primitive world from which we all originally came. There is a technical snag to this fable. An eye surgeon tells me that no owl, however wise, could look into a hotel room after breakfast. The owl, it seems, is a kind of hotel dick in its own right and can look into hotel rooms only at night. I see that Audubon noted this over a hundred years ago. 'Owls', he wrote, 'seem to us a dull and stupid race, principally because we only notice them during the day, which nature requires them to spend in sleep, the structure of their eyes compelling them to avoid the light and seek concealment in hollow trees, in caves and obscure retreats.'

What started out as a children's story, then, full of sweetness and light, is in fact a near-tragedy. This bird was lost and plunging through a blinding world of light and saw a barn, an obscure retreat, which turned out – pitifully – to be Room 2752 of a New York skyscraper.

This is the kind of story that could only happen in the fall. There is, indeed, a special anxiety that overtakes bird-lovers then, when the great migrations to the South begin. Many fine species have not yet heard about the invention of the skyscraper, and some ordinary birds are even wildly attracted to it. The starlings, for instance. It is a happy fall during which flocks of starlings don't smash into the Empire State Building, which is four times the height of the tallest California redwood and higher than any building anywhere, even – I'm afraid – in the Soviet Union. (When the jet aeroplane came in, there was a more perilous hazard from the starlings. In several crashes, it came out that they had been sucked into the engines.) These accidents have a poignant appeal to anyone who, in the fall, has to work in a city and who knows that beyond the city limits lies a world crammed with colour and beauty and old habits that unfortunately play no part in the European picture of that detested 'American way of life'.

The day before the barn owl flew into the hotel, I was reading a piece in an American magazine by Mr Cyril Connolly, a writer with whom I feel a strong sympathy and never more than in this piece, which was about the widespread Americanizing of Europe. What are those influences which many Europeans think of as all America has to offer, and which they wish had stayed on this side of the Atlantic? Connolly lists them: 'jazz, gangster stories, bad films, tales of violence, science fiction'. I could add some others, especially the compulsion to break up the relics of London as an eighteenth-century country town and riddle them with chromium-plated fronts and dingy 'American' snack bars and amusement arcades and the tattiest attempts at modern 'American' architecture. Not to mention the Cockney's surrender to what he imagines is American slang, the frantic imitation bebop, the transatlantic zoot-suiter. The point is that these influences, picked up I suppose from the movies, are almost always bad imitations of crummy originals. What is alarming, and what the European seems unaware of, is that they are often planted firmly in a solid English background, in the sort of place they would not be found in the American background. They do not have chrome cocktail bars along the noble stretch of North Street, in Litchfield, Connecticut, or snack bars at the bottom of Zion Canyon. Along the new motor parkways of New York and New England they do not even allow the petrol companies to build their own pumps. The stations, like the overpasses, must conform to a design sanctioned by the commissioner of parks or highways and be made of the local stone. And the fences that bind the parkways are the same for a hundred miles or more and are made from a pine that fits the landscape. It is an unexpected and admirable thing about the development of the automobile age in America that Americans have developed a sense of style as watchful as that of the men who gave us the urban style of eighteenth-century London and the country style of eighteenth-century New England. (The billboard lobby and the freeways are now doing their damnedest to date this compliment.)

I sometimes think that a European deploring the horror of Pittsburgh and Detroit and St Louis and 'your Midwest cities' is not really criticizing the Midwest or American cities but the nineteenth-century city anywhere. But it is also a fact that though American towns may, and do, seethe with the random horrors that are now so faithfully transplanted to British towns, it is almost easier over here to get away from them. My European visitors are always surprised to discover how much virgin forest there appears to be on the edge of town. Theoretically, there are only two big stands of the forest primeval in this country, one in the Cascade Mountains and the other in the Bitterroots, both far out on the northwest Pacific Coast. But I'm thinking of long-settled country. I have taken Englishmen in a car fifteen minutes from where I am talking to you and once beyond the George Washington Bridge they are weaving around great rocks and little woods as dense as the New Forest. A half-hour from Times Square (all right, then, two hours in the rush hour) they can be in something that looks like Fenimore Cooper country, and it is not hard to imagine on dark nights an Indian slipping through the trees, slinking across the six-lane divided highway and standing as aghast at the lights of Manhattan as I am when I see what the 'developers' have done to Regency Mayfair.

For nearly two centuries now, there has been a continuous argument, sometimes amiable sometimes bloodthirsty, about which country was influencing the other the most. Until about fifty years ago, the example was all one way, and the way was east to west. But it has been changing very fast. Every world power leaves indelible imprints even on countries that pretend to hate it. And as Europe comes to admit, which it soon will have to, that the United States is now the ranking world power, its customs and gadgets and manners and literature and ways of doing business will powerfully influence the young. They may reject it later on, as Europe pulls itself around and asserts again, as I don't doubt it will want to, its own pride and independence.

But in the meantime, Britain still retains an advantage which will not pass over to America, I think, for a long time to come. It is this:

Americans who have not been in Europe tend to imagine what is best about her, Europeans who have not been in America tend to imagine what is worst. Ask a few simple Americans what Britain means – ask a schoolgirl, a farmer, a shopkeeper, an elevator man (I have just tried it) what comes to mind when you say 'Britain' – and they will say something like: 'Oh, old buildings, more easygoing than us, I guess, beautiful countryside, tea in the afternoon, Shakespeare'; and, as my elevator man added, 'And I understand they are very dignified, very strict, they tell me, in their law courts.'

This may sound very naive to you. But it picks up a flattering myth and not, like the other way around, a libellous one. My own daughter, 14 years old, swings violently between wanting to go to England and being afraid to. Why does she want to go? Because she imagines the place peopled with Mr Pickwick and Romeo and Juliet and Robin Hood, not to mention Laurence Olivier; and because she is crazy about the tables that Sheraton designed and the chairs and desks of Hepplewhite and imagines that every little house in England would throw out anything less graceful. She has, indeed, heard rude things about the cooking. But I tell her that this is steadily improving. I tell her also that it is true about the parklike countryside and the fat cattle, and the sheep as big as buffaloes in Scotland, and it is due as much as anything to the fact that the grass pack of English dairyland is five times as dense as the proud grass pack of Iowa. She thinks the English countryside must be heaven. (By the way, she takes entirely for granted the stupendous beauty of the Tetons and the desert and Yosemite, which leave Englishmen feeling that they have come face to face with their Maker.)

And why *doesn't* she want to go to England? Well, she explains, wriggling nervously, 'Everyone would expect me to be on my best behaviour, they are so polite and – everything.'

This is quite a reputation the British have built up. And the other tourist countries of Europe are not far behind. We read here about the exquisite care the French take over their food, and the dedicated way they tread on their grapes, and the devotion they bring to their public buildings. We do not hear about the really garish modern housing that begins to sprout in the Parisian suburbs, or about the alarming incapacity of the French for self-government. We read about the ruthlessness of the Mafia as it goes about its business in New York or New Orleans but not about its stranglehold on the enslaved slum of Sicily. From Italy we read rather about the preciousness of a new Roman 'find' in Tuscany or about the charm of the Appian Way, not about the clutter of billboards that disfigures it.

It will surely be a great day when you ask an Englishman what comes to mind at the mention of the word 'America' and he replies: 'The white villages of New England and the eighteenth-century houses, the neighbourly warmth of the Midwesterners, the contributions of American scholarship, the buffet meals that young American house-wives whip up, the style and colour of so many American homes, the outdoor life of California, the god-given glory of Bryce Canyon and the man-made marvel of Hoover Dam.'

Getting Away from It All

11 September 1953

The real end of the American year is not 31 December, but the old festival of Labor Day. It is the day when the summer is put away, the swimming trunks squeezed for the last time, the ashtrays in country cottages filled with mouse-seed and rat-paste, the storm-doors hammered into place, the lock turned for the last time on your private world of sun and sand and picnics and the pride of growing children. Labor Day brings you back to the world of schools and offices, to sniffling colds and insurance policies, to taxes and radio commentators, to dark nights and the dark horizon of politics.

We sat around for the last time in our cottage at the end of Long Island. We had brought in the furniture from off the porch and the rusty barbecue grill we haven't used in four years but always put out in the sun at the beginning of summer as a symbol of our pioneer instincts. We had phoned the electric company to turn off the current.

Called the phone company to disconnect same. Left a note for the garbage-man, same for the milkman. What else has to be done? Defrost and clean the refrigerator. Draw the curtains across the windows on the east and west sides. Sprinkle moth-flakes on the rugs. Try to hide a smelly fishing rod in a dark closet, and fail – your wife coming at you saying, 'Could this be bait?' It is. It is a poor, dried-up piece of squid that was chewed on by a whole school of porgies and sucked dry.

We sit around finishing a last bite. The baby is snoring placidly in a house reeking of camphor and good old mouse-paste. We bury and burn the last load of garbage. We pack the car while we wait for the baby to wake. Some of the grasses on the dunes have started to turn the fall colours. So children who normally treat them as considerately as bulldozers now develop a collector's passion for bayberry and pine branches and feather-grass. Somebody sees a gramophone record worn so grey you'd think it had been played with a poker. It is 'Good Night, Irene', and it too is suddenly an object of tenderness. We finally leave, with the rear end of the borrowed station wagon looking like an army camouflage squad, bushes and plants and a bedstead growing out of each side of 'Good Night, Irene'. We are on our way.

We stop and say goodbye to Mrs Horton, who sells eggs and collects antiques and whose family has farmed the same plot since 1649 – not so hot, perhaps, to a European, but impressive to us. We wish a good winter to the Ryskos, who sell groceries; to Grathwohl, the builder and sometime carpenter; to the Doroski brothers, who run a gas and service station; to Josie Wanowski, the little bent old toothless Polish woman who has taken in washing these many years and for many of them kept a crippled husband, and who raised four astonishingly handsome children, two straight beautiful girls with shining teeth, who might be movie starlets but are in fact a nurse and a schoolteacher; two boys, one in college, one ex-army air forces.

It is much the same as any other leave-taking in the fall. But there is an ominous note or two. The bank manager is off to Riverhead: there is a meeting of the new civil defence evacuation committee – a committee, that is, to plan the evacuation of doomed New Yorkers to the potato-fields of Long Island. A young man who came out of the Navy four years ago, who chose to be a potato-farmer the year of the big drought and went into debt for $2,000, is not around any more.

His troubles were all scattered by a letter one morning from the President of the United States, beginning – 'Greetings!' – a cordial invitation to come back into the service, or else. Eddie, the boy who drives the grocer's delivery truck, says 'Well, I'd better say goodbye', in a strange, shy way. He too has had his call.

These little things give you a shock, and you wonder about them on the way up to the city. Everything looks like the familiar fall, the maples turning, a milky stream of smoke from burning leaves curling up into a blue, bottomless sky. But as the swift twilight comes on we are at the end of the parkway, past La Guardia Field, over the Triboro Bridge, and there are the vertical city and the plunging spires: New York again, splendid as ever in the autumn light. Not quite the same, though. We curve round and down off the bridge and pass a billboard advertising a new de luxe apartment building somewhere. The big sign has stars against the features it is specially proud of: thermostat heat control in each flat; all-electric kitchen, with deep freeze, laundry and dish-washing machines, and garbage-disposal unit; air-conditioned units available in summer; two bathrooms for every four rooms. The last item, the last star, says: 'Adequate sub-basement atomic bomb-shelter'. One of the children reads it aloud, and it makes a pompous sound, so that the baby claps her hands and chortles like a wise old man. And we all laugh.

Back in the city, people with copper tans who ought to be congratulating themselves on being able in the first place to get away from the New York summer, began in recent years to find themselves fingering the real-estate sections of the Sunday papers and peering through advertisements for 'desirable country houses'. Why should lucky and comfortable people be so fretful and restless for more idleness? It was not idleness such people sought but a more dreadful thing: safety. Lately the phrase 'getting away from it all' has taken on a sadder and more furtive meaning in the minds of parents who live in industrial cities. It needs no winks or meaningful glances to arouse a fear that everybody feels and a few talk openly about. It is the padding fear of the atom bomb.

I heard of a man who lives in Washington who had quit his job, fallen back on his savings, bought a little place deep in the hills of

Arkansas and gone off there to farm with his wife and five children. Far off in the Black Hills of South Dakota, some pessimist as thoughtful as Noah has bought a mountain cave and invited prudent couples – one male, one female – to abandon their regular lives and batten down underground at an annual cost of $2,500 per person, all found. This may appear to be the furthest pole of lunacy. But during the San Francisco organizing conference of the United Nations, the citizens of the Black Hills, bidding for a lasting fame as the chosen headquarters of the United Nations, challenged the delegations with maps (Dakotas projection) to find a spot anywhere in the United States more swiftly accessible by air to Moscow, Cairo, Tokyo or London. Maybe this pessimist was acting from the same melancholy discovery.

Then in the late 1940s businessmen caught the epidemic. Businessmen, I should say, who have factories in the East, in the ring of cities round the southern rim of the Great Lakes, or out on the Coast. An aircraft company in Bridgeport, Connecticut, announced it had decided to move bag and baggage to Dallas, Texas. Now, this is quite an undertaking. The company worked on 1.5 million square feet. Its factory cost $10 million. It employed about ten thousand people. The company invited its skilled workers to go with it. As an American migration, this one would not be without its epic and humorous side. Bridgeport is a typical New England industrial city, except for the untypical fact that it has a socialist government. Its workers are mostly of Italian and Czech, Hungarian and Polish stock. They are used to cold winters and New England ways. It would be quite a sight to see them in West Texas, mimicking the Texas accent, being baffled by the Mexican foods, wondering when the hot dry winds of spring and the steaming misery of summer would ever end in – as the song says – 'that Texas town that never seen ice or snow'. For a few excitable weeks, the unskilled men had a happy time joshing their superior brothers who had signed up to go. They bandied around the nicknames Sagebrush, and Tex, and 'Hi, there, Dallas!' Jokers appeared in ten-gallon hats and called a work-gang 'you-all'. But however gay the workers felt, the company's announcement caused a nasty jolt to other defence industries along the East Coast. Any company that would make a move as dramatic and costly as that must, they figured, have 'heard something'. The Defense Department was rattled by telephone enquiries verging between anxiety and hysteria. The callers were told in as non-committal a way as possible that there was no 'immediate' plan to go underground, to move industrial cities, to decentralize the basic industries that surround the Great Lakes. It was made officially plain that the Bridgeport company had made up its own mind and the National Security Resources Board had given its nod. The company's work had to do with testing jet-planes, and the directors had decided that the congested seaboard was a poor place to accommodate, without an expensive new airport, the special and alarming habits of jets. The Texas central plain is – if Texans will pardon the expression – flatter than Kansas. It seemed just right. But many industries, big and little, leaped to the conclusion which they dread and which – by the peculiar chemistry of deep fear – they half-hope to have fulfilled.

The telling point about the Bridgeport story is, I think, the current emotional disposition to believe the worst. The atomic age offers us the raw material of a civilization larger, more efficient and more humane than any that has gone before. But this promise and this challenge are lost sight of in the energy that goes and must go into making weapons of war. This energy has the real excuse that never before in history have free men faced the threat of a tyranny so large, so merciless and so painstaking as that with which the Soviet Union confronts us. Dangling between these two unique worlds – a world of unequalled slavery and a world of incomparable riches – we build the storm-cellars and hope for the best.

Most men find the problems of political power insoluble and tend to despair before a world that has shrunk in scale and enlarged in complexity, so that the knowledge of how it behaves seems more and more to be open only to the specialist. There never was a time, except perhaps in the fearful pestilences of the Middle Ages, when men hungered more for a decent private life, and when they are tempted to match in their joys the intensity of the sorrows all around them. I believe that this impulse, far from being an escape, is the only right way of asserting that human dignity which gives sense to the phrase 'an appetite for life'. What reasonable hope can an ordinary man have for himself and his family? Must we oscillate like crocodiles between panic and apathy? What more adult way is there of coming to terms with the alternatives of the atomic age?

I should like to have the wisdom and the knowledge to suggest something at once practical and noble. But all I can think of is an incident from the American past that comes nearer to home every day and seems to me as sensible as anything written since Hiroshima.

The time was 19 May 1780. The place was Hartford, Connecticut. The day has gone down in New England history as a terrible foretaste of Judgement Day. For at noon the skies turned from blue to grey and by mid-afternoon had blackened over so densely that, in that religious age, men fell on their knees and begged a final blessing before the end came. The Connecticut House of Representatives was in session. And as some men fell down and others clamoured for an immediate adjournment, the Speaker of the House, one Colonel Davenport, came to his feet. He silenced them and said these words: 'The Day of Judgement is either approaching or it is not. If it is not, there is no cause for adjournment. If it is, I choose to be found doing my duty. I wish, therefore, that candles may be brought.'

Ladies and gentlemen, let candles be brought.

The Court and the Negro

20 August 1954

When I first went South, I was in the South but didn't know it. I was on my first visit to the home, and the home country, of my first American college friend, who is now a doctor in Maryland and was brought up on the edge of a beautiful valley outside Baltimore. (Today only a couple of golf courses hold the landscape against the encircling post-war suburbia and a maze of freeways.)

This man holds a special place in the history of my friendships because in the early 1930s he was a tolerant and amiable teacher about all things American. He instructed me in the wry, and often barefaced, realities of city and state government. We had a common interest in jazz and maintained it against the prevailing conviction of ninety-nine college boys in a hundred that Ellington, Louis Armstrong, and other combinations were 'dinge stuff', that is to say a minority fad indulged in by Negroes. He had an affectionate knowledge of the local trees and flowers and first showed me something of the variety of American oaks, and introduced me to the pink and white dogwood and the Maryland golden aster. He was also responsible for my first taste of crab cakes and terrapin stew and for easing me into the pleasing custom, on hot summer nights, of spreading a newspaper on a table on the back porch at midnight, slicing a watermelon into quarters, and lolling back and burying your face in a quadrant till you came up for air with a drooling sound and paused to spit seeds at the moths.

Many of these pleasures came our way through the stealthy solici-tude of Miss Minn. Miss Minn was the cook, first maid, second maid, laundress, nurse, cleaning woman, mother confessor and hub of the household. She was the first Negro I ever knew and to this day is a great mystery. Even twenty years ago she admitted to no age. She was rumoured to be a grandmother, though she never seemed to know how many times. She was not so much an employee in the house as a presence, like a clock that never tells you it's there until it strikes the hour. And hours would go by without any thought of Miss Minn, for she made no noise at all until you began to search for a newspaper or felt hungry or thought aloud that a glass of beer would be just the thing. At such times she would amble through the room or the garden like a forgotten ghost, accidentally bearing the newspaper or a tray with two beers. She was never called and was never out of reach, giving the impression – whether you were upstairs or downstairs, in the garden or the kitchen – that the house was loaded with Miss Minns.

She had no politics, no grievances and – I almost said – no life of her own. But much of the raillery and lazy banter that went back and forth between the family and Miss Minn was about another existence, the echoes of which drifted to us from the edge of our world and the beginning of hers. It was – to us – a very vague, timeless world that sounded, from the hints she dropped, like the libretto of a low-life opera; in which husbands came and went, forgotten sons turned up from distant places, stayed over a carefree weekend and consumed festival meals of snapper turtle, whole crabs dunked in beer, steaks as big as doormats, and then left and showed up again a month or a year later as buck privates, or on crutches from a car crash, or with a new wife and two children. Miss Minn never went into this side of her life for more than a couple of sentences and I honestly don't know when she managed to live it except on certain weekends, when she was off and the family was reduced to camping out of the icebox. Her own style of talk conveyed that these sons and lovers and erupting relations were creatures of the imagination who flitted like elves or stray animals through a shadowy forest.

Miss Minn had been with my friend's family for thirty years and expected to die with them. She is the last of an ancient breed. I don't believe that if you put the question to her she would have had any notion what you meant by 'the Negro problem'. She might have asked, 'Which Negro?' For all her vaguely suggested problems were about a particular person in the here and now. To me, a new arrival in the country, Negroes were at once a rooted part of the landscape and a fascinating novelty. The 'white' and 'coloured' signs on the doors of waiting rooms, toilets, and the automatic retreat of coloured people to the back of buses and theatres were a shock, but this was the Americans' country and maybe they knew best.

If this sounds callous now, let me say that the mass of people at any given time are rarely better than their lights. And I picked up the attitude of my friends, which in the North was one of lumping the Negroes with poor people everywhere and overcoming the unconscious discomfort of this attitude by praising with particular warmth any Negro who had pulled himself out of the morass of his race with a special talent: a Negro pianist, dancer, poet.

My friends in the South had a quite different feeling. The Negroes were close to their lives, the essential servant, handyman, labour pool, but also confidant, childhood friend, licensed clown, grumbler. The great mass of Negroes who grew the cotton and tobacco and ploughed their squalid little farms were off there somewhere over the horizon. Their lot was wretched but we didn't think about it too much; the legend was passed down from generation to generation that they could put up with squalor much better than us (they had to) and that they mostly maintained a happy-sad temperament with bouts of fine singing.

The experience of the South was to come later, but Maryland is of the South if not in it, and just now I might have been talking about the Miss Minns of Louisiana or Alabama. I wasn't aware of this at the time, and the distinction between the North and South didn't come up until one night we were cruising around the countryside in the north of the state and I happened to remark to my friend that there were no Negroes around, in any of the small towns where I had seen them by day. My friend said, 'No? Let me show you something.' He turned down a side road and circled back to town, and just where the open country was planted with the first outposts of the suburbs he stopped the car, and where four roads met he beckoned me to a tree. Nailed to a fence was a wooden board and on it had been crudely painted: 'Nigger, don't let the sun set on you here.'

We were very close to the northern boundary of Maryland; we were, in fact, standing at the Mason and Dixon line, which divided the slave states from the so-called free soil to the North before the Civil War. This imaginary line is named after two English surveyors, Charles Mason and Jeremiah Dixon, who in 1767 settled an old colonial boundary dispute by defining once for all the southern border of Pennsylvania. This is a precise explanation, but to any American you might stop on a street today, the Mason and Dixon line is the division between two Americas, two worlds, two social systems.

Maryland was neutral in the Civil War. It is a border state. Many industries and customs are Northern, but once you get south of Pennsylvania, the vowels are slurred, the voices are less strident, the coats come off in the summertime, the Negroes are everywhere, and the white man is boss. He is, with shuddering exceptions among the poor whites, a more indulgent and considerate boss than the more vocal Northern liberals could ever be. They like to storm about the smugness and insensitivity of the Southerners, but they do not often get within hailing distance of a Negro they might help to take for a friend. Perhaps one Negro is the wrong unit, because self-conscious liberals and literary bohemians have regularly made a point of cultivating any pet Negro who is foolish enough to stand in as a sop to their conscience.

Now of the many Southern words that reflect the separate life of the South, none has been more taken for granted than the word 'segregation'. I know Southerners who have been brought up to give time and money and pride to the legal protection or the neighbourly defence of the Negroes who work for them. Their children and the local coloured children are close playmates (in a way that Northerners rarely are) up to the age of puberty. But if you ever suggested that their children should go to the same school as the Negroes, they would throw a fit. Well, they're going to throw a fit.

For, as everyone has heard by now, the Supreme Court of the United States has just (17 May 1954) handed down a judgement that I should think is going to cause the most revolutionary change in American social life since, eighty-six years ago, the Court decided that Negroes were American citizens like any other and were entitled to the equal protection of the laws of the United States. The Country was saved from the thunderbolt that has just descended on it by a reservation that the Court made: the status of the Negro was to be equal 'but separate'.

But today the Court recalled the famous phrase of an old judge who defended that earlier ruling. 'The Constitution', he said, 'is colour-blind.' So it is, but the people who hope to live by it are not. And in the Southland, whose sad and profound culture antedates the Constitution by nearly a hundred and fifty years, many generations of Americans have been brought up not necessarily to believe that the Negro is an inferior human being (no Southern Catholic, I hope, would be brought up to believe any such thing) but to believe with Abraham Lincoln that 'the physical differences between the white and black races (I believe) will for ever forbid the two races living together on terms of social and political equality, and inasmuch as they cannot so live, while they do remain together there must be the position of superior and inferior ... I am not, nor ever have been, in favour of making voters or jurors of Negroes, nor of qualifying them to hold office, nor to intermarry with white people ... I, as much as any other man, am in favour of having the superior position assigned to the white race.'

That was spoken nearly a hundred years ago and it is, no doubt, unfair to Lincoln to imply that he would feel the same way today. But it is not ridiculous to think so. Millions of decent – should we now say 'otherwise decent'? – Americans think and feel so, in the South and far from it.

It is hard in a few minutes to take up this challenge to the instincts and traditions of a whole region without doing its people a clumsy injustice. From much travel – and stopping – around the United States, I have to say that I respect more the considerate relations that many Southerners have with the Negroes around them than the glib 'social consciousness' of Northerners and Westerners whose daily life has a guaranteed immunity from Negro problems, either because there are few of them around or because they exist conveniently in some tight, slummy corner of the big city. It is one thing to talk about equality in New York or Oregon and live it in Alabama, where one person in three is coloured, or in Mississipi, where there are one million whites and one million Negroes.

So, in the South, and in the Deep South most of all, the mere force of numbers is a threat, if only in the minds of men, to the political and social dominance of the white man. When people, even the gentlest people, fear that they might be terrified or intimidated, they tend to take terrifying precautions. I am not thinking of the understandable misgivings of those Southerners who remember, through the books or through a grandfather, the Negro soldiers who patrolled the beaten South or the state legislatures run in the main by Negroes. I am thinking of something simpler and more universal. In the places where there are many Negroes the black man is invested with the force – the threatening force – of a myth. The daily experience of white people may deny this myth but in their secret heart it has great vitality. It is an image of a black man who is a little slow in his wits, terrible in anger, and above all potent (there's the rub). The scientists have proved this to be nonsense, but, even after a Supreme Court decision, human beings trust their intuition more than the demonstrable truth that their intuition is moonshine. Some of this fear of the Negro may be only the cover-up for the guilt the white man feels for the way he has treated the Negro. But I think the central fear is something else, a fear so embarrassing that white mothers whisper it to each other and intellectuals fretting over 'the Negro problem' will not deign to consider it. It is summed up in the old folk question, muttered behind the palm of the hand: 'Would you want your daughter to marry a N-E-G-R-O?'

The revered Lincoln saw only one solution to the problem of the Negroes' suffering: colonization somewhere in an unsettled land. The late, detested Senator Bilbo of Mississippi saw two possible solutions: 'Separation or Mongrelization'. At the moment, it would be difficult to advocate or argue these solutions and be taken seriously. But it seems to me, at least, frivolous and superficial not to face the fact that after a generation or so of mixed schooling, social barriers will tumble, young people will pick their friends for themselves, they will fall in love, as they do everywhere, with the girls and boys around them.

This is a consummation which is at present being devoutly ignored. The traditions of American life are strong enough, *so far*, to make intermarriage prohibitive in the thirty-one states where white and coloured do go to the same schools. Oddly, it is in the South, where the races are separated in school and church and in theatres, that the Negro is woven deep into the texture of society. And it is in the South that the test will come of whether the white man can live and work with the black man as a social and political equal and create a new kind of American society which has at last relaxed the powerful tensions of three hundred years. In the exhilaration of the Supreme Court's trumpet call, we should not, I think, expect too much of whites, now or later. We can only say that to proclaim the attempt at a new American society should give tremendous pause to the racial propaganda that rages over Asia. If it works, 1954 will come to be a date in history as momentous as the year of Magna Carta.

The Colonel of the Plains

21 April 1955

When Colonel Robert McCormick, the publisher of the Chicago *Tribune*, died in Chicago even his enemies among the Midwestern papers couldn't suppress a sigh over the passing of their feudal baron. Right or wrong, he was their man, the son and champion of that part of the country that is variously known as the Midwest, the Heartland, the

Farm Belt, the Isolationist Belt, and the Cow Country. Local pride in America is a complicated emotion, which permits – at different times – the separation and the overlapping of different loyalties: to the town, the county, the state, and the allegiance that embraces and swallows them all – regional pride. For, if I may say so, this is a big country; more, it is a continent and its natural regions span four time zones and a range of terrain from true desert in the Southwest and semitropical swamps in the Southeast, up through semi-desert and high plateau country to wheatlands and lush pasture country and, in the West, to the forest primeval, until the whole northern verge of the country shears away to Canada and on to tundra. A man from the state of Maine, who lives on the rocky edge of a glacial coastline, can be as much of a stranger to a man from southern California as a Laplander is to a Hawaiian Islander.

Nowhere is regional pride so jealously upheld as in the mid-continent, whose capital is Chicago. Colonel McCormick was born there and he liked to think of himself as the chosen monarch of all he surveyed. He was, in fact, not chosen at all. He was the self-appointed defender of the Midwest against its perpetual legendary rival and persecutor, the financial East. He saw himself fondly as the original pioneer, the valiant son of New England who had the get-up-and-go to desert the effete comforts of New York and Philadelphia and hack through the forest and emerge at last to build a plain, brave, wholesome life on the vast Central Plain. So he thundered through a long life against the New York bankers who supposedly held the Midwestern farmer in thrall. He half-believed that industry was born in the Mid-west. He was quite sure that self-reliance and honest-to-God American-ism were. Till the day he died he never ceased to lament that New York and Washington and Boston were little better than British outposts drugged by the decadence of Europe and periodically perverted by a loyalty to Britain which he considered little short of treason.

I have deliberately painted no picture of Colonel McCormick himself but rather let off a volley of his favourite gunfire in the hope that through the clearing smoke you could picture for yourselves the honest, granity outline of him: a rugged, downright rough diamond, unaffec-ted, unlettered, but unbowed, the very archetype of the Irish and Germans and Poles and Swedes and Czechs who built the railroads and ran the factories and sowed the prairie soil and intermarried to produce a new man in the world whom we know as the Midwesterner. Well, let me now give you a closer look and unveil the details of this splendid statue of a man. It is true that his grandfather was the same McCormick who developed the McCormick reaper, which reaped the grain and raked the cuttings off the platform and bound the sheaves in a mechanical operation. This great invention guaranteed an historic development of wheat farming on the endless high plains, where the climate had always been ideal but where there were never enough human beings to harvest it by hand. It also guaranteed that the next generation of McCormicks would be very nicely taken care of.

So the first thing is that young Robert Rutherford McCormick was born in the lap of luxury that he came to despise. His father was a diplomat who was sent, when the boy was only 9 years old, to serve in the American Embassy in the hated colonial capital of London, England. Consequently, the boy had a rather lonely childhood, and his humiliation as a native Midwesterner began very early in life. For he was first sent to school, and to a fashionable prep school, in England. From there he went to Groton, in Massachusetts, which in those days was considered, and still might claim to be, the American Eton. There, by the way, he met another little boy, not at all a solitary type, a genial, sunny, slightly dude-ish Easterner. This boy was to become his lifetime enemy, a symbol of everything he disliked about the eastern United States: the effortless assumption of breeding, the rather prim, la-de-dah manners, the mawkish concern for old Europe and the tendency to run to her aid in time of trouble. This other boy's name was Franklin Delano Roosevelt. At Groton, McCormick was one form ahead of Roosevelt, so by the stern code of schoolboys he was able to regard young Roosevelt as a junior and a whippersnapper. In later years, it was something to be grateful for.

From school, McCormick passed on to Yale, which was then hardly a plebeian retreat. By this time, his family was in what used to be called Petrograd and is known to us as Leningrad. The boy had the best reasons to feel neglected and put-upon. His family lived abroad and the apple of its eye was his eldest brother, who was being trained to succeed his grandfather as the publisher of the Chicago *Tribune*.

Suddenly, in 1910, the brother died and Robert Rutherford inherited the paper. In the next ten years, he transformed it into a technically brilliant production. He bought up huge forests in Canada. He always regretted having to secure his pulp from the country which, he calculated, would be the jumping-off ground, or staging area, of the next British invasion of the United States. But, on the Salvation Army principle that the devil's money is as good as any, he imported the forests and downed his pride. He took the incoming immigrants under his wing, much as William Randolph Hearst did in New York; and it must be said that he shared a forgotten virtue of Hearst in his early days: which was that he understood profoundly the social plight of the shoals of newcomers, from central Europe especially, who poured into a new land with a new language and strange habits, different in different places, and who were already too old to go to school and learn the language or the elementary facts of American history and American customs. Hearst deliberately set out to teach them and to make his newspapers family newspapers in the novel sense that they helped to make the immigrant feel like a member of the American family. Of course, this entailed a good deal of flag-waving and bombast; but Hearst, and McCormick after him, took to heart the remark of the other Roosevelt (the 'manly one', as he was sometimes known in the family to distinguish him from Franklin the dude). America, said Theodore Roosevelt, was too far-flung already to be able to afford millions of what he called 'hyphenated Americans'. If all these strangers were to be melted into the pot of a single powerful brew, the sooner the better for people to stop identifying German-Americans, Polish-Americans, Italian-Americans, and so on. What Hearst tried to do for the workers of the cities of the East, Colonel McCormick did for the new Chicagoans and the Midwest. They rewarded him by buying his paper. And the Colonel – he earned the title in the First World War and never afterwards dropped it – quadrupled the circulation of the *Tribune* and chose, about twenty-five years ago, to call it flatly 'the world's greatest newspaper'. In case there was any doubt about it, he printed the slogan as a subtitle at the top of the front page.

The Colonel lived in what was called 'quiet luxury' in a thirty-five-room house. He had a bony long rectangle of a face, a guardee's moustache, the quizzical gaze and the slightly bloodshot eyeballs of a retired Indian officer or a master of foxhounds. He wore two wristwatches, one on each hand, for he was always afraid of anyone getting the jump on him; and in his crusade of saving America for the Americans and setting it free from all foreign entanglements, it was always later than you think. He took tea at precisely 4.30 in the afternoon, a custom indulged in in this country only by the most rabid Anglophiles. His voice could hardly boast a single Midwestern vowel, uvular *r* or cadence. In horrid fact, he had more than a trace of a British accent. So that if you went to Chicago looking for that archetypal Midwesterner you would never have found him. He looked indeed like a Tory clubman, a Bond Street polo player, of the vintage of 1912. Freud, thou shouldst be living at this hour!

How is one to explain this remarkable contradiction between the spirit and the flesh? Well, I have talked about him because, although he was rare enough to be that rare thing, an American eccentric, he yet embodied a conflict in the Midwestern character which usually throws up no signals on the surface. It lies in the sort of dislike that involves a strain of envy. Colonel McCormick, I think it fair to guess, was secretly angry with cultivated Easterners and Europeans of his own type because they were so obviously and irritatingly more self-assured than the Midwestern natives and immigrants with whom he had thrown in his lot. But make no mistake, his feeling for the Midwest and its destiny was very genuine. I got the impression from him that he wished American history might jump a hundred years so he could demonstrate that the Midwest had just as many good clubs and representative museums and fine universities and civilized people as the detested East. His criteria of civilization were the same as the Easterners, in spite of his prodigal's embrace of the farm and the factory and the honest uproar of the streets. If he had only known it, he was Colonel Don Quixote tilting at windmills that had collapsed long before he died. For the first thing a foreigner has to learn when he arrives in this country is that it has no unchallenged capital city. Washington is the capital of government, New York of publishing and show business and fashion. But the vast, and vastly separated, regions, like the old Greek states, have their own capitals. And in the hundred years of its growth, Chicago need hardly bow to any other American city for the quality of its medical schools, its art collections, its social amenities. It is actually a national leader in advanced engineering, agriculture, and Oriental languages. It was the cradle of modern American architecture. It was to Chicago that Sir William Craigie came to edit, on the model of the great Oxford dictionary, the dictionary of American English. Chicagoans know all this but they still fear that they are best known for Al Capone and the railroads and the endless troop of livestock, who come into Chicago as cattle and go out as steaks or tennis racquets.

As you push west from the eastern seaboard, it is impossible not to notice the Midwestern chip on the shoulder, which Colonel McCormick elevated to the dignity of an epaulette. Old de Tocqueville, over a century and a quarter ago, spotted and pinned it in two marvellous sentences. Writing about the bleak New England coast where this nation was born, he says, 'This tongue of arid land was the cradle of those English colonies which were destined one day to become the United States of America. The centre of power still remains here; while in the far backwoods the true elements of the great people to whom the future control of the continent belongs are gathering almost in secrecy together.' Secrecy is the word. In Midwesterners, of whom Colonel McCormick was an ideological caricature, there is always the secret fear that perhaps the Midwest has not in fact achieved 'the control of the continent' or the grandeur it imagined for itself in its youth.

HLM: RIP

3 February 1956

The other night, the most famous man who has ever come out of the city of Baltimore (pronounced by all natives Bawlamer) showed to the door an old friend from the Peabody Conservatory of Music, came in to say good night to his brother, who had lived with him through the twenty years since his wife died, and went upstairs to bed. It was just after 9 o'clock. And for a man over 75 who had had a stroke seven years ago, and a heart attack two years later, 9 o'clock was the witching hour when the good things of day – and at that age, alas, of life itself – begin to droop and drowse.

A little man, a stocky man with a bull neck, eyes as blue as gas jets, white hair parted exactly down the middle in the fashion of the early years of the century, and tiny hands and feet that added four surprising grace notes to the solid theme of his body, which was that of an undersized German pork butcher. The Sage of Baltimore, they called him, after they had forgotten the furious years in which they had called him every scurrilous name they could coin for a rebel against respectability, gentility and the social order he chose to call 'the church, nobility and commons': a chuckler at all bankers, bishops, politicians, Methodists, feminists, city fathers, labour leaders, and 'every other sort of faith healer' – a lifelong unbeliever. This little man was in the flesh a genial and even kindly sceptic, and he was very much at home in the society of which he pretended to be the scourge. He was, to those who knew him, Mickey Mouse playing Tamburlaine the Great.

He yawned and doused the stogie of his last cigar and he ambled slowly up the two storeys to his bedroom. He turned on the radio to hear some music. There was a programme that night of Beethoven, whom he had worshipped all his life and who combined, he wrote, 'The glory that was Greece, the grandeur that was Rome'; and Bach, whom he summed up in the single metaphor, 'Genesis 1: 1'; and Mozart. Since the two-hundredth anniversary of Mozart had let loose on the night air a silver flood of his music, let us hope that it was mainly Mozart. If so, no more angelic sounds could have been arranged for the end of an old man who seven years before had roused himself in an oxygen tent long enough to say, 'Bring on the angels.'

Around 11 o'clock, his brother passed along the corridor and heard him snoring, with the music still on. Next morning, a coloured houseman, one Rancho Brown, having prepared the coffee and laid the breakfast table, went upstairs and knocked on the old man's door. 'Eight o'clock,' he said. 'Eight o'clock, Mr Mencken, sir.' But Henry Louis Mencken did not answer and never would again. He had departed what he called 'the cosmos we all infest' sometime in the night and embraced without any struggle the end he had groaned for these many years. When all your life is bounded by books and ideas, and you yourself have a magic way with them, it is a bitter judgement on a man to find for his last seven years that he can neither read nor write and is reduced – by an affliction they call a semantic aphasia – to a vegetable, contemplating other vegetables in his small back garden, laying a brick or two, shambling off in the evening to the one entertainment he had always despised: the movies. The fact was, or came to be, that they provided the most animated and passionate contact he had with human beings (about twenty years after everybody else he fell violently in love with Myrna Loy), but he could not bear to renounce the anathema of a lifetime, and he explained his fondness for the old movies they showed around the corner on the muttered grounds that 'their imbecilities amuse me'. In the fall of 1948 he had come down with a cerebral thrombosis, which left him paralysed and babbling for a time, but, to everyone's surprise, the paralysis left him and one morning he woke up and demanded a boiled egg and a stein of beer.

His old enemies lamented that he might have been stricken but he was not yet cowed. He went home to the row house on the edge of Baltimore where he had lived since he was 3, where his brother, August, a retired engineer, nursed and did for him. And H. L. Mencken, the American Bernard Shaw, the cheerful juvenile delinquent of genteel American culture, the three-volume-classic authority on the American language, the man who could read at a glance a page of anything – theology, criticism, medicine, law, the news – the man to whom the English language was green pasture to romp in, a three-ring circus to perform in to the delight and terror of the onlooking 'boobs': this man got home and extended his index finger and, at the prompting of a patient nurse, learned to identify it like a 3-year-old. He learned all over again the simple physical nouns and the things they stood for. 'Fin-ger, finger,' he repeated, and 'plate', 'spoon', elbow', 'chair', 'floor' and, worst of all, 'book'. For it turned out that the damage had settled in the part of the brain that synchronizes sight and meaning, the ability to see and the ability to make sense of what you see. This disability never left him. He could focus the written page but what he saw was an orderly array of meaningless symbols. So he never read again. He could see and he could talk, pretty much as he had always talked, with sass and pungency and scornful humour. The last time I saw him he made little of the then general fear of the Russians. He had been out on the streets looking at the billboards and store signs. 'Why do they fuss about the Russians? It appears to me,' he said, 'that the Chinese have already taken over.' But sitting in his library with several thousand books buried on the walls, he was like a crippled castaway surrounded by the mocking ocean, the one element he had loved and mastered.

Henry Louis Mencken was the grandson of a German who had deserted the troubles of 1848, settled in Baltimore, and left to his son a prosperous cigar business. Young Henry was meant to take it over but he was temperamentally unfitted to following in anybody's footsteps. As a boy in the 1880s he lay on his back on the kitchen table and shot lemon rind from a catapult at the flies which, in the days before fine-mesh door and window screens, camped on the ceiling. 'The hired girl,' he wrote, 'when she was in an amiable mood prepared us enough of these missiles for an hour's brisk shooting, and in the morning she had the Red Cross job of sweeping the dead flies off the ceiling.' Having tasted what he called 'the red mammalian blood that leaked from the biggest horseflies', he looked around in adolescence for fatter fry. For a time he masked these bloodthirsty instincts in a bookish stoop, which alarmed his father so much that he sent his son off to a gymnasium hoping – said Mencken – 'to make a kind of grenadier of me. If so, he was in error, for I remain more or less Bible-backed to this day and am often mistaken for a Talmudist.'

When he was 9, young Mencken read *Huckleberry Finn* and it opened up to him astonishing vistas of life in the world outside. He decided a little later on that to be a newspaperman would offer the priceless opportunity, as he put it later, 'to lay in all the worldly wisdom of a police lieutenant, a bartender, a shyster lawyer, and a midwife'. At 19 he descended on journalism with a whoop. He was extremely spry and industrious and he very soon went from a reporter to a city editor and rollicked in the absurdities, the pomp, the small scandals and big bores with which any self-respecting big city abounds. 'The days chased one another,' he wrote, 'like kittens chasing their tails.'

Now, he looked around for the horseflies. He found them in public life and in the late-Victorian beliefs which, before the First World War, gave life its earnest meaning and society its complacency. He had developed a stinging prose style and an essentially humorous view of human idealism. Like Voltaire in one country and Shaw in another, he let fly at his own. And for about ten years, through the prime of his forties, he skinned every respected institution in the land which he thought had grown fat and uncritical. He regretted the arid theology of the puritan fathers and debunked the heroes of the Revolution. George Washington himself he thought would be today 'ineligible for any office of profit or honour' in the Republic, and he begged the American fiction of the 1920s to cure itself of its 'marshmallow gentility'. The new young realists swarmed to Mencken like Polish underground refugees to London during the Blitz, and he started a magazine and printed their first, and then considered pretty revolutionary, work. O'Neill, James Farrell, Dreiser, Sherwood Anderson, Ring Lardner, and more. They were the rude natives he defended at the gates of the Governor's garden party. Through the 1920s and until the Depression gave people simpler and more urgent troubles to think about, Mencken was the rebel god of American letters. Soon after that his influence wilted, for he was suddenly a gadfly in a charnel house, and he turned to his work on *The American Language* and to the writing of his enchanting memoirs. Every four years he would enjoy a ribald excursion into his old never-never land by way of reporting the Presidential nominating conventions.

This outrageous, cocky, gallant, cynical, sentimental, greatly gifted man went out suddenly last Sunday without even a coughing fit, snoozing in his bed as the dawn came in over the city he had loved and terrorized. If he could have seen the way he went, you may be sure he would have fired off a final impenitent chuckle. For it contradicted something he had noticed long ago: 'The human tendency to make death dramatic and heroic has little excuse in the facts . . . A man does not die quickly and brilliantly like a lightning stroke; he passes out by inches, hesitatingly and, one may almost add, gingerly . . . the abominable acidosis sneaks upon us, gradually paralysing the adrenals, flabbergasting the thyroid, crippling the poor old liver, and throwing its fog upon the brain. We pass into the blank unconsciousness of infancy and then into the blank unconsciousness of the prenatal state and finally into the condition of undifferentiated protoplasm . . . the dying man doesn't struggle much and he isn't afraid. As his alkalis give out he succumbs to a blest stupidity. His mind fogs. His will power vanishes. He submits decently. He scarcely gives a damn.'

Living or dying, it was Mencken's special glory that he didn't give a damn. He was all of a piece, from the boy on the kitchen table firing slingshots at horseflies to the old man whose last political comment to me was that the old soldier, General MacArthur, 'is a dreadful old fraud but he appears to be fading satisfactorily'. 'All of a piece' is a phrase we seldom hear any more; we prefer the solemn word 'integrity'. It may be the word I am looking for, though it is taken as a Christian concession to allow the word these days to men who are wholly dull or wholly predictable because they give no rein to the warring impulses in all of us, to men who would better be called conventional, or prudent, or obstinate, or plodding, or enslaved by the codes they never made. Mencken was an original with the courage to live by his sometimes outrageous convictions. Like all writers of surpassing talent he was offered huge sums to do some other man's bidding. But he early on turned down the big money and never wrote a piece he didn't want to write. In a persuasive plutocracy, he was impervious to the seductions of the rich because he liked his life and was devoid of envy. 'In the face of another man's good fortune,' he once wrote, 'I am as inert as a curb broker before Johann Sebastian Bach.'

Of the advice he gave me as a starting newspaperman in the late 1930s, I have always been grateful for one rule, or rather three, which a reasonably honest man might get to respect but only after a long convalescence from painful bruises: 'Never accept a free ticket from a theatre manager, a free ride from the chamber of commerce, or a favour from a politician.' He lived absolutely by this rule. He wanted to have his say, and he knew that a very gifted man who isn't interested in money is very hard to tame.

With his father's admiring help he became an agnostic as a boy and stayed one for the rest of the seventy-five years, four months and eight days of his life. There was no weakening at the end, no yielding at last to lifelong temptations to throw in his lot with this sect or that, religious or secular, no sloppy concession that there are no atheists in foxholes. As old age came on he was noticeably more tolerant, even of types he abominated, like evangelists, city politicians and golfers. He was challenged towards the end by an old opponent to confess what he would do if he discovered there was an afterlife by the simple fact of finding himself in one. He replied that if he did indeed 'fetch up beside the Twelve Apostles, I should simply say to them: Gentlemen, I was wrong'.

He prepared for his end with singular sprightliness and care, appealing in his will for no parsonic 'whooping and heaving' at the grave, a little poetry perhaps but nothing that would offend his irreligious scruples. In an astonishingly well-ordered life, his secretary was asked to appear at the same split second every morning. He answered every letter by return of mail. He took a daily nap at the selfsame hour. He locked away his files at six precisely, and they were as elaborately card-indexed as the personnel records of the Pentagon. As the sun faded from the front parlour he mixed the martinis, for he was ready to observe the second half of another lifelong rule: 'Never accept a drink by day or refuse one by night.'

In such a life it would have been an odd oversight if he had not prescribed the proper sentiment to go on his tombstone. Since he ordered that there should be no fuss or ceremony at the end, he was cremated, and the only service was a reminiscent get-together of a few friends. But he had not overlooked his epitaph. He wrote it over forty years ago. It is chiselled on a brass plaque that greets you today in the lobby of the Baltimore Sunpapers building. This is it: 'If, after I depart this vale, you ever remember me and have thought to please my ghost, forgive some sinner, and wink your eye at some homely girl.'

The Road to Churchill Downs

8 May 1956

I was recently invited to go down to Kentucky as a house guest for a few days and wind up with a front seat at the Derby. In the early days of May this is about as sure a guarantee of heaven as a city dweller, or even a countryman, could ask for on this earth.

Kentucky is technically a border state, lying poised between the North and the South, but it deserves far more than its neighbour, Ohio, the description, 'a Northern state with a Southern exposure'. Being not quite in the South it has striven to be very much *of* it. There are no Southerners quite so Southern as the professional Southerners of Kentucky, and by practice as well as by blood they have taken on the legendary pace of Southern life, its customs and cookery, the slow twist of vowels into diphthongs, and that attractive Southern irony which is prepared to believe the best of human beings and expect the worst.

It was a little warmer than usual the day I tumbled down into Kentucky, but the Ulstermen, or as they say here the Scots-Irish, who settled here a century and a half ago soon accustomed themselves to a semitropical drowse that would have choked their cousins in Aberdeen. It was at Aberdeen, by the way, that I crossed the Ohio River, and along its banks the Judas trees were in full flame. The town is terraced high on the steep slopes of the hills as they crowd down to the river, as if rushing to make a last stand before they give way to the rolling meadows of the Bluegrass country.

I tossed in the word 'Bluegrass' there in a casual way, but have no fear that it is going to go unexplained. This whole talk, if it takes the turn I hope, is going to be about the Bluegrass region, which for a hundred and seventy years has bred the fastest, proudest, most gleaming of America's racehorses. On top of the Fayette County courthouse is a weathervane in the shape of a golden stallion. It is no more possible to go through the Bluegrass country and ignore the horses than it would be to go through Nevada and ignore the slot machines. From Maysville, the first town across the Kentucky line, down to Lexington, the capital of the Bluegrass, is sixty-three miles, and there are some interesting oddities. There are handsome houses overlooking the river that were built in the spacious times when the steamboat minted fortunes as fast as the railroads that superseded them. But this was, and is, trapper country. The first white men who really roamed this hinterland were the French, the fur trappers and traders who made the most of a huge continental landscape where, unlike Europe, the mountain ranges ran from north to south, and the rivers also. There is hardly a river in the main river systems of the American mainland that has not left the relics of the French fur trappers, for they extended Napoleon's empire up the Mississippi and the Missouri and the Ohio to places far in the north. Even Chicago, it may strike you, is pronounced 'Shick-ago' and not 'Chick-ago' because the first people to come on it were French rivermen. Chicago is an Indian name, but the French had trouble with the 'chi' sound, as they still do (they can't even say, 'Goodnight, chairee'), and they had to say it 'Shick-ago'. The incoming Yankees picked up the pronunciation and it has stayed that way ever since, except, of course, out of the mouths of Englishmen, who live eighteen miles from the French but have had little truck with them.

But in this first valley that I went through, the French had been quietly obliterated by the Scots-Irish, who have a habit of taking over any place they settle in; and if they don't absorb it, they preserve the gift of not being absorbed either. Until I arrived on the edge of the Bluegrass all the names were such as Cochran, McConnell, Marshall, and Keith and Duncan. In a charming small town called Washington one of the houses that is a required stop for tourists is a two-storeyed Georgian brick house. It was built at the turn of the eighteenth century by a man who had loaded a large family on a flatboat, sailed down the Ohio, and made a home here. The point of visiting the place today is that in the grounds many of the Marshall family are buried. And there stands still the modest tombstone of a certain Mary Keith, who turned out to be the mother of John Marshall, an early and great Chief Justice of the United States Supreme Court. The epitaphs on Scottish tombstones are not, as I recall, very flowery, not even when they were written in the eighteenth century, which both in old England and in New England consigned its beloved to the care of Providence with grand flourishes of the language. But some of these Kentucky leave-takings are as chilly as the Highlands. That of the mother of Chief Justice Marshall is no exception. It reads, 'Mary Randolph Keith, born 1737, she was good, not brilliant, useful not ornamental, and the mother of fifteen children.' The mind reels at the size of her progeny if she had been ornamental.

Well, by the middle of the afternoon I had come to the end of the winding river-bottom roads and was on a long, undulating upland and the true Bluegrass country. You will want to know, as everybody who has never seen it does, if the grass is really blue. It is not. Even the natives admit that it is merely green in summer. But no matter how much the Kentucky guide insists that 'only in May do the blue anthers of its blossoms give the grass a distinctly steel-blue tint', a stranger needs to wear special tinted glasses to make it appear so. The way not to disappoint your friends is to photograph it in colour in the very late afternoon, when the slanting light of the entire Western hemisphere spreads a film of milky blue on anything, even the complexion of your favourite girl. It is only fair to say that you do notice the greenness of the grass, but it would not startle an Englishman or an Irishman and it would not be much of a surprise to a native of Oregon. However, let's not be hoity-toity about this local product. It is as indigenous to this region as the Monterey cypress is to that small coastal stretch of central California. It is not matched as turf, and as pastureland is surpassed, I should guess, only by the two famous sections of eastern Pennsylvania and southwestern Belgium, which a League of Nations survey chose as the finest in the world.

The Bluegrass is a small central plain, less than eight thousand square miles, which lies on a bed of limestone and is richly veined with underground water. And this is the perfect – they say essential – recipe for the two glories of Kentucky: fine horses and bourbon whiskey. It is the limestone which endows the waters that pass through it with phosphorus and calcium. Which, as every stable boy knows (and I just learned), are two ingredients of bone and rippling muscle. This is why the Kentucky thoroughbreds are strong and fast and beautiful to look upon. This is why, as you drop south from the eroded hills of southern

Ohio and up on to the downs of the Bluegrass country, the road signs change from advertisements for familiar gasolines and cigarettes to elegant signs by elegant stud farms that say: 'Brood mares, boarding and training'; 'Track entrance, 100 feet'; and 'Blue Grass Seed'.

In deference to people who were brought up in my own self-denying faith, I will quickly explain the essential ingredients of Kentucky's second famous product and then pass on. It may be regrettable but it is also true that the water that courses through the limestone has a distinctive flavour. There are simple, strong people who slake their thirst with the natural product alone and go on, I'm told, to live blameless lives. But there are others, the first of whom was one Jacob Spears, as long ago as 1790, who looked on the Kentucky water as the merest raw material for a confection that has done the state some service. The United States abounds, as you may have heard, in maize, so much so that like the English with their wheat, the Scots with their barley, and the Australians with their oats, they have adopted for it the usual counter-word for the staple crop: corn. Mr Spears earned the gratitude of uncounted generations by having the wit to take the maize and grind it and mash it and add the magic limestone water, and then distil the compound and age it. And that's how bourbon was born, so called after the name of the county that gave birth to this splendid firewater. Not surprisingly, Mr Spears' first distillery was in Paris. And the heart of the Bluegrass country is between Paris and Versailles.

These towns were so named, as were many others near by, in grateful remembrance of a stripling boy, a 19-year-old Frenchman, the Marquis de Lafayette, who offered himself in the service of the American Revolution to General Washington and beat you know who, and has ever after symbolized the special one-upmanship that the French enjoy in America. This is nothing to dwell on, but you surely can't expect me to toss off the remark that I have just driven from Paris to Versailles without explaining that we are still in Kentucky.

It has a wide, undulating, green horizon, strikingly devoid of ever-greens but spotted here and there with those jetting, fanlike American elms, which, alas, have been blighted by the Dutch bug all the way from Ohio to the New England coast. The Bluegrass is rich country in more senses than one, for it must cost a modest fortune to maintain even the five-barred white wooden fences that ring the paddocks and enclose the fields and swing like switchbacks between you and the horizon. Inside these pastures is practised that strange and compelling ritual of breeding racehorses which so obsesses the insider and leaves the outsider feeling that he has been mistaken all his life about what a horse *is*. In sickness and in health, in affluence and depression, no babies anywhere in Kentucky are so jealously and delicately cared for. After the weaning comes the precisely regulated diet – a mixture of oats and corn, bran and flax seed and vitamin extracts – then the trimming of the feet, the breaking to the halter, the gentling into the paddock routine, then the exploratory trotting and cantering, and then the speed trials; all this going on for two years or more before the magic truth is revealed or exploded: whether or not the blood of the horse's ancestors and the skill of his training will merge to produce a true racehorse, perhaps a great one.

In the late winter and early spring, you could have seen on the doors of some stalls record charts – for temperature, diet and other clinical peculiarities of the tender patient inside – which are as anxiously consulted as those in a surgical ward; because no discipline is too fussy, no care too excessive to the men who match their knowledge of bloodlines and skill in training methods in the gaudy hope that one day the people may flock to see their ward run on the first Saturday of May in the Derby at Churchill Downs. And there can be few Kentucky owners and breeders who do not nurse a faint hope that later on the people may troop to a second shrine comparable with Kentucky's first.

And what is that? It is Faraway Farm, outside Lexington, and to some knowing people it is as much of a pilgrimage as Lenin's Tomb to an obedient Russian. Up against the sky and standing on a small hillock is a handsome statue of the greatest racehorse of his time, who won nineteen times in twenty-one starts, collected a quarter of a million dollars in only two seasons, sired two hundred and thirty-six horses, one hundred and seventy-six of whom were winners: the fastest, the most beautiful, the proudest son of Kentucky – Man o' War. You amble up to the statue with your hands in your pockets and a few other visitors come up, and the men take their hats off. You are surprised to find that you have done the same.

*

All this, you will have assumed, is an easy build-up to the climax of a holiday in Kentucky: the breathtaking spectacle itself, the Derby. Well, to be quite honest, I can think offhand of a dozen other spectacles that catch my breath quicker. A hooked bluefish, for instance, a glass of lager, the dimple in the chin of Ava Gardner. For I was shaken to discover that if while the race is on, you lose your programme or have a coughing fit you can miss it altogether. If anybody had asked me, I should have guessed that the Kentucky Derby was something like the bicycle race around France, and that we were going to sit through the last day of it. It turned out it takes two minutes, and for this the whole population of Louisville, and several hundred train and plane loads of gamblers from the East and West, and breeders from Ireland and Argentina, and 'kinfolk' from the South, make plans for a year, dicker for tickets, pay regal prices for a bed, and line up for food – for a hundred and twenty seconds on the first Saturday in May. Other people's enthusiasms are always a riddle, but I shouldn't take kindly to a sneer at mine. So I will say that the reason for my being in this strange place was a promise I had given, in a wild moment a year before, to my 10-year-old daughter. By the peculiar grace of God, she has not yet become aware of one half the human race – I mean boys. That being so, what else is there on earth to rave about but horses? Her weekends are spent bouncing round the park, the only dress catalogues she handles feverishly are ones for riding gear, her room is plastered with more ribbons and horse prints than a Presidential Convention with campaign buttons. She flew in on a flawless day over the velvety pastures and the rolling farms and the gleam of horseflesh, and she said at once, 'Why can't we live in Kentucky?' I said, 'I'll tell you why. Because a little later on you'll discover that they breed boys in other places than the Bluegrass.'

The object of this trip, then, was up at dawn and out with Ned, a slim young man in blue jeans and a high-buttoned shirt, with tendons as bowed as the horse he couldn't sell. There was a choice of colts, fillies, ponies, for this was a working farm, and a working farm for other less favoured beasts. Cows sloshed their tails around in the heat of the day, and at night sheep complained to the moon and the air was dense with birds that trilled, barked, whistled, shrieked and glucked. The sun came up like a yellow rose and fell like a sweating orange. It was 94 degrees the first day, 92 the second, 96 on the great day itself. But the tempo was easy and nobody was going anyplace but Churchill Downs. We lay on the grass and had lunch of Kentucky chicken hash and potato pancakes and the best succotash (corn and lima beans) I'd ever eaten. We had a box overlooking the finishing post, and for the first time since 1880 there was a challenge from the losing jockey, and a very tense pause before the stewards decided that in the stretch Tommy Lee and Sword Dancer were bumping each other in a rhythmical and entirely legal way.

Some people, I don't doubt, will be sensing with suspicion or disfavour the sort of society I seem to be sketching: a horsey, arrogant, vowel-chopping – or vowel-smearing – upper crust. Not your cup of tea perhaps? Not mine either, I assure you. While I feel like a vaudeville clown in the presence of dignitaries of the Church and State, I am practically T. S. Eliot in the presence of horsey people. I know less about a horse than – certainly – a horsefly. An Argentinian, in a mad attack of mistaken identity, asked me if I'd brought any promising fillies along. I said I had brought a ten-year-old filly with me. My daughter hopped to my side and growled in a whisper, 'You can't be a filly if you're older than four.' How about colts? I asked. 'Same thing,' she said and blushed for her city-slicker father. The Argentinian thought he was in the wrong town and wandered off.

But the great surprise, and the delight, of this interlude in the Bluegrass was to mix with a lot of people who were expert and hospitable and easygoing with their knowledge, and impossible to grade socially. You never knew whether the young tow-haired man in the corner was a Yale sophomore or a groom. For three great days, Jefferson's original image of America was restored – that of a pastoral Republic where the rich, the poor, and the in-between mingle, eat, drink, joke together, have the same manners, the same idioms, and an overriding gentleness and naturalness. A small, uncorrupted society united in a lovely landscape by a genuine love of the same thing – a horse. I discovered, much too late in life, that the same sense of an innocent community can be guaranteed by the pursuit of a ball with a liquid centre.

On the plane coming home, my daughter rattled on in ecstasy till she had to catch her breath. I jumped in with the damping reminder that it was wonderful but it was not at all like life. 'What d'you mean?'

she said. 'Well,' I said as we looked down on the approaching industrial landscape of the Jersey flats, 'we might have had bad seats, or stayed in a crummy motel, or keeled over from the heat, or been bedded down in Louisville, or there might have been no horses to ride. Everything was perfect,' I said, 'but it isn't always so.'

'I don't get it,' she said, and fell asleep.

Politics and the Human Animal

7 December 1956

As sometimes happens, I was chided the other morning, in a letter from an indignant correspondent in England, for having given a talk about the complexities of American football when I might better have given a sermon about the complications of the Middle East. Men were dying, he reminded me. Empires were tottering. A tyrant was squeezing the lifeblood from Britain's lifeline in the Suez Canal. In a word, I was fiddling while London, Cairo and Washington burned.

If I believed this, I should be embarrassed to talk at all about one country to another. But in all these talks I have gone along on the original theory that people are permanently curious about how other people live, and that all the politicians and propagandists in the world working on three shifts a day cannot for ever impose their line on two people sitting alone in a room. They are the only proper audience for a letter. I grant my correspondent that there are vast heavings and resettlings of power around the world; that there is a ferment in Asia and Africa; that there is a periodic flow of bad blood across the Atlantic; that the rich grow richer and the poor poorer with consequences that could end in world famine and revolution. I can only reply that I still feel no embarrassment in maintaining, in a warlike time, a civil tongue.

If this sounds impertinent in our present troubles, let me repeat a few sentences I wrote as the preface to a collection of these talks that was put out some years ago: 'Politics will undoubtedly bedevil us all till the day we die, but ... even the prospect of early annihilation should not keep us from making the most of our days on this unhappy planet. In the best of times, our days are numbered, anyway. And it would be a crime against Nature for any generation to take the world crisis so solemnly that it put off enjoying those things for which we were presumably designed in the first place, and which the gravest statesmen and the hoarsest politicians hope to make available to all men in the end: I mean the opportunity to do good work, to fall in love, to enjoy friends, to sit under trees, to read, to hit a ball and bounce the baby.'

Am I saying that the world is too much with us, and is incurable anyway, and that we should gather roses while we may? I am saying no such thing. I *am* saying that when the nations rage furiously together we should not be misled by their hullabaloo into thinking that the world's anxieties, however grave, are the fundamental things in life and that all else is a bauble. It happens, merely, to be my daily chore to sit and watch and listen to the chief actors on the political stage, domestic and foreign, and I am struck by many things. By the ease with which a nation does something from instinct and justifies it by reason. By the careerism and vanity that dog the ambition of most politicians and statesmen. But I am struck most of all by the absence of humour, which as much as any other solvent could relax the protagonists in any quarrel, however international, and halt them in their race to murder each other from the highest motives. Most of the chief delegates to the United Nations are hard-working men but because they are trying to handle the world's conflicts they are not thereby or necessarily the most serious men around. Some of them are certainly the solemnest men around.

And however splendid the United Nations Charter may be, there is nothing inherently noble about the United Nations delegations. I suggest that my critic is making this sort of mistake. He is mistaking the label on the tin for the contents. Most first-rate comedians are in private life more serious than most politicians and all of them are melancholy men. And what may be essential to one's self-respect may not be essential to a friendship, whether at the other end of a loudspeaker or at the other end of a room.

I have, for instance, a close friend, a merry, kindly and simple man, very able in his special field of finance. I feel agreeable in his presence and I admire his human qualities. At the shabbiest period in recent American history, when the fear of domestic Communists was most paranoid, this friend was a strong, even a devout, McCarthyite. He used to load my morning mail with the transcripts of all the testimony before the Senate Subcommittee on Government Operations, over which the late Senator Joseph McCarthy presided with – by my lights – such indignity and malevolence. Of course, McCarthyism was a fundamental issue of the time, not only an American political issue but fundamental to any man's notions of justice and decency. You might guess, therefore, that my friend's admiration for McCarthy marked the parting of the ways for us. Well, it was an embarrassment, but not to our affection or continuing association. Of course, if by some convulsion of history (a sudden depression, say, and twenty million unemployed) McCarthy had become an American dictator, my friend and I would probably have said goodbye and retreated to opposite sides of the barricades. Nobody has sharpened this point better, in my view, than the late Justice Holmes when he said that the purpose of civilized argument between friends is to arrive at the point where you agree that some day it might be necessary to shoot each other. Until that day is unavoidable, 'the democratic process', both in public and in private, is no more but no less than an acceptance of the notion that in important issues you may be wrong.

My first mentor in journalism in this country was a man who had no use for democracy at all, except in this crucial belief. 'Democracy', he once wrote, 'is the theory that the common people know what they want, and deserve to get it good and hard.' But he also wrote, 'What I admire most in any man is a serene spirit ... when he fights he fights in the manner of a gentleman fighting a duel, not in that of a longshoreman cleaning out a waterfront saloon.' We had a tacit understanding that while I allowed him to shoot off his face about the fraudulence and guile of Franklin Roosevelt, I should then be allowed to go off and vote for him. This division never interfered with a friendship that was amiable at all times.

I believe this to be not only a sane approach to politics but essential to all the things that lie outside politics.

I hope that the blood pressure of my critic is still holding. Politics, I grant, is of great importance to us all, since it affects our survival and the future we plan for ourselves and for all the countries that lie outside our own. It is admirable, though not, I believe, compulsory, for people to take an interest in politics. But first things first. How much politics is there in the greatest novels? In Flaubert, Dickens or Dostoyevsky? How much in the greatest poetry? In Shakespeare, Yeats, John Donne or whoever? Surely nobody will deny that poets and novelists, poets especially, deal with human experience at its most intense and most profound. Was Thomas Hardy indifferent to the great issues of his time because he chose to look steadily and long at the life of a few Dorset villages? Is the poetry of Robert Frost trivial because it deals with a bit of pasture or the death of a hired man? Frost, by the way, had his own recipe for the end of the world. It would not come, he thought, in the shock of avenging armies but either by lust or by hate.

> Some say the world will end in fire,
> Some say in ice.
> From what I've tasted of desire
> I hold with those who favour fire.
>
> But if it had to perish twice,
> I think I know enough of hate
> To say that for destruction ice
> Is also great
> And would suffice.

You may say that a first-rate poet, because he is a rare bird, rarer than a first-rate politician, has earned a special exemption from the obligations of politics. Not because of his special gift, he hasn't. That would be like saying that all wars should be fought by the poor and the ungifted. And although a mere journalist cannot achieve the intensity or profundity of a good poet, he still has the obligation to see things as he sees them and not as he would like to, or as somebody else says he should. If paying tribute to Caesar is not his main business in life, he must pay his citizen's due and get on with what really interests him.

What do you suppose the Secretary General of the United Nations turns to when he goes home at night? Mr Hammarskjöld is, he likes to say, 'the curator of the secrets and prejudices of seventy-nine nations'. That should be enough to fill the waking hours of any conscientious man. But it evidently is not. When he steps off the high wire of his diplomatic circus and comes down to earth, does he agonize all over again about Suez or the Congo or the seizure of Hungary? He settles to the permanent things. He reads Eliot and Robert Lowell and André Gide and his favourite novelists – Mark Twain, Hemingway, Stephen Crane – and most of all the man whose high seriousness and perfect accommodation of his style to the thing he wants to say makes him, in Hammarskjöld's opinion, the modern master of serious English prose. James Thurber.

So let us take our stand on the Middle East, or Vietnam, or whatever, and in the process perhaps lose a friend or shoot a friend, or agree to differ and do neither. Then let us get down to life and living.

General Marshall

16 October 1959

It has been a habit of these letters to honour, as W. H. Auden put it, 'the vertical man', the Americans in all their variety who are up and doing. But Americans themselves are great celebrators of their eminent dead. And when the calendar reminds us of a great one who was born or died fifty or a hundred years ago, he is obediently honoured in the tomb by people who would have feared or hated him in the flesh. For Americans, an impetuous but ceremonial people, are soon ready to pay tribute to a man once the wind is out of him.

Lately we observed as a holiday the date kept aside as Columbus Day, which celebrates the discovery of this country by a man who neither discovered it nor ever saw it. And a few days later we nodded respectfully in the direction of Harpers Ferry, West Virginia, where –

a hundred years ago – John Brown, a near-lunatic with a hot eye and a single purpose, started on his wild and brief campaign to set up a free state in the Appalachians as a sanctuary for escaped Negro slaves. Next day, a man died who had been born just across the Pennsylvania border from Harpers Ferry who had an equally single purpose but who was so prosaic, so deeply disdainful of drama and public exposure, that not one American in a million would have recognized him on the streets, and not even his close friends knew a pungent or delightful story about him. He was almost impossible for a newspaperman to know, for he winced at the word 'newspaper' and he therefore acquired no public personality, not even a couple of identifying adjectives in *Time*. In the last few years of his life he used to drive downtown most days from his small house in Pinehurst, North Carolina, buy his groceries in the supermarket, tote them to his car to the accompaniment of a nod from the townspeople, a bit of gossip with the drugstore clerk, and then get into his car again, receive the flourish of a salute from the traffic cop, and drive home again. Yet on a bright day, wherever in the world the American flag flies, it was lowered and flown for him.

I hope I won't be misunderstood if I say that he was a most un-American figure because he was so remarkably self-effacing. The United States has as many people as anybody afflicted with self-effacement, but it usually springs from social discomfort, or genuine shyness, or that other form of shyness which, as somebody wisely said, is a sure sign of conceit. This man was not shy, but the subordination of self to teamwork was almost an instinct with him, and I suppose few men who take to soldiering took to it for a better reason. Most Americans were willing to credit the reports of his eminence but it was something they had to take on trust; for General George Catlett Marshall, of all the great figures of our time, was the least 'colourful', the least impressive in a casual meeting and the least rewarding to the collector of anecdotes. He was a man whose inner strength and secret humour only slowly dripped through the surfaces of life, as a stalactite hangs stiff and granity for centuries before one sees beneath it a pool of still water of marvellous purity.

He was always uncomfortable when anyone mentioned the great Plan that bears his name, the plan to repair the fabric of European life after the devastation of the Second World War. He took no credit for it, and he was nearly right. For it was first conceived by underlings in the State Department and seized on by Under-Secretary Dean Acheson when he realized that all the largesse of UNRRA and Bretton Woods, and the loan to Britain, and other loans to Greece and Turkey, were far from enough. It was time to jettison Europe or to throw out a lifeline. Acheson developed the Plan, and it was worked on in the White House, and he floated it as a trial balloon in a speech at Cleveland, Mississippi. No one in the country took particular notice of it. Marshall had been in Europe and when he came back, Acheson told him about it, not without misgiving, for Americans had not marvelled at his trial balloon, and a sudden Communist stab at Hungary might puncture it once and for all. Marshall, it must be said, now saw the necessity of speed and a public forum and contrived within two days to speak at the Harvard commencement. He was no orator, and the dramatic novelty of the Plan went unnoticed by everybody except a trio of British correspondents and the British Foreign Secretary, Ernest Bevin, who sat by his bedside in England and heard a transatlantic broadcast and responded to it at once as 'a lifeline to sinking men ... the generosity of it was beyond our belief ... we grabbed it with both hands'. So it is not for the Marshall Plan that we honour the General.

Imagine now a sturdy, well-knit man, stiff-necked it would be fair to say, certainly in the physical sense, with sandy hair and mild blue eyes and a homely, underslung mouth from which issued unspectacular remarks in a throaty voice. A student of war, from the books and the maps but also from the arms contracts and the quartermaster records, and from a personal knowledge of the battlefields picked up on private walks when the bones of the dead were long overgrown.

It is possible – we shall never know – that in his private imagination he was another Robert E. Lee who dreamed dreams of high deeds in the cannon's mouth. But for almost fifty years he was fated by his superiors and, in the crisis of his career, by his own conscience to return as always to the drawing board, to revise the training methods of a tank corps, to compute the comparative tactical efficiency of a 55-millimetre machine gun in close combat and in desert warfare, to gauge the competing need for anti-aircraft of the slums of Chungking or the docks and ports of Iceland. A high subordinate who worked with him assures me that in the history of warfare Marshall could not have had his equal as a master of supply: the first master, as this West Point colonel put it, of global warfare. I suppose we must defer to this expert judgement. It was enthusiastically seconded by the three or four senior British generals during the Second World War. But to most of us, unifying the command of an army outpost or totting up the number of landing barges that could be spared from Malaya for the Normandy landings is hardly so flashing as Montgomery's long dash through the desert, or MacArthur's vigil on Bataan, or even the single syllable by which General McAuliffe earned his immortality: 'Nuts!'

A layman is not going to break out a flag for a man who looks like a stolid golf-club secretary, a desk general who refused an aide-de-camp or a chauffeur and worked out of an office with six telephones. Even though 1984 comes closer every day, this is not yet an acceptable recipe for a hero. Though no doubt when Hollywood comes to embalm him on celluloid, he will grow a British basso, which is practically a compulsory grafting process for American historical characters in the movies. He will open letters with a toy replica of the sword of Stonewall Jackson (who was, to be truthful, a lifetime's idol).

But in life no such colour brightened the grey picture of a man devoted to the daily study of warfare on several continents with all the ardour of a certified public accountant. In a word, he was a soldier's soldier. Nor, I fear, is there any point in looking for some deep and guilty secret to explain his reputation for justice and chivalry. There is, however, one voice that has been silent. No syllable of praise or criticism has come from a soldier who can coin resounding epitaphs when he so chooses. General MacArthur has said nothing, and I dare to wonder about his silence only because it reflects a conflict of character and temperament that was conducted on both sides with shattering dignity. It will by now be no surprise to learn that on Marshall's side it was a most undramatic quality: the gift of making at fateful times sensible decisions that elevate another man and swing the spotlight away from you.

We have to go back to February 1956 for the last public word about Marshall by General MacArthur. 'General Marshall's enmity towards me', he wrote, 'was an old one.' Discounting the word 'enmity', let us say that the original row – the sort of thing that elephants and politicians never forget – goes back to the First World War, when Marshall, a colonel on the Operations Planning Section of the American Expeditionary Force, was planning the recapture of Sedan, the historic town which three German armies in the last century have broken through to lay waste the lands of France. Marshall's plans did not allow for the impetuous ambition of a young brigadier general to summon his own division and take Sedan at a bound. The brigadier general was, need I say, MacArthur. He leaped through a loophole in the Marshall plan and took Sedan in his dashing stride. From then on he vaulted ahead of Marshall in everything but prudence. By 1930, when he became chief of staff, you would have had to scan the army lists with binoculars to see what happened to Marshall.

After the First World War, you might have thought that his appearance at the side of General Pershing as a personal aide would have assured a flashier or more enterprising type some quick preferment, but it was downhill again for another fifteen years. As late as 1933, for instance, he was appointed senior instructor to the Illinois National Guard, an appointment that would have thrilled a scoutmaster. But for an able soldier, 52 years of age, it was the pit of his career. Once MacArthur retired, in 1935 – and it may be no more than coincidence – Marshall had his feet on the ladder again. Two days before the Germans swept into Poland he was made chief of staff.

I said that in the supreme crisis of his career it was his own conscience that sent him back to the commanding obscurity that was his habitat. Nobody has told this incident better than the late Henry Stimson, Roosevelt's Secretary of War. In a letter to the President in August 1943, Stimson wrote, 'I believe the time has come when we must put our most commanding soldier in charge of this critical operation [that was to be the invasion of Europe]. You are far more fortunate than was Mr Lincoln or Mr Wilson in the ease with which that selection can be made . . . General Marshall already has a towering eminence of reputation as a tried soldier and as a broad-minded and skilful administrator.' The British had, in fact, suggested him. Churchill assumed he was already picked and Stalin had vouchsafed a wily nod of approval. There came a day in Cairo when President Roosevelt and Marshall lunched alone. It seems to be accepted among Marshall's close friends that he had all his life yearned for a combat command.

The most majestic command in history was his for the asking. Roosevelt had already made up his mind but, as usual, allowed himself room to manoeuvre (and lament) if things didn't turn out his way. He asked Marshall whether he would prefer to stay in Washington as chief of staff or take the supreme command. Stimson kept some notes, made from Roosevelt's account of the lunch, and in them he says that Marshall declined the gambit. It was, he said, entirely for the President to decide. He warned the President that if he was chosen to go to Europe, there was only one man he could think of to replace him in Washington. It was the new general, Dwight D. Eisenhower, who had commanded the North African landings. The President decided that Eisenhower had neither Marshall's grasp of worldwide strategy nor his familiarity with Congress. So he picked Eisenhower, and Marshall congratulated him, and the lunch was over. At the end of it, Roosevelt said, 'I couldn't sleep nights, George, if you were out of Washington.' (Roosevelt is the only known man who ever called General Marshall 'George'.) When Stimson heard of this he was, he said, 'staggered'. He gave to his diary the note that 'at the bottom of his heart it was Marshall's secret desire above all things to command the invasion of Europe'. But Marshall himself had advanced the deciding argument. Who else would oversee the war of supply, who would review the war in both oceans, from the necessary desk in Washington? He never by any sign showed that the President's decision was not the perfect one. The British too were staggered and apprehensive, and it was a British official who put down in his journal: 'In Marshall's presence ambition folds its tent.' Stimson put down an order sentence he had once quoted about Marshall: 'He that ruleth his spirit is better than he that taketh a city.'

When the dust and the glory came blowing up over the battlefields, Marshall was the father confessor and guru to Eisenhower. To MacArthur he was still a sullen office figure, smarting at long range over the humiliation at Sedan, but it was Marshall who urged on Congress the award to MacArthur of the Medal of Honor. Twelve years later, when Eisenhower was campaigning for the Presidency in Wisconsin, he deleted – at the personal urging of the late Senator Joseph McCarthy – a passage in praise of Marshall from a speech that he was about to give. Not a word ever passed the lips of Marshall about this dismal episode, and when McCarthy called him a traitor for the failure of his post-war mission to China, all Marshall said to a personal friend was: 'The hardest thing I ever did was to keep my temper at that time.'

There is a final story about him which I happen to have from the only other man of three present. I think it will serve as a proper epitaph. In the early 1950s, a distinguished, a very lordly, American magazine publisher badgered Marshall to see him on what he described as a serious professional mission. He was invited to the General's summer home in Virginia. After a polite lunch, the General, the publisher and the third man retired to the study. The publisher had come to ask the general to write his war memoirs. They would be serialized in the magazine and a national newspaper and the settlement for the book publication would be handsome indeed. The General instantly refused on the grounds that his own true opinion of several wartime decisions had differed from the President's. To advertise the difference now would leave Roosevelt's defence unspoken and would imply that many lives might have been saved. Moreover, any honest account might offend the living men involved and hurt the widow and family of the late President. The publisher pleaded for two hours. 'We have had', he said, 'the personal testaments of Eisenhower, Bradley, Churchill, Stimson, James Byrnes. Montgomery is coming up and Alanbrooke, and yet there is one yawning gap.' The General was adamant. At last, the publisher said, 'General, I will put it on the line. I will tell you how essential we feel it to have you fill that gap, whether with two hundred thousand words or ten thousand. I am prepared to offer you $1 million after taxes for that manuscript.' General Marshall was faintly embarrassed, but quite composed. 'But, sir,' he said, 'you don't seem to understand. I am not interested in $1 million.'

The 1960s

Beizbol

13 October 1961

One of the most reliable clichés of American newspaper writing is the opening phrase: 'The eyes of the nation were focused today on . . .' There is one day of the year when this is true. It is the first Wednesday in October, the opening of what is majestically called the World Series. On that day the champions of the two major leagues play each other to decide which team, by winning the best of seven games, shall be declared to be the world champions at the old Russian game of beizbol.

We never, by the way, seem able to make up our minds whether Russian propaganda is too subtle or too crude. But it was a shrewd move of theirs in 1952 to look into the origins of the American national game and, after a severely scientific survey, conclude that it started in the Ukraine sometime in the Middle Ages. Of course, the best way to meet these objective Russian surveys is to make one of our own. And that is what we're going to do. In fact, it has been done for us – twice. Once by a commission set up in 1908, and again by a learned and curious librarian who had strong reasons to doubt the commission's findings.

In the country south of the Mohawk Valley, in the setting for several of the stories of James Fenimore Cooper, there is a town called – not unnaturally – Cooperstown. It is now a regular port of call on the tourist route because of a museum, sacred to the memory of one Abner Doubleday. He, it says here, was the only true inventor of the national game. The museum has a lot of early relics. It has a homemade baseball supposedly used by the great man himself. It preserves prints of Union soldiers playing baseball in North Carolina during the Civil War. It has bronze plaques bearing the names of retired heroes of the game who have been voted into the so-called 'hall of fame' by 75 per cent of the members of the Baseball Writers Association. Tap an American anywhere between the Canadian and Mexican borders and ask him who invented baseball and he will reverently pronounce the name – Abner Doubleday.

Let me begin by quoting the official account as it is quite briskly told in the federal guide to New York State: 'Baseball grew quite informally from Old Cat, a favourite boys' game in Colonial days, played by a thrower, a catcher and a batter. In 1839, Colonel Abner Doubleday, a student in a local military academy, later a major general in the Civil War, limited the number of players to eleven, outlined the first diamond-shaped field and drew up a memorandum of rules for the game which he named "baseball".' That is the version confirmed by the investigating commission I referred to after its researches in 1908. It was not, by the way, a government commission, as most baseball fans like to assume. It consisted of a sporting-goods manufacturer, a bunch of baseball managers and one United States Senator who was mad about the game. Even the *Encyclopaedia Britannica* (a Chicago publication) says about this commission: 'It was appointed ostensibly to investigate the origins of the game but really to "prove" its exclusively American origin.'

Well, by 1908, any other inventor of the game who could challenge the Doubleday legend was dead and gone. Cooperstown, New York, was naturally delighted to be singled out for glory. And the commission's findings passed into the record books and the tablets of sacred Americana. However, there is another name rarely mentioned by baseball scholars, and it is not surprising, because he is a dissenter and a sceptic; once you have picked and immortalized a public hero it is an awful nuisance to discover that he is a fraud. The name of the Doubting Thomas is Robert W. Henderson, a quiet fellow who, true to the requirements of his job as a staff member of the New York Public Library, doesn't like to take things for granted. Down the years he had poked around into the baseball story and by 1939 he was ready to launch a shattering offensive against the legend of Doubleday and Cooperstown. He confirmed, for instance, that Abner Doubleday went up to West Point in 1838, the year before he invented and named baseball at Cooperstown while he was presumably on leave from his military education. But at that time, cadets never got any leave in their second year. Mr Henderson also doubted that Cadet Doubleday managed to grow into a colonel in one year as a student. Luckily for the legend, the records of that investigating commission were lost in a fire. All that's left is a small file of papers quoting the main witness. He was a resident of Cooperstown bearing the suspicious name of Abner Graves. He laid it down that his namesake invented the game and that the runner was put out by the fielder hitting him with the ball. Since this doesn't happen in baseball, and granting that the man was telling the truth as he had observed it in many a stretcher case, Mr Henderson began to cast around for a game in which it did happen. He found that it had been the normal practice of an English game for a couple of centuries. He then started to go through the English records.

He found out – what even the Oxford dictionary had overlooked – that the word supposedly coined by Doubleday is first mentioned in 1744 in a letter of Lady Hervey in which she writes about the habits and pastimes of the then Prince of Wales: 'The Prince's family divert themselves at baseball, a play all who are, or have been, schoolboys are well acquainted with.' Jane Austen in one of her novels writes about a heroine who 'had nothing by nature heroic about her . . . she preferred cricket, baseball, riding on horseback . . . to books'. Mr Henderson began to pile up a mountain of documentary evidence from English literature, mainly from notebooks and journals and the like, to show that baseball – and so called – was a very popular children's game in England in the early eighteenth century. In the same year as Lady Hervey's letter there appeared a children's book of games, one letter of the alphabet for one game. B stood for baseball, and it has a picture of the player at the plate, a pitcher, a catcher and two posts for bases. The book was a best-seller and was reprinted twice in America. And in 1828, when Abner Doubleday (if he ever existed) was 9 years old, the *Boy's Own Book*, published in London, had a whole chapter about the game and illustrated it with a picture of a diamond, with bases at each corner. Many a rearguard Doubleday man will concede that perhaps Abner did not invent the game but certainly invented the diamond. Not old Abner. Colonel Jane Austen, maybe, but not General Abner.

What came out of Mr Henderson's subversive labours was that a game called baseball, which looks very much like a rudimentary version of today's American game, was played everywhere in England in the eighteenth century; and that it was called 'baseball' in the southern counties, 'rounders' in the West Country, and 'feeder' in metropolitan London.

From all this there emerges the solid, objective and bitter truth that baseball was invented not in the Ukraine, and not in Cooperstown, New York, but in England; was at first an amusement of the landed and leisured gentry of the southern counties; and that they called it baseball. Now since such people, when they emigrated to America at all, shunned the rude and pious New England shore and joined the more congenial Virginia colony, they brought over the game and the name. It developed several varieties here; and six years before Abner Doubleday, that charlatan, invented it, it was being played throughout the tidewater South and later in New England. In Philadelphia there was a full-fledged club.

All right, say the desperate Doubleday partisans, forced back now into the Catskills like guerrillas, so Abner may not have invented the game or the name but he surely drew up the rules of the modern game. Well, they too must have been lost in the fire. Because the only documentary record of a complete set of rules, on which the contemporary game is based, is one printed in 1845 by the Knicker-bocker Baseball Club of New York. And this version of the game grew into modern baseball through the accident, if we may so call it, of the Civil War. There were over fifty clubs enrolled and competing in a national association as early as 1850. The invincible champions of that year, who never seem to have lost a game, were the renowned Excelsiors of Brooklyn. All these clubs were composed of amateurs. It is not too much to deduce that baseball followed the precedent of other sports, blood sports especially, that now belong to the honest working man, whether in the Ukraine or elsewhere. They start out as the amusement of the rich and leisured until one day the squire finds himself in a tough spot and there is an onlooking groom, stable boy or gillie with a mean left-handed curve ball.

Well, the club games stopped with the Civil War. But the Union armies spread the Knickerbocker game through the border states and the South and played everywhere behind the lines. By the time the war was over, and the survivors went home in all directions, the only possible competitor to the New York game, played with a hard ball, was a softball game, played by small boys and Bostonians, who invented it (and let's not go into that).

The New York game was, then, the core of modern professional baseball. Amateur baseball may be the glory of the high schools but in the colleges it is rapidly on the wane. Baseball has suffered from the usual afflictions of an easygoing amateur diversion that turns into a high-pressure professional business. It has a very complicated system of buying and selling, of contracts and franchises. Twice in its modern history tremendous financial scandals have almost destroyed its reputation. But let us confess that in its present form it would alarm and astonish Jane Austen and the Prince of Wales, as well as the rude outfielders of the Ukraine. It is *the* characteristic American athletic spectacle and combines in its marvellous standard of fielding and the cunning flight of the ball through the air all the invisible (I mean subtle) skill of cricket and all the very visible competitive frenzy of the English national game, which I take to be association football.

A baseball stadium is a far cry from the fields and the lowly vacant lots of its origins. And baseball bears almost no resemblance to the game which Americans make a point of deriding and ignoring: cricket. If the Atlantic alliance is to hold on the playing fields, we shall have to act on the suggestion of the late Robert Benchley, who bravely suggested that it would be better to abolish cricket and baseball and 'start all over again with a game that both countries can play – preferably baseball'.

Robert Frost

1 February 1963

It was a splendid day in Vermont when they buried Robert Frost, the sky without a cloud, the light from the white landscape making every elm and barn as sharp as a blade, and the people crunching quietly through the deep snow and squinting in the enormous sun.

It is a harmless sentimental custom to bury men who have been supreme in some craft with a visible symbol of their mastery: one thinks of composers whose tombstones are inscribed with a lyre, and cricketers who were laid to rest with a floral wreath of a bat and a ball. Few men must have gone to their graves amid such an exhibition of the tools of their trade as Robert Frost did the other day. From the smallest object on the horizon, a clump of evergreens or a mountain top, to the most domestic scenery that was close at hand – a maple tree, a country store, a spade – everything the mourners saw or passed among had been the subjects of his poems and the objects of his lifelong meditation. He was once called 'an original ordinary man', but whether we ordinary men are ready or able to understand an original among us is another question. And I wonder how many Americans could have honestly agreed with President Kennedy that Frost had 'bequeathed this nation a body of imperishable verse from which Americans will forever gain joy and understanding'. Because if his poetry was as plain as its surface, it was very ordinary indeed. And if it was as deep and difficult as his best admirers said, the understanding audience for it must have been as small as it always is for great poetry.

However, President Kennedy had taken him up, and in the last year or two he became a sort of unofficial Poet Laureate, more honoured, I suspect, for his connection with the White House than for any spontaneous response of the American people to the body of his work. At any rate, when he died, either 87 or 88 years of age (no one is quite sure), his last days were full of honour, love, obedience, troops of friends, as his early days had been full of menial farm chores, odd jobs that never paid off, and easygoing obscurity.

He was born in San Francisco of a New Hampshire farmer and a Scottish mother. His father died when he was 10, and his mother took him back East to settle in Lawrence, Massachusetts, and he became and remained a New Englander. From his nineteenth year to his thirty-eighth he managed to get only fourteen poems into print. In the meantime, he had tried and failed to be a student at Dartmouth College, but he did later stick out two years at Harvard. In the five years between these two grim efforts to be formally educated he was a bobbin boy in the mills, a cobbler, a smalltown editor, a schoolteacher, and at last a farmer. But the soil of New England, as he came to reflect later, is a glacial relic, for most of the year the victim of alternating fire and ice. For this reason, or possibly because he was too obsessed with the natural objects of the countryside to be a good farmer, he had to eke out a living; which he did by going from his chores to teach English at one country school and to try teaching 'psychology' (a new fetish discovered by William James) at another.

So in his thirty-seventh year he was neither a prosperous farmer nor an accepted poet. From his long meditations on the country life and landscape of New England he had shored up two small books of poems: *A Boy's Life* and *North of Boston*. Neither of them found a publisher until he moved to England in 1912 with the set intention 'to write and be poor without further scandal in the family'. There he lived and walked in the West Country and was befriended and admired by Wilfrid Gibson and Edward Thomas, two early Georgians with whom he seemed at the time to have a lot in common. He had left America with a family reputation as a dilettante, but when he came back he was greeted, by a small audience, as a pro. He had no more trouble making a modest living, and for nearly thirty years, on and off, he lived on another farm, was the so-called 'poet in residence' at Amherst, and did other agreeable stretches as a teacher at the University of Michigan, Harvard, but mostly at Middlebury College in Vermont, and then again at Dartmouth. He put out his books of poetry at about five-year intervals until the 1940s saw him at the peak of his productivity and his authority, bustling around 'collecting sticks' – as he used to put it – for what he would ignite as annual 'poetic bonfires'.

From 1924 on he took the Pulitzer Prize for poetry at regular – about six-year – intervals. This habit, because it set him up as a solid establishment poet, made his more intellectual admirers begin to think that there must be less in his work than met the eye. Indeed, Frost suffered for a long time from the incapacity of the critics to overcome certain stock responses to the various schools of poetry that were then in fashion. Because he had been a friend of the English Georgians, he was for too long taken by some people to be an over-simple rebel against the developing technology of modern life, an expatriate cricket-and-ale rustic. And because, when he got back to America, he met the high tide of the 'new' poetry of the Chicago school, he had to be looked on as a New England Sandburg. And because, in the 1930s, he maintained his lifelong lack of interest in politics, the socially conscious writers of the New Deal dismissed him as a cranky escapist. We never seem to learn – though the evidence is stacked high in any library – that contemporary prejudices about a writer very rarely seem relevant in the long view. Frost was, in fact, as absorbed, and in some ways as difficult, a poet as Emily Dickinson, whose entire meditations on life were conducted inside the house in Amherst, Massachusetts, from which she barred all visitors and rarely stirred in more than twenty years. Frost was, let us say, an outdoor Emily Dickinson, which is a curiosity almost too bizarre to bear thinking about. Even when he was writing what later was admitted to be his finest poetry, his admirers were again of the wrong sort to satisfy the literary lawmakers. The people who called him 'our classic New England poet' also tended to see Will Rogers as the Mark Twain of the 1920s, and Pearl Buck as the travelling George Eliot of the 1930s. This is a kind of reverse sentimentality and a usual reflex of highbrows, who are often more concerned to validate a man's reputation than to enjoy him. It never troubled Frost much, and it would be a mistake to think of him at any time as a martyr. But for many years it made good men back away from him.

Other people, who were willing to be impressed, were put off for more honest reasons. They turned with pleasurable anticipation to his work, and what did they find? They found verses as flat and bare, and frequently as limp with bathos, as the verses on a country calendar. But if you persisted with him, you found that he had persisted ahead of you. Sometimes he reads like a man with no poetical gift whatsoever who is determined to slog his way through some simple fact of nature and discover, at all costs, some universal truth. But what ought to give pause to the unwary is that there *is* always a mind at work, a wriggling, probing and in the end, a tragic mind. The very titles of his poems are deceptively ordinary. 'The Cow in Apple Time', about a cow drooling cider, sounds like a humdrum cheerful thing. But it is not. Listen.

> Having tasted fruit,
> She scorns a pasture withering to the root.
> She runs from tree to tree where lie and sweeten
> The windfalls spiked with stubble and worm-eaten.
> She leaves them bitten when she has to fly.
> She bellows on a knoll against the sky.
> Her udder shrivels and the milk goes dry.

It was not until after the Second World War, when the flame of the Harriet Monroe revolution had died down, and left so many of its fiery figures mere cinders along the way, that another generation of critics noticed Frost still there, still writing his knotty monosyllables. They began to be excited by the suspicion that here possibly was an American Donne, or a Yankee Theocritus, or – a harder thing to grapple with – Robert Frost, an original. The idea that a huckleberry or a birch tree, or the games a boy played with that birch tree who was 'too far from town to learn baseball'; the idea that these things could bear the most unsentimental and profound contemplation was at first frightening, until the reader inched his way through the roughness of the underbush and, like 'The Soldier' – in Frost's poem – discovered that

> the obstacle that checked
> And tripped the body, shot spirit on
> Further than target ever showed or shone.

By the time that he was being accepted as a pure and gritty-minded pastoral poet, about as far removed from the Georgians as Thomas Hardy from Brer Rabbit, he himself was rejecting the physical world as a treacherous harbinger of winter and sickness. You could say more simply that he was a genuine poet and the oncoming of old age stirred him:

> Petals I have once pursued
> Leaves are all my darker mood.

At the age of 70 he was ready to upbraid God for the fate of Job and for His general cruelty to the human race. This challenge, in 'The Masque of Reason', was too much for him, but by now the critics were ready to grant that unlike any poet before or since, Frost had used the ordinary vernacular of a New England farmer to probe a few fundamental doubts. In poetry that is subtler in structure even than most vernacular, he transmuted rocks and flowers, wind and berries and hired men, and striking mill-workers, and boys swinging on trees, into the purest symbols of what is most hardy but most perishable in the human condition.

To the great mass of Americans, I suppose, he was simply a noble old man, said to be a great poet, who had come to be a colourful human adjunct to the refurbishing of the White House, rather like one of those plain hooked rugs, woven by a grandmother, with which wealthy New Englanders or Virginians living in exquisite colonial houses will sometimes pay a small tribute to their origins. He must have learned to live with the knowledge that to most of his countrymen he was known only by a couple of lines from one poem, 'Stopping by Woods on a Snowy Evening', just as John Donne must groan in his grave at all the twentieth-century people who know him only by the thought that 'No man is an island'. In our time, which is the age of mass marketing, we have to package our great men as quickly and simply as possible to make them acceptable to the family trade.

At the end, though, there was a lucky occasion on which his true readers and his uncomprehending large public could see him alike for what he was. In the icicle brilliance of Kennedy's inauguration he stood in 12 degrees of frost and tried to read aloud a poem specially written for the great occasion. The sun stabbed at his failing eyes, the wind slapped at him, the white light from the snow was too much for him, and he finally gave up and spoke out, stumblingly, what he knew, his fingers kneading his palms in a secret fury and his white hair blowing in sloppy waves against his forehead. It was an embarrassing moment for the President and the officials who had brought him, and for the huge crowd. But it was as good an end as any he might have imagined: an old farmer stripped down at last to a blinded oak of a man, tangled in his own branches, made foolish by the sun and the cold and the wind, by the simple elements he had once rejoiced in but which now he had come to mistrust as the mockers of humankind from Eden to Washington, DC.

The Father

22 February 1963

A simple way to turn an honest dime in a small company of Americans is to ask them on a bet how many national holidays are observed throughout the United States. They will usually count to no less than five: the birthdays of Washington and Lincoln, Independence Day, Thanksgiving Day and Labor Day. There are in fact only three. Labor Day, invented in New York as a trade union celebration, is not among them. Nor is the birthday of Lincoln. Only thirty-two states of the Union pause on 12 February to commemorate the most impressive life in the American experience. It was natural, however, that the defeated South should have taken a sour view of Lincoln for many decades after his death; and to this day, from Virginia round the whole bend of the South, through Louisiana and Texas, his birthday is officially disregarded. Once you cross the Texas line and enter New Mexico, you can begin to honour Lincoln again.

This leaves, therefore, only one American in history whom the entire country delights to honour. On every 22 February the offices and factories close down. The hundred and seventy elevators that serve the sixty thousand wage-slaves who work every day in the little plot of Manhattan ground known as Radio City – they run not at all, and the wind whistles through the shafts. Over the Post Office building, looking out on a tropical sea in San Juan, Puerto Rico, an American flag is run up and languishes in the hot air. And five thousand miles to the north and west, in a forest lookout tower in the snow-capped Cascade Mountains, another flag goes up and slaps against a frozen pole. Over every public building in this country and its territories and possessions the flags are raised, and the schools are closed.

There is a Fifth Avenue dress house that always, on this day, takes away its early spring models and loops its windows with purple draperies, beneath which, in a pool of light thrown by a single high spot, stands a lump of cool white marble: the bust of a big-faced man with a big aquiline nose, a considerable chin, an eighteenth-century wig, and the drooping eyelid that novelists prescribe for what they call a patrician gaze. It is of course an effigy of George Washington, to whom once a year all sorts of men pay all kinds of tribute. Even the *Wall Street Journal* is not published on the sacred birthday, though the day before I see there was inserted a chaste two-column advertisement for a jewel firm. Its copy consisted of a single sentence: 'If, to please the people, we offer what we ourselves disapprove, how can we afterward defend our work?' An oddly moral remark, you might think, for a jeweller. But the quotation was from none other than the father of his country.

Washington towers over the generations of notable Americans as Shakespeare towers over the literature of England. He is acceptable to everybody for at least one of the same reasons: we don't know too much about him, or what we have learned we have idealized, so every man can construct a Washington in the image he likes best. From time to time, most recently in the 1920s, snide authors come along to try and show that Washington was a promoter of stock companies, an exploiter of mines and timber, a man 'who knew more profanity than Scripture . . . had no belief in the wisdom of the common people but regarded them as inflammatory dolts'. But these scandals never seem to take. They get the same reception that they had from Calvin Coolidge when he was asked in the White House what effect a particularly scurrilous biography of the first President would have on his reputation. Coolidge swivelled round in his desk chair and biliously looked out the window at the soaring Washington monument, which is raised over the capital like the sword of the Archangel Gabriel. 'He's still there,' said Coolidge.

At this late date, it would be almost tasteless to compose a picture of Washington as a great if frail human being. Every nation has to have one or two blameless legends, and Americans feel as uncomfortable today to hear that Washington was a land grabber as an Englishman would be to hear that King Alfred was a cannibal or the late Queen Mary a secret drinker. Washington's birthday is as close to a secular Christmas as any Christian country dare come this side of blasphemy. I hasten to throw in quickly that the United States, though founded in the main by Christian men, was not set up as a Christian nation, since its creators had had their fill of the established Church that hounded their forebears. It may explain why, when Americans are sorely troubled, they turn for official inspiration not to the the Koran or the Bible but to the the colonial scriptures, to the sayings of the Founding Fathers, most of all to the speeches of Washington.

There is today a pronouncement of his that they linger over with a great yearning. It is regularly reprinted and blazoned in newspaper editorials on any 22 February that Americans feel about to be tricked into a European war or seduced into an alliance. It is a passage from Washington's so-called Farewell Address, which he gave as he took leave of the Presidency. It reads today rather like a commentary of General de Gaulle on the 'special relationship' between Britain and the United States. This is it: 'A passionate attachment of one nation for another produces a variety of evils. Sympathy for the favourite nation, facilitating the illusion of an imaginary common interest in cases where no real common interest exists ... betrays the former into a participation in the quarrels of the latter, without adequate inducement or justification.'

It does not quite have the swing of 'Tell me where is fancy bred' or 'My luve's like a red, red rose'. So, down the centuries Americans have tended to shorten this unmemorable, and unlearnable, passage into a snappy single phrase: 'No entangling alliances.' When it is pointed out that this is a misquotation, that the phrase actually came from the lips of Thomas Jefferson, the sensible retort is that, anyway, that's what old George meant to say.

Now that we have the effigy and its legend pretty well established, let us come down to the man himself.

His family came from England and he was born in Virginia in 1732. His father was what you might describe as a substantial small squire, a status that made him possibly a grander figure in the Southern colonies than he would have been in the old country. Almost anybody who owned land in Virginia led a life which was a curious combination of a farmhand and an aristocrat. (I am aware that grooms and the like were all, until the First World War, elements of the aristocratic system – 'all part of the same show', as a Prime Minister of England eloquently put it; but except in the rituals of blood sports their habits were not interchangeable.) Washington learned all that could be learned about the farming and management of his father's estate, which had passed to him from a half-brother who died young. He raised cattle, he was out in the fields growing tobacco, he shot wild turkey and ate it on the bone. He had taught himself a lot of mathematics and on his surveying trips he was always adding to his land. He rode by day and often by night, he brushed up against the Indians from time to time, and a scalp was as natural, I imagine, as a cow-flop.

He served in the French and Indian wars as a general's aide, had horses shot out from under him and acquired an enviable, though local, reputation for a blank refusal to panic. Then quite suddenly his health failed him and he resigned his commission and retreated, for what he thought would be the rest of his life, to a fine stretch of land overlooking the Potomac River where he had built an elegant and charming white house with a little Wren tower, a colonial façade, and a long portico supported by slender columns. (It is now a national shrine and, along with the Spanish mission at Santa Barbara, California, used to be one of the two handsomest colonial relics in America. But both of them have been refaced and at close quarters look like something out of Disney.)

He was in his bearing and looks and manners an eighteenth-century British soldier and landowner; and if he could be resurrected he would undoubtedly alarm a great many Americans by sounding and seeming more British than the British. He had, for instance, very decided ideas about the relations of one class with another. In the towns, at any rate. In the country it was another thing: he was with many conditions of men who were 'part of the same show'. Not only did he not slap backs, he made a point on becoming President of not shaking hands. He thought it was unbecoming for the President of a great state to touch the flesh of his subjects. The Senate used to bristle over this characteristic, and when he was inaugurated as President in New York – an early and transient capital – he came down the Hudson in a great barge and he clattered to the ceremony in full-dress uniform with a flourish of outriders. As he took the oath of office, the impressive silence was cracked only by the growl of a Senator from Massachusetts saying to his neighbour: 'I fear that we may have exchanged George the Third for George the First.'

You would think, then, that there was little in this reserved and lordly man to provoke the famous compliment that was spoken on his death: 'First in war, first in peace, first in the hearts of his countrymen.' Six feet three or four (the tape measures vary), imperious, self-sufficient, contemptuous of jolly human relations, his sword at his side, a big face serene to the point of complacency but pitted with smallpox, a frosty eyebrow under which rolled a sleepy blue eye, which, however, was said to rouse itself a little at the sight of a pretty woman – I think he must have been one of those people, not always appealing, whose greatness was simply the triumph of character over the flesh. Perhaps he was British enough by instinct to rise at the same qualities in his country's rulers. He had been, remember, a militiaman in the British army and had been the victim of some very overbearing officers. Not unnaturally he came to attribute arrogance to the land of their birth. He detested the strict and pettifogging restrictions on American trade that were soon to cause a war, and to cause, in fact, the United States of America. He organized the resistance in Virginia to the English Stamp Act and the Tobacco Act. He was a Virginia delegate to the first meeting of the colonies which met to decide, and did decide, to fight the mother country. He was chosen, not at that time by the mark of his obvious superiority but by a political deal, as the commander-in-chief of the rather miserable army that undertook to defend the American continent against the British.

How did it come about that in five short years he was able to break through the strong chrysalis of a Virginia gentleman and take wings and become a name which in its day combined the authority of Napoleon with the magic of Franklin Roosevelt? The answer seems to lie not in any personal charm but in his iron resolution to keep the American army united when it was all but ready to fall apart from incompetence, indifference, corruption and starvation. What an army it was! For every trained soldier there were three half-trained and ten mechanics, farmers, illiterates, half of them pressed into service or bought into service, deserting in droves, buying their way out when the going was rough.

According to Jefferson and other reliables, he often failed in the field and was not, in the military sense, a great general. But for eight years, and through many defeats and constant betrayal, he was as cool as an icicle and as impressive as God. He believed in his men long after they had ceased to believe in themselves. He fought with and for them even when the Congress thought of calling off the war. And in the famous winter of 1777 he was lucky to rescue from two thrashings by the British the ragged remnant of an army, so puny and bedraggled that the word went to Britain that the war was almost won. He pulled together a few thousand men, many times outnumbered by the crack troops of the enemy, and he camped in a rolling, bare valley in Pennsylvania. Less than half his men had arms, most of them had neither shoes nor shirts. The Congress took flight into the mountains of Pennsylvania and there was great rejoicing in London. During that winter, it is not too much to say, whatever was mortal in Washington was absorbed and elevated into the legend. He lost men from disease, desertion, treachery, and very many simply starved to death. Congress was so out of sympathy with this bitter-ender that it reorganized the War Department without his say-so. But he kept his camp at Valley Forge through the racking winter. And in the spring the French lined up with the rebels, and the rebellion held.

So Valley Forge was no victory. It was a pitiful siege. But it explains the veneration in which Washington came to be held, then and ever after, for of all the battles of the war Valley Forge was the proudest. It was the heart of the Revolution, the thing itself. No great general has ever been remembered so exclusively by such a defeat or by such a homely place name.

When he died, Napoleon was observed to bow his head, and in the English Channel the British fleet fired a salute of twenty guns.

The Assassination

24 November 1963

By now it may well be impossible to add any sensible or proper words to all the millions that have been written and spoken about the life and cruel death of John F. Kennedy. Those of us who have ever sat down to write a letter of condolence to a close friend know what an aching task it is to say something that is pointed and that touches the right vein of sympathy. But I hope you will understand that there is no other thing to talk about – not here. At three thousand miles it may be easier to speculate about policy, the new administration – not here. For I cannot remember a time, certainly in the last thirty years, when the people everywhere around you were so quiet, so tired-looking, and for all their variety of shape and colour and character so plainly the victims of a huge and bitter disappointment. That may sound a queer word to use, but grief is a general term that covers all kinds of sorrow, and I think that what sets off this death from that of other great Americans of our time is the sense that we have been cheated, in a moment, by a wild but devilishly accurate stroke of the promise of what we had begun to call the Age of Kennedy.

Let me remind you of a sentence in his Inaugural address, when he took over the Presidency on that icy day of 20 January 1961. He said, 'Let the word go forth from this time and place to friend and foe alike that the torch has been passed to a new generation of Americans, born in this century, tempered by war, disciplined by a hard and bitter peace, proud of our ancient heritage and unwilling to witness or permit the slow undoing of those human rights to which this nation has always been committed . . . Let every nation know, whether it wishes us well or ill, that we shall pay any price, bear any burden, meet any hardship, support any friend, oppose any foe, to assure the survival and the success of liberty.'

This is, of course, the finest rhetoric, worthy of Lincoln, but what made it sound so brave and rousing on that first day was the clear statement that a young man was speaking for a new generation. It concentrated in one scornful sentence the reminder that the old men who had handled the uncertain peace and the Second World War had had their day and that there was at hand a band of young Americans ready not to ignore the wisdom of their forefathers but to fight for it.

It would be hard to say more exactly or more bravely that it was a fresh America that would have to be negotiated with, but that, as always, liberty itself was not negotiable.

Now, even in the moment of knowing that the promises of an inaugural address are bound to have a grandeur very hard to live up to the morning after, this remarkable speech, which the President had hammered out, sentence by sentence, with his closest aide and companion, Theodore Sorensen, did strike a note to which the American people, and their allies everywhere, responded with great good cheer. Of course we knew, older men and women have always known (what in their youth they blithely rattled off as a quotation from Shakespeare) that 'golden lads and girls all must, as chimney sweepers, come to dust'. But it is always stirring to see that young people don't believe it. We chuckled sympathetically then at the warning which Senator Lyndon Johnson had chanted all through the campaign: that the Presidency could not safely be put in the hands of a man 'who has not a touch of gray in his hair'. John Kennedy had turned the tables triumphantly on this argument by saying, in effect, that in a world shivering under the bomb it was the young who had the vigour and the single-mindedness to lead.

If we pause and run over the record of the very slow translation of these ideals into law – the hair's breadth defeat of the medical care for the aged plan, the shelving after a year of labour of the tax bill, the perilous reluctance of the Congress to tame the Negro revolution now with a civil rights law – we have to admit that the clear trumpet sound of the Kennedy Inaugural has been sadly soured down three short years.

Any intelligent American family, sitting around a few weeks ago, would grant these deep disappointments; and many thoughtful men were beginning to wonder if the President's powers were not a mockery of his office, since he can be thwarted from getting any laws passed at all by the simple obstructionism of a dozen chairmen of Congressional committees, most of them, by the irony of a seniority system that gives more and more power to old men who keep getting re-elected by the same states, most of them from the South. But that same American family, sitting around this weekend, could live with these disappointments but not with the great one: the sense that the new generation, 'born in this century, tempered by war, disciplined by a hard and bitter peace, proud of our ancient heritage and unwilling to witness or permit . . .', was struck down lifeless, unable to witness or permit, or not to permit, anything.

When it is possible to be reasonable we will all realize, calling on our everyday fatalism, that if John Kennedy was 46 and his brother only 38, most of the men around him were in their fifties and some in their sixties; and that therefore we fell, for a day or two in November 1963, into a sentimental fit. However, we are not yet reasonable; the self-protective fatalism, which tells most of us that what has been must be, has not yet restored us to the humdrum course of life.

I am not dwelling on this theme, the slashing down in a wanton moment of the flower of youth, because it's enjoyable or poetic to think about. It seems to me, looking over the faces of the people and hearing my friends, that the essence of the American mood this very dark weekend is this deep feeling that our youth has been mocked, and the vigour of America for the moment paralysed.

It is, to be hard-hearted about it, fascinating – when it is not also poignant – to see in how many ways people express the same emotion. Many of the memorial photographs in the shop windows have small replicas of the Presidential standard on one side, and a Navy flag on the other, recalling the incredible five days' gallantry on that Pacific island which Kennedy himself never recalled, except to the men who were with him and survived. A young socialite, whose life is a round of clothes and parties and music, bemoans the fact that the Kennedys will leave the White House and take with them 'the style, the grace, the fun they brought to it'. An American friend from Paris writes: 'I think his death will especially be felt by the young, for he had become for them a symbol of what was possible, with intelligence and will.' An old man, wise in the ups and downs of politics, says: 'I wonder if we knew what he might have grown to in the second term.' A child with wide eyes asks, 'Tell me, will the Peace Corps go on?'

There is another thing that strikes me, which is allied to the idea of a young lion shot down. It is best seen in the bewilderment of people who were against him, who felt he had temporized and betrayed the promise of the first days. One of them, a politically active woman, rang me up and what she had to say dissolved in tears. Another, a veteran sailor, a close friend and a lifelong Republican, said last night: 'I can't understand, I never felt so close to Kennedy as I do now.' This sudden discovery that he was more familiar than we knew is, I think, easier to explain. He was the first President of the television age, not as a matter of chronology but in the incessant use he made of this new medium. When he became President-elect, he asked a friend to prepare a memorandum on the history of Presidential press conferences. He wanted to know how much the succession of Presidents since Wilson had been able to mould the press conference and how much it had moulded *them*. What he received was a plea, disguised as a monograph, to abandon Eisenhower's innovation of saying everything on the record for quotation and letting the conference be televised. He looked it over, at his usual rate (of about a thousand words a minute), granted the arguments but said simply: 'Television is now the main personal link between the people and the White House. We can't go back.' He allowed his press conferences to be televised live. He also made another decision which ran counter to the wisdom of all incumbent Presidents. No man who is in power invites a debate with an opponent who is out of power and who can speak not of the things he's done but of the things the incumbent has done wrong. In spite of knowing well that next time he would be the man with his back against the wall, he had decided that the television debate was now an essential element of a Presidential campaign.

So for three years and more, we have seen him, at the end of our day, on all his tours – in Vienna, in Dublin, in Berlin, in Florida, Chicago, Palm Beach, in – alas – Dallas, in his own house talking affably with reporters, rumpling up the children, very rarely posing, always offhand and about his business, talking to foreign students in the White House garden, making sly, dry jokes at dinners, every other week fencing shrewdly and often brilliantly with two hundred reporters, and sometimes at formal rallies stabbing the air with his forefinger and bringing to life again, in his eyes and his chin and his soaring sentences, the old image of the young warrior who promised 'the energy, the faith, the devotion that will light America and all who serve her'.

The consequence of all this is that the family, the American family, has been robbed, violently and atrociously, of a member. When Roosevelt died, the unlikeliest people, the very young who thought of him as a perpetual President, and some of the very old who hated him, confessed that they felt they had lost a father. Today, millions of Americans are baffled by the feeling, which seems to have little to do with their political loyalties, that they have lost a brother, the bright young brother you are proud of, the one who went far and mingled with the great, and had no side, no pomp, and in the worst moments (the Bay of Pigs) took all the blame, and in the best (the Cuban crisis) had the best sort of courage, which is the courage to face the worst and take a quiet stand.

This charming, complicated, subtle and greatly intelligent man, whom the Western world was proud to call its leader, appeared for a split second in the telescopic sight of a maniac's rifle. And he was snuffed out. In that moment, all the decent grief of a nation was taunted and outraged. So that along with the sorrow, there is a desperate and howling note over the land. We may pray on our knees, but when we get up from them, we cry with the poet:

> Do not go gentle into that good night.
> Rage, rage against the dying of the light.

LBJ

28 November 1965

One of the occupational burdens of a foreign correspondent is the request from the home office for a piece which the home office has already composed in its head. Many years ago, an English magazine asked me for an article and an accompanying photograph 'doing something American, preferably sporting'. I was briefly fascinated by the thought of what the editor imagined a sporting American to be (a rodeo rider? a Las Vegas gambler? a golfer in two-toned – or as they used to be called, 'co-respondent's' – shoes?). For almost at once I came on a photograph taken by a friend on a hot summer's day on the south shore of Long Island. At that time I was mad about surf-casting, and here was a tanned and lithe fellow, young and black-haired, casting the long line with a masterful arc. I was in shorts and my knees were buried in the froth of the surf. It seemed just the ticket. I scribbled in a suggestion for a caption: 'Cooke casting for striped bass on Long Island'. Incidentally, I was in left profile facing the ocean, which was on the left of the picture.

When the magazine sent me a complimentary copy, I was in right profile and the ocean was on the right. This was not an error, though it involves a rather laborious photographic trick. I thought, Why print the negative? The editor wrote back, 'If the ocean is on your left, it will look as if you were fishing in the Pacific – very confusing.' But the printed caption alarmed me more. It said, 'Cooke fishing in Florida'. The editor had an answer for that one, too. 'The English,' he wrote on a crisp postcard, 'know certain elementary things and we mustn't upset them. The Pacific is where Hollywood is; fishing would seem a waste of time. Cowboys come from the West. Fishing is in Florida – no use puzzling them by bringing up Long Island, which is where rich men keep their yachts.'

It took me years to work up the nerve to write for a British audience about fishing. I still wanted to correct that caption, thoug. undoubtedly the only living person who remembered it. I v to say that though they do surf-fish in Florida – and catch inconsequential stuff as snook, permit and various snappers – it i: loot of the deep seas, the white and blue marlin, and the inshore ִed and mutton snappers, the pompano and other lurid and tasty monsters, for which Florida should be respected; and that it is we in the North who have the thundering surf through which striped bass as weighty as thirty or forty pounds knife their headlong way till they are practically beached at your feet, and wheel around and beat it out to sea. It was all too late to explain. No use even mentioning to a transatlantic audience that striped bass is probably the most succulent of our eating fish. If it does not swim in Europe, it's probably tasteless.

❡ This early episode provided my initiation into the war between correspondents and their editors. Lately, I have had another. Very soon after Lyndon Johnson took over the Presidency I had a cable from an English editor saying, 'WOULD APPRECIATE ARTICLE ON TEXAS AS BACKGROUNDER JOHNSON STOP COWBOYS COMMA OIL COMMA MILLIONAIRES COMMA HUGE RANCHES COMMA GENERAL CRASSNESS BAD MANNERS ETC.' I promptly declined this assignment since the whole piece would have had to show that the editor was wrong at the start, and the end. If cowboys, oil, millionaires, huge ranches, and general crassness were the true background of Lyndon Johnson, or even the elementary things about Texas, clearly the editor could have written the piece himself.

My first thought was: cowboys there are, west of the Johnson country, which is central Texas, a landscape of pulverized granite planted with mesquite, very congenial to armadillos and other armoured divisions but the pasture otherwise so poor that the sheep eat the wild flowers and the goats must nibble for the rest. Goats, they say, can live where all other four-footed animals would starve. And this is goat country, and that is why Lyndon Johnson as a Congressman, or some other Congressman from nearby, would be pretty certain to be on the House Military Affairs Committee, because goats produce mohair, and mohair produces army uniforms.

All right – oil. It used to be smart to say that Texas has traded its open range for a sea of oil beneath. But it is very likely that most of the people in and around Johnson City and the Pedernales River have never seen an oil man. The great oilfields lie to the east and the north, and to Johnson's family and neighbours they are another world. In his early days, in fact, Johnson had to fight the oil lobby on behalf of the poor farmers around him, and you could say that the unceasing struggle of the farmers against drought and floods, their need for some elementary conservation and electricity – these were the hard facts of life that first pushed Johnson into politics.

By now I hope I don't need to say that millionaires in Johnson country are as scarce as they are in northern Scotland. Huge ranches? I must say that this magazine editor had an uncanny knack for picking on the very attributes that aren't there. The celebrated King Ranch, from which this preconception springs, is in the extreme southeast of the state, right on the Gulf. It is the largest ranch there is, just under a million acres, and it is spectacularly atypical. The average Texas ranch is two hundred acres, and the ranches (meaning the farms) of the Johnson country are smaller still.

General crassness? Certainly there are crass people in Texas, as there are in Maine and Berkshire and India and France. But when I read to the end of this sorry cablegram, what came perversely to mind was a remark of the late Lord Halifax when he was ambassador to the United States. Whenever he could snatch a weekend or a few days away from Washington, he would go down to Texas and his Texas friends. It was his favourite state, and about its people he said, 'They have the finest manners of any foreign people I have ever known.'

Manners? Lyndon Johnson? In this, perhaps, he is an original, and only a week or two after he succeeded to the Presidency, an old American statesman, an intellect and a wasp (in more senses than one), told me that 'the problem the American people are going to have with him is to recognize that his "country manners" do not preclude genuine compassion and a first-rate mind'.

So, if you are going to write a piece filling in the background of Lyndon Johnson there are some essential things that you have to picture. The granite soil, with actual high mounds of granite slabs; the heat and the barrenness of the country; the stern and tidy life of the nearby German town of Fredericksburg; the strong hold of the Methodists and Baptists on the Texas state legislature – hence no alcoholic mixed drinks are served in Texas from one end of its 800-mile stretch to another, and millionaires must tote their booze into a fancy restaurant in brown paper bags. The boyhood spent with people of Scots-Irish descent, known there as Anglos, because the other neighbours are Germans and Mexicans. The Germans are a Republican pocket on the plain, and as a boy Johnson saw many old friends suffer cruelly in the First World War because of their ties of blood.

The most important mark of this part of Texas is its classlessness, of a special, highly regional kind. Thus, Johnson could be at one and the same time a small farmer, once a very poor one, and yet be well connected as to family (his father and grandfather could be high in state government and yet be close to bankruptcy). He is a country boy with Southern talk and Western habits. He knows the Old Testament as well as he knows the soils of Texas. And throughout his childhood, college was a distant thing to aim at but not to take for granted. The enduring ambition of his boyhood was that of his friends: the passionate desire of a poor farmboy to own his own farm and call it a ranch. The now famous LBJ ranch is a modest place, as such things go. And when Johnson first bought it and took old Speaker Rayburn down there to show it off, Mr Sam said: 'Lyndon, you told me you'd bought a ranch, why it's nothin' but an itty-bitty farm.'

The pride of Johnson in these origins is something we shall all have to reckon with. What has already emerged from his Presidency is the force of his remark, long buried, that he was 'a Roosevelt man, lock, stock, and barrel'. Roosevelt took to the young Johnson in the pit of the Depression and sent him to his own people to reclaim thousands of unemployed young men from the streets and the farm patches. It was, Johnson later said, 'the most satisfying job I ever did have in my life'. This remark attests, I think, to the genuineness of his so-called war on poverty, which the opposition said was a cynical election-year ploy. As a Roosevelt radical he was well hated by the oil and insurance interests when he first ran for Congress. And if we say that he was allied rather with 'the ranching interests' they include very conspicuously the interest of the small farmers, the Mexicans especially, in having sheep that stayed alive, electricity for their kitchens and pumps, feed for their cattle, not to mention food for their families.

There is another aspect of this regional pride that is bound to affect

Johnson's approach to negotiation both with friends and foes. He delights to look on southwest Texas as a training ground and a horoscope for the world outside. He strongly believes that if a man can learn to harmonize the conflicting interests and prejudices of Mexican bean-farmers and German bakers and Anglo retailers and Jews and real-estate men from Austin, he can approach foreigners – men from India and prime ministers from Westphalia – on the same basis. He always provokes a stranger to talk about his past and his origins, so as to gauge the real forces that commit a man's heart before his head is involved. He startled a German delegation, on its first visit to the ranch, by saying that the German demand for a milk subsidy, the Italians' concern for protecting their rice and olive oil, the Netherlands' need for a margarine tax, all composed not the dangerous battleground of the European Common Market but the common ground on which they would have to weave these necessities into a system. 'He talked to us,' said one goggling German, 'as if we were his constituents.'

It remains a great question whether this instinct for what he calls 'creative compromise' will provide the proper magic for talking to the Russians and the British about Europe, or the South Vietnamese – and maybe one day the Chinese – about Southeast Asia. There is another large question. It is whether a conservative country in a revolutionary mood (I mean the United States) will be willing to let 'a Roosevelt man, lock, stock, and barrel' finish the liberal revolution of Roosevelt's New Deal that was only halfway along when it was rudely arrested by the Second World War.

It is not simply to bolster your spirits on a dark anniversary that I have attempted this little session on the couch, but to warn the intelligentsia, which mourns too inconsolably the bad day at Dallas, that it should watch and wait. Lincoln, too, was considered an oaf by the intelligentsia and actually dubbed 'the Baboon' by the best-informed men in London, including the editorial writers of *The Times*. He fooled most of the people most of the time he was alive. But he didn't fool history. So it could be with Johnson.

Has the World Gone to Pot?

15 April 1966

Anyone like me who was brought up in Britain had used the slang phrase l.s.d. ever since he could remember. It was one of the last souvenirs of the Roman occupation and was the normal phrase for pounds, shillings and pence. It naturally held a fascination for the smallest tot who ever stood on the wrong side of the plate-glass window of a candy store. But the initials never had the sinister fascination they now spell out.

A letter from the federal government to two thousand university and college officials reminded me at first of the comparative innocence of my own boyhood, and then by free association of two blind men, James Thurber and Aldous Huxley. Most of all, it reminded me of a walk I took with Huxley, around Christmas time 1959, along the road and around the garden of his house high above the bowl of mountains which encloses Hollywood at its rim and Los Angeles in its huge basin. Aldous Huxley was not a poet himself but a man of fine insight into poetic experience. He was also a man who held grimly on to some rather rum superstitions, and I don't think it's unkind to say that southern California was at least one congenial room in his spiritual home.

I mention both these characteristics, one of which is a kind of parody or excess of the other, because they both applied to something he said to me as we walked high up in the hills and he began to tell me about an experiment he was making with a certain drug. It excited him greatly. He called it lysergic acid, and I presume it was an early compound of the one that is now known as LSD-25. Huxley was, so far as any ordinary person could see or sense, a blind man. He could read through very thick lenses when he held the paper almost to his eyeballs. He could, he said, distinguish intensities of light. Sometimes his eyes were better and sometimes worse but not so that an acquaintance would notice. You had to guide him on a walk and you could believe he had any sight at all only when he went into his own house and moved easily around its familiar geography. It is necessary to go into the seeming limits of his sight because he was, during our walk, talking about the essential thing in a poet, his ability to see physical things more penetratingly than most of us, and to feel more deeply.

I remember we were treading carefully along the road, and I gathered that Huxley could not possibly see more than dim shadows and shapes farther than a few feet in front of him. He had just said that D. H. Lawrence had the most acute sensitivity of anyone he had known to the texture and tactile character of animals and birds and flowers. 'Well,' he said, in his gentle and intense way, 'I have found out that with this drug one can be granted for a while a kind of exquisitely heightened sensibility, so that' – he said, as the gravel crunched under our feet – 'every stone or piece of gravel on this roadway, for instance, comes to look like a separate and marvellous jewel.'

In the past week or so, more than six years later, I have dared to wonder whether the drug quickened and improved the sense he had almost lost or whether it did, in fact, replace his loss with a vision. I put it this way because we have lately heard some sad and shocking testimony about the effect of LSD-25 on college students, who, in the present fashion, seem to take all sensation for their province, including the further reaches of consciousness, and unconsciousness, induced by drugs. LSD is absurdly cheap to make. It is one of the company of drugs now known as hallucinogens, and there is no doubt that in some people it produces exquisite visions. The big question is whether they are of the outer or inner world, whether in fact they heighten and deepen reality or fool the taker into believing that the kind of vision a madman sees is the real world that convention, habit, or sheer blunting of instinct hide from him. At any rate, the experience of a dose sometimes passes off with a few bad effects that are noticeable. (We ought to say 'noticeable at the time, and to the outsider'.) There now appears also to be no doubt that LSD can, and often does, induce mental aberrations and psychotic states that may last several hours or days; that it may plant a chronic psychosis, or do temporary or permanent damage to the central nervous system. Sometimes, though apparently rarely, it drives the taker to suicide, murder, or death.

It was the director of the Food and Drugs Administration who sent this letter to the presidents and deans, principals and science departments of the colleges and universities, warning them of the 'extreme danger' of these 'hallucinatory drugs', in particular of LSD-25, one-tenth of an ounce of which can provide 100,000 tiny doses, each big enough, in the government's opinion, to be called 'exceedingly dangerous'.

This radical move was called for by the great prevalence of pep pills, barbiturates, and other drugs among college students. Lately, we have had scary news about the prevalence of LSD, in California especially. It is the kind of news about which it is almost impossible to make a helpful comment. Older people deplore the pathological extremes which this generation of college students seems to touch in its hunger for experience. Doctors shake their heads, but the addicts don't go to doctors unless they are thoroughly alarmed; with LSD, the government suggests, the alarm may sound too late. The hope about LSD is that it will be more often terrifying than exalting, and it will be dropped, even by neurotics who are tempted to go beyond the euphoria of pep pills and the weed grown in back gardens known as marijuana. (Marijuana is always lumped with the other dangerous drugs, but the day may come when we have to consider it as a special case. The state laws are strict against its possession, on the general assumption that it is a narcotic. But the scientists are agreed that it is not, as – for instance – cigarettes are. It spreads the time sense in some people, so that an oncoming truck may seem to be a mile away instead of its actual few hundred yards. In most people, I'm told, it produces much the same sense of confident well-being and happy talk as a couple of dry martinis, which are not so far, thank God, banned from American life.)

Whenever the LSD topic comes up, most of us – if we have children of college age – are forced to ask ourselves whether we are taking a merely reflex, stuffy view of the failings of the young. We tend to lump drugs with the active rebellion of the young against what they call the establishment and we call society. I don't know the answer to this. But there is one comment I should like to make. The generation just ahead of me, which was young and dashing in the 1920s, was certainly indicted by *its* elders. It was told it had violated the whole moral code and was fast destroying family life. (If you were chic in the 1920s having children was considered naive or, since birth control was a prevailing fad, clumsy.) In this country, the brazen young defied the Noble Experiment of prohibition with a flask of bathtub gin in the hip pocket. There were, in every city, whole benches of magistrates to bemoan that the young were leading the world into decadence and damnation to the wailing of the newly revived saxophone and the shameless gyrations of the charleston.

Well, I suppose that these people, who are now in their mid-sixties or beyond, produced their quota of pleasure hounds and even drug addicts. A remarkable number of them wrote remarkable books, painted memorable pictures, composed so many charming and bouncy songs that without them any band that plays for old-time dancing (what you might now call 'square' dancing) would have to fold long before midnight. Other family-wreckers turned into statesmen, architects, businessmen, conscientious plumbers and builders, doctors, scientists, and the majority into law-abiding citizens and devoted parents who, only a few years ago, provoked the amazed admiration of their grandchildren by teaching them how to do the charleston.

The irresistible thing is to say that old people always lament the morals and manners of the young and are always wrong. The fact that is often overlooked is that sometimes the old people have been right; and the trick is to know when you are living in one of those times. An old Roman codger who lamented in the fourth century AD that the empire was going to rack and ruin was absolutely correct. A Greek doctor who, let us say, in the first century AD feared that his trade of medicine was seriously declining would no doubt have been ridiculed as a fogey. But he could hardly have been enough of a pessimist to guess that for the next twelve or thirteen hundred years, medicine would flounder in a dark age of quackery and superstition before it again enlisted the early scientific method or the insights of Hippocrates, who knew the difference between the fever of tuberculosis and the fever of pneumonia, though he had never heard of a micro-organism. Or consider an old English playgoer, in about 1630, grumbling that the best tragedies had all been written and staged in his youth. Another fogey, no doubt, but neither he nor the young who scoffed at him could possibly have imagined that no decent tragedies at all would appear in English for another two hundred and fifty years.

It's an old cliché, but annoyingly enough it's a true one, to say that Americans are obsessed with the idea that progress is inevitable, that – as a faith healer of the 1920s used to say – 'every day and in every way we are getting better and better'. The belief in progress is certainly a stimulant to achieve it and is responsible for the tenacity of, say, American industrial research (applied research, to be precise) and for the national delight in new things, as well as (I've been hinting) for the complacency of seeing virtue only in what is new, whether it's a plastic or a poem or a new way of talk. But it does disguise from us the truth that civilizations have their ups and downs and all of them, at last, snuff out. Because we can 'hang' glass buildings on a steel frame does not necessarily make us the superiors of John Nash, or Palladio or Louis Sullivan. The fact that we've seen in our time – in the last thirty years only – the birth and glory of the great age of bacteriology is no gurantee that it's going to go on. As a political fact, simply, it has guaranteed the survival of more people than can be decently fed and housed.

I put the question, and I do not stay for an answer. Just in time, another medical item came off the ticker and may help us to hang on with our fingernails through this barrage of brimstone. A research scientist from the Neuropsychiatric Institute at Princeton, speaking before an impressive gathering of experimental biologists, has come up with the pronouncement that the only drug that some of us will ever take with a steady hand and a clear conscience is not only a painkiller but has very positive properties to relieve anxiety. The man has been measuring brainwaves, of course, and he finds that this magic drug has more reliable and harmless effect than the tranquillizers. It is called aspirin. When it is 'buffered', he says, it will soothe you and strengthen you against 'the real anxieties of the world'.

Fortified by two of these little white placebos, I look out of my window and on to the park and, whether it is there or not, I can see the forsythia at last is out, that the cherry is starting to blossom. I have a vision of the sap rising in the trees. I am humbly grateful for the faculty of sight. And I recall suddenly that James Thurber, in his brave, crotchety way, used to maintain that writers can actually be handicapped by sight. We were sitting out on the terrace of his house in Connecticut and I asked him what he meant. 'Well,' he said, 'you are constantly distracted by the sight of the flowers and the buds bursting. I can sit here and I don't get distracted by flying birds or the sight of a pretty girl going by. Of course,' he said after a thoughtful pause, 'I can still *hear* a pretty girl go by.'

John McLaren's Folly

24 June 1966

The idea that San Francisco is a beautiful metropolis, if not the most beautiful big city in America, is one to which, I should think, most Americans and all San Franciscans are delighted to subscribe. I hate to crab our conversation at the start, but it seems to me that the appeal of the place is its cosy, small-town quality, which a huge bay and nine rambling hills cannot convert into a metropolis. San Francisco is not a beautiful city any more than a homely girl standing on a beautiful mountain top is a beautiful girl. There is a plain reason for this, and we will examine it and then pass on to something of which the San Franciscans, or more accurately the Scots, have a right to be proud.

The city, as everybody knows, was destroyed in what historians and visitors call the earthquake of 1906. There is a firm superstition among the natives which makes them refer instead to 'the fire'. San Francisco, like much of northern and central California, sits precariously on the rim of a geological fault, the San Andreas fault. On the morning of 18 April 1906, the fault gave a strenuous heave, and certainly there was an earthquake, the most damaging that has been known in North America in modern times. But whether you have in mind the enormous shudder, or the devastation of the subsequent fire (which had Enrico Caruso running out of the Palace Hotel screaming, 'It is worse than Vesuvius'), the truth is that the centre of the city was totally demolished. Its rebuilding came at an unfortunate time – I mean unfortunate in the history of architecture, either domestic or foreign. After a century of peace in Europe, and forty years of it in America, it was a comfortable, smug and earnest time, relieved by heavy whimsy in the arts, and these qualities were reflected in laborious and whimsical ideas about beauty in brick and stone. Accordingly, San Francisco is dense with thousands of the most clumsy, formidable, comical gingerbread houses and hospitals and other public buildings you can imagine.

The great thing about San Francisco is not its parts but the sum of its parts seen from a long way off. In other words, the precious thing about it is its site. Like the plain girl standing alone on the beautiful mountain top, its outline, its profile, has a dignity and charm which only rarely belong to any of its lesser attributes. The city itself is hillier than Naples, more intimate than Hong Kong. It is founded and spread over nine great hills overlooking a fine bay, and in any city that ever knew ice or snow it would have been an impossible hazard to life and limb to build houses over the hills and have streetcars or automobiles run up and down them. But San Francisco has had a flurry of snow twice, I think, in forty years; and though its nights are very often cool and clammy, the thermometer does not drop below freezing and not often into the forties. In fact, San Francisco has one of the narrowest ranges of daily temperature, winter and summer, of any city in America. So the buildings topple all over the hills, and the streetcars are pulled up by cables running through slots in the middle of the roadway, and the first necessity of an automobile is flawless brakes. When you park your car on a slanting street, you must turn the wheels to bank against the sidewalk kerb. If you do not, you get a ticket. You drive very often straight at the sky and when you come to the crest of a street that crosses a main thoroughfare you have to pause at an angle of 30 degrees or so until the crosstown traffic lets you nudge your way over the hill before you plunge down a block or two and begin the next ascent. The steepest streets have steps cut into the sidewalk, and the tourists goggle at the hills and giggle at their own attempts to walk up and down them. But the residents pant and pause at half a mile an hour and totter down a house-lined mountainside to do their day's shopping. This gives the place a solemn but rollicking air.

The land breezes are very dry and the ocean winds very clean. So it is a sparkling city much of the time, except when the fog from the ocean comes sliding in as solid as a freight train, especially in the foggy, cold days of July and August. Until the Second World War, when industry began to disfigure the whole littoral of the bay, smog was something that God in his wisdom had visited only on the vast, blowsy city four hundred and forty miles to the south – the city of the angels (a misnomer if ever there was one): Los Angeles.

Seen from any distance in the late afternoon of one of its crystalline days, San Francisco is a white city rolling over these great hills, and certainly it is unlike any other city of the United States. It is also a place of succulent and rare vegetation. And this is the miracle of the place that I want to talk about.

When San Francisco was founded, in the mania of the gold rush, it was nothing but a collection of huge sandhills overlooking on one side a great inland bay and on the other the Pacific Ocean. The earliest prints – I'm thinking of the fine ones they made in the 1850s – show fleets of decorative sailing ships in the harbour but not a tree in sight. Soon the Nobs – the makers of the earliest gold fortunes – built large houses on the highest hill, which was consequently known, and still is, as Nob Hill. Like the others it was a mountain of shifting sand. And when the winds blew in from the Pacific, the mountains appeared to move inside the orbit of their outline. It was like the Sahara in a storm, and the people staggered blindly up and down the hills holding handkerchiefs over their mouths and noses. The more chic residents patronized a shop started by a Frenchman (it is now a prosperous store) and bought from him one of his first products: a cotton-gauze mask intended to protect you from the suffocating fogs of blown sand.

This was accepted as a fact of life for twenty years or so. Then the city fathers had an agreeable new idea. They had by now acquired the essential amenities of a city – a red-light district, pretentious houses, a concert hall and a police force, in that order (after some violent years in which the most responsible citizens, outraged by the rapine and murder that infested the place, took the law into their own hands as a committee of vigilantes). Now the city fathers thought that they would have a park. This would be rather like Holland thinking it ought to have a mountain. It was plainly an impossibility.

Nevertheless, the city council set aside 1,017 acres of high flat land near the ocean which was, most of the time, a windswept desert. The fathers laboured to plant seedlings and flower beds but found that they promptly choked and died. After three years of this noble experiment, the daily newspaper of a small town in a grassy valley to the north wrote a chuckling editorial: 'Of all the elephants the city of San Francisco has ever owned, they now have the heaviest in the shape of "Golden Gate Park", a dreary waste of shifting sand hills where a blade of grass cannot be raised without four posts to support it and keep it from blowing away.' It was almost literally true. In the seventeen following years they had managed to plant and hold – with many sorts of structural braces – a thin forest of trees and some grassy spaces on the eastern, the leeward, side. In 1887 the park commission, still regarded as a bunch of visionaries, appointed a new superintendent, a Scotsman, John McLaren, a young landscape gardener, then 29 years old. The commission gave him, with his assignment, a prescription in the following gaudy language: 'Mr McLaren, we want you to make the Golden Gate Park one of the beauty spots of the world.' An English visitor to the city took home this sentence as a prime example of the American's gift for windbag rhetoric. But young McLaren was neither boastful nor amused. As he received his certificate of office, and as thousands mocked, he replied: 'With your aid, gentlemen, and God be willing, that I shall do.'

His first task was not to move mountains but to arrest them. And for that he needed what San Francisco did not have, a steady source of fresh water. Even then the salt water of the bay backed up and percolated all the surrounding land. McLaren did not ignore this disability but he fought it for a year or two. He was a Scotch type familiar to most of us, a rather grim poet of a man with the single-mindedness of a mule. He would often, as he later wrote, 'go out into the country and walk along a stream until I came to a bonnie brook. Then I'd come back to the park and try to reproduce what Nature had done.'

So he started out with what you would expect a Scot to start with: barley. It normally grows fast and dense. But not in San Francisco. He turned to native lupine. Same thing. Then he recalled the tough beach grass of Scotland, and it was the first plant to put down rapid roots and grow, on top, fast enough to give a green fringe to the dunes which the blown sand could not bury. Then he looked around for a couple of species of trees, one to hold the contours of the sand, another to build up soil as well. He found both in Australia and imported them: the tea tree and the Australian acacia. Eucalyptus, the gum tree as Australians call it, came from there too and did pretty well, though it had a habit, and still has, of blighting the growth of anything within its shade. From the nearby valleys and the canyons of the peninsula he brought in two of the loveliest of the small trees of California, the manzanita and the madrone. I make it sound as if McLaren were a slogging, purposeful type who knew what he wanted and got it. In fact, for several years he seemed to be undertaking a missing labour of Hercules. His task had its satisfactions but its despairs also. One time he planted a thousand trees, and a few months later they looked like the markers for new-formed sand dunes. He dug them all up and he tried again, and again. Fertilizer was a constant problem. It cost a lot of money to ship in from southern California, and his original budget was slimming fast. So he asked the Mayor if the sanitation department would collect and deliver to him the horse sweepings from the streets. Without too much publicity it was done.

One of his faults, as a public official, was that he was immune or allergic to political finagling – something that any man who wants anything from those in power must learn to accept and exploit. He would no doubt have been horrified at Franklin Roosevelt's remark about a big city Mayor, a gruesome character but a Democrat, from whom Roosevelt expected a landslide of votes in a crucial election. A squeamish member of the Roosevelt team was afraid that Mayor was too crafty to depend on, and anyway he was, the man said, 'a son of a bitch'. 'Yes,' said Roosevelt, flashing his most endearing smile, 'but he's *our* son of a bitch.'

Young McLaren, on the contrary, would not truckle or hire or pay patronage to influential men he disliked. The police superintendent was one. And after some rude rebuff McLaren found three of his proudest trees had been hauled away overnight by the police from in front of their station house. John McLaren summoned his staff the same day, had the new cement shovelled away, and planted three new oaks. They stand today in front of the San Francisco police station.

But as he asserted himself, and the park began to grow into a visible thing of beauty, the San Franciscans came to think of him as a precious city asset. It was a time, remember, when rich men expected to die in their fifties and accordingly retired at 40 to live it up a little before the end came. Sixty was then the rather late, but compulsory, retiring age of all civil servants. But when McLaren got there the people of San Francisco insisted that he stay on. And when he was 70, they insisted again. After that he was given a perennial waiver of retirement. And he died, still the superintendent of the park, at the age of 95, in 1943.

Long before that time the Golden Gate Park – with its lush meadows and artful wildernesses, its sheep pastures and Japanese tea garden, its peacocks on little lawns, its waterfalls and great evergreen forests, its protected buffalo and deer, its five thousand varieties of plants, its daisies from South Africa, cypress from Kashmir, abelias from the Himalayas, its hundred-odd types of conifer, its rhododendrons from Tibet and Siberia, its playgrounds and its foxes, its dozen lakes and its myriad blackbirds – it had become indeed what McLaren promised to make it. Certainly, in my experience, the most beautiful entirely created city park.

I thought of John McLaren this week because he was doing his damnedest to hold the first trees just at the time, around 1895, when a dozen other Scots came over to teach Americans the game of golf. The United States Open Championship was held in San Francisco last week, and the great bane of the big hitters was the trees, the forty-three thousand cypresses and pines and eucalyptus planted in John McLaren's early time and tended, at one time or another, by him. Arnold Palmer, the most heroic of the new breed of America's millionaire golfers, lost the championship by driving constantly into the fronds of a great overhanging cypress. His collapse and his tragedy could all be put down to Scotland. You could say that one Scotsman gave him his living and another took it away from him.

The Well-Dressed American, Man!

30 October 1966

A few years ago, when my son had about a year and a half to go before he graduated from college, I was mildly astonished to hear myself saying to him what fathers of college boys have said for generations. 'I have a proposition to make to you,' I said. 'You've worked pretty hard and well. Keep it up for the next eighteen months and come out with a halfway decent degree and I'll give you the fare for a trip to Europe.' I was a little uncomfortable making this traditional speech, because I had not always been the father of a college boy. I am, in fact, in my fifties for the first time in my life. But I heard myself sounding like the fathers I knew in my time, all of them, I then believed, professional fathers born into middle age.

Of course, I expected my son would fall on his face in gratitude. Instead, he cocked his head and looked at me with that peculiar tenderness that 20-year-olds reserve for the naivety of their parents.

'Are you kidding?' he said. 'I'll be off to Europe a month from now.'

'Indeed,' I said, icing up very fast, 'and where do you expect to travel?' (I almost said, 'And, pray, where do you expect to travel?')

'Oh, a little time in Rome and Florence, a month or so in Paris, I guess, maybe a stretch in Tangier.'

I wondered how he expected to live on his frugal allowance. In staggered disbelief he explained to me, with great simplicity and patience, some facts of life that had been kept from me. The summer vacation before his last academic year was coming up, and the university laid on several charter flights to Europe, leave a certain date, back a certain date, at something less than half the commercial fare. My son is a cagey mathematician where rent, food and expenses are concerned and he had done a calculation on which I could not fault him. Even allowing for the cost of the transatlantic fare, he could live noticeably cheaper for three months in Europe than he could by staying in his rooms in Cambridge, Massachusetts. Uncounted thousands of American college boys and girls have discovered the same thing. Most of them, even on the home ground, live much like cave dwellers. A room as we knew it is by no means the same thing as a pad. We were, I now realize, painfully fastidious in my day. Whatever the cut of our political or social jib, we required such things as beds actually raised above the floor, curtains in windows, chairs for sitting on. These things, I am told, are now looked on as establishment fetishes. American and European college boys of today are throwbacks to the wandering minstrels of the Middle Ages. They live from hand to mouth, and friend to friend, and pad to pad. They have a universal uniform: one pair of trousers, one shirt, a guitar, a pack of Gauloises, a jacket (maybe), and a toothbrush (sometimes). The motto of my old school would serve them well. It is *Ubi bene, ibi patria*, which being roughly translated means, 'Wherever there's a handout, that's for me, man.'

All the countries of Europe, and some of Africa, are now peopled by these identical types. They rustle around the continents like cockroaches, and you can never be sure, when you see them on the Spanish Steps, or in the Uffizi, or along the docks at Casablanca, or in the streets of East Berlin, whether they are American, English, Swedish, German or even Russian. Every place they go they are at home with other wanderers from other lands. The language barrier does not exist, for I am told by a very earnest sociologist that this generation is passing beyond the need of speech into a *lingua franca* of gestures, grunts, shrugs that establish – and I quote – 'a subtle and vital form of identity-communication'. No niceties of dress disturb them. On second thoughts, I'm not so sure of that. However, *our* niceties of dress are as alien and meaningless to them as the elaborate hierarchy of military orders among South American generals who have never seen a puff of cannon smoke.

Of course, today we all pretend to be unfussy and informal about clothes, and to have abandoned the social distinctions that they once used to signify. I doubt very much whether this can ever be so. I have lately been in London for a spell, and then in Devon, Dorset and Surrey, then back to New York for three days, and am now in California. I am struck by the weirdly different uniforms that the inhabitants of any one place take for granted. A man lying on a beach at Brighton would not alarm anybody if he wore a cap, a tweed coat with an open shirt (the collar folded carefully outside the coat collar), a pair of dark grey flannels, and boots. A woman coming to dinner in Surrey causes no alarm by appearing in the outfit in which a woman in Minnesota plays golf. Some of these distinctions are obviously imposed by the climate. And to prepare for the jaunt I have just enjoyed calls for some pretty thoughtful packing. Yet even here when people are in doubt they tend to disbelieve the travel-guide warnings and stay with their own prejudice. Every time we go to San Francisco, I tell my wife that she should pack warm clothes for the evening and that a fur coat is a blessing for the fog-swept, chilly nights of July and August. This is so plainly ridiculous if you were born and brought up in the East that she dismisses my advice as raging hypochondria and later complains that she has not been warned.

But providing for the weather is comparatively easy. The really subtle challenges set in when you travel between the same social strata in different countries. My last three evenings in London were spent respectively at a toney dinner party, at a cosy supper with my step-daughter, at a 'happening' in a railroad yard in a dingy London suburb. No problem with my daughter: she is acquainted with my tastes and I with hers. I wore a suit she once admired and a tie with little tigers snarling on it, and which her friends might well mistake for a white hunter's special. At the socialite dinner party, whose hostess had casually mentioned 'black tie', I had to fake it by wearing a black business suit and a black dress tie, which I always carry against such a sudden summons to the tables of the mighty. Nobody noticed the difference, except a modern young siren with eyelashes like quills who must have seen black wherever she went. She congratulated me on the cut and style of my dinner jacket, so much 'cooler', she thought, than those old-fashioned silk facings. 'Where did you get it?' she asked. I bunched up so as to hide the breast-pocket label that said, 'New Haven, Conn.' Spain, I said. She purred.

The 'happening' was something else. I wore a suit – matching coat and trousers, that is – a necktie and a dark-blue topcoat. I looked, I was later told, like a fugitive from the Foreign Office. Everybody in sight was in jeans or stretch pants, in silver lamé, blue velvet, fuchsia corduroy, and monk's cowls, dhotis; and many of them sported beards, leather jackets, and rhinestone necklaces or beads that jangled around their thighs. They were a tolerant lot. No one, I was assured, was outraged by me. The friendly attitude seemed to be: 'If this cat wants to dress like an American ambassador, then okay, so long as he keeps his trap shut about Vietnam.'

Dressing in America is trickier, for in a country of this size each region incorporates the prejudices of a separate country. I know exactly how New Yorkers of many social types dress for winter, spring, summer and fall. I know, for instance, that it is necessary to warn a visiting Englishwoman that no New Yorker with the smallest pretension to style wears white shoes, in summer or any other time, in the city. But dressing in Hollywood so that you won't look stuffy, or flashy *in the wrong way*, is a separate trick that not one Easterner in a hundred ever masters. Because they have at the back of their minds a preconception of Hollywood – bikinis, fat cigars, picture ties, Klieg lights, two-tone shoes, Swiss silk suits, V-necks cut to the navel, summer prints of a psychedelic garishness. They know for sure that Beverly Hills is more informal than, say, London. Not so. Only in the movies. You arrive at a Hollywood dinner party in a smart blue blazer, light blue shirt, sleek slacks, a club tie and black loafers, a costume that would be entirely acceptable at a summer drop-in dinner at the Garrick Club. But in Beverly Hills you find yourself surrounded by men entirely in dark suits, white shirts and tiny patterned ties. The women, it is true, have a licence to wear evening dresses or canary-yellow slack suits. Yet I suspect that this licence too prescribes some nuances and forbids others.

Santa Barbara is only ninety miles from Hollywood but it is one social band of the stratosphere away. Although October is a hot month there, fashion obeys the calendar and dictates that it is the fall. The women put on warmer clothes, darker colours, paler shoes. At a Santa Barbara dinner the other evening there was a ravishing New Yorker present wearing a melon-pink suit of Thai silk. It became her greatly. We sat out on a terrace where it was around 75 degrees, and she stood out like a firefly in the night. She was thought by her hosts, I later discovered, to be attractive but odd.

That same evening I mentioned to my host a little detective work along these lines that I had done while driving in an airport limousine on the way from the beautiful coastline of the Carmel Bay to the Monterey airport. The only other people aboard were a handsome couple in, I should guess, their middle forties. The woman was pretty and effortlessly chic and clearly a Californian, for though the day was blinding she wore an exquisitely fitting light-brown cashmere dress and alligator shoes. Her husband, though – lover, perhaps? – was a puzzle. He had on pencil-thin well-cut slacks of a tiny hound's-tooth pattern; a dark-blue jacket; a mini-hat – a rakish deerstalker, also of a tiny hound's-tooth pattern, and in the brim was tucked a little swirling black feather. If he had been an Easterner, I cannot think what sort of man he could have been. A very well-heeled advertising man, possibly, on holiday. But he sounded too relaxed, too professional; he looked with a steady, matter-of-fact gaze at the blue-brown headlands, the writhing Monterey cypresses, the foaming blue, blue ocean. A little wily conversation at the airport drew out from him that he was a distinguished gynaecologist – but from Beverly Hills. He could not possibly, I told my Santa Barbara host, have been a gynaecologist in the East. 'Nor,' he responded, 'in Santa Barbara either.'

To many people this may appear to be a very trivial theme in the great day of social upheaval and the equality of man. But, I am told at the United Nations, even in China the uniform of Mao Tse-tung has details that escape us which signify to the faithful that his worker's smock is not any worker's smock but the costume of the All-Highest. The Russians, once they were well over their revolution, got out a blue book for their crack regiments patterned after the blue book which once laid down for a British Guards officer the correct civilian uniform for every place and time. And my son now tells me that my own observation of Carnaby Street distinctions is naive and unseeing.

It will be said that these are snobbish preoccupations. And so they are, and important to go into, since we are all snobs. All of us draw social inferences from the way people dress. In this, fishermen and farmers are just as snobbish as debutantes and hippies. And there is no one, however regal, however humble, who is not put off by some detail of dress he personally dislikes. I well remember the morning that one of President Kennedy's aides came in wearing a button-down shirt, an item that started in America in the very early 1930s as an Ivy League fad. It remained so until a few years ago but was swiftly abandoned when it spread to bond salesmen and airline executives and then to Midwesterners, and then to cattle ranchers in convention, and finally to Englishmen. It is still retained by ageing country-club types who have not noticed that they suddenly look old-fashioned. 'For Heaven's sake,' said Kennedy to his bewildered aide, 'take off that shirt. Nobody wears those things any more, except Chester Bowles and Adlai.'

By remarking on these tiny things, John O'Hara for once cornered for himself a small but subtle and memorable view of life. For the rest of us, they can be invaluable signals and telling symptoms of what lies behind the appraising glance and the guarded handshake.

A Lonely Man

26 May 1967

On a Saturday afternoon at the end of May, a single-engine plane, looking very like something out of the early comic strips, wobbled and ducked over Roosevelt Field, one of the earliest airports around New York, and buzzed the tower. A small crowd of people on the ground looked up and waved and clapped, and then somebody unveiled a marker. And they all retired to an old hotel in one of the oldest country suburbs on Long Island and joined other crowds who had jammed the bars and the assembly rooms all day long to celebrate the same event.

It had been forty years to the day since a skinny, flat-chested, blond, 25-year-old Midwesterner had left Long Island on a most peculiar journey. He had stayed the night of 19 May 1927 in the same hotel where all the carousing and celebrating were now going on. He had ambled out on a miserable day, through rain and heavy ground mist, to an aeroplane he had built himself, at a total cost of $6,000. There were not great crowds that time. There was a wet and restless pack of newspapermen who kept sloshing in the drizzle between three planes, which were sitting there in a film of mud waiting for favourable weather to take off and have a shot at a $25,000 prize that had been put up by a New York hotel owner. There was no question which of the three competitors would make the most impressive copy. He was Lieutenant Commander Byrd, who had been to the North Pole and was already a national figure. But the lonely one, the skinny young man from the Midwest, was more challenging if only because he was so preoccupied with his plane, tinkering with it, frowning, wading back for a monkey wrench or a screw, smiling little, talking less. The reporters had all heard of him, of course. He had been a flying cadet in the Air Service Reserve, as it was then called. He had been a mail-pilot. He had made small items in the papers as a parachute jumper. Only a week before he had flown this crate from San Diego, California, to St Louis to Long Island in the breathtaking time of twenty-one hours and twenty minutes, which was a new record for a coast-to-coast flight. They had heard about his wild ambition to make the coming flight alone. He was known as what they called a stunt merchant, a flying fool. He was about to live up to his nickname, for he decided on the wretched grey morning of 20 May that the time was now. The weather reports, such as they were in those days, said that there would be fair skies over most of the Atlantic. He decided to risk it. He arranged his long limbs in the tiny cockpit, pulled his goggles down, and splashed off through the rain puddles on the runway. He wobbled into the air and bounced back on the ground again; up again and then down. At the end of the runway, to everyone's relief, he was airborne. None too soon, for he just managed to clear the telephone lines at the end of the field.

I suppose, at 8 o'clock on that May morning, not one American in a thousand was preoccupied with his name, and in most other countries not one person in a hundred thousand had ever heard it. The wire services noted that he had taken off alone, in a home-made plane, with the mad ambition of being the first man to cross the Atlantic alone. I can't recall ever having read about anyone who swooped so suddenly into world fame. It is strange to look back to the morning papers of 20 May and hunt for the first stories about him; and then turn to the evening papers and get the impression that Alexander the Great had reappeared on the earth and was headed straight for you. It was not necessary to know anything about flying. The farmers rang through to the nearest newspaper office, and the telephone switchboards were clogged on three continents. Stockbrokers and parsons and racing touts and new brides and politicians and intellectuals and steelworkers had been galvanized in a few hours. By what? There had been trans-atlantic flights before. There had been the dramatic close call of Alcock and Brown. As long ago as 1919 a British dirigible had flown thirty-one men from Scotland to Long Island and turned around and flown back again. Only three years before, two American army planes had crossed by way of Iceland, Greenland and Newfoundland.

There were two new things that combined to stir the imagination of people everywhere. He was not going to hop islands or countries. No Newfoundland to Ireland for him. He was going for the whole stretch: New York to Paris. And he was going alone.

He had not publicized these dramatic facts, though they were known to the sponsors of the prize. But what catapulted the populations of America and Europe into a two-day delirium was the shock of the news, not that he was going to take off but that he had already gone. That night, there was a championship bout in Yankee Stadium (Sharkey was fighting Maloney). Before the fight started, the announcer stood in the ring and bawled at an audience of forty thousand fans and asked them to rise and pray for the flyer. Like some vast chorus in an open-air performance of *Guys and Dolls*, they stood and bared their heads. By then, nobody knew where or how he was.

Today, we should hear about him every mile of the way. But he had no radio, no radar, no sextant, only an instrument panel slightly less impressive than the dashboard of a modern car. You remember when John Glenn fired his retrorockets, and we heard a scramble of talk about heat coming up from somewhere? And the long crackle of radio waves and he'd gone? You remember we'd been told that the fearful heat of re-entry could bore through the nose of his capsule – and for five minutes there was the chance that he'd been burned to ash? Five minutes! This boy was lost to us for nearly thirty hours. It was the agony of Glenn diluted but stretched over a day and a night. Then the headlines boomed that he'd been seen over Ireland, then that he was crossing over England. Then he was over the Channel. Then the night fell. From his own account, he experienced the most enraging episode of the flight. He knew he was over France but he did not know the way to Paris. He sputtered along in a daze of exhaustion and at last he recognized Paris. Now he had to find Le Bourget. After half an hour more, which he later said felt like another night, he was struck by a curious broad shaft of fog, a sort of pathway of diffused light. Of the hundred thousand Parisians who were thrashing around down there, a hundred or more had cars and they'd been told to turn their lights on. This was his rudimentary glide path. And he came on it and bumped in and trundled to the edge of the field. And then an ocean of humanity broke around him. 'I', he said, 'am Charles Lindbergh.'

There was never any need, anywhere in the world after that, for the next forty years, to introduce himself. I was at a party in Nairobi two years ago, a diplomatic affair, and the main room of an ambassador's house and the terrace outside were flashing with all degrees of political grandees. But they were as excited, in a subdued way, as a gaggle of teenagers in the lobby of a hotel housing the Beatles. I sensed this restless curiosity but I didn't know the reason for it. Pretty soon a dark, fragile, handsome woman came in and at her side was a very tall, very clean, very tanned, white-haired man with the same boyish face, now matured and fully modelled. It was, of course, Lindbergh. Diplomats don't normally rush at a great man for his autograph, because it's impolite and because they are always rather hoping that somebody will rush at them. There was no fuss, no vulgar staring. The Lindberghs fell in with a little group, but at their coming there was a kind of rustle of pleasure, a palpable feeling among these eminent men that they were really hobnobbing with the famous.

By now the gruesome and the distressing periods of Lindbergh's life have been forgotten – the kidnapping of his child, the obscene trial, the exile in England, and the later incarnation as the hero of the isolationists, the cat's-paw of an American nationalist party. This weekend, it was nothing but the unique flight of 20 and 21 May, forty years ago.

You mention it today to people who were alive at the time and, as with the death of President Kennedy, they will tell you at once where they were when it happened. I was in school in England, and the morning after the great night scene in Paris, our science master skipped the lesson and recalled his own heroics in the Battle of the Marne. The geography master took on a special glow of pride and demonstrated over and over again that he was the living expert on the geography of the North Atlantic. Everybody paid Lindbergh the most naive and sincere form of tribute: they wanted to be in on the act.

So, on this Saturday morning, the crowds milled around the Garden City hotel on Long Island, and till long past midnight they toasted Charles Lindbergh. He was not there. He had turned down the invitation. He is an acutely shy man with an acute loathing of crowds. Perhaps the first huge night at Le Bourget was a trauma. He was thoroughly secluded, across Long Island Sound, in Connecticut. At 65 he has three absorbing interests. He is the technical adviser to a famous airline. He has long been interested in the construction of an artificial heart. And all the rest of the time he spends between here and East Africa. His great concern is to preserve, in the jet age, the lonely leopards and the wildebeest and the gazelles of the Serengeti Plain.

Vietnam

22 March 1968

There was once a British ambassador to this country, a good man, now dead, who – like most of his predecessors, with the blinding exception of Lord Bryce – had much trouble understanding the difference between a parliamentary system and a federal system. He could not understand why the Cabinet didn't sit in Congress, nor why the legislature and the executive were completely separate. No one, I'm afraid, had explained to him the Founding Fathers' pressing fear of a military dictatorship, of a king with a private army, and the precautions they took to frustrate it by setting up the President and the Congress as natural enemies. Or you can say that they set up the President as the chief executive of the state and then provided for a permanent pack of watchdogs to check his every move. The ambassador wrote down in his journal this conclusion: 'This leaves the President's press conference as a poor substitute for the regular cross-examination of ministers at question-time in the House of Commons.'

Well, the President's press conference does seem to be the obvious counterpart. It is obvious but it is wrong. And many an American Cabinet officer could wish it wasn't. For occasional exposure in the House of Commons to a rasping question or even a guffaw is not to be compared, as a form of executive torture, to an all-day inquisition by a standing committee of Congress. The Congressional inquiry, I'd say, is the nerve system of what Americans like to call 'the democratic process'. And nowhere is it seen to more terrifying effect than in the cross-examination of a Secretary of State by the Senate Foreign Relations Committee. This committee has the power to reject ambassadors and treaties proposed by the President.

In the spring of 1968, then, it was anxious to recall the President to his constitutional duty to seek the 'advice and consent of the Senate' on a war that had got away from both of them: the undeclared war in Vietnam. So the Secretary of State, called as the President's understudy, was subjected to the third degree by the representatives of the people. If that sounds a little lurid or sentimental, let me remind you of the cast of characters that sat like a court of judges there and challenged Secretary Rusk from ten in the morning to six-thirty one day, and from nine to two the next.

The lives and labours of these men may not represent (as advertising executives like to say about their wives) a 'cross-section of the American people'. But they made up an impressive sample of the variety of the millions who chose them. There was a farmer from Vermont, a mining engineer from Montana, a Rhodes scholar from Arkansas, the schoolteacher son of a hardware merchant from South Dakota, an electric-products manufacturer from Missouri, a stockman from Kansas. The mining engineer wound up as a professor of Latin American and Far Eastern history. The electric products man was a former Secretary of the Air. The schoolteacher was also a famous fisherman. There were six lawyers, not too many to reflect the preponderance of lawyers who sit in Congress and who do, after all, make the laws. None of these men had been in the Senate for less than twelve years; the farmer had been there twenty-eight years and two others for twenty-four years. Five of them were veterans of the First World War.

One saw action in the Second in Burma and China. Another was a survivor of the Normandy invasion. Two of them had, and have, enough ordinary vanity not to give their ages in the *Congressional Directory*. If you think of them in this variety you will be less inclined to imagine a cartoonist's Star Chamber of Neanderthal men bearing the tag 'Senate Committee'.

Secretary Rusk had resisted this call for two years. But there was a well-substantiated rumour that General Westmoreland wanted another two hundred thousand troops. And suddenly the world expressed its distrust of American policy by losing its confidence in the dollar. So the Secretary yielded and agreed to go before the committee and talk about the administration's request for foreign aid. But the committee had brought him in to expound and defend the administration's policy on Vietnam, the excuse for ignoring the main theme being that you can't guess how much money will be left over for any other dependent country until you've gauged the expense and the probable scale of the war in Vietnam. For two days Secretary Rusk was questioned and quizzed and lectured to and pleaded with by a committee whose old ratio of hawks to doves was significantly shrinking. The role of Chairman Fulbright as a scold and ironist could now be presumed. So could the ringing patriotism of Senator Mundt of South Dakota and the troubled curiosity of young Senator Church of Idaho and the holy wrath of Senator Wayne Morse of Oregon, God's favourite maverick.

But at these sessions only Fulbright and Morse stayed with the usual script. The others were sufficiently disturbed to think aloud with more honesty and eloquence than they had shown before. And all of them maintained an unfailing gravity and courtesy such as men do when they are scared, when they are losing an attitude and acquiring an anxiety. Nothing was more startling than Senator Mundt's forlorn suspicion that elections in South Vietnam were not alone worth the ensnaring of half a million Americans into the continental bog of Southeast Asia. And a bugle sounding the retreat is not more ominous than the confession of Senator Symington, a resolute hawk, that he was now a prey to misgiving. Senator Symington had been saying for years that the war had better be won or written off, since the day was coming when the United States would have to weigh the cost of it in gold that wasn't there. He has always been indulged by his colleagues and friends as a man riding a comical hobby horse. This time, he had the sad satisfaction of being taken seriously.

We have not talked lately about Vietnam, whereas once we talked about little else, because everything that could be said has been said. Families, friends, and the workers at the same bench either ran with their own kind or resigned themselves, as so many bad marriages do, to a kind of despairing truce. But now we were measuring, with quite a new sort of alarm, the eleven and a half billion dollars in the Treasury that covered our stock of gold against the twenty-six billion a year that was being spent on Vietnam. And, at last, the American casualties in Vietnam surpassed those of Korea: a turn which, I suggested a year ago, would be the hardest test of the people's tolerance of the war.

So we were shaking ourselves out of the stupor and the truce, and starting all over again with the fundamental questions. How had it come about? Was it indeed a crusade or a vast miscalculation? Would Asia crumble to Communism if South Vietnam fell? Was it the wrong war in the wrong place, or the right war in the wrong place? Was the United States the only man in the boat rowing in time?

A hundred books and a thousand editorial writers have recited and disputed the political origins of the war and enlarged on the human tragedy of its conduct. What matters, or will come to matter to most people, I think, is not any new balance we can strike in the old argument; but the realization that America, which has seldom lost a war, is not invincible; and the very late discovery that an elephant can trumpet and shake the earth but not the self-possession of the ants who hold it. So when I say how did it come about, I am not thinking of splitting the hair between the SEATO treaty's pledge to resist 'aggression' and the American protocol that stipulated 'Communist aggression'. I mean, how did the American people move from their early indifference or complacency to the recognition of a nightmare?

Well, the war crept up on us with no more menace than a zephyr. South Vietnam was only one of many strange place names that joined the noble roll-call of countries which America, in the early glow of its world power, swore to protect and defend. If Russia, that atomic monolith, could be scared off Iran and Greece and Turkey and foiled in Western Europe, it never crossed our minds that we couldn't intimidate

Asian Communists who fought with sticks and stones. Certainly it would have been churlish to deny these brave little countries the handful of American 'technicians' they needed to train their armies. (We presumed, without doing much detective work, that – as with Belgium and Finland at other times – the democratic credentials of Thailand, Pakistan, Laos, Cambodia, Vietnam and the other signatories could be taken for granted.) In 1962 we moved troops into the Mekong Delta and the Pathet Lao withdrew. And that took care of Laos.

Johnson came in, and for a year or more the shadow of Vietnam failed to darken the bright procession of legislation he drove through the 89th Congress. It dawned on us very slowly that the American technicians were turning into American soldiers. Then we admitted that the men were off to the rice paddies and not the desks and hospitals behind the lines. The draft felt the chill, and the college boys, and the Vietniks were born. It was not with most of them a conscientious objection to war itself. Most, I think, would have admitted that Hitler had to be stopped and that Korea, the first United Nations war, was a good war. But they were baffled by the morality of this war, which killed more civilians than soldiers and devastated the land we were sworn to protect: a war in which there were no attacks at dawn, no discernible lines, and few human restraints either of rules or weapons. 'Napalm' and 'fragmentation bombs' came into the language and sickened us, though our own 'strategic bombing' of Dresden in the Second World War had been worse than Hiroshima, and millions of women and children had been routed from their homes in Europe too. War, the administration could only remind us, was hell. So we piled up the forces and piled on the force and dropped more bombs than all the bombs dropped in Europe and Africa in the Second World War. The American forces rose from thirty thousand to fifty, then to a hundred thousand and then to half a million. And the latest word was that perhaps seven hundred thousand might in truth fulfil the promises of the generals, whose estimates of when and how the turn might come had dreadfully paralleled the expert predictions of the French generals before them.

These and many other doubts and disasters were aired and tossed before Dean Rusk. The administration's position had something of the straightforward grandeur of Bach, if only Bach had been the tune that were called for. The theme was that the war in Asia was a continuation of the European struggle, first against Hitler, then against the Russians. The United States was pledged to resist aggression against free nations. If one pledge was betrayed, then the other wards and dependants would panic and succumb to Communism. The countries of Southeast Asia are a stack of dominoes and if one falls so will they all.

Down the years, the administration has offered us many warning historical examples of what happens to a strong power which yields to an aggressor bit by bit. The favourite analogy is Munich, and it has been reinforced by the old tag about nations that know no history being doomed to repeat it.

But many people have looked at this analogy and rejected it, as they have rejected, also, the analogy of Korea, where there was a clear aggression, so defined by all the sitting members of the United Nations Security Council. The New Left has a bad-tempered analogy of its own in the white man's treatment of the Indians in this country: the determination to obliterate him for his own good and resettle him on permanently protected 'enclaves' of bare land on which no white man could exist. I myself keep thinking of Napoleon's disastrous adventure in Haiti. The ideology and the excuse for this overseas expedition were quite different from ours. On the contrary, Napoleon moved to denounce and destroy the extension of self-government to the natives. But strategically, the adventure so far from home has a lesson for us. To put down the native peoples he dispatched an expedition of seven warships and forty-five thousand of his crack soldiers; which, at the time, must have seemed every bit as formidable as our half-million and their bombers. But there was a native general, Christophe, who revived a tactic used originally by the Tunisians against the Arabs and later known as a 'scorched earth' policy. More successful still was his practice of 'guerrilla warfare', so called. Not all the armament and skill of the most modern army in Europe could suppress these roving guerrillas, who were friends by day and enemies by night, who never stood and made a front, who could live on the forage of the fields, and take yellow fever or leave it, who pounded prepared positions and dissolved into the earth. A ragged native population whipped the best of France. It was enough to turn Napoleon against any more campaigns at four thousand miles and to decide him against conquering North America; with the happy result, for us, that he sold the huge reaches of the Louisiana Territory to Jefferson for $15 million.

These analogies are dangerous to press, because you are always faced with a situation in which what is new hurts more than what is familiar. Still, I think that the view of the United States as Napoleon in Haiti is better than the view of Ho Chi Minh as Hitler in Europe.

There is one awful possibility that was put to me, when the war was only beginning to warm up, by the late Pandit Nehru. It is that a Western power, finding itself deep in Asia, might simply refuse to believe, as the Romans did, that its Roman might could possibly be disabled by a primitive people. 'You see,' said this bland Indian, 'the trouble with Westerners is, they hate to lose face.' It was too early in the game to reflect that a Texan might hate it more than anybody.

Yet it seems to me that anyone who ridicules the domino theory is obliged to say how and why it is wrong, and to suggest some better way of, as Dean Rusk put it, 'organizing the peace' either through the United Nations or through some alliance that can guarantee preponderant power. Preponderant power – that has always been the true deterrent, in spite of the Christian rhetoric that breathed so piously through the preamble to the Treaty of Westphalia (1648) and through the preamble to the Charter of the United Nations (1945). All these favourable balances of power have expressed that power through their willingness to use their ultimate weapon. With the British it was the Navy, and it was through their Navy that they could patrol the seven seas, put down wars in Asia, confine all big wars to Europe, and backstop for landbound allies. Today the United States is the world's greatest power only through its nuclear power. But, what is never acknowledged, the universal taboo against the use of this power disarms America at a blow and leaves it a large and rich but far from omnipotent power, capable of fighting one or two unconventional wars with conventional weapons.

This, it seems to me, is the real American position in the world today and the reason why its best aims are frustrated. The United States has one hundred and thirty-two military bases abroad and solemn treaty 'commitments' to come to the aid of forty-three nations if they are attacked or, what is more likely these days, disrupted from within. The earnest and gentle Senator Church put his finger on this Achilles heel by asking the Secretary if the great conflict was not between 'commitment and capacity'. In other words, America may be right, but is she able?

How did it come about that this country, led successively by a soldier, then by an alert foreign affairs student, and then by the shrewdest of politicians, committed itself to play St George to forty-three dragons? We must go back, I think, to what I called the 'early glow' of American world power, in the early 1950s. That is when the pledges were given, and when the cost of them was never counted. The Communists, not to mention the nationalists, and the millions of Asians who simply want to see the white men leave their continent for good, had not attempted a test of American power. As late as the day of Kennedy's inauguration, the United States was still flexing and rippling its muscles for lack of exercise. And on that day, the President delivered himself of a sentence, magnificent as rhetoric, appalling as policy. Secretary Rusk, very much moved, recited it to the committee as the touchstone of America's resolve: 'Let every nation know, whether it wishes us well or ill, that we shall pay any price, bear any burden, meet any hardship, support any friend, oppose any foe to assure the survival and the success of liberty.'

This is fine to read but fatal to act on. It may be the wish of a strong nation to do this, but in reality it will not support any friend or fight *any* foe, or support the burden, say, of a civil war in its own land, in order to rush to the aid of forty-three friends and fight forty-three foes. Vietnam, I fear, is the price of the Kennedy Inaugural.

A Bad Night in Los Angeles

9 June 1968

It does not seem nearly so long ago as thirty years that the trade of the foreign correspondent caught the fancy of the Hollywood producers. And for good reason. Hitler was on the loose, and Europe was crackling with crises and atrocities, and some of the best American reporters of the time – John Gunther and Vincent Sheehan and Ed Murrow – always seemed to be on hand. They came to look like heroic agents of the American people, who were fascinated and repelled at long distance by the violence of Europe and who, I must say, indulged a good deal of self-righteousness in parroting the ancient American lament about 'old, sick Europe'.

Well, I was saying, the foreign correspondent was in vogue. And soon Hollywood created a romantic stereotype of him. First, in the Boy Scout version of Joel McCrea in a trench coat; and then in the subtler variation of Bogart, who acted so tough and seemed as tricky as Goebbels but who – for all his smoker's cough and his cynical appraisal of passing females – was secretly on the side of all good men and true.

This attractive stereotype was not only larger than life but luckier than any journalist living or dead. He followed unerringly in the tracks of dictators and tipped off foreign ministers marked for *anschluss*. He was behind a curtain when a king signed an instrument of abdication. He knew the man who shot the prime minister. He decoded the vital message that gave the date of the invasion. He was always where the action was.

In life, it is not like that. Only by the wildest freak is a reporter, after many years on the hop, actually present at a single accidental convulsion of history. Mostly, we write the coroner's inquest, the account of the funeral, the reconstruction of the prison riot, the *trial* of the spy, not the hatching of the plot.

On the night of Tuesday, 4 June 1968, for the first time in thirty years, I found myself, by one casual chance in a thousand, on hand: in a narrow serving pantry of the Ambassador Hotel in Los Angeles, a place that, I suppose, will never be wiped out of my memory as a sinister alley, a Roman circus run amok, and a charnel house. It would be false to say, as I should truly like to say, that I am sorry I was there. It is more complicated than that. Nothing so simple as a conflict between professional pride and human revulsion, between having the feelings and having to sit down and write about them. Yet, because I saw it for once not as an event to comment on but as a thunderbolt assault on the senses, my own view of the whole thing, now and later, is bound to be from the stomach up to the head. Visceral, as we say. I don't imagine that if your hand falls on a live wire you are in any condition to measure the charge or judge the sense of the public safety regulations or moralize about the electric company's dereliction of duty.

So my view of this miserable episode is probably strange and I ought not to ascribe to anybody else the shape or colour of the opinions that floated up later from my muddled sensations. I warn you about this, because I feel unmoved by some ideas that others feel strongly, and on the other hand I have some fears that others may not share. So, since this is a more personal talk than I could have hoped, I had better tell you how it came about.

On that Tuesday afternoon, I was in San Francisco, on one of those jewel-like days that are revealed when the wrapping of the morning fog has been lifted. I had no great urge to fly to the vast spread of Los Angeles. On the contrary, I had hoped to spend the day padding down the fairways of the Olympic Club, which run like cathedral aisles between superb stands of cypresses. But it was election day, and Los Angeles is now the hub of California politics, if only because, of the fifty-eight counties of California, Los Angeles County alone accounts for 48 per cent of the vote. For the purpose of an election dateline, San Francisco, four hundred-odd miles away, was not much better than New York City. So it had to be done. I was going to have to report the general atmosphere of the winner's camp and the loser's.

I had seen scores of these election night entertainments. They are amiable but blowsy affairs. But to give me a fresh view of a ceremony that had staled by familiarity, and also to make some compensation to a hostess who had offered me a bed, I had asked her if she would like to mooch around the town with me and see what we could see. She was agog with anticipation, for just as a foreign correspondent thinks a movie actress must have a fascinating life, so a movie actress thought a correspondent's life must be glamorous in the extreme.

So, high in the Santa Monica hills, amid the scent of the eucalyptuses and the pepper trees, we sat for a while after the polls closed and waited for a sign of the outcome. You don't have to wait long in these computer days. The Oregon result was exactly predicted by the Big Brain twelve minutes after the polls closed, when the returns already in were less than 1 per cent. Somehow, the Brain was having more trouble with California. Party politics are, for various historical reasons, very loosely organized in that state and, for one thing, its northern end tends to contradict the verdict of the South. So when the early returns from the North showed McCarthy in a commanding lead it proved nothing. Los Angeles County, with its heavy working-class vote and its swarms of Negroes (or blacks, as we are now more respectfully meant to say), and its Mexican-Americans, was fairly certain to go heavily for Kennedy. Pretty soon, the gap between McCarthy's tally and Kennedy's began to shrink and it became clear that, saving a miracle, McCarthy would not be able to withstand the avalanche of Los Angeles votes that began to move in for Kennedy. The computers were silent, but the writing was on the wall.

Just before eleven, then, we took off for the McCarthy hotel, and there was no doubt when we got there that the college boys and the miniskirt girls and the wandering poets and the spruced-up student leaders and the chin-up McCarthy staff were whistling in a graveyard. There was a rock band that whooped it up all the louder to drown out the inevitable news. They would pause a while, and another ominous statistic would be flashed, and an emcee would shout, 'Are we down-hearted?' And the ballroom crowd would roar its defiance of the obvious.

The Ambassador, a comparatively venerable hotel miles away on Wilshire Boulevard, was the Kennedy headquarters. And that was the place to be. We took off, and so did lots of other people, so that when we turned into the long driveway we lined up behind scores of cars containing all those sensible people who love a winner. At last we got into the hotel lobby and a tumult of singing, cheering, and happy hobnobbing. Election parties give out innumerable tickets and badges to keep out the rabble, but no one is more aware than a winning candidate that on such occasions the rabble are the people. So you can usually drift with the multitude and nobody asks for a credential.

It was not so at the Ambassador. Guards and cops blocked the entrance to the ballroom, and I doubt that a passport and a birth certificate and a personal recommendation from Senator Kennedy could have got you in. My own general press credentials were useless. The lobbies were too packed to lift an elbow and too deafening to talk in. My companion and I screamed at each other through the din of all these happy people and we decided that the whole safari had been a mistake. We turned and started down the corridor for the outdoors and for home.

On our left, about fifty feet along, was another door to another room and a pack of people trying and failing to get through. There was a guard shaking his head continuously and pushing people back and behind him a young Kennedy staff man turning down everybody. This man shouted over the bobbing heads, 'Mr Cooke, come on, you can get in here.' We were folded in through the mob and emerged, as from a chute, into an open place: a cool, half-empty room, a small private dining room of the hotel stripped and fitted out as a press room. There were newsmen I knew and a radio man untangling cables, and a swarthy photographer in a sweatshirt locking up his cameras, and one or two middle-aged women and a half-dozen Western Union girls, and a fat girl in a Kennedy boater, a young reporter in a beard and, I guess, his girl.

It was a perfect private way through to the ballroom. But one of my reporter friends said, 'You don't want to get in there. It's murder in there. Anyway Pierre [Salinger] has promised that when Bobby gets through his speech he'll come through in to this room and talk with us.' It was an unbelievable break. We sat down and had a drink and heard the telegraph girls tapping out copy and tried not to wince at the television set in a corner that was tuned up to a howling decibel level.

A few minutes later the television commentators gave way to the ballroom scene, and Bobby was up there with his beaming helpers and his ecstatic little wife, and he was thanking everybody and saying things must change, and so on to Chicago. It was about eighteen minutes after midnight. We were standing outside the swinging doors that gave on to the serving pantry he would come through, on his way from the ballroom to us. These doors had no glass peepholes, but we'd soon hear the pleasant bustle of him coming through greeting the coloured chef and various waiters and bus boys who had lined up to shake his hand.

Then. Above the bassy boom of the television there was a banging repetition of sounds. Like somebody dropping a rack of trays, or banging a single tray against a wall. Half a dozen of us were startled enough to head for the doors, and suddenly we were jolted through by a flying wedge of other men. It had just happened. It was a narrow lane he had to come through, for there were two long steam tables and somebody had stacked up against them those trellis gates, with artificial leaves stuck on them, that they use to fence a dance band off from the floor. The only light was the blue-white light of three fluorescent tubes slotted in the ceiling.

We heard nothing but a howling jungle of cries and obscenities and saw a turmoil of arms and fearful faces and flying limbs, and two enormous backs – of Roosevelt Grier, the football player, and Rafer Johnson, the Olympic champion – piling on to a pair of blue jeans or chinos on a steam table. There was a head on the floor streaming blood, and somebody put a Kennedy boater under it, and the blood trickled down the sides like chocolate sauce on an iced cake. There were splashes of flashlights, and infernal heat, and the button eyes of Ethel Kennedy turned to cinders. She was wrestling or slapping a young man and he was saying, 'Listen, lady, I'm hurt, too.' And then she was on her knees cradling him briefly, and in another little pool of light on the greasy floor was a huddle of clothes and staring out of it the face of Bobby Kennedy, like the stone face of a child's effigy on a cathedral tomb.

I had, and have, no idea of the stretch of time, or any immediate sense of the event itself. Everybody has a vulnerable organ that reacts to shock, and mine is the stomach. My lips were like emery paper and I was feeling very sick and hollow. I pattered back into the creamy, green genteel dining room. And only then did I hear somebody yell, 'Kennedy's shot, they shot him.' I heard a girl nearby moan, 'No, no, not again!' And while I was thinking, 'that was in Dallas', a dark woman suddenly bounded to a table and beat it and howled like a wolf, 'Goddam stinking country! No! No! No! No! No! No! No!' Another woman attacked the bright television screen and the image of the placid commentators, who had not yet got the news. My companion was fingering a cigarette package like a paralytic. I sat her down and went back in again. Everybody wanted to make space and air, but everybody also wanted to see the worst. By now, the baying and the moaning had carried over into the ballroom, and it sounded like a great hospital bombed and in panic.

It may have been a minute, or twenty minutes later, when a squad of cops bristling with shotguns burst through the swinging doors of the pantry our way with their bundle of black curly head and the jeans, and the tight, small behind, and the limp head, and a face totally dazed.

Well, the next morning, when I saw and heard the Pope in his gentle, faltering English, I still could not believe that he was talking about the squalid, appalling scene in a hotel pantry that I had been a part of and would always be a part of.

I don't doubt that such an experience is a trauma. And because of it, and five days later, I still cannot rise to the editorial pages and the general lamentations about a sick society. I for one do not feel like an accessory to a crime. And I reject, almost as a frivolous obscenity, the notion of collective guilt, the idea that I or the American people killed John Fitzgerald Kennedy and Martin Luther King and Robert Francis Kennedy. I don't believe, either, that *you* conceived Hitler, and that in some deep unfathomable sense all Europe was responsible for the extermination of six million Jews. With Edmund Burke, I don't know how you can indict a whole nation. To me, this now roaringly fashionable theme is a great folly. It is difficult to resist, because it provides emergency resuscitation to one's self-esteem. It deflects the search for a villain to some big corporate culprit. It offers cheap reassurance, cut-rate wisdom, but is really a way of opting out of the human situation: a situation that includes pity for the dead Kennedys and the living, compassion for Sirhan Sirhan, and sympathy for the American nation at a time when the vicious side of its frontier tradition (to which it has owed its vigour and variety) is surging up again, for reasons that no one has accurately diagnosed.

I said as much as this to a young friend. And he replied, 'Me too. I don't feel implicated in the murder of John or Bobby Kennedy. But when Martin Luther King is killed, the only people who know that you and I are not like the killers are you and I.'

It is a tremendous sentence and exposes the present danger to America and its public order. The more people talk about collective guilt, the more they will feel it. For after three hundred years of subjection and prejudice any desperate black man or deluded outcast is likely to act as if it were true: that the American people, and not their derelicts, are the villains.

Making a Home of a House

26 January 1969

It obviously takes a little time to be able to judge the political style of any new President, because he suddenly has more power inside the White House than he'd ever guessed. But less power outside the White House than he'd hoped.

In the meantime, there are other changes, from one White House-keeper to the next, that are more likely, I believe, to fascinate more people than those who are interested only in political programmes. I mean, quite simply, the way the man lives, or is made to live by what we call 'maintenance' and once called a wife. What he does with his day, the gadgets and objects he likes to have around him, the sort of midnight snack he chooses to steal from the icebox.

Five Presidents and thirty-five years ago, the chief White House usher brought forth a book of reminiscences covering nine Presidents and forty-two years in the White House. 'Ike' Hoover, as he was familiarly known, was a sharp-eyed man who had quiet but definite ideas on dignity, eccentricity, what was becoming in a President and what was not. His book is a mine of offhand observation not unlike, I imagine, the notebooks that Dickens kept on names, characters, foibles, for novels he died too soon to write. Ike Hoover's is a proper book and anyone looking for keyhole confidences or coy sexual innuendo is going to be disappointed. Ike Hoover would have despised such stuff. Nevertheless, what stays in my memory more than all the Cabinet crises or the state dinners are his small observations about character and taste. He never hesitates to draw comparisons. Such as, that Wilson was the only President who cared for the theatre (though Harding 'liked vaudeville'), and that nearly all of them were voracious readers of detective stories. As for diversions, he records – without irony – that whereas for Wilson it was 'much motoring, golf, and solitaire', and for Harding 'golf, poker and lots of company', Coolidge indulged in 'some smoking, sleep and jigsaw puzzles'.

Ike Hoover puts down whatever comes to mind always with propriety but never with censorship. It will be hard to forget the offhand note that Herbert Hoover seldom noticed the staff and never said 'Good morning', 'Good evening', 'Merry Christmas' or 'Happy New Year'. Ike Hoover also seemed to feel a historian's responsibility to deliver a final judgement on every man he served. He announced that 'The nine Presidents whom I have known seem to me just about average men.' But having obliterated them under a blanket of ordinariness, he then pulled them out again and assigned them marks for human qualities that meant much to him. Egotism? Coolidge had most, Hoover least. Self-control? 'Those who saw Coolidge in a rage were simply startled for life.' Laughter? Taft was a hearty laugher. Hoover, he says, never laughed at all. Fondness for the ladies? 'Theodore Roosevelt was a man's man, through and through. Taft was a ladies' man, pure and simple. Harding was a sporting ladies' man.' Food fads? 'Harding liked fancy food . . . Roosevelt would make a whole meal on pork and beans . . . Coolidge enjoyed cheese and would eat it by the slice like pie . . . Hoover just ate.' Sleeping habits? Teddy Roosevelt never slept by day, Taft 'could sleep at any old time', Wilson could take a nap 'when he had large affairs to deal with . . . [he could] go right to sleep as soon as he lay down on the couch. It was part of his plan of self-control.' The report on Calvin Coolidge amounts to a revelation. He went to bed at ten and got up between seven and nine. 'In the afternoon he would without fail take a nap lasting from two to four hours, going from one-thirty to . . . sometimes five o'clock.' I have forgotten many things about Calvin Coolidge, but I shall not readily lose the picture of a President of the United States who on principle slept between eleven and fifteen hours a day.

Well, Ike Hoover is long gone, and we shall never have the pleasure of his clean but odious comparisons between, say, Truman and Eisenhower. Even though we've had a spate of memoirs and torrents of gossip, we still don't have as memorable a domestic picture of the newcomers.

A few of us were sitting around the other evening indulging a fantasy that millions of Americans must have been enjoying in secret this week: what would you do if the impossible office came your way? What's the first thing you'd do if you moved into the White House? A pretty brunette with a fine chin knew at once: 'I'd get rid of those damn Remingtons.'

Frederic Remington was an American painter and sculptor of the old West, born just at the right time, the year of the outbreak of the Civil War, to see the last upsurge of the old boisterous life on the plains. If he'd been born out West, he no doubt would have taken for granted the old corral, and the trail herd, and the branding, and the buffalo range, and the occasional Indian massacre. But he was born in New York State and, following the rule that no true believer is so bigoted as a convert, he did over two thousand seven hundred paintings and drawings of horses, cattle, cowboys, Indians, soldiers, and horses, horses, horses. They were done with almost painful realism, every hoof and muscle and lariat and nostril painted as if by a photographer who was not satisfied with the print until he had pencilled in all the creases. Yet Remington prompted in strong, simple men the thrill of recognition that comes to yachtsmen when they see a painting, good or awful, which reflects the sunset light on ballooning sails.

Today, Remington's pictures bring incredible prices. Two of them were loaned to the White House at the insistence of President Johnson and hung in a room outside his big office. It was a compulsory routine, if you were a visitor to Johnson's White House, to be led at the end out of the office and planted in front of these broncos and urged to admire them. The President would look at them as other men look at a Rubens or a photograph of their grandmother, and a tear would form in the corner of one eye. He would sniff like a gusting wind and brush away the tear with the back of a hand the size of a cod.

Now, if one thing is more certain than another in the transfer of power from Johnson to Nixon, it is that the style and flavour of White House family life will change. It always does, of course, though there have been new occupants too timorous to change anything for a while. Mrs Truman was one. For six weeks, she nibbled away at cold, hard dinner rolls of a kind surely very familiar to English-speaking and French-speaking people. But she'd been brought up in Missouri and inherited the Southern taste for hot, crumbly rolls. It was only on the command of President Truman that her recipe was passed on to the chef, and the Trumans reverted to breaking the bread of their fathers.

I don't suppose any of us would dare to say yet what changes the Nixons are likely to make. In spite of the loving work done on the Nixon image by advertising men and similar plastic surgeons we really know very little about his tastes and private prejudices. He was so anxious for so long to be all things to all men that he seemed to have no preferences whatsoever. In, for instance, food. On his campaign trips his enthusiasm was carefully prepared for the regional food that came his way. In Idaho, he simply craved a baked potato. In the state of Washington, he couldn't get enough apple and boysenberry pie. In Maryland, he drooled to get at the crabs (and in that, we must admit, he was at one with the best crab-fanciers on earth). In his native state of California – which grows an alarming variety of food – he knew enough to be pretty spry. Praise an orange in Merced County, for example, and you're likely to lose the votes of all the Armenians who pack apricots. When in doubt he settled for plastic hamburgers everywhere, and in southern California, his home ground, he made a big thing of wolfing chilli con carne in the Mexican districts, even though it is a Texas and not a Mexican dish. But now he's in his own large home, and he can do what comes naturally, and it must be an immense relief.

First thing he did was to throw out those Remingtons, or rather send them back politely to the museum. Within twenty-four hours, he struck some other blows for liberty that wiped out the more theatrical memories of the Johnson reign. First, he announced that he's not comfortable working in a large, pretentious office. The President's office is a sumptuous and beautiful white oval room. It has two or three superb portraits of earlier Presidents, some elegant eighteenth-century furniture, and a great sofa, in front of which Johnson planted a massive white console. It looked like the computerized dashboard of a nuclear submarine, with many winking lights signifying all the people at home and abroad who were dying to phone the President. He used to gaze at it fondly, as a Roman emperor might have gazed at the roaring Colosseum begging him to elevate his thumb or invert it. Away off, and facing the sofa, were three television sets, each tuned to a different station, for if ever there was a man yearning to know what the world was saying about Lyndon Johnson on three networks, not to mention Telstar, that man was Lyndon Johnson.

Well, the console has gone, and so have the television sets. Mr Nixon hastened to remark that he was not against television. He just wants to turn an IBM headquarters into a home. The Oval Office will be used for ceremonial occasions. Mr Nixon has taken over a small office, where he can put his feet up and – a moving touch – have a fire, with the air conditioning turned way up, even on the blistering days of midsummer.

These changes will be applauded, I believe, by both the citizens who voted for him and by those who didn't. Nixon is a small-town boy, and in spite of the trappings of power that have surrounded him since he came to the Vice Presidency sixteen long years ago (he has been at the top or close to it as long as any politician in American history) he likes small surroundings and homely things. There is an anxiety among some old courtiers from Camelot that the Nixons will tear down the French eighteenth-century wallpapers, and dispose of the fine paintings, and otherwise reduce to a suburban 'den' all the other elegant fixings with which Mrs Kennedy did over the White House in the splendid Federal style. There's no sign of this at the moment.

But a President has considerable say in how he wants to have the house look while he's in it. Theodore Roosevelt, another New York convert to the muscle-flexing life of the Far West (and the jungles of

Brazil), did over several rooms into menageries of moose and bison heads. His successor couldn't wait to ship them away and be free to walk through the place standing up straight. Harry Truman loved to sit in an old rocker in the evenings and face the lawns behind the White House. What he missed was a porch to rock on, so after a squabble with Congress and the architects (who said the second floor would look like a big Missouri back porch), he had some construction done under the back portico. It looked like a big Missouri back porch.

And how about the Vice President? Agnew is his name. In spite of the usual promise that he will be given vast new sovereign powers, he is tucked away in a tiny office he has commandeered from a secretary. He thus gives substance to Mencken's definition of a Vice President: 'He is a man who sits in the outer office of the White House hoping – to hear the President sneeze.'

Telling One Country about Another

2 March 1969

A year or two ago, I had an invitation to go and talk to the cadets at West Point, which is the Sandhurst or St Cyr of the United States. The letter was signed by a general. It was the first time a general had invited me to anything, though more years ago than I care to say I did get a letter from the President of the United States which began: 'Greetings!' – with a cordial exclamation mark, too.

The general even sent a car to drive me up the Hudson. If I'd been going to talk to the Arts Club, or whatever, of Long Beach, California, I'd have put on a pair of golfing slacks and a blazer. But I was not going to be found guilty, at West Point, of what my headmaster called 'the supreme act of rudeness: casualness' and I decked myself out in a suit and a tie bearing the three cocks (the cock crowed three times) and weeping crowns of Jesus College, Cambridge. This badge offered the only possibility open to me of pulling rank. I also practised saying 'Yes, sir', 'No, sir' and 'Not at all, sir'.

When I got up there, I was the one who was called sir. The commanding general, it happened, was about five years younger than I and on the verge of retirement. He wondered if there was anything he might do to make me comfortable. This alarming deference made me think back to an afternoon, in 1962, aboard the USS *Kitty Hawk*, a super aircraft carrier. I was along with the White House press corps at a demonstration of missile firing being put on for President Kennedy. When it was all over, and the twilight was dropping over the Pacific, I was nearly knocked down by a hefty slap on the back. It came from the Admiral of the Pacific Fleet. 'Hi, there!' he said, 'You old bastard.' I had known him twenty years before as a humble lieutenant, and we had had one or two memorable raucous evenings together.

There seem, indeed, to be fewer men around than there used to be to whom I feel I ought to defer. By the same token, there are more and more men, going from grey to white at that, who come to me and seek advice. It is a mixed compliment. I now get calls from incoming foreign correspondents who wonder how to go about acquainting themselves with the Presidency, the Congress, investigating committees and the rest of it. The other day, one of them asked me to tell him the main differences between reporting the America of today and the America of thirty years ago. It is worth a passing thought or two.

To begin with, I could say, and truly, that the job is always the same: to say, or write, what you see and hear and relate it to what you know of the country's traditional behaviour. 'Traditional behaviour' may sound a little clumsy. But I'm trying to avoid the trap of what is called 'national character'. Whenever you are really baffled, it is always safe to put it all down to national character. I have come to think that a strong belief in national character is the first refuge of the anxious. For the moment, we'll let that pass.

A foreign correspondent, then, is both an interpreter and a victim of his subject matter. He must be aware of his own changing view of the country he's assigned to. And the danger here is that of assuming that the longer you stay in a country, the truer will be your perspective.

As the Pope said to the earnest visitor who wondered how long he ought to stay in Rome to know it well: 'Two days, very good. Two weeks, better. Two years, not long enough.'

More important still, the reporter must always have in mind the settled view that his readers or listeners hold of the country he's writing about. The home reader, whether a simpleton or an intellectual, a Socialist or a Tory, wants – like a tourist – to find what he's looking for. He doesn't want to be startled out of his preconceptions. It is the correspondent's job to startle preconceptions. And, I must admit, sometimes to say that they're right.

There was, twenty-odd years ago, the instructive case of a Hungarian refugee from his Communist country. He had been a Communist himself, till he saw Communism in action. Then he escaped to Britain. He was a journalist, a brilliant intellectual, and a Jew. When, after the Second World War, the British Labour government had to try and establish a policy for Palestine, a British editor decided that this man was the ideal outsider to report on the anarchy and ill-will that had set in between the British and the Jews. The editor gently suggested that it would be a fine thing if he could incidentally expose the 'lies' that the Palestine Jews were spreading abroad. The 'lies' included the notion that Mr Ernest Bevin, the Foreign Secretary, in trying to hold on to Palestine, and the support of the Arabs, and the goodwill of the Jews, was attempting an impossibility that was involving him in ruthless treatment of the Jews. The Hungarian was told to spend a few weeks feeling his way into the situation and then to begin filing his series of articles. He stayed a month, five weeks, six weeks, and nothing was heard from him. When the editor cabled, 'What happened? Where is the series?' he cabled back, 'Sorry, no series, all the lies are true.'

Luckily, no such bad blood has soured the relations between Britain and the United States in the past thirty years, except during the first three or four years of the 1950s, when the British view of the late Senator Joseph McCarthy blew up the only blizzard of disgusted mail I have ever received. But, more recently, there have been delicate problems involved in reporting a first-rate power that was once a second-rate power to a second-rate power that was once first-rate. For many years after the Second World War, Britons refused to acknowledge their fading influence. And for a blazing month or two the most

AC in the BBC's New York studio, reading one of his Letters, *circa* 1953.

At the White House in 1941, just before FDR announced the signing
of the Lend Lease Agreement.

AC reviewing the troops along a line of New York City mounted police in the early
1960s, probably here the Columbus Day Parade held every October.

AC (with Susie, foreground) in front of the general store in Cutchogue, Long Island, going through the morning paper.

Keeping in touch and afloat with the news, AC drifts past a neighbour's house at Nassau Point, Long Island, *circa* 1952.

AC filing a story to
England from his teletype
machine in Nassau Point
while Susie waits patiently
so they can go to the
beach, *circa* 1952.

AC with his son John in a
New York studio,
preparing for a broadcast,
circa 1945.

AC never visited a barber shop after he met Jane. Here Jane does the honours in their bathroom at 1150 Fifth Avenue, *circa* 1952.

'Domestic Interior', at 114 East 71st Street, with AC, Jane and Susie, June 1950. The family moved to more spacious quarters at 1150 Fifth Avenue in December of that year.

AC typically enjoying
himself while discussing
the Hollywood film
business with
colleagues in 1949.

An elegant evening
with long-time friend
Lauren Bacall.

Always curious about the public's reaction to any given event, Cooke delighted in talking to the cabbie, the butcher and the man on the street.

AC with Jane aboard
Cunard's *Queen Mary*,
circa 1962.

AC delighted and
relieved to be
nearly home and
back in New York.
Here, in the
airport, late 1960s.

unpopular American in Britain was Dean Acheson, simply for having expressed his glimpse of the obvious: 'Britain has lost an empire and not yet found a role.'

When I arrived in Washington in the late 1930s, I was one of only four British correspondents. Today, there must be forty or fifty, if you count reporters on particular assignment, and the enlarged radio and television staffs of the BBC and the British commercial television companies. This trek followed a simple law of politics: the best reporters, like the best chefs, gravitate toward the centres of power. (The Australians today complain, as Americans did fifty years ago, that the foreign press corps in their country is unreasonably small.) When Britain really ruled the waves, in good King George V's glorious reign, London was the capital of foreign correspondence. The Foreign Office briefings were attended by a pack of correspondents from nations big and small. And the Foreign Office, being the repository of all wise and relevant information, felt no call to bandy debating points with the press. The Foreign Office distributed handouts, no questions asked. It did not justify its policies. It announced them. And I remember how American correspondents, newly arrived in London, used to fume in their impotence when they found it was not possible to have a private word with a Cabinet minister. To have invited him to lunch would have thrown him into a coronary.

A young Texan, a journalist, who is now a distinguished American magazine editor, stayed with me in London when I was back there in the early, dark spring of 1938. He was an inquisitive and typically courteous Texan, and one night he had a message from his New York office asking him to look into a rumour, a correct rumour as it turned out, that the Nazis were about to invade Austria. It sounded pretty melodramatic to me, but in those days we were not yet accustomed to the idea that gangsterism was a working technique of international politics. My friend mulled over the cable from New York and his instincts as an Associated Press stringer got the better of him. He asked to use my telephone and he rang up the Foreign Office, an impulse which to me was as bizarre as phoning Buckingham Palace. When the FO answered he asked to talk to Lord Halifax, who had just then become the Foreign Secretary. I was agog with admiration. I was at the time a political innocent, a film critic, but I knew my Hitchcock movies well enough to know that that was exactly how Joel McCrea in a raincoat went about his business.

It was soon obvious that my friend was having a rough time with the other end of the wire. 'Yes, sir,' he kept saying in courteous variations, 'I know it's very late in the evening, but this is not the sort of rumour the Associated Press can just forget.' Somehow, he managed to get Lord Halifax's home number, a remarkable feat in itself. He re-dialled and there was a crackle and a pause and a respectful fluting sound from the other end. It was the butler, who had a strangulated moment or two while, I imagine, he was being revived by the rest of the household staff. At last, he pronounced the definitive sentence: 'I'm sorry, sir, his Lordship is in his bath.'

This is still not an approach I'd be inclined to take, though in failing to be so brash I no longer feel merely courteous: I feel I'm neglecting my duty. Because I now take for granted the ease of access to people in government in America. Americans had, and have, a quite different feeling about the press. In many countries, and Britain used to be one of them, a reporter is a potential enemy. The Americans, however, feel it is better to have a friend in print than an enemy. And this, too, is a great danger, for nothing castrates a reporter so easily as flattery. But the main thing is, the politicians tend to look on you as a camp follower through the maze of politics, and if they can help you find your way out, without trading the Pentagon secret file, they will do it. Nowadays, of course, even dictators have to pretend to welcome cosy conversations with television interviewers.

America, from the beginning of my time, was an open book to a reporter. The people were there to mix with, and the landscape and its troubles and pleasures, and a reporter with the most modest credentials could get to talk to everybody from the Governor, the local Congressman, the Chamber of Commerce, the saloon keepers, the local madams. Huey Long stretched out on a bed barefoot in the Roosevelt Hotel in New Orleans and picked his toes while he enlarged on the glorious future he had in mind for Everyman and Everywoman in Louisiana. I once asked the late Governor Talmadge of Georgia how the (since abolished) 'county unit' system worked in his state. He sucked his teeth and ordered up a car, oddly – it seemed to me then – a humble jalopy. We jumped in and he drove me into the corners of three counties that fringed Atlanta. In each of them he dropped in on a couple of farmers on the pretence of needing to relieve himself. When we were back in the city, he said, 'I got myself six unit votes right there, and them students and doctors and Commies in Atlanta can shout themselves hoarse – it's more votes than they have.' Once, I was driving across Nevada and noticed from the map that I was close by Hawthorne, and that it was the site of the US Naval Ammunition Depot. I asked to look in on it, and I did. I am a little awestruck now to reflect that a Japanese reporter could probably have done the same right up to the eve of Pearl Harbor.

In the 1930s you required no confidential sources to straighten you out on the condition of the country. The country was racked by Depression. On several trips around the United States, in the South more than anywhere, I was physically nauseated by the people I saw in the country towns and in the workless cities: the absolutely drained look of mothers nourishing babies at shrunken breasts, the general coma of the rural poor, with the telltale rash of scurvy or pellagra on the back of their necks. Today there is very little, if any, scurvy or pellagra in the South, because they varied the crops and learned about green vegetables, and the cities turned to textiles. They were no longer doomed to plates of rice and corn and potatoes and hominy grits – a feast, whenever it was a feast, of nothing but starch.

The first year I drove around the whole country, about one family in four was on the breadline or just above it. Yet, while we totted up the grim statistics, we wrote little about these things for foreign consumption. The foreign consumers too had their silent factories and marching miners, and they had bemused and stumbling leaders. The great news from America was that the country was galvanized by the new President into a prospect of greener pastures. The story was the exhilaration of the Roosevelt era: the public works, the dams and new housing, the first national network of concrete highways, the poor boys planting millions of trees. These things excited us more than the conditions they were meant to cure depressed us. If 30 or 40 per cent of the population was then at some stage of need, today only 11 per cent falls below the government's rather generous definition of a subsistence income of $2,200 a year. And though that may sound like small pickings, there has never been a time in this country's history,

ps in human history, when more people in one nation were
ff, never a smaller percentage of two hundred millions who
be called poor. Yet there is less complacency, I believe, than
ver was. As I talk, the cities tremble and the countryside groans
over the shame of it.

In case my drift is being misunderstood, let me say that this trembling
and groaning is a good thing too. If God observes the fall of one
sparrow, it is right in a prosperous time that we should feel not only
that we are our brother's keeper but that our brother is the whole of
society. I think it must be the first time in history that the so-called
civilized nations have felt this way. Why? Are we more humane, more
sensitive than we used to be? I think not. The world's population of
the starving and near-starving at the height of the Victorian age must
have been beyond our imagining. But the point is, the Victorians had
to imagine it, or read the fine print, or take the progressive magazines
or dig out – from some encyclopedia – the infant mortality rates.
Statistics make few people bleed or weep. Today all of us, in a castle
or a cottage, can see every night the warped skeletons of the children
of Biafra. Thirty students up at Columbia University paralysed for a
time the education of several thousand, and it looked and sounded, on
the evening news, like the siege of Mafeking. A hundred cops go
berserk on an August night in Chicago, and next day it's the scandal
of the world. Television, whatever its faults and banalities, is the new
conscience – or nagger – of mankind. I am frankly relieved to reflect
that in the early Hitler days we had no television. The news dispatches
of brave men had to be read by choice. The television scene of Nazism,
as filmed by the devilishly skilled Leni Riefenstahl, could have recruited
millions of disciples. It might, of course, have made people stop and
listen to Winston Churchill, who went on and on, a croaking old
orator, about the threat of a frightful regime he had evidently pictured
in his mind.

This, I am sure, is the single greatest change that has come over our
society's awareness of what is going on everywhere. The sight of
violence has quite likely upset our sense of proportion just as badly as
the assumption of general calm upset it by default. If so, we are upset
in the right way.

The effect on the foreign correspondent has been revolutionary. All

newspaper reporters, whether they know it or not, are comp
the television news, which has a daily audience bigger than
famous newspaper correspondent ever dreamed of. The she
gency of television, of the thing seen, invokes not meditatio
partisanship: that is to say, instant ideology. The newspapers, to
solvent, try to match this emotional appeal. The result is that – in
Britain, for example – the best papers are more and more turning into
daily magazines of opinion, and the worst make the crudest, the most
blatant, appeal to the seven deadly sins.

Consequently, while the scope of a foreign correspondent has not
been narrowed (he's still expected to take all knowledge for his province) the reader's expectations of him are narrower, more ideological.
When I began, it was possible to present the awkward complexity of
a political story without any side being taken. And then to move on to
any number of what were called 'colour' pieces: on the landscape, the
livelihood of a region, sport, odd characters, the history of this custom
and that place. Today, you write about these things and the partisan
oldsters say you are fiddling while Washington or Chicago burns. The
young say you've got a hang-up on whimsy.

A year ago, I was talking to a forum of Californians about the rape
of their beautiful landscape by the developers. The tidal wave of
new arrivals. The mania for city ways. The universal obsession with
industry as the only true form of progress. When it was over, a
handsome, 19-, 20-year-old girl came up to me and said, 'I understood
most of it except for one thing.' What's that? I said: She said, 'You
have a thing about trees, don't you?' That's right, I said.

In these talks, and at the risk of seeming callous or whimsical, I
propose to go on having a thing about many other matters than Soviet
expansionism, and the plight of the cities, and the nuclear arms race,
and who – after the next Presidential election – is going to be the lord
and master of us all.

Pegler

29 June 1969

I'd like to tell you about an outrageous man who was one of the best American humorists of any time and even at his worst handled the American language with a freewheeling audacity that has rarely been matched since Mark Twain.

Westbrook Pegler died suddenly the other day and I was saddened. I am puzzled to say why this should be so. I was never close to him, he was 74, he'd been sick in more than a physical way for years, and he had not been seen in print much in a decade or so. Scurrility was his trade, you might say, and in the 1930s and 1940s, it was a breathtaking thing to see how close he could sail to the wind of the libel laws. Long before the end, he lost all skill in coming about when the wind was raging. He grossly libelled an old newspaper friend by describing him, among other repulsive things, as a coward, a war profiteer, a fugitive from the London Blitz in the bowels of comfortable hotels, 'an absentee war correspondent', and he wrote also that the man had once gone 'nuding along the road with a wench in the raw'. This spasm of whimsy and malice cost Pegler's employers $175,000 in the biggest libel settlement awarded up to that time.

He was always a scornful man, but after that his scorn turned rancid and he babbled on and on about old enemies, about both President and Mrs Roosevelt long after they were dead. His last years seemed to have been spent in fuming total recall of all the Presidents he had watched, from the first Roosevelt to John F. Kennedy, whom he called 'a mean, ratty, dough-heavy Boston gang politician'. Towards the end, even the monthly magazine of the John Birch Society found his last piece, on Chief Justice Warren, too raw to print.

You would think that here was the case of a great talent gone to seed. And as a man, certainly, he was for years simply thrashing in deep water and making incoherent sounds before he went under. Why, then, should I have felt sad at his going? It is because, I think, of a fact of relativity not mentioned in Einstein's theory. Some people are so bristling with life that when they have been dead for years they still seem to be on call, whereas many sweet but pallid people who are up and about have nothing more to offer.

Pegler, newspaperman, is the man I am talking about, and he had a lion's share of the vitality that outlasts its time and place. Picture him first. A big hulking man but erect as a guardee, with glimmering blue eyes that flashed an ultimatum to all simple believers and all secret slobs. A grim, mischievous Irish mouth. Two shaggy, forked eyebrows, to stress that the message – via Western Union – came from nobody but Mephistopheles. Plainly not the kind of reporter to be brushed off by a handout, or a telephone call, or a Presidential 'no comment'.

He was what they used to call a muckraker, and in his middle years he was the best. Once, over a drink in Denver, when I asked him what he was doing so far from his den in Connecticut, he said he'd heard that a couple of insurance companies had suddenly shown alarming fat profits. 'The trail led out here,' he said, 'and I thought I might come and – sink a pick. Could be pay dirt.' I imagined every insurance man in the West out of bed and doctoring the books.

When, soon after, he appeared in Hollywood to look into the way the motion picture unions worked, his hosts should have been warned. At that time, a man named Willie Bioff was the labour boss of the movie unions and a man highly thought of by the bigwigs of the New Deal. Pegler threatened nothing and nobody. He mooched around the studios and the houses in Beverly Hills and dingy offices downtown, and picked up a private scent that led him to Chicago and on to other, obscurer, towns in the hinterland. He pored over police blotters and old newspapers and tramped off to interview this anonymous old man and that forgotten old madam. And after six months of pick-sinking, he wrote a series of searing columns. The first began with the firecracker of a sentence: 'Willie Bioff is a convicted pimp.' Period. By the time Pegler was through, so was Bioff, whose shady past Pegler had reconstructed with the tedious accuracy of one of those picture puzzles in a hundred bits and pieces that emerges at last as the Taj Mahal. Bioff went to jail. So did the national president of a building employees' union, and the prison gates closed behind him on the whining phrase: 'I've been Peglerized.'

Pegler was born in Minneapolis, a skinny little runt, irascible at his first gasp. He delivered newspapers as a boy in the paralysing northern winters, and one day he was shoving his little wagon along in Chicago when the Arctic wind whistling in across the lake blew his papers away, and while he was chasing them his route book too took off in another direction. He was disgusted. He tore off home and when the route boss called him up and said, 'You're fined three dollars,' he shouted back, 'Oh, shut your face!' And that was the end of his first job.

He was the son of a newspaperman and he never thought there was any other trade to follow. He started, at 16, as a $10-a-week cub reporter and described himself as 'a raw kid as freckled as a guinea egg'. He was transferred to St Louis and at 22 was in London as a fledgling foreign correspondent. Then he went into the Navy in the First World War and after that turned sports reporter and in no time showed that he had a rowdy, biting style that was to make him a star. He moved up to a sports column, and when nothing much was happening he wrote about this and that and found himself sounding off about the cost of living, the gangsters and the man in the White House. In 1933 he set up shop as a national columnist with no illusions about the pretensions of the breed. He called all columnists 'myriad-minded us ... experts on the budget who can't balance an expense account, pundits on the technological age who can't put a fresh ribbon in their own typewriters, and resounding authorities on the problems of the farmer who never grew a geranium in a pot'.

The first fifteen years of his column were the great years. He wrote about everything with the unsleeping scepticism of a man in the bleachers who had watched many a dumb-bell turn into a national hero on the baseball mound, who had seen many a horse race fixed and who was therefore quite ready to believe that a labour leader, a Governor, a Secretary of the Treasury or even a President might be no better than he should be.

He refused to be dazzled by the vocabulary of the sociologists or distracted from his own horse-sense by the hushed pronouncements of the Walter Lippmanns and the Arthur Krocks – what he used to call 'double-dome' commentators. Mussolini, for instance, at one time had very vocal admirers and detesters in the United States, but the role of his Blackshirts in the Spanish Civil War was thought to be a topic for exclusively military experts. To Pegler it was all very simple: 'In most invincible legions, the front rank is regarded as the post of maximum peril and honour. But at Guadalajara, when Mussolini's brave Black-shirts encountered the enemy, the men in the rear rank found them-selves overwhelmed by the impetuous dash of their comrades in the forward positions . . . it is reliably reported that most of the Blackshirts casualties were caused by hobnails.'

Off in Florida covering some labour conference, he took a day to explore the expensive magic of deep-sea fishing. He was not impressed. Listen to this: it might be out of *Life On the Mississippi*.

We were going after tarpon and they kept telling me the water was absolutely reeking with all kinds of fish with queer names like dace, mace, plaice, reach, peach, gudgeon, mullet, grommet and shovel-nosed duebills . . . we anchored in the barley water beside a channel and rigged up a lot of tackle with hooks the size of those on which they hang half-cows in butcher shops . . . we didn't catch any fish on the first day or the second . . . the third day we were burned as red as fire engines and the mosquitoes were coming up in clouds . . . I can't play golf either . . . when I was a kid, I was a punk ball player. Poker – the same story. I try to live right and follow the instructions, but it never makes any difference. Maybe this is what makes me so mean.

Well, in time Pegler's meanness got to be a national scandal, and the obituary writers made much – too much I think – of his almost psychotic hatred of the Roosevelt family, and his ornery conviction that practically all Americans of Slavic origin were probably Commu-nists. In life, in fact, he was most of the time, and in a private room, an amiable and surprisingly soft-spoken companion. But the path to his prose led through the bile duct. He had a perverse love of demoting all current heroes in a single phrase. Vice President Henry Wallace was 'old bubble-head'. J. Edgar Hoover, when everybody thought of him as the national scourge of all evil men, was put down as 'a nightclub fly-cop'. Mayor Fiorello LaGuardia, the plucky Little Flower to the citizens of New York, was to Pegler 'the little *padrone* of the Bol-sheviki'. And though it may seem odd, his devotion to Franklin Roose-velt till America got into the war was an expression of this same contempt for people in power, for he saw Roosevelt as the champion of 'the hired help' against 'the meanness of a complacent upper class'.

He was brought up in the tough and talented school of Chicago reporters when Chicago was the best newspaper town in the country. And when he came East, he carried with him this air of being a prairie lad permanently unfooled by the rich, the genteel, the powerful and all foreigners. He must have adopted the manner early on, possibly as a small fry's defence against the jeering reminders of his gang that his father (a diligent and respectable Cockney immigrant) was English, and his mother was Canadian: Irish-Canadian but still Canadian. Like many other Midwesterners, Pegler was specially on his guard against any beguilements that came from England and the English. But unlike some Midwesterners, he was not exasperated by an English story that defeated the usual American preconceptions.

There was an unforgettable evening just after the Second World War when I was dining with a Midwesterner who had made a fortune in New York as an advertising tycoon. He was the son of a poor parson and he remained a lifelong rural Republican, and a fervent anti-Royalist with a very pat view of Europeans as the lackeys of kings and courts. The only other guest was Pegler. I had just returned from London and the bleakness of England in the winter after Harry Truman had abruptly cancelled the blessings of Lend-Lease. In material comforts the British were, if anything, worse off than they'd been during the war. But I had been struck, as all visitors were in those days, by a new and rousing social equality that the war had – you would almost say – enforced on the country: an equality of want. Pegler and the tycoon politely doubted it. I told them how I'd been invited by the Lord Privy Seal, no less (fifth in line of precedence after the king) to look over the bomb damage to the House of Commons and other ancient memorials. They visibly sniffed at my dragging in such a title. I couldn't think why I'd been chosen for this flattering grand tour until the Lord Privy Seal began to speculate aloud about the type of Englishman who might be best qualified to be the next ambassador to the United States. I said only that I wished for once he could be plain Mr Somebody, and not knighted beforehand, since Americans were fuzzy about titles and tended to think that even a knight was an eighth earl accustomed to whipping the peasants. Pegler and the host glared at their plates as if to challenge me to produce one common man in a society so notoriously class-ridden. Well, so what did Lord What's His Name say to that? He replied, I said, 'Ah dawn't want to goa to't friggin Stairs, we've got a bloody sawcial revolution goin' on 'ere.' (The Lord Privy Seal was a poor boy from the woollen mills of Yorkshire.)

There was a long bristling silence. Then the tycoon said grimly, '*The Prisoner of Zenda* was the last good book to come out of Europe.' The tycoon glowered while Pegler bellowed. He told me much later he'd never forgotten it.

It's true that Pegler often got angry about many foolish things and never forgot a grudge. But just as often his indignation was nobly directed against unfashionable targets and sometimes his scorn made Dean Swift read like Lewis Carroll. He bucked the Ku Klux Klan when it was dangerously powerful, and he belaboured the ruthlessness of union leaders when their power was sacrosanct. He wrote withering pieces out of Nazi Germany, which was more than many resident correspondents did, but when Hitler was everybody's Evil Eye and Stalin was his benign counterpart, Pegler saw Stalin as at least an equal monster. Defending the American police in the gangster days against invidious comparisons with Scotland Yard, he pointed out the comparative amateurishness of English criminals and the probity of English courts, and ended with this blazing sentence: 'So the British hang their simpletons and Scotland Yard takes credit for another triumph, all to the great inferential disgrace of the American cops, who have to fight it out with Dillingers and Harvey Baleys and Vincent Colls and crooked lawyers, low-grade governors, sentimental juries and courts beneath contempt.'

If the spiritualists are right, and Pegler is somewhere within the sound of these words, he is certainly tearing at his robes and bashing in his harp. But those are the kind of opinions for which he is to be honoured. All you can do with the talent is envy it.

'Eternal Vigilance' – by Whom?

19 October 1969

The other day I had a long talk with an attractive young American. The conversation divided between long sarcastic monologues on his part, and grunts of approval – more often of doubt – on mine. He was bemoaning, as we all should, the noisy and smelly flood of scandal and corruption that fills the papers these days, defaces the brightness of the television screen, and makes television commercials seem more smug and fatuous than ever. We touched on street crime, on the army sergeants swiping huge profits from overseas service clubs, the continuing proof about risky short cuts in the manufacture of automobiles, the deep inroads the Mafia is making into big and respectable business. And so on and so on.

What bothered me was that he put all these things down, not to the corruption of any class but to 'middle-class values' in themselves. Before we come to that, I'd like to say that it was not only the substance of his jeremiad that upset me, the blanket indictment of a whole country. It was the muddy language that drooled from his lips. Nobody burgles a house any more: 'A kid I know was burglarized.' None of the statesmen we brought up ever met or tangled: they were involved in 'a confrontation'. He talked of 'interface' and 'feedback'. People were either 'committed' or 'alienated'. I said goodbye and went off. I believe he thought I was shaken and impressed. I was glad I'd not said what I was tempted to: that the whole burden of his song had been sung long ago – 'It's the rich what gets the pleasure, it's the poor what gets the blame.'

I suppose that one way of explaining this unpleasant get-together (confrontation?) was the so-called 'generation gap'. Well, in some things it is a fact, and always will be. In many more disputes, and strained relations, the generation gap is a lazy excuse for the age-old suspicion between parents and children. And today, certainly, there is a widening gap between the language the generations use. I throw it out as a suggestion merely that this may be due to the sudden eruption, in the past twenty years or so, of technology – the passing over, into ordinary speech, of the special vocabularies of advanced mathematics and computers, and the new and respectable status now given to the ghastly language of sociology and psychology. Most of the horrors that now befog the speech of students and politicians, not to mention advertising men, are a special lingo that the layman doesn't understand: like 'input', 'orientation', 'parameter'. 'Parameter' is a good example. In mathematics, it means a quantity constant in a given case, but one that varies in different cases. It is used by politicians and pundits to mean no more than limit, or boundary.

No wonder they talk about a failure of 'communication' (another stopgap word between two thoughts) when they spend so long using words like 'communicate' and 'verbalize'. Only a year ago, I heard a qualified psychiatrist declare that his 2-year-old was already talking. But he didn't say it that way. He said, 'Children of his age group don't usually verbalize at this stage.' Especially if there's a verbalizing sibling in the familial situation. A gabby brother, that is.

Well, by way of thoughtful reacting, I can only say that things are bad and they'll probably get worse. There's just one point I'd like to make to people who despair of American society – and I have to confess it's a point I often forget myself. In a self-governing Republic – good government in some places, dubious in others – three thousand miles wide, eighteen hundred miles long, with fifty separate states which in many important matters have almost absolute powers – with two hundred million people drawn from scores of nations, what is remarkable is not the conflict between them but the truce. Enough is happening in America at any one time – enough that is exciting, frightening, funny, brutal, brave, intolerable, bizarre, dull, slavish, eccentric, inspiring and disastrous – that almost anything you care to say about the United States is true. You can make a case for thinking this the best, the worst, the most abject, the most alert democracy ever invented. Of course, this reflection doesn't help people bleeding in a riot or languishing in a sloppily run hospital at an outrageous daily rate. The great need for anyone in authority is courage. And the requirement for a reporter, an onlooker, is horse-sense and the ability to strike a true balance. I don't know any good reporter who would confidently claim these qualities.

Yet there is one whole class in America, and that is the largest, which claims them and thinks of itself as the balance wheel of the American system. It is nothing more or less pretentious than the middle class. In America, it is not only huger – proportionately and absolutely – than anywhere else. It is not simply a large group of people who qualify by reason of income and social habits. It includes all the people who aspire to be in it, or think they are already there. In nearly forty years, I have never heard an American say, 'I am a working-class man.' I have often heard people say, 'So-and-so is looking out for the ordinary guy like me', but that's not quite the same thing.

In all the great conflicts of the past ten years – of race, student rebellion, street crime, pornography – the middle class has not been much heard from. It has been, in fact, the besieged, the ridiculed victim – of the black leaders, the student leaders, the film makers, the intellectuals, all leftists and many liberals. Yet middle-class standards, as they were planted and have grown everywhere in this country, are the ones that have kept America a going concern. It is time to grit the teeth slightly, prepare for a shower of eggs, and say what those standards are. Fair wages for good work. Concern for the family and its good name. A distrust of extremes and often, perhaps, a lazy willingness to compromise. The hope of owning your own house and improving it. The belief that the mother and father are the bosses, however easygoing, of the household and not simply pals. A pride in the whole country, often as canting and unreasonable as such patriotism can be. Vague but stubborn ideas about decency. An equally vague but untroubled belief in God. A natural sense of neighbourliness, fed by the assumption that your neighbour is much like you and is willing to share the same lawn (hedges are rare in American towns) or lend you a mower, a hammer or a bottle of milk.

Did you ever hear of qualities less heroic? Helpless laughter must be bellying up from almost any group of young people who happen to be hearing this recital. But there are signs, tentative and fumbled signs, that these people – who for too long have been called 'the silent majority' – are tired of being laughed at and frustrated. In desperate times, the meekest people show alarming symptoms of defiance. And, in the early races for the autumn elections, I notice that policemen are being elected as the mayors of cities. It should not yet give us cause to splutter. It is possible, I dare to say it is common, to find policemen who are fair, brave and level-headed.

However, it doesn't seem to me a good thing that the middle class, weary of violence and mockery as it may be, should turn to policemen as rulers, any more than that we should turn the government of the military over to the military. If war is too important to be left to the generals, the government of the people is too serious to be turned over to the police.

There is a more disturbing sign of the turning of the worm. Some cities are beginning to form vigilante committees. The most famous instance of this drastic remedy for lawlessness and disorder happened in San Francisco in the first furious years of its life as an El Dorado, after gold had been discovered nearby. San Francisco had been a shanty town on whistling sandhills. Then suddenly hundreds, and shortly thousands, of people from many states and several lands, came hurtling in to pan the rivers and get rich quick. The vast majority never made it but stayed. The garrison down the Peninsula deserted. The farmers quit. The shop-keepers closed down, and the laundries. The lucky new-rich sent their shirts to Hawaii – or even to China – to be washed.

When the ordinary, and pretty rude, services opened up again, the town was a combination of a doss house, a street bazaar, a mush-rooming suburb and a brothel. At nightfall gangs roamed the streets, invaded stores, taverns and houses and beat up the inmates, especially if they were foreigners, and robbed them and quite often shot them. In two months, among a population of only twenty-five thousand, there were over a hundred murders, and no one had been executed. In the end, the silent majority rose up, held mass meetings, elected officials and formed what was known as the Vigilance Committee of San Francisco. In short order they tried, condemned and hanged all the notorious criminals they could catch.

Inevitably, the lust for justice, and quick justice, can be as insatiable as any other lust. When California came into the Union, it became possible within a year or two to suspend the committee and hand the law over to the State government. Not all San Franciscans thought this was a sensible, or even a decent, thing to do. In a report I have in front of me, written in 1856, the author has this to say about the Vigilance Committee of that year. It is quite an end-of-term report:

Scorn and applause, exoneration and abuse, indignation and sympathy, have been the expressions of the civilized world in speaking of the Vigilance Committee of San Francisco. To law-loving and worthy people, it did seem strange that such an organization which usurped, as it were, the laws of the land and inflicted the severest penalties, should exist without molestation at this time . . . yet from this power California recognized her only protector of life and property, her only security for peace and virtue. Such was the object of the Society of Vigilantes. The remedy was violent but the result was good.

The other day, the *Wall Street Journal* carried a long report on the growth of vigilante societies around the country. At present they take the form of night patrols. They mean to make the streets safe. Mostly, they go unarmed. But in some small towns they tote guns, and in others they are sufficiently in league with the police to ride around in police cars. In one place their targets are robbers or muggers, in another Negroes or radicals or homosexuals. Most of them protest that their aims are innocent. Conceivably, these are simple and just men who, like the sheriff's deputies in the old Western towns, feel they must fill in for the failure of law and order. Needless to say, the courts and the police and the Governors in most states are dead against them. Vigilantism is at best a mischievous pretension, at worst a seedbed for civil chaos.

It is a small, and understandable, but ugly symptom. It would be a tragic thing for America if the middle class, the silent majority, provoked by some appalling wave of rioting and violence, found its voice and used it not to preach but to improvise law and order. Those last three words have become a catchphrase, used by the Right to argue for arbitrary restraints on the freedom of people you don't like. But the phrase has been taken up too by the Left, as a sneering put-down of ordinary people who question violence and the abuse of 'peaceable assembly'. I say, a plague on both your houses. Any society that hopes to be stable must surely yield its most passionate prejudices in the cause of getting law and order by consent of the majority. The only alternative is to get a very tough form of law and order imposed by a powerful minority. Sometimes, a minority of one.

The 1970s

The Letter from Long Island

4 August 1970

We have just seen for the first time a film made in Japan exactly twenty-five years ago. It is about what happened on that fine, hot August day to the city of Hiroshima. It was shown here now, I suppose, as a bleak reminder, and a commemoration of the 120,000 dead or injured. Two things struck me all through the film. One was the remarkable bravery – or phlegm – of the cameramen. The other was the thought that this gross nightmare should have happened to a people who have always been noted for their delicate fine touch, whether in the growing of a tree or the making of an optical lens or, as here, following the tracery of a score of wounds on a single human being.

It was enough to lacerate us, and it started up again the controversy, which will never be settled, about President Truman's decision to drop the bomb in the first place. Without raising more dust over the bleached bones of Hiroshima, I should like to contribute a couple of reminders. The first is that the men who had to make the decision to pass on to the President – General George C. Marshall and the Secretary of War, Henry L. Stimson – were just as humane and tortured at the time as you and I were later. And secondly, that they had to make a choice of alternatives that I for one would not have wanted to have to make for all the offers of redemption from all the religions of the world.

What the President and his advisers did not know, and what we rather confidently know now, is that by August 1945 the Japanese were at the end of their rope. The plans were going forward for a step-by-step invasion of the Japanese home islands, where the Japanese had a million men under arms, apart from another three million if the worst happened in the rest of the Far East. The best estimates, put together by the staffs of Marshall and Stimson, were that an invasion would require five million American men, that it would probably not succeed until 1947, and that the casualties, of Americans, the fighting Japanese and Japanese civilians, would amount to something between one and a half and three millions. When the invasion was being planned, the bomb had not been tried. But once it went off in New Mexico, the question was whether the Japanese should be given an ultimatum and a warning 'technical' demonstration, on uninhabited land, of the bomb's power. The atomic scientists in New Mexico delivered their opinion: 'We can propose no technical demonstration likely to bring an end to the war; we see no acceptable alternative to direct military use.'

With that judgement in their hands, Marshall and Stimson and Co. looked over the proposed targets. They ruled out the old cultural capital of Kyoto and in the end decided on Hiroshima, as the headquarters and main arsenal of the Japanese army defending southern Japan; and Nagasaki, a seaport and a centre of the war industry.

I suppose we must all have wondered, in a distraught way at some time or other, how it all started. To be painstakingly historical about it you could, of course, take it back far beyond Einstein and Rutherford and the quantum theory. If you really got going, you could find yourself in the fifth century BC with Empedocles, who worked on the assumption that an atom is the smallest indivisible particle of matter. But let us leap, say, twenty-five centuries forward to the spring of 1939 and the slowly dawning idea, in the minds of a few physicists, that an atomic bomb might be made. It was left to a scattered band of Jewish refugees from Germany – some in Sweden, most in the United States – to realize that the bomb might get into the wrong hands, namely Hitler's. Three of these refugees, all Hungarians, lived here in the obscurity that is the lot of scientists whose speciality is so exotic that neither the statesmen nor the public knows that it exists.

These three men were named Szilard, Wigner and Teller. They kept up with what was happening in their work abroad through letters from old friends, Jews mostly, who had been driven out of Germany into Belgium and Britain and Sweden. By the winter of 1938–9, the three began to hear that the Germans were working on something called 'the uranium problem'. In March 1939 an Italian physicist, Enrico Fermi, had actually called on an American admiral in the Navy Department and had touched on the possibility of an atomic bomb.

Evidently it was an interesting, wild, passing thought, like the possibility at some remote time of a man landing on the moon. Neither the Navy nor any other branch of the government gave it another thought. Then the three heard that a meeting of physicists had been called in Berlin to discuss the possibility of using something called 'nuclear fission' to drive an automobile.

Maybe they were reassured about the German intentions. But not for long. The summer came on and they had a letter from a woman scientist in Sweden who told them something that, even if it had been circulated in the Foreign Offices of London and Paris, let alone the American State Department, would have meant nothing at all to anybody outside businessmen with an interest in metal stocks. Germany had suddenly banned all exports of uranium ore from Czechoslovakia, which it occupied. There was only one other European country that stocked uranium ore: Belgium, which got it from the Belgian Congo. Szilard, Wigner and Teller, it is safe to say, were the only trio of friends anywhere in the United States who were alarmed by the news. They felt they must get the warning word to somebody in American government. This was a problem. They were unknown refugees; only Wigner was an American citizen. They had cause to distrust the military mind, because of its ingrained habit of preparing to fight the last war. They had no more standing with the White House or the State Department than any ordinary person who writes a crackpot letter to the President. (The Secret Service and the FBI between them screen several hundreds of such alarms every week.) They saw what was ahead. And suddenly they thought of 'the Old Man', who was world-renowned and who, if he wrote to the Belgians – that was their first idea – might be able to get them to hold on to their stocks of uranium. They must get to the Old Man.

So it began, on a drenching hot midsummer day in July 1939. Two of the refugees, Szilard and Wigner, woke one morning and got out a map of Long Island. They knew that the Old Man had rented a cottage for the summer from one Dr Moore. That's all. They had been lately so out of touch with him both in their work and their social contacts that they didn't know where the cottage was. Long Island is a hundred and twenty miles long and choked with place names, English and Indian. But the Old Man had named it on the telephone. Wigner was his associate at Princeton. He looked over the map. It was something with a 'P'. Way down on the south shore of the island, he saw the name – Patchogue. That was it. So they drove off. They got out to Patchogue and asked in stores and gas stations for the whereabouts of Dr Moore's cottage. Nobody had ever heard of him. They got back into the car and sweated over the map. Could it be, said Szilard, looking up across the bay to the North Fork of the island, could it be Peconic? 'Peconic,' said Wigner, 'that's it, I remember.' So they drove north and east forty-some miles, along the North Fork, and came to the minute town of Peconic, which to this day consists of one small saloon and the clearing of what was then a crumbling wooden railway shelter. Dr Moore, please? Dr Moore was unheard of.

It was one of those hideous northeastern midsummer days, of a grey leaden sky, and the wet heat up in the nineties, and the map was like a towel in their hands. They were irritable and pretty much in despair and they turned, to drive the hundred miles back to the city. Less than two miles from Peconic, on a two-lane road, you have to come back through a one-street town called Cutchogue. They stopped at Mr Kramer's drugstore to get some trifle or other. They saw a boy, about 7 years old, standing in a corner with a fishing rod in his hands. The Old Man was a great fisherman. 'Sure,' said the boy, 'he lives in Dr Moore's cottage.' He climbed in and he led them over a causeway and along a narrow peninsula called Nassau Point and they came to the cottage.

The Old Man came out in his slippers, and they told him their news. They had a hot hour explaining to him what it all meant, or could mean. Szilard, with whom I checked the facts of this trip years later, said he was surprised to realize that 'the possibility of a chain reaction had not occurred to the Old Man'. But they convinced him, and together they agreed that the best thing to do would be to write a letter to the Belgian government and send a copy of it to the United States State Department. Then Wigner and Szilard drove back to New York.

And there they began to have more misgivings. The Belgians might not respond. The copy might vanish in the yawning files of the State Department. They began to grow tense over the likelihood of a long delay. Maybe they should persuade the Old Man himself to write to the President of the United States, no less. They made discreet inquiries of other friends, other refugees, and came on a German economist who knew a banker who was a personal friend of President Roosevelt. Maybe the banker could be the courier. They sat down and drafted a much bolder and simpler letter.

And on 2 August, they drove off again. 'They', this time, were not the same couple. Wigner had gone on his holiday in California. Szilard, a scientific brain beyond our comprehension, couldn't drive a car. So Szilard invited Teller to drive him down the island. With no fear, this time, of losing the way. Not Patchogue, with a 'P', not Peconic, but Cutchogue with an 'ogue'. An easy mistake. Our weekend guests make it all the time.

The Old Man was ready for them, and they went from the porch into his study and read him both a German draft and an English translation they had typed. At last the Old Man nodded, and put his pen to it. Next step, on to the middleman banker and the White House.

It read:

Nassau Point,
Peconic, Long Island.
August 2nd, 1939

F. D. Roosevelt,
President of the United States,
White House,
Washington, D.C.

Sir:

Some recent work of E. Fermi and L. Szilard, which has been communicated to me in manuscript, leads me to expect that the element uranium may be turned into a new and important source of energy in the immediate future. Certain aspects of the situation which has arisen seem to call for watchfulness and, if necessary, quick action on the part of the Administration. I believe therefore that it is my duty to bring to your attention the following facts and recommendations:

In the course of the last four months it has been made probable – through the work of Joliot in France as well as Fermi and Szilard in America – that it may become possible to set up a nuclear chain reaction in a large mass of uranium, by which vast amounts of power and large quantities of new radium-like elements would be generated . . . by which, my dear Mr President, it might be possible to unleash an immense destructive force.

The President got the letter from the banker, but not before the following October, and maybe he thought it interesting enough, though mysterious. Not until two years later, in the fall of 1941, did he appoint a committee – of the Vice President, and the Secretary of War, and General Marshall and two scientists – to look into it. He put aside some hundreds of dollars in executive funds for this study, which, later on, were increased to the tune of over $2 billion.

The Old Man, who put his signature to the Nassau Point letter, was, of course, 'A. Einstein'.

Give Thanks, for What?

25 November 1972

A week ago I was on one of the islands that the English had a rough time settling, because it is whipped at all times by high winds around a rocky and treacherous coastline. It is made of coral, which is not hospitable to swarming algae. So the sea around it does not present the usual blue-grey goulash that slops up against the islands of the North Atlantic. It is clear water, and even on overcast days it's of a light and shimmering aquamarine or turquoise colour. This beautiful sheen disguises the many perils of the rocks and helps you to forget the winds and the fact that in the late summer the island is in the path of the hurricanes that are brewed in the tropical Caribbean. I am talking about Bermuda, which Shakespeare vividly and accurately called the 'vexed Bermouthes'.

Well, I was rambling over the hills and dales of a hundred-odd acres of this island thoughtfully set aside for the pursuit of a little white ball with a liquid centre. I was accompanied by one of the most celebrated

brooders in America, a man who denies himself the pleasure of chasing
the ball for about 363 days in the year because, like the unflagging
Calvinist he is, he feels a prior obligation to his job as a journalist of
the most awesome kind: a daily preacher whose duty is, in the good
old phrase, to 'comfort the afflicted and afflict the comfortable'. I
cannot think of any more forgivable auspices under which to play
any game whatsoever. Playing a round of golf with this man is as
comfortable as drinking double martinis with Billy Graham.

His routine of self-sacrifice would not be praiseworthy in a golfing
duffer. In fact, to most of us, wrestling with the problems of inflation
or foreign policy is a good deal easier than guiding the damn ball into
a hole 425 yards away. But this old Scot (and the fact that he has spent
the last fifty years in this country has not pacified his conscience in the
least, he is still the dour little – well, large – preacher from Clydeside)
– this old Scot was once, I believe, the junior golf champion of Ohio.
He was, in other words, at one time that forever forbidding figure, a
scratch player. (For the uninitiated, may I say that golf is one game in
which you do not start from scratch.) James Reston began on the
sports desk of the Associated Press. In his late twenties he heard the
call of John Calvin or John Knox or John the Baptist, it doesn't matter
which, and turned to politics during the London Blitz, and then to
Washington. Since when he has been urging us, on a syndicated basis,
what to believe about Europe, the Soviet Union, Cuba, China and all
fifty of the United States.

If all Mr Reston's powerful sermons were lost, he would still be a
large footnote in history. Because, on his visit to China (it was typical
of him that he got there before Mr Nixon) he came down with appendi-
citis and had the useless organ removed by a top team of Chinese
surgeons (they may be seven thousand miles away but they know that
you don't leave the appendix of the chief columnist and vice president
of the *New York Times* to a horse doctor). While he was under the
anaesthetic influence of acupuncture, he wrote it up, and when he
could amble around, he and his wife were allowed to watch several
operations, during which – so he claimed – the patient who'd just had
a brain or a lung removed said, like the boy in *Pickwick*, that he
'wouldn't lie there to be made game of, and he'd tell his mother if they
didn't begin'.

So Mr Reston returned with the glad tidings of the wise men from the East who stick needles in you and lo, you feel no pain and, practically before the bandages are wrapped, you get up from your bed and walk. The news of this miracle was syndicated in papers around the world, and in this country we are now in the full flush of the belief, or the fashion, or the superstition, that there is no human ill that cannot be cured in a trice by a Chinese sinking in a needle. Many an American doctor, and non-doctor, is already preparing to moonlight with acupuncture and pick up a little pin money, so to speak, on the side.

I've built up Mr Reston's considerable credentials as a seer and prophet – not beyond his due – because I wanted to assure you that I don't spend my time loping around a golf course with heedless bums. We would fall silent occasionally to ponder the nasty stance required to pitch to a pulpit green from squirty crabgrass. But we would then get down to the business in hand and fall in together (as, we are told, the British ambassador and the Emperor Franz Josef used to do while in pursuit of the stag in the old days) and ponder tremendous matters. Even when Mr Reston is pursuing the little white ball, he is pursued in turn by a deadline.

Much on his mind, that beautiful afternoon, was a column he had to write on the eve of Thanksgiving. What, he wanted to know, had we cause to be thankful for? It was a problem. He stood to the ball, reminding himself to imitate the immortal Bobby Jones, whose swing was said to have 'the drowsy beauty of a summer's day'. Reston then unloosed the tornado of his caddie swing, which has all the drowsy beauty of a pneumatic drill. 'Well?' he said. 'Come to think of it,' I said, 'I can't think of anything we can be grateful for.' I moved over to my ball and performed my own ritual swing, which I have often thought bears a striking resemblance to Tom Weiskopf in the take-away and to Henry Cotton in the finish. A recent series of stop-action pictures, however, shows a man who, at the top of the backswing, is either taking off a sweater or putting on a lifebuoy.

'Come now,' said Reston, fluffing a three-foot putt, 'there's a lot of things to be thankful for.' 'Name one,' I said, and dispatched the thing ten feet into the back of the cup. 'Well,' he said, and he now had his pipe out, which is always an impressive accompaniment to a stalling mind. Come on, come on. 'Why, sure,' he said, ambling off down the next fairway like Barnacle Bill the sailor. All I could think of was the demonstrable fact that Mr Nixon, like him or loathe him, had done something that no Eisenhower, Kennedy or Johnson had done before him. He had not conquered inflation but he had held it remarkably in check. The economists knew it, and praised him. The bankers knew it, and rejoiced. Even the liberals knew it, and grunted reluctant approval. More important, the housewives knew it, and they had voted for him.

I was giving Reston time to digest his column. He brooded some more and put two balls in the drink of a long water-hole. Which is ridiculous in a former scratch player, though playing twice a year does not tend to maintain the handicap at a single figure. Then I teed up majestically, thought about Thanksgiving, and with incredible accuracy placed two balls in exactly the same grave as his. After that, we jokingly decided it was only a game and, anyway, we were still wondering what to thank the Lord for.

Mr Reston's column appeared duly on the eve of Thanksgiving and it betrayed no smitch of strain, no hint of the writhings that had seized him as he peered all over the rolling course looking for blessings to count. He put up a brave show. There may be five millions unemployed, but there are eighty-two millions in jobs. More than half of all American families, families not individuals, have an annual income of roughly $12,000. Vietnam, they say, is close to a ceasefire. The campuses have cooled. There is, he believes, 'a calmer atmosphere between the races and the generations'. America may be relatively less powerful than she was but there is 'less danger and fear of a major clash between the nuclear powers than at any other time since the start of the Cold War'. Mr Nixon, he believes, has at least 'bought time to arrange a kind of truce between the Communist and the Western worlds'.

In the main, I believe that this is, with one big reservation, fair enough. Nobody ever expected a Republican President to introduce compulsory price and wage control in peacetime, but it seemed to work. A Democrat and an economist, who takes a generally dim view of Mr Nixon, has just written: 'He hasn't mastered it, but it's working, and that's something when you look at South America (Chile has reduced its inflation in the past year from a hundred per cent to eighteen per cent). And in Europe, the British inflation is disastrously out of hand.'

Also, one has to grant, if there had been a Democrat in the White House, the liberal press would be sounding hosannas for the courage of the visits to Moscow and Peking and the shrewd recognition that they both need money and trade and good crops more than they need arms. (The Russians are doing very well building their own mammoth navy, thank you, and the Chinese move on deferentially, with charming smiles, towards their own nuclear capability.)

My reservation is about the calm between the races and the generations. I devoutly hope it is so. But I cannot see how the widening gap between the prosperous majority and the poor and bitter minority will keep the minority from protest. All the groups that raised Cain in 1968 are still there. The colleges may appear to be beginning to share authority with the students, if that's a good thing. True, a black boy has a better chance of going to college here than practically any boy in Western Europe. Yet, one black boy in three between the ages of 16 and 22 has no job and very little prospect of ever getting one. The cities groan quietly, and the President promises not to soften them by 'throwing dollars at problems'. The powerful malcontents – the young, the black, the radicals, the Mexican-Americans – who were told to work within the system tried it with McGovern and it got them a stone. We may have cause to give thanks, but we should leave as an open question whether militant America is calming down once for all or whether it is pausing. Anyone who has ever been in the eye of a hurricane knows the blessed feeling of relief when the damage is done, and the clouds are scudding, and the blue is breaking through, just before everything goes leaden and hissing again, and the fury is let loose from the other side.

This is just to say that I think there's a danger in the present lull of overlooking the hazard in front of our eyes. As Reston and I teed up on that long water-hole (we had to carry about 160 yards before the dry land) the caddie said, 'Forget the water, just pretend it's all smooth grass.' It would be nice to do this, looking out across the United States and seeing only the green haven beyond the drink. We shouldn't forget, though, that both of us, disdaining the briny deep in front of us, drowned in it – twice.

The Duke

31 May 1974

'When it is finished,' says the guidebook, 'it may well be the largest cathedral in the world.' I am always leery of sentences that contain the phrase 'may well be'. But it is certainly a very large cathedral: namely the Episcopal Cathedral Church of St John the Divine on the Upper West Side in New York City. Its foundations were laid in 1892. They've been building it ever since, and the end is not yet.

On Monday, 27 May 1974 St John the Divine housed a ceremony that would have flabbergasted its architect and its early worshippers. Every pew was filled, and the aisles were choked, and there were several thousands listening to loudspeakers out on the street. And when the ten thousand people inside were asked to stand and pray, there was a vast rustling sound as awesome, it struck me, as that of the several million bats whooshing out of the Carlsbad Caverns in New Mexico at the first blush of dawn.

It is not the size of the crowd that would have shocked the cathedral's founders (they might have taken it jubilantly as a sign of a great religious revival). It was what the crowd was there for. A crowd that ranged through the whole human colour scale, from the most purple black to the most pallid white, come there to honour the life and mourn the death of a man who had become supreme in an art that began in the brothels of New Orleans. The art is that of jazz, and the practitioner of it they mourned was Edward Kennedy Ellington, identified around the world more immediately than any member of any royal family as – the Duke.

The Duke's career was so much his life that there's very little to say about his private ups and downs, if any. He was born in Washington, DC in 1899, the son of a White House butler, and perhaps the knowledge that Father had a special, protected status inside the white establishment had much to do with the Duke's seeming to be untouched, or untroubled, by the privations and public humiliations we should expect of a black born in the nation's capital. Certainly, he must have thought of himself as belonging to one of the upper tiers of black society. But his upbringing could be called normal for any of the black boys who were to turn into great jazzmen. I'm thinking of men like Earl Hines and Fats Waller, the sons of coloured parsons or church organists who, almost automatically as little boys, were hoisted on to a piano stool. The Duke took piano lessons but also took to sketching and thought of a career as an artist. This dilemma was solved by his becoming a sign painter by day and running small bands by night.

What got him going was the nightly grind and the daily practice. It is something that nightclub habitués seldom credit, it being assumed that while classical pianists must follow a daily regimen, people like Ellington, Hines, Waller, Tatum simply have a 'natural gift' and just rattle the stuff off on request. Nothing could be more false. I remember ten, fifteen years ago running into an old and engaging jazzman, a white who was employed in a poky little jazz joint in San Francisco. Muggsy Spanier, a sweet and talented man who had had a long experience of the roller-coaster fortunes of a jazzman: one year you are playing before delirious crowds in a movie theatre or grand hotel, three years later blowing your brains out before a few listless drunks in a crummy roadhouse off the main highway in some place called Four Forks, Arkansas, or New Iberia, Louisiana. Just then Muggsy was in a lean year playing in a small band with Earl Hines, who was also at a low ebb (this was before Hines, the father of jazz piano, had been discovered by the State Department and the Soviet government, or been rediscovered by a new generation). Well, Muggsy had left his trumpet in this dreadful nightclub and found he needed it, on his night off, for some impromptu gig or other. So he had to go into the nightclub next morning, always a depressing experience, what with the reek of sour air and spilled alcohol and the lights turned down to a mainten-ance bulb or two. He told me that one of the unforgettable shocks of his stint in San Francisco was coming from the bone-white sunlight into the smelly cave and squinnying through the dark and seeing Hines sitting there, as he did for two or three hours every morning, practising not the blues or 'Rosetta' or 'Honeysuckle Rose' but the piano con-certos of Mozart and Beethoven. To the gaping Muggsy, Hines looked up and said, 'Just keeping the fingers loose.' To be the best, it's a sad truth most of us amateurs shrink from admitting, you have to run, fight, golf, write, play the piano every day. I think it was Paganini – it may have been Rubinstein – who said, 'If I go a week without practice, the audience notices it. If I go a day without practice, I notice it.'

This digression is very relevant to the character and the mastery of Duke Ellington. He was at a piano, but he was there as a composer, day in and night out. For a man of such early and sustained success, it is amazing that he not only tolerated the grind, after one-night stands, of the long bus rides through the day and the pick-up meals, but actually cherished them as the opportunity to sit back and scribble and hum and compose. He did this to the end.

I knew all the records of his first period when I was in college, from 1927 through 1932. And when I first arrived in New York I wasted no time in beating it up to the Cotton Club to see the great man in the flesh. But apart from a nodding acquaintance in nightclubs, and becoming known to him no doubt as one of those ever-present nuisances who request this number and that, I didn't meet Ellington alone, by appointment so to speak, until the very end of the Second World War. I went up to his apartment on the swagger side of Harlem. There is such a place, in fact there are as many fine shadings of Negro housing through the hierarchy of Negro social status as there are shadings of pigment from the high-yaller to the coal-black. Ellington was at the top of the scale, in a large Victorian building looking out on a patch of greenery.

The date had been for two in the afternoon. In my mind's eye I had the picture complete: the dapper figure of the Duke seated in a Noël Coward bathrobe deep in composition at a concert grand. For those were the days long before band leaders got themselves up in gold lamé and sequins. The big band leaders wore dinner jackets. The Duke wore white tie and tails, and was as sleek as a seal.

Well, I was shown into a large and rambling apartment with a living room that had evidently seen a little strenuous drinking the night before. Off from the living room behind curtained French doors was a bedroom. The doors were open and there in full view was a large bed rumpled and unmade. Beyond that was a bathroom, and out of it emerged what I first took to be some swami in the wrong country. It was the Duke, naked except for a pair of under-drawers and a towel woven around his head. He came in groaning slightly and saying to himself, 'Man!' Then *his* man came in, a coloured butler, and they went into the knotty question of what sort of breakfast would be at once tasty and medicinal. It was agreed on, and the Duke turned and said, 'Now.' Meaning, what's your business at this unholy hour of two in the afternoon?

The breakfast arrived and he went at it like a marooned mountaineer. To my attempts to excite him with the proposal I had come to make, he grunted 'Uh-huh' and 'Uh-un' between, or during, mouthfuls.

At last, he pushed the plate away, picked up his coffee cup and sat down and slurped it rapidly and nodded for me to begin again. I had come to suggest that he might like to record a long session with his band for the BBC. This was, remember, the peak period of his big band, and I suggested that we record him not, as we now say, 'in concert', but in rehearsal. He shot a suspicious glare at me, as if I'd suggested recording him doing five-finger exercises. But slowly and warily he began to see my problem and to respect it. Simply, how to convey to a listener (this was before television) the peculiar genius of the Duke, since it was unique in the practice of jazz music. Which was somehow to be, and feel, present at the act of creation when it was happening to the Duke standing in front of the band in rehearsal. Everybody knows that the best jazz is impossible to write down in the usual musical notation. You can no more make a transcription of Hines playing 'I Can't Give You Anything but Love', or, worse, Art Tatum playing any of his cascading variations on 'Tea for Two', than you can write down three rules for the average swimmer to follow in doing the two hundred metres like Mark Spitz. Jazz is always improvisation done best by a group of players who know each other's whimsical ways with such mysteries as harmonics, counterpoint, scooped pitch, jamming in unison. Alone among jazz composers, the Duke's raw material was the tune, scribbled bridge passages, a sketch in his head of the progression of solos and ensembles he wanted to hear, and an instinctive knowledge of the rich and original talents, and strengths and perversities, of his players. They were not just trumpet, trombone, clarinet, E flat alto sax, and so on. They were individual performers who had stayed with him for years, for decades. One of them, Harry Carney, played with the Duke on his first recording date in 1927, and he was with him on the last date, in Kalamazoo, Michigan, last March. In 1927, Ellington had created a weird, compact, entirely personal sound with his band. It was weirder still and richer, but it was just as personal at the end.

Eventually, the Duke appreciated that what we wanted was not just another performance. He agreed, and we had a long and unforgettable session, in a hired studio on Fifth Avenue, where we recorded the whole process of the number dictated, the roughest run-through, with many pauses, trying this fusion of instruments and that, stopping and starting and transferring the obligato from one man to another, the Duke talking and shouting, 'Now, Tricky, four bars!' and 'Barney, in there eight.' And in the last hour, what had been a taste in the Duke's head came out as a harmonious, rich meal.

The Duke was nicknamed as a boy by a friend who kidded him about his sharp dressing. He was an elegant and articulate man and, as I've hinted, strangely apart from the recent turmoil of his race. Not, I think, because he was ever indifferent or afraid. He was a supremely natural man, and in his later years devout, and he seemed to assume that men of all colours are brothers. And most of the immediate problems of prejudice, and condescension, and tension between black and white dissolved in the presence of a man whom even an incurable bigot must have recognized as a man of unassailable natural dignity. He had a childlike side, which – we ought to remember – is recommended in the New Testament for entry into the kingdom of Heaven. He was very sick indeed in the last few months. He knew, but kept it to himself, that he had cancer in both lungs. A week or two before the end he sent out to hundreds of friends and acquaintances what looked at first like a Christmas card. It was a greeting. On a field of blue was a cross, made of four vertical letters and three horizontal. They were joined by the letter 'O'. The vertical word spelled 'Love' and the horizontal 'God'.

He has left us, in the blessed library of recorded sound, a huge anthology of his music from his twenty-eighth birthday to his seventy-fifth. He began as a minority cult, too rude for the collectors of dance music. For much, maybe most, of his time he was never a best-seller. He never stuck in the current groove, or in his own groove. He moved with all the influences of the time from blues to bebop and the moderns and transmuted them into his own, and at the end his difficult anti-phonies and plotted discords, the newer harmonic structures he was always reaching for, were no more saleable to the ordinary popular music fan than they had ever been. Most people simply bowed to him as an institution.

In 1931, a college room-mate of mine who was something of a pioneer as a jazz critic, on the university weekly, was graduating, and he wrote a farewell piece. He recorded the rise and fall – during his four-year stint – of the Red Hot Peppers, and the Blue Four, and McKinney's Cotton Pickers, and Bix and Trumbauer. He ended with the phrase: 'Bands may come and bands may go, but the Duke goes on for ever.' Ah, how true! We thought it a marvel that the Duke had ridden out all fashions for four long years. In fact, his good and always developing music lasted for forty-seven years. And we have it all.

So, I am inclined to paraphrase what John O'Hara said on the death of George Gershwin: 'Duke Ellington is dead. I don't have to believe it if I don't want to.'

The End of the Affair
11 April 1975

Throughout the nineteenth century and on into our own time, military disasters were reported to the home front as, at worst, military set-backs. Thanks, I suppose, to strict censorship at the front and the unquestioned existence of official secrets acts and such, which con-cealed the unvarnished truth for so many years that by the time it was open for inspection, the people at home had other things on their minds. It was left to the historians to analyse and thrash over the ashes of once burning issues.

I think of the ill-fated expedition to Dakar in the Second World

War, and the ill-conceived British landings in Norway. True, they caused a rumpus in the House of Commons, since the brave invaders quickly came home again. But there were no nightly pictures on the television to show, for instance, our men landing in Norway without skis, on the assumption of generals bred in a temperate climate that the men were going off to fight a rifle-to-rifle battle in Surrey or on the fields of northern France.

The enormous catastrophe of the Dardanelles campaign in the First World War was, I well remember, reported to us as a difficult but heroic undertaking. And when it failed, the tiptoe evacuation of all our forces was glowingly represented as a triumphant success. In those days, they did not publish the human cost. Only the schoolboys of a later generation learned to be dazed by the news that Gallipoli cost each side a quarter of a million causalties. And those of you old enough to remember Dunkirk will recall how the relief at the evacuation of so many men from beaches under aerial bombing was turned by the government of the day, by the newsreels, and then by Hollywood, into a glorious thing. Until Mr Churchill brought us to our senses with a speech in the House of Commons in which he bluntly declared, 'It is a colossal military disaster . . . wars are not won by evacuations.' But there can never have been a time like that of the mid-nineteenth century, not in Britain anyway, when the romantic legend of our brave chaps out there was so deliberately separated from the reality. The dreadful idiocy of the Battle of Balaclava was celebrated – by the Poet Laureate no less – as an act of epic valour: 'Theirs not to reason why/ Theirs but to do and die.'

Well, the United States has just suffered the most unmitigated defeat in its history, and we know it. The cost, in casualties, and money, and pride is being counted *now*. And everybody is arguing 'the reason why'. What Kennedy started with the quiet infiltration of 'military technicians' is about to end, fourteen years later. It would no doubt have ended much sooner if the United States hadn't believed in the beginning that it had a duty to stem the advance of Communism in Asia and, what turned out to be more fateful, believed it had the capacity to do it. The most unrepentant hawks will maintain on their deathbeds that the United States did have the capacity, by a general invasion of North Vietnam or by the use of tactical atomic weapons.

But none of the four Presidents who bore the burden, and the curse, of the Vietnamese war was ready to do that. All of them knew that if America could keep its treaty commitments only by means of even a limited nuclear bombardment, America would be a monster's name everywhere on earth.

So the country is just now in a stew of recrimination. No doubt in time the arguments will straighten themselves out and people will come to take up one of two positions, which won't necessarily be closer to the truth because they've been over-simplified.

The most striking thing to me about this turmoil of public opinion is the way, while the Right is holding its ground, the Left is shifting its ground. The leftist and liberal commentators who have been against the American presence in Indochina more or less since the beginning have always tended to stress the corruption of the South Vietnamese government and the brutality of its treatment of prisoners and political dissidents, but has always turned a blind eye towards – or refused to credit – the Hanoi government's brutal treatment of prisoners and political dissidents (if any were ever known to speak up). The Left has always said that if the United States got out, and if South Vietnam capitulated, then the people of South Vietnam would receive their conquerors with relief and, after thirty years of nothing but war, would settle down peaceably to be ruled by them.

But now that we've seen thousands of bedraggled and wounded civilians fleeing from their homes and jamming every escape route to the south, the Left is saying how shocking that we didn't evacuate these people sooner instead of leaving them to the mercies of the oncoming armies. This shock implies a belief in something that the leftists and the liberals have never been willing to concede: that vast numbers of the population of South Vietnam have been and still are terrified of the Communists and want to get out.

In other words, since the United States is no longer there as a military force, it has got to be blamed for something. And it is now being blamed for deserting the South Vietnamese in their hour of need. Some reporters, especially foreign correspondents who throughout the war have been privileged to enjoy the luxury of neutral high-mindedness, have written dispatches burning with indignation at the thought of President Ford playing golf while babies were being bundled into planes and flown to camps in the United States (and – something I've not seen in an American paper – to homes in Britain and Australia).

Well, it was maybe a tactless time for the President to be practising his backswing, but the inference of these angry men is that President Ford and his advisers callously refused to send in planes, and the old Marines, to arrange a mass evacuation when the Central Highlands were about to be overrun. But neither the President nor the Pentagon, nor an American military mission on the spot, seems to have been given much notice of President Thieu's independent decision to abandon the Central Highlands. The White House and the Pentagon seethed with their own sort of indignation when it happened, and had to improvise a makeshift Dunkirk operation. Naturally, they said hard words about President Thieu. And their anger gave him a god-sent excuse to declare that the United States had betrayed its ally.

In turn, the conservatives here who have gone on thinking of President Thieu as the poor man's Chiang Kai-shek were only too eager to pick up his accusation and turn it, not so much against President Ford, whom they've come to consider a well-meaning drifter, as against the Democrats' majority in Congress. Certainly, if the retreat of the South Vietnamese could have been held up by more millions of dollars from Congress, then those Democrats in power are to blame. At this point, the country is heard from. Over 70 per cent of the American people are convinced that South Vietnam and Cambodia would be lost, sooner rather than later, no matter how much money the Congress voted.

Meanwhile, less positive people – middle of the roaders, weary newspaper students of the long war – are going back to see where the rot set in. Who was to blame? President Johnson blamed the doubters for having little faith. President Nixon called his opponents traitors. President Ford is going back to Kennedy's line – a rather forlorn battle cry so late in the day: that the United States has 'solemn commitments' and must honour them. He blames Congress. And he's helped by Henry Kissinger who sees, in the Congressional echo of public sentiment, a dreadful determination 'to destroy our allies'. Others again, looking pluckily on the bright side, say that the administration is making a fundamental error in confusing the collapse of Indochina with America's real interests. They say that to let Vietnam go is no proof that the United States would let Japan go, or Israel, or Europe.

However, it is possible to recognize a pall forming over all this dissension in the reports that are coming in from Thailand, and Malaysia and Israel and other places whose governments – rightly or wrongly – are beginning to wonder whether the United States is an ally you can depend on. Hardly reported at all are the fears of the Australians, to whom what we call the Far East is the Near North, against which they had better prepare their own defences.

And through this bedlam of charge and counter-charge, a still small voice rises, from people who were once dogmatic, and from people who are merely puzzled: what if, after all, the domino theory is correct?

I'm All Right, Jack

21 May 1976

Somewhere, in Shakespeare certainly, but maybe also in some simple nursery rhyme, there must be a wincing reminder that when a small painful thing happens to you and me, it blots out a catastrophe that staggers the headlines. Nobody has made a keener comment on it than James Agate in a passage of his 'Ego' diaries. He had been to watch a day in the trial of an architect's wife and her lover. She was 38. The chauffeur-lover was 18. Came the day when the husband was hit over the head with a mallet. The couple was on trial for his murder.

It sounds like a humdrum, squalid business – except, of course, for the accused couple. Anyway, Agate was in court when the woman was asked what was her first thought when her lover came to her and told her what he'd done. She replied, 'My first thought was to protect him.' It's the sort of surprising line that a dramatist would give his right arm – a dollop of his royalties, anyway – to have thought of. Agate remarked it was the kind of thing that Balzac would have called 'sublime'.

In the following days, Agate couldn't get the woman's reply out of his mind. And just then, there was an immense earthquake in Quetta, in India. Agate wrote in his diary: 'This trial has moved me immensely, probably because I saw part of it, while the dreadful affair at Quetta makes no impression. The 20,000 said to have perished might be flies. I see no remedy for this; one can't order one's feelings, and to pretend different is merely hypocrisy.'

I imagine that we all have secret ways of compensating for this awkward truth. I make it up to myself by admiring immoderately those people – hospital volunteers, the Salvation Army, most of all people who work every day with the disabled: the people *who do something about it*, even though they obviously have lives and troubles of their own. I think I was saved from living the life of a secret slob by my father-in-law, an austere old New England puritan. When I came back to the United States for keeps, he explained to me – as you might to a child about to receive its first weekly allowance – how 'we Americans' divide the breadwinner's salary: 'You try to pay between a fifth and a quarter of your income for rent, never more than a quarter, and you set aside 10 per cent of your income for charity. The rest goes for food and savings.' For a time, I followed this punctiliously, for I had applied for citizenship and took it to be a requirement of the Constitution. Later, I regret to say, rents went up, and so, but not for a long time, did the income.

Well, the past two weeks have reflected once again the embarrassing truth that the downfall of a dictator is significant, but a toothache is an emergency. I ought to be talking about Dr Kissinger's decision to resign as Secretary of State after the next election. I ought to go on about the recent earthquake in the Soviet Union, which had a force one-third as great again as the 1906 San Francisco earthquake. There is a lot of room for comment in the fact that the Russians have been very tight-lipped about it. But Dr Kissinger and the Russian earthquake fade away like ghosts at dawn before the sentence shouted at me during the past fortnight by my wife whenever I am on my way out. 'Don't go out,' she'd scream from some distant room, 'without taking down the garbage.'

What is this? Am I moonlighting as a spare-time dustman – or, as we slangily say in the United States – a sanitation department employee? Of course not, though there must be scholars and clerks and other members of the sedentary professions who are greatly tempted by the report from San Francisco that the dustmen of that city successfully struck for a guaranteed high wage of $27,000 a year.

No, what has been happening here is a strike of handymen and the other 'maintenance personnel' of our apartment houses, or blocks of flats. (By the way, although I'm always maintaining, in the presence of Americans, that the British still hold to Anglo-Saxon English in contexts which Americans fog up with pompous Latinisms, I am bound to say that it is the British who have succumbed to the euphemism of 'industrial action'. In America, they still strike.)

Well, the men who keep things humming in the big apartment houses walked out two weeks ago. So it was left to the tenants to run the lifts, stoke the furnace, stack the garbage, sort the mail, guard the front door and work in shifts round the clock keeping tabs on all visitors and demanding to see their identity cards, if any. If not, the house phone rings and a voice – plainly not that of the regular doorman – says, 'There's a gentleman down here who claims to be Mr Tim Slessor and says he has a date with you.' And you answer, according to mood, 'Send him up,' or 'Throw the bum out.'

It was a trying time for us tenants. But we learned some useful things. A friend of mine phoned me one morning. He'd been running his elevator for four hours that day. He said, 'D'you know something? It's not true that being an elevator man is an unskilled job – you have to know all about the weather.'

Well, it's over now. The strike ended at 4 p.m. and at five the men were back in uniform helping old ladies out of cabs, carrying bags, handing out mail and recognizing friends and tenants without peremptory challenge. They struck – as almost everybody does these days – for more pay and a shorter working week. They didn't get what they asked for, since it's well understood that the first increase they demand (it's always 'demand') is like the first price a Persian quotes to you when you admire a rug. You simply walk round the block, get a second price, go out to lunch, come back and settle for the third price.

In most strikes today, the non-striking people on the outside, commonly known as the public, make an assumption, I think, which a friend of mine in California tells me is very naive. I find it hard to label his profession, since it is a comparatively new one. Not quite a labour lawyer but a contract adviser or, as he puts it, a hassle soother.

Sometimes he's hired by a company, sometimes by the union, either to draft the next contract or, if things are already out of hand, to help settle a strike. Most of his adult life has been spent in bargaining between the two contending parties about such things as time and a half, pension payments, redefining overtime, pregnancy benefits, a new recreation ground, redundancies (another British euphemism, by the way, for men you no longer need).

According to this cunning negotiator, the naive assumption we all make is that in every strike the dispute is between the employer and the employee, a conflict which is dramatized in the newspapers either as a fight between the ruthless union and the company going broke, or between the ruthless boss and the ground-down faces of the workers. He says this is 'a bunch of – er – nineteenth-century ideology'. He says that almost invariably both sides *want* the strike. Generally, to prove their need of recompense – more wages or a fairer profit margin – to some third party: the government, the city council, or even the consumer himself. Well, it was strongly hinted in our apartment strike that both the union members and the landlords were eager to prove to the state government in Albany and the city fathers of New York City that rent control has to go.

I think I'm right in saying that no other city in America still retains the rent control laws that were imposed nationally during the Second World War. There are many thousands of apartment houses in this city – rundown buildings, modest blocks of flats, handsome big apartment buildings – which must conform to the rents set by a city control board. This board yields, about once a year, to the landlords' plea that their costs – of fuel, insurance, staff, maintenance in general – far outrun the biggest rents they are allowed to charge. The rent control board yields them an extra seven and a half per cent a year. And though I ought to keep my mouth shut, I must say I feel a little sheepish when I run into a young couple in an uncontrolled building who pay for two rooms what I pay for eight. When a baby comes, they do not tie pink ribbons, they wring their hands.

If they are in 'the professions', they go to their boss and say, in some dudgeon, 'An electrician earns more than I do.' They become – what miners become, and nurses, and truck drivers, and all of us when we feel the pinch – 'a special case'. In fact, it sometimes seems to me that an ever-soaring inflation rate was guaranteed the day that the ordinary citizen, who is against both inflation and strikes on principle, started to say that his case was different.

Until ten or twenty years ago, I think it was as true in America as in less affluent countries, the socially sanctioned scale of wages has held since the nineteenth century. I say *scale*, not wage rates. It was an unwritten law that working people, so called, could earn only a certain maximum, which stopped short of the general level of wages paid to the professions. This is so obvious that it's either not worth saying or it's one of those simple discoveries that nobody thought of before Aristotle. It's so obvious, anyway, that nobody seems to have said it. We have gone on, down all the years during which labour–management relations have grown more complex and more acrid, talking about the labourer being worthy of his hire, while the industrial and craft unions have been developing a wholly new view of their monetary worth to society. While the professions – the learned professions especially – have gone on living on the old assumption that being upper- and not lower-middle class, they must be living better than the average skilled factory worker. They slowly and sadly learned that it is not so, that they – along with the old and the pensioned professionals – are the worst victims of inflation. It is odd that the more educated should have done nothing to define or justify their relative worth, while the less educated – with the help of such as my labour negotiator in this country, and the shrewd shop steward in other countries – have done everything.

No Cabinet Officers Need Apply

24 December 1976

One of the most curious but absolutely dependable chores of political journalism in the United States is undertaken around Christmas time once every four years. Whenever we are only a month away from the inauguration of a new President, the papers are full of speculation about who is likely to be a Cabinet officer, and of profiles of people who've already been picked. I say it's a curious custom because the American Presidential system is not a Cabinet system. This is something that Cabinet officers usually discover, to their chagrin, rather late in the day. The system puts all the responsibility for a riot, say, not on the Secretary of the Interior (the British Home Secretary) but on the President. A cruel budget is not attributed to the Secretary of the Treasury but to the President. If there's a public outcry about selling wheat to Russia at bargain prices, the howls are piped into the White House, not into the Department of Agriculture. And so on.

But there is one Cabinet appointment just made that has set off a tremendous uproar, especially among the blacks. The concern is not particularly ideological, though while Mr Carter says that the new man has a 'superb' record on civil rights, the black leaders says he has a very dubious record indeed. What has aroused the blacks is a provocation which I don't think would come up in other white democracies. The appointee is Mr Griffin Bell to be Attorney General, who – as the head of the Department of Justice – is therefore the chief law enforcement officer of the United States. Mr Bell is an Atlanta lawyer and a close friend of Mr Carter. The sin with which he is charged stresses once again the vigilante role of the American press that makes the life – the private life and public life – of any man or woman an open book. To sharpen the contrast with Britain, say, let me put it this way. When you hear that John Wallaby has been made Foreign Secretary, or Richard Stretchford Chancellor of the

Exchequer, do you instantly wonder how many companies he has shares in? Are you impatient for the newspapers to list the clubs he belongs to? Do you, every now and then, expect questions to be asked in the House, and have them followed by a regretful little speech from the Prime Minister withdrawing the appointment? I think not.

Well, Mr Bell had been Attorney General designate for no more than twenty-four hours when the diggers of the press dug up the hair-raising fact that he was a member of two private clubs in Atlanta that have no blacks or Jews as members. What amazes the politicians is that Mr Carter should not have routinely questioned his appointees about such affiliations. Because when it comes out, it always triggers a shock wave, which always subsides when the appointee regrets the insensitivity of his past life and resigns from the club or clubs. Which Mr Bell, after a little self-defensive hectoring, will undoubtedly do.

When Mr Carter heard about the sin of Mr Bell he said rather wanly that he 'hoped' all his Cabinet officers would give up their membership in any society that discriminated against minorities. (In California, it may soon become a scandal if you belong to a club that does not admit Chicanos, that is to say, Mexican-Americans, whose vote is large.)

This has brought up in the minds of many people the question of whether it is legal today to form a club with any sort of exclusive membership. Well, yes, it is, no question. You can form an Irish-American club, or a rifle club, or a tennis club, or a drinking club *provided* you don't meet in a building, or on land, or employ services, owned by your city, your state, or by the federal government. All the test cases that have come up before the Supreme Court since its integration decision of 1954 have challenged the right of exclusivity of any organization that is supported in any way by public funds: schools, restaurants, buses, toilets, housing projects, recreation grounds, clubs and so on. The grounds here are always the same, and the Supreme Court has reiterated them again and again: that such discrimination violates the Fourteenth Amendment to the Constitution, which says, 'No state shall make or enforce any law which shall abridge the privileges or immunities of citizens of the United States ... nor deny to any person within its jurisdiction the equal protection of the laws.'

No one, I think, has yet tested the right of private clubs to exclude people on the grounds of race, religion or whatever. And I doubt they're likely to. Mr Bell's clubs were privately owned. Like most such clubs everywhere, they were organizations of congenial people who shared a certain interest, people who are like-minded, like-coloured, alike in their enthusiasms or even their prejudices. Senator John F. Kennedy belonged for years to a private and very exclusive club in Washington which, in the most gentlemanly way in the world, quietly excluded Negroes. When he became President, he resigned at once. Similarly, Mr Bell is not up against the law. He's up against the strong public feeling that anyone who chooses to become a government official, dedicated to the service of the whole country, should not be associated with any group that bars any sort of American.

We had, a few years ago, a prime example of the power of the press to embarrass any public man with ambitions to govern into shedding a lifetime's fellowship with his own kind. When Mr Nelson Rockefeller came out for the Presidency, the press discovered overnight that he was a member of an exclusive New York City club that had never had a Jewish member and never seen a Negro, except one bearing a tray. 'What?' cried Mr Rockefeller, 'no Jews or Negroes?' He was shocked to his marrow and he got out at once. It then came out that one of his sons – I believe it was the littlest and the last, a toddler – had a sizeable block of shares in the club. Well, I never – said Mr Rockefeller, and scrupulously and immediately sold it.

Within a matter of days, Mr Richard M. Nixon let it be known that he too was thinking of the Presidency. So the press obliged by discovering that he was a member of a famous golf club in New Jersey that might have heard of Jews or blacks but had never seen one out on the course or on the receiving end in the clubhouse. Mr Nixon's approach was, as you might expect, less hasty, more thoughtful, more humane. Mr Nixon said 'Ah, yes,' he was well aware of the discrimination but he was 'working from within' to end it. This admirable crusade, which he had naturally not publicized, was brought to an abrupt end when – within a day or two at most – Mr Nixon resigned.

This, by the way, was the club that was chosen, in 1967, as the site of the US Open, the American national golf championship. I remember it well, because I was called on by my paper to cover the championship at the last minute. It seemed that our golf expert, the eminent Pat

Ward-Thomas, was detained in Britain on other business. This put me in a bind. The Security Council of the United Nations had been meeting night and day over the Arab–Israeli war. Its last session finished considerably at three in the morning of the day the United States Open was to start. And I recall the puzzlement on the face of the most artful of American sports writers, a prose demon named Red Smith, when he saw me on that first morning, before the play had begun, bent over my typewriter in the press tent banging out a couple of thousand words. What could I possibly find to write? Then he looked over my shoulder, saw that the dateline was 'United Nations, NY' and he relaxed with an 'Oh, that. I thought you knew something the rest of us didn't.' This was my last dispatch on the Middle East.

The tournament was played in one of the most drenching heatwaves even of an American summer on the infernal Eastern seaboard. On the last, the fourth, morning of the championship, it was 112 degrees inside the press tent. At some sweating pause, in mid-morning, two or three of us were standing around looking up at the scoreboard that blanketed one wall of the tent. The scores are recorded cumulatively, so you can see at a glance who is leading. You look first for the players whose scores are up there in red: the ones who are playing the course under par. At the end of the last round, there was only one name in red. It was that of an unknown, a fellow named Marty Fleckman. As we were goggling over this, and hoping for some official to come through with a quick, potted biography of this redoubtable Fleckman, an old stockbroker who cuts a considerable figure in the administration of American golf, an old gaffer not famous for his tact, followed our gaze and barked out, 'Who is that Fleckman in the lead? Is that that Jewish boy from New Orleans?' 'The same,' somebody said. Somebody else said, 'Boy, wait till the Arabs hear about this!' Red Smith said wistfully, 'Forget the Arabs, wait till the club hears about it!' This funny remark is something which, in the United States today, you'd have to be careful to pick your audience for.

The ironical thing about discrimination, against Jews in particular, is that it is practised with the quietest tenacity by white professing Christians of the genteelest kind. It's a rueful thought, at this time of the year, that they would have been the first to blackball the founder of Christianity himself.

Christmas in Vermont

31 December 1976

I spent a four-day Christmas with my daughter in northern Vermont after flying out of New York City on one of those brilliant blue winter days that ring like a bell. There was not a smidgen of snow anywhere. But very soon after we flew over Long Island Sound and into Connecticut, the smears were lining the roads, and by the time we were over Boston every lake and pond was a white rectangle and the forests were as leafless as a storehouse of telegraph poles, the towns collections of little wooden boxes strewn around bare ground. Then the real snow came in, first fringing the mountains then blanketing them, and as we veered and banked over the white-peppered evergreens the only bare land you could see was the long curving ribbons of cement, of the federal highways snaking through a planet of snow.

When you're not used to it, it's always a shock to get out of a plane and feel that somebody's slapped you in the eyes with a towel. This is simply the first adjustment to the blinding northern light. I went padding towards the tiny airport taking deep breaths of oxygen as sharp as ammonia. I was met by my daughter and son-in-law and grandson, a grinning Brueghel trio if ever I saw one. It had been 14 below zero when they woke up, and though it had gone up to a suffocating 20 above, their outlines were thickened by the snow boots and the billowing pants and those parkas that look like balloons but weigh about an ounce and are warmer than all the wool and sweaters in the world. My family, in short, looked like the first family of spacemen out there to greet a wan man-creature from remote New York.

With suspicious casualness, my daughter told me to put my bag in the back of the station wagon. I found it was impossible, because rearing up there and making a frightful honking sound were two of the fattest geese outside the *Christmas Carol*. About twenty minutes later, when we'd arrived at the graceful little white wooden eighteenth-century box they call home, I should say not more than ten minutes after we'd arrived, the two fat geese honked no more. They had departed this life, having had their necks wrung by my son-in-law and my son – a flown-in refugee from another distant planet, California. I didn't see these two for the next hour or two, which is just as well for a squeamish city type, since they'd been busy cleaning and plucking the birds against the Christmas feast.

The kitchen, which on any working farm is the centre of things, was dense with odours and tottering with platters and bowls, and my wife and daughter up to their elbows in parsley and onions and forcemeat and chanterelles, and pans bubbling with morels (plucked, according to a sacred tradition of my children, from dark corners in the woods by the light of a waning moon). The only time I ever saw anything like it was in rural France when I was invited to see what was brewing in the recesses of one of those country restaurants that manage to snag three stars from the Parisian dictators of such things.

My daughter and son-in-law lead a hard – but on these occasions and strictly to an outsider what looks like an idyllic – life. The food is not everything in some families but it happens to be my daughter's passion. And why not? After all, she has a lot of time hanging on her hands. She gets up before six, feeds, dresses and civilizes two small children, then goes out to see to the chickens and – in summer and fall – the raising of the fruits and vegetables. All that's left is to clean the house, stack the wood for the stoves, clean the barns, shovel the knee-high, fresh snow into parapets so as to be able to get to the big sleeping polar bear which tomorrow, the next day maybe, will turn into an automobile. Ferry the 4-year-old over the ice and snow to school, and put in an hour or so campaigning for the public (non-commercial) television station. So this leaves her ample time to prepare three meals a day, which are never snacks, at any time of the year. The first night, we started – started, mind – with a platter of smoked bluefish, one of a dozen thirteen-pounders her husband had caught in the summer off the end of Long Island. We smoked them within hours of the catch and they froze beautifully. After that came the irresistible piece of resistance: venison. Ten days before, my son-in-law had shot a doe and I'm happy to say I was not on hand to watch him and my daughter spend the next six hours skinning, de-gutting and butchering it before leaving it for the statutory week or so to hang.

I ought to say that I've had venison in farmhouses in Scotland and in lush restaurants in London and Paris. And, with an immense to-do and gaudy promises of food for the gods, in Texas. Texas does not, like any other region, simply have indigenous dishes. It proclaims them. It congratulates you, on your arrival, at having escaped from the slop-pails of the other forty-nine states. Welcome to Texas, and the incomparable three dishes of the Lone Star State: venison, chilli con carne and rattlesnake. (To the goggling unbeliever, they say – as people always say about their mangier dishes – 'But it's just like chicken, only tenderer.' Rattlesnake is, in fact, just like chicken, only tougher.)

Well, about venison and its hunters and preparers, I can only say that they all wag their fingers against their noses and confide to you, as a privileged guest, their dark and secret recipes for hanging and cooking and having it 'come out just right'. And it's always smelly and gamey and a little tough. In a restaurant, you can let the whole thing go with a sickly nod at the waiter. But the Texans are nothing if not considerate and eager hosts. They always beg you to tell them truthfully if you've ever eaten venison like that. The true answer is yes, unfortu-nately, always. But they are kindly people and you have to think up some variation on old Sam Goldwyn's line when he was pressed for an opinion by a brother film producer who'd just shown him his latest masterpiece in a sneak preview. 'Louis,' Goldwyn used to say, looking the man square in the eye, 'only you could 'eff made a movie like thet.'

Well, I want to tell you that that first evening I had naturally assigned the venison to Christmas Day and the big feast. I started to slice into a very fine tenderloin steak. It was so tender you could have eaten it with a spoon. But a round of uh-ums alerted me, rather late, to the fact that this was the venison. With delicate chanterelle sauce. A salad with raw mushrooms. Then Susie's fat and creamy cheesecake, with some of the fruit of the two hundred and seventy strawberry plants I'd seen her putting in earlier in the year, up to her knees in mud on some idle day. Just to keep things in the family, the wine was a remarkable claret from the vineyard my stepson farms in the beautiful Alexander Valley eighty miles north of San Francisco.

Well, it went on like that. And on Christmas Day, we had the geese, succulent and very serene in death. And a billowing cheese soufflé. And from time to time, there wafted in from the kitchen the scent of the four sorts of bread my daughter had baked. I once said to her, 'Any day now, Susie, you'll be making your own soap.' It was too late. She'd done it.

At the Christmas feast, with old Thomas Beecham whipping his orchestra and principals into proving once again that he is the Handel master of all time, I was asked to turn it down a shade while my son-in-law – a New England version of Gary Cooper – proposed a toast. He is not a gabby type, and this extraordinary initiative must have been inspired by the Alexander Valley grapes. Anyway, he said he didn't know what a proper toast should be but all he could think of with – 'well, pride I guess you can call it' – was the fact that everything we'd eaten in three days had lived or roamed or been grown right there, or in the woods that rise from the long meadow that goes up to the hills. Nothing, as they say in New England, had been 'store boughten'. And, he ended, 'If it doesn't sound pretentious' – wriggling at the fear that it might be – 'I think we should drink to the bounty of nature.' A very weird thing to toast in the last quarter of the twentieth century, when you can hardly buy a tomato that hasn't been squirted a chemical red, and chickens are raised in little gravel cages, and since they are immobile from birth and failing fast, must for our protection be injected with antibiotics and God knows what. (I know a very knowledgeable food writer in France who says he now recalls that the last time he tasted a chicken – a real free-range chicken – in a restaurant was in 1952.)

That evening we sang carols, in close if creaky harmony, with the 4-year-old Adam piping 'God Rest Ye Merry, Gentlemen' right on pitch. Next morning, I woke up and he was out on his skis. They are small skis and he got them a year ago. He was plumping up the hills and skimming down them with the poles helping him on the turns. And I thought, what an extraordinary childhood. He was born in 20 below zero (outside; of course he was born inside). Winter brings about 100–120 inches of snow. May is the squishy month, when the thaw sets in. Summer bangs in with 90 degrees. Fall is a fountain of scarlet and gold, and inky forests of evergreens on the mountains. And here, at 4, he's skiing over the deep and crisp and even like a Disney doll. And this is all the life Adam knows.

One day he will grow up and, I'm afraid, taste of the forbidden fruit. One day, he will read the *New York Times*. And Adam will be out of the Garden of Eden, out of Vermont, for ever.

Mr Olmsted's Park

8 July 1977

My workplace is a study that has the great luck to be perched on the fifteenth storey of an apartment house that looks out over the reservoir and the enclosing trees and meadows of Mr Frederick Law Olmsted's Central Park.

Olmsted was a remarkable Connecticut Yankee who wrote the classic, and still the fairest, account – on the verge of the Civil War – of life in the slave states of the South: *The Cotton Kingdom*. During the war, he ran the Union's sanitary commission. But before that, after a lively knockabout career, he had settled down as a landscape architect. When the city fathers of New York were thinking, in the 1850s, of having a city park, and when – naturally – the real-estate men and the cement contractors and the politicians were trying to guess at the likely location and buy up every acre in sight, Olmsted's plan won out over the plans of thirty competitors. Maybe, I suspect, because Olmsted brought great relief to the realtors by placing his park on empty, bosky ground way out of town. In fact, Oliver Wendell Holmes, the father of the great Justice, wrote a satirical essay wondering why Olmsted should have christened the proposed park 'Central' Park, since it would be about two miles north of where everybody lived.

Olmsted had out-foxed them all. He privately, and correctly, figured that the next great lurch of residents would be north of the limit of populated Manhattan, which in the 1850s was the streets in the Forties. By the time the park commission had voted on the site and ordered the twenty-year job to begin, it was too late for the realtors to do more than buy up the surrounding fringes of what would become a precious breathing space in a jungle of cement and steel. Olmsted showed remarkable foresight in other ways. His original plan allowed for meadows and a lake for recreation, for a wriggle of footpaths, for carriage paths, and for so-called 'transverses' that would at three banked intervals allow the invisible passage of crosstown horse-buses. When the internal combustion engine arrived, nothing radical was required to adapt the original plan to the 1920s or the 1970s. The carriage paths and the transverses were paved over, and today the automobiles skim their winding way through the trees and meadows and the buses and trucks cut through and under the bridges without entering the park. Olmsted went on to lay out three more parks in New York, and the grounds around the Capitol in Washington, and those around Stanford University in California, and the now splendid lake front of Chicago. His masterpiece, to my mind, is the little-known but exquisite estate of trees, lakes, lawns, and rolling hills that now houses Emory University bang in the middle of Atlanta, Georgia.

Well, as I was saying, I have the luck to look out on Olmsted's first great work and, in moments of furious idleness, when I am trying to work up a little creative thought, I stare at the stark trees of the winter against the snowfields, or the heartening fuzz of the breaking spring, or the rioting forsythia and dogwood and cherry, and then the vast blobs of the summer's full foliage before the yellows and scarlets of the fall come on. I am just at the height of a plane coming in for a steady landing, but I am low enough to sit and envy the kids down there – in winter the little Brueghel dolls scudding downhill on their sledges, but now – in the steaming mid-summer – tossing balls, lolling under trees with girls, gobbling ice-cream cones and, on the diamond off to the right, playing baseball.

Which gave me an idea. What has occurred to me, sitting here and weighing several leaden statements of the world's rulers – of Mr Brezhnev and Mr Carter and Mr Sadat – is that all the people I've ever known who are able to maintain an absorption with politics in the summertime don't play, or even watch, games. Of course, they can't stop governing through the summer – though in the blissful days before the United States became the Big Guy, the Congress of the United States managed it. But because great statesmen are almost wholly unfamiliar with games, they are unacquainted with such simple truths as that you win one, lose one, and begin again. This incapacity makes them fail to realize that politics – government, too – is a game.

I remember in the bitter Presidential campaign of 1932, in the pit of the Depression, when President Hoover was saying that prosperity was just around the corner, and Governor Roosevelt was saying that Hoover and his kidney had betrayed America, the rhetoric got so sharp and malicious that Will Rogers, the cowboy philosopher, wrote one of his three-sentence columns saying: 'Who do these fellas think they are, telling us who owns the Republic, and who is ruining the people? If we lost both of them, we'd get along. Why don't they shut their traps and go fishing?' Such was the popular prestige of Will Rogers that within days the news agencies received two photographs and printed them. One was of Roosevelt hauling a swordfish over the stern of a yacht. The other was of Hoover fly-fishing in a creek.

I hope it's not flippant to wish that Mr Sadat and General Dayan and Mr Carter could find some game they all played – cricket, say – and work up a healthy sweat and then sit down and talk about the future of the occupied territories, and the security of Israel, and the possibility of a Palestinian homeland. Instead of looking at the elements of the game, they all hammer away at a thesis. Which is to say, they are obsessed with their own ideologies. They are like a man who agrees to play a game but only on the understanding he shall win. Consequently, they have no disposition to begin by saying what and where are you prepared to lose? We've just had a particularly depressing example of what happens to idealists, ideologists, or – as we now say – ideologues when their ideology is reinforced by fear.

Let's admit that the problem of limiting the manufacture, and stockpiling, of nuclear arms is immense and maddeningly complex, and hard to simplify. You may remember that one powerful speech of Mr Carter – which had much to do with his election to the Presidency – insisted on beginning to limit nuclear arms and then working with the Russians to scrap them all. The Russians responded to this by saying that Mr Carter was saying just what they'd been saying all along. At the same time, to show the wickedness of Mr Carter's Republican opponents, who were always equated with 'the imperialist, war-mongering ruling classes', the Russians disclosed to their astonished people that thirty cents in every American tax dollar went for arms. What the Russians didn't tell their people was that: first, in Kennedy's day, it was closer to sixty cents in the dollar and, second, that they themselves accounted for rather more without any Russian being aware of it.

But the Americans, from the beginning of the SALT talks, have laboured under the hobbling difficulty of a democratic press, which lays out all the facts, supposed facts and rumours, and leaves them open to all sorts of benign and malign interpretations. During the Presidential campaign, the Democrats were quite willing to let the Russian characterization of the Republicans stand. Then along comes Mr Carter, who – the Russians delightedly recalled – had promised during the campaign not to go ahead with the B-1 bomber, which is superior to anything the Russians have. However, a couple of weeks ago, the word got out that he would, after all, go ahead with the B-1. The Russians said they knew all the time it was a campaign promise. Then he *did* ban it. Now the Russians say this only shows how foxy he is, and probably he'll manufacture it in secret. But so he won't be thought to be a fall guy for Russian bullying, Mr Carter says that, by the way, he *is* going ahead with the air-launched cruise missile, which is years ahead of the Russian missile. This had been agreed upon, but now the Russians are howling that America has in the White House an even more warlike, imperialist leader than Nixon.

This is what in diplomacy is blandly called an impasse. Now the administration announced that it has successfully tested a neutron bomb, and must therefore put up its umbrellas against a downpour of abuse not only from the Russians but from its liberal critics. Useless for Mr Carter to explain that the new bomb would greatly reduce the area of contamination in its job of killing off a military force inside a circumscribed place. What the Russians are going to say, and the liberals are saying already, is a phrase overwhelmingly attractive to ideologists, because it is so sharp and tangy. It is that at last we have a 'clean' bomb: one that protects the real estate but murders the inmates. As far as thought – and sarcasm – can reach, it's going to be a very tough ideological game to win.

In this impasse, I look out on Mr Olmsted's park again. And what do I see? Not people tossing balls, lolling under trees with girls, gobbling ice-cream cones, or playing baseball; all of which are honourable occupations. I see joggers. To be frank, I see them every morning, winter, summer, in sleet and Arctic cold, in the brisk fall and the furnace of the summer: these panting, slanting figures, in shorts and T-shirts, jogging, jogging, jogging around the long circumference of the reservoir. They are all very earnest, and so they are all ideologues. For earnestness is the only soil in which ideology can grow.

They used to make me feel guilty. But no more. Because I have to hand a copy, flown in here overnight, of the London *Times*. And in it is a short letter which, as far as I'm concerned, disposes once for all of the insanity of jogging. I don't know if there is a medical consensus about jogging, though in California – as you'd expect – there are psychiatrists, physiotherapists and other druids who, for a fat fee, promise to supervise your jogging by way of curing loneliness, depression, arteriosclerosis and hypertension, and restoring hair, fallen arches and failing marriages. I incline, myself, to the wisdom of three doctor friends of mine, one in San Francisco, one in Baltimore, the third in New York. The San Franciscan says that to jog over the age of 50 is madness, too much of a strain on the heart. The Baltimorean – who keeps his windows shut night and day, winter and summer – says more people have died of what they call 'fresh air' than any other noxious gas. The New Yorker, a man of great experience and some important original research, says that two martinis will cure anything.

Well, however that may be (and these are medical findings we should by no means dismiss without exhaustive testing), I can only say that the gentleman who wrote to *The Times* made a simple point worthy of Aristotle or Sir Isaac Newton: that is to say, he discovered an obvious thing which many people may have been dimly moving towards but which nobody ever said before. Let us not be coy about the identity of this great man. I have never heard of him, and it is possible that not many people have ever heard of him outside Blackheath – which is where he writes from. But I put his letter in a file of human wisdom that contains such gems as Aristotle's 'A play has a beginning, a middle and an end', Dr Johnson's 'Much may be made of a Scotsman if he be caught young', Mark Twain's 'The human being is the only animal that blushes, or needs to', and H. L. Mencken's definition of self-respect: 'The secure feeling that no one, as yet, is suspicious.'

The great man's name is Mark Godding. And this is his admirable brief chronicle: 'Sir – Regarding the current enthusiasm for jogging to extend one's life, may I point out that if one jogged ten miles a day then, having lived to the ripe old age of eighty – one would have jogged for approximately nine years . . . Is it worth it?' Here in a nutshell is revealed the absurdity of seeking to prolong life by a process that shortens it, by nine years, during which you might better have been reading, playing games, flirting, shutting windows or drinking martinis.

A year or two ago, a doctor in California planned a book on How to Avoid a Heart Attack. Before he'd finished writing it, he had a heart attack. The main thesis of the book was that human beings fall into (yet another) two opposing types – A and B. A is highly strung and, therefore, subject to heart attacks. B is placid, less subject. Recently, this doc was approached about jogging. 'Well,' he said, 'I really hate to have a jogger for a patient. Because a jogger is, by definition, a type A.'

PS About ten days after I broadcast this talk, I had a letter from London. It said: 'Dear Mr Cooke, I was very pleased that you mentioned me in your talk. Would you kindly send me your autograph? Sincerely, Mark Godding (aged 15).'

The Retiring Kind

9 September 1977

Americans, successful Americans most of all, are always talking about 'getting out of the rat race'. The rat race can mean any working routine that has started to bore you. I've heard this ambition voiced – bitterly, wearily, wistfully – by businessmen big and small, lawyers, big-time golfers, small-time grocers, university lecturers, burlesque strippers, journalists, ranchers, once, I remember, by a parson. He was a Southerner and he said, 'I've had ma fill of savin' souls, I'd just like to hole up in some dogpatch and nurse ma own.'

Englishmen, in my experience, go about it in a far less irascible way. They assume, or maybe they're taught from birth, that any job carries with it daily stretches of boredom. So they jog along for thirty, forty years and patter off sweetly or seedily into an inadequate pension, and then they are galvanized into doing what they've secretly wanted to do: to catch butterflies, collect stamps or book matches, read all of Trollope or grow turnips. An old lady wrote to me a year or so ago from Dorset, a lady plainly engrossed in her singular hobby. 'My retirement,' she wrote, 'which came in my sixty-fifth year, has made it possible for me to pursue my hobby: to catch *The Sound of Music* wherever it is being shown. Sometimes, I sit through all three performances. So far, I've seen it seventy-nine times, and I hope the end is not yet.'

The English live a life of boredom and then switch to mania. With Americans, it's the other way round. They are paranoid for years about the grind and horror of their jobs till they get to the pension, and then they mope and putter and mutter and confront their wives with a new ordeal – the daily nuisance of having to cook a lunch for a hanger-on.

These thoughts came to me when I recalled the pleasure this summer of visiting an old friend, an American newspaperman, who got out of the rat race with a bang one day, no notice given. He had never seemed to complain about the grind, even though he was the always-on-tap head of the Washington bureau of a distinguished Midwestern newspaper, even though he hated the fetid heat of Washington, which was odd in a boy born in the blistering heat of the prairie. It blisters in summer and petrifies in winter.

I imagine we all have a picture in our minds of how and where our friends will retire, the kind of set-up they've been used to and may now be expected to modify, or the kind of retreat they've always yearned for. If anybody had asked me, I could have improvised pretty quickly the ideal haven of my friend in retirement. I had known him best in the Kennedy days. It was a time when the White House press corps was more eager to be at the President's side than at any other time before or since. Not because Kennedy had loads of charm, which he had, but because he chose Palm Beach, Florida, as his winter White House. Let me explain.

Roosevelt's winter White House was the White House. His summer White House was the family home in Hyde Park, New York State, up in the steaming Hudson Valley. After him, Truman slaved away in the White House winter and summer, but he did take quick winter safaris down in Key West, which is frowsier than the travel brochures indicate. Anyway, Truman lived with the Marines at their base, and the accommodation for the press was makeshift at best. Eisenhower simply didn't like the press around anywhere. But then came Kennedy. The moment it was known that he would be hopping off all the time to use his father's mansion in Palm Beach as the winter White House, the rush to become a White House correspondent was indecent. I myself remember writing a fast note to my editor, a cagey Scot with an unpleasant gift for distinguishing between a call to duty and a call to pleasure. I put it to him frankly: my conscience had been riven for some time. We never covered the President except when he was in Washington. Had not the time come for me to attach myself to the White House press corps, however much inconvenience it might entail? I would be the only foreign correspondent so accredited, and think of the opportunities for a scoop: ('President Kennedy today played sixteen holes of Seminole, the famous course named after the local Indian tribe which can be seen, on a clear day, watching things closely from its encampment – on stilts – in the swamp of the Everglades.') The time had come.

Kennedy, you remember, was elected on a promise to settle something called the New Frontier. Well, they had some pretty splendid shacks down there on the New Frontier, which, to all intents and purposes I've ever been able to figure, began and ended at Palm Beach. This was just one of the facts of life we had to face. For the news of the world outside we watched the Miami *Herald*. We were put up in a glittering, medium-size hotel overlooking a lagoon. The palm trees dozed in a blinding sun. The little boats skimmed along. There were some very lively fish, and there was the finest golf course in the South (Ben Hogan once said, 'Play Seminole and die'). The ambulating girls were tanned and nubile. There was nothing we wouldn't do to conquer the New Frontier.

Well, this is where I first met the man I've been talking about: later chief of the Washington bureau, then White House correspondent of the *Chicago Sun Times*. He was tall and languid-dapper, silver-haired, good looking in a wry way. If it hadn't been for his absolutely slack, unhurried manner (a deadline was a daily chore, like washing the dishes, never a seizure) you might have thought of him as a Navy man. I once noted his striking resemblance to a Riviera admiral in an old Jerome Kern musical.

If you'd asked me then what sort of place he'd retire to, I'd have said he'd get himself a very comfortable, split-level, ranch-style house overlooking a golf course, with easy access to a plush bar, and a snappy clothier's and a good book store down the road. One day, in about 1970, I think, years after the New Frontier had been abandoned, or absorbed, he went to his suburban home from his Washington office and announced to his wife that he was quitting. 'To where?' she asked. I see him now, slowly licking his thumb and turning at a turtle's pace the holiday ads in the *Saturday Review*. There was a tiny one, in two lines. It said baldly: 'Cottage for rent, three weeks, Glandore, Ireland.' That's it, he said. They thought they'd begin by using this unseen cottage as a tenting base for roving trips around Europe. They'd look around, in time they'd pick their Shangri-La and have their things shipped there. So they packed up everything – the furniture, clothes, books, records, kitchenware, stereo deck, golf clubs, bird seed, the lot – and put them in a warehouse in Washington. They are still there.

They took the cottage for three weeks, and for the past seven years it has been their only home. It is what they'd call in Scotland a crofter's cottage: one door, one combination living room, kitchen, dining room, study, pantry, with three chairs, a bench, a stove, a lamp, a kettle, some pots and pans. Upstairs, two bedrooms, and a partitioned alley-way with a hole in the ceiling, through which drips a dribble of water known as a shower. From the downstairs room, they look out on a seven-foot-high white-washed wall. They sit and look at that, why I don't know, except it does shut out the thought that over the horizon is another assignment, another deadline. From their bedroom, they look out over dropping headlands and a bay and the sweeping Atlantic, which shores up again at the Antarctic.

At intervals, they read a paperback, bake the gritty, chewy Irish bread and take it – according to my Irish doctor's prescription – with refreshing swigs of the poteen. They breathe in and out. They have an old bone-shaker of an American car, not – so far as I could see – bearing Irish licence plates. If they occasionally infringe the law, like parking near a fire hydrant or picking up a pint ten minutes after closing, they are not apprehended. As my friend says, 'The great thing about this country is – there's always somebody who doesn't care.'

This should be an improving lesson to all of us who fret about retirement and the upkeep of the mortgage payment, and how to stretch the pound or dollar, how to maintain on half-pay our lifestyle, as we now preposterously call any way of life whether it has style or not. The moral is something an old schoolmaster told me. I thought it sententious at the time, as schoolboys think all general reflections on life are bound to be, since they seem meant to deny the particular schoolboy way of life. 'Never', said this middle-aged Welshman, 'let your wants outstrip your needs.' This is no sort of advice to give to a 16-year-old, who's lusting after a new cricket bat, or the latest Venuti-Lang record, not to mention what's left over with which to finance the local bird at the cinema, the tea-dance or wherever.

But it's a good line to say to fretful oldsters on the verge of a pension. And I should have guessed that nobody was more in need of it than my dapper, high-living (on his paper) Jerome Kern admiral. So what happened? Well, with – I suspect – a firm push from his beguiling wife, he became one of the few people I ever knew who got out of the rat race and managed with obvious content to *reduce* his wants to his needs. It is all the more remarkable in that it happened to an American couple, for Americans, as all the world knows, are alternately harried and cushioned from the womb with every brand of material comfort. Not, I hasten to say, like the British who, as we all know, want only to sit by a broken teapot and meditate and grow a flower.

What was at the back of my mind when I began, what got me off on this high moral theme, was the fact that a couple of years after I first met the admiral, I was invited to dinner in Palm Beach by a new United States Senator who was down there to celebrate his victory at the polls with a holiday. He was an old friend of mine. He'd been Governor of his state twice. And because he'd jumped aboard the Kennedy bandwagon about four years before anybody else, he was rewarded by becoming the first man to be appointed to the Kennedy Cabinet.

This dinner was the first time I'd seen him since his translation from Cabinet officer into Senator. I asked him why he'd made the switch. Why quit the Kennedy administration, in which he might have gone onwards and upwards (he'd actually had an offer of a seat on the Supreme Court)? He was very firm about it. 'You know why?' he said. 'You want to know why?' (He sounded for a moment like Jackie Gleason about to browbeat Alice.) 'Because now, goddamit, I'm my own man.' Go on, I said. 'Well,' he said, 'let me put it this way. When you get to be a Cabinet officer, you think you'll have the President's ear every day. I had great plans for a health and welfare bill, worked on it for months. I drafted it and sent it up to the President. I waited for the phone to ring. Hell, I didn't see him, except casually, in two months. Finally, I got a call from the *real* President of the United States.' Who dat? I drawled. With extraordinary venom for a normally benevolent man, he shouted, 'The Director of the Bureau of the Budget, that's who. He told me they'd looked over the bill. Fine, just fine. Great job. But they thought they'd have to whittle it down, the costs I mean, from – oh, I don't know – maybe twenty-five millions to two millions! End of bill. Never forget, my friend, the effective President of the United States, when you're in the Cabinet, is the Director of the Budget. What'll you drink?'

Well, it sometimes takes the wheel a long time to come full circle. In this case, fifteen years. The Director of the Budget has changed his title, but not his authority. He's now the Director of the Office of Management and Budget. But he's the same quietly dictatorial figure, unknown to the public, who decides what the President's budget is to be, how much will be spent on what. As I talk, the big man is one Bert Lance, an old, dear friend of the President and, naturally, a Georgian. He is now accused, or suspected, of all sorts of shenanigans with his own bank, and with his securities and investments. Four government agencies and three Congressional committees are looking into these dark matters. The key committee – the one that can save him or break him – is the Senate's Governmental Affairs Committee. Its chairman thought he had enough evidence by mid-week to urge Mr Lance to resign. Either way, this chairman's judgement could be decisive. And his conduct of the Committee hearings was, for him, unusually severe. He is normally gentle, forbearing, wistfully inviting sinners to repentance. In these hearings, he was almost an inquisitor. Very odd. Perhaps it was due to an impulse to get in some final legislative licks before he retires, at the end of his present term.

So who *is* the chairman of that Senate Committee? He is that Senator who discovered to his chagrin, fifteen years ago, who was the 'real' President of the United States. He is the handsome, the able, senior Senator from Connecticut: Abraham Ribicoff.

Two for the Road

23 December 1977

At the risk of seeming to take a short trot through a graveyard (something that only Dickens in one of his familiar morbid moods would do at Christmas time) I should like to say something about two tremendous figures who recently went off – along with Johnny Mercer – into immortality. Or upon what Mercer, the most poetic of jazz lyricists, called 'the long, long road'.

I hope there was no moaning at the bar over the death of Groucho Marx. He was very old, and for several years he had had only short lucid intervals in which he knew much about what was going on.

My first contact with him was about twenty-five years ago, when he wrote to me to say he would very much like to be on a television show that I was running. We were delighted to start negotiations, and at one point we thought everything was sewed up. Then, mysteriously, he backed out. In those days, television was done 'live' (no taping beforehand) and movie stars were petrified by it since they'd have to memorize a whole part instead of thirty-second bits. By the same token, stage actors were eager for exposure over a national network, and you could hire the best of them for a few hundred dollars. Groucho evidently didn't know this. And I soon heard from our business manager why Groucho wouldn't be with us: he had asked an enormous fee. We regretfully declined his services. There was an awkward interval of silence at both ends. Then he wrote to me: 'Like Sam Goldwyn, I believe in art. But my agent, a coarse type, believes in money. And who am I to argue with such a baboon?'

Shortly after that, I was in Hollywood. He invited me to lunch, and ever afterwards, whenever my wife and I were out on the Coast, we saw him and enjoyed him as the slap-happy anarchist he was in life just as much as he was in the movies. The great pleasure in him came from his finicky, and funny, respect for the English language. That, at first hearing, may sound incomprehensible. But whatever his comic style was like when he started out in vaudeville, he had the luck in Hollywood to fall in with the supreme American humorist, S. J. Perelman, who wrote one or two of the early Marx Brothers movies. I dare say nobody alive has a quicker ear for the oddities and absurdities of the language that can spring from taking words – taking the tenses of English – literally. This gift passed over to Groucho and he made it his own. So much so that when I wrote a piece about Groucho's gift to the Library of Congress of his letters, I suggested in it that S. J. Perelman's scripts and letters should be sent along too. Groucho, whose laughable view of human pomp did not extend to his own vanity, kicked up a great fuss and swore our friendship was an unpleasantness from the past. A vow he forgot the next time he embraced me.

The most memorable example I can think of this language game happened when we were lunching with him at the most luxurious of Jewish country clubs in Los Angeles. When the menu was passed around, I raised an eyebrow at what even then were outrageous prices. 'Fear not, my friend,' said Groucho, 'it's only money. The initiation fee at this club is $10,000, and for that you don't even get a dill pickle.' When the main course was over and the waiter came to take the dessert order, he stumbled several times over who was having what. Finally, he said, 'Four éclairs and four – no, four éclairs and two coffees?' Groucho whipped in with, 'Four éclairs and two coffees ago, our forefathers brought forth on this continent a nation dedicated to the proposition – skip the dedication and bring the dessoit.'

On the way out, Groucho lined up to pay his bill behind a fat and fussy lady who was fiddling around in her bag for change. The young cashier gave a patient sigh, and Groucho – his cigar raking the air like an artillery barrage – said, 'Shoot her when you see the whites of her eyes!' The large lady turned around in a huff, which dissolved into a delighted giggle. 'Would you,' she gasped, 'be Groucho Marx?' In a flash, Groucho rasped out, 'Waddya mean, *would* I be Groucho Marx? I *am* Groucho Marx. Who would *you* be if you weren't yourself? Marilyn Monroe, no doubt. Well, pay your bill, lady, you'll never make it.'

The other great man was a world apart from Groucho – in geography, upbringing, temperament and talent. I'm talking about Harry Lillis Crosby who, for reasons as obscure and debatable as the origins of the word 'jazz', was known from boyhood on as Bing. Some years ago, a friend of mine, a publisher, thought of persuading Bing to sit down in several sessions with a tape recorder and put out a book of reminiscences. My friend was very steamed up about this project and came to me one day and said he'd got the main thing, he'd got the title. He narrowed his eyes and said very slowly, '*My Friends Call Me Bing.*' Four words too many, I said. And truly, I don't suppose there are more than half a dozen people in the world who would be instantly recognizable by a single word.

It's been just over fifty years since we were first exposed to the Rhythm Boys and their lead tenor, who provided the first happy breakaway from the ladylike sopranos and resonant baritones of the London and New York stages who were singing Youmans, Gershwin and Rodgers as if they were still commuting between Heidelberg and Ruritania. Then the Rhythm Boys' tenor, never identified on the record label, broke loose on his own, and the word ran through the English underground that a genuine jazz singer – and a white man! – had appeared in the unlikeliest place: breezing along on the ocean of Paul Whiteman's lush 'symphonic' sound. For about six precious months, as I recall, from the fall of 1927 through the spring of 1928, Whiteman, of all people, permitted a small jazz group – Bix Beiderbecke, Frank Trumbauer, Eddie Lang and Crosby – to be given its head. And on the long spring nights, the punts drifting along the Cambridge Backs gave out the easy, vagabond phrases of Bing and the lovely codas of Bill Challis' orchestrations.

For several years after that, the underground went into mourning for the apostasy of Bing Crosby, who turned into a gargling crooner. We abandoned him as a traitor, until after the war years he relaxed again into the unbuttoned troubadour, the mellower jazz singer, known from El Paso to El Alamein as the Groaner, Der Bingle and always Bing. For thirty years or so, there appeared a parade of male singers, from Russ Columbo through Como and Sinatra and beyond, who could never have found their own style if Crosby had never existed.

By then, Bing had done everything he wanted to do in music and movies, and having wisely appreciated the approach of the gentleman with a scythe, he countered him by developing other talents and went off to fire 3-irons in Scotland and repeating rifles in Africa. Never a man to push himself, at twilight or any other time, he crooned only to himself. Then, fifty years after his first record, he cut a final album. Well into his seventies, he was the same Bing, because he had the great good sense to know the right keys, the navigable modulations, where to go and where not to go, unlike some other star-studded egos who like to fancy that the rules of mortality have been suspended for them alone.

I first ran into him on the set of one of the Hope–Crosby 'Road' movies, and I think I picked up a false impression of him right away. Because he was saucy, mischievous, almost gabby when he was work-ing, especially with Hope. They ad-libbed so much and broke down in chuckles so often that at one point Bing turned to a writer who was sitting with the director and said, 'If you hear any of your own lines, shout Bingo!' Of course, Bing was witty, in a droll, tired way (nobody else would have described his face, with its flapping ears, as looking 'like a taxicab with both doors open'), but the movie image of Bing was a very high-pressure version of the man off the set. Once the lights dimmed and the director said, 'It's a take,' Bing visibly drooped into a character so shambling and low key that I got the impression he'd had a sleepless night and would soon be off for a nap. People used to ask me, 'What was Bing like playing golf, I'll bet he was uproarious, right?' In fact, he was relaxed to the point of boredom, good-natured boredom. It's true he always looked you in the eye, but he did it with the grey, tired eyes of a man who had seen everything – a lot of fun but also a lot of grief – and was never going to be surprised by anything said or done.

From his early success days with the Rhythm Boys and on into his movie career, there'd been all sorts of problems in and around his family: sickness, death, the bottle, truancy, spats and sulks with his sons. Until he came into port at last, after some stormy seas, with his second wife and his new family. It is possible that he talked about these things to very close friends, but even his butler couldn't recall any. To everyone, except some missing confidant, he put up the quiet defence of offhand, easygoing small talk.

I can't think of another man of anything like his fame who was so unrattled by it and so genuinely modest. The accursed foible of show business people is prima donnaism: the massive ego, the implication that the whole world is revolving around them and their new picture, their new plans – which they pretend to find delightful but embarrassing. Not Bing. He was in this more mature than any actor or actress, author or musician, statesman or politician I have known in coming to sensible terms with great fame. His mail must have been staggering, with its appeals for favours and money from every charity and every crackpot in the world. He never mentioned it. He was polite to every nice fan, and every child, and every moron who hailed him. All his later concerts, and pro-amateur golf tournaments, passed on the receipts to a raft of favourite charities.

When he died, there was a spate of film clips and replayed old interviews and the like. The most revealing of these was one done shortly before he died by the news interviewer Barbara Walters, who does have a knack for asking the childlike questions we'd all like to ask but don't dare. She asked him to sum himself up, and he allowed that he had an easy temperament, a way with a song, a fair vocabulary, on the whole a contented life. And she said, 'Are you telling us that's all there is – a nice, agreeable shell of a man?' Bing appeared not to be floored. After the slightest pause for deep reflection, he said, 'Sure, that's about it. I have no deep thoughts, no profound philosophy. That's right. I guess that's what I am.'

It was so startling, so honest, and probably so true, that it explained why he'd been able, through hard times, to stay on an even keel. Perhaps he was one of those people who, though not at all selfish, are deeply self-centred: what they call 'a very private person'. Because he couldn't identify with other people's troubles, he was able to appear, and to be, everybody's easygoing buddy, and forget death and disaster in a recording date or a round of golf. He was the least exhibitionist celebrity I have ever known. And because death is so dramatic, so showy, some of us cannot believe he won't show up in the locker room tomorrow and say, 'Well, skipper, how's tricks?'

The Spy That Came Down in the Cold

10 February 1978

We have just followed the first story of general interest to come out of the vast tundra of Canada's Northwest Territories since the Klondike gold rush.

It came at us first as a scare story, like something out of *Dr Strangelove* or *Star Wars*. Then it turned into a technological puzzle as remote from the interests, or competence, of ordinary people as the workings of a breeder reactor. So that, more or less out of boredom, we were ready to sink back into the soap opera or the insurance policy, when the *New York Times* published a long piece that suggested, for the first time in print, appalling possibilities for all of us. The White House promptly denied the gist of the story. And then the whole thing was surprisingly dropped.

What I'm talking about is the Soviet satellite that fell out of its orbit into the earth's atmosphere, burst into flames and disintegrated above North America. For a day or two, the main concern of Canadians and Americans was to know if the accident had happened over any well-populated part of this continent. But once it was run to ground in the empty pinelands surrounding Canada's Great Slave Lake, everybody breathed again, and we all chuckled and quoted the man who said, 'Chicken Little was right.'

Yet the Russian satellite was admittedly a spy, whose job was to orbit the earth a hundred and fifty miles above it and keep track of the movements of all the ocean-going American warships – what we now call defence ships – including submarines deeply submerged. The satellite carried a load of radioactive materials, and that was what caused the fright. The debris from the disintegration rained across a two-hundred-and-fifty-mile stretch. But once it was established that none of the sample fragments picked up was radioactive, the scare died down.

It shows how far we've come in eighteen years, how far in stoicism, or a sense of reality, maybe. In May 1960, when an American spy plane was shot down over the Soviet Union, President Eisenhower denied that American reconnaissance planes ever flew over Russia. Then he broke down and said, 'Well, you do it too.' This happened just when the Big Four leaders had assembled in Paris for a summit meeting. But in the uproar over the American U-2 plane, Mr Khrushchev, the Soviet Prime Minister, stomped off home. The other three looked foolish and packed their bags. And the summit never took place.

If we have acquired a new sense of reality, it is no less than a rather fearful admission that we are in a steady *warm* war with the Soviet Union – and at a time when we go on talking about the progress of détente. Whatever it is, it has nothing to do with a change of heart, or with policy, or, indeed, with Mr Carter or Mr Brezhnev. It is due to the inescapable fact that spy planes can now fly too high to be reached. The U-2 reconnaissance planes flew at 65,000 feet, which is roughly twelve and a half miles up. From that height the Americans at least had – so long ago as 1962 – cameras that could define with astonishing accuracy objects as small as a woodshed. The Russians must not have known this. Because when they were shown, in the Security Council of the United Nations, the American reconnaissance blow-ups of the Russian missiles being installed in Cuba, they blustered and swore that the pictures were fakes. But the photographs plainly showed missiles mounted and unmounted, all the paraphernalia of bases and launch pads that could not possibly be mistaken for woodsheds. So it was not so much the initiative of President Kennedy that persuaded the Russians to abandon their bluff and dismantle their bases. It was the cameras of the U-2s with their nine- by eighteen-inch negatives and their incredible twenty-six-inch lenses.

Well, by now, photographs of landscape from 65,000 feet are so taken for granted that NASA, the National Aeronautics and Space Administration, puts out infrared prints (you can buy them) of every section of the United States, in reaches of country thirty or forty miles across, on which you can see the sharp divisions of streets in cities of several million population. Obviously, these pictures would not be made public if they represented the known limit of the technical resources of reconnaissance, or spying. Clearly, since 1962, enormous advances have been made in the ways that one nation can scan the land and the industry and the defence establishment of another. We now spy, not from twelve miles up but from a hundred and fifty miles up. Neither the Russians nor the Americans deny it. In fact, since this scanning through radar has passed over into space, we have a situation that could have been imagined a hundred years ago only by W. S. Gilbert and Jules Verne working in tandem. Through several accidents, the two superpowers have become so aware of the lethal consequences of mismanagement in space that they keep each other posted on the movement of their spy ships, the orbiting satellites that are monitoring each other's military movements.

The crash of the Soviet satellite, Cosmos 954, provided the ordinary citizen with, I believe, the first glimpse we've had into this involuntary partnership. I say involuntary, because whether or not the Pentagon or the Soviet Defence Department wants it, the possibilities of accidental devastation from satellites floating *untracked* through space are too awful to be ignored. So it's worth taking a look into how it works. And today it can be done quite openly and the findings published without so much as a squeak of protest from the North American Air Defense Command, whose headquarters are buried deep in the granite of the Colorado Rockies.

Six years ago, I was doing a television programme about the working of the Strategic Air Command's underground headquarters in Omaha, Nebraska. We were given extraordinary freedom to film the whole process that could lead to the President's final cue for a nuclear attack. But there *were* things that were off-limits. We were not allowed to guess at the number of missiles the Americans had at the ready.

The perils of free-floating satellites have changed all that. Today, we know – and the Soviets know – that there are 4,600 machines of various sorts in space and precisely 939 satellites. Perhaps, now, 938. Somewhere in the Urals or wherever, Soviet technicians are tracking them. And, in the bowels of the Rockies, American technicians are doing the same. They marked the launching of Cosmos 954 on 17 September last. They knew its job was to scan the oceans with its radar and tell Soviet ground stations what it saw by way of ships and submarines. The Americans knew that its penetrating radar equipment was powered by a nuclear reactor.

Three months after it was launched, in mid-December, Cosmos 954 began to sag out of its prescribed orbit. The Russians ordered it to break into three parts and dissipate. Evidently it didn't obey. It stayed intact, and every time it went round the earth, it swung a little nearer. In early January, the Americans figured it would fall into the earth's atmosphere over North America. The Soviet ambassador was invited to a secret meeting in the White House, and the Russians were asked for all relevant information. The American anxiety was over the amount of uranium on board the satellite and its chances of disintegrating on or above the earth. Teams of observers and decontamination experts were flown out to likely points of impact. The afternoon before it crumbled, the men of Air Defense Command watched it go across Australia and then the Pacific and then on into northern Canada. When a Canadian Mountie reported a meteorite, they knew it was all over. The fragments were tested, and it seemed certain that the satellite and its nuclear power cell had burned up completely on re-entering the earth's atmosphere. The Air Defense Command relaxed. The newspapers cooled down. All was well.

Not quite. What came out a few days later was the admission from space scientists that the location of the crash was not contrived by human skill or the magic of computers. It was sheer luck. They calculated that if the satellite had managed to hobble once more around the earth, it would have come down somewhere close to New York City between eight and nine in the morning. This afterthought was not published. The official story was all over, except for a plea from President Carter for a law, an agreement at least, to ban from space any satellite that contains nuclear reactors. The Secretary of Energy said amen, but he couldn't quite see how it was to be done. Mr Brezhnev made the stunning comment, 'There must not be another war.' Ah, so. Apart from that, the Russians said nothing. However, the doubt remains whether any satellite, like Cosmos 954, would be able to spot the movement of submarines unless its radar was powered by a nuclear reactor. In other words, the evidence is undeniable that we are already embarked on the military uses of space. And just how far we've gone was chillingly exposed two days later by a front-page piece in the *New York Times*. It recalled that the United States had become the first nation to put a spy-satellite in orbit, in 1959. That, more recently, Mr Carter became the first President to admit that both countries are developing weapons meant to destroy each other's satellites. And that the Defense Department is well aware of Russian experiments in space with laser weapons.

Then the *Times* dropped its bombshell. It reported that the Russians have outstripped the Americans, probably by several years, in developing what are known as 'hunter-killer satellites', which 'could knock out the Pentagon's ability to communicate with, and give orders to, ships, planes, submarines, missile silos and ground forces around the world'. Now, this, of course, means that the United States could be paralysed from outer space and rendered impotent even to order an act of retaliation if she were attacked.

The subject was evidently too touchy for security experts in the White House and the Pentagon. They wouldn't talk about it. But the recently retired Chief of Air Force Intelligence would and did. He is General George Keegan. He said that eighteen years ago, a Russian spy working for the allies in the Kremlin warned Washington that the Russians were about to invest on a grand scale in military space research. He says the man was ignored. But two years ago, American experts were startled when the Russians put into orbit a hunter-killer that could destroy a target on earth after making only one pass around it. General Keegan says the threat is 'grim'.

And what does President Carter say? He brushed the story off at a press conference. How could he have said anything of substance? To say, 'Yes, the Russians have them and we don't' would have dealt a crippling blow to the morale of the people.

What we have to face is that whether it's true or not, it is going to be. We are already far gone towards preparing for the kind of war that H. G. Wells conceived as scientific fiction half a century ago, and that Bertrand Russell, twenty-two years ago, foresaw as the almost certain consequence of American and Russian nuclear research. It surely should give an aching urgency to the coming talks on how to limit strategic arms. For, if the wind out of Canada has blown any good, it is the warning that satellites are already beyond absolute human control, that the technology of war is acquiring a momentum independent of national policy or the men who make it. Like that ghoulish computer in an old 1969 movie, the hunter-killer may come to have a mind of its own.

A Letter from Long Island

18 August 1978

As you may have heard, all the New York City newspapers – all three of them – are on strike. How, then, am I going to acquaint you with what is being said, and thought, and speculated about all the great issues of the day? I am not. It may be cold-blooded to say so but this seems to me to offer a golden opportunity to disclaim all responsibility for being well-informed, or informed at all. I could spoil it for you – and for me – by remarking that the television networks are doubling and tripling their coverage from New York and of the local controversies that spring from the strike. So it's possible to sit down at 6 p.m. and emerge four hours later choked and dizzy with facts and fancies.

In the middle of a sweaty August, it seems to me to be a mistake not to make the most of the surcease from the *New York Times*. Far better, I hope you'll agree, if I retreat to where I belong and tell you something about life as it is lived at the end of Long Island. I don't mean to give you the romantic notion that the end of the Island – we are precisely one hundred miles from door to door – is a romantic haven devoid of all involvement with the modern world. On the contrary, it would be possible for a nosey reporter to make it over into a miniature of the nation's plight.

The county politicians voted not to raise the pay of our local sheriffs, so for a day or two the prison guards called in to say they were all feeling very poorly. Rural crime has increased by 3 per cent in the past year – up in our village from ten robberies to – presumably – ten and a third! There is a mild hullabaloo about a proposal to build an atomic plant in the middle of our potato fields. The groundwater supply, our only source of water, is becoming polluted with nitrates from fertilizers used by farmers and golf clubs, and it's going to cost a quarter of a million dollars to keep the water safe for humans. And so on.

Enough. You must picture the island as a fish, a very long fish with its snout on the left and its tail on the right. Its mouth is hooked to Manhattan and its body reaches into the Atlantic in a direction more easterly than anything, for about one hundred and twenty miles. Its tail is divided into two flukes, which enclose a bay about thirty miles long, five to six miles wide. This is called Peconic Bay (the Peconics were a tribe of Indians, fishermen, whom the refugees from Suffolk came on in the seventeenth century).

There are certain places of the earth I would rather be than anywhere else, at certain times of the year. In the fall, there is nowhere I would rather be than Vermont, for the beauty of its scarlet and gold landscape – except Long Island, for its shining days and its miraculous draught of fishes. In fact, there is nowhere I know – not the Mediterranean, or the Crimea, most certainly not California – where, between May and November, there is such a succulent haul of so many kinds of splendid eating fish. We are just at the point where the northern cold-water fish nibble at our shores and where the warm-water fish abound. First, for the gourmet, are the noble striped bass, and the bluefish. Then the swordfish, and the flounder, and the lemon sole. But there are also other very tasty species, which city people either don't know about or despise out of genteel ignorance. In the summer months, the fat flat porgy is always mooching along the bed of the bay. It is very easy to catch by bouncing a sinker on the bottom and stirring up enough sand and mud to blind it. It is a paranoid species that feels it's being chased by submarines and so comes to the surface along a zigzag course, as if in convoy during wartime. Baked porgy is delicious, and I simply have no idea why it never appears on restaurant menus.

Then there is the blowfish, known to the local tots as the swell-belly, for the exact reason that when it's grounded it blows itself up like a balloon in the hope of disposing of the hook. It is regarded by week-enders as a pest fish, but it has down its backbone a slim triangular fillet of firm flesh, the closest thing we have to the delicious rubbery texture – I'm afraid there is no other word – of a Dover sole. More remarkable still is the city's non-acceptance of the weakfish. I have caught it and savoured it for forty years. It is so called because it has a weak, papery mouth, which it cheerfully – I presume – rips in order to dislodge the hook. It then swims off and grows its mouth together again. Maybe its name is the snag. Some years ago, droll Italians who owned fish markets on the South Shore took to laying out weakfish and marking them with a sign saying, 'Sea Trout'. They were out of stock within an hour of piling up the weaks.

The island, like all other bits of geography, has its own local lingo for its different districts that will not be found on maps or in atlases. Thus, the northern fluke – where I live – is known as the North Fork. But the southern fluke is known as the South *Shore* (never mind that some old families over there try to retain the South Fork). The natives of the North Fork say they are going 'South Side' whenever they are disposed to do so, which is not often, for reasons I hasten to explain.

The South Shore used to be the exclusive monopoly of early Dutch and English landowners. One of the latter, William Floyd, was a signer of the Declaration of Independence and achieved a very late badge of immortality by having a motorway named after him. The early settlers were a little miffed, at the end of the nineteenth century, when some of the robber barons and their heirs moved in. One of them, name of Vanderbilt, visited Scotland and saw the natives playing the peculiar game known locally as 'the gowf'. He accordingly imported some clubs, hired a landscape man, or golf architect, and commissioned him to lay out the first twelve-hole links course in the United States.

Until the Second World War, the fashionable resorts of the South Shore – Southampton, Bridgehampton, Easthampton – were pretty choosy places. But following the immemorial custom of all Western societies, the latest batch of the new rich moved as close to the old rich as possible in the hope of having some of their effortless poise brush off on them. In the past twenty or thirty years, these once fussy compounds have been invaded by brokers, interior decorators, bankers, chic painters, actors and actresses, television producers, and infested by ten-percenters of all kinds.

If you detect a note of inverted snobbery in this account, your instinct is correct. I have summered and autumned (fallen?) on the North Fork for forty-two years. We stand out on our hundred-foot high cliff or bluff and look across the five or six miles of the quarantine waters that separate us from the chic, the bad and the beautiful. The North Fork is not chic. It is not rich. I doubt there are more than half a dozen residents whose combined securities could match the portfolio of any one of several hundreds of the denizens of Easthampton and Southampton. The North Fork was for two and a half centuries the province of English settlers from Suffolk, and you can follow the family lines through platoons of tombstones, the victims of seventeenth-century epidemics, and all the wars since the Revolution, in the local graveyards or what – in my village – is known as 'the burying ground'. I know old people, and not so old, who only once in their lifetime have made the hundred-mile trip to New York. They didn't like what they saw, and went no more.

Shortly after the robber barons invaded the South Shore the North Fork was invaded by immigrant Poles: Catholic farmers. Like all immigrants, they had a nostril tuned to the smell of their native soil. And the North Fork, planted as far as the eye can see with potatoes and cauliflower and corn, is interrupted only by a few old colonial churches but more conspicuously by squat wooden churches with blunt spires. The Fork could be used today with great accuracy as the location for a film about central Poland.

The Poles were industrious and very thrifty and in no time took over the big duck farms, which had been run in a comfortable way by the Anglos. So now, our Fork is populated mostly by the descendants of the original English and by third-generation Poles. And in the manner of long-settled rural communities, the North Forkers tend to take a dim view of the South Shore. But then, the South Shore takes no view at all of the North Fork. In fact, friends of ours on the South Side have lived and died there without having the faintest idea where the North Fork was or how to find our point, though it's clearly visible from the Peconic shore of their side. I still have friends who ask us every summer, 'How are things at your place in Southampton?' Which is like asking a proud Lancastrian, 'How are things in Bradford and Leeds?'

Our point is called Nassau Point. After the English occupation it was rechristened Hog's Neck, but it reverted later on to Nassau since, under the Dutch, it had been designated as a sliver of crown property by King William (Prince, you'll recall, of Orange and Nassau). Since then the Point has managed to remain unmentioned in the history books or even in the newspapers. In fact, we are so obscure that when Nassau Point achieved the fame of a new comet, nobody noticed it. It needed no newspaper strike to leave us unhonoured and unsung. But that is another story. Another letter.

The Presidential Ear

8 December 1978

The newspapers and the television commentators have just paid their annual respects – or regrets – to the Japanese attack on Pearl Harbor on 7 December 1941, a day, President Roosevelt said when he went before Congress, 'that will live in infamy'.

However, two days before that was 5 December 1978, a night which will surely live in American history. For there occurred an event that has never before taken place in the history of the Republic: an incumbent President of the United States took his seat at the opera. The doors of New York's Metropolitan Opera House – either the old or the new – have never been darkened, or lit up, by the presence of a President.

Nothing ought to be made of the fact that the opera was *Aida*, an opera on an Egyptian subject commissioned by Ismail Pasha and first performed in Cairo, though it's possible something may be made of it by ill-meaning journalists in and out of Israel. In which case, the President could make amends by commissioning a performance of Handel's *Israel in Egypt*.

The fact is that President Carter is something of a freak among the long line of American Presidents. He is a music lover. I don't mean that he has his favourite tunes (as haven't we all). President Eisenhower, I believe, let it be known that he had an album of favourites, which he liked to have piped in so that he could hum to them, as George V on a memorable occasion – his fifth visit to *his* favourite opera, *Rose Marie* – sat in the royal box and, having conquered his favourite song in the whole of music, accompanied the chorus singing 'Totem tom tom, Totem tom tom.'

I mean that President Carter is the phenomenon of a very hard-working President who yet makes time every morning – every dawning, I ought to say – to listen to a half-hour or so of Mozart or Beethoven. It is hard to think of a better prescription for rinsing out the mind before the growing cacophonies of the day. It is fascinating, though perhaps not very instructive, to wonder why politicians, who regularly acquire some strange bedmates, should so rarely relax with the muse of music, with classical music, that is. Franklin Roosevelt and John F. Kennedy would have paid any price to avoid a symphony concert. Disciples of the late Harry Truman will be bound to protest that he actually played the piano, chopped his way through bits of Chopin, and at all times was ready to give a soulful performance of 'The Missouri Waltz'.

But, having heard him and followed his tastes, I must say that his range was that of the excerpts we staggered through on the piano when I was a boy: a series of what was called 'The Three Star Folio', which incorporated the more swinging bits from the *Poet and Peasant* overture, 'Zampa', Handel's 'Largo' and the 'Four Indian Love Lyrics' of the immortal Amy Woodforde-Finden. They were conveniently known as middle-brow classics.

And I'm sure that out of Texas will storm the reminder that whenever at a barbecue or other local festival Lyndon Johnson heard 'The Eyes of Texas', the tears flowed down the clefts of his endless cheeks. President Nixon, too, was almost as eager to get to any piano in sight as was George Gershwin, about whom a close but clear-eyed friend said, 'No question about it, an evening with Gershwin is a Gershwin evening.' Nobody thumped away with more zest and pleasure than President Nixon, and I imagine he treasures as one of the precious mementoes of his Presidency the evening when, in full view of a delirious audience, Duke Ellington kissed him on both cheeks – the last time, I believe, Mr Nixon was ever kissed in public, except by next of kin.

In case any overseas listener is beginning to preen himself on the superior cultivation of his own politicians, as distinct from the rude American kind, I beg him or her to take thought. Name offhand, or even after much boning up, any politician of the first chop who is or was a known lover of classical music. Apart, that is, from the blinding exception of Mr Edward Heath. Mr Gladstone, my father told me, was properly reverent when called to Buckingham Palace to listen to performances of sacred music commissioned by Queen Victoria. He would have been a brave Prime Minister who dared to refuse *that* royal command to listen to any music, however sacred, however stupefyingly dull. But I don't remember from the memoirs that Balfour, Lloyd George, Asquith, Bonar Law or any of their generation had the slightest interest in music. In the many volumes of the works of Winston Churchill, I can't recall a reference to any of the top-flight or even third-flight composers, though Mr Churchill was also known to weep whenever the 'Battle Hymn of the Republic' was played. As for the succeeding generations of British politicians – and I hope I do them no insult – I cannot find either that Anthony Eden was an accomplished bassoonist or that Mr Callaghan devotes his spare hours to reading the scores of the Bach fugues. I do recall, and was actually present once, when the astonishing thing happened: the first Lord Birkenhead was tone deaf and had to be nudged whenever the band went into the national anthem.

Going back for a minute or two to the startling event that provoked all this meditation, I must say it seems very unlikely that some President, at some time or other, did not find it expedient, let alone pleasurable, to attend the opera. A friend of mine, who knows not only all the obscure operas of the great composers but all the mediocre operas of the obscure composers, did a little digging and came up with the nugget that in 1918 President Wilson did appear at the Metropolitan Opera House. But it turned out that he was there, as usual, not to listen but to perform. Not, so help us, to sing, but to make a speech before a rally called to stir up popular support for the League of Nations. There is also an unauthenticated rumour that at another time, President Wilson dropped a hint to the authorities that he might come up to New York to attend the opera, but when he discovered that it was to be performed on a Sunday, he was shocked into withdrawing his request.

Further painstaking research at last reveals that there is one other President who not only had the wild impulse to go to the Met but yielded to it. Not, however, in New York. The Metropolitan company was on tour in the winter of 1905–6, and when it appeared in Philadelphia President Theodore Roosevelt – in the full flush of what had been till then the biggest popular majority any President had ever had from the voters – took himself off to see and hear Enrico Caruso. Roosevelt must have slipped into the house – if a mountain can ever be said to have slipped in anywhere – or he had not tipped off the company. Because when the performance was over and he went backstage to greet the great man, the other great man, Caruso, we are told, believed for an awkward time that he was meeting an impostor. But when he realized that he was indeed being visited by the one and only T.R. or Teddy, he threw his arms around the President and – anticipating Duke Ellington – smacked a kiss on each cheek. There was a photographer present – a small fact I mention because the following April Caruso was performing in San Francisco, and early in the morning of the 18th he was asleep in his regal suite in the Palace Hotel. Just before dawn, the bed started to shake and the chandelier to swing and, in a word, the hell of the famous earthquake was let loose all around him. He dashed out, like all the other guests, in a nightgown into the courtyard of the hotel and begged for any form of transport that would take him to the ferry, which in turn would take him to the railroad and save him from disaster. In what must have been an agony of conflict, between egotism and self-preservation, he tried to think of some single possession he could not bear to lose. My opera historian records – and who is to question him? – that what Caruso rescued was the photograph of himself with Teddy Roosevelt.

I was pondering on this unexplained mystery – why politics apparently works through the nervous system to produce an allergy to first-rate music – when one of the television networks ended its nightly news roundup with a five-minute visual essay on two minority peoples, most of whom live outside China but some of whom spill over the northern and southern borders: namely, Mongols and Thais. This piece was put on, I imagine, partly to tell us more about our now Communist friend, and partly to offset the chill of the twenty-year treaty of friendship that the Soviet Union has just signed with Afghanistan.

These two ancient peoples are, of course, resident aliens, or what the Bible calls 'strangers within the gates'. They have their own strong cultures, and we were assured that the Chinese in no wise want to reform them. To keep them friendly, on both sides of the borders, we were told that the Chinese allow them to live – I quote – 'independent lives according to their own customs, within the framework of Chinese Communism'. I must say this sounded to me like saying that the Jews were 'allowed to live independent lives, according to their own customs, within the framework of the Third Reich'. Anyway, what we saw mostly was young children dancing to charming music, and I was told later that this was not any Oriental equivalent of rock or pop but classical folk music. It was very pleasing. And because these were the only films we'd ever seen of these people, we got the impression that they did nothing else but dance to classical music. It was as if American propaganda films sent to China showed the American people as one mammoth Mormon choir singing the *St Matthew Passion*.

The shock was in what the delightful children were doing to the music. The Mongol tots danced with rifles, the Thais with rifles and fixed bayonets. Evidently, there are some nations whose rulers have learned how to soothe the savagery of their system by marrying music to politics. For export only.

The 1980s

Bringing Up Baby

2 January 1981

You wake up under a strange ceiling and pad over to a strange window and look out on a sun just chasing the night away and suddenly lighting up a landscape that blinds your eyes. The valley's bone white and the forests on the mountains like stockades of thistledown. Every branch of every tree is bearing a sword of snow. The road that curves past this old farmhouse and up into the mountains is gleaming with ice. A car comes scudding by, and if you were brought up in what they call a temperate climate you may wonder for a moment how any car could hold a foot of the road. But in this part of the world, work and life have to go on in a planet of snow, and you couldn't drive anywhere if you didn't have snow tyres and four-wheel drive. You go off to the bathroom and take a peek at the two-way thermometer in the window. On the left column is the indoor temperature, on the right the outdoor. The left says 70 degrees precisely, and that's what the thermostat says, set for every room in the house. The outdoor temperature is ridiculous. Below freezing, the column turns blue. Below zero, it turns red. Well, something must be wrong. Turn on the radio and hear the man giving the ski conditions and then the weather forecast. He says, 'Twenty-eight inches base, six inches of fresh powder, the lifts are holding.' That's something you've never heard before. Lifts holding! My son-in-law tells me that means 'no downhill skiing'. A very rare prohibition, I gather. Why? The man goes on: 'Happy New Year, people. The temperature stands now at 34 degrees below zero and that's considerably warmer than it was during the night. But cross-country skiers should be warned that the wind chill factor is such that it feels like 80 degrees below zero.' This is so preposterous that it's impossible to take in, until you go out later in the brilliant midday light. We go out in turns, my son-in-law having warmed up the car. Ready, Adam, go. Zeb, go. Next their mother with a ten-week-old baby, a fat, faceless bundle of clothes. Then grandma. Then the old man. We're off, to call on a neighbour.

You'll gather we're in northern Vermont, and one of the striking things about life here during the Christmas holidays is that people shop and visit and hardly mention the weather. Any more than people in the Caribbean mention the temperature of the sea they swim in. This time, though, we did shake hands with this neighbouring family, and an old man said, 'a little nippy out there'. A young relation, visiting from Alaska, says, 'it's almost a relief to me. Where I come from it's been 60 below zero every day for the last three weeks.' The old man, if *I* call him an old man, he's an *old man*. He reminisces. He's a Vermonter, and he recalls the most biting cold he ever experienced. 'Once,' he says, 'I was in Scotland in July. It was my first and only time there. And we were in a little hotel by the sea. Well, it was a holiday, so what do I do but go in swimming. Holy smoke!' he says, 'you ever tried that? I went and bought a thermometer. I couldn't believe it. The water was 55 degrees – 55 degrees! I was out of that water quicker than a dog with fleas. It left a lifelong impression.'

This is my contribution to the theory of relativity. All such words as hot, cold, sweet, sour, dry, wet have no absolute meaning at all. They depend on what you heard from your parents in the place you were brought up in. You do wonder how they, the English, of all people, ever colonized and settled northern New England (a famous photographer once said that if America had been discovered at California and the colonizers had then moved east, New England, with its glacial soil and Arctic winters never would have been settled). But living up here for some days, you don't wonder that there's little talk about Mr Reagan's Cabinet appointments, or the hostages, or who's going to be or maybe has just been appointed Secretary of the Interior. Survival is all.

Missiles and laser beams are another matter. The first morning I came down to the kitchen, I found on the icebox (the refrigerator) door two notes, one practically a thesis written by my grandsons. The 8-year-old has printed his thesis out with painstaking precision. It says: 'The Cosmos is ever expanding, even as a tree grows, as a rocket is zooming through deep space, as a satellite is launched. There are more wonders on space, like we will send men to Saturn. We'll send people to stars or other universes. The vast Cosmos has more stars than there are single grains of sand on Earth. Isn't that unbelievable?' He's obviously hooked on Carl Sagan. The other note is from the 5-year-old and has been there since Christmas morning. It says: 'Mother, I am thankful for my X-wing fighter, my brown suit, my Millenium Falcon, and Eliza.' (Eliza is the new baby.) Both the boys are hipped on *Star Wars* and in all the reams of political stuff that comes on the evening television news. There's only one sort of item that makes them perk up: anything about the M-X missile or the proposed deployment of a new intercontinental what not. I set this down as a fact, without comment, except to say that I was once close to a scientist, a very good scientist and a sweet serious-minded man and devoted father. He forbade his sons ever to play with toy pistols or soldiers. One boy was frightened for life. The other went into the Marines.

I suppose every generation of young parents proceeds on a theory of bringing up children. I have in my time watched the waxing and waning of several fashions, but may I whisper to grandparents that it's important never to use that word in relation to the serious business of how to bring up a child. Every first-time mother is grateful for the fact that after centuries of trial and error, her generation has arrived finally at universal truth. I go back to the dark ages when babies were slapped for wetting their pants; then to the time when mothers stayed in the hospital with their newborn for about ten days. Then the pendulum swung and mothers were told to sit up and dangle their legs the first day and get out the third day at the latest. I am ashamed but secretly relieved to say that, in my time, the father stayed home and brooded, whereas it is now compulsory for the expectant father to attend fatherhood classes for several weeks beforehand and assist in person at the birth. My children's baby doctor was an enormously tall, gangling bony man with an amiable loose-limbed manner who regarded nothing that happened to babies as odd. He seemed to us, anyway, to sweep away, with his affable presence, dense fogs of Victorian superstition and old wives' tales. His physical presence did, however, terrify my daughter for a time. But we were as dogmatic as all young parents and thought he was one in a hundred. His name was Ben Spock, and I understand he went on to make quite a name for himself.

I don't know how far we've come from old Ben, but my daughter is up on every new movement in diet, environmentalism, baby care and the rest. And I must say I was astonished, when the baby cried, to see at hand an object which I thought had been banished since about 1920. It was what we in England called a dummy, and what Americans called a pacifier. The wheel, one of the wheels anyway, has come full circle. Thirty years ago, it was thought to be the most witless, primitive and ruinous device ever given to a baby. It was said to pull the upper teeth out, and it may well have been the reason why some of my college friends, otherwise fairly handsome, came to resemble Bugs Bunny. Well, Eliza has a dummy, but it is an orthodontic pacifier, approved by dentists. It is not just a blob of rubber. It looks more like the snout of a dolphin, curving up to stay under the upper gum without requiring too much outward pull to keep it in. (I hope they're right about this one.)

You'll gather, from these intensely domestic concerns that Washington, which is only six hundred miles south of here, seems as remote as Peking. I feel like Captain Scott at the Pole, except that if Captain Scott had had central heating, as well as a Swedish stove, and snow tyres, and an electric typewriter, a word computer, not to mention lashings of shrimp, pâté, chicken, geese, cakes and a huge plum pudding (because of grandpa's English origins, this un-American item is considerately included in the Christmas fare), Captain Scott would have retired to the House of Lords and died in bed.

Since we do not choose to drive into the village in what is now 31 degrees below zero to pick up the *New York Times*, we must fall back on the local paper, which is delivered to the door, come 30 below or 90 above. It is a journal not to be sneezed at. Apart from the usual international and Washington stories, and the numbing pictures of the hostages, there is a local item that makes a four-column headline. A federal court has struck down a law, which banned highway billboards in the neighbouring state of Maine. This disturbs Vermont, whose extraordinary beauty has gone unsullied since 1968 when it passed a law banning every form of outdoor advertising throughout the state. The court's ground is that outdoor advertising is a form of freedom of speech, guaranteed by the Constitution. We can only hope that if it goes to the Supreme Court, the nine old men will decide that the screaming defilement of the highways and byways and valleys and mountains is not a form of free speech the Founding Fathers were eager to preserve.

The art students of the local high school have put on an exhibition of a life-size group of Jimmy Who, Donald Duck, Richard Nixon, Abe Lincoln and Mick Jagger playing a silent hand of stud poker. And the local church of the Nativity has still on display a crib to remind us of what Christmas is about. If this is rather a humdrum thing, we see on the television that in Bethlehem, there were soldiers (in full battledress) on duty at the site of Jesus' birth, to keep an eye on the crowds flocking around Manger Square – which is now a parking lot. Well, as the taxi drivers say, 'You can't stop progress, can you?'

Attempted Assassination of President Reagan

3 April 1981

Our plane was coming in from San Francisco, nosing in through endless layers of cotton wool, with the rain streaming against the windows and no land in sight, till we suddenly spun out of a ground mist and hit the runway. As the brakes roared on and the plane slowed to make the long taxi to the terminal, the captain came on the public address system. He said there was something he wanted to tell us, 'not by way of sensationalism' (he said), about something that had happened in mid-afternoon. I assumed there'd been some trouble with the plane, and he had sensibly waited to tell us about it till we were safe and sound. He was mumbling very low into his microphone. I think he didn't want to sound 'sensational', but unfortunately he could hardly be heard. It was something about the President and a secretary. Then he said a little more clearly that two and a half hours ago an assassination attempt had been made on the President, and he was now in surgery in a Washington hospital. It was something he thought we ought to know.

At Kennedy (which used to be Idlewild Airport before the assassination of that President), people waited for their baggage, and I don't think the most imaginative or hyped-up reporter could have seen anything different in the behaviour of the people, from that of any other day. Maybe there was less jocular small talk. Most people looked tired and patient. Perhaps by now we are resigned to atrocity, as infantrymen get used to seeing dead bodies.

We happened to get possibly the only Chinese cab driver at the airport who spoke little English and had no radio. So it was nearly an hour before we were home, and turning on the television and seeing there – almost like a cruel replay of Dallas, 1963 – startled Secret Service men, people falling to the ground, and a sudden scrum of men huddled over a young man.

Fortunately, for the country, the anxious hours were blessedly few. The first authoritative spokesman, the man who conducted an evening press conference at the hospital, was one Dr Dennis O'Leary, the dean of clinical affairs at George Washington University Hospital. By great good luck, he was one doctor in a thousand, in that he had an immediate air of candour and authority; he sensed in a flash what sort of language would enlighten people without alarming them. He had humour, when it was appropriate to have it; he was responsive to intelligent questions and courteously non-committal to idiotic questions. And he was able, as doctors very rarely are, to translate the abominable jargon of his trade into sensible and even subtle English that any of us could understand. Of course, the fates were with him. The President had been jaunty about his wound, he had the luck of what Dr O'Leary called 'fine physiological health . . . a very young 70-year-old', and the bullet had stayed inches away from a fatal point of entry. Still, looking back on it, I think we all owe an enormous debt to Dr O'Leary. He is young enough to have come to take for granted what actually scandalized an older generation: the expectation that the press would want to know all the medical details and had a right to have them. This tradition is very new, though we were already inured to the historical shift in journalistic practice when President Eisenhower had his heart attack. Day after day in Denver his doctor came before the media, and described everything in great detail, down to the consistency of the President's bowel movements. Ever since then, a public man hides from the press the symptoms of any affliction, however mild, at his peril. Obviously, it has become harder and harder for a doctor to instruct the layman in the facts without leaving little loopholes through which the dumber sort of journalist will fish out lurid inferences.

So what Dr O'Leary did, on the evening of the wounding of the President, was to restore the morale of the country in a decent and authoritative way. He was helped, of course, by being able to report the heartening fact that the President had shown an almost puckish bravery of spirit. Dr O'Leary deserves the Medal of Freedom – especially because the scene in the White House, where you would properly expect authority to take hold, was a muddled, and for a time, a faintly alarming one. I'm afraid the culprit here was General Haig, the Secretary of State. It is quite true that he was, very shortly after the shooting, the senior member of the Cabinet who happened to be on hand. He at once decided that since the Vice President was flying back from Texas, he – Mr Haig – was now in charge of the government. Of course, he wasn't; President Reagan was, until either the President declared himself disabled to continue in office, or the Vice President and a majority of the Cabinet told (in writing) the pro tem President of the Senate and the Speaker of the House that the President was unable to discharge his duties. Then, and then only, the Vice President becomes Acting President. This is all set forth quite precisely in the 25th Amendment to the Constitution. And suppose that the President dies, and after him – or with him – the Vice President, the succession then goes to the Speaker of the House. *He* is third in line. But Mr Haig, when all about him might have been losing their heads, rushed on to television with darting eyes and a sweaty forehead. He was nervous and he was dogmatic. He was, he said, 'in control'. He could have been in control in a purely practical sense at the moment, but his fatal remark came when he was asked why. He mentioned the Constitution and repeated the gaffe that the Secretary of State succeeds after the President and the Vice President, thus showing, as one commentator put it, 'an incredible lack of understanding of constitutional succession'.

There is, however, another line of succession, which has to do with the command structure of the military, the Pentagon. When Mr Haig got away from his unfortunate performance on television, he went back to what is known in the White House as the Situation Room, the place where crucial military decisions are made, invariably in the presence of the President, who, we should remember, is the Commander-in-Chief of all the armed forces. There, the Secretary of Defense, Mr Weinberger, felt it his duty to tell Mr Haig that he was not in charge of that structure either. The command passes from the President to the Vice President and then to the Secretary of Defense – nobody but Mr Weinberger. Altogether, an acutely unhappy time for Secretary Haig. But he, and the people, were put right at once by the chief Washington correspondents of two networks.

One of the more stupid but I suppose inevitable questions put to Dr O'Leary, of all political neutrals, was whether or not there was evidence of a conspiracy. He wouldn't think of commenting on that. And from what we know, and we know a great deal about the life and character of the pathetic John Hinckley, he was no more of a conspirator than the equally pathetic 18-year-old bartender who fired twice on Constitution Hill at the very young Queen Victoria and missed. Edward Oxford (this was his name) did not have a repeater. Unlike John Hinckley, he did not have the means to spray half a dozen shots in two seconds at several targets. Hinckley, at this time anyway, appears to be a sick, and lovesick, young man acting out a fantasy with a girl he had never met, and meaning, more than anything, to make himself important by a violent act.

Inevitably, old arguments have been brought up and old morals have been drawn. The campaign for stricter control of handguns (Washington, DC, by the way, has one of the strictest laws, as strict as anything that might be written into a federal law) takes on new strength, through indignation, after every murder or attempted murder of a prominent person. It raged after John Kennedy's death, then waned; raged again after the assassination of Martin Luther King, Jr., the paralysing of Governor George Wallace, the death of Bobby Kennedy, the shooting of John Lennon. But these crusades always fade away, not, as many angry people charge, because the rifle lobby is very powerful in Washington, which it is, but because millions of Americans are scared enough of violence on the streets and against their homes to feel that a law to ban handguns would render the citizen helpless against the criminal, who will always get a gun somehow. At any rate, there is not likely to be much success in the next crusade, since President Reagan himself is strongly against gun control. His solution, as Governor of California, was, and still is, a compulsory sentence of from five to fifteen years in jail for anyone committing a crime while in possession of a gun.

I leave the grave and undoubtedly sincere moralizing about the sickness of this country, of our time, to others. If violence is indeed a special sickness of our age, it is universal, and nobody so far has come up with a cure. But I will end by reminding you that such characters as John Hinckley seem to be around at all times, especially in a country which offers to a fugitive the escape-hatch of a continent. The proper comparison between violence in America is not with any one country but with the whole of Europe. On any given day, the Protective Research Section of the United States Secret Service has on file the names of not less than fifty thousand persons who have written threatening or obscene letters to the incumbent President. Fifteen hundred new letters are added every month. Repeaters are tracked down, simply from their letters, and the Secret Service claims an average of 98 per cent of such people are apprehended, many of them tried and put away. John Hinckley, it appears now, was one of the 2 per cent who slipped through the net.

The Fourth of July

2 July 1982

Next door to my apartment house, or, if it helps, block of flats, is a small three-storey house in a French style, what used to be called a carriage house. Thirty years ago or more, it was owned and lived in by a wealthy New York eccentric. His most endearing habit was that of dressing up, as men did in those days, dressing up in white tie and tails for the first night of the Metropolitan Opera season, going down there and standing on his head on the sidewalk outside the opera house. This feat was always received with applause by the passers-by. Well, he died years ago, and the Metropolitan openings have never been quite the same since. His house was sold and turned into a school. It was the first private school in Manhattan that truly integrated whites and blacks. Through the 1950s and 1960s there'd been several so-called progressive schools (disciples of the theories of John Dewey) which boasted a few token blacks who were there if their parents could afford the fees. This massaged the social conscience of the whites and presented the black children with the unenviable task of pretending to belong to the upper-middle-class white WASP culture, without emotional strain. But the people next door, the young couple who twenty years ago set up this mixed school, started with something like 30 per cent black children and now the races are about equally divided; I mean integrated. The blacks come from – I was going to say all sorts of backgrounds, but the social range of blacks anywhere in this country is pretty narrow. (I don't want to seem to be making a snide comment; we should still not forget that at the last count I'm aware of, about ten years ago, more black children went to college in this country than white children in the British Isles.) However, whereas the first lot of black children next door were nearly all from poor Harlem families, by now there's more than a sprinkling of the new black middle class, whose parents work in offices, banks, the professions, all the places where, thirty years ago, the work force was uniformly white. How do the majority of these poorish black children get to the school? They are there on financial support, scholarships and the like, raised by the school itself.

Well, I was coming along the block to my entrance the other morning and could barely thread my way through a pile-up of duffel bags and kitbags and battered little suitcases and string bags and – bags. Sitting on them were the tots, holding hands or sulkily refusing to hold hands, with their mothers. But most of them were hopping around as merry as crickets. They were waiting for a bus, a bus half the size of a city block, which eventually glided up. It looked like an air-conditioned mausoleum with its dark brown tinted windows. It had printed on the side 'Adirondack Bus Tours Inc.' I knew then what the children were doing with their duffel bags. They were off like a vast army of young New Yorkers between the ages of, say, 7 and 12, to summer camp. And this lot was off to the Adirondacks: a lush, mountainous region of upstate New York, much of it protected by state law, where 4,000–5,000-foot mountains are carpeted – bristled would be better – with forests of spruce, pine and hemlock and tower over a couple of hundred lakes, naturally, a summer mecca for tourists and campers and school camps (a winter mecca, by the way, for such things as Olympic skiing).

The sight of all these small fry bundling themselves and their bags into the bus was a gladsome one and a sharp reminder that school was out everywhere, and that this is the weekend of the Fourth: Independence Day – the Fourth of July, falling this year on a Sunday and therefore, according to recent custom and union insistence, making Monday a holiday too. The Fourth is understandably the oldest of American national holidays, since it celebrates the adoption by the original thirteen colonies of the Declaration, signed two days earlier, that proclaimed their independence of England. Of the especially American national holidays, there are only three that are truly national: the Fourth, George Washington's birthday and Thanksgiving. Columbus Day, hailing the discovery of the New World itself, is not celebrated in Alaska. Certainly the word has got there by now, but at five or six thousand miles from old Christopher's landfall, it must seem unreal. Lincoln's birthday, a stranger might assume, is a cause for national celebration, but to this day it is politely ignored in the South. George Washington's birthday, you would swear, is celebrated in all the fifty states. And so it now is, but only since 1955, when the Governor of Idaho had to be nudged, by yours truly, with the sinister reminder that his state was the only one in the Union that failed to recognize Washington's birthday as a legal holiday. I'm proud to say that I have in my possession, suitable for framing, a letter from the then Governor with a hasty postscript, in his own hand, which says: 'A bill is now before me for signature. It will have my approval, and February 22nd, 1955, will be a legal holiday in Idaho. – Robert E. Smylie, Governor.'

But there have been no such oversights about the celebration of the Fourth of July. The Fourth of July is for everybody. Within a year of the signing of the Declaration, the main cities of the thirteen emancipated states got busy with parades, the firing of guns, ringing of bells, the explosion of fireworks. Boston started the custom of getting things going with a prayer. Charleston, South Carolina, was I believe, the first city enlightened enough to require the drinking of thirteen toasts by way of saluting the independence of the thirteen colonies. Philadelphia twisted the knife in the wound of the British lion by forcing a German band to provide the music. (They were Hessians, and the Hessians, unlike the French and, at the last minute, the Spanish, had bet on the wrong winner. The Hessians had been hired by England to fight the colonial rebels, and the Philadelphia band was made up of musical prisoners of war.)

After the new nation got its second and its permanent form of government, with the adoption of the Constitution of the United States, the custom of high jinks on the Fourth spread to smaller towns. And by the time, during the next sixty-odd years, that pioneers had pushed through the Appalachians, across the prairie and the Rockies and the High Sierras, the annual festival had reached California. Once the festivities spread to country towns, the celebrations became less formal and less grand, but no less fervent. The bawling politician, who made a heyday of the Fourth, came in and only gradually faded away. But there were everywhere picnics, potato-sack races, and contests in eating the most watermelons or catching the greasiest pig. Most of this has gone now and been supplanted by rock concerts, jazz festivals, in the Western states by rodeos, and in California by giant barbecues, log-rolling contests, Hollywood Bowl Super-recitals, and supermarket specials of two jumbo burgers for the price of one.

An early piece I dug up, from a historical dictionary, says: 'Throughout the two centuries, however, fireworks, great and small, have held a foremost place.' So they have, but not without much hand-wringing from the city and state fathers. Fireworks, including even crackers and sparklers, are illegal in New York, New Jersey, Connecticut and many more states.

But this is a fact of life that most people consider, as they considered the prohibition law, more of a nuisance than a prohibition. There's something grave and dotty, and typically American, it seems to me, about a government commission (the Federal Consumer Product Safety Commission) and the statement it put out this weekend. Fireworks are illegal, right? Right. So, the commissioner says: 'Fireworks sometimes do things they are not supposed to. People should be extremely careful.' Last year more than eleven thousand Americans were treated in hospitals for injuries from fireworks that did things they are not supposed to. The Commission, acting responsibly in the knowledge that fireworks are illegal, has now put out seven rules or precautions to help people set off fireworks safely, such as: make sure the fuses are attached; don't use leaky fireworks; have adults on hand to supervise fire-cracking children; ignite fireworks outdoors. And, my favourite: 'Call the local police or fire department if you are unsure about the law.' The law, that is, that you are going to break.

Of course, I guess the big deal on the Fourth of July weekend for most Americans is neither a watermelon contest nor a rodeo nor a rock concert. It is flocking to the stadiums to watch baseball, or, and I should guess many more millions are doing it, sitting in the living room with two or three buddies, getting out the six-pack of beer, pulling down the shades against the intrusion of the noonday sun and *watching* baseball on the box. A big minority will be watching the Wimbledon finals on the box, and a smaller minority will be watching golf. A smaller minority still, say no more than fifteen million, will be banging a tennis ball or scuffing a golf ball, and wishing they'd stayed with tossing horseshoes.

An odd minority, showbiz stars and agents and such, at the end of a winter run, will be off to open up their houses at the end of Long Island. This is the weekend they used to trek like homing pigeons to the Adirondacks where the little blacks and whites are going. That reminds me of a story involving the great musical comedy, rather operetta, composer: Sigmund Romberg. He had a summer house up there in the Adirondacks. He was a bridge addict, and had a favourite partner. One time, they played through the night, and as the final hand was dealt, Romberg and his pal gambled all or nothing on the last hand. They were about to make a killing. The partner picked up his hand. He had one heart, leaned back, and as airily as possible, started to hum the tune of Romberg's great hit: 'One Alone'. No visible recognition from Romberg. They lost. The furious pal took Romberg in a corner afterwards and said, 'Rommy, what's the matter with you? I gave you the sign!' What sign? 'I started to hum, "One Alone", my heart was yours, for Pete's sake.' Romberg, a vain man, said, 'Ach! Who knows from lyrics?'

Old Man Reagan

12 October 1984

We have just over three weeks to go to the Presidential election, which is always the first Tuesday in November. And while all the reporters travelling with both camps, and all the commentators and all the pollsters, have unravelled and re-ravelled every possible 'issue' that might decide the outcome, suddenly, out of the blue, there comes looming up an issue that was dead and buried four years ago. A man from Mars who knew nothing about American politics might have guessed at it as an important issue, but that would only have shown his charming ignorance of the whole subject. It is the issue of President Reagan's age.

Surely it's always been there. Well, no, it hasn't. Of course, when Mr Reagan was nominated by the Republicans four years ago, it was a lively theme. Here was a man who, if he was elected, would within a month or so of his inauguration be the oldest President ever to have lived in the White House. In other words, no other President, at the very end of his term, had been older than this one would be at the beginning of it. The issue no sooner came up than it gradually, and then quickly, began to disappear. Let me remind you how this happened. Many of you will recall what turned out to be the crucial television debate between President Carter and Mr Reagan. Mr Carter was then 56. Mr Reagan was 69. Many months before that debate, in the late winter when the primary elections were getting under way, the Democrats were going around with mock glum faces masking secret giggles and saying, 'Just think, by the end of this man's first term, he'll be 73.' Mr Reagan's campaign team, whom nobody knew much about at the time (except the California politicians who knew it was a very smart team indeed), quickly thought up an artful tactic. They encouraged Mr Reagan, as he barnstormed around the country, to bring up the issue himself, in the form of chuckly jokes. He'd say something like: 'Neither George Washington nor Thomas Jefferson would have stood for the abuse of government we've been seeing in the past twenty years. I know, because both of them told me so.' Things like that. It was a winning ploy in both senses of the term. The clincher was the Reagan team's decision, just before the New Hampshire primary, to organize and advertise public celebrations of Mr Reagan's sixty-ninth birthday, when he was seen on television acknowledging well-wishers and cutting a cake with a comically shaking hand. That ploy dissolved the issue in the most effective way that a grave topic *can* be dissolved – in laughter.

Of course, the Democrats went on mumbling warnings about the enormous strains of the Presidency and what it was likely to do to the health of a man over the turn of his seventies. Anyway, we'd all get a good long look at both men in the coming Presidential debates. What I've called the crucial debate was the one in which Mr Reagan responded to warnings from Mr Carter of what life under Reagan might be. Usually Mr Carter would hint at a statistic which Mr Reagan would then disarm, suggesting Mr Carter had got it all wrong. The telling, the triumphant phrase, accompanied by a regretful, almost a forgiving shrug was: 'There you go again.' But what was far more powerful, far more reassuring as a sign of Reagan's health, and blitheness, was the sight and sound, the demeanour of Reagan matched against the demeanour of Carter. What we saw was Reagan as a natural optimist against Carter, a cautionary school principal. Reagan, the confident purveyor of half-truths (and sometimes of howling boners) against a Carter insisting that life is real and earnest and painfully complicated. Reagan the broadcaster, who had learned through years of practice and as many as fourteen speeches a day on the road as a salesman for General Electric, had learned to be his best self talking to neighbours in a room, against a more thoughtful but verbose lay preacher addressing a congregation. And – here was the rub – a seeming young Reagan against a seeming old Carter.

None of us enquires about a man's age before deciding how bright or healthy or vigorous he is. We react to his appearance of life, and only then ask how old he might be. And, those of us who know 60-year-olds doddering in mind or body or both never get the feeling, watching President Reagan, that he is any special age at all. At least, we didn't get the feeling until last Sunday. That's when 'the issue' raised its wrinkled head again.

The debate. The television debate between the two principal nominees – the so-called Presidential debate – is by now not only a fixture every four years, it has become as compulsory a duty as if it had been laid down in the Constitution. It is, of course, a new thing. I don't know why I say that! Those of us who were already mature or sentient, shall I say, in 1960 must realize with a shock that there is a generation, already in its mid-twenties, that was imbibing mother's milk when the first television debate took place, between Vice President Richard Nixon and Senator John F. Kennedy. What most of us recall from that debate is the *appearance* of Nixon against the appearance of Kennedy. There were other debates after that first one, but the contrasting appearance of the two men, and what their appearance implied, was as the lawyers say, controlling. Before we saw them together, Kennedy was suffering from the age issue, in reverse. He was only 43. If he won, he would be, after Theodore Roosevelt, the second youngest President, on the day of his inauguration. Mr Nixon was 47, a fact that now shocks oldsters to recall, because on television he looked a generation older than Kennedy. Mr Nixon, that first and, as it turned out, fateful, evening had been campaigning between the Pacific and the East Coast. He'd had a very short night. The make-up man had failed to mask what was then known as a five o'clock shadow, but which looked at the time more like a three-day shadow. In short, Nixon looked like Bela Lugosi. Kennedy looked like a choirboy. Even President Truman had wondered whether the Republic could be safely entrusted to such a youngster. Lyndon Johnson, who had lost the nomination, felt similar misgivings about the safety of America in the hands of what he called 'eh beardless youth'. Well, in the result, Kennedy's boy-scout appearance worked for him: he was completely unintimidated by the expertise of the Vice President. His grasp of facts and policies was at least as firm. So the impression he left was that of a boy prodigy.

Last Sunday, before the Reagan–Mondale debate, I didn't read anything by way of commentary, or speculation, that even hinted the age issue would rise and dither from its grave. If we had a preconception about the failings of both men, it was one summed up in a cartoon. Two boxed pictures: one showed Reagan asleep at a Cabinet meeting; the other showed Mondale addressing his potential Cabinet, and the Cabinet was asleep. The public image of Mondale, which has bedevilled him since the start, has been that of an earnest speaker, chop-chopping away at his opponent, one stroke at a time, with no emotional rise and fall to a long speech. Everybody knows by now what is most successful about President Reagan: the ease, the intimacy, the emotion rising almost against his own wish, the directness and simplicity. Reagan turned from a 'B'-film actor into an 'A'-film actor of the quality of Gary Cooper.

Well, on Sunday we saw a new Mondale: a courteous and firm debater, gutsy and graceful at the same time. We saw a Reagan, as an incumbent President must always be in these debates, on the defensive. He had no script beautifully printed on a wrap-around, invisible teleprompter. He was on his feet and on his own. And he was nervous, and hesitant. And when he pulled out of the bag his old, famous line 'There you go again', Mondale was ready for it, like an outfielder ready for the catch that would clinch the World Series. Mr Reagan did not know (until later) that the Mondale team, working on a mock debate, had given Mondale six different ways of reacting to just that line. In the event, he leaped in with, 'D'you know when you said that? D'you know when you said that? When President Carter said you were going to cut Medicare. And you said, "oh no, there you go again". And what did you do right after the election? You went out and tried to cut twenty billion dollars out of Medicare!' (In fact, 'right after the election' was two years later. It didn't matter on Sunday night.)

So, the result has been a whole literature, from columnists, and gerontologists, and various medical men, on the quality of physical stamina and mental alertness to be expected from a man, a President, between the ages of 73 and 77. The White House pretended, for a day or two, to regard the whole thing as frivolous. But on Wednesday it released the latest medical report on the President, backing up its assertion of a robust physique and a sharp mind with enough statistical details to satisfy the fussiest clinician: from alkaline phosphotase through segmented neutrophils to mean corpuscular haemoglobin. This means he's in great shape! But what Sunday's debate recalled to me was not the physique, it was Benjamin Franklin's 'By my rambling digressions I perceive myself to be growing old'.

The consensus of the pollsters that Mondale was the overwhelming winner last Sunday has certainly brought a spark of life to Mondale's campaign. It will tantalize a larger audience for the next, and last, debate between the two men. It probably won't in the short run of three weeks cut significantly into Reagan's handsome lead. It may, however, stir new misgivings in a lot of people about the *image* of President Reagan they'll be seeing in the long run, two, three years from now.

Inaugurals – On and Off

25 January 1985

'Beautiful but dangerous.' It's a phrase that's been used, I imagine, about every siren from Cleopatra to Ava Gardner. I doubt it has been used before, as it was last Monday morning, about Washington, DC. Thomas Jefferson was one of the old colonials who were disgusted with the choice of Washington as a capital city. He called it 'That Indian place in the wilderness'. More often it was called a swamp, or 'a notable hotbed of vapors and disease'. These nasty words objected to the fact that Washington is nowhere more than a few hundred feet above sea level, and being on a river on the edge of the South, it has, in summer, such a humid stew of a climate that for many years – it may still be so – the British Foreign Office gave the ambassador to Washington and his staff a special tropical allowance, the idea being that they could retreat in summer to a hill station, which they did, to the Blue Ridge Mountains of Virginia. Since the arrival of the jet aeroplane, however, they've tended to escape to the hill stations of the Cotswolds.

In winter, as all the books and the records will tell you, Washington has a mild, damp, shivery climate, much like London, somewhere in the high thirties, low forties Fahrenheit, rarely getting very much below freezing. But last Monday it went to 34 degrees below freezing, or 2 below zero Fahrenheit. A high wind on Sunday evening and a whirl of snow flurries reduced the feel of the air, what we now call the wind-chill factor, to about 15 below zero. It's no weather for man or beast, and especially not for five thousand participants – half of them youngsters – in uniformed jackets and miniskirts. On the Sunday morning, one or two hardy detachments of these high school cheerleaders and bands had been out on the streets rehearsing for the great inauguration parade. They didn't stay there long. Some of them discovered that if you don't have ear muffs, or a ski mask, and something to cover the nose, it would take only about five or six minutes for the first burning sensation that precedes frostbite. The valves on wind instruments froze up. The skin of several drums cracked. Rifles jammed. An ensign had the unique experience of watching the standard he was bearing snap and break in mid-air.

So, on Sunday evening, the President sadly called in the Senator from Maryland who was in charge of the Presidential Inaugural Committee, and they sat down with a doctor or two, and the whole thing, the four-hour outdoor triumphal parade, was called off. The doctors were not thinking primarily about the President – he would be cosy in a heated reviewing stand behind a six-inch layer of bulletproof glass. They were thinking of the five thousand soldiery, the teenagers on floats, the marching delegations from most of the states, the need for fleets of ambulances and heaven knows how many people carried indoors for emergency treatment. The only delegation that could be confidently certified as fit for public exposure was an Alaskan dog-sled team. And, of course, they were gung-ho and ready to go. But it would have been odd and pretty funny, to have only the Alaskans mushing down the vast emptiness of Pennsylvania Avenue. So the word went out, only a little before midnight, that the huge festival, which took three months to plan, was off, and that a makeshift demonstration of high school and other bands would be put on in a sports arena outside Washington. A hundred and forty thousand spectators were instructed to turn in their tickets for a refund. Every one of them would have been required, on Monday morning, to pass through the sort of metal detectors they have at airports. The loss of money from the intending spectators was figured at about two million dollars. Anyone who has ever put together even a band concert in a town square can only guess at the hundreds of organizers who got no sleep on Sunday night. The most frantic of these insomniacs were the presidents, or more probably, the executive vice presidents in charge of sales at the television networks. In all, more than a hundred sponsors had to be re-slotted or reimbursed. The only consolation for thousands of people from the hinterland who had flown into Washington over the weekend, and were now comfortably marooned in their hotels, was that they were not back home. For most of the continent, including, freakishly, the South all the way down to the Gulf of Mexico, was assaulted by an atrocious storm, in the South worse than anything this century. The happiest refugees I talked to were from Chicago, where it was 27 below zero Fahrenheit – the whole city cloaked in ice – even the fire engines and their gear petrified to look like huge abstract sculptures from the Ice Age.

I must say, speaking as a tucked-up viewer in a warm room overlooking the ice of the Central Park reservoir – that the effect of taking the inauguration ceremony indoors, inside the Rotunda of the Capitol, was to give this usual circus an unintended dignity. Only about eight hundred people could be got in there. And the sequence of events – a prayer, a hymn, the swearing in first of the Vice President, then of the President, his speech, the Lord's Prayer, a benediction. I think it's one of the very few Inaugurals, perhaps the only one of modern times, to which old Thomas Jefferson would have given his blessing. Jefferson, the third President of the United States, but a young man very much in on the founding of the Republic – he did the final draft of the Declaration of Independence – had very firm ideas about the limits of ceremony and public display that were proper for a republic. George Washington, the first President, arrived for this first Inaugural in full dress military uniform. He had a coach flanked by outriders. It was a small, smart military ceremony, but by our lights not much more elaborate than a performance by an amateur dramatic society. Nevertheless, it was too much for Jefferson. And, when soon afterwards, Washington held levees, made a formal speech to the Congress, and enjoyed watching the procession of Congress in a body to reply to it, Jefferson was so upset by what he took to be 'symptoms of a change of principle' that he wrote to the President saying that (these things) 'are not at all in character with the simplicity of republican governments, and looking as if wistfully to [the practices] of European courts'.

When the time came for Jefferson's own inauguration, he renounced all such pomp. He got on his horse, rode up to the Capitol, tethered his nag, went inside, made his speech – almost inaudibly – went out, mounted his horse and rode off back to his boarding house, where finding the places at the head of the dinner table taken, he sat down below the salt.

I suppose the last glimpse we've had of anything like such 'republican simplicity' was the memorable scene, at the inauguration of Jimmy Carter, when he got out of his gleaming limousine and walked down Pennsylvania Avenue hand in hand with his wife. A gesture such as that would not possibly be allowed today, when two or three millions of those inauguration dollars went on electronic and weapons security the like of which there has never been before but which there will certainly be again.

When it was all over, the television commentators – deprived of the parade, and the Cadillacs and the chinchillas and the crowds and the clothes and uniforms and bands and general glitz – these poor professionals, found that the cameras stationed all over town could show nothing but the enormous wide avenues in the sunlight empty of all humans, as if the bomb had dropped. They checked in from time to time with their own roving commentators on the streets. They were there, muffled to the eyebrows, lonely steaming sentinels. 'Anything happening out there?' one anchorman cried hopefully. The man came back: 'Nothing out here but us electronic chickens.' It was sad and comical. All these millions gone to erect miles of stands nobody would sit in, the grandeur of a block-long reviewing stand, with nobody there to review except, just for a quick darting moment, I noticed, one small, bewildered sparrow.

So the commentators had to fall back on talking about the mostly invisible hero of it all. Ronald Reagan. The enormity of his landslide. How come this 'B'-movie actor had swept the country twice? Old liberals who had spent four years scorning or pitying Reagan now thought again. The most interesting of the rafts of big men brought in to meditate was the old Governor of California whom Reagan had trounced seventeen years ago, Edmund 'Pat' Brown. 'We Democrats in California', he said, 'made the mistake the whole Democratic party made a dozen years later: we mightily underrated him as a politician, as a leader.'

And now that the party's over, the most beetle-browed writers and commentators are looking at inflation, down to an eighteen-year low, unemployment holding steady, employment up at about 350,000 a month, the promise, at least, of talks with the Russians. But mostly, the old pros and the old politicos look at him and listen to him and have come to envy his effortless gift for being, like no other living politician, as natural, and easy, and affable in public as he is in private, before a crowd or before two or three. So that when they hear him say, looking all of us straight in the eyes, that his own vision of America is of a country 'hopeful, big-hearted, idealistic, daring, decent and fair' well, we forget much of the dubious shenanigans of some of his Cabinet, and the CIA. We see Ronald Reagan standing in for Jefferson, and Lincoln, and Gary Cooper as the marshal, and Robert Redford as a fearless reporter, and we say, as an ageing Washington friend of mine said, 'I hunger to believe – or hope – it's so.'

Memories of 11 November

15 November 1985

As I sit down to record this talk – a little earlier than usual, since I am in San Francisco, six thousand miles away from its destination at Broadcasting House – I cannot help noticing the bizarre coincidence that it is the one thousand nine hundred and eighteenth talk in this series, and that it is being recorded on Monday the 11th. So, if this were a newspaper dispatch, it would bear the dateline 'Letter from America 1918, the 11th of November.'

I suppose that is a date which now has to be taught in schools, since most of the people who lived through it, in France, in Russia, in every part of Australia, India, New Zealand, not to mention Germany and Austria and Turkey – are dead and gone. But for those of us still around, it is as solemn and as indelible as any date in our lifetime. On the eleventh hour of the eleventh day of the eleventh month, in 1918, what *we* called the Great War, and then the World War, and then ruefully, the First World War, and now what is known to younger generations as simply 'The 14–18 War' was all over. I was up at the first flicker of dawn, because our newspaper had promised the day before that it would print on the 11th the terms of the Armistice. I took out several pages of what we then called cartridge paper, and, in a laborious but pretty fast script for a 9-year-old, I copied out the entire document. I gummed the pages together in a long scroll, rolled it as stage plays and early movies had taught us to believe was the proper shape of a diplomatic document, tied it with a little red, white and blue ribbon, and marched off around our seaside town, my left hand in my mother's hand, my right clutching this state document. (It should have been to the neighbours an early warning signal of the emergence of a ham.) It was, I recall, a crisp and sunny November day. But the only other memory, which is as sharp and mouth-watering as last night's dinner, is a shop window. After our walkabout – on the way home – we passed by what was then called the confectioner's. I imagine today they are called pastry boutiques, just as in Paris, the chicest boutique I know calls itself simply Le Shop. Anyway, a confectioner's window was, of all shops in wartime, the most barren, the most pitifully denuded of all shops' windows. Sometimes, there were two or three loaves of brown bread. And sometimes, there was none. But, on that still, blissful, bright November morning, there stood, glistening in the centre of the empty window, a cut-glass cake stand. And on the stand stood a bun, a round bun. And on the top of the bun was a circle of snow? Ice? No, of white icing, something I had never seen before. It was an iced bun, what Americans call a cupcake. It was, for the long moment we stared at it, a thrilling symbol of the fact that we had come through.

Last Monday, I paused in this reminiscence, as the clock of San Francisco's nearby Grace Cathedral struck eleven. I paused and looked out down on the graceful little rectangular park that surmounts Nob Hill. The hour struck, but nobody else was pausing. Two tots were being pushed on the swings. Two mothers were chatting away. An old Chinese man in a black suit was doing his morning exercises under a tree in the grave, slow-motion dance style of his race. The cars whisked by. People bent forward, staggered up the practically vertical incline of Taylor Street, or leaned back and pattered down. Nobody went in or out of the cathedral. I felt uncomfortably like a visitor from another planet, another century. I don't know for how many years, at that hour, on that day, and in how many countries, everything stopped for precisely two minutes. Streetcars, buses, motor cars, people – the men doffing their hats, everybody standing stock-still. There was the most unearthly silence in all great cities. And two minutes later, everything started up and soon the cities were roaring again. It must be twenty years, at least, since this stunning and admirable custom ended. Perhaps it isn't admirable, after all, or after a time. To forget old enmities, old wars, is necessary for the sanity of the living. At any rate, the two-minute silence is long gone, and I should guess, forgotten by most of the world's peoples. And, you can't go on for ever calling 11 November Armistice Day. In this country, it has been re-christened Veterans' Day, to commemorate the veterans of all the American wars, from the first, the triumphant one that ended two hundred years ago, to the last, Vietnam, the bitterest lost one. And on Sunday in Washington, on a balmy morning, several thousand men and women and children, a silent troop of unforgetting mothers and widows and sisters and fathers, took their turn to touch what is surely the boldest and most sombre of all war memorials, the vast, black stone wall on which are chiselled 58,022 names, the men who died in combat in Vietnam.

In the past day or two, I have read a lot of newspapers. Because of its place in the time zones, San Francisco can offer you at breakfast not only the *Los Angeles Times* as well as the local newspapers, but also that morning's *New York Times* and London *Times*. I have read, or scanned, hundreds of pages but only here in the *San Francisco Chronicle* have I seen a piece devoted entirely to recalling the first Armistice Day, the eleventh of November, and what it meant to a generation or two that is now white-haired or gone for good. This was a piece by Herb Caen, a local columnist, who is San Francisco's resident Mr Pepys. He remarked on how the importance of the day has waned and added regretfully that 'too many of our [national] holidays are disappearing or becoming homogenized. As school kids, we were so proud to remember the 12th of February as Lincoln's birthday, and February 22nd as Washington's, but now they have been telescoped into a long weekend, so much better for business, so much more convenient.'

This is literally true. Whatever day of the week 22 February fell on, the entire nation used to close its businesses and schools. Store windows displayed pictures or busts of George Washington and gave him a swag or drape of the Stars and Stripes. (I ought to tell you, though, that while on Lincoln's birthday many states performed the same obeisance for old Abe, 12 February was never a national holiday; and no President ever dared proclaim it as such, so long as the South retained its own resentful image of Lincoln as a tyrant at worst, at best a Northern conqueror. To this day, one hundred and twenty years after the end of the Civil War – most Southern cities and towns, and they are embraced by a third of the nation's geography, don't exactly make a fetish of ignoring Lincoln's birthday: they pay it the passing tribute of a nod, and go about their business.) So it seems that while many decent solemn dates dim and vanish, the bitter taste of others keeps its tang.

I noticed in the long spring commemoration of the end of the Second World War in Europe, the hideous fate of the Jews in the Holocaust was, properly, retold and mourned over till, however, there came a point when I, for one, began to feel uneasy that this necessary but prolonged act of remembrance might have the opposite effect to what was intended: to stir, in sullen or bigoted people, their old anti-Semitic impulses. This is not the sort of fear that respectable commentators put into print or over the air, but I mention it because several friends, mostly Jewish friends, confidentially felt the same way. The fear came very vivid to me when, after one of the many documentaries we saw (about six million people being treated like pigs on a spit), one New York television station showed a family of Armenian-Americans cele-brating, or bemoaning, their own particular annual festival. It was the seventieth anniversary of the infamous massacre of the Armenians by their Turkish conqueror. It had been going on since the 1890s, but in 1915, the Turks, in a final spasm of hatred, slaughtered all the able-bodied Armenians in sight and drove the rest out into the Syrian desert on the wholesale charge that all Armenians existed to help the Russian armies. Hundreds of thousands of Armenians died in the desert of starvation and/or sunstroke, and in the end the official estimate of the Armenian dead was over a million. This outrage was, of course, thoroughly reported at the time in Britain, all the more colourfully since Turkey was a fighting enemy. But after the war the indignation cooled and the war hatreds eventually languished and died – in Britain, I mean, but not in America, where there were, and are, large colonies of immigrants from every part of Southern and Central and Eastern Europe. They feel acutely the sufferings of their relatives, partly no doubt from the guilt of not being there to share them. When I came to this country in the early 1930s, small children everywhere were scolded for not cleaning their plates: 'Think', the parents used to say, 'of the starving Armenians.' And in several great cities, and in one valley of California almost entirely populated by Armenian immigrants, the old grievance against the Turks was nursed and kept green. But not, I should have thought, into 1985. However, on the television pro-gramme I mentioned, a great-grandfather and a grandfather were, on a night last spring, instructing their small grand- and great-grandchildren, slowly, patiently, as you might teach them a nursery rhyme, in hatred of the Turks.

I don't know why this scene horrified me, whereas the recall of the Nazi Holocaust seemed timely and right. Do an extra thirty years make all the difference? When will the Germans feel free from the stigma of the swastika? They are, to me, unanswerable questions.

One thing was painfully clear last weekend. The war in Vietnam ended ten years ago, but the wound to American morale is only partly healed. It was the first great military defeat in the country's history. The Veterans' Administration calculates that between 300,000 and 400,000 of the men who served are still afflicted with what they call 'post-trauma stress disorder', what in the First World War was more bluntly called 'shell shock'. One veteran who touched the black stone last weekend called it 'a memorial to desolation'. So, Veterans' Day this year did at least remind us of the tenacity of old hatreds, and leave us with the uncomfortable question: when will the Turks, and the Germans, and the Vietnamese, be welcomed back as equal members of the human family?

Miss Much – No Regret

3 January 1986

I hope I'm not stretching to find good news in a wicked world when I say that the happiest sentence I've read in the New Year comes from an anonymous – until now – office worker in his mid-thirties who has a wife and a 12-year-old son. His name is Gadany. He lives in Moscow. 'Quite frankly,' he told a British newspaperman, 'we were amazed when we turned on the 9 o'clock news and saw this friendly face staring out at us, speaking what sounded like a genuine message of peace.' It's not too much to say that the man was in shock, in the pleasantest way. He went on: 'My family noticed [too] that despite what we have always been told, he looked friendly and quite normal.' This may not be an earth-shaking confession to most of us, but consider who was saying it, and about whom. The 'friendly face' which appeared to be that of a 'normal' human being was none other than that of Ronald Reagan. Mr Gadany is an ordinary Russian, intelligent, educated – we are told – but yet he was amazed by this strange, this wholly unexpected face and manner. We know it well, but consider the weight of that phrase 'despite what we have always been told'. Mr Gadany, and surely millions of other ordinary non-official Russians, had never before been talked to by this President of the United States and, on a New Year's Day, they discovered that he does not have horns and fangs. Other correspondents in Moscow, both British and American, confirmed the general amazement at seeing the leader of the other superpower as nothing like what – since 1980 – 'we have always been told'. Namely, a leering warmonger with a six-pack of missiles in his hand, a figure hardly less terrifying to the Russian people than Attila the Hun. I'm not joking. I don't know where the suggestion came from that the two leaders should go on television and talk to each other's people. But whether it came from the American side, or the Russian, the decision to let Reagan be Reagan in full view of the Russian people could not have been taken lightly in Moscow. Only the resident fly on the Kremlin wall could tell us whether it was the result of intense discussion and back-and-forth arguments by Mr Gorbachev's inner circle, or whether it was a single bold decision by Mr Gorbachev himself. And what amazes me, as distinct from Mr Gadany, is the subsequent decision to permit the whole text of Mr Reagan's talk to go unedited, most of all to allow him to be seen and heard saying that 'both the United States and the Soviet Union are doing research on the possibilities of harnessing new technologies to the cause of defense'. This means, meant, only one thing: that both superpowers have been busy working on a strategic defence initiative, on what – in the teeth of Mr Reagan's pleas to drop the term, has been, and will always be, known as Star Wars. I suppose that the phrase 'harnessing new technologies' was thought sufficiently vague by the boys in the Kremlin to mask what it means to us.

Another passage in Mr Reagan's talk must have given them (the

Kremlin elite) thoughtful pause. It was this: 'Our democratic system is founded on the belief in the sanctity of human life and the rights of the individual.' That's all right; from everything they've been taught, the Russian people could take this to mean that the Soviet state is most concerned for the right of its people to have free education, free health care and a home, however humble. But then the President went on: '. . . the rights of the individual, such as freedom of speech, of assembly, of movement and of worship.' Perhaps 'freedom of speech and assembly' are untranslatable as new and daring freedoms to a people who from birth have never known them. I'm sorry to say that neither Mr Gadany nor any other man in the street appears to have been questioned on this vital difference. I certainly wish some correspondent, on our side, or anybody's side, would go around Moscow or Leningrad or Yalta or wherever and ask the people: 'What do freedom of speech, freedom of assembly, of movement, of worship mean to you?' There must be a confident, plausible answer that any Russian official could give, because in most of his or her contacts with the West, they hear it from their point of view, ad nauseam. Well, it's not ad nauseam to us. And I dare to think that it can come as a revelation, of a wholly new kind of life, to a Soviet citizen who for one reason or another is allowed to leave his native land and take up life in another.

This brings irresistibly to mind a cab driver I rode with a couple of months ago. I've often thought back to him and felt at one time I must talk about him. My problem here was that to give the flavour of the encounter, I should have to be able to mimic his thick and floundering English as well as it could be done, by, say, Peter Ustinov. I can't do this, and if I could, I'm afraid that he would inevitably come out as a comic vaudeville character. I think I ought to have a shot at it, mainly because it moved me, and it moved me to think again about this very topic that most of us take for granted.

Quite simply, I hailed a cab at my door, as I do every week at the same time, to drive downtown to the BBC to do my talk. A cab drove up and I was not merely nodded in, but welcomed in by a driver who smiled and even managed to bow in his seat. This is not standard practice among New York cab drivers, however amiable they may be. I did notice the man's name on the registration that is fixed above the dashboard. It was a Russian name. I've forgotten it. No matter. In an accent like molasses trying to pour itself through a tea strainer, he wanted to know 'Where, please, pleasure to be taking you.' We didn't exchange any words for a few minutes, till this sturdy middle-aged man, who was jolly and intense at the same time, half-turned over his right shoulder and said: 'Please, sir, to be telling me if you long in America.' A very long time, I said, but that like him I was born and grew up abroad. 'Ah, England,' he said, and nodded approvingly. 'And how about you?' I said. 'One year only,' he said. Then he was off, or rather he struggled to give me his story. About 50 (a bad time, I should guess, for a national of any country to emigrate to another), he had two children, grown. Not much to go on there. Then a traffic light changed, a cab in the adjacent lane squealed to a halt and just missed a carefree pedestrian. The driver, the other driver, snarled some obscenity, and my man gave a shrug, halfway between a chuckle and a sigh. 'Some', he said, 'very rude, very sharp, some very nice. But no can tell. No sure what manners may be for all.' It was, you can guess, heavy going. I'd already sensed that this man was a sensitive, nice man incapable of a cliché and anxious to express his difficult feelings in a language that stretched before him like a marsh of alternating bogs and hidden islands. I made a quick mental resolve to reduce my own part in the conversation to words of one syllable and to the simplest English idioms. The trouble here is the assumption that the English he'd learned had started with plain talk. A man who has landed here and never heard anything but having his wages 'inflation-indexed in the shortest possible time frame' is not likely to know what you're talking about if you say, 'And do your wages go up as soon as there's more inflation?'

Anyway, after several hopeless, strangulated pauses, we managed to hit on an understandable common language. He sensed I was on his side. And his story came out, in a wonderful, thrashing, staggering, procession of sentences. He *was* 50. It was a hard decision to make to leave Russia, his own country which loving very much. Missing very much. The people. The friends. All people, ways, food very different here. Very troubling. He was not Jewish. He was not political. But his two children, a son, a daughter, were now getting to college age. Both were very bright. But he saw no future for them except in some branch of the civil service and in Moscow. This would not have upset him, but he caught stuff on the big radio of his brother on the Voice of America. He also, to my alarm, said he had also listened, when it was not jammed, to an Englishman who did a talk from New York. It was called 'I think, Letter – Letter from America'. Believe me, I wasn't going to take the blame for yet another soured, embittered immigrant. Truthfully, I said I'd heard of him, but he was not heard in America. This amazed him. He went on. Why had he left? Because he'd heard children – studious ones – could try in America many colleges, could travel to get in, and could then choose what to do. He even heard, from that man, that it was a common thing for New York taxi drivers to take a week or two or a month off in winter and go to Florida. He had a distant cousin in New York. He and his wife took the risk. Now, his daughter was at Hunter College, didn't have to say yet what she wanted to be. His son was in premedical, going to be a doctor. But life was hard, he so missed Russia, the country, the people, the 'ways I brought up'. I asked him if he regretted the move. And he swivelled round in something close to alarm. 'No, no, no, no,' he said, 'miss much, but no regret.' Why? Why? 'How can I tell you? Listen, please. I talk to cab drivers. I visit the store. I meet on the street. People talk, all the time, they argue. On the TV. People fight in words. Like the government, don't like the government. Say good things, bad things. Say anything. Nobody follows. Nothing happens. My daughter no like Reagan. I like Reagan, I think great man. He say all the time why I here. What you call it?'

He was writhing in his seat reaching for some difficult impossible word. Freedom, I hinted. He positively shouted, 'Freedom!' I saw that his face was streaming with tears. I sniffed myself. 'I do know what you mean,' I said. Though, as I say, we take it for granted. This naive, shaken man did not.

Expert Witness

27 June 1986

Some years ago I had the extraordinary – for me, unique – experience of appearing as an expert witness before a judge. I immediately hear prim old gentlemen saying, 'And pray, what expertise can you claim in any field whatsoever?' A good question. A journalist, a foreign correspondent especially, is expected to pick up something across as wide a range of knowledge as possible. He is by definition a jack of all trades. And so, to complete the definition, he is assumed to be master of none.

But nobody is a born journalist. And before I was stricken by the urge to enlighten the general public on every conceivable subject, from medicine to golf, from professors of religion to practitioners of politics (which is about as wide a gamut as exists in our society), I was a scholar, in a special field of study. It was linguistics. Which is not quite the same as being a linguist. Linguistics is the scientific study of how languages come about and how they change. Why the Greek 'k' goes over into English as a soft 'c' and kinema turns into cinema. Why do the French put a circumflex accent in the word 'côte'? To show that between Old French and later French, an 's' got dropped, and the original word was the one that passed over into English as 'coast'. How did it happen that the Spanish looked at the basic Roman word for a sheath and turned it into 'vanilla'? Look that up and you are in for a startling discovery.

Well, my special study was pursued under an American linguistic scholar who was, in his time, the American Henry Higgins (you'll see in a minute why that name came up). My special field was the history of the English language in America, following, most obviously, the growth or development of a new vocabulary to describe the new landscape, and the effect on English of having daily contact – first with Indians, then with the Spanish and the French, and then the Dutch and arriving Germans, and in time, Poles, Russians, Hungarians, Italians and so on, all of whom contributed words to the English of America.

But the most fascinating part of the year I spent doing practically nothing else, was the history of the seventeenth-century *pronunciation* of England – among incoming lawyers, divines, carpenters and mechanics. Offhand, you'd say it would be impossible to know about this because there were no movies, no recordings of sound anyway. Well, yes, there was. We have the written records of the earliest town meetings, two in Massachusetts, one on Long Island. The town meeting was, still is, in almost all small towns and villages, the basic body of democratic government. Anybody could come and have his or her say, on any topic that was disturbing or exciting the neighbourhood. They were conducted in the early days usually by the lawyer or the parson – by the educated types. The record, in longhand abbreviated, was usually kept by a farmer or mechanic. And the pronunciations of the chairman were, naturally, written down in a rude phonetic way. So when the English parson, or whoever, said 'lib-rairy', we know that that's how educated Englishmen of the time spoke the word. That pronunciation, like many another old English pronunciation, stayed on in America, while down the years, the centuries, it changed in England. More often than not, that was the story: the Americans retained the old English pronunciations, and the English changed them.

Well, to my expert appearance. An old friend of mine, a theatrical lawyer, was planning to revive in New York the masterpiece of his long-time client, the late Alan Jay Lerner. That masterpiece, as at least three continents are well aware, is Lerner and Loewe's adaptation of Bernard Shaw's *Pygmalion*: *My Fair Lady*. Whenever you decide to bring an English play to New York, or an American play to London, you instantly have trouble with the actors' unions. The general rule here is that an Englishman will be allowed to play his part in the American production if it can be demonstrated – before the actors' union – that he is sufficiently distinguished to be irreplaceable by an American playing the part.

This is not a regulation restricted to actors. It is a regular requirement of the immigration service (same in England). It applies to a doctor, a carpenter, anyone of foreign citizenship seeking to do a temporary job in the United States. The immigration service gets in touch with the appropriate union, and if the union agrees that the man, the woman, has some skill not likely to be matched by an unemployed American, he, she, will be allowed in. This applies all the way from labourers to nuclear physicists, though it would probably not be hard for the Pentagon and the President's chief scientific adviser to prove, or maintain, that Herr Schmidt or Joe Parkinson is uniquely qualified to take on the job they have in mind. For instance, there would be no ban on a nuclear physicist from any (non-Communist) country who knew why cockroaches are immune to radiation (and don't think there aren't in many countries men bending over test tubes and microscopes and bits of cockroach tissue trying to solve that puzzle).

When it comes to proving here that an English actor or actress can play a role with unequalled skill, that is a tougher assignment. There are, after all, not only unemployed American actors who would like to strut their stuff but also, in or around New York, literally hundreds of English actors at large (resting, as they say) who also have the prime requirement of being American citizens. Well, in this case, in this play, *My Fair Lady*, Mr Lerner and my lawyer friend wanted to bring over Ian Richardson as Higgins and a young Englishwoman who had been chosen from a series of auditions, given in London, to over thirty English applicants for the part of Eliza Doolittle. They'd also had extensive auditions here, among Americans, but couldn't find one as good as the Englishwoman they chose.

The immigration service telephoned the actors' union. The union, after some thought, was quite willing and quite right too, to let Mr Richardson play Higgins. But they balked at the Englishwoman. The procedure then is to call for a so-called arbitration meeting, at which one arbiter, chosen by the union, will hear the case from the author's/ producer's side, on why the Englishwoman could play Eliza better than any of the Americans who'd been auditioned. The union challenged this assertion.

Came the great day, for the first and only time in my life, of the confrontation (one on one) between the union arbiter and the 'expert' that Mr Lerner and his lawyer had decided could best sustain their preference. A few other members of the union, as well as Mr Lerner and his lawyer, were allowed to sit in. The lawyer presented the credentials of the expert, never, to the arbiter's surprise and curiosity, mentioning such things as journalism or broadcasting, except to say that their man had been here for many, many years, had closely followed the theatre in both countries, but mainly because he had started, and pursued, down the years a special study of British and American speech.

Very good. Now proceed. I was required to detail the work I'd done at Harvard, and the fieldwork on a mighty work of sound (in both senses) scholarship called *The American Linguistic Atlas*. And so on. All this led to my contention that I could think of no living American woman who was capable – in a play uniquely about the social significance of spoken English – who was capable of moving without effort from genuine Cockney to believable Mayfair. The arbiter, at the peak of the discussion, called off American actresses he obviously admired, and challenged me to question their great gifts. I turned 'em all down as tactfully as possible, while expressing my own passion for his favourites on other grounds. At last, he looked at me, as the song says, square down in the eye and pronounced a name which (he probably never knew) was mentioned mockingly on Broadway, fifty years ago, as the name of a non-actress but who, down the decades, has been elevated into a pantheon all her own. He mentioned the English and Scottish roles she had played, from Mary, Queen of Scots down – or up. How about, he said, Katharine Hepburn? 'Impossible,' I said, 'was never any better than an upper-middle-class New Englander trying strenuously to sound British.'

At the end, he thanked me profusely, said he was impressed, and he would let us know the verdict within twenty-four hours. I blushed becomingly, and the lawyer and Mr Lerner took me out to a celebration lunch. 'Tremendous,' they said, 'We're in.' They saw me off with gaudy expressions of admiration and promises of lifelong devotion. Next day, need I say, the arbiter turned us down. The part would have to be played by an American. And so it was. And she was good, more than adequate. But the Cockney was studied, and the Mayfair could just as well have been Kensington or Bette Davis.

When it was all over, and the three of us met again, we fell to talking about the opposite problem: how to find English actors who can talk American. To Americans, it is an equal problem. Many British actors are wonderful mimics – of Cockney, North Country, West Country, whatever. Peter Sellers and Peter Ustinov could do Spanish-English, Italian-English, and German-English. But the best of them, for some reason, never exactly discovered or could do more than one sort of American. And whether they were being a judge, an ambassador, a president, a Southerner, a cab driver, it always came out – to Americans – sounding like George Raft, or some other gangster's henchman.

Last weekend, a great friend, an Englishman who has lived here for a dozen years or so, shed a beam of light on this dark problem. 'Even good English mimics', he said, 'are not prepared to think of Americans as individuals. They think of Americans as one type of variation on Englishmen. They are always the same: tough, Midwestern. They act out a theory in their heads, that Americans are nasal and rough-hewn. They don't listen.' So it was, and is, and no doubt for ever will be. Ah, me – and amen.

The Drugs Blight

19 September 1986

One of the sparkling sights at this time of year, around the equinox (it can vary by a day or two), is to see the boats go out from the marinas and inlets into the blue expanse of Peconic Bay, which divides the forks at the end of Long Island. The boats are owned by the so-called 'bay-men' and what they go out now to garner is the first harvest of a delicacy about which a friend of ours, a visiting Frenchwoman, once said: 'If they were as fine as this in France, tourists would come from all over the country.' The delicacy is the tiny Peconic Bay scallop, in its maturity no more than an inch in diameter. And on the first day of the season, the bay-men usually bring in hundreds of thousands of this tender, delectable, bivalve mollusc, which is not matched anywhere.

The Peconic harvest provides more than 30 per cent of the bay scallops, seared, just in butter, in restaurants around the country. At any time of the year, you can see 'bay scallops' printed on menus everywhere; but the fresh Peconic variety is not available before the third week in September. What you get at any other time is either frozen scallops or calicos from the Carolinas. Most often the title 'bay scallops' is a cover-up for the large sea scallops cut up into small chunks.

Well, this past weekend it was a sad sight on the shores of the Bay. The four hundred bay-men, whose livelihood depends on this late and abundant harvest, stayed home. No boats went out, for the simple blunt reason that there are no scallops. None. Or to be fussy, one boat did go out, piloted by one Christopher Smith, a marine specialist. 'We were out in Orient Harbor,' he said. 'Normally, you'd find hundreds of thousands of scallops, both young and adult, in there. We find two. It was like we were holding nuggets of gold.'

This is the third autumn of our discontent. In the late summer of 1984, we'd look out from any cliff or bluff and see something new and puzzling: instead of the blue waters lapping in, we looked down on what we came to call 'the brown tide'. It was the first invasion in human memory of what the marine biologists call a bloom of algae, so microscopic and so dense that we assumed we were the late victims of some pollutant, of spreading industrial waste, which has deprived us, for instance, of our finest eating fish: the noble striped bass. They spawn in the Hudson River in what are now polluted stretches, but even when they swim out along the ocean line and into the bays along a hundred miles of Long Island, their catch has been prohibited.

But this is not the case of the bay scallop. Nobody knows where the brown tide came from. One marine scientist has a theory, but is ready to admit it's only a hunch. He thinks it's meterological in origin, and follows on a succession of dry winters and dry springs. But we've had – we had in the mid-1970s – three or four such dry seasons. We also had a million scallops later on.

There's no mystery, however, about what the algae do. They choke out the normal phytoplankton, the microscopic plant life on which the scallops feed. So, simply, they starve to death.

In the fall of 1984, the scallop harvest was pitifully small. Last year, there was none. Same this year. The expert theory, not a very cheerful one, is that in some mysterious but dependable way, the scallops would learn to overcome, or enjoy, the algae and would recover on their own, but not much before the end of the century. So, at the understandable pleading of the four hundred bay-men, who together will lose the two million dollars they earn at the dock, New York State has done something about it: an experiment conducted with skill and crossed fingers. Last Monday, in the late afternoon, a single-engined plane flew into Montauk, the last – the most eastern – settlement on Long Island. It had come from the state of Maine. It carried eight hundred thousand minute bay scallops taken from a nursery on a river in Maine at eleven in the morning. They were packed in foam coolers, and the pilot was nervous about their expectation of life, for they can live outside salt water for no more than eight hours. He landed at Montauk just after 4.30. That left two and a half hours to get them into pens in a saltwater lake on Montauk Point. It took two hours to unpack, separate and open up the scallops. In the last half-hour, the divers started plunging into the lake. By 7 o'clock, just when the sun was sinking (as it does at this latitude, as fast as the divers), and to everybody's relief, the minuscule molluscs were feeding away in their new home. It is a re-seeding project, and the hope is that if it works, and *if* the brown tide that killed all the native scallops doesn't come back next summer, there could be a sizeable crop of these mature immigrants by the fall of 1988.

I appreciate that the sudden impoverishment of four hundred men and their families is not a matter of great pain to 99.9 per cent, or more, of my listeners. But it was happening to us. And as we all come to know, four hundred thousand people killed in an earthquake in China is a horrid, but bearable, statistic. A child you saw killed by a motor car is a memory that stays with you for life.

There is one form of pollution that is drastically affecting this whole nation. And if it's true, as somebody said, that 'in America we see our future, good and bad', then this blight will soon overtake the other countries of the Western world. In fact, there's lots of evidence that in Germany, in Scandinavia, in Britain, in Holland, it has already started. I mean the drug blight, which sixty years ago was a small sinister symptom of the decadent 1920s in Hollywood, and among the arty-society Bohemians of London. (Dorothy Sayers wrote one of her novels, an untypically tart one, about them: *Murder Must Advertise*.)

But now, we are talking about a country, this one, in which one high school pupil in five has tried cocaine, in which one in twenty or thirty is likely to become an addict. A treatment programme in Florida, which has over six hundred teenagers under treatment, found that most of them had started a drug habit by the age of 12. As against 7 per cent of a similar group that had used cocaine in 1984, today 63 per cent have done so. Two in three of them used drugs of one sort or another before their parents suspected it. Most – 70 per cent – were introduced to drugs, not on the street or by pushers, but by friends.

Cocaine has become the drug of choice of the middle-class teenager (not to mention, of course, prosperous yuppies, rock performers and showbiz parasites, and an alarming minority of star footballers and baseball players), and finally President Reagan has decided to propose a national battle against drugs. 'Finally' is not meant to imply a sneer. Mrs Reagan, since the first month she was in the White House, has devoted all her spare time to travelling far and wide, talking to youngsters in and out of school, in and out of treatment centres, about drugs. And, consequently, her husband is probably more aware of the blighted lives of the young than most husbands.

And of course, the White House, through the Department of Justice, has for long had a programme of trying to stop the importation of drugs into the United States from South and Central America. It's an effort which – in view of the size of the country with its enormous wriggling borders, the impossibility of patrolling the twenty-five-hundred-mile southern border of the United States with anything like enough radar-equipped helicopters, the ruthless ability of South American growers and organized crime to mount fleets of small boats and larger fleets of private aeroplanes on secret night-flights, in view of this tidal wave of drug entry into the country – has so far been about as effective as mopping up the ocean with a pocket handkerchief. One official, trying to plug the innumerable gateways to Florida by air, by sea, by every sort of roadway from four-lane motorways to dirt roads, said that the plugging-up process was like squeezing a balloon: 'You press in one place, and it bulges out in another.'

What the President has now done, in a determinedly dramatic appearance with Mrs Reagan on national television, is to announce what he called a national 'crusade' against drug abuse. It went far beyond the long battle with foreign importers, suppliers and pushers. For the first time, it turned to the users. It was a powerful sermon against drug abuse and a warning, especially to the young. As such, people who have spent half a lifetime with addicts doubted that the young – temperamentally curious and likely to try drugs – will be stopped by sermons, however eloquent or well-intentioned. One stoical youngster spoke for what I suspect is a large percentage of actual or potential users when he said: 'Nothing can be done for my drug-using friends. They do it for fun.' And when you say, 'Don't they realize it will ruin their lives?' they say, 'Well, it hasn't happened to me yet.'

The Presidential programme, which must go before the Congress, would stiffen the laws against drug-related crimes; give more money for research and treatment centres; and – in its most controversial proposal – require about a million government workers in sensitive jobs to take drug tests. That means routine urinalysis. This suggestion at once provoked an outcry in Congress, from civil libertarians, and from one government union that has already filed a suit. They all protested that compulsory testing would violate a citizen's constitutional rights by invading his or her privacy. The House of Representatives, which is controlled by the Democrats, no sooner heard about the President's forthcoming address than it rushed, three days before the address was given, to prove quite suddenly it was more alert than anybody to the nationwide drug abuse. It passed, helter-skelter, its own anti-drug programme. It was more specific than the President's, and tougher on two counts, both of which had other Congressmen and civil libertarians protesting against an unconstitutional use of the military, and a federal return to the death penalty. The House bill proposes the death penalty for pushers of drugs to children. And it sanctions the use of the military, instead of only the local police and the FBI, to stop illegal drugs coming into the country.

I'm afraid both the House bill and the President's crusade represent less of a considered cure than a rush to righteousness. The entire House of Representatives comes up for re-election in November. And a Congressman voting against a drug-abuse bill today would be about as popular as a Congressman who voted against mother and Santa Claus. Maybe, when the election is over, both houses of Congress will sit down and look at all the facts, ponder, and write a thoughtful, effective programme. At the moment, the government's anti-drug pro-gramme and the House's response to it have been launched in the headlong, vote-catching atmosphere that characterized the passage of the 18th Amendment, which prohibited 'the manufacture, sale or trans-portation of intoxicating liquors'; and which plunged the country into a fourteen-year orgy of self-righteousness, hypocrisy and prosperous crime.

Time to Retire

16 January 1987

A letter from a friend in England caught me napping between two emotions. It was the sort of letter that normally calls for congratu-lations. But in the moment of writing back to say, 'Well done, good luck!' I felt something of a fraud, because my first emotion was one of shock, verging on alarm. I suppressed this feeling in the interests of common courtesy.

So, what was the letter about? It simply announced with evident pleasure, not to say pride, that he was retiring. What do you say to a friend who retires? There are so-called greetings cards available at every stationer's in this country, and I don't doubt in many other countries, for every conceivable and inconceivable occasion. I recently had a flock of them on my birthday; my favourite being one that came from my daughter. On the outside, it showed a drawing of a simple, cheerful-looking dope. And above the drawing, the inscription: 'At your age, you've got a lot going for you.' Turn the page, and on the inside, it said, 'Your eyes are going, your back is going, your knees are going, your hearing is . . . Happy Birthday.'

But there are no greetings cards for people about to retire. For in a nation that coined the phrases 'over-achiever' and 'under-achiever', a man who retires has announced that from now on, he's going to be a 'non-achiever'. Not quite a disgrace, but nothing to cheer about either.

I can best explain my feeling of shock at the news of this vigorous, dapper man on his way out by recalling one of the last acts passed by the expiring 99th Congress (which died in December). It was a measure which received so little publicity here that I didn't think to remark on it at the time: a federal, a national, act which forbids an employer to require anyone to retire at the age of – wait for it – 70. Unless the person can be medically pronounced to be incompetent or disabled from doing his or her job, if he or she wants to go on, so be it.

I don't know what the law or custom is in France or Mexico or the Australian outback, but Englishmen, at any rate, will now appreciate my shock. My retiring friend is about to be 60. I mentioned this to many friends here – from the naive to the sophisticated – and they too either registered shock or suggested that I'd got it wrong. One determined sceptic practically demanded proof, so I got out *Who's Who* and looked up various men we knew, or knew of, who had been in the Foreign Service. Subtract their birth date from the retirement date, and sure enough, the answer was always 60, except for one or two brave entries which briefly stated 'called' or 'recalled' out of retirement to take on one more job for old England's sake. How about Churchill, somebody asked, who formed his last ministry in his seventy-seventh year, which is what Ronald Reagan will enter in another three weeks. Doesn't apply, I said, to elected officials.

It's an interesting difference between the two countries, because it reflects such a dramatically different view of the limits of a person's stamina and usefulness to society. A sharp American friend of mine immediately asked what is the normal expectation of life in Britain, because that would seem to be the most realistic gauge of how long you can do your job effectively. The answer is, of course, that in Britain and America the expectation of life at birth (the only true measure of a nation's increasing or decreasing lifespan), is just about the same, give or take a percentage point. And because in both countries, as also in the Scandinavian countries – in fact all of Western Europe, I believe – people are living very much longer than they did eighty, even fifty, years ago, the actuarial tables of insurance companies have been adjusted accordingly. My friend assumed, and so did I, that the general view of a proper retirement age has similarly changed.

Of course, the age at which you officially become one of the old folks, or as we now ridiculously say, a 'senior citizen', remains, in this country as elsewhere, 65. And that's the age when you get a card from the government entitling you to medical benefits – by Act of Congress (Medicare) – and the age at which, even more agreeably, you start receiving a monthly cheque to return to you the benefits that have accrued from your payments under the Social Security Act of fifty years ago. One even more agreeable novelty which I still don't quite understand is that when the male of the family reaches 72, his wife, whether she has ever been employed in a salaried job or not, also gets a cheque. I imagine it's the same in all countries: communications between a human being and his government are so impersonal that you never know whom to write to, either by way of gratitude or protest. Such communications normally have no signature. They are printed. They do manage to print your name at the top, but everything else is a form letter that could have gone to anybody. Sometimes there's not even a date. Imagine, then, the comic shock we had when, about a week after my seventy-second birthday, a letter – nay, a telegram, a Mailgram as it's called – arrived for my wife. She tore it open hoping it was no bad news about any of the children, who live three and six thousand miles apart, or any of our brood of grandchildren. It was, in fact, a telegram from the government. Remember, there'd never been any 'Dear Mr C' or 'Dear Sir' or any recognition of me, in previous correspondence, except as the bearer of Social Security number 066-34-1674. This Mailgram said, with almost weepy intimacy, 'Dear Jane, now that Alistair is 72 you will be entitled to and will receive a monthly Social Security check.' In the interest of not getting my block knocked off, I stopped myself saying: 'What have you done to deserve this?' The answer, of course, is everything: from bearing, rearing, maintaining, nursing, feeding, schooling, laundering, etc., etc., a family. This carries the official status on government documents as 'non-working housewife', which recalls the memorable question, at Christmas time, of a vivacious young woman at a small, quick party which my daughter, mother of five, was able to attend for an hour or so. 'Tell me,' asked the vivacious one, 'do you work?' 'Sort of,' my daughter replied, 'from about 4.30 a.m. to 10 p.m.' 'Really,' exclaimed this vivacious dumb-bell. 'What at?' No answer.

Still, it's a pleasant surprise to know that both of us will, till death do us part, get a monthly cheque from the government. And mine keeps going up. I don't write to the government and ask them why. Like every other concerned citizen, I believe that the administration should drastically cut the budget, so we can do something about our appalling $150 billion deficit, but wherever else they make the cuts, we're dead against reducing *our* slice of the pie.

Well . . . expectation of life. That certainly would seem to be the logical test of when people should retire. At the turn of the century, I mean around 1900, and on – certainly until the First World War – successful businessmen usually retired between 45 and 50, since the expectation of life for men was then between 55 or 60; for women, a few years longer. When the American Social Security system was started, a regular percentage was taken out of your pay-cheque, on the understanding that it would go into a giant piggy bank in which all those withheld payments would sit and collect interest until the accumulated money would be paid back in the form of retirement benefits. This is the general understanding, and it is false. No wonder this is the popular myth, because the system, when it was first established, was called 'an intergenerational income transfer program' to which most beneficiaries replied: 'How much is in it for me when I'm old?' What it meant, and means, is that in the beginning and now, active workers have a part of their salary withheld in order to support people already retired. And when today's workers retire, they in turn will be supported by a future generation of workers. I remember at the time – the mid-1930s, at the peak of Roosevelt's New Deal – the President translated 'intergenerational income transfer program' in a masterly way, using one of his typically homely figures of speech. 'The Social Security system', he said, 'is no more and no less than a national attempt to observe the Fifth Commandment: "Honour thy father and thy mother."'

It worked fine for about forty years. The trouble began about ten years ago, when it was recognized that more people than ever were living longer. Today, the expectation of life at birth, here and in most of the Western world, is 69 point something for males, 74 point something for females. So, except for the early years of the Great Depression, the system used to take in more money than it paid out.

But increasingly, during the past decade, because there are millions more retired than was originally figured on, the system is paying out much more money than it's taking in. Therefore the government keeps drawing and drawing on reserves. It's got to the point where something like 40 per cent of the national budget is devoted to Social Security. No Senator or Congressman dares say it must be cut. The popular cry now is to cut military spending, which is a little more than half of Social Security. Maybe the federal extension of the compulsory retirement age (it's been extended twice in the past twenty years) is, in essence, not so much an assertion of the rude health and vigour of Americans as a rather desperate way of taking in more deductions from the old in order to help the older. It's a brave effort, anyway. I can't imagine what the burden is going to be on the working population of the young in Britain who pay to maintain, in pensions, all those sturdy people who have to retire at 60. I forbear from mentioning the medical fact that men, at least, who retire in their prime tend to keel over; or the social fact that they amaze their wives by suddenly becoming household nuisances, wanting, for instance – lunch!

Martin Luther King – the Black Washington

23 January 1987

If you had arrived as a stranger, in just about any American city or small town last Monday, you'd have been puzzled to see some banks open, some not, some offices closed. Over public buildings, flags flying at half mast here, and there, a flag flying high and free. In New York, in San Francisco, the two financial centres of the East and West coasts, there was no trading on the stock exchanges. If you had been in Phoenix, the capital city of the Arizona desert, you would have seen a march of thousands of people – fifteen thousand was the police count – leaning into freakish, freezing winds and trudging towards the state capitol, the Arizona legislature. The march there was led by the former Governor of the state, a Democrat. 'Let's all keep coming back here,' he said, 'until we have in Arizona a holiday in his memory.'

The memory they were invoking was that of the Reverend Martin Luther King, Jr., the black leader, who was assassinated in the spring of 1968, and who would have been 58 last Monday. That day, 19 January, has been designated by the Congress, in a bill signed two years ago by President Reagan, as a national holiday: a federal holiday, that is for all workers in the federal government. Most of the states, well over forty, have seconded the motion and declared it a holiday for all workers in state government. Last Monday was the second national observance of Martin Luther King's birthday. Why then the to-do in Phoenix, Arizona? Because, it is the only state that first followed the federal government and then, last November, elected a new Governor who has rescinded Martin Luther King Jr. Day as a state holiday. It has produced an uproar and, inevitably, charges of insensitivity and racism. The new Governor says he has no prejudice, no emotion at all about his act. He says that a state holiday may only, in law, be declared by the legislature, and therefore the former Governor did wrong in proclaiming it on his own initiative. 'Let the people decide,' says the new Governor. (Arizona has a population of just over 5 per cent blacks.)

When the idea of a national holiday was first proposed, several years ago, there was, remarkably, not much opposition. And it came, mainly, not from old segregationists; of course it came from pockets of declared white Christian supremacists and the small, frenzied remnants of the Ku Klux Klan. But in the main, it was from a Senator or two, a Congressman or two (in states not dependent on considerable black populations), who pointed out, quite correctly, that Dr King was about to be given a distinction which, in the whole of American history, has been accorded only one man: George Washington. True, Lincoln's birthday is a legal holiday, but only in twenty states, nowhere I believe, in the South, in any of the states of the old Confederacy. To be absolutely accurate about the custom, and the procedure, there are no national holidays in the United States. The President and Congress can legally designate holidays for government: federal employees only in Washington, that is, its district, the District of Columbia. Each state has the right to follow suit or not to.

So, while thirty states still hold out against Lincoln, there are no more than half a dozen that do not officially recognize Dr Martin Luther King Jr. Day. Of course, federal government workers everywhere take the day off. But as the first objectors pointed out, there is no Jefferson Day, no Benjamin Franklin Day, no Madison Day, and no Franklin Roosevelt Day. Why, they asked, should one man be singled out, above a roster of distinguished Presidents, for this amazing honour? The answer cannot be minced into fine legal English. The answer is simple and resounding. Dr Martin Luther King, Jr., in his late twenties, thirty-one years ago, led a black boycott against a bus company down in Alabama and that led to other boycotts, and marches, and jailing for Dr King and others, and a vast rebellion that we call the Black Revolution. This happened, by the way, two years after the United States Supreme Court came through with its historic ruling that segregation was, at last, unconstitutional.

There was instant and formidable resistance to the Court throughout, at first, the whole South. The little matter of the Montgomery bus boycott turned out to be the spark that ignited the revolution. And in that little matter, as happens in every nation, one obscure person, as obscure as Wat Tyler or Ned Ludd, lit the charge. Her name was Rosa Parks. Let me reach on the shelf and look over a very browned-off page of a newspaper. It is eerie to read it now, because it was written, from Montgomery, Alabama, by a reporter who had not a flicker of foresight about where this humdrum incident would lead. It was written by me. It was written in the spring of 1956, and was in the main about a church service, or rally, which I attended as, by the way, the only white in the congregation. But it went back to the beginning of the boycott, which was still going on five months later. It goes like this:

On December third last, four Negroes went aboard a city bus and sat in its forward section. This is a flexible area marked off by cards that snap on to the central poles; they may be moved back and forth according to the racial majority that lives along the bus's normal route. The bus driver asked them to move back into the colored section. All but one, a woman, complied: one

Rosa Parks. The driver acted in accordance with a city law, which may be flouted at the risk of fine and imprisonment and the loss of the city's operating franchise. The bus driver tried again, and failing, called in two policemen. When the woman still refused to move, they arrested her. The same afternoon thousands of printed handbills mysteriously dropped on the doorsteps of colored homes urging a boycott of the bus line, to start two days later. It accordingly began on Monday the 5th.

Well, it was still going five months later when I was down there to cover the story, which by now was a national concern. It would not have grown so, I believe, if it hadn't been for the man who kept coming back there to strengthen the resistance of the blacks, all of whom went on, day after day, month after month, walking to work. In the evening of that spring day, I went to the service – a sort of service of rededication – in a shambling coloured section of town, a squat, ugly Victorian church, the Mount Zion African Methodist Episcopal church. The place was jammed to the doors. For an hour or more, there were chants and hymns, and single figures rising as the spirit moved them, to shout and 'testify' in many a Bible sentence sung in the minor chords and heaving melancholy of the blues. Then they all sang 'Old Time Religion' and there was a rustle of leaders at a side door, and out came three parsons who prepared the way for the coming of the leader. The side door opened again, and the roar might have been for Victory in Europe. He was a young man with solemn good looks. The roar eventually died into a breathless silence, and this young Dr King read out a petition that was to be, he said, 'a constitution for our cause'. At the end, I walked out with one of the clergymen. 'Tell me', I said, 'about Dr King.' With a steady look and absolute seriousness, he said: 'God took time to prepare him a man. God had to find him a Leader. And having looked, he chose Him a man, young, dynamic, wise and Christian. He is second only to Lincoln as the Great Emancipator.'

Well, it was a rousing, seething evening, not to be forgotten. But the rhetoric did seem a little heady at the time to one reporter who was moving through the South to see how well or badly the states, the cities, the country towns were complying with the Supreme Court's already famous judgement.

Since that evening in darktown Montgomery, Dr King's so-called

302

'constitution', which meant only to demand equal treatment in public transportation, came to force equal rights across the whole social span of American life. He stands alone as a black leader, and he triumphed with no more, but no less, than the weapons of Mahatma Gandhi: steadiness, unwavering courage, jail terms, abuse, patience, an absolutely iron refusal to meet violence with violence. When the resolution came before Congress to declare his birthday a federal holiday, there were very few Congressmen who dared oppose it. President Reagan himself was against it, and when asked at a press conference if the thought (it was a common, scurrilous rumour) that Dr King was a Communist, he replied: 'Well, in about thirty years or so, I guess we'll know, won't we?' When the resolution was passed, the President signed it. And last Monday, he spoke movingly about the lessons we had learned from Dr King, a man who united us in tolerance and understanding. Down in Atlanta where Dr King was buried, there was an ecumenical church service, from which Mr Reagan's Secretary of State, Mr Shultz, took Dr King's message out to South Africa. 'Our objective', he said, 'is to encourage the extension of the full benefits of citizenship, which white Americans so rightly cherish, to all their countrymen.'

There have been, around the time of the King birthday, some sporadic flares of racism – whites beating up blacks in a New York City borough; one small county in Georgia swears it will let no black family live there. This county is now practically under siege. Thirty years ago, it would never have made the news. There would have been thousands of counties all over the country similarly minded.

So, the revolution has been won? No. So things are much the same? No. Black unemployment is still twice that of whites. Four black families in ten have no man in the house. But beyond any other white society I know, blacks are no longer the obvious pool of menial labour. They have spread their ablest through every sort of profession and job, up from businessmen and bank clerks to editors, sheriffs and mayors – of five of the seven biggest cities – to the Supreme Court. No cause yet to crow. But it is a vastly different, more colour-blind society from the one I took for granted when I left Montgomery that spring evening thirty-two years ago, and waited for my train in a waiting room marked, 'Whites Only'.

Fred Astaire

26 June 1987

Movie stars don't make it. Nor statesmen. Not Prime Ministers, or dictators unless they die in office. Not even a world-famous rock star, unless he's assassinated. But last Monday, none of the three national television networks hesitated about the story that would lead the evening news. On millions of little screens in this country and I don't doubt in many other countries around the world, the first shots were of an imp, a graceful wraith, a firefly in impeccable white tie and tails.

And for much longer than the lead story usually runs, for a full five minutes on NBC, we were given a loving retrospective of the dead man, ending with the firm declaration by Nureyev that 'He was not just the best ballroom dancer, or tap dancer, he was simply the greatest, most imaginative, dancer of our time.' And the newsmen were right to remind us of the immortal comment of the Hollywood mogul, who, with the no-nonsense directness of an expert, reported on Fred Astaire's first film test: 'Has enormous ears, can't act, can't sing, dances a little.'

That Hollywood mogul, long gone, spent his life ducking round corners, to avoid being identified as the oaf who looked in the sky and never saw the brightest star. However, that expert opinion was, as the lawyers say, controlling at the time and in Astaire's first movies, there was no thought of allowing him to act or sing. But not for long. And thanks to the invention of television, and the need to fill vast stretches of the afternoon and night with old movies, it has been possible for my daughter, for instance, to claim Fred Astaire as her favourite film star from the evidence of all the movies he made fifteen, ten, five, three years before she was born.

When I got the news on Monday evening here, and realized with immediate professional satisfaction that the BBC had smartly on hand a musical obituary tribute to him I put together eight years ago, I couldn't help recalling the casual, comic way this and similar radio obituaries came about.

I was in London at the end of 1979, and Richard Rodgers – one of the two or three greatest of American song writers – had just died, I believe on New Year's Eve or the night before. Britons, by then, were getting accustomed, without pain, to making what used to be a two-day Christmas holiday into a ten-day much-needed rest. For all laborious research purposes, the BBC was shut up. And there was no retrospective programme on the life and music of Richard Rodgers in the BBC's archives. Of course, in a gramophone library that looks like an annex to the Pentagon, there were hundreds, perhaps thousands, of recordings of his songs. The SOS went out to a writer, a producer, and – I presume – a man who had the key to the gramophone library. The silent place was unlocked, and the three of them laboured through the day to put together an hour's tribute to Richard Rodgers. It was done. It was competent enough, but rushed to an impossible deadline. This hasty improvisation happened just when my own music producer and I, who had enjoyed working together for six years or so on American popular music, were wondering what we could offer next. We'd done a sketch history of jazz, through individuals. We'd gone through all the popular music of the 1920s, 1930s and 1940s, and were stumped for a new series, at which point I asked if we mightn't go and talk to the head of the channel, network or whatever. We went in, and the genial boss asked me what we had in mind. 'A morgue,' I said. A what? 'Where', I asked, 'is your morgue?' He was not familiar with the word, a newspaper term. 'Well,' I said, 'all newspapers have them.' 'How d'you mean?' 'If', I explained, 'Mrs Thatcher died tonight and you woke up and read a two-sentence obituary, you'd be rightly outraged. But if you saw a two-page obituary, you'd take it for granted. When d'you suppose it was written?' 'That's right,' he said thoughtfully. What I was proposing was a morgue of the Americans eminent in popular music and jazz, so they'd not get caught short again. A splendid idea, the man said; pick your stars. We made a list and were commissioned to return to America and finish all of them. Naturally, we looked at a calendar, and birthdates of Hoagy Carmichael, Earl Hines, Harold Arlen, Ethel Merman, Stephane Grappelli, Ella Fitzgerald. But then, in a spasm of panic, we thought of two giants – if the word can be used about two comparative midgets: Irving Berlin and Fred Astaire. Berlin was then 91. And Fred Astaire was just crowding 80. The boss man, to whom the idea of a morgue had been, only a few minutes before, quaint if not morbid, wondered what we were waiting for. Better get busy, at once, on Berlin and then on Astaire. I remember doing the Astaire obit, then and there, while I was still in London. Meanwhile, we'd simply pray every night that the Lord would keep Irving Berlin breathing till I could get home and get busy. I remember being picked up in a car by a charming young girl to get to the BBC and record my Astaire narration – there wasn't a moment to lose. She asked me, in the car, what the script was that I was clutching. 'It's an obituary', I said, 'of Fred Astaire.' 'Fred Astaire,' she shrieked, 'dead?' and almost swerved into a bus. 'Of *course*, he's not dead,' I said, 'but he's going to be one day.' She, too, was new to the institution of a morgue. I recalled that when I was a correspondent for a British paper in the United States, and when for example, Dean Acheson was appointed Secretary of State, the first cable I had from my editor said, 'Welcome Acheson obituary soonest.' How ghoulish, she said.

I imagine that to two generations at least, it's assumed that Fred Astaire, this slim, pop-eyed newcomer to Hollywood who couldn't act, couldn't sing, danced a little, only made a fool of the mogul through the movies he made, with Ginger Rogers, in the mid- and late 1930s. But long before then, from the mid-1920s on, he was already an incomparable star – as a dancer – to theatre audiences both in New York and in London. Perhaps more in London than anywhere, certainly in the 1920s, with the early Gershwin hits, *Funny Face* and *Lady Be Good*, and lastly, in 1933, in Cole Porter's *Gay Divorce* (which was the title of the theatre show; Hollywood would not then allow so shocking a title and called the movie version, *The Gay Divorcee*). Of all the thousands of words that have been written this week, and will be written, there is a passage I went back to on Tuesday night which, I think, as well as anything I know, sums up Astaire's overall appeal – the appeal that takes in but transcends one's admiration for his dancing and for his inimitably intimate singing style. This was written in November 1933, by a theatre critic who had so little feel for dancing that he marvelled why London should go on about 'Mr Astaire's doing well enough what the Tiller Girls at Blackpool do superbly'. The critic, the writer, was James Agate, the irascible, dogmatic, opinionated but brilliant journalist, and I believe the best critic of acting we have had this century. He is writing his review of *Gay Divorce*, after declaring yet again his contempt for musical comedy as an entertainment for idiots, deploring the play's plot and the acting and hoping 'Micawberishly, for something to turn up'. 'Presently,' he wrote, 'Mr Fred Astaire obliged, and there is really no more to be said.' Except – 'a very distinguished colleague began his criticism of this show by asking what is Mr Astaire's secret. May I suggest that the solution hangs on a little word of three letters? Mr Astaire's secret is that of the late Rudolf Valentino and of Mr Maurice Chevalier – sex, but sex so bejewelled and be-pixied that the weaker vessels who fall for it can pretend that it isn't sex at all but a sublimated projection of the Little Fellow with the Knuckles in His Eyes. You'd have thought by the look of the first night foyer that it was Mothering Thursday, since every woman in the place was urgent to take to her bosom this waif with the sad eyes and the twinkling feet.'

As for the unique quality of Astaire's dancing – something impossible to put into words – I think the near-impossible has been achieved by an American critic of films and jazz, the late Otis Ferguson. He wrote: in reviewing *Top Hat*: 'He has given the best visual expression that has been generally seen of what is called The Jazz, as a man who can create figures, intricate, unpredictable, constantly varied and yet simple, seemingly effortless. Whenever the band gathers its brasses and rhythm section and begins to beat it out, he is unequalled any-where, with his soft-shoe sandman number, and when before the line of men with top hats, he swings up the steps . . . Fred Astaire, whatever he may do in whatever picture he is in, has the beat, the swing, the debonair and damn-your-eyes violence of rhythm, all the gay contradiction and irresponsibility, of the best thing this country can contribute to musical history, which is – the best American jazz.'

Origins of American Slang

14 August 1987

In the spring of 1984, there was a new television commercial, for one of those three or four fast-food chains that compete savagely and endlessly like religious factions in a holy war, for the favour of teenagers who seem to survive mainly on hamburgers, French fries and gaseous soft drinks. This short, I think, only thirty-second ad, was an audacious exercise in a new type of television commercial in this country which doesn't cry up its own product so much as cry down the product of its competitors. Very often, this type of ad names the chief competitor and sneers at its claims, a technique that, a dozen years ago, would have appeared likely to offer grounds for a libel suit.

In this particular ad, you saw two women looking down at a very meagre hamburger, and at their side a little old lady with a craggy face. You sensed at once from her scowl that she was the representative of the chain that was making the ad. She was, apart from her angry carbuncle of a face, tiny: in life, only four feet ten. So all we saw of her, above the counter, was her bobbing angry face. She had obviously had enough of the pitiful object her friends had been served. And she suddenly barked at them: 'But where's the beef, where's the beef?'

It touched the hearts of those millions of us who, when eating out, very rarely come on the genuine article, a plump patty of chopped sirloin or filet, but more often a sliver of a patty that could be mistaken for a coaster to rest your drink on, and composed usually of pounded cereal and other foreign bodies impregnated with a shred of meat. The line 'where's the beef?' must have been echoed in a thousand lunch counters and roadside restaurants. It suddenly, however, became a national idiom when Mr Walter Mondale, in a televised debate with Mr Gary Hart, another contender for the Democratic nomination, listened a while to Mr Hart's visionary, and rather vague, blueprint for running the country (Mr Hart's rhetoric was always a little short on substance). Mr Mondale heard him out, but then turned to him and said, 'Yes, but where's the beef?' It brought the house down, and the director of the hamburger commercial said later, 'If Walter Mondale could have said the line like Clara, he'd have been our president.'

Clara was Clara Peller, a child immigrant from Russia, and for most of her life, a manicurist, who in her sixties, got into television commercials as a non-speaking, practically invisible, extra. In 1984, when she was 83, her head appeared above that lunch counter, and she barked out her famous line. She died in Chicago the other day at the age of 86, and achieved the dignity of a two-column obituary in the *New York Times*. A clip of her ad, and another of Mondale's adoption of it, was shown on all the national networks.

Clara Peller's famous three words are a reminder that the television ad is only the latest source of American popular idiom. I can now think back to a dozen or more catchphrases in the past ten years or so that came out of television commercials and, since millions of people heard them, passed into the language, for the time being. American slang, especially, has traditionally sprung from what is most character-istic in the experience of people doing different jobs in different cli-mates. From the timber workers in the Northwest, we got 'on the skids' – planks of saplings on which the logs could be rolled down the river. The cowboy gave many expressions to the language, and one of them – I should guess the last of them – remained into my own time. I remember when I first came to Yale, if you asked somebody to do a favour which might be troublesome, he'd say: 'No trouble, it's a cinch.' This came from the cattlemen in Texas who, a century ago, rounded up their yearling calves for the long trail to the feed lots in the lush pastures of the Midwest, where they would be fattened up for you and me. When the whole company, the outfit, was ready for the journey north, the cowboys strapped up the belt around the girth of their horses, the saddle girth, and were on their way. In Spanish – and remember, the Southwest had once been New Spain – in Spanish a saddle girth is a 'cincha'. So, 'it's a cinch' came to mean, ready to go, and then by extension, as we now say, 'No problem.'

However, the word is long gone and I doubt that any American under 40 has ever heard of it. It appears that once an idiom no longer calls up a picture of the condition that bred it, it dies. And the cowboy and the cattle kingdom and all their customs and talk are dead and gone. Hence, young people are the first to drop their parents' slang and catchphrases because they don't recall the life that spawned them. I'm not sure whether this is so true in older countries. There must still be old gentlemen in England who talk about somebody being 'hoist with his own petard', but I'm pretty sure that few of them get a mental picture of what is meant by the phrase, and fewer still who know the very rude origin of the word 'petard' from the French. I've heard even young people, in England, say they were 'on tenterhooks', but I'll bet only young Lancashire men or Yorkshire men with fathers or grandfathers who were in the mills know what a tenterhook is and why it produces tension.

In my early time here, the Prohibition gangsters of the early 1930s splattered the language with phrases that, through the early sound movies, passed over to England and were used, often with unconscious comical effect, even by respectable officers of the BBC. Staff members who were sacked were said to have been 'taken for a ride' or 'bumped off'. Somebody getting quickly out of an awkward situation decided to 'take it on the lam'. But certainly, what you might call the classical language of the gangsters has passed away with the gangsters of the Chicago vintage. You'll notice I don't say with the gangsters. They are still with us, but today they are not crude and flashy. They dress austerely, like the conservative businessmen they are. Their sons have probably gone to Princeton or Columbia. They don't merely eat at fashionable places, they quite likely own them. Their offices are not in suburban warehouses. They are in Wall Street. They run such diverse and essential enterprises as – in some cities – the building industry, the docks and waterfront stevedores' unions from Maine to New Orleans. They have a hand in such seemingly innocent fronts as ski resorts and pizza parlours (which have proved to be wonderful cover-ups for drug sales). Only the sleazier heirs of the old Capone days specialize in the gambling and prostitution rackets of Las Vegas and Atlantic City. For the others, whatever slang they generate is indistinguishable from the daily jargon of takeovers and insider trading.

Prison slang has always been a very fertile source of the American vernacular, and all of us use, quite innocently, many of the jailbird's expressions, the original meaning of which the most brazen of us would blush to learn. We won't go into that. New York City itself added new words to the language in the beginning because the Dutch had owned the place before the English. And such words as the 'stoop' (of a house) and 'cruller' as a kind of cake have stayed with us, and every child who learns to say 'faist' and pronounces turmoil as 'toimerl' knows that Brooklyn is an English corruption of Breucklein. But the main source of new entries into New York English was the fact that in the past hundred years this city has been the port of entry for immigrants from many countries of Europe. And because about half of all the Jews who arrived here settled here, many Yiddish words passed into everybody's slang. I hadn't been here a month before I knew what a schlemiel was, and when playing cards, learned to watch out for kibitzers. The cloak-and-suit business alone produced catchphrases that are still with us.

Coming up to today, I was going to say that since the administration was taken over by Marines and Navy men, but that would be an outrageous exaggeration. However, in the recent testimony before the Iran-Contra committees, we kept hearing naval expressions from three ex-Marines: Secretary Shultz, former Chief of Staff Don Regan, not to mention the third man – what's his name? – Colonel North. At one point, Mr Shultz differed with Admiral Poindexter over the meaning of the phrase 'stood down'. The Admiral had said that there came a time when the Iran arms deal was 'stood down', by which he implied it had been put, for the time being, on the shelf. Mr Shultz said that when he was told it was stood down, he assumed it had been abandoned. Why, he was asked, the difference in understanding? Because, he said, 'I'm a Marine, not a Navy man'. Out of those hearings there has come an old phrase which will for ever be attached to what the President now calls the Iran-Contra 'mess'. 'The buck' comes from poker. It was a marker, often a silver dollar, to show who had the next deal, and it could be passed by someone who didn't want the responsibility of dealing to the man on his left. Hence, 'passing the buck'. President Truman made the word immortal when he made it clear that the President alone is responsible for his administration. 'The buck', he said, 'stops here.' In this administration, and in its 'mess', we had come to believe that the buck stopped with Admiral

Poindexter. 'Not so,' said Mr Reagan on Wednesday, 'it stops with the President.' It will send a huge sigh of relief throughout the country. After nine months of doubt, we know now that the President *is* the man in charge, and that he is responsible for what happened, as the old Marines kept saying, 'on his watch'.

Mayor Koch at Work

12 August 1988

The other morning, caught on Fifth Avenue in a hopeless traffic jam, the driver and I panting away in the furnace of his taxi which must have been well over 100 degrees, the driver said, 'If you'll excuse me, mister, but I'm going home.' I didn't blame him, paid him off, and padded down the Avenue with all the alacrity of an infantryman tiptoeing through a minefield.

Later in the day, I had occasion to be going by Gracie Mansion, the Mayor of New York's graceful colonial house that sits in a little park on the edge of the East River. The ordeal of the morning, the traffic jam, and the sight of the Mayor's white house bristling like a mirage among the trees made me think back to a time, I think the last time, I was a guest in the house with the then Mayor, and one or two of his young aides. We were going on about the increasing traffic density everywhere in the city, and I was complaining – as I've been doing ever since – about the meaningless signs, posted every two blocks, on Park and Fifth Avenues, which said, in bold print: 'No Commercial Traffic.' No truck driver I can remember has ever been stopped. I suggested there was an enormous amount of revenue available from a campaign to enforce the signs and hand out hefty fines. The trucks and vans, I said, go ten, twenty, forty blocks, two miles down Fifth Avenue and nobody does anything. The Mayor shook his head: 'It's not possible', he said, 'to do anything anymore. You'd have unholy congestion on every avenue that allows commercial traffic.'

That must have been twenty years ago, and presumably Mayor Koch feels the same way. As we tilted our drinks that evening long ago, and gave up yet another local issue as a bad job, I suggested, 'Why don't you do what they did in Rome? Prohibit all commercial deliveries between dawn and sunset.' Say, said the youngest of the aides, how about that? The Mayor looked pityingly at this young, this very young politician and said, 'Oh, great! First, you'd be paying golden time, triple pay, to all the truck drivers. The price of everything would shoot up. Then you'd have protest marches about the city's inflation rate being way above the national average. Pretty soon, I can imagine somebody in Albany getting out a bill – Teamsters Marriage Compensation Act – for all the drivers whose marriages went bust through the guy sleeping by day and being out all night. The Parent-Teacher Association would move in on that one. And citizens' groups protesting all those delivery vans and trucks barrelling through the streets in the dead of night. And extra help needed at the toll stations and the tunnels across the rivers, at double pay. Shall I go on?' 'Well,' said the young aide, 'they did it in Rome.' 'When?' asked the Mayor. 'I think,' I said, 'it was around 30, 40 BC.' Another bright idea bit the dust.

The other night, I watched the present Mayor, the beleaguered but indestructible Ed Koch, in a packed schoolroom up in Harlem doing what he does once a week, which is primly described as the Mayor's question-and-answer show, on the city's television station. You might have thought you were present at an interrogation session on the West Bank between Israeli soldiers and a pack of young Palestinians. Everybody was fanning themselves in the atrocious heat. The Mayor was continually mopping his face and neck with a handkerchief the size of a tablecloth. And the questioning, so-called, a screaming siren of protests, about the drug pushers taking over this bit of park, no street lights in that lady's block on Staten Island, an old man threatened with eviction and what was the Mayor ever going to do about extra night police at such an intersection, and why was a big condominium – a high-rise for the well-off – going up by a tenement that had no water pressure. The questions were very rarely put as questions. They were defiant, disgusted speeches, bawled at this sweating figure on a rostrum, and the Mayor never paused or backed away: 'Listen, lady, if you'll listen, when this meeting is over, get a hold of Commissioner So-and-so, he's right here, and give him the details. You, no the man in the red shirt, okay, okay, lady, that's enough, shut up. Next: the young woman over there, what's your complaint?' She was the one screaming about the street lights on Staten Island, and she also joined in on the water-pressure problem, which the Mayor said was 'absolutely unavoidable with the enormous draw on the power grid in this heat – you'll be lucky if you don't wake up one night with all the lights out'. The young woman, a Hispanic with blazing black eyes, howled: 'My father tell me don't go live New York, it's hell on earth.' She was screaming on and the Mayor cut in: 'Okay, listen to your father next time. You – the old lady in the corner. Yes, Madam?'

There are many mayors of cities, governors of states, who regularly submit to the questions of citizens from all over but in the air-conditioned sanctuary of a television studio with an emcee monitoring the incoming calls, and the questioners, the attackers, at the long, safe, distance of a telephone wire. I don't know of another politician who goes through this face-to-face, nature-red-in-tooth-and-claw perform-ance more than once in a while, as an unpleasant necessity of political office. But to Mayor Koch, it's a necessary weekly joust which, he fervently believes, is the essence of his being: being a politician. When the meetings are over, within a few days his office is flooded with letters from people who saw the show on television, and the various officials who stood warily beside him that night are confronted by the complainers who were told to take their troubles to the responsible department. This is, of course, a mere item in the Mayor's daily grind, which starts at dawn and is lucky to end at midnight. Just now, today for instance, he's trying to recruit seven hundred new policemen in the narcotics division of the city force to stem the outrage over open drug dealing in the streets of many neighbourhoods. He's just apologized for the excessive force he believes the police used in putting down a demonstration against a curfew in a small but dangerous park. He's just begged people to stop giving money to street panhandlers and contribute instead to city charities. He's ordering the hospitals to report on their methods for disposing of hospital waste, which has been washing up in noxious quantities along some of the Jersey and Long Island beaches – and now, by the way, has appeared lapping the shores of Lake Erie, seven hundred miles inland in Cleveland, Ohio. That has spurred the United States Senate to get out a bill prohibiting, from 1990 on, the disposal of hospital wastes in all seas and lakes.

Meanwhile, the Mayor faces a constant battle with the people in every borough who want new prisons but don't want them in their neighbourhood – just like the aroused citizens of several New England states who believe, in principle, in nuclear power but have mobilized to resist having an essential nuclear waste dump in their neck of the woods.

Two or three evenings a week, the Mayor has, in theory, time off, which means attending a dinner to distribute to eminent immigrants the city's medal of freedom; the ducking into an Italian-American dinner; then a Puerto Rican dinner; an Irish protest meeting about his outrageous remark that the British in Northern Ireland did not constitute an army of occupation. That observation alone probably lost him a hundred thousand Irish votes; in the next year's election, he backed off. And, the unreal, the incredible thing is: he wants to run again, after eleven years of presiding over this seething cosmopolis, and after two years of fighting charges of corruption in his administration. During that time, several of his closest aides and city officials have gone to jail, resigned under fire or committed suicide. He has, by his own admission, too often put his trust in the wrong people.

Why would he want a shot at another four years? Because, I think, after all the wear and tear of trying to take care of seven million people, he remains an irrepressible romantic, who has had the tonic experience of sometimes seeing romance turn into reality. He did pluck New York from the brink of bankruptcy and is not going to let you forget it. But unlike President Reagan, another romantic, he does not cling to an old and simpler picture of America and yearn to restore it. He gets as excited over the prospect of housing a hundred homeless families in a rundown Harlem hotel as Mr Reagan does over the vision of Star Wars.

Mayor Koch, in his racy, egotistical and never dull autobiography wrote:

The City of New York included nearly two hundred religions, races, and national groups. It used to be said that New York City was a melting pot. It never was, and it isn't today. Our fathers and mothers, and some of us, wanted to believe we had lost our own racial and ethnic traditions and had become homogenized. That never happened. What happens is, you gain respect for the traditions of others but don't lose your own. Today, black is beautiful. Spanish is the language of the future. Women want to be astronauts, and are. Jews play golf. God made us whatever we are. Being Mayor of the City is a very special experience, and I'm lucky.

By the way, the Mayor – one of the leading Democrats of the nation – did not go to the Atlanta Convention. Sobbing rhetoric and a thousand balloons are not his style. As for the weekly brawl with those rocking, bawling, aggrieved citizens, the Mayor finds it a stimulus. If nobody had ever invented the now worn-out phrase, he could truthfully say: 'That's what government is all about.' If he were a demagogue, which he isn't, he might call it 'democracy in action'. As it is, if you put it to him, he'll say, with a stoical smile, his eyebrows up, and his shoulders shrugging: 'Well, it's nothing else.'

Hurricanes

23 September 1988

If you can imagine yourself in an aeroplane flying from the tip of Cornwall to the north of Scotland, or more accurately, from the toe of Italy up the seven hundred and fifty miles to Milan, and seeing the greater part of the land you flew over under water, you would have an idea of the monstrous scale of Hurricane Gilbert after it had done its frightful wrecking job on Jamaica, the Yucatan peninsula, and the Mexican towns on the Gulf coast. Most of central Texas and on through western Oklahoma had, in twenty-four hours, between 10

In the studio, 1970s. AC was always relieved and relaxed once the recording was completed.

AC and President Eisenhower share a light moment during the filming of 'General Eisenhow on the Military Churchill' at Eisenhower's Gettysburg, Pennsylvania, home, August 1967.

AC on the dais with Attorney General Robert Kennedy speaking, at a luncheon meeting of members of Congress in New York City, February 1968.

Adlai Stevenson's 54th birthday: Stevenson receiving a cake from the
New Yorker book critic Clifton Fadiman, with AC on the right.

AC interviewing LBJ about Vietnam, August 1965, photograph signed and
dedicated to AC by LBJ.

AC at his favourite 'twilight' time of day – when conversation and whisky flowed. Here, in his study at 1150 Fifth Avenue, in 1972.

AC putting in the long gallery at 1150 Fifth Avenue, where numerous carpets were replaced over the years owing to divots.

AC left the apartment, crossed Fifth Avenue and practised his swing in Central Park, regardless of the time of year.

AC chipping out of a bunker at Island's End Golf & Country Club, Inc.

AC after a round with Bing Crosby and Robert Cameron (aerial photographer), June 1973.

On the roof of 1150 Fifth Avenue, overlooking the reservoir – the view he saw from his desk every day. 1972.

In the living room of 1150 Fifth Avenue, adjacent to a window providing the same parkside view. 1972.

Portrait by long-time friend Roddy McDowall, who captured AC as only a good friend could. This picture remains one of Jane's and Susie's favourites.

and 18 inches of rain. Something like 32 inches is the annual quota of London and, by the way, New York. The result, of which we saw only 30-second glimpses, was of an endless landscape of little Venices with people wading or getting from here to there on improvised rafts. The only good (for the United States) that blew in with this ill wind was a deluge of rain dumped on the farm states of Kansas and Nebraska and Iowa (we are now fifteen hundred miles north of Yucatan), whose immense crops have withered in this summer of unrelieved drought.

As for Mexico, the plight of hundreds of small towns and villages is hardly to be pictured. The heartbreaking item was the fact that the worst casualties, now mounting two hundred, were of people who'd had the sense to flee from the coast and were already a hundred and eighty miles inland in Monterrey, when their buses were overwhelmed by the roaring flood waters.

For a storm that was a thousand miles in diameter when it crossed the Gulf of Mexico and packed winds of over a hundred and fifty miles an hour, it must appear that the casualties were astonishingly, blessedly low. And so they were, compared with, for instance, a hurricane that swooped on to the coastal city of Galveston, Texas, in 1900 and took six thousand lives in that small city alone, one-seventh of the population, leaving, the official report said, 'not a single house undamaged'. Well, even if all the people had fled, I suppose the physical, structural damage would have been the same. But the death rate was due to a simple failure, incapacity of the time: the inability to see it coming. The weather forecast for 8 September 1900 in the Galveston papers read, 'Sunny and warm'. And so it was for all the great recorded hurricanes from 1938 back to 1848 – a monster that destroyed much of Florida and did damage for the next thousand miles of its northward trek.

All that people knew, for the years that records had been kept, was that these hurricanes arise in August and September in the West Indies and move north or northwest. The meteorologists could track them only when they hit land. Not until 1932 did a radio station in Florida, working with a couple of the university's engineers, and financed by the WPA (the New Deal agency for the unemployed) start a rudimentary hurricane research station whose job was to maintain short-wave radio communication with Puerto Rico. Even then, they were dependent on reports from the West Indies of what people had seen happening to them. The course and intensity of the storms, once they got up into the Gulf, were a mystery. Only in the past thirty years have we had a National Hurricane Center in Florida, now on permanent duty, a staff of hurricane experts equipped with high-tech devices and, the really new and vital adjunct, a crew of Coast Guard pilots trained to fly over and then drop into the eye of hurricanes and to bring back the details of their forward speed, rotary speed, and their course. Even then, even now, after Gilbert was buccaneering into Oklahoma, the head of the National Hurricane Center remarked that we can accurately predict the direction of a hurricane only for the next twenty-four hours. Beyond that, we still do not know if it is going to turn, and where, and why. So, once the thing had torn through Jamaica and across the Yucatan peninsula, the Hurricane Center could do no better than suggest the evacuation of the coast populations round an arc of the Gulf from northern Mexico along all the Texas and Louisiana Gulf coasts, a broken stretch of over five hundred miles. By Friday of last week, about half a million people were on the move. As Gilbert stubbornly maintained its west-northwestern course, the alarm was called off for New Orleans and the Louisiana coast.

By the way, last weekend I asked a young European who broadcasts to his native land if he had, at any point in his early reports, said what a hurricane is. He was startled. Surely, he said, everybody knows that. Yet, I've noticed, even some of my friends imply that a hurricane is a very high wind, high in the sense of speedy. I was told by English meteorologists that the great storm which ravaged southeastern England last autumn was not technically a hurricane, which must be scant consolation to the curators of Kew Gardens. We have weathered six hurricanes on Long Island in the last fifty years, and while they've detached shingles, broken windows and let the rain in, it was not a hurricane but a simple though ferocious northeast wind that five years ago ripped off the whole bayside porch of the house, crashed it through the roof and deposited much of it in the living room. Luckily, we weren't there. We were sitting in a hotel room on the coast of California watching pictures of people in boats ferrying between houses and flooded shops. 'Wonder where that can be?' we said. 'Riverhead, Long Island,' the announcer obliged. 'Poor old Riverhead,' we said. When

318

we got back to New York and drove down to the Island, we said, 'Poor old us!'

The main point about a hurricane is that it is not a furious, fast and damaging wind moving like an army. It is shaped like a doughnut, a doughnut whirling around anti- or counterclockwise at speeds above 73 miles per hour (Gilbert got up to 180 at one point). The hole in the middle of the doughnut is the eye and the eerie thing about it is that it is dead calm. The forward movement of the whole system is very much slower, usually not more than 20 miles per hour. The damage comes from the whirling motion, and the worst damage happens to very tall trees, which can be spun and plucked up by their roots.

It's an odd coincidence that even if there'd been no Gilbert, I'm pretty sure that this week I should have talked about hurricanes – about one hurricane, the memory of which made those of us who came through it shudder a little last Wednesday. Just fifty years ago, on that day, I was sailing to New York on the great French liner, the *Normandie*. The sea was a little choppy, and the sky was overcast and stayed so the next morning when we woke up to receive the breakfast tray and the ship's newspaper. Those of you who have ever taken a cruise or sailed the transatlantic ships in the old days will know what I mean when I say that a ship's newspaper could be a source of much hilarity. Scraps of international news picked up by radio overnight – most of the copy about fashions or sport. Spelling mistakes abounded, pieces stopped in mid-paragraph. So, when we saw a headline, 'Hurricane à New-York', we knew that the French had got their information badly fouled up. We did not have hurricanes 'à New York'. But I read on, and it talked about the devastation of towns on 'le Fork du Nord' (the North Fork, which is where we live) and the lifting of a cinema on the Fork du Sud (the South Fork) at Westhampton out to sea. They were right – twenty-odd people at a matinée, and the theatre, projectionist and all, landed two miles into the Atlantic and drowned. There was flooding of Providence, Rhode Island, huge destruction of the forests of New England, and so on.

Next morning, we were practically jolted out of our beds, and the public address system announced that nobody must try to go on deck. The hurricane blowing out across the Atlantic had hit us. What I most remember, for an hour or two, was that the *Normandie*, the second largest (I believe) transatlantic liner afloat, simply got up out of the water, shook itself in the air like a drenched mastiff and plunged back into the deeps. On and on. Five people out of close to three thousand went down to dinner.

The following morning, as always seems to happen, was a brilliant and beautiful day, and we sailed up the bay and into the harbour, and there my father-in-law was waiting for us. A ramrod-straight, austere old New Englander who scorned ever to show emotion for any hurt done to him, he told us briskly with a moist eye about his ninety wooded acres, 'a lifetime to plant, a few years, perhaps to clean up and plant again'. Well, it wasn't quite that bad, but it was about ten days before we could drive through the main street of our nearest village, Southold. The towering American elms had been whisked and plucked and brought up by their roots and the sidewalks with them, so that the streets were trenches with tilted pavements as their walls. The devastation everywhere was indescribable. A third of the American feather-duster elms through Rhode Island and Massachusetts were destroyed, half the New Hampshire stands of white birch. More than six hundred people were drowned. The *New York Times* weather forecast, on the morning of 21 September 1938, said: 'Cloudy, chance of rain'.

My sharpest, the most indelible memoir of a hurricane, which to me dramatized the wind force more than a hundred panoramic shots of toppled trees and floating houses, was my recollection of a pencil-thin something that had pierced the bark of a tree and lodged deep in there like a struck arrow. It was a straw.

Chaplin – the Last Word

21 April 1989

About a month, six weeks ago, I was surprised to get a call from a newspaper – and in the following weeks pursued by a flurry of calls from other papers and television stations, all asking the same question. Would I like to contribute to the coming great celebration, the centenary of the birth of you know who? I knew who, but I put them off by saying: 'Oh, so you're going to do a big feature on Hitler?' Everybody was baffled. Hitler? Why Hitler? Because, I said, 20 April 1889 is a date that will live in infamy. They may have changed now, but none of them at the time had any plans to observe (shall we say), if not celebrate, the hundredth anniversary of the arrival on the continent of Europe of the human who did more than anybody in this century to shatter it.

No doubt by now, this weekend most of the media will be making up for this omission. It would be an omission. After all, most of us who live through the exploits of our youthful heroes and villains go into middle and old age remaining constantly amazed that the next generation, or the one after that, has never heard of them. I well remember the envy I felt for the bliss of my daughter's ignorance when, thirty-some years ago, when she was about 6, she had been watching a television programme and came running into my study saying, 'Daddy, what's Hitler?' What's? Wonderful! She learned.

Of course, the man I was being solicited to talk or write about was none other than Charles Spencer Chaplin. I turned them all down on the ground that I had written, in a book, just about everything I should want to say about him. Most of the telephone callers were amazed to hear this. One knowledgeable girl said, 'But we understand in this office that you once worked with him on a movie about Napoleon?' 'That's right, it's all in the book,' I said. 'Thanks for thinking of me, but goodbye.'

However, in reading just now the reams of tributes, potted biographies, critiques of every film, from the Essanay shorts to the final, dreadful *Countess of Hong Kong*, it struck me that everybody I read was picking up stories they'd heard, or read, or making a big deal out of a single meeting. Why? Were they being devious, dishonest? Not at all. They were doing what I should do, what I do regularly if I'm writing about Disraeli or Lloyd George or Jack Hobbs or anyone else who was in his glory days when I was a tot, or not yet born. All the writers, even the greybeards of film criticism, were – the awful truth dawned – too young to have known him. And their knowledge, too, of practically every film up to *Modern Times* had come from reverent little pilgrimages to film clubs or Motion Picture Museums, which, in Britain and America, are growing like mushrooms.

So, I thought, maybe I should, here and now, and only here and now, have a last word about this extraordinary, irascible, generous, conscienceless, thoughtful, mischievous, overwhelmingly charming man about whose work the young and the old generations, I gather, now agree to differ. At my end of the calendar, it is now established as gospel that Chaplin was the first genius of film comedy, its inventor, and that nobody has touched him for weaving together slapstick and pathos in artful ways. (I ought to say that way back there in my twenties I had a friend, a sly unfooled Irishman, who enjoyed Max Linder and Buster Keaton and the Marx Brothers, but found Chaplin from the beginning arch, self-conscious and nauseatingly sentimental. But old Heb Davidson, still, I hope, of Donard Demesne, County Wicklow, was always an exception, a wicked dissenter from all conventional wisdom.) Now I gather – from the young critics who have paused to celebrate the anniversary – that Buster Keaton is the resurrected god and that Chaplin, as comedian, is sorry stuff. I have not seen any writing of this kind about him here, but it appears to me a standard view in Britain, among, that is, the intelligentsia, who were, sixty years ago, the first people to rescue the early Chaplin from the masses who adored him and suggest he was almost too good for them. The new view, surprising to me, was put crisply last week by *The Economist*, which – remarking correctly that Chaplin's comedy was rooted in the Victorian music hall, both in its slapstick and its maudlin sentimental songs – concluded that this is why today his comedy 'is so unfunny and manipulative'.

Well, that's all that need or can be said about the comedian. For although it is possible – indeed, it happens all the time – that people can be taught to enjoy a composer, a painter, a writer (what are our arts schools for?), there is absolutely no way that anyone can be instructed, beguiled, persuaded, to find someone funny whom they find unfunny. The most useless arguments between friends are about which writer or performer is or is not funny, and which food is or is not delicious.

But how about this man, who one day in 1934 wrote to me (a miracle, that: he rarely wrote to anyone) asking me to go out to Hollywood and help him with the script of a projected film on Napoleon? I have written at length on how I got to know him – that the previous year, as a graduate student cruising around the United States, I had a commission from a London paper to interview him, that I went to his studio to meet him; that he took me up to his house; and that the rest of the summer I was up there most days and many evenings. He was then 44, a tiny, dapper man, a graceful golliwog in an angora sweater, topped by a remarkably handsome face of almost sculptural bone structure. I was 24, lean and gabby, hipped on the movies and certainly, at first, dazzled to be taken up by the most famous man in the world – an obvious title when you remember that, since his movies were silent, the natives of about a hundred and fifty countries had seen and laughed at him. The old cowboy philosopher Will Rogers put it in a nutshell: 'The Zulus knew Chaplin better than Arkansas knew Garbo.'

So in the second year, 1934, I drove off across the country, landed in Hollywood and reported to his funny little rundown bungalow studio. Next day, we retired to a small workroom, a shabby place (he always said he was uncomfortable working in lavish surroundings) with peeling wallpaper, worn oilcloth on the floor, three straight-backed chairs, a plain table, an upright piano out of tune. The room was a shock, an interesting reflection of something noticed about other rich men who had been born in dire poverty. It was not there to recall the poverty, but to remind you that perhaps the new money was not there for keeps. It explained, too, I think his habit of never carrying money. He either signed restaurant bills or got his assistant director or another employee to pay for him.

Most days I spent the afternoons in the local library, boning up on books about Napoleon's life in exile on St Helena. Next morning we would go over the stuff, and Chaplin would start to create scenes, in mime: a row with his British doctor, a complaint dictated back to Britain, daydreams about a battle or Josephine, or an imperial attack of indigestion. That latter bit could have come straight out of *The Immigrant* or *The Gold Rush*. In fact, I think I knew then the project would never work. Mostly he would stomp or slouch around the room mumbling incomprehensible dialogue, and look thoughtful or indignant or sombre, and he had an astonishing gift to look more like Napoleon than Napoleon (or, for that matter, more like any of the many real people he mimicked). But he instinctively couldn't help making the point, in dumb show, that an emperor with a hiccup or a burp is just as helpless as a baby. Several times, in the weeks we worked on this rough script, a serious scene – Napoleon rewriting his will – would gradually turn into a piece of comic pantomime that had us helpless. The third member, brought in as the public stand-in to try things out on, was the old shambling Swede, Henry Bergman, who had played in practically every Chaplin comedy. We'd give up, and go chuckling off to lunch. One day, I went up to the house to dinner. We sat and played, as a duet, the song 'Titine', which he was to use in *Modern Times*. He broke off for a telephone call and when he came back, I remember, he had a toothpick. He sat back on a sofa and picked away. 'By the way,' he said, 'the Napoleon thing. It's a beautiful idea – for somebody else.' We didn't discuss it. Nobody discussed a personal decision made by Charles Spencer Chaplin. On the way out to dinner, he said, 'Nobody pays to see Chaplin do an artistic experiment. They go to see the little man.' Nothing more was said, ever. A week or two later, I packed and took off East. I'm sure he was right, as some later impersonations proved.

This is not the place to go into his exile to Switzerland. It had little to do with his politics. He was never more than what in those days was called 'a parlour pink' though he was accused of every radical crime in the book by malicious gossip columnists who resented his holding on to his British citizenship. It had much to do with paternity suits and his cavalier way of ignoring subpoenas on other womanly matters, and the instructions of the courts. The administration hounded him, and found nothing indictable, but when they rescinded his re-entry permit as he was on the Atlantic on his way to Europe, he had had enough, and abruptly decided to stay in Switzerland for life. It was a sad end to his long American adventure. He loved this country, but he never forgave the Truman administration's final, abrupt and shabby treatment of him.

Those paranoid years are long gone, and luckily the generation that doesn't know much about him will know even less of his old age. He remains, as W. C. Fields described him, better than he meant, 'A ballet dancer', the universal homeless waif, over-sentimental at times, certainly, endlessly inventive, as Fred Astaire was inventive, often touching, and to some of us still uniquely – funny.

San Francisco Earthquake

20 October 1989

Sometime in the middle of the First World War – it must have been towards the end of the dreadful year of 1916, after the nightmare slaughter of the Somme – an aunt of mine, whose husband was a soldier in France, announced that she didn't believe a word of what she read in the papers. She was going to write to her husband to find out for real what was going on on the Western Front. This showed, first, a touching ignorance of the censorship of letters, both ways. But eventually he replied. All he could tell her about the way the war was going was what life was like in a muddied trench he'd been living in for a month or two. And what a blasted 200 yards looked like between him and the German trenches. The whole war for him shrank to dampness, lice, chilblains, rats, bully beef, the sight of two ruined trees, and would she please send him some chocolate and cigarettes.

On Tuesday night and Wednesday of this past week, it struck me that the constant irony of the San Francisco earthquake, in this, the wonderful age of worldwide communication was that – compared with the people of Europe, Australia, India, wherever – the only people who hadn't a clue to what was going on were the people of San Francisco and other neighbouring cities, without power. From the first rumble and shudder of those wracking fifteen seconds, and on for a couple of days, they had no power, no television, no radio, no newspapers. A reporter who had flown in from the East on Wednesday wrote that it was a strange, embarrassing feeling to stand in almost any part of the city and tell these gaping natives about Candlestick Park, the Nimitz Freeway, the damage in the Mission district, the collapsed shopping mall ninety miles away in Santa Cruz, the buckled highways, the astonishing range of pictures she'd seen on television overnight. Mainly transmitted from that station in Atlanta, Georgia – CNN – which the irrepressible Ted Turner started years ago and which pulls in through innumerable saucers live coverage from everywhere on earth, and broadcasts without a pause, twenty-four hours a day. On Tuesday night in the East, when the scene jumped to President Bush at a dinner to give us the latest word, the CNN anchor people charitably left him as soon as possible: he was already well behind the times. He had not been at home watching CNN Atlanta.

It was an eerie break for millions of Americans settling down across the country at 5:00 Pacific time, 8 p.m., in the East, that they were about to have the privilege of getting a vast panorama of the scene below, of the course, the baseball stadium, and the surrounding city, as seen by a blimp that is always on hand, on high, for such sporting occasions. All these fans were settling in, as I was, with a friend and a beer, to watch the third game of the baseball championship of the World Series. It was 5 o'clock, and we'd seen the 62,000 rustling away down there, and inevitably, they always like to set the stage, long panning shots of the enchanting bay and the great bridges glistening in the falling sun. We saw the pitchers warming up in the bullpen, the managers and teams chewing away, gum, perhaps, more often tobacco, in the dugout. We were ready for the introductions, the national anthem, then all but one of the batting team would trot back to the dugout, and the fielding team would spread for the first pitch, and there'd be a raucous roar of the Oakland fans who had come to see the Christians, the Giants that is, mauled.

Back to three anchormen in their booth. They chatter. One of them looks behind him and down, as if a friend had called. Then he looks up. Then the second deck of the stadium at Candlestick Park – well, the camera must have been clumsily handled, the deck seemed to sway and sag a little. I don't believe we knew this as a fact till it was over. And, providentially, the huge crowd didn't seem to catch on either. In fact, after the first rolling wave there was a cheer, and a big cry of 'Play Ball'. And then a stranger wave, of a vast human sigh or gasp. And then the players broke up, their wives appeared on the field, and soon they were cradling bewildered children or walking quietly off with arms around their wives. To this day, the blessed, the unexplained truth is the absence of panic, I thought for a time the umpires had not turned up, some other failure of the usual arrangements. And then we heard. And in no time, the great blimp took off, and as the night came on soared and was seeing the incredible sight of a collapsed span of the Bay Bridge over the huge blacked-out city with smoke plumes rising there down toward the bay, and then the plumes turning into flames and the beginning of the fire. The pictures, picked up now from all around the bay, swam with menacing slowness all through the night, till at daybreak we saw, as I'm sure you did, wherever you were, the collapsed upper deck of the Nimitz Freeway on the Oakland side, the sudden ghastly appearance of what somebody called the concrete sandwich. Hasty guesses were made about the numbers of cars and people trapped in there, and overseas papers grabbed at a figure – 250 – which the police here first deplored, saying that after many hours only seven bodies had been dragged out. But on Thursday morning a reporter close by pointed to the compression of the upper deck of the highway on the lower and banished any hope of survivors by remarking that the visible space between the two decks was at most 18 inches high.

Apart from the strange, almost casual, departure of the 60,000 baseball fans, it must be said that the other great and unanticipated blessing was the comparatively minute damage done to the city of San Francisco itself, accordingly, little loss of life, compared, that is, with

April 1906. This reading on the Richter scale, as you'll have heard, was 6.9, exactly the measurement of last year's earthquake in Armenia, which took 25,000 lives. That difference is easily explained. Since 1906, California, northern California especially, has lived always with the prospect in mind of another great quake, and in 1907 drafted its first new building code, devised for the first time by structural engineers working with architects. It required bracing systems and reinforced masonry. And until the Second World War, the city withstood innumerable shocks, minor by Tuesday's reckoning. In 1946, another, tougher code went into effect. By 1965 we had a wealth of new building materials and by then, also, San Francisco was, lamentably, about to put up its first high-rises and downtown skyscrapers. So another more elaborate and stricter code was made to apply to all new building. In the early 1970s, by the way, they decided that the concrete decks on the two-tier bridges might, in an earthquake, be too heavy for the vertical supports. They reinforced them. The Golden Gate Bridge and two others across the Bay held firm this time, though engineers now suspect that the sustaining verticals on the Bay Bridge proved too skinny. One expert in earthquake engineering went so far – after the Nimitz disaster – as to doubt whether any more two-decker highways should be built.

What was most impressive was the speed and harmony that marked the mobilization, within the hour, of the National Guard, the Army Corps of Engineers, the California state authorities, the city fathers, the police, engineers, the Red Cross, and a resource that San Francisco is unique in being able to call on: a permanent, steady earthquake medical team. Not to forget the heartening sight of thousands of ordinary citizens up from their beds in the middle of the night helping the teams at the collapsed highways or forming human ladders with buckets at the Marina fire, before they were able to rig up the system of pumping water from the Bay itself. All these volunteers, in San Francisco, were warned to go home and stay there, the great fear, once the fire started from burst gas mains was the fear that was devastatingly fulfilled in 1906, the gas leaks from other mains and the eruption of hundreds of other fires. When I first went to San Francisco, fifty-six years ago, and for several decades thereafter, old San Franciscans would wince at a gaffe regularly committed by visitors: to any mention of the Earthquake. It was always, the fire – the great fire. And it's true that while immense damage was done by the initial shock – 8 points – on that April morning, the ravaging of the heart of the city was done by fire. So insatiable was the fire's appetite, raging over four square miles, that to save the northwestern part of the city, the army was called out from the Presidio, dynamited the whole cross avenue of Van Ness and held the fire.

Well, this time, there were no aftershocks to burst other mains (aftershocks can happen days or weeks or months after the first jolt). And all these helpers, expert and amateur, came together under the government's central authority: the Federal Emergency Management Agency, which it so happens held a simulated earthquake drill throughout the city only two months ago. FEMA's main job is the granting of low-cost loans to people who have suffered loss of property or injury. FEMA just now suffers from a cruel disability; most of its national team is off in Puerto Rico, the Virgin Islands and South Carolina, working sixteen hours a day helping to repair the wrecked lives of over quarter of a million victims of Hurricane Hugo. A disaster insurance expert with FEMA brought us a timely, if grisly, reminder on Wednesday, that Hugo is a far greater human catastrophe than the earthquake. At this moment, FEMA is trying to handle 20,000 applications for help in the Virgin Islands, 45,000 in and around Charleston, South Carolina and 200,000 in Puerto Rico. FEMA's resources have touched bottom, and the man stressed for all of us who feel compassionate about San Francisco that cash – for Hugo, from people, anywhere – is still the main burden of their appeal.

The 1990s

Presidential Ghosts

23 February 1990

Of course, the most moving event of the week was the appearance, and the speech, of President Havel of Czechoslovakia before a joint session of both houses of Congress. Time and again, cries of 'Bravo' went up, and five times he was accorded something that happens to a Presidential address only once, at the end of it: namely a standing ovation. An extraordinary thing about the speech was noted in press and television reports of it. He wrote it himself!

This astounding fact was mentioned only a day or two before the publication of a book by the young woman who is more responsible than either President Reagan or President Bush for the popular view of their characters. She is Peggy Noonan, a witty, lyrical Irish troll, who wrote the speeches through which we came to believe we were seeing the true, the charming, the inspiring Ronald Reagan and George Bush. In fact, there is an alarming discovery available in Miss Noonan's book. It is that practically all the most famous, the most winning, the most characteristic utterances of both Presidents – were composed by her. From 'You ain't seen nothing yet' and 'Make my day!' to 'Read my lips' and 'a kinder, gentler, nation'.

For Mr Bush, especially, Miss Noonan was the alchemist who at a stroke, in the nomination acceptance speech at New Orleans in the summer of 1988, transformed our picture of George Bush from that of an intense wimp, a rather awkward speaker, into a generous, kind and surprisingly eloquent practitioner of English prose. There was never a poll directly charting the effect of that speech on the voters, but there were two polls that parallel the remarkable change in the popular view of Mr Bush's character. Before the New Orleans speech, Mr Bush was running a few points behind Mr Dukakis as the general choice of President. After it, Mr Bush went ahead in comparative popularity and never looked back. And even when Miss Noonan left him and the White House, the remaining speech-writers, who had questioned and hounded the style she had composed for him, adopted it as best they could and maintained the character she had created. So that, or perhaps not so that, but either by accident or more likely as one natural consequence, Mr Bush today finds himself approved by a solid 70 per cent of the nation, a lovable peak achieved in our time only by John F. Kennedy in his first term. President Kennedy, I ought to say, also had his Henry Higgins. His immortal, incessantly quoted Inaugural speech, was written by Mr Theodore Sorensen, who stayed with him and on all formal occasions, impressed ever deeper on our ears and our consciousness the figure of a young, gallant and moving orator.

I emerged from Miss Noonan's book with mixed feelings – of wonder and distress. The distress arises from the growing discovery that I'm not sure I know, even now, the true character of either Ronald Reagan or George Bush. As a famous journalist once asked about a dozen celebrities he tracked down for private interviews, 'Are they the same at home?'

So, it was a shock, and a pleasant one, to realize during the hour that the Mr Havel who spoke here was both the private and the public man we were listening to. At one go, the first time we ever heard him, he provided the sort of rare satisfaction that must have come to people listening, for the first time, to Abraham Lincoln or Winston Churchill.

Which reminds me of a time, less than a month after the United States came into the Second World War, when, at Christmas time, Prime Minister Churchill arrived suddenly (his voyage was, of course, unannounced) in Washington to stay with President Roosevelt. These two had met, incidentally for the first time, to survey the theatres of war and sketch out a common strategy. Towards the end of this now famous visit, the two leaders agreed that, within a few days of Mr Churchill's safe return to London, each of them would go on air and broadcast to the peoples of the new transatlantic alliance his own inspiring version of their discussions. There was a firm but unwritten agreement that the two broadcasts, on radio of course, would fall on the same evening. The American radio networks were made privy to the arrangement, and while Churchill was flying home, Roosevelt wasted no time in summoning three of his most dependable and gifted ghosts, Judge Sam Rosenman, the poet Archibald MacLeish, and the playwright, Robert Sherwood, to compose as soon as possible (and in view of the formidable competition, no less than Churchill himself) a piece of memorable prose. They were, next morning, not much further along than a first draft when they had a telephone call from London, to the effect that Mr Churchill was safe at home and was going on the BBC that very evening. He was requesting the President to have the American networks clear a circuit for simultaneous broadcast. Roosevelt was appalled at this cunning betrayal. It seemed that during the boisterous thirteen-hour homeward flight, Mr Churchill – bouncing through murky weather (with no jets in those days) and sometimes while taking over the controls of the bomber – the traitor Churchill, with no other points of reference than a map of the world, had dictated a masterly conspectus of the global battlefronts. The tapes, or cylinders, were delivered to a secretary in Downing Street, typed up, the BBC was alerted, and the Prime Minister went on the air with his rumbling, majestic cadences.

In Washington, there were at least four despondent listeners. 'How,' moaned President Roosevelt to his slaving ghosts, 'how can he do it? How *did* he do it?' It was the playwright Sherwood who gave the melancholy answer. 'I'm afraid, Mr President,' he said, 'he rolls his own.' It was nothing but the truth.

Well, the rare, if not unique, pleasure of listening to President Havel sprang from the knowledge that 'he rolls his own'. It is a pleasure that was bound to be felt most acutely by writers, by actors, by voters who have a prejudice in favour of men who have a way with words. On the other hand, speech-writers in the White House are known – half enviously, half contemptibly – as 'wordsmiths'. Once the writer's draft has been submitted to fifty government departments (fifty!), and questioned and torn apart, and returned, it is assumed that the body of the speech, the substance, the right stuff, is all there, like the structure of a new house. Now it is up to the wordsmith to perform his or her particular function, which is that of a decorator. No wonder Miss Noonan lasted less than four years. The record of the corrections, rejections, of her originals, the stuffing of them with clumsy jargon, all the pretentious buzzwords that hang like a cloud of bees over the Pentagon, the State Department, the Office of Management and

Budget, the almost paranoid fear by government types of simple idiom, homely phrases, natural humour, pungent lines. Once this long agony has been endured, the writer submits a final draft. Then the chief of staff must look it over and then, at least, hand it to the speaker, the puppet, the President, no less. And then the writer, Miss Noonan, sits with her fingers and her talents crossed, and listens to the speech itself, and hopes and sighs (so *that* had to go) or hugs a friend (they left it in, they left it in!). And next week, the Challenger shuttle will explode in mid-air, and she must begin again – and did – to compose that most touching and poignant of all President Reagan's eulogies to American dead.

Mr Havel spoke sometimes in English, warm, resonant, simple English; more often, he spoke in his native language followed, paragraph by paragraph, by the translation. I just said now that writers, people who enjoy words and the handling of them, are the ones most likely to have enjoyed Lincoln, Churchill and now President Havel. There is a catch here, and Mr Havel made us know that he is aware of it. People with a fondness for writing and eloquence always vote for a candidate who seems to have the gift of words over one who doesn't. Hence the deep disappointment of legions when Adlai Stevenson lost to General Eisenhower. Intellectuals tend to vote for intellectuals, whenever they appear as political candidates. Mr Havel noted that the men who declared American independence and wrote the Constitution and the Bill of Rights – Jefferson most of all – were intellectuals. He noted this fact almost wistfully. He must know that, apart from that astonishing and unique generation, intellectuals have a very poor record as politicians. He himself, a playwright, made quite clear that he is not a politician and does not mean to be.

The End of the Eighties –
Great or Greedy?

27 April 1990

esday morning, a brilliant spring day, saw an extraordinary scene
downtown Manhattan that was variously described by newspaper
orters as the curtain call on the 1980s and, in a paper long known
its good, grey prose, as the last public appearance of 'the premier
ancial swindler of all time'.
There was a big restless crowd already on the sidewalk outside the
deral District Court when a black car slid up. The man himself, a
ry tall slim man in a dark suit, an affable-looking man with a tumble
black hair, unwound himself out of the car and had a rough time
tting through the crowd, which was now surging and bubbling
ound him as it might for a movie star. In a way he is a movie star,
at the same moment on a sidewalk in the mid-1970s on the East
de, there was another crowd, watching the filming of a character of
ich our man entering the courthouse was the prototype. The movie
at is being shot here is an adaptation of Tom Wolfe's *Bonfire of the
nities*, a Balzacian coroner's inquest on the life and death of the
80s. And the character the cameras were training on was Sherman
cCoy, who thought of himself as the King of the Jungle (the Wall
eet jungle, that is) and who would, before the movie ended, get his
el but just reward. At the same time, down in Federal Court, the
iginal of Sherman McCoy was being asked how he pleaded to six
ony counts: of conspiracy; filing false information with the Securities
d Exchange Commission (which polices the stock market); securities
ud; violating the Commission's reporting requirements; mail fraud;
d aiding and abetting in the filing of a false tax return. It has taken
e United States Attorney General's office years to track through a
ngle of documents and letters and memos and audits in order to

present the case at Tuesday's hearing. In a simpler world, they might have been spared their sweat. For in no time at all in the courtroom, the tall man, all his affability dissolved, was sobbing: 'I realize by my acts I have hurt those who are closest to me. I am truly sorry.' The judge allowed him to dry his tears and then asked him, 'Mr Millken, how do you plead?' Through a cracking tone of voice, Michael Millken replied, 'Guilty, your Honour.'

Mr Millken has been known as the King of the Junk Bond, which may be very starkly defined as a perilously high-risk but (if it works) high-yield security. Junk bonds have undoubtedly helped many small firms through generous grants of credit, to survive and prosper. But more often than not, they have paper-financed giant takeovers, pushed them at once on to preposterous levels of debt and ruined them, along with legions of investors. However, none of the crimes to which Mr Millken pleaded guilty involved the junk bond market. He was charged with other crimes on that count, but the charges were dropped when he agreed to pay $200 million in fines, and set aside another $400 million to satisfy civil claims filed against him – a remarkable break for a big-time swindler. The crimes he admitted were, in general, illegal acts performed with accomplices which were intended to enrich Mr Millken's enormously prestigious firm, Drexel Burnham Lambert, whose prestige, whose existence, vanished with the wind with its collapse into bankruptcy less than three months ago. Mr Millken will be sentenced on 1 October. So he will have five months to enjoy himself at large. It is not likely to be a greatly restricted, or impoverished, life. After paying out those $600 million, he is reliably reported to be left with a little over $1 billion.

The exposure and ruination of a banker or other prominently wealthy man is always a fascinating story and – let's admit it – to most of us a meanly satisfying story. In a Depression, there are scores of them. They come, they excite us, they go. But every so often, the sudden decline and fall of one man sounds more like a general warning, a fire alarm, than a personal calamity, whenever the fallen man is seen as a symbol of a system that has gone awry. In the depth of the Great Depression, in early 1932, it is hackneyed to say that most ordinary people had lost faith in the bankers and the banking system. But of the big men that we thought had let us down, the financiers and statesmen

o promised us that 'prosperity was just around the corner' – most
re guilty of bad judgement, of myopic foresight. Their misdeeds
re well within the law. Then on a March day in that year, a Swedish
ancier, one Ivar Kreuger, known as the Swedish match king, put a
llet through his chest. The news rocked the newspapers of the world.
euger had been celebrated, in awesome prose, by some of the most
ute and serious journals in many countries. *Time* magazine called
n a 'Titan' of finance. When his story came out, what we had to
nfront was an unbelievable record of financial crookery on a splendid
ernational scale. I doubt that the columnist in last Wednesday's
w York Times, if he had stopped to look over the story of Ivar
euger, would have called Michael Millken 'the premier financial
indler of all time'. Kreuger, in his grave, must be registering a
orous dissent.

But Millken is in the same league with Kreuger, certainly as a symbol,
a symbol of what has been called 'the me decade', of what Tom
olfe called 'the burning itch to grab it now'. The sentencing of
ichael Millken will drive the last nail in the coffin of the junk bond
d send a shudder through the millions of ordinary citizens who lost
eir shirts in the mass bankruptcy of the savings and loans, the
ilding societies.

The day that Michael Millken came to court, a headline in a news-
per literary section read, 'In Books, Greed Is Out'. It topped a survey
the best-seller lists and revealed that a trend in public taste that we
essed would soon be on its way out was already dead and gone.
roughout the 1980s, the non-fiction lists were headed by the auto-
ographies of self-made men, by titans like Lee Iacocca, the phoenix
the automobile, by Donald Trump, the young, bouncy, blond tycoon
ose aspirations to take over hotels, casinos, airlines, resorts, cities
why not the country? – appear to be boundless. Along with these
nfessions of success, the non-fiction best-seller list was for many
ars filled out by 'How To' books, but mostly *How to Make a Million,*
w to Gain Comfort and Luxury in Early Retirement, How to Live
American Dream in Two Years Flat. There has been a general
reat of such stuff from the stores and from the publishers' lists. A
ole raft of the spring offerings suggest almost a concerted act of
nance for the Reagan years we once so loved to praise. How about

– The Politics of Rich and Poor: Wealth and the American Electorate in the Reagan Aftermath? And *Disorder and Decline: Crime and the Spiral of Decay in American Neighborhoods.* And *The Worst Years of Our Lives: An Outsider's View of the '80s.* Notice that these titles all carry emphatic subtitles, just to drive home the point that the author was never deceived and is about to indulge a full-throated lamentation for the fool's paradise of the 1980s. One publisher, who – I should guess – didn't anticipate the new trend and probably has several self-made heroes lined up for public exposure, sighed: 'What businessmen as heroes have we left?'

Well! What happened to the measured but shining tributes to Ronald Reagan the day he left office? Or the long eulogy of George Will, the sharpest and most thoughtful of conservative commentators? Listen: 'Reagan's aim has been to restore the plain language of right and wrong, good and evil for the purpose of enabling people to make the most of freedom ... The world seems less dangerous than it did in 1980, and Reagan is partly responsible ... By knocking the budget into radical imbalance, he has placed a restraining hand on the 1990s, but it will not restrain the growth of the Welfare State ... in 1981, America needed reassurance. It needed to recover confidence in its health and goodness. It needed to recover what was lost in the 1960s and '70s, the sense that it has a competence commensurate with its nobility and responsibilities. Reagan, like Roosevelt, has been a great reassurer, a steadying captain who calmed the passengers and, to some extent, the sea.'

And now, the community song has turned into a song of lamentation, a dirge and an indictment, of Greed and Decline and Disorder and Corruption. Reagan is now, suddenly, not a second Roosevelt but a second Harding, another very popular President in a prosperous time, who is now chiefly remembered for the shady financial shenanigans of his Cabinet. I wonder how the old man feels; sitting up there in his office tower in Beverly Hills, to hear and read from the sprightly new 1990s authors that he was presiding over a corrupt administration and a failing country. Surely the verdict of history, even in the short run, won't be so damning, or so lyrical. It all depends on which events stick in the public memory: the lowest unemployment rate and lowest inflation, or Iran-Contra and Michael Millken. There's no rule, no formula to guarantee the remembrance of the good things. President Herbert Hoover was – for one – a remarkable American in many ways, not simply an engineer of international repute, but the man who saved Europe, after the First World War, from mass starvation. John Maynard Keynes said of him at the Versailles Peace Conference: 'He imported into the Councils of Paris . . . precisely that atmosphere of reality, knowledge, magnanimity and disinterestedness which, if they had been found in other quarters also, would have given us the Good Peace.' But Wall Street crashed during Hoover's reign and he is remembered cruelly as the author of the Depression.

Mr Reagan claims to know the American people well. I hope he knows that their frantic affection for every new crooner is only matched by their impatience for the next one. At the moment, he is the victim of an associated American trait: the yearning to anoint a new President as a Moses, and when he turns out not to be Moses, to dump him and look around for another one.

Fighting in What?

30 November 1990

Well, we've had four months of haphazard debate over Saddam Hussein, of amateur prophesying, of fuzzy Presidential rhetoric, of snatched analogies with Vietnam and Hitler, and of – compared with the 1960s – surprisingly little mockery from the colleges. At last what was always serious and relevant from the beginning has come out into the open. It has to be said that one of the obstacles to defining and arguing the real issue or issues in the Gulf has been President Bush's variety of explanations as to why the American troops had been dispatched there in the first place. Almost as if his advisers had set up a bargain basement of reasons, and he had wandered through it trying this one out for size on the American consumer, next day trying another one, or two.

At first, right at the beginning of August, Mr Bush said the United States had responded so promptly with the first big wave of troops because Saudi Arabia was at imminent risk of being invaded. So it was, and both parties in Congress and a national poll gave the President a thumping 85 per cent approval. At the same time, in the very early days Mr Bush told the people – that's you and me – that Mr Hussein had performed an act of 'naked aggression', and the day was long gone when we could permit dictators to do such things. Mrs Thatcher, who was over here at the time, prompted him and stiffened him, and echoed him in the same language. So now we knew, to our temporary satisfaction, that the United States was not going to tolerate – anywhere, it was implied – tinpot dictators marching into little countries, even though we had not jumped into Ethiopia, Angola, Cambodia.

It was at that time, in August, that we heard the first mention of Hitler again – a crude analogy with a tyrant who gobbled up little countries. There was a brief flurry of debate (between old historians for the most part) about Hitler and Mr Hussein: some saying Hussein was, if anything, more evil, more ruthless, and a tyrant with frightening ambitions to dominate, first the Middle East and after that, what? And their antagonists who said the comparison was ridiculous, that Saddam Hussein was, as a world threat, a midget compared with Hitler, not a man with a great nation in thrall.

Then people, country people, college students, professional cynics, began to say: the whole thing's about oil. Are we going to die for the oil companies? The administration jibbed at that one, and, it seemed to me, missed a great opportunity. Mr Cheney, the Secretary of Defense, did, I recall, on his first mission to the Gulf come out bluntly and say, yes, it's about oil, repeating a figure much banded about at the time: that, if Mr Hussein invaded Saudi Arabia and overran its shoreline, he would, could, control 42 per cent of the world's oil supply. But the President, though mentioning oil from time to time as almost an embarrassing necessity, didn't stress it or ever say, 'You bet, it's about oil.'

Neither he nor anyone else in or out of the administration, that I heard of, recalled what had been the one, great, persisting fear, that the Soviet Union would eventually, one day, soon or late, march south, bestride the Mediterranean, control the countries that border the Persian Gulf: in a word, control the source of Western Europe's energy, and, therefore, of its economies, its prosperity, and, very soon, of its survival as a continent of sovereign nations. I remember a hot argument with an old friend – this must have been twenty-five years ago – who had a strong but blinkered vision of the Soviet Union solely as a direct military threat to Western Europe; and a third party saying that if the Soviet Union did come to control the Gulf and patrol the Mediterranean, there would be no need for one Soviet bomb to drop on Western Europe: the Kremlin, having strangled their economies, could simply indicate to Britain, France, West Germany, all the NATO partners, that they had better get themselves governments agreeable to Moscow, and all would be well. I believe this nightmare was always present throughout the Cold War.

So, what I'm saying in accusing the Bush administration of missing a great opportunity for popular education was its failure to take up the jeering view of the oil threat and point out how many great wars in history start, if you like, with the Egyptians' chronic lack of wood, the whole of Western Europe's lack of spices to make food palatable, how often wars have been fought precisely because of the lack or denial of the raw materials by which you can live and prosper. Perhaps Mr Bush and his spokesmen ducked the vital question of access to Middle Eastern oil, maybe because people began to remind him how much less dependent the United States was than Western Europe and Japan on Middle Eastern oil.

At any rate, by that time we were now, I'd say, in September, October. People, the Congress, the pollsters, were saying that the President's support was slipping because he had not come out in public with one strong, clear explanation of why the United States was there, in such huge numbers, in the Gulf. The President did speak out from time to time, with that earnest hesitancy of his, which suggests that any minute now he's going to come up with the real reason. By then we were in the Gulf, the President assured us, to maintain American values, to sustain our way of life. Some of these random, additional reasons puzzled people: it was surely a little risky to go on about championing American values. How about democracy, free speech, representative government? Because everybody knew by then that Kuwait was a medieval kingdom run by sheiks, and so were an Arab ally or two.

There were never, as with Vietnam, two strong opposing sides to what we call the national debate – never a rigid body of hawks, a dogged body of doves. Most people still seemed to agree that something had to be done about Mr Hussein in Kuwait, but they disputed under what provocation, and when force (war) should be used. Surprisingly few people (judging from the national polls) were against fighting Saddam Hussein under any circumstances. As the fall came on, the regular snippets of television interviews with the men and women 'out there' had been put on, I suppose, as morale builders, these interviews or little pep talks to the folks back home. They began to turn testy, grumbling. The commanders of the forces in the desert must have groaned many times at the decision of the networks to start these bright, chirpy interviews. But, there you are, it's a democracy, isn't it? We can't go back to the frontline censorship of the First and Second World Wars – of all wars before Vietnam, when, once for all, I imagine, microphones and cameras were allowed in foxholes; and troops who cursed the war in the morning were seen by the whole country in the evening.

The grumbling among the men in the desert was an inevitable consequence, I believe, of America's long innocence of war on the home front (one hundred and twenty-five years) but also, in the short run, of the peculiar experience of war instilled by the Reagan and Bush administrations. Libya. Grenada. Panama. No debate, no angry appeals to the exclusive right of Congress to declare war. The decision was made in the White House one day, and next day the announcement of the bombing, of the swift invasion, of Grenada, of Panama. Then an anxious day or two, perhaps, but in a week, two at most, the war's all over, and most of the boys are on their way home.

I called these experiences 'peculiar' just now. They are certainly atypical of the experience of war by any great nation you can think of. The great, the dreadful, exception was, of course, Vietnam. And I believe the rising impatience of the American desert troops, the reported decline in morale, is due to the view – in the minds of the young men who may have to fight this war – that there are only two kinds of war: the quick, manageable Grenada–Panama war that they watched or followed in their teens, and the ghastly, prolonged, failing war of Vietnam that they have only read about or seen in the movies.

So it would be a natural puzzle in the minds of the men hunkered down there in the desert that, since this is plainly not Grenada or Panama, what is it? Mostly, we are told, they want action or they want out. A former Chairman of the Joint Chiefs of Staff, Admiral Crowe, remarked the other day: 'It's curious that some expect our military to train soldiers to stand up to hostile fire but doubt its ability to train them to occupy ground and wait patiently.' Well, I'm pretty sure that most of the men who've been dispatched to the Gulf in the past four months did not expect to occupy the desert and wait patiently.

The last opinion anticipates the change, or movement, of opinion. The big change in the mixture of opinion, the hardening of attitudes barely arrived at, came with the President's decision, two weeks ago, to send another 150,000 American troops, at a time when we were being told that the economic sanctions were working, and that the United Nations Security Council was moving towards a resolution setting a deadline for Saddam Hussein to get out of Kuwait, and permitting the member nations to use other 'necessary means' to make him ('necessary means' being taken by everybody to mean 'go to war'). The President's boosting of American forces to a staggering 400,000 (just short of the total forces deployed in the Korean War) gave many, perhaps most Americans the idea, the fear, that the President was hell-bent on war, now or very soon. The shock of his action immediately precipitated, in the chemical sense, attitudes that had been invisible, wet, in solution. A cry goes up in Congress to have the President call Congress in special session. There are loud reminders to the President that, under the Constitution, only the Congress can declare war. (Nobody has yet mentioned the fact that the last time Congress declared war was forty-nine years ago! – the declaration against Italy in December 1941.) The Senate Armed Services Committee is called into a series of hearings (which are going on now), and every expert and former defence official and pundit and his brother is called to testify. The upshot, the loud, important upshot is that two of America's former military chiefs (chairmen of the Joint Chiefs of Staff), Admiral Crowe and General David Johns, have urged the President to pause in his belligerent rush, to give sanctions at least a year to work. The other attitude that has come out of these hearings is a body of opinion, in the Senate, to persuade the President to institute a rotation system for the dispatch and maintenance of American troops in the desert. Four months' duty, six at the most, is being suggested.

So this is where we were as the Security Council sat down on Thursday to vote on the resolution, sanctioning further 'necessary measures'.

But, there is one big, nasty fact that has at last emerged from the writings of one or two columnists who were ignored or declared to be alarmists way back there in August, when they suggested that Saddam Hussein was on the way to building a nuclear weapon and might have it within two or three years. That was what led some lonely conservatives to say that the choice was to fight Saddam Hussein now, or fight a stronger, nuclear-equipped Saddam Hussein two, three years from now. That suggested a, for once, *relevant* Hitler analogy.

Even President Bush has picked up the omen of this threat in recent speeches and remarks, which has led some 'experts' to say nonsense – it will be ten years before Mr Hussein has a destructive nuclear capability. This denial roused the dozing nuclear missile experts from their many think tanks. The President said the other day that the first Iraqi bomb could be months away. Senator Edward Kennedy, the arch-liberal who, if there was only one dove in Washington would be it, spoke in the Senate Armed Services Committee hearings. His followers and idolaters surely expected him to say what we all want to believe, that Saddam Hussein is years, maybe ten years, away from a nuclear capability. Senator Kennedy said, 'The best estimates, I imagine, are eight or nine months'!

So, we are back to where we came in, in the middle of August, when I first reported this minority, almost secret fear of Saddam Hussein's nuclear potential. Reduced to a stark, practical alternative, the choice is in fact, a dilemma – a choice of two courses of action, either of which is unsatisfactory: (1) to give the sanctions a year or more to work, by which time he may have the bomb or, (2) to fight him now – with, ahead of us, unpredictable possibilities of massive casualties, the break-up of the United Nations alliance, civil war in the Middle East – at best a long, long war.

Riots in Los Angeles
1 May 1992

It was one of those evenings, last Wednesday, when you or I take a break from the world and its woes: out to dinner with a friend, talk golf and tennis mostly, and marvel at the news of that 10-year-old shrimp of a Russian girl who has boggled the experience of the veteran Florida teachers, is aching to turn professional and go out and slaughter Seles, Capriati, and any other young genius who thinks she's a prodigy.

And then home, and, as I always do just before turning in, to flip through thirty-two television channels – it's now fifty – and light briefly on Channel 24, which is Atlanta's CNN, the television world news station that is most often there, as the general said, 'fastest with the mostest'. I see a helicopter shot of a street intersection and stalled truck, and what looks like a man sprawled on the ground – one or two other men running around, making gestures. They are all so tiny, seen from the air. It's probably a random shooting somewhere, most likely in Harlem or Los Angeles, maybe. We see at least one every night. Something's hurriedly spoken about a verdict. So to bed, to read a new book which claims, and for once maybe rightly, to have solved after a hundred and four years the identity of Jack the Ripper. So to sleep.

Thursday morning, and – the first words I heard from an announcer in Los Angeles were, 'worse, much worse, than Watts'. Because we can now see it was historically the forerunner of dreadful things to come two, three years later, we had better look back to Watts. Watts was that frowsy but not slummy suburb of Los Angeles where a white policeman's arrest of a black youth started a rumour that the black man had been shot. The rumour grew: he'd been wounded, no, killed, in cold blood. Within an hour, a full-scale riot was thriving in that black neighbourhood, and within twenty-four hours the whole suburb was ablaze, loud with guns and happy looters. There was a time when it appeared the chaos might not be controlled by the ten thousand men of the National Guard, who'd been ordered in by the Governor of California. The National Guard is the civilian reserve militia which every state has on call, and which can, in a war or other emergency, be mobilized as regular army under the regular military command. I try to clarify the function of the misleadingly named National Guard because we'll come to look at their part in this week's riots. By the end of that dreadful week in 1965, Watts was a large, gutted suburb. And it was mentioned the other night that after twenty-seven years, it is not wholly recovered or rebuilt.

Well, if the horror of Watts was triggered by a tiny casual arrest and a ballooning false rumour, what triggered the rage of south central Los Angeles last Wednesday night? Let's go back as calmly as we can and look at what started it all.

On the night of 3 March 1991, a black motorist was seen by a police car whizzing along a boulevard at a breakneck pace and the police pursued him. It took quite a time to catch up with him, by which time other police cars and many other policemen had come to form almost an impromptu posse, twenty-three in all. When they did catch him, two other men in the car gave themselves up without resistance; they were handcuffed and taken off into custody. The driver remained defiant and aggressive, so freewheeling with arms and legs that one of the policemen said he assumed the man was high on some drug.

Anyway, what came next would doubtless have been buried in the police records but for a unique accident that made what happened on that night-time street something for all the world to see. A man who lived in an apartment overlooking what was now a scene on the street was aroused by the noise of the police siren and the following scuffle. He picked up his video camera, stood (on his porch, I imagine) and cranked away. His film lasted for eighty-one seconds, and horrified everybody who subsequently saw it, and saw it, and saw it, on television. Four police officers were flailing their batons and flogging the driver, writhing and squirming on the ground. It's true he wasn't going to lie down and take it – he wriggled, but his body also jerked in reflexes, of pain, surely, from the beating he was taking. In eighty-one seconds, almost a minute and a half, there were fifty-six counted beatings.

Eleven days later, a Los Angeles grand jury indicted one police sergeant and three police officers. They pleaded not guilty. The Attorney General of the United States responded by ordering an immediate review of complaints of brutality against the Los Angeles police. The review expanded to cover the whole nation – that was thirteen months ago – and the report has not been published. The Mayor of Los Angeles, a black man who's been in office for an unprecedented twenty years, appointed a commission to investigate the Los Angeles police department. There was for a time a wrangle over the chief of police, a white man, who was charged with insensitivity and condoning bad police behaviour. A month or two later, he promised to retire this spring. He was still there this week. A month or so after the beating, the driver, Rodney King, and his wife, filed a federal civil rights suit against the city of Los Angeles. Three weeks later, Mr King was discovered in a parked car with a transvestite prostitute. He failed to get away but after two months all charges were dropped.

Meanwhile, the grand jury brought no charges against the nineteen police officers who were bystanders. But the four men who were seen to do the beating eventually, after many legal manoeuvres, came to trial a year to the day after the event. By the way, on the motion of the defence which maintained that the four policemen could not get a fair trial in the black-dominated quarter where the incident took place, the trial was moved to another suburb (which, it's important to remark, is almost entirely white and is called home by about two thousand policemen and their families). Although one or two blacks were called for jury duty, they were quizzed and excused by the defence, which is its privilege. The sitting jury consisted of ten whites, one Hispanic, one Asian. On 23 April the case went to the jury. We gather from the jurors themselves that their verdict was arrived at within an hour or two (an astonishing feat for an American jury, which can battle it out for days and weeks) but took another three days to argue, and was eventually hung, on one count against one officer.

So it was this past Wednesday evening when the stunning verdict came – actually over the television, for the trial was televised throughout. The four had been found not guilty, of brutality and of excessive force (that is, going beyond the needs of the cause). In interviews after the result, the jurors willing to speak said the amateur motion picture was crude (so it was, it was filming a very crude event), did not express the physical threat Mr King posed, and that much of the flailing was into the thin night air.

It's fair to say that a vast majority of the country will refuse to believe a word of it. That first shot I saw, of a stalled truck and a prone man and one or two running around, was the beginning: a white truck driver dragged to the pavement and beaten up by blacks. I'd better say at once that in all the following burnings and lootings were done by blacks and poor whites, who now had what everybody told them was just cause to vent their long-suppressed rage and disillusion in the equality that wasn't there, and the jobs that weren't forthcoming.

In the beginning, what we saw were the flaming suburbs by night, and black people complaining that it had taken the fire department twenty minutes to answer their call. On any night, the average calls to the Los Angeles fire department are ten. Last Wednesday night, over a hundred and twenty fires blazed in central and south central Los Angeles, and then beyond. And the firemen were being attacked, along with the police and the paramedics. Los Angeles is not a skyscraper city but a huge collection, connection, of ninety suburbs over five hundred and fifty square miles. Sunset Boulevard alone runs for twenty-two miles – through sections that could be in Hong Kong, in Mexico, in Korea, in Kansas City. On Thursday night forty fires burned, out beyond by miles, up into the rich and by now – I should guess – terrified habitat of the film and television folk: the designers, the yuppies, who mean no harm.

By Friday noon, the President had sent a light infantry battalion into a 'staging area' near Los Angeles, to be used if the National Guard and the police cannot control things. By Friday, the worst we feared had happened: the rioting, looting contagion had spread to San Francisco, to Atlanta, to Seattle, and in a smaller way to other towns thousands of miles apart. There were peaceable black demonstrations in Kansas City and on the campus of a college in Baton Rouge, Louisiana.

In Watts, before the end, there was the awful fear that ten thousand of the National Guard might not be enough. If the violence from the poor and the hoodlum packs and the juvenile gangs takes over many cities, the President and his generals may have to worry whether there'll be enough troops to contain what could become a race rebellion.

There's one discernible piece of good news in all this. Now that the

State of California has exhausted its legal procedure (the verdict is the end), the federal government can move in, and it could institute a new trial but not on the same grounds. That would run the risk of double jeopardy. The Justice Department, through the Attorney General, has revived a criminal investigation into the incident of the beating to see if the constitutional civil rights of Mr King were violated. It's the ground on which, just a year ago, the Kings filed their suit against the city of Los Angeles.

White House Style

6 November 1992

When I became the chief American correspondent of a paper whose mission, way back then, was to prompt and protect the thinking of one city, Manchester, I was disturbed at the thought that I was going to have to move myself and my family from New York to Washington. Washington, of course was where all the chief foreign correspondents were based. To my great relief, I soon had a letter from my editor – a small, canny, spiky-haired, bespectacled imp of a Lancashireman. He wrote quite simply: 'No, I don't want you to move to Washington. I don't want you to report Washington, except from time to time. I want you, *all* the time, to report America. New York is the best news base, and the best home base for travel.'

That wise and wily sentence is one that might not only be passed on to editors of papers around the world. It would serve a useful purpose if it could be engraved or done up in needlework, framed and hung in the Oval Office of the White House. It would remind every President of a truth which every President, especially in his second term, is in danger of forgetting: that the White House is not home or anything remotely like the homes of the two hundred million people he is there to represent. The White House is a temporary Versailles and not the best place in which to maintain what Teddy Roosevelt called 'a sense of the continent'.

You have to have been in the White House as a guest to appreciate its elegance and patrician comfort, and to have been treated like some venerated old monarch in luxurious exile, in order to feel the benign truth behind the phrase coined by the historian Arthur Schlesinger, 'the Imperial Presidency'. He was referring to the White House – I almost said the court – of Richard M. Nixon. And certainly there's been no Presidency in our time, or perhaps in any time, when the White House more resembled a royal palace. Mrs Kennedy had done the place over into an eighteenth-century French mansion more exquisite than most royal palaces. Mr Nixon added some folderols of a monarch's office as imagined by Hollywood. He summoned for ceremonial occasions a row of trumpeters in uniform with tight white pumps and knee breeches, looking for all the world like the wedding guard of honour designed for King Rudolf of Ruritania (Ronald Colman) and Princess Flavia (Madeleine Carroll).

The television pictures of this absurdity evoked such hilarity and mirth (not least in the British Royal Family) that these yeoman of the guard were soon disbanded. But what Mr Nixon had revealed, in exaggeration, was a perception of himself to which a President after a year or two is in danger of succumbing: that he is in charge of – that he rules – a nation and that the word is handed down from the White House, not up from the people. It may be said that every Prime Minister probably feels the same in his official residence. I doubt it. Once, at a White House dinner, I sat next to the son of the British Prime Minister, who was at that moment the President's guest of honour. The son had been received, as everyone is, by a young Marine officer in a spanking dress uniform. His lady companion took the Marine's proffered arm. They were led through a small suite with a small orchestra playing waltzes by Strauss. Other beautiful rooms or galleries they passed through were ablaze with gilt and glass. On into the main reception room; more Marines, more impeccable manners – the reception line – the shaking hands with the king – I mean the President – and the First Lady. Cocktails and smiling chatter. And on into two linked dining rooms, and a splendid banquet sparkling with a hundred candles. A soothing fountain of music showered from another room. 'Home', said the Prime Minister's son, 'was never like this.' And, in truth, by comparison, No. 10 Downing Street is a modest upper-middle-class town house.

Apart from this beautiful protective shell in which the President lives, there is the constant human situation, in which he is surrounded by people who defer to him and who pass on to him every day their own view (which might be as blinkered as his) of what is happening, what is being felt and thought, on the Great Outside. The outside is the United States and its people. Only in the past month or so did Mr Bush attempt to listen to their troubles, to emerge from his cocoon of complacency ('yes, there are people having a bad time but the economy's growing, ninety-three million at work – things are getting better all the time'). This reminded me of the fatal 1932 assurance Herbert Hoover issued from the White House to millions shivering in tar-paper shacks down by the rivers, and to the quarter of the working people of America who had no work: 'Prosperity is just around the corner.'

Some of you may have expected me to talk about the failures of the Bush campaign, for, only two days after the election, the papers are full of reasons and excuses and explanations by Republicans about failures of technique: he should have had sharper figures, he should have been more insulting earlier, he should have used more women, he should have hired as mean a man as the one who invented the infamous Willie Horton television commercial last time. (He was the Massachusetts black man who, given parole by Governor Dukakis, promptly raped a woman.) One bitter intimate who could enjoy the frankness of having left the administration came a little closer to the central truth when he moaned: 'He surrounded himself with second-rate talent and clones. He was only comfortable with a white-bread crowd, a bunch of white male Protestants and number-crunchers.' I can sympathize with that man's view. I and my generation *are* probably more comfortable with WASPs (and a Catholic friend or two) than with the polyglot, white – black – Latino – brown – Asian, multi-cultural society that America has increasingly become. But Clinton has reached out to it, and listened to it, is at home with it, his generation is a link with it.

This was never clearer than on Thursday morning, when the *New York Times* carried a front-page photograph of the President-elect with his mother and pals at a friend's house. Clinton in threadbare jeans, a check wool shirt, unzipped windbreaker, bulging Reeboks. Mostly young pals in laughing bunches similarly dressed, or undressed. Not a suit, not a necktie, not a button-down shirt in sight. 'Well,' I said to my wife, 'can you believe this? There is the next President of the United States and his buddies.' I wasn't suggesting that Mr Clinton was putting on an act, as poor Mr Bush had to do when he wolfed a hamburger at the local lunch counter and said, 'Gee whillikins, this is great.' 'Clinton', said my wife sternly, 'is the President of those people and he dresses like them.' Quite right. Unbuttoned, one way or another, is his natural style. Along with the passing of George Bush, we shall see, I fear, the passing of the blue blazer.

The Irish in New York City

19 March 1993

A year or two ago, the brouhaha about the St Patrick's Day parade began – as many other social conflicts have done – with the coming out (their term) of homosexuals. I suppose that means it's been about twenty years since men and women in large numbers asserted that homosexuality was a lifestyle of choice, not, as for many centuries it had been, 'the sin that dare not speak its name'.

To the Catholic Church, however, whether or not it speaks its name, it is still a sin. And that belief is at the root of the never-ending wrangle in this city, between the Church and the homosexuals who claim to be good Catholics. The City of New York, its government, its laws and ordinances, theoretically stands in between, though, according to who's Mayor, it goes along with one side or the other. Last year, our first black Mayor, Mr David Dinkins, marched in the parade under the banner of the so-proclaimed Gays and Lesbians. He was often booed along the way, and he had several kinds of refuse thrown at him. He has survived. This year he stayed home, respecting a decision of the courts – which came only on the eve of the parade – that denied the homosexual group a permit to mount their own separate parade.

I'd better stop talking about homosexuals in general because they are not, as such, a party to the dispute, any more than are all New York's Irish. The adversaries in this contest are the ILGO – the Irish Lesbian and Gay Organization – and the most venerable of Irish Catholic societies in this city, the Ancient Order of Hibernians. The Gays and Lesbians, whom from now on we shall call the ILGOs, were organized only a few years ago and are said to have one hundred and twenty paid-up members. The Ancient Hibernians and their order go back to 1836, to a time when the prevailing Anglo-Americans began to be alarmed at the thousands of Irish immigrants pouring into New York from Liverpool and Cobh (only twelve years later the flood would arrive, the starving refugees from the Irish potato famine). The Anglo-Americans were greatly bothered by the noisy and effective Irish entry into local politics. In 1835 Irishmen had organized to drive the local Whigs from the polls, and when the Mayor and a sheriff's posse tumbled along to restore law and order, they were put to flight with blinding showers of green confetti and the threat of a brawl. The city fathers consequently retaliated with ordinances, just short of laws, that sharply discriminated against the Irish in housing and employment. The year after that Keystone Kops chase between the Irish and the Mayor and his henchmen, 1836, the Ancient Order of Hibernians was founded.

They have always been the sponsors of the St Patrick's Day parade here. And, after the disruption of last year's parade by angry onlookers resenting the marching homosexuals, the Hibernians were first in line to claim an exclusive right to sponsor and organize this parade, but also announced they would not tolerate a homosexual group. The city granted the Hibernians a permit but ignored their threat to ban the ILGOs. Whereupon, the ILGOs appealed to the city to declare that the Hibernians had no constitutional right to ban them. Everything, you'll notice, from playing a radio in public to selling films of close-up sexual intercourse comes down, sooner or later, to the First Amendment – the free press – right of the Constitution. Well, the city couldn't at that point take on the Constitution. In the end, the whole row went to the courts. The ILGOs had thought up what they took to be an even-handed, fair solution: they asked for a permit to hold a separate parade, an hour or two before the big one. The judge said no, too big a risk of a literal meeting of the minds and bodies, what we call a confrontation, especially if, as the ILGOs wanted, they marched south and, at the end, met the oncoming Hibernians.

So, now denied any legal right to march in the big parade or to stage one of their own, what were they to do? On the eve of the great day, they announced that they would defy the court and the Mayor and the city and – most of all – Cardinal O'Connor, the head of this diocese, who always, except last year, stands under a canopy outside St Patrick's cathedral nodding and blessing all the groups, the marching bands, the societies, the local units, the drum majorettes, all the emerald-tinged bodies that go by: 198 units, 120,000 paraders.

Not surprisingly, when the nasty, grey, drenching day dawned there were over four thousand police at the ready, more than eight hundred more than last year. As the Hibernians were assembling down at 42nd Street and Fifth Avenue, the ILGOs set up in marching order and waving banners ('Cardinal O'Connor Is a Bigot in a Dress', 'ILGOs Against Bigotry and Intolerance', 'Freedom for ILGOs'), and they marched in triumph. Exactly one block. At 43rd Street they approached a wall of policemen who, like trainers routinely leading the horses into their stalls, quietly arrested over two hundred, which was just about the total muster of the ILGOs brigade. There wasn't a truncheon, a flailing of a stick or a visible bully. The ILGOs, whatever their words said, kept to the promised deed: they practised civil, not to say deferential, disobedience. In about fifteen minutes, the homosexual rebellion was all over. The big parade began and for four, five hours, the endless troops of the faithful plodded through rain coming down, as they say, like stair rods. On the sidewalk outside St Patrick's cathedral, were onlookers under umbrellas still roused by the Cardinal's stinging peroration at the early Mass: 'Neither respectability nor political correctness is worth one comma of the Apostle's Creed.' There were some present at the Mass who, however, had other sinners in mind. 'A pity', grumbled a Republican and Hibernian, 'the day doesn't focus on the key issue: the British presence in Ireland.'

This tremendous argument – about the Hibernians and the ILGOs

– has been going on for months, and debated with eloquence, with absurdity, with – on both sides – bigoted charges of bigotry, in the City Council, in the pubs and clubs, on television endlessly. But it strikes me: two points were never made, not anyway in my hearing or reading. One is ironic and not likely to be made much of by the faithful. It is: who was St Patrick? He was a Scot, kidnapped at the age of 17 by the brutal Romans in one of their press-gang raids, whipped off to Ireland to be made a pig-keeper, which he hated, but, being an apprentice saint, endured for six years until he yearned to get back to his native land, and did so. But at some point he had a dream in which he was urged, by the Almighty, to fulfil his true mission, to return to Ireland and preach the gospel. He did. He made himself a bishop, he baptized converts, and he ordained priests and allowed them to marry (how about that, Cardinal O'Connor?). So, his mission in life was not to glorify the Irish but to save them from perdition.

The other point is the legal decision of the judge, which was no more and no less than to approve the Ancient Order of Hibernians' constitutional right to bar the ILGOs. The propriety of this ruling was never gone into by the ILGOs, who stayed with heated protests against bigotry, homophobia, fascism and the like. One angry man brought up the analogy of McSorley's Tavern, an old Irish pub downtown that, in the discrimination battles of the 1960s, had at last to let in women, two women, as it happened, who were determined to invade any public place where men liked to be with men. But note the word 'public'. McSorley's Tavern is public – so is any land or property owned by the city or the state. In such places, you may not, under the law, bar anyone on account of race or religion. But, the judge pointed out, the Ancient Order of Hibernians is a private society. Like any other private club or society owning its own premises, it can legally keep its membership to men, to women, to whites, to blacks. It can bar anybody it likes, bachelors, Italians, Englishmen, left-handed people. This is the simple truth in the law the ILGOs couldn't bear to face.

In spite of the Hibernians' announcement that they welcomed open homosexuals in the parade but not marching under a banner that proclaimed them as something special and different, the ILGOs didn't want that. They wanted to use the parade not as a celebration of St Patrick but as an advertisement for open homosexuality.

Why do the Irish – Irish-Americans (perhaps most immigrants) – get so much more inflamed about such issues than their relatives in the homeland? Well, for the Irish, there's the long history of discrimination against them. Mainly, though, I think that when any immigrant or ethnic group comes into the welter of this seething, polyglot city, they make an extra effort to show they're different and to water, or exaggerate, their roots. An old Irish friend of mine, whom I've known for over sixty years, wrote to me the other day. His letter arrived coincidentally on the morning of our parade. He wrote: 'As soon as an Irishman leaves home and enters America, he ceases to be whatever he was but behaves rather more so.'

'Give me your tired, your poor . . .'

25 June 1993

There can hardly be an American born here who cannot recite the five thundering lines inscribed on the Statue of Liberty: the hectoring command – 'Give me your tired, your poor, /Your huddled masses yearning to breathe free, /The wretched refuse of your teeming shore. –/Send these, the homeless tempest-tossed, to me: /I lift my lamp beside the golden door.' Generous words, almost arrogant in their bravery. Whether they constitute fine poetry or doggerel, they touched the hearts and minds of millions of Europeans – always the poor, often the persecuted, very often the fugitives from military service. They were spurred to pack a few belongings, often no more than a blanket, a cooking pot, a prayer book, a corset, to climb aboard box cars deep inside Russia or Hungary or Lithuania or Germany and be carried to the great ports: Constantinople, Piraeus, Antwerp, Bremen, and then put aboard. There, in enclosures outside the embarkation city, they were bathed, de-loused, fed, their baggage and clothes fumigated. They were prepared for the land of the free.

We are talking about the routine procedures employed with the ourteen and a half million immigrants who arrived here, mainly New ork or Boston, in the first two decades of the twentieth century. ooking up in awe to the bosom of the colossal lady peering out owards Europe, they would very soon find out that the physical outine of getting into the United States was not quite what a poor oundling might expect of a new, compassionate mother.

Coming across the Atlantic, they were not so much allotted space s stowed aboard, as many as nine hundred in steerage. Sailing slowly p the lower bay of New York City, they would spot their first mericans climbing aboard from a Coast Guard cutter, two men and woman: immigration inspectors, whose first job was to look over the nip's manifest and see if the captain had recorded cases of contagious isease. Considering the frequency and unpredictability at the time of avaging epidemics across the continent of Europe, they looked out rst for signs of cholera, typhoid, tuberculosis. If you showed any sign f these fearsome diseases, you were at once taken off to quarantine n an island in the bay and got ready for early deportation.

Once the newcomers had been herded into a large reception hall, ney would be tagged with numbers and grouped according to their ative tongue, which for the vast majority of them was the only one ney spoke. They moved, shadowed by interpreters, in lines past a octor in a blue uniform, a man with a chalk in his hand – an instant iagnostician. He was certainly a fast one and had the confidence that omes from not knowing anything about CT scans, or MRIs, or PSAs. Ie saw an ageing man with purple lips and chalked on his back: H – ossible heart disease. Separate this man! Children in arms stood down o see if they betrayed the limp of rickets. T on the back was the xpulsion sign of tuberculosis. Two other doctors dipped into a bowl f disinfectant and folded a suspect eyelid back with a buttonhook. rachoma – very prevalent in Southern and Eastern Europe and a sure arbinger of blindness. You, too, were on your way back home.

We won't follow the release of most of the healthy rest to railroad gents, con men, honest bosses and sweatshop owners looking for, nd getting in luscious numbers, an army of cheap labourers, for most f whom the prospect was better than life in the homeland.

The expectation, among the mass of the settled population, was that these strangers would settle in too. But with every wave of new immigrants there was always a booming counterwave of protest, from the people who'd been here a long time, two, three or more generations of what we now call the Anglos and their collateral Nordics – Swedes, Norwegians, Germans. They had run the country, its government, its institutions for a hundred years or more. So every breaking wave of new immigrants made a rude sound to the residents, and they protested, then they discriminated. Often Washington legislated, as it did in the 1920s and again in the 1950s against what were called 'undesirable types', meaning Orientals, Southern and Eastern Europeans. Even as late as the time I first came here, in the early 1930s, there were still pasted on shop windows and employment agencies stickers left over from early in the century: 'No Irish Need Apply.' But now, equally new to me, just outside the entrance to an apartment building was a sign: a wooden post surmounted by a rectangle, a sort of mahogany plaque, very handsome, a meticulously printed sign of gold lettering on a black background. It said 'Apartments To Let, Three To Six Rooms. Restricted.' That last word was not put in as an afterthought. It was printed in the same fine style as the rest of the announcement. 'Restricted', I discovered, was shorthand for 'No Jews Need Apply'. This was standard practice here in New York, in Manhattan especially; the other four boroughs, getting most of their business and work from the legions of incoming Jews, could not afford to be so particular. That rather callous sign vanished. It came to be made illegal in the late 1940s, when a Republican Governor of New York, Thomas E. Dewey (who had two failing shots at the Presidency against Franklin Roosevelt), pushed through the state legislature the first (in this country) fair employment and fair housing Act. (The practice of exclusion was not totally abandoned. It continued in parts of the Upper East Side, unofficially, without the dreaded word, discreetly, on tiptoe, in the English manner.) Today there are no signs, except scurrilous ones painted by hooligans. But in the teeming boroughs, in Queens, Staten Island, the Bronx, Brooklyn, blacks glare at the successful Korean fruiterers, the pious religious Jewish sects watch their step, people who once went to Chinatown for entertainment and exquisite cheap sandals now stay away, after hearing of boatloads of smuggled Chinese brought in here to swell the active army of gangsters.

It is news to most of us that there have been for some time ruthless and very active Chinese gangs working profitably in – what else? – drugs.

But at the moment the victim, the scapegoat, everybody's feared interloper, is the Haitian. I mentioned lately the drastically changed ethnic composition of the fleet of New York's taxi drivers. Where once taxi drivers were first- or second-generation Irishmen, Italians, Germans, now, they are Puerto Ricans, Haitians, Russians, Israelis. Why should the arrivals from Haiti be so feared?

Well, since the Haitian military overthrew President Aristide almost two years ago, about forty thousand Haitians have fled from what is quite plainly a particularly brutal tyranny. They came floating in across the Caribbean and on to Florida, and hundreds, perhaps many thousands, of them never made it. Simply fell off their miserable little boats or sank with all hands. President Bush decided to apply the existing immigration laws which offer legal haven if you can prove that you are a political refugee escaping likely persecution. If you simply sought a better life, but could give no proof of past or pending persecution, you were returned to Haiti.

During the Presidential campaign, Mr Clinton called this policy illegal and cruel and swore to reverse it and let in the Haitian masses huddled in their leaky boats. Tremendous joy throughout Haiti! At once, over a hundred thousand people helped to build more leaky boats. In the face of this totally unpredicted tidal wave, President Clinton reverted to the Bush policy. A national howl of pain from Haiti and cries of outrage from American liberals.

Last Monday the Supreme Court, nodding regretfully at the mention of the word cruelty, nevertheless ruled by 8 to 1 that this policy, intercepting the unpersecuted ones, was constitutional. Just before this ruling was handed down, a hundred and twenty-five refugees from Haiti, who had been judged to be true political refugees, were released from the American naval base in Cuba and flown to Miami – some to New York – there to be allowed to be absorbed into the American way of life. They were designated a 'special group'. What was so special about them – apart from an unconscionable long time they had been detained, is that they were all HIV positive, infected with the virus that causes AIDS.

So, in one action, freedom is available to diseased people who will at once be entitled to free medical care, to a home, to an interpreter, to daily maintenance. But in the more sweeping action, affecting all the boat people, the Supreme Court has added a phrase to Emma Lazarus's soaring invitation: 'Give me your tired, your poor, your huddled masses yearning to breathe free – but see they carry a return ticket.'

Thirtieth Anniversary of Kennedy Assassination

26 November 1993

I've always thought of 'anniversary' – the turn of the year, or literally the return of the year – as a happy word. But there've been one or two lately that considerably bruised the idea of anniversary as a festive time. I'd say that ten years ago – less – most Americans, asked to respond offhand to the prospect of 1992, the five hundredth anniversary of Christopher Columbus limping ashore on this hemisphere, would have looked forward to it as an all-American fiesta. But in the meantime, a literature of disillusion had been spawned, and when October 1992 arrived there were very few fireworks and – from one end of the Americas to the other, many memorial parades, many trooping Indian tribes observing 12 October as a day of mourning.

What they were mourning was their experience, the native experience of the conquistadors. The very name says 'conquest', and in the fifteenth century the conquest by any European nation of a native society meant subjection, enslavement, rapine, often torture and suppression of the native religion. It took about four centuries for intending conquerors (the French and the British are the best examples) to have the sense to let the subject peoples keep many of the mores and all of their religions.

The sudden revelation of all this, last year, in books and in magazine and newspaper pieces can only mean that for a couple of centuries or so the white man's settlement, the conquest of the Americas, must have been very badly taught in schools. The 'truths' revealed last year were always true but quietly relegated to the shadows, while the big spotlight was turned on the European view of Columbus as a master sailor, an extremely courageous explorer, a remarkable commander, a visionary and a devout Catholic, all of which he was.

However, once the brutal side of the Spanish conquests became common knowledge, became in the past two years something of a publishing industry, it was not possible to say, 'well, too bad, let's forget that part', and on the great October day enjoy, as John Adams recommended for the Fourth of July: 'fireworks, parades, bands, and general rejoicing'. In fact, when Columbus Day was over, the Governors and Mayors, not to mention the members of Congress, expressed sighs of relief that the few riots and eruptions of violence happened in only three or four countries and they were in Central and South America.

Well, I have to say that I believe very many Americans young and old will be greatly relieved that 22 November is over, not from any fear this time of protest marches or riots, but relief from the sheer din of morbid nostalgia. Thirty years ago, 22 November 1963, was, as surely everyone listening now must know, was the assassination of President Kennedy. If disillusion with Columbus was a publishing industry, *two* industries based on the life of John Kennedy have flourished and overwhelmed us this past month or so. One is what you might call the Camelot industry, the perpetuation and embroidering of the beautiful myth taken from Tennyson – of an ideal, small nation whose 'shining hour' was the time it was presided over by a brave young king. The other, a growth industry that gives no sign of stopping growing, is the Kennedy conspiracy industry.

To say much about it would only massage the sales representatives of this feverish speciality. Let me just say that I have no peculiar or privileged knowledge of the affair. I have fairly creditable credentials: I was there at the time. I practically wrote the next day's issue of the English newspaper for which I was at the time the chief American correspondent. I read every word of the Warren Commission's report (which, by the way, was a Commission of able, inquisitive and honour-able men, none of them, so far as I know, crippled by a hobby horse). Subsequently, I read the early books and a summary of the – was it 1974? – House Committee's renewed inquiry. And of course, like everybody who was at the time a sentient adult, I have paid attention to most of the later reports and theories and revised versions. I do not believe that the President was killed on the orders of the Kremlin, Fidel Castro, Lyndon Johnson, J. Edgar Hoover, Mao Tse-tung, Generalis-simo Francisco Franco, Carrie Nation or Dr Crippen. I lean to the belief that a very forlorn, agitated, lonely psychopath named Lee Harvey Oswald did it, without help or coaching. And as for the maze of motives that the conspiracy boys and girls would have you thread through, it seems to me that the likeliest is one small enough to seem trivial to the big apocalyptic revisionists but big enough to have inspired some of the world's greatest literature – including *Othello* and *Madame Bovary*, – namely, Oswald's suspicion, which his widow says plagued him at the time, that she adored Kennedy and was at the same time, sleeping with an FBI agent. So far as I'm concerned, there is no more to say.

About the mythical kingdom of Camelot, which during the run of the fanciful musical of the same name came to be merged with the fact of the Kennedy Presidency, we can only say now, it must show that nations, like individuals, have a constant yearning for leaders who are larger, more heroic, than life. And John Kennedy and his wife arrived as something quite new in the history of the Presidency: a beautiful young couple. So what was wrong about having a handsome young President with a beautiful wife? Nothing, except we went on from there to romanticize their public lives (the private life seemed blissfully right – a delusion that was not shared by the White House press corps, but in those days one of the taboos that was observed and never discussed was against writing about the sexual peccadilloes of the President, if any). A White House butler, who wrote – fifty years ago – a memoir of the Presidents he'd served, described President Harding as 'a ladies' man' but only in the opposite sense to his characterization of Teddy Roosevelt as 'a man's man'. Fortunately for John Kennedy, the taboo against writing about or publicly disclosing sexual habits of

ιe public man was still in force. If it had not been so, I doubt he'd
ver have been able to run for public office.

As it was, after the grim years of the Second World War, and
ιe unexpectedly bitter ordeal of the Korean War, and a stretch of
overnment by a late-middle-aged man, it was a tonic to see a young
andsome President up there on his brilliant, frosty inauguration day
ιying, 'the torch has been passed to a new generation', even though
ll the equals he had to deal with were the old men of the recent wars.
Ve readily embraced the glitter and charm and promise of a kind of
hivalry in the Presidency. This romantic hunger was so strong that
·hen the ill-conceived and wretchedly executed invasion of Cuba
ιiled miserably, and Kennedy said he was sorry for it, his popular
anding in the polls went soaring.

A journalist I know wrote movingly the other day about his boyhood
iew of Kennedy as a magical 'little guy on a black and white television
et, who, although he was a rich politician from Boston, I believed
epresented me and understood me. This boy enjoyed chanting over
·hat he called the sing-song aphorisms of Ted Sorensen – he was the
uthor of the Kennedy Inaugural speech. "Ask not what your country
an do for you; ask rather what you can do for your country."' The
ame journalist – now, I guess, crowding 50 – wrote on this 22nd:
Kennedy was the first great fraud of the post-modern era. He was the
urprised and grateful object of a mass delusion, he came from a state
·here electing Irish politicians by fraud was an art form. His father
·as a bandit and a profiteer . . . JFK never won a majority in a national
lection; it seems likely that the election of 1960 was stolen for him by
ιe Daley machine in Chicago.' That is, I think, almost certainly true.
ut as for the other judgements, they are too brutal; they are the
ynical outcries of a disappointed sentimentalist. We should not now
lame Kennedy for our misplaced romanticism. He brought to the
residency the energy of an optimistic spirit. On the initiative of a
Congressman from Wisconsin, he invented the Peace Corps. He got us
eeply involved in Vietnam. In the early assertion of the civil rights of
lacks, he did use the National Guard with, as he would have said,
·igah' where Eisenhower had used it with reluctance. He had wit and
low-key gift for Irish blarney. He was disorganized and acted too

often on impulse. He had no gift for cajoling and nudging and arm-twisting the Congress. He once called Congress 'the enemy'. When he died, there were something like ninety bills that were dead or dying. Luckily, he was succeeded by Lyndon Johnson, no charmer but the best con man ever to convert an enemy, who got more than two-thirds of those bills through the Congress in the following six months.

It has been remarked that when an American President dies, a halo descends on him and stays there with his memory. This is not true of McKinley. It's very true of Lincoln and Kennedy. The debates about their true worth still go on, or, perhaps, only about Kennedy. Lincoln has almost been sanctified, and the bad and arbitrary things about him are buried in his grave. Let it be so, once and for all, with John Fitzgerald Kennedy.

Boston

11 March 1994

'The Bostonians, almost without [an] exception, are derived from one country and a single stock. They are all descendants of Englishmen and, of course, are united by all the great bonds of society – language, religion, government, manners and interest.' That was written by the President of Yale (then known as Yale College) in 1796. Quoting that sentence in a federal guidebook in 1936, the writer says, as for this 'legend of ethnic homogeneity, it is so much pernicious twaddle'.

I lived across the river from Boston just sixty years ago and it could be truly said way back then that 'five minutes' walk from the State House will take the visitor to any one of several sections of the city where English is a foreign language . . . every third person you meet on the street is foreign-born, and three out of four are of other than English descent'. This guidebook, again, mind, quoting the census figures of 1930, begins with another bit of demolition prose, to wit:

366

'The modern fable that Boston is now an "Irish city" is no better founded than the English Puritan myth. Of Boston's quarter of a million foreign born, the largest number come from Canada – 45,000. Ireland, 43,000. Italy, 36,000. Russia (mainly Jews), 31,000. From the UK, 22,000. The rest come from Poland, Norway, Denmark, Germany, Greece and Lithuania.'

I bring up that accounting of sixty years ago in order to add a note which Americans of English origin, no matter how distant, tend to believe is still true or ought to be, namely, 'The old New England stock still largely controls leading banks, business enterprises, museums, hospitals and universities, but numerically is insignificant.' Today no minority but a spread of minorities controls the banks and businesses. When I was there, the Irish, though powerful in local politics, had hardly begun to challenge, on the national political scene, the Cabots and Saltonstalls and Lodges and Forbeses. Today the three main federal, that's to say United States government, buildings (employing 35,000) are called the Thomas O'Neill Federal Building, the J. W. McCormack Building and the John Fitzgerald Kennedy Federal Building.

There is, so far as I know, no James Michael Curley Building, an extraordinary oversight because, more than any other man this century, Curley marked the political triumph of the immigrant Irish over the entrenched old Yankees. A tall, dapper, handsome Irishman with, for those days, longish grey locks and flashing eyes, a black Irishman if ever there was one, he spent over a quarter of a century in politics, eight years in Congress, two as Governor, sixteen as Mayor, two spells in jail, during the second of which he was still Mayor and ran the city competently from his cell. The knowledge of all this, which dropped on me like a thunderbolt at the beginning of my year in Boston, was something that Bostonians, I mean the old Yankees, were almost proud to show you, through the example of Curley and later the recently dead Speaker O'Neill (of the United States House of Representatives), that Boston could still produce men of sap and mischief. The corollary is also true: that the Anglo-Saxon minority of Boston, no longer calling themselves the old Brahmins (Curley called them 'our Brahmin overlords'), are pale, respectable shadows of the originals.

What sparked these thoughts about Boston and what we'd now call its ethnic composition was an item reported the other day in a quiet nook of my newspaper: that in one state alone, California, there was a sudden flurry of lawsuits from Hispanic children protesting that they are not receiving a bilingual education. Ten years ago, there was something of a national debate on whether any school should teach in two languages. Now there's a move, throughout all the Southern border states, Florida, Louisiana, Texas, Arizona, California, to make it illegal *not* to have bilingual education. In two ways Hispanic (or what we're now supposed to call Latino) children are suing to be taught basic subjects in their native Spanish, and English as a second language. Meanwhile, English-speaking children are protesting that the basic education at their school is given in Spanish, which they don't understand, so they want basics in English, and Spanish as a second language. This is plainly a movement that will, in time, overtake all elementary and secondary education. A freakish offshoot of this movement (I think it was in Chicago) was where black children – who at home, on the streets, at play, speak their own brand of Black English – are beginning, through their parents and the nearest lawyer at the ready, to demand that in school, the basics should be taught in Black English, and that Formal English, or what you and I call English, should be taught as a second language.

It used to be the case, before and after the Second World War, that immigrants from any country were, willing or not, tossed into the ocean of English speakers, the immersion method. They learned, pretty soon, that so long as they spoke only the language they'd arrived with they would be doomed to swell the pool of cheap labour. Learn English, and you are already on your way from what today is called your 'entry profession', meaning first humble job, janitor, dustman, trucker or messenger. What has happened throughout the second half of the century is that the immigrant, especially the Spanish-speaking immigrant, has acquired a new self-respect as a special type of independent American. Many of them don't want to mix in, though I think these lawsuits will reflect a truth which sooner than later they panic to discover: that the only way you can rise into the middle class over most of the country is by way of the English language.

I find it striking that, so far anyway, we've not read of this kind of lawsuit coming from the Asians. Very conspicuously, more than any other type, they come, they flounder for a while with the new language, but, whether or not their parents pick up any rudimentary English, the children are at the grindstone every minute of every school day, and in a year or two are fluent and – it's a byword by now – markedly superior in learning to other nationals. They bloom sooner than anybody into clerks, office workers, then businessmen, doctors, lawyers, most notably as scientists and medical researchers. They are, naturally, greatly resented for the palpable superiority. And in some cities, New York is one, there has always been – in neighbourhoods where blacks and Asians live side by side – the prospect of boycotts (of Asian merchants) and, as you'd sadly guess, of riots.

My trip to Boston, in the first place, was not, however, meant to be mainly about immigrant tensions. It was about a remarkable model of a fish, up above the Speaker's chair in the House, known as the Hall of Representatives. There stands, or hangs, or gapes against the wall what is known as the Sacred Cod. It is the emblem of the item that saved the economy, and hence the foundation of the state – the Commonwealth of Massachusetts. Boston is still known to lisping children as 'the home of the bean and the cod'. Last week, the Governor of Massachusetts put in a plea to Washington – help! – a plea for emergency financial aid from the federal government for the industry that kept Massachusetts on the map. This is only one chapter of a story that takes in the whole country, from the far northwest, Seattle, in the state of Washington, across to New England and down all the East Coast to the Gulf of Mexico. A friend of mind – a Bostonian by the way – called me in horror the other day, alarmed to hear that the cod are dying in the polluted ocean. Polluted ocean? Yes, that's what we are only now beginning to accept as a true fact of life. She asked me if I'd read the long scare story in the *New York Times* and complained, rightly, that some government department, after saying nothing for years, suddenly spews at us a flood of statistics that proclaim a national crisis.

Quite simply, the fact is that – take New England first, and its principal port of Boston – after three hundred and fifty years, the oldest American fishing ground is almost barren of the fish it caught and sold and traded and lived by: haddock, cod, flounder. Last week, on one day, the fishermen in Boston Harbor tooted their boat horns.

They wanted as much government help as they might get after an earthquake. Somebody said that the honking of the horns sounded like a funeral dirge. But down three hundred miles to Chesapeake Bay, what native son Mencken called 'the vast protein factory of Chesapeake Bay', and on and all the way down to New Orleans, there are few groupers, and no more red snappers, which were the main catch of the southern East Coast. On the Pacific Coast, where I started, the great port of Seattle reports that the decline of the famous Pacific salmon is 'catastrophic . . . threatening to wipe out not only whole industries but also cultures and communities that depend on the catch'. The fishermen, both commercial and sporting, have been warned that unless there's a dramatic improvement from some unknown source, there may be a ban on all salmon fishing along the – what? Fifteen hundred miles of the American Pacific Coast. Now they tell us! 'Government officials', it says here, 'say that most of the commercial fishing grounds outside Alaska are in trouble, and that of the world's [not America's, but the *world's*] seventeen principal fishing zones, thirteen are in trouble.'

This widespread shortage is not something the normal fish-eater has begun to notice. Here in the East, we wish we saw more of the noble striped bass, our finest eating fish. But I get splendid salmon. Of course, I realize, on second thoughts, that it's Norwegian. Both Norway and several South American countries are making a killing here with imported farmed fish, raised in pens. The killing of course forces down the cost of the local article.

It occurs to me that if New England is losing the thing that helped the first settlers survive, Virginia and the Carolinas are fighting to keep the thing that helped *them* survive after a false start with glassmaking. And what was that? The tobacco leaf. That's another story, hilarious or tragic, according to your interest.

Trick or Treat

4 *November 1994*

On the evening of Monday, 31 October, millions of doors were knocked on and opened in response to the cry: Trick or Treat? If there is one Irish institution, other than the practice of charm, or blarney, that came into the United States and conquered, it is the secular festival of Hallowe'en. I stress secular because, so far as I can discover, few secular, or, if you like, pagan festivals passed so solidly into Christian practice.

It was originally a Celtic festival called Samhain, and Celtic scholars or crossword buffs, perhaps, will no doubt be eager to translate it for me. Samhain was the Celtic harvest festival, but also thought of as the time when the spirits of the dead came back to their old haunts, I suppose is the proper word. Until the ninth century, it seems people were content to accept these visitations as the return, from the underworld, of demons and goblins and other monsters. How and why the Roman Catholic Church managed in eight hundred and something AD to introduce this weird festival and its usages into the Christian liturgy is to me a remarkable mystery, and must remain one pending an explanatory fax from Rome.

Anyway, the original pagan festival became All Saints Day (now it was saints and not demons that came back) and 31 October became All-Hallows Eve.

I believe there is no record of daubing faces with soot or red dye, mask-wearing, tricking and treating in this country until the middle of the nineteenth century and the arrival, in lively multitudes, of the Irish. The interesting switch here is that apparently right from the start, except among the extremely devout, they cast off the religious elements and turned it into a children's holiday, as somebody said, of trick or treating and general mischief-making. If so, the mischief-making was pretty innocent. And, wherever they settled, the Irish, for a generation or two, were always the poorest people in town. No wonder they sent children off (very often their own) to knock on the doors of the comfortable and say 'trick or treat' – in the full expectation that nobody wants to have a scary trick practised on them, and would willingly cough up a cake, a pie, a candy bar or some such.

So last Monday, inside the lift in our building, there was posted a sheet of paper, with two parallel lists written on it. On the left, a list of tenants willing to subject themselves to the knockings and giggling of children in the building and to provide them with a treat. On the right was a list of children willing to offer themselves up for the reception of these goodies.

You'll have noticed the phrase, 'children in the building'. It's the first sinister change in the once general custom of kissing your tots goodbye and good luck and sending them out into the night to roam and knock and garner a cornucopia of treats. Kids used to love to do this the way we, when a little older and in another country, set out into the darkness of Christmas Eve with four or five other songsters and jogged around the town till all hours, carolling outside houses that were well lit, and looked prosperous, and might – did – have you in for a mince pie.

But to send your – and anybody else's – children out on the town without a protective adult these nights would be taken in some quarters as a heartless form of child neglect punishable in the courts. For more years now than I care to count – ten, twenty – the last thing on any parent's mind is to send small children, or, for that matter, young teenagers, out at night for any purpose, secular or holy. And as you no doubt know, in some cities, there are curfews for people under 18. I don't need to tell you that the painful restriction of Hallowe'en to one apartment building in cities, or one street block under adult patrol in the countryside, is yet another response to the growing and seemingly incurable affliction of random public crime. Most crime, as you've no doubt heard, is committed between members of the same family (most homicides, at any rate), or between close friends or members of one family feuding with another. And always, and dependably swelling the homicides in Los Angeles, Miami, Detroit and half a dozen cities we'd never guess at, are the ritual murders of teenage gangs who have replaced life, liberty and the pursuit of happiness with the triple pledge: respect, reputation and retaliation. Which means, pitifully, once you're initiated into a gang, you earn respect by a serious mugging or attempted shooting, reputation by clocking up a record of shootings, and retaliation by avenging the wounds, or murders, of your own gangsters by another murder, on the principle of an eye for an eye.

But in spite of this remarkable closed circuit of crime, which eats away at the decent community life of this country, there is a great deal of random street crime. And what could be more appetizing, likely to be safer, than a swift assault on a gaggle of small children? There's been enough of it in the recent past to have some cities post warnings, in the week before Hallowe'en, urging parents to forgo Hallowe'en altogether; a cruel blow, surely, to the aspirations, pleasures, of the young. Such parents are, usually, fundamentalist Christians, who dislike very much, or detest, the clause in the Bill of Rights First Amendment that dictates the separation of Church and State. The extremist wing of them longs to make this nation a Christian nation, against the lively presence of so many other religions here, and against the unwavering rulings of the United States Supreme Court. They take every opportunity of introducing Christian customs, symbols, feasts into public places; and just as resolutely, and just as tiresomely, the civil liberties maniacs (not just civil liberties upholders) grimly fight and oppose the militant Christians – and usually win. As, for instance, whenever a church or any Christian religious group mounts a Christmas crib in, say, a village square, up jumps the American Civil Liberties Union, goes to court and is conceded yet another victory by pointing out that the crib is on display on public property, maintained and paid for with the taxes of Muslims, Jews, agnostics and heathens.

But now Hallowe'en, the latest bait to the religious right. In at least five states, they have this year begged or urged or tried to order families to abandon Hallowe'en or change its rituals drastically and celebrate it as a sacred Christian festival. Because, they insist, they've just discovered, perhaps, that all these years, for a century and a half, America has been practising without shame a purely pagan festival and perpetuating, in the innocent young, a belief in the most wicked and primitive superstitions. Black cats. Witches. Ghosts. Scary monsters. Death's heads made out of pumpkins, that healthy, pure, Puritan fruit, if ever there was one. So in Maryland, New York, Ohio, Georgia, California, only of course in certain places bouncing with Christian fundamentalists, the public-elementary schools, fearing the prospect of litigation, have reluctantly told children to come to school in their normal dress and forgo the innumerable comic or ghastly masks available. Of course, the first protests have come from the manufacturers and retailers, in hot Republican territory, of masks, lifelike but in this context sinister, of Bill Clinton. I myself was about to appear as Madonna if we had stayed in New York, but we were flying off to family. Still, I was cheered to arrive at the airport and duck under a great sweeping sheet of something swaying slightly in the atmosphere, like a giant cobweb. It *was* a giant cobweb, reaching, without explanation, from one shining pillar to another squeaky clean wall or counter. Candle-lit pumpkins everywhere; one or two small passengers who plainly, from their scarred or deformed faces, had just arrived, or were on their way, to the underworld. It was very rousing. And, I must mention, on the last day of the American golf tour championship in San Francisco, marching up the eighteenth fairway was a very athletic figure with a skeleton's head. It was the super-golfer Greg Norman, doing his bit to defy the hysterical Christian right. In some cities, the brethren announced that Hallowe'en night would be replaced by 'Hallelujah night' and prizes would be given – to tots, mind you – for the best biblical costume. Not much public sympathy, I'm afraid, for the prim little one who chose to come as David instead of Dracula. The way around this, in some wicked places, was to appear as a ferocious Goliath or, so defying the parents too, as one or other of the more disreputable inhabitants of Sodom and Gomorrah.

The television stations, I'm happy to say, paid no attention whatever to the reformers. Of our seventy-two operating channels, I'd guess that at least forty were drenched with blood last Monday night: every horror film ever made, an actual revival of such old Saturday night series – serieses – as Chiller Theater, and the more vivid films of Hammer Productions and the Japanese company that gave us the incomparable Godzilla. Also, a public station notable for its nightly one-hour profiles, biographies, of the famous (and very well done, from Julius Caesar to Sigmund Freud and Humphrey Bogart, Charles Darwin and Charles Laughton), came out with a piece that drained the previous horrors away with a documentary life proving – and it was quite true – the essential lovability of Vincent Price. It was a kind of final purge of pity and terror, worthy of the Greeks.

Fiftieth Anniversary of VE Day

5 May 1995

This weekend, I suppose every nation that fought in the Second World War will be recalling 7–8 May 1945 and the general jubilation that greeted the end of the fighting in what an American Navy commander I knew called 'the European sector'. It's a phrase, I imagine, that could never have occurred to the armies and the people of Europe. But it's an oddity worth mentioning, because although it is a touch stilted, it spoke volumes for the American view – here on the Pacific Coast – of VE Day, as distinct from a European view. That sailor friend was in San Francisco at the time, and so was I. And, more to the point, so were thousands of soldiers, sailors and Marines having a brief final fling before shipping out through the Golden Gate and into the huge Pacific towards the Japanese islands, where most of them expected to be fighting or dying through the summer and fall. Indeed, given the Japanese's fanatical capacity for holding their ground till the last man – the expert guess was that we could not expect to invade the main islands before the spring of 1946. General Marshall debated with the Secretary of War and with General Omar Bradley whether the price to be exacted by that distant VJ Day would be one or two million lives.

When the certainty of VE Day was reported here (there'd been a false alarm two days before in a dispatch filed by an over-eager American agency reporter), when it really came, the whooping it up was muted but delayed here, because while Londoners were aswarm along the Mall, and New Yorkers, early risers anyway, were pouring into

Times Square to watch the illuminated news ticker, we here in San Francisco (and we were the delegates of fifty-one nations and about three or four hundred press, and radio reporters, in the second week of the cumbersome, the immensely tedious business of setting up the various bodies of a new League of Nations, christened – before he died by Franklin Roosevelt – the United Nations), we and the rest of the San Francisco population, were in bed and snoozing at four in the morning. By the time we woke, there were small crowds out on Market Street. But by 9 o'clock, the delegates to the founding conference of the United Nations were assembled in plenary session in the Opera House here, chatting animatedly, brought to order by the gavel of the temporary Secretary General, and an announcement was made. The Nazis had surrendered. There was a short wave of polite applause, the generals and the statesmen all sat down, and the business was resumed of writing the UN charter to, as it says, 'save succeeding generations from the scourge of war'. A great and noble aim, and in the brilliant spring of 1945, it was, believe me, thought to be an achievable aim.

I sifted through the delegations and buttonholed many soldiers and politicians and civil servants from many countries. And I don't remember any one of them who made a wry face when that memorable phrase was recited or when we looked ahead to the prospect of a long peace. I don't believe the most cynical delegate present would ever have guessed or predicted that by the fiftieth anniversary of the United Nations, the world would have endured, by the UN's own count, something like two hundred and forty wars, and, in this anniversary year, a half-dozen very active and murderous ones.

But even if idealism was rampant in San Francisco in 1945 (and it was), what was so markedly different about VE Day here and the rejoicings in the capitals of Europe was the looming prospect over the Pacific horizon, of worse to come. At the end of the celebratory week, I was sitting in a movie theatre with a Marine officer; the European and New York newsreels (of course, there was no television yet) had been flown out to the West Coast, so we saw the surging, reverberating crowds around Buckingham Palace, the Royal Family there on the balcony, and the squat, rosy-faced figure of Churchill making the V sign. My Marine officer said, no resentment intended, just casually, almost amused: 'You'd think the war was over.' And of course, to the peoples of Europe, so it was. But my Marine's offhand remark was one I would never forget. He shipped out within the week, and was soon fighting on the island of Okinawa, which was thought vital to take a hold as the first stepping stone, a launch pad for the mass bombing and invasion of Japan eight hundred miles away. One-third of all the American Marine casualties of the Second World War were counted in the taking of Okinawa. My Marine officer was one of them.

We have only just now, last month, celebrated the landing on Okinawa. I suppose 'celebrated' is the word, but the anniversary ceremony involved most conspicuously the widows and family survivors of the dead. And this time, which marks the fiftieth anniversary of so many great events, the urge toward hilarity and joy is rebuked by the uncomfortable fact that the victory, the successful battles, the liberating of the Holocaust victims, coincided with so many other dreadful and humiliating events. So, in no more than a month or so, we've been commemorating some events we'd rather forget.

I have atop a bookcase in my study a postcard, about three times the normal length. I bought it in 1931 after I'd walked along a street of many children, walking skeletons with bulging bellies. (We'd never heard in Britain about the actual famine and deep despair of the famished, one plausible cause of Hitler.) I walked along and came to a marble arch, a high wall and steps going up to the entrance of the most breathtaking horizon of architecture I had ever seen then, or have ever seen since. It was a vast, far-reaching palace, with four majestic sides, *the* masterpiece of northern Baroque. I'm sorry I found this postcard – a few weeks ago – on the fiftieth anniversary of the firebombing of Dresden, when 120,000 (mostly civilians) were burned alive or drowned in the river they plunged into. British and American bombers pelted Dresden, in two waves, over a night and a day. Possibly our most ignoble act of the war, it was certainly nothing to celebrate.

Last weekend, there was no way for Americans to avoid the news of another mighty celebration in the city that we knew as Saigon, now Ho Chi Minh City, capital of a united Communist Vietnam. What was being celebrated (not by us) was the twentieth anniversary of the surrender of South Vietnam in the long, eight-year war that America lost, after President Kennedy's military advisers and technicians turned into President Johnson's American soldiers and sailors and airmen, and in the end, into half a million fighting men. There's no need to go on, to stress what we've been saying throughout those twenty years, that Vietnam was a wound from which the United States has never wholly recovered. So this week's pictures and reports, all they did was turn the knife in the wound. Another twist of it was given by Lyndon Johnson's Secretary of Defense, who – throughout his service in that office – was the super-hawk, so much so, it was by many people called McNamara's War. Now he has written a tearful memoir saying he knew early on the war was wrong, the war should never have been fought. He stops short of the rueful verdict of another former hawk, the late Secretary of State Dean Acheson, who said at the end: 'Vietnam was worse than immoral – it was a mistake.'

Mr Robert McNamara has lit up a fiery controversy by his agonized confessional. He has been challenged by the obvious question: Why did he stay on? Why didn't he resign if that's the way he felt? Anthony Eden resigned when he couldn't square the government's policy with being Foreign Secretary. Mr Cyrus Vance resigned as President Carter's Secretary of State when his conscience wouldn't let him conceal from the allies Mr Carter's disastrous adventure in the desert to rescue the Iran hostages. Lord Carrington resigned as Foreign Secretary when Argentina invaded the Falklands, not because he was responsible, he said, simply he ought to have seen it coming. Mr McNamara's excuse is his loyalty to President Johnson. It's exactly how Colonel Oliver North defended his running a secret, underground foreign policy in the Iran-Contra affair. It's a strange excuse. No Cabinet officer, nobody serving the government, takes an oath to the President. He or she takes an oath only to 'uphold the Constitution of the United States'.

So you see, this fiftieth anniversary, commemoration, has more properly justified the American word for commemoration: 'memorializing'. We're sorrier for more millions than we're happy for.

And now, the act of commemoration itself is being performed. Where? Amazingly, in Moscow, in the building where Stalin's man, Molotov, signed the treacherous pact with Hitler's man, Ribbentrop, that brought on all this woe and the devastation of Europe. There's one, only one, anniversary I now look forward to, one to *celebrate*. I hope I'm here for it: 5 June 1997, the fiftieth anniversary of another spring morning when General George Marshall, on the initiative of his successor, Dean Acheson, announced the breathtaking American plan to invest $17 billion in Europe, to do what Dean Acheson said it was meant to do, and which it did: 'to repair the fabric of European life'.

O.J. – the Verdict

6 October 1995

The Congress suspended business for fifteen minutes, airlines delayed flights, bank tellers stopped counting bills, empty streets were remarked on in the big cities across the country, as, just before ten in the morning in California, and 1 p.m. in New York, the television commentators started what one called 'the countdown' which was – this time – not a word clocking the launching of John Glenn's capsule through 81,000 miles, as thirty-three years ago, but the calling off of the minutes as they ticked away towards the verdict in the case of 'The People of California vs. O. J. Simpson', not so long ago a folk hero, sometime actor, the greatest running back in the history of American football. But, from the moment of his arrest almost sixteen months ago, the Los Angeles District Attorney's office, the prosecutor, chose rather to cast him as an American Othello, a man whipped by jealousy to the point of murdering the woman he loved not wisely but too well.

In the beginning, in June 1994 (seven months before the trial began), everything we heard that might be evidence in the trial ran against O. J. Simpson. Quite simply, here is an outline of the undisputed plot. After midnight of Sunday, 12 June 1994, Mrs Simpson was found savagely slaughtered with many stab wounds, outside her house in a posh section of Los Angeles. By her side was a young man, a waiter who had come to return some eyeglasses Mrs Simpson's mother had left, the evening before, at his restaurant. About an hour before, a chauffeur had picked up Mr Simpson at *his* house (the Simpsons were

379

separated) and driven him to the airport to keep a long-planned business date in Chicago. Of course, he flew back shortly after he arrived at the Chicago hotel. After the funeral, police charged him with the double murder. He agreed to turn himself in, but instead he disappeared, leaving behind a sad, rambling letter protesting his innocence, conceding he had had a good life, and saying goodbye. The police eventually tracked him in a white car speeding at a great rate along one of the Los Angeles highways. A friend who was driving him reported over a cellular phone that Simpson was holding a gun to his head and threatening suicide. The car followed a roundabout course and at last went back to Mr Simpson's home, where he stayed slumped in the car for an hour before police managed to coax him out. He was taken into custody and two days later pleaded not guilty and was held without bail.

The trial was set on the docket for late in the year, but it took for ever to choose a jury, and various other niceties of the California criminal code had to be observed (remember, this was not a federal trial) – a code that is in some ways more stringent that most, and stuffed with precedents which counsel are quick to cite on very fragile pretexts. (This meant, in the long run, that the trial itself would have a very long run.) Finally, in the middle of January this year, it started, and ended nine months later, by which time the court had lost ten jurors in all, through sickness, minor misbehaviour of some sort, admitted prejudice; one or two, I feel fairly certain, hadn't thought too deeply about the meaning of sequestration, and under whatever pretext, were silently crying, 'Let me out of here.'

Sequestration! In California, a judge may, and in this case did, order the jury's exile from normal life to a degree that a dictator held under house arrest would very likely protest before the International Court of Justice. The jury, after interminable challenges, queries and manufactured indignation from both sides, and subsequent excuses or dismissals, consisted of nine blacks, two whites and one Latino. They, along with the originals, had been told the trial might last three or four months. They must brace themselves to obey the rules. They would be sequestered in a hotel, separated from the other guests. They would be led to their meals. They were not allowed to read newspapers or magazines, listen to radio, or watch television. Movies were chosen for them, which they saw together. The married were from time to time allowed conjugal visits.

When at last the jury began their deliberations, at 9 o'clock last Monday morning, the commentators – shoals of them, mostly lawyers, legal scholars, former prosecutors, notable defence attorneys and so on – settled down to speculate and guess at the verdict. The overwhelming consensus was that the jury would take a week or two to declare itself a hung jury. Suddenly, in the middle of the day the word went to the judge: we have reached a verdict. That was a stunner for everybody. But the judge said the secret would remain sealed overnight.

This gave us all time to guess now what evidence had been decisive. The DNA analysis of the bloodstains? Although this excruciatingly complex stuff (which possibly a few hundred people alive understand) took four days to explain to the jury, my own sense was that, in general, juries distrust medical expertise, especially when there are conflicting theories, and that this jury might well have believed the defence's contention that the Los Angeles Police Department had been sloppy in analysing the blood samples, might have contaminated them.

The prosecution's main case was that Mr Simpson was the only villain, a known wife-beater who, once he knew for certain that he had lost her, and she was living her own life, couldn't bear the loss of his control over her. One June night, he went berserk, left his house, drove off to her house, murdered her and Mr Goldman, drove home, changed, buried or hid the clothes and the weapon, took a shower, dressed and packed for Chicago. (The defence said, by the way, that by the prosecution's estimate of time, he would have had to do all that in five minutes.) But the chauffeur had to wait forty-one minutes for him, and when he appeared, he said he'd overslept and had to take a shower. The prosecution maintained that nobody saw Simpson for over an hour, and he had ample time to commit the murders.

Since there were no witnesses, both sides had to stress the physical evidence, of which there were two items all agreed were crucial. One was a bloody glove, the other a bloody sock, both found by the police in Simpson's home. It was not disputed that the rescued droplets belonged to nobody in the world but Mr Simpson. And that, for the prosecution, was conclusive proof of his guilt.

But the defence lawyers touched the nerve of all doubt when they asked who found the glove, and when. The answer was, one Mark Fuhrman, a detective who, without a warrant, climbed over the fence to Simpson's home and later produced the glove, the blood still moist seven hours after Mr Simpson dropped it, if he did (a chemical impossibility, two doctors testified). And why did it take two months for the bloody sock to appear, after two months of exhaustive search of houses, gates, grass, cars, furniture, everything? The defence contention, which seemed very melodramatic when it was first launched, was that this same Fuhrman was a racist who chose, with one other detective, to frame Mr Simpson and actually planted the glove and smeared the sock. Mr Fuhrman was challenged on the stand as to his reputation as a racist. He denied any hint of it. In ten years he had never used the word 'nigger'. I must say he sounded plausible at the time, and the prosecution ridiculed the whole macabre nonsense of a conspiracy contrived by two or more of the Los Angeles Police Department which we should not forget – the jury didn't – has had an unsavoury reputation over many years for its powerful minority of race-hating cops.

Alas for the prosecution's ridicule. In a turn that marked the collapse of their case, a screenwriter was found who had, over three years, recorded many hours of taped interviews with Detective Fuhrman, in which he used 'nigger' forty-three times, in which he told of police initiatives in framing blacks. At one point he had wished all the blacks in America could be piled up and burned. (It seems to me very naive to say that these disclosures from a foul-mouthed bigot would not deeply affect a jury with nine black members, however high-minded their final discussion.) Off in retirement in the mountains of Idaho, former Detective Fuhrman was quoted as saying, 'If I go down, the case goes down.' And so it was.

All our analysing and judgements made in retrospect were swept away by the one item of evidence (out of 45,000 pages of it) that the jury had asked to be read over. It was the testimony of the chauffeur, who picked up Mr Simpson and drove him to the airport. It came out that in the first two minutes of their gathering, they voted 10 to 2 for acquittal. But they decided to take Ms Clark, the chief prosecutor, at her word, that the nub, the root, of the evidence was the time-line: the jury's decision whether or not Simpson had time to drive to Mrs

Simpson's home, perform the double murder, get home, clean up, hide the clothes and the weapon, shower, dress and be ready for the waiting chauffeur.

The jury trooped back. They heard the chauffeur's testimony. He got the time of arrival at Simpson's house wrong by an hour, but corrected himself. He didn't see O.J.'s car (because the prosecution held he had not yet driven it back). The jury cut off the rest of the chauffeur's testimony. They had heard enough. They went back and reached a not-guilty verdict within the hour.

There is a point that worried some of us from the start who were inclined to believe in Simpson's guilt. It is the ferocity of the murder, calculated by both sides to have taken more than ten minutes: thirty-two stab wounds in Mr Goldman (did he put up a fight?) and Mrs Simpson practically decapitated. Yet Simpson revealed after his arrest not a bruise or a blemish on his body. And no blood on anything he subsequently wore. Altogether, the incriminating blood evidence was very sparse – the jury thought sparse enough to have been planted.

When the verdict was announced, and had travelled in seconds the length and breadth of the country, there was great and thunderous rejoicing among blacks everywhere, from the most famous black university to the seediest inner-city slum. There is one consolation for the people who think justice was denied. There were no riots, anywhere.

The Old Rocking Chair

3 May 1996

Early on a fine June morning, under a blue, blue sky, we took off from Point Mogu, a Coast Guard base in Southern California, and we clattered off in a small fleet of helicopters out on to the huge, sail-less Pacific. 'We' were the travelling White House press corps, which in those days consisted of no more than, say, fifteen or twenty correspondents, plus yours truly – the only foreign correspondent present. Not more than ten miles offshore, there loomed up a monster of a ship with a flat top comprising, it seemed, several football fields. It was the aircraft carrier, the USS *Kitty Hawk*.

We were to see a performance of missile-firing, both by day and by night, from the *Kitty Hawk*'s yawning deck, an event that had been postponed, for one official reason and another. But now the Navy was ready, and the President, who had flown on ahead of us, was ready. And the day was perfection. What we were to see was how missiles from the carrier's deck swooshed at impossible speed off to the horizon to pinpoint drag targets – large, flying red banners (which looked to us no bigger than handkerchiefs). They were red to imply that they were Soviet targets. The daytime performance was brilliant indeed. Enormous, sleek missiles whooshed up from below. They were Phantoms, so called, and they skimmed across the bow and were lost to sight in a matter of seconds. Then, coming up on elevators like a sudden plague of wasps, was a fleet of little, manned jets, a hundred or more of them. They unfolded their wings and whizzed off over the blue water till they were recalled and came hurtling back at a hundred and fifty miles an hour to be retrieved with a jolt by their arresting cables.

But, for beauty and theatrical impressiveness, nothing could compare with the night show: the great ship immovable in this most motionless of oceans; the last, long, red streaks of the sun dissolving into the horizon; and the coming on of an eerie sort of darkness, an encompassing purple twilight; and a long silence, suddenly punctured by horns and buzzing sounds, punched up by coordinators on an immense console winking in several colours in the darkness of the upper bridge. What I was doing there will appear in good time. In response to these winking orders, small armies of figures in phosphorescent uniforms came running and advancing and retreating across the deck down below, like bright clockwork toys. At intervals, there was a deep rumble, as of underground steam pressure, and a huge missile exploded out of the ship's belly, rose like a flying submarine, and could just be seen in pursuit of an illuminated flying target far away. There was a faint, tiny explosion, the target fell like a shot bird, the missile vanished like an expiring cinder, and we all clapped. We had hit the

viet target! We hit all the targets that night (of course) and the
esident was well pleased.

Before the show started, we had been the guests of the officers at
inner, in an underground dining room about twice the size of the
ueen Mary's. Then we were led along many decks and corridors
ward a lower bridge, where, we were told, we should have a privi-
ed view of things. The most privileged view of all, of course, would
 given to the President alone, sitting with the admiral on the topmost
idge. As the reporters were pattering on our way I felt a smart slap
 my shoulder, an affectionate oath spoken from behind, and lo! – a
end from the very beginning of America's war in the Pacific, a young
icer I'd known and had merry evenings with back in February 1942
en I was assigned as a correspondent to San Francisco, the Seventh
val District, and, most secret, never to be written about, the Net,
 underwater net across San Francisco Bay. The young officer had
oadened and grizzled slightly (hadn't we all?) and was now vice
miral of the Pacific fleet. With a quick pull on my arm, he said, 'You
n't want to go up there. Follow me!' We snaked up a narrow,
nding stairway, came to a small door, knocked three times, and
re appeared a junior officer with what Britons call a torch, and
nericans, less frighteningly, a flashlight. He cupped it with one hand,
 it would not disturb the surrounding blackness of the enclosed
dge. As we ducked in and crept into the only two seats in this tiny
om, half of which was a semicircle of the console, there was one
houetted figure that was as still and sharp as a cut-out – the back of
 man's head resting against the high back of a most extraordinary
air to be in this tiny cockpit. It was a rocking chair, and the head
s, of course, the head of President John F. Kennedy.

Later, I asked my old friend about it. I'd thought I knew everything
out the physical condition of President Kennedy, and how much of
was, by an unspoken agreement in those days, kept secret. I recalled
 brief uproar during the primary campaign, when Senator Lyndon
nnson was running against Kennedy, and the Johnson team put out
 scurrilous news that Senator Kennedy had Addison's disease (so
 had) which explained the yellowish pigment in his skin sometimes.
 also occasionally appeared to have a hump (known, I discovered
er, as a cortisone hump). We noticed these things at the time as,

simply, on and off days of a very busy public man. Anyway, there was then a code, unwritten, never brought up, which would have made it tasteless to mention such things. As for Kennedy and Lyndon Johnson's foul accusation, the Kennedy camp promptly denied it, and no more was said.

So, as I say, after the brilliant and sombre missile show that June night in 1963 in the Pacific, I asked my old sailor friend, 'How about the rocking chair, where did you get it?' 'Oh,' he said, 'it's his, nobody else's. They fly it everywhere. Seems he has to have it. He can't walk for too long without either taking a bath or going to work in the rocking chair.' More than a year later when I was making a memorial album about President Kennedy, compiling many recorded interviews with every sort of person who'd known him, I mentioned to Mrs Kennedy that when he didn't have that slightly waxy complexion he always looked as if he'd just emerged from a hot bath. She said, 'So he had. He took them all the time. It was the only place, the only time he didn't feel the pain in his back.' (That was from his naval war wound.)

You can see now why the most vivid memory of that memorable night on the *Kitty Hawk* was not the magic of the soaring missiles, leaping like dolphins at play in the apocalypse, but – that rocking chair. First, it made me realize how drastically the conventions, you might almost say the courtesies, of reporting have changed in thirty years; some might say deteriorated. The first hint I had of a new – not a new convention but you might say a new feeling – a completely new emotion among a new generation of reporters, was in 1958, just five years before that night with Kennedy in the Pacific. There had been, I recall, a long debate in the United Nations Security Council. Mr John Foster Dulles, who was Eisenhower's Secretary of State, long after midnight finished a speech and went off home. He didn't go home. He went straight to a hospital. Within a day or two, there appeared as a banner headline, on the front page of the *New York Daily News* (a tabloid but then a good and responsible one): 'Dulles Has Inoperable Cancer.' I wrote for my paper next day, 'No mention has been made in this country about the unique break with tradition implicit in the publication last Sunday of his doctor's bulletin.' We had come a long way since the case of President Grover Cleveland, more than a century ago, who woke up one morning with a sore throat which persisted. One of his doctors, smarter than the rest, correctly diagnosed cancer of the throat. So one day the Presidential yacht was commissioned for a weekend cruise. They went out to sea, the cancer was operated on, the President returned, convalesced for some days, a week or more in the White House. There were no press conferences in those days. He never had to see anyone he didn't choose to see. Nothing was put out, nothing was, in fact, known. About thirty years after he'd died, it came out.

And then in our own time, there is what I'm now told is the even more unbelievable press silence about Franklin Roosevelt. It is true that (I should guess) throughout thirteen years, 95 per cent of the American people never thought that their President was paralysed from the waist down. Maybe 60 per cent would have said they knew, if they'd been reminded that, way back in his fortieth year, when he was Governor of New York, he had had poliomyelitis. But what the people of every nation saw throughout his unprecedented long reign was the strong upper body, the bull-like stance, the hands gripping a lectern, the confident, inimitable tenor voice rousing and consoling the people. Nothing was ever said or written (and all photography was banned) of his being lifted into a chair, the wheelchair he lived his life in, the daily ordeal of simply getting out of bed. I think it was an admirable convention the press observed. Today, it would be thought an outrageous suppression of free speech.

And, last week, we saw that Kennedy rocking chair on the stage of an auction house in New York, not in a museum: an artefact of a President, and a time, and an affliction. Its historical value is beyond price. Its value at auction was – $453,000. Responding to this and other monstrous bids, an auctioneer's representative said: 'Well, they are buying pieces of history.' Not so; this audience were buying a faded vision, the myth of the first Presidency to be cast in Hollywood – the handsome, war-hero President, and the beautiful, delicate, elegant wife. Somebody called it Camelot – which is not history but myth. And people paid dearly to recover some symbols of the myth, and pretend it was a historical fact.

Silver Watergate

20 June 1997

Americans seems to be celebrating, or at least recalling, more anniversaries than anybody these days. And I think it must have much to do with the never-ending increase in television channels, and the constant problem of filling them with programmes throughout the day. Most stations, like most newspapers, employ somebody to consult every day one of those big books like the *Time Tables of History*, which record in parallel columns what was happening around the world in government, science, the arts, sport, literature, inventions, exploration, medicine and so on, from prehistory to Only Yesterday. But last Tuesday there fell an anniversary that all the networks seized on because they had whole libraries of tape, of film about it: the outstanding American scandal of our time, certainly the greatest constitutional crisis since the Civil War.

Like most viewers, I suppose, I hadn't noticed anything particularly significant about the date, 17 June 1997. It flashed on my retina with the opening shot of the evening news: a late-middle-aged man standing on aeroplane steps, swarthy, grinning, arms spreadeagled like a new dictator just arrived to a thunderous welcome. But this man wasn't coming. He was going. A student in his early twenties, watching, said, simply, the incredible sentence: 'Who *is* he?' He was Richard M. Nixon, the only President in American history to resign in disgrace. I suppose the young man might be forgiven. Tuesday was the twenty-fifth anniversary of the event that brought Mr Nixon down, a year or two before this young man was born. I myself at his age would have had a hard time recognizing General Botha, Britain's enemy in the Boer War, which had also happened – to me – in the very distant past, namely six years before I was born.

It occurred to me that since this otherwise bright young man didn't recognize the famous, the infamous, President Nixon, twenty-five years might also have dulled the memory of a lot of people who were alive and sentient at the time. The event was to be for ever known as Watergate; and this week many Americans dated their distrust in and cynicism about Washington and government itself from Watergate. So I think it's worth looking back and retelling as simply and clearly as possible the tale of the rather ridiculous burglary that began on 17 June 1972 and ended on 8 August 1974 with a heavily jowled and heavy-hearted Richard Nixon announcing over television that he was resigning the Presidency there and then, that his rather astonished Vice President, Mr Gerald Ford, would be sworn in next day, and he would fly home, once and for all, to California.

Two o'clock on a hot morning, then, in Washington. In June, at a large apartment complex known as the Watergate Building, a guard was making his nightly rounds. As he passed by the offices of the Democratic National Committee, he noticed a tape on the lock of their door. He thought this odd and he smelled a rat, five rats. He called the police and they hotfooted it over and caught, inside the Democrats' office, five men, two of them Cubans. They had cameras and electronic gear for bugging telephones. It looked like – it was – a clumsy attempt to bug the Democrats' phones.

It drew only comical attention in the papers, but naturally the press guessed that the raid must have been staged by the Republicans, maybe by enthusiastic Nixon fans. It was a Presidential year, and the campaign was hotting up. Next day, Wednesday, the White House announced that the burglars were 'operating neither on our behalf nor with our consent'. That word came from Mr Nixon's re-election campaign manager, his Attorney General, later a convicted felon sent to jail. For a week or two, facetious references continued to be made about what the papers called 'the Watergate caper'. Then the silly story was forgotten, but not by two reporters on the *Washington Post*, later to become nationally if not world-famous as a brilliant investigative team; two reporters in their late twenties, Woodward and Bernstein. After about six weeks of mooching around, digging into lots of apparently irrelevant documents, reports, memoranda, and interviewing all sorts of people (they worked on an average about sixteen hours a day), on 1 August they published a piece in their paper asserting that the Watergate break-in was not, as everybody had come to take for granted, a wild partisan escapade by a couple of loony Cubans and helpers who feared that, if Mr Nixon's Democratic opponent was elected in November, Fidel Castro and the Communists would take over the United States. The break-in, they said, was linked financially with a Committee to Re-elect the President, known later as CREEP – which of course, was a proper legitimate organization.

Political parties must report the source of their campaign contributions. But the Democrats, and the two reporters, discovered that $114,000 was missing from President Nixon's reported contributions. It was, the reporters said, the exact amount paid out by CREEP's finance chairman to – guess who? – the leader of the burglars' gang. They went on to reveal it as a down payment of what was meant to be a massive campaign of espionage and sabotage against the Democrats (and even against reporters secretly listed as 'Nixon enemies'). The day after the discovery of the secret fund, President Nixon denounced the *Washington Post* for 'mudslinging' and 'shabby journalism'. But Woodward and Bernstein had picked up a scent which led from the break-in and the secret fund and the laundering of great sums of money in Miami and other places. And the trail led nearer and nearer to the President's men in the White House. By the spring of 1973, a former CIA official and several Republican Party officials had pleaded guilty, and co-conspirators in this whole plot and the President's two senior advisers (who by now must have known that Woodward and Bernstein had their number) decided to resign. We would hear much more from them at a special Senate investigating committee set up as the Woodward–Bernstein plot grew thicker and murkier. The chairman of that committee was a courtly old Southern lawyer (Senator Ervin) but his roguish charm did not soften his legal jabs or his curiosity in wondering 'What did the President know and when did he know it?' At one of these hearings, a minor White House official, testifying in answer to a question, said, 'Oh, that was all on the tapes'. The tapes? What tapes? Oh, didn't they know? The President secretly taped all and every conversation in his White House office. The Committee at first gasped and then rejoiced. They requested the tapes from the White House. Mr Nixon claimed 'executive privilege'. Senator Ervin retorted, 'Executive poppycock! I could send the Sergeant-at-Arms up to the White House, and say, with Shakespeare, what meat doth this Caesar it that he grows so fat?' The Supreme Court ordered the tapes to be surrendered. First, a batch that Mr Nixon had edited. Then another batch, unedited. The tapes were an appalling revelation. Apart from showing up Mr Nixon as a remarkable practitioner of foul language, there were masses of conversations about the secret fund, about first paying off the burglars so they wouldn't blow the whistle on the White House people involved.

But in all the thousands of discussions and private plotting and arguing about the whole smelly business, there was no single speech or confession from the President's own mouth that he had known about the raid early on and tried to cover up the consequences. By the spring of 1974, the Watergate scandal had grown so serious and Mr Nixon's part in it so conspicuous, if still not specific, that the House Judiciary Committee met to consider Articles of Impeachment against him. At the beginning of August 1974 Mr Nixon was forced by the Supreme Court to release one last, very early, tape. There, as gross as a manacle, was the missing link: the President himself telling an aide to get busy at once and stop the CIA and FBI from investigating the break-in. That sentence was spoken only six days after the break-in itself. It showed that Nixon had known all along, had relentlessly covered up, and lied steadily and unblinkingly to the Congress, the Press, the people, for two years. The Committee voted for his impeachment, mainly on the charge of obstruction of justice. On 8 August, he resigned, rather than stand trial before the Senate.

Looking back on it now, through all the tortuous complexity of the conspiracy, I believe there were two fateful moments fatal for the conspirators. One was the moment the Watergate guard saw the Democratic National Committee office's door-lock taped. The other was the offhand remark of that minor White House official that the President taped everything talked about in his office – and forgot to turn off the machine! The guard's name was Frank Kelly. The White House official was one Alexander Butterfield. Kelly and Butterfield will have their names permanently inscribed as footnotes to the historical record.

The only other consequence of the whole business that strikes me as having had a lasting influence on journalism is the fame of Woodward and Bernstein. They were pioneers of investigative reporting: diligent, serious and extremely careful. Unfortunately, they have inspired a whole generation of reporters in the English-speaking countries who take very little interest in the movers and shakers of their time, but are brought up on the idea that unveiling a personal (preferably a sexual) scandal is the whole purpose of good journalism. It's true, and it's awful.

The End of Civilization

25 July 1997

I don't know which cliché to avoid and which to fall back upon. The end of an era, shopworn for centuries. During the Second War, we used to be told: 'If we don't fight Hitler, it will be the end of civilization as we know it.' Well, last Friday the bell tolled, and it sounded the end of civilization as I, and I'm sure many of you, came to know it. In a simple, brutal phrase: last Friday, F. W. Woolworth's announced it was closing down all its four hundred stores in the United States. Whether the paralysis is to spread to Europe, it didn't say.

For once, some older people may be shocked to notice, I am able to use a trade name without the risk of a scolding from the powers above. To younger people that sentence will probably be double Dutch. But I went into journalism when – and for many years thereafter – it was forbidden to use a trade name in an ordinary descriptive piece, either in your newspaper (if it was a serious paper and not a rag) or, over the air – when the BBC *was* the air. An example or two. Once, I covered the very rare event of a cricket match got up between Yale and Harvard. There were three spectators in a field till there bounced on to the scene, just to show that some corner of a foreign field is for ever England, a parson carrying (it was a chilly day) a thermos. It never crossed my mind that in the very upright (in those days) *Manchester Guardian*, you could not outrage the readers by writing a trade name. I frankly had forgotten, if I ever knew, that 'thermos' was one. The alert A. P. Wadsworth, an editor never to be caught napping, saw that it was

anged. In the published piece, what the parson was carrying was a
cuumatic container'. I must say, my sentence sort of lost its swing.
other time, I innocently wrote that someone applied for some good
son, a smear of 'Vaseline'. Old A.P. was again on the alert. What
man smeared, in print, was a dollop of 'petroleum jelly'.

Happily, for some of us, that austere custom has died. Anyway, I
uld not be able to do this talk at all if I were forbidden to use trade
mes. So, again, I remark to everybody over, say, 45, 'the bell tolls
d it tolls for thee'. No more Woolworth's!

They are closing those ancient, incomparable discount stores for the
st obvious reason: they've been losing money for years. Last year,
y reported an operating loss of $37 million. Anyway, one hundred
d seventeen years was a long life for any institution, and, considering
revolution that's happened to the business of making and market-
household necessities, it's astounding that Woolworth's survived
long: during a half-century in which discount stores were absorbed
larger chains, by shopping malls, by huge stores built not in town,
ce an actual majority of the population ceased to live in cities, but
the highways close to thriving suburbs. The same thing happened
en to Woolworth's bigger competitors, not to mention what one
iter memorably dubs as 'hundreds of local chains that have faded
o the collective memory of a nation warmly nostalgic for old stores
t not willing to shop in them any more'.

However, this is not to be a nostalgic piece. It's to recall a special
nerican impulse of which Woolworth's was a prime example. Let's
call something of the world in the year that Woolworth and several
her bright boys started something new in 1879! I'm skipping, if
u'll excuse me, the enormous events recorded by all historians: like
war between Chile and Bolivia; the founding of the Irish Land
ague to campaign for independence from Britain; the founding of
ristian Science; the collapse of the Firth of Tay bridge in a winter
rm. I'm thinking of America only, and of smaller things that would
ve a bigger influence on more people everywhere.

In 1879 a Scottish-American immigrant, Robert Gair, a paper-bag
aker, invented a machine to produce cheap cardboard cartons
eady cut and creased and folded. It raised Robert Gair's normal
oduction of 50 paper bags an hour to 7,500 cartons.

A saloon keeper in Dayton, Ohio, Jake Ritty, took a sea voyage for his health, noticed a device on the steamship that recorded the revolutions of the propeller, and so gave an accurate daily record of the ship's speed. Hmm, he thought, it gave him an idea. He patented it as 'Ritty's Incomparable Cashier', the first cash register to keep a cumulative record of the day's transactions which later elevated a plate so both the clerk and the customer could see the figure.

An early electrical engineer thought the telephone shouldn't remain a company luxury. A company switchboard: that would do it, first in New Haven, Connecticut. It would make the telephone available to small stores, to families, perhaps soon to everybody. In 1879 there were fifty thousand American telephones; by 1890, a quarter of a million. Also in 1879, in Brooklyn, New York, a dairy company delivered milk in bottles instead of measuring it from barrels into housewives' jugs. Wow! It took thirty years for the practice to start in England. In December, one Thomas Edison announced he had invented a light bulb that would burn for one thousand hours. To the jeers of the gas lighting experts and the intelligentsia, he said electric lighting would become so cheap that only the rich would be able to afford candles.

And in 1879, in a small town in upstate New York, a shop assistant, 27, urged his boss to install a single counter, at which all the goods were to be priced at five cents each. To pacify this lunatic, the shopkeeper agreed. Then this young Frank Woolworth borrowed from a businessman the vast sum of $400. He opened his own store, in which everything was priced at five cents. His store failed. But the same lender liked Frank's courage and staked him a store in a Pennsylvania small town which would, however, have two divisions of goods: one at five cents, another at ten cents. It was the first of its kind. It worked. Young Mr Woolworth had one ambition: to build a chain of stores where poor and working people could find open-shelf self-service, and everything to buy for a nickel or a dime. It came to be called the Five and Ten. It started with a five-cent fire shovel, and went on to egg-whisks, pie-plates, moustache cups, puzzles, clothes, locks, keys, galoshes, a soda fountain, chirping household pets, full meals, everything. In 1913 Frank built the world's tallest building, sixty storeys high. He died in 1919, leaving over a thousand Woolworth's stores in the United States and hundreds more in other countries. He thought, as everybody did, it would go on for ever.

What these half-dozen men had in common was not merely an inventive spirit. What I called a common 'impulse' was the idea of enlarging the possessions that working people could afford. The thirty-five years after the end of the Civil War, that's to say from 1865 to 1900, were the golden time of American inventiveness. Half a million patents were granted. But it's true to say that many if not most of them, successful or not, were attempts to do something that half a century later was best summed up in a sentence by a poor boy from Indiana who ran for President, and lost, against Roosevelt, Wendell Willkie. 'It is the destiny of America', he said, 'to turn the luxuries of the rich into conveniences for the many.' So, George Eastman didn't want to invent a camera that would make the Germans envious. He wanted to make a cheap, family camera, and did it; and everywhere, in many languages, it was known as Ein Kodak. There was Singer's cheap, home sewing machine. The typewriter was so tricky and imper-sonal. Authors thought it took the soul out of writing. It took fifty years, after it was invented, to catch on.

It's worth remarking that most of these – what you might call popular inventors – were originally poor. A one-room schoolhouse, or none. Edison's total education was three months in an elementary school. They knew in the flesh what it was like to lack the finer necessities, so there was a special pride in, as Woolworth put it, 'applying democracy to human needs and desires'. Automobiles were for the rich. Is that so? Henry Ford invented the assembly line and made the first *volkswagens* – cheap cars for everybody. An American clockmaker was just as appreciative as you are of the delicate work-manship of a Swiss watch. But what he wanted to do was to make a *dollar* watch. 'But does it work?' facetious Europeans would ask. It did. Just as today, hearing that most Americans can tap, on cable, sixty or seventy television channels, 'But is there anything you can watch on them, tee hee?' The answer is yes; in my case, I tap over forty channels and wish I had more than five hours every evening to give over to the magic tube. Hotels were for the rich. So, how about motor courts, later motels? Same with paper and napkins and, with half the work-force now women, frozen dinners, take-out food, etc., etc., etc.

So, what were first known as variety stores gave birth to Woolworth's and bigger chains still, and more mail-order catalogues offering more and cheaper goods than, if possible, the blessed Sears Roebuck catalogue, another casualty. And the deep freeze in every home eventually killed off the beloved soda fountain: you could make your own sundaes, parfaits, milk shakes. And now the huge shopping malls on the highway are beginning to tremble. Computer systems are leading at a breathless rate to computer shopping. Soon, tedious grandfathers will bore their kin with tearful memories of the days when they got in the car and drove off to the supermarket in the shopping mall on Highway 58.

In the meantime, there is no pause in the unstoppable movement to, as Woolworth said, 'apply democracy to people's desires'. This is a prospect that doesn't alarm me, for one. What I have called the American impulse lifted more millions out of a threadbare living, and gave them a better material life than all the generations before them. So, on the demise of a famous business, I say, let's hear it for Frank W. Woolworth and Robert Gair and Jack Ritty and George Eastman – and remember what the teacher said: 'Never forget, children, that if it hadn't been for Thomas Edison, you'd be watching television by candlelight.'

The Kennedy Missile Tapes

24 October 1997

Thirty-five years ago this Sunday, 26 October, I woke up here in New York City, and looked out of the window at a sparkling and, I felt then, a god-given scene. A dazzling, crystalline day in late fall, looking over Central Park's forest of light green, yellow-golden foliage to the West Side skyline and, above it, a cloudless sky. The forest ends down to the left, and gives way to a large blue lake, a city reservoir. And, on at shining morning, a seagull came winging in from the ocean and ared high over the reservoir and the park and was gone off to the orthern horizon to tell its marvellous story. Did I say a seagull? Of urse, but for a happy split second it seemed to be a dove, to announce e blessed tidings: that we had overnight emerged unscathed from a rospect which, the previous night, the President of the United States ought would be avoided only by the mercy of God, or what we call uck: the prospect, in a day or two, of a nuclear war.

Even people – temperamental scaremongers and bloodshot journal-ts – who are given to the most lurid view of any event may recoil, I ink, at such a grandiose sentence. But we have only now become rivy to the taped private discussions of President Kennedy and his dvisers, and the desperate communications with the Soviet leader hrushchev. I'm sure that blood-chilling sentence is nothing but the uth. I say 'only now' made privy, because there has just been pub-shed, for all to read, the transcript of the tapes recorded in the White Iouse of the two weeks of discussion between President Kennedy and is advisers on what to do about the alarming discovery by American econnaissance planes of nuclear missile bases and launching sites in uba that could have been planted there only by the Soviet Union.

Some listeners may still be reeling in disbelief at the simple mention f 'the Kennedy Tapes'. Wasn't it Mr Nixon who taped conversations the White House, a record that eventually proved he had covered p the Watergate scandal and bribed participants to stay mum about ? Yes, but lately it turns out other Presidents taped conversations ith cronies and visitors and only *they* knew they were doing it. yndon Johnson's most private thoughts and pep talks are now avail-ble. We hear that Franklin Roosevelt had a crude taping system, ntirely at the touch of his own inclination. And only last week, resident Clinton released tapes – videotapes, talking pictures, no less of meetings with foreigners and one or two shady characters, many f whom gave large sums of money to the Democratic Party.

It's enough to make you, in retrospect, feel actually sympathetic owards President Nixon. His big mistake, not made by his prede-essors or successors, was that he forgot to turn the machine off. The vay our experience of Presidential shenanigans is going, it may soon e that the big act of 'obstruction of justice' (a ground for impeachment) will be turning off the tape recorder in the White House. I ought to say, after these disheartening revelations, that President Truman didn't make secret recordings. Neither did Eisenhower. And a former Clinton aide who is now free to feel relieved, said chucklingly the other Sunday, 'Nobody in the White House today dare scribble a date in his appointment book, let alone write a memo.'

But you'll have guessed that, in this unexpected and unpredicted flood of Presidential tapes, the now-released 'Kennedy Tapes' (the two weeks of secret talks in the White House between Monday, 15 October and Saturday, 27 October) are at once the most historic and most blood-curdling. For they record an event that has been called, without melodrama or exaggeration, 'the single most dangerous episode in the history of mankind'.

It began for me on – I can't swear to the date but it must have been – the Saturday before Monday, 15 October 1962, in an aeroplane: the press plane that goes on ahead of the Presidential plane, wherever he's off to. He was going off to Chicago to give a needed lift to a Democratic Senator, I believe, who was up for re-election in a few days' time. Nineteen sixty-two was what they call an 'off year' – not a Presidential but a Congressional election year. We were winging along when suddenly there came striding in from the cockpit the President's press secretary, Pierre Salinger. He had serious news for us. He had just been in radio touch with the President's plane. The President was showing symptoms of the flu, and we were all going to turn around and go back to Washington.

I don't know how many days we, the press, enquired about the flu or how soon we came to know better. But we now know – it must have been while the President was heading west to Chicago – that he heard from the CIA the thundering news that an army reconnaissance plane had taken pictures over Cuba, that the pictures had been developed, and, clear as a flower petal, were missiles and launch pads and all the paraphernalia of missile launching grounds.

On Monday the 15th Kennedy put together a committee of the Secretary of State, Secretary of Defense, Chairman of the Joint Chiefs of Staff, National Security advisers, and one or two other men who'd been close to the conduct of foreign affairs. That first meeting is the first recorded session of the two weeks' discussions about the

eveloping crisis. And I ought to say now that the tapes were techni-
ally infinitely inferior to the Nixon tapes of a decade later: a low-
itched drone of hissing, crackling sounds, not to mention the
verlapping voices that you get in any recorded conversation of a
oomful of people. It took two Harvard professors more than a year,
ith the help of expert court reporters, to improve the sounds and
ake all but a fraction of the dialogue understandable.

At the start you may wonder why Mr Khrushchev was able to install
uch hugely visible technology without being spotted. At the time, the
White House was absorbed, even obsessed, with the likelihood that
e Soviets were going to seize Berlin, and Cuba was not being routinely
atrolled by reconnaissance planes. Mr Khrushchev's mistake (it now
ppears) was not to know that American reconnaissance had got to
e point where photographs taken from 30,000 feet could count the
aves on a tree. The Soviet ambassador was called in and assured the
resident to his face that whatever his planes saw, they could not be
issiles or missile pads, since the Soviet Union was quite innocent of
uch a plot. President Kennedy didn't contradict him, just bowed out
nd went back to his committee meetings.

The problem of what to do with these installations was not complex.
was very stark and simple, and so were the responses the committee
atted back and forth. From the start, there was no general agreement
n a course of action, but in the beginning it was agreed that one of
ree things could be done: a sudden, unannounced air strike to 'take
ut' (destroy) the weapons; a wide aerial attack, covering airfields and
torage areas; thirdly, to mount as soon as possible a full-scale invasion
f Cuba.

Kennedy heard all alternatives, tapped his pencil, made only one
ositive assertion: 'We're certainly going to do number one, we're
oing to take out those missiles.' Through the next six days and nights,
e discussions probed all the likely Soviet responses to any and all
ilitary action. To delay, or tip the Soviets off to a chosen form of
ction, would hasten their building work and probably make them
ove the missiles underground somewhere. To delay while making
artial sounds in Khrushchev's direction might make him come out
ore defiantly in support of Fidel Castro, a position from which he
ould not then retreat. It took a week for a fourth alternative to

grow and become one favoured by the President: a proclaimed naval blockade of Cuba – this too was ferociously debated. It's remarkable that the Senate's king of the doves (when later it came to Vietnam), Senator William Fulbright, was dead against the blockade because it would announce a direct confrontation with Khrushchev. Kennedy's brother called it a slow form of death. Fulbright, like the top military, was all for 'an all-out invasion'.

After the President announced the blockade over national television, everybody waited for Russian ships on the way to Cuba to turn back or risk attack. Khrushchev offered to remove the missiles if the United States would promise not to invade. Then he suggested removing the Cuban missiles in exchange for the American removal of allied missiles in Turkey. To do that, Kennedy thought, would invite the outrage of the NATO allies and perhaps mark the end of NATO itself. All this while, new photographs showed the Russians were hectically installing missiles. At the end of the second week Kennedy, having gone ahead with the blockade and secretly amassed in Florida an invasion force larger than anything since D-Day, called in the Congressional leaders of both parties and wearily told them not to expect a peaceful solution. 'If we stop one Russian ship, it means war. If we invade Cuba, it means war. There's no telling.' He went to bed on the Saturday night fairly convinced in his own mind that a war was imminent, and that it would begin with the Russians firing tactical nuclear weapons on Florida. He said goodnight to the committee, the machine was turned off, and he hoped he'd see them tomorrow. 'None of us might ever see each other. Now it's up to luck.'

At dawn, the marvellous news came in that the Russians' lead ship, the *Grozny*, had turned back from the blockade. That was the Sunday morning that, against a clear blue sky, the seagull flew in from the ocean looking like a dove.

The Evolution of the Grand Jury
31 July 1998

A few weeks ago, I realized that I had spoken a sentence that must have been totally incomprehensible to most listeners – in the United Kingdom, anyway. I don't know about India, Australia, New Zealand and other countries that inherit the tradition of the common law from England. What I'm saying is that it occurred to me, rather late in the day, that when I said, 'so far, in the case of the President and Miss Lewinsky, so far seventy witnesses have appeared before the grand jury', it's unlikely, to be polite, that one British listener in a hundred under the age of say, 85 or 90, has any precise idea what a grand jury is, since the institution was abandoned in the United Kingdom in 1913 and formally abolished in 1933.

I'd better start and say how the grand jury came about in England, centuries ago, how and why it was so eagerly taken up by colonial America, how in fact it was used as an opening wedge in the War of Independence, and how it has developed here since.

One of the greatest English lawyers called the grand jury 'the glory and the greatest invention of English law'. It took about four hundred years from its rude birth to turn into its modern form. Edward III was the inventor and 1368 the crucial date. He decided to choose twenty-four men in each of the English counties to form a board that would report on and watch out for crimes in the county: a sort of clearing house or detention centre for criminals who might then go to trial. From the beginning, it was an accusatory body. It took another three hundred years for the grand jury to perform the function it performs today. First in England, the grand jury turned into, usually, sixteen neighbours who knew the man accused of a crime. Judges, riding 'on circuit' coming into town, would collect the sixteen and say, 'John Doe is accused of stealing ten pounds. Is he the sort of man who might steal money?' The neighbours, men who knew him well, would say, 'Not the sort' or 'Well, perhaps'. They'd vote, and if a majority said 'Yes, possibly', then John Doe would go to trial. Otherwise, no case. This all sounds very simple and artless. But the grand jury was the first protection the citizen had against gossip, malicious charges, hearsay, political prosecutions.

Of course, the grand jury crossed the Atlantic with the first English settlers and took root in American law. It was greatly prized, especially by the colonists who were growing more and more outraged by the arbitrary behaviour of the king's ministers here. It was the Governor of each colony (or his underlings) who charged people with crimes and mounted prosecutions in the king's name. There came a time, about forty-odd years before the Revolution broke out, when one grand jury had the nerve to refuse to accept the charges brought against an editor by the king's prosecutor. And thereafter the rebellious colonials used the grand jury as an instrument of resistance to the over-reaching authority of the English governors. A twentieth-century American judge called the grand jury, in retrospect, 'the first arm of democratic self-government'. And the blessing of this protection was not forgotten when they came to write the Constitution, or rather the Amendments called the Bill of Rights. The Fifth says, 'no person shall be held to answer for a capital or otherwise infamous crime, unless on a presentment of indictment by a grand jury'.

By now, in all federal courts, the grand jury is compulsory, but only about half the states stick with the system as a preliminary hearing. The other states authorize a magistrate, which, inevitably, brings us to England, what happened there, and why it fell into disuse and was abolished. If there is one man who was more responsible than another for killing off the grand jury, it was a young Lancastrian – a Liverpudlian, son of an army sergeant major – who got a scholarship to Oxford, dazzled every examiner he ran into, became a devastatingly brilliant, witty and arrogant barrister, and at the age of 46 became Lord Chancellor: F. E. 'Freddy' Smith, subsequently the first Earl of Birkenhead.

He it was who mounted the case against the grand jury in its present form and wrote a devastating attack on it. First, he said, since grand juries were recruited from people on the voting registers, it was preposterous in a city of seven million to keep up the pretence that the chosen jurors would know the man well enough to say if he was likely

have committed a crime. Next, an institution which had been the
otector of the liberties of an accused person was now a prosecutor's
eapon with which to beat a jury into the conviction that the accused
is guilty before he could be tried. Today, in America, this is truer
an ever. The public prosecutor (the District Attorney, or in our
esent crisis, the special prosecutor) can come before the grand jury
th a team of lawyers (which Mr Starr has done) and call all the
osecution witnesses he wants, which he has done. Mr Starr has
eady had over seventy accusers of President Clinton appear. But
e accused is not permitted a lawyer or any witnesses. Birkenhead
aintained, with his own savagely wounding sarcasm, that this protec-
r of a citizen's liberty began the protective process by recruiting
ery accuser, every gossip-monger, every hearsay miscreant (to this
y, hearsay is allowed), to trap the accused in a machinery of guilt
d then invite him to wriggle his way out. In other words, it's become
preliminary trial in which the accused is to be proved guilty before
has a legal chance to prove himself innocent.

Birkenhead wound up by saying that the grand jury system, once
e genuine guardian of a citizen's innocence, had turned into an
quisition – the creature of the prosecutor – which was authoritarian,
idemocratic and a monstrous anachronism. His argument was so
mpelling that the grand jury was, to everybody's relief, formally
olished in 1933. Better leave it, the consensus became, to a magis-
ate or a tribunal of magistrates, with their knowledge of the law and
human beings. They might be, some of them, blinkered, but they
uld, on the whole, do better at deciding whether an accused man
ght to go to trial.

To this day, in America, all that a grand jury is meant to do is to
cide if there is a case, if the accused ought to be tried. Yet I assure
u I've been saddened down the years to discover how many Ameri-
ns, and I'm thinking of educated people as well as illiterates, see a
adline in the paper: 'John Doe Indicted For Fraud', and at once
gister the emotion that John Doe has been found halfway guilty, as
a grand jury indictment was a preliminary trial.

The thing which sticks in the throat of libertarians is the curious old
ct that the accused is not allowed a lawyer or any witnesses. So, this
ings us to the serious, possibly dire, condition in which, suddenly,

the President finds himself. Mr Starr, the special prosecutor, had the gall, or the courage, to issue a subpoena on the President to appear before the grand jury that has been looking (till it's almost blind) into the relations between Miss Monica Lewinsky and the President.

This act, of subpoenaing the President, happened only once before, way back when a man was being tried for treason. Thomas Jefferson was subpoenaed. He didn't appear but he delivered relevant documents, as did Nixon. Other Presidents – Ford and Reagan – have videotaped evidence. But in none of these was the President the accused. In the Lewinsky case, the target is President Clinton. And the question of whether a sitting President can be prosecuted before or after Articles of Impeachment had gone to the House of Representatives, whether simply, a sitting President can be subject to criminal prosecution, is a question that last week had constitutional lawyers arguing furiously pro and con. Happily, the problem became irrelevant. Mr Clinton did not accept or reject the subpoena. Mr Starr, the special prosecutor, exercised a unique gesture of magnanimity, and agreed to withdraw the subpoena if the President would testify on videotape in the White House before his (Starr's) lawyers. And, breaking the most baffling, some say the most undemocratic provision of the grand jury system, the President will be allowed to have a lawyer present.

So, two weeks from now, the leakers are going to discover whether the President will go on stoutly denying he ever had a sexual relationship with Miss Lewinsky. But she has suddenly been given immunity from prosecution by Mr Starr, so she can tell the truth without fear or favour, leaving us in stark fact to decide which of them is lying. (She's already said yes, they had sex. She can prove it with a stained dress.) The root question is not whether Mr Clinton had sex with Miss Lewinsky (amazingly about 65 per cent of the country thinks so, while the same number think he's being a good President!), which Mr Starr has been aching for six months to have answered, but: Did the President try to persuade Miss Lewinsky to lie if she ever appeared before the grand jury? As you'll see, her grant of immunity gives her the freedom to tell a truth that could bring the President down. Because if the grand jury finds that the President did take part in a cosy conspiracy to withhold the truth, then he could be guilty of one of the high crimes stated in the Constitution that provide grounds for impeachment: obstruction of justice.

This is the perilous position the President finds himself in as he mingles this weekend with his jet-set supporters on the south (the fashionable) shore of Long Island. In the meantime, and as Hamlet said, 'looking before and after', there is a case to be made, that so far as I know has never been made or is likely to be made in this country, against the *existence* of the grand jury system.

The President Will Address the Nation

21 August 1998

'The President will address the nation at 10 p.m. this evening, Eastern Daylight Time, 9 Central, 7 Pacific.'

Of all the times a similar announcement has come over the radio or the television I can't recall a time when more Americans mentally made this date with history – as they did last Monday, this time, more than sixty millions of them. Whatever the outcome from that four-minute speech of the President, Monday, 17 August 1998 will be remembered as long as there is a television station with an unfaded videotape, not to mention a living American with a memory of the time.

Looking back on the days before the fateful hour, it strikes me now that, semi-consciously, vast numbers of people had the feeling, the hope too, that this would mark the end of the affair. This only showed how much we've been brainwashed by the movies. In the real drama, of Prosecutor Starr versus President Clinton, it was at best only the beginning of the end.

I ought to say, though, why even some veteran politicians of both parties hoped that the President's address to the nation would put an early end to things. The chairman of the Senate Judiciary Committee, who would be the man to arrange the trial of the President (if the House voted articles of impeachment), an old hand at such hearings and a political opponent, said just before the address that if the President made an outright, from-the-heart, candid confession of his relationship with Miss Lewinsky, and gave convincing word that he had not conspired or cajoled anybody into covering it up or otherwise lying about it, if he then threw himself on the mercy of the American people, he could most likely be forgiven because, as the Senator put it, for the good of the nation and our form of government, nobody wants to impeach him.

When the President had finished, the Senator, that same Judiciary Committee chairman, was – like many members of both parties – aghast with anger and disappointment. They felt, as the overwhelming editorial opinion of the country expressed it, that he had spoken from a legally contrived script, that as a confession it was feeble and inadequate. Several of Mr Clinton's Cabinet rallied with urgent pleas to move on and carry out the nation's business. But the President's leaders of his own party were as dispirited as the press. The House Democratic leader: 'I am very disappointed in his personal conduct.' The Democrats' Senate leader: 'A more complete explanation of his relationship should have come earlier.' One of the senior Senators of the two most populous states, California and New York, both Democrats, Senator Moynihan of New York, remarked that he had made no adequate apology to 'an awful lot of people he has put through terrible times'. These 'people' must have referred mainly to his loyal staff – not least to Mrs Clinton whom, the President said, he had 'misled', which turned out to mean that only last Sunday, the night before his address, did he tell his wife that he had lied about the Lewinsky affair. Then the senior Senator from California, the most politically powerful of all the states with an essential mass of votes to offer in any election, Senator Diane Feinstein – who stood at the President's side on the famous, or infamous, day in January when he wagged his finger at us and swore to the nation he had had no sexual relationship with Miss Lewinsky – after Monday night, Senator Feinstein said she was blazing with anger. 'I believed him. I felt betrayed.'

So, if finally so many influential people, papers, Democrats, have changed their mind and lost their loyalty, why does the great body of the Democrats in Congress stay mum so far? Because of the puzzling fact that while 70 per cent of the voters believed the President had lied before Monday evening, over 60 per cent say he's been a good President and shouldn't be impeached. This contradiction is, especially for the politicians of both parties who are running for re-election in November, the great, awkward stumbling block to the free exercise of their conscience.

What was it about the speech, apart from its brevity, and lack of open-hearted candour, that left so many with the complaining word 'inadequate'? Well, before it was written, and finally transcribed to a teleprompter, the substance and style of the speech had been fought over, we are told, up to the last hour on Monday evening, by two factions: the President's White House political cronies, and his legal advisers. The polls told him his one chance of redemption was a heartfelt, complete confession, an apology to many supporters, with no mention of the special prosecutor or the length of the investigation; then throw himself on the people's mercy. The politicians lost. The lawyers had convinced themselves that his best chance of survival was to contrive a careful legal evasion of the whole truth. So the speech was a lawyer's extra-delicate exercise in weasel words. I cannot think whom these characters imagined they would fool by having the President go back to his deposition (in the Paula Jones case), after which he gave that little speech to the press and said, 'I swear to you I did not have a sexual relationship with that woman, Miss Lewinsky.' So on Monday night he says that phrase in January was 'legally correct', but in the next sentence, his lawyers had him say: 'Indeed I did have a relationship with Miss Lewinsky that was not appropriate.' Mr Clinton left it to the sixty-odd million viewers to figure out the difference between a sexual relationship and an inappropriate one. Incidentally, and very much incident to Presidential crises, 'inappropriate' has become (since Mr Nixon used it frequently twenty-five years ago) the adjective of choice for defendants, for men accused of practically any crime in the book. Nixon, till the day he abdicated, never said he did wrong; he left office because he did not have 'sufficient political backing in the Congress'. His actions had been, he feared, 'inappropriate'.

Once Monday's speech was over, the first effect that the sharpest White House reporters noticed was on the faces of the staff, the close advisers who could be seen next morning. One who used to be there, and very close indeed to the President, said it was heartbreaking to see these aides, and to the end fervent supporters, loyalists of the President, restraining their disappointment and humiliation. They had forgiven him Gennifer Flowers, with whom he'd sworn he'd never had any sex, then said months later, sorry, sorry, just once. She said, with hours of taped telephone calls to give weight to her claim, that they had been lovers for twelve years. All forgiven. Paula Jones and the self-exposure incident in the hotel, long ago, which even the judge in the Paula Jones case said was, if true, gross behaviour: the judge threw the case out, not for disbelieving Miss Jones, but for finding no evidence that she had suffered grievous harm, professionally and privately.

But over Miss Lewinsky, they trusted him, as did many, many more. It came out in the past few days that Mr Clinton, before a grand jury, refused to answer most questions on the Lewinsky matter, about which, we reliably hear, he was amazed to discover how much detail Mr Starr knew – presumably from the grand jury testimony recently of Miss Lewinsky. Accordingly, Miss Lewinsky was called back to the grand jury this Thursday.

Well, having waded through this welter and foam of cross-currents of opinion, whatever the final consensus, we have to confront the root question of self-government: what is meant by moral authority and does a leader need it? At the bland, the non-caring end of the political spectrum are modern, secular so-called 'progressives' of several genera-tions, who say the President's sexual habits are none of our business, and if they don't interfere with his policies, then everything is hunky-dory. A lot of people feel this way.

Moral authority in a leader, as old man Aristotle pointed out two thousand and more years ago, resides in a leader because he is a better-than-average character. Moral authority does not mean sexual behaviour. It means the capacity for being trusted, to have the people believe the word of the leader in many things and be ready to follow him when he judges what is the right thing to do. It means Lincoln declaring that a civil war had to be fought not to free an enslaved race but to preserve the Union. It meant Franklin Roosevelt taking the

United States into the war against Hitler and Japan, not because it was legal (he did something that brought cries for *his* impeachment) but because it was right. It was Harry Truman declaring that since the League of Nations failed because the Western Europeans were too cowardly to stop Mussolini in Ethiopia, the United States had a moral duty to save the United Nations by going into South Korea to stem the Communist invasion from the North. It is the pattern of lying in Mr Clinton that the prosecutor is investigating, and that has offended and bewildered the country.

This may still leave unexplained the discrepancy between the 60 per cent of the country who believed he lied about his sexual relations with Miss Lewinsky, as with Paula Jones, as with Gennifer Flowers, and the 60 per cent who say still he's a good President and shouldn't go. There is one pungent voice that is worth at least listening to: an old politician from Connecticut, not a party man, a maverick and a retired governor who now teaches politics at the University of Virginia. Asked how it comes about that about 60 per cent think Clinton lied, and about 60 per cent want him to stay, Governor Lowell Weicker, implying that this reflects the sad moral climate of our time, said: 'That 60 per cent – those people are equally to be condemned with the President' as having no sense of the moral side of leadership.

So, after the four-minute confessional on Monday, there are only two opinions that are shared by the great majority of the people. One, that this investigation is by no means over, that the President's troubles reach forward certainly to the day of Mr Starr's delivery of an impeachment report to the House. The other consensus, which sympathetic and even forgiving people are reluctant to come to, is that if he survives, Mr Clinton will be a limping leader through the remaining two years of his Presidency.

New Words for Objects New and Old

16 October 1998

An old friend of mine, an Englishman, was saying how close British English and American English have come together compared with the days, say, of my boyhood when nobody in Britain, except kings, statesmen, ambassadors and bankers had ever heard an American speak. I was 21 when sound (what we called 'talking pictures') came in, and I remember the shock to all of us when we heard the weird sounds coming out of the mouths of the people on the screen.

And of course, quite apart from becoming familiar with the odd pronunciations of Americans of all sorts, we began to notice differences in the usage of words; we became aware for the first time of the great changes and unknown additions to the language that had been made by Englishmen who had been settling in America for three hundred years. It occurred to most of us rather late that this was bound to happen when Englishmen arrived on a new continent, saw a new landscape which had to be described with different words (tidewater, creek), new foods, new habits of life and work, not to mention the adoption, first from the Dutch, of new words for objects new and old: Englishmen who'd eaten buns found themselves eating crullers, and sitting out on the stoops of their houses. If you want to follow the impress of Spanish, Russian, German, Italian, Hungarian, Czech and the other European languages on the English of America, all you have to do is go to the library and take out the 2,400 finely printed pages of Mr H. L. Mencken's massive work, *The American Language*. And that will take you only as far as 1950.

The point my old friend was making was that after almost seventy years of talking pictures, and with the radio and television now becoming universal media, nothing in American speech or writing surprises us any more and the two languages have rubbed together so closely for so long that they are practically indistinguishable.

Well, there's much in this. But there are still little signs in any given piece of American prose playing a mischievous devil's advocate. One time last year I wrote a piece of English prose, quite guileless stuff, a page of fiction about a single mild adventure of a young man in New York. I asked this same old Englishman to go over it and strike out words which proved that, though the locale of the story was New York City, and the presumption of the story and all the fixings was that it had been written by an American, there were lots of little signs which showed it could not have been written by anyone but an Englishman. I'll just say two things: that my friend missed them, and that most Englishmen would have, too.

Just last week there was printed in the *New Yorker* magazine a phrase about Californian wines, proving that the writer or the copy editor was English. No American talks or writes about Californian wines. California wines. 'California' is the adjective. 'Californian' is a noun: a native or resident of California. The other most gross and most frequent trick which not one Englishman in a thousand ever seems to notice is this: I say or write, 'I have a friend in England called Alan Owen.' That is an immediate giveaway. No American could say or write it unless they'd been corrupted by long close association with the Brits. Americans write and say, 'I have a friend in England *named* Alan Owen.' Maybe he's *called* Al. 'Called' would refer to a nickname. 'Named' is used where the English use 'called'. In other words, a President named William Jefferson Clinton is called Bill Clinton. 'Named' always for the baptismal name . . . right?

We went on to discuss American words, phrases, usually slang, that are picked up in England (E. B. White said it usually took fifteen years) and there go wrong, quite often assuming an opposite meaning. A beauty close to home is the word 'bomb'. When a book, a play, a movie flops with a sickly thud, it is said to have bombed. 'It ran a year in London, but bombed in New York.' Inexplicably, it got to England and took on the opposite meaning. I shall never, you'll appreciate, forget a telephone call from my daughter in England when a book of mine, a history of America carrying the succinct title *America*, had just come out. 'Daddy,' she shouted across the Atlantic, 'your book is a bomb!' I very much prayed it wasn't so. Indeed, the fact it wasn't is one reason why I'm sitting here talking to you at this late date – in comfort.

All this amiable light talk sprang from a darker happening: the passing of a great American writer, who received a large, worthy obituary in the *New York Times* but, to my surprise and dismay, did not rate a mention in the news magazines. I'm afraid it's because the writers of literary obituaries are too young to have remembered the splendid prime and great popularity of the man. His name was Jerome Weidman, and, if we were living in the 1930s, 1940s or 1950s and he had died, you would no more have been ignorant of his name than today you would say, Who is John Updike, Martin Amis? (Who, asked a contemporary of a grandson of mine, who was Ernest Hemingway?) There you have it, the frailty, the treachery, of fame. Jerome Weidman was not just a popular novelist, in the sense that James Michener or Dorothy Sayers were popular novelists. Jerome Weidman was a popular novelist who greatly impressed the literary world of New York with his first novel. He was 24 years old and earning $11 a week as an office boy and starting secretary, when in the spring of 1937, he published *I Can Get It For You Wholesale.*

Here was a story mining a new vein by a young man who, even at that tender age, knew the subject, the terrain and the people inside out. It was about Manhattan's garment centre – the hub and vortex of maybe half a million New Yorkers who whirled every day around the making of pants and coats; a mainly Jewish industry, because so many immigrant tailors originally had set it up.

Jerome Weidman's mother was Hungarian, and his father a young Austrian who, like George Gershwin's Russian father, was alerted to the prospect of America and the immigrant ships by hearing the sound of a bugle, the call to fight for the Austrian emperor, which didn't mean a year or two of military service but a semi-life sentence. He hopped it to New York City and went at once, on the Lower East Side, back to his only trade: he made trousers, pants. His son Jerome maintained against all comers that his father's unique genius was for making better pants pockets than any other tailor on earth.

Jerome was brought up on the Lower East Side, with the sights and sounds and idiom of the garment men and their families. That first book created a character, Harry Bogen, a shrewd, quicksilver scamp who in several disguises was to appear in his later books. All the best ones were about this life he knew as well as Dickens knew the East End of London. What was new and liberated the American novel from gentility (or the Hemingway flat protest against it) was the running talk, the exact sound and sense of these lowly characters – the first-generation immigrant sons striving to be free.

Now you'll see why such a man, such a writer, prompted our whole talk about the American language. Jerome Weidman was the first American street-smart novelist. (There – there's another one, turned in England often into 'street-wise'; nobody's wise on the streets, but Jerome Weidman and his swarming characters are nothing if not street-smart.) He never adopted this language, but it came so naturally that when he chose titles for his subsequent works he fell as naturally as Ira and George Gershwin did into simply taking over some prevailing bit of American idiom slang. After *I Can Get It For You Wholesale* came *What's In It For Me?* and *The Price Is Right* – marvellously constructed short novels that made guessing the next turn of character as tense as tracking down a murderer. His last book, written in 1987, was a memoir, and the then senior book editor of the *New Yorker* magazine headed his review with the single, simple word: Pro. So he was, the complete professional, as Balzac was a pro, and Dickens. Indeed, it's not reaching too far to say that Jerome Weidman was the Dickens of the Lower East Side (throw in the Bronx, too). He never started out with an ambition to be a writer. He was going into the garment business, and then, he thought, law school. Then he read Mark Twain and saw how he made literature out of the humblest material. All you needed was insight into character and an ear for the character's speech. 'Life for me on East Fourth Street', Weidman once wrote, 'when I was a boy was not unlike what life on the banks of the Mississippi had been for young Sam Clemens of Hannibal, Missouri. Guileless, untrained and unselfconscious, I put the stories down on paper the way I learned to walk.'

After a fine rollicking success as a novelist, he wrote a musical play about the incomparable, cocky, little Italianate reform Mayor of New York City, Fiorello LaGuardia. It was called simply *Fiorello*. The most prestigious theatre prize in this country (as also for fiction, history, whatever) is the Pulitzer Prize. On a spring day in 1960, in his forty-eighth year, Jerome Weidman was deliciously thunderstruck to hear he had won it with *Fiorello*. I should tell you that if another famous novelist had lived on a year or two longer, you may be sure that one of the first calls of congratulation would have come from him: Jerome's old friend, the late W. Somerset Maugham. As it was, the first call came from his mother. Neither Jerome's father nor mother was comfortable with English. They were of that generation that was forever wary of the outside world they'd moved into – the world of America and Americans. Jerome Weidman recalled with pride, and typical exactness, what his mother said to him in that telephone call: 'Mr Mawgham was right. That a college like Columbia University, when they decided to give you a price like this should go and pick a day to do it that it's the twelfth anniversary of the founding of the State of Israel. If you listened to me and became a lawyer a wonderful thing like this could never have happened.'

He will be rediscovered, and revived, and read, when many, more famous and fashionable American writers, big guns today, are dead and gone for ever.

Jerome Weidman, born Lower East Side, New York City, 1913. Died Upper East Side, New York City, October 1998. RIP. Jerome, Harry Bogen, and Momma and Poppa Weidman.

Loneliness, Male Companionship and the Hunt

30 July 1999

Here are the opening sentences of two novels, both published in 1933.

They drove uncertainly along the avenue that led to the house ... The navy-blue car was built high off the ground and the name on its bonnet recalled a bankrupt, forgotten firm of motor-makers. Inside, the car was done up in a material like grey corduroy, with folding seats in unexpected places, constructed liberally to accommodate some Edwardian Swiss Family Robinson.

Here is the opening of the second novel, written the same year:

You know how it is there early in the morning in Havana with the bums still asleep against the walls of the buildings, before even the ice wagons come by with ice for the bars. Well, we came across the square from the dock to the café to get coffee and there was only one beggar awake in the square and he was getting a drink out of the fountain. But when we got inside the café and sat down, there were the three of them waiting for us.

The first passage is a piece of considered literary prose that could have been written in 1923 or even 1913. It was written for an audience rather like the writer: literary, sensitive, leisured. The second passage has all the leisure of a ticking time bomb. And in 1933 it was a shocker. The reader is addressed as an equal but there is no suggestion of a literary man anywhere. It's more like an anecdote a travelling salesman is telling to a buddy sitting up at a bar.

What shocked most literary folk, both in Britain and America, in 1933 was the baldness of the writing. Not an adjective or an adverb in sight. Just plain nouns hitting plainer verbs. And yet, as one or two critics reluctantly admitted, in no more than a sentence or two a picture has been painted that is vivid, arresting, of a time and a feel for a place. And a note of suspense is struck at once: 'There were the three of them waiting for us.'

Well, it had taken most of twenty years for the author to be able to fashion such a sentence to his own satisfaction. The writer was Ernest Miller Hemingway, who was born a hundred years ago this past week in a Chicago suburb. In his teens, he already had the itch to write and skipped college to work on a newspaper in Kansas City, Missouri. He'd hardly got his hand in at reporting when America was in the First World War, and the 18-year-old Hemingway joined an ambulance unit attached to the Italian infantry. He was badly wounded four months before the Armistice, and when that happened he was still convalescing in a hospital in Milan. In little more than a year, a Toronto paper took him on as a foreign correspondent – the dashing life he'd hardly dreamed would ever come his way. He travelled far and wide in France, Italy, Spain, Switzerland and Germany. Two years after the signing of the peace treaty, he was on the road in and around Greece, following a surging population of refugees much like the beaten families we saw deserting Kosovo. One dispatch reported: 'In a staggering march, the Christian population of Eastern Thrace is jamming the roads towards Macedonia . . . An old man marches bent under a young pig, a scythe and a gun, with a chicken tied to his scythe. A husband spreads a blanket over a woman in labor in one of the carts to keep off the driving rain. She is the only person making a sound. Then his little daughter looks at her in horror and begins to cry. And the procession keeps moving.'

The oddest thing about him was a descriptive gift, expressed with such plainness and simplicity. It was something he worked on consciously while he was still a newspaper reporter. Based, in his early twenties, in a room over a sawmill in Paris, he appeared to belong to the circle of newly arrived American expatriates. But, from the start, it has not been much remarked, he shrank from their dilettantism. He was a professional writer who meant to achieve something new in the American language. What moved him most in those early days were memories of the shooting trips he had taken with his father into the Michigan woods, and it cannot have been simply an amazing coincidence, rather an impulse welling up from his unconscious, that his first stories, about those boyhood excursions, contained the elements of the romantic situations to which, for the rest of his life, he would be most susceptible: loneliness, male companionship and the hunt – especially the hunt – whether in the infantryman's first experience of hand-to-hand combat, or in stalking game amid *The Green Hills of Africa*, or in the bullring, with its tension between human mettle and an animal's courage.

However, it was not the themes that obsessed him, so much as how they were to be written about, the ambition he held for his writing: 'To put down what really happened in action, what the actual things were which made the emotion and which would be valid in a year or ten years.' He wrote hard and long, rarely more than two hundred words a day and spent the next day paring them down. He'd already found out that, for him, adjectives and adverbs, when they were describing action or emotion, were devices of delay, of tapping the teeth while getting ready to find the right word. His idol Mark Twain had had something to say about that. (I have to throw in a background note that in America what in England is known as a firefly is in America more familiarly 'a lightning bug'.) Mark Twain wrote: 'the difference between the right word and the nearly right word is the difference between lightning and a lightning bug.'

The critics did not take kindly to Hemingway's first books. They thought that here was an author who had for no discoverable reason created a self-conscious, tough-guy, no-nonsense style. That's probably because most of the influential critics lived in London and New York, in a metropolis, and didn't have in their childhood background the vernacular that Hemingway distilled and refined into a personal style. It was nothing more mysterious or synthetic than the ordinary speech of ordinary people of the Mississippi Valley, as bare as the prairie and as sinuous as the fifty-four rivers that feed it, just the speech you will hear all around you any day in the smallest spurts of conversation of farmers, garage mechanics, shopkeepers, salesmen, soldiers, gardeners, merchants, anywhere from Cairo, Illinois, to Duluth, Minnesota. But it was what the mass of Hemingway's readers, a new generation of young non-critics, recognized as themselves and their emotions nakedly and truly expressed. In time, even some of the intelligentsia came to concede that Hemingway had managed, in a very bare idiom, to show that the emotions of ordinary, even illiterate, people were just as fine and complex as their very own.

Like all true originals, Hemingway was too often judged by people who didn't know the difference between the true Midwestern vernacular and the crude imitations of it which were soon being practised – thanks to Hemingway – everywhere, from Glasgow to Hollywood. Striking proof that he had achieved 'the real thing', extracted from that Midwestern ore and passed on as something original and precious into literature, is suggested by the fact that in the Nobel country itself, which gave him its literature award, his example, they say, transformed Swedish fiction. As for the English-speaking world, it seems to me that no one since Dryden has so revolutionized the English narrative sentence of his time.

For myself, I would add a little to those three elements I said were at the root of his view of life: loneliness, male companionship, the hunt. I would add that he brings to relationships between the old and the young a certain touch of tenderness. And there is always that strain of suspense.

The best way I can express my own admiration for Hemingway is to do an outrageous thing. Years ago, an American monthly magazine ran a competition for a parody of Hemingway. I entered it, and I did not win. I got a letter back from the judge saying, 'this is preposterous – this isn't a crude parody, which our readers would recognize – this is too true, this is essence of Hemingway. Which book did you steal it from? Sorry.' Maybe it will say more in fewer words than I have used to convey what to me is touching, dramatic, comically grave and suspenseful about his writing. This is a very short story about an old man and his grandson in Florida, stopping at a lunch counter to get a hamburger.

A FIRST TIME FOR EVERYTHING

The old man and the boy went in and sat down on the swivel stools and behind the counter there were two of them waiting. One was a black man in a white apron and the other was a big blonde with corn-colored locks. It was the boy's first time down there in Florida

418

and his hands showed up on the counter like baby whitefish against the brown arms of the old man that were blotched with the benevolent skin cancer.

The old man nodded without speaking, and the black man who knew all the signs dropped on the shiny stove something that looked like a red coaster you'd put a drinking glass on, and later would look like a brown coaster. Then he lifted his arm high and snatched from a shelf a fat white roll between his splayed thumb and little finger the way he would receive a throw cleanly like in the high school play-offs. The boy looked up at the old man.

'They are the rolls,' the old man said, 'first baked by Macdonald of the Isles, a Scottish chieftain who in the manner of the Scots called them baps with their floury but crisp outsides. But these are closer to what the English call buns, which are softer but not as soft and delicate as the good buns they made in the old days in the Basque country. Basque buns are best.'

'Will they come together to enclose it?' the boy asked.

'They will enclose it good,' said the old man.

The black man had finished now and scooped the coaster between the two halves of the bap and slid the whole onto a clean white plate. The big blonde extended her right hand and whisked the plate with a single turn of her buttocks in front of the boy. It reminded the old man of the way the great Manolete performed a veronica in the forgotten afternoons when the sun went low in the good times. The boy lifted the thing to his lips.

'Now,' said the old man, 'you are having your first Big Mac.'

'Truly?' asked the boy.

'Truly,' said the old man.

Park Avenue's Colourful Christmas

24 December 1999

The curious thing about a city that boasts extravagantly about its best features, as well as some of its worst, is that there is a never-mentioned little miracle in New York City. It is the railed-off plots of grass that for almost three miles run down the middle of Park Avenue and divide the uptown and downtown traffic. Along this whole stretch (fifty-four blocks from 96th to 42nd Street), what is a constant delight and surprise is the regularly changing character of these more than fifty little gardens. And they're not so little: each, one city block long and about fifteen feet wide.

You drive down this avenue one season of the year through a great ripple of crocuses. Another time, tulips from here to infinity. Sometimes you notice that at each end of each garden there is a new young tree, a hundred or so of them from the 96th Street entrance down to where the Avenue ends at Grand Central Station. Or maybe next time, they are locusts or London plane trees. At Christmas time, as now, they've been replaced by small firs.

I suppose we take it so easily for granted (and thousands of the true city types never notice the changes at all) because the very large workforce that performs these magical transformations works by night and by stealth. In fifty years of living round the corner from this long divide of Park Avenue I have never seen any of them at their remarkable labour of creating, along three miles, complete variations of miniature landscapes about, it seems, once every few weeks.

I know they're at it, because I once tactfully guessed at the fortune it requires to employ them and to maintain this city perquisite. I happened to know the possessor of the fortune, a lady named Mary Lasker (heiress of an advertising multi-millionaire, a self-effacing, absolutely non-socialite doer of many unadvertised good works of which the Park Avenue divider is the only conspicuous one). At Christmas time, especially, it makes me think again, with gratitude, of the late Mary Lasker. For now each tree, a hundred or so, is lit at twilight.

By Mrs Lasker's request, and, thank God, this confirming dictate of the Park Avenue property owners, the trees are not gaily decorated with red bulbs and green bulbs and purple bulbs and yellow bulbs – illuminations that make so many city squares and streets look like amusement arcades gone berserk. Each of the Park Avenue firs is decorated with about five hundred tiny oyster-white bulbs. So at twilight, you look down from the small eminence of 96th Street at this three-mile stretch of small, small fountains of light. All the way down, the only colours are the alternating reds and greens of the traffic lights at the fifty-odd intersections. Now, by day it used to be that the long canyon of Park Avenue was majestically closed at the southern end by the great gold dome of Grand Central Station. Then they built behind it a towering, flat monolith of a skyscraper which blotted out the dome (or indeed the outline) of Grand Central. This defiling obstacle tower has been ingeniously made to evaporate by the night – at Christmas time. As the dark comes on, and both Grand Central and the monolith behind it fade into the black sky, there appears by magic a great white cross. This is achieved by leaving on the lights of so many offices on one floor to form the horizontal bar and many more offices to form the vertical bar.

Simple and sublime; but in the past year or two, I'm afraid, it's been an object of sporadic controversy. From whom? From that fervent bank of First Amendment protestors who sometimes sound as if there were no other clauses in the Bill of Rights: 'Congress shall make no law respecting an establishment of religion.' This has been taken in many court appeals in many states to forbid every expression of any religion – by word, decorating, symbol – on *public* property. This argument has been going on for years and years and is effectively won, mainly in places where agnostics or atheists speak louder and longer than the true believers in any religion popular in a given town. So far, by the way, there have been no protests against the dozen performances of *Messiah* and a half-dozen of Bach's *Christmas Oratorio*, even done in public auditoriums or theatres. The board of ACLU (the American Civil Liberties Union) appears to be slipping.

There are some states, however, that can afford to be more blasé or unintimidated by the First Amendment fanatics, for an interesting *new* reason. What is it that Florida, Texas and California have in common that favourably affects the practice of the Christian religion and, say, tends to discourage the march of an army of atheists with banners? The answer: they are the states (Southwestern states) into which more South and Central American immigrants have arrived in the past quarter-century than in the rest of the country put together, the vast majority of them practising Roman Catholics. What they have brought to Christmas is a colourful and quite different tradition of Christmas decoration. Whereas most of the United States picked up the English nineteenth-century trimmings – Prince Albert's Christmas tree, holly and ivy, green and red and so forth, while Britain picked up from New York (via the Dutch settlers) the idea, the well-known figure, of Santa Claus – the Mexicans especially have given us the most colourful and original variations. This week, the Governor of Texas, one George W. Bush, gave a little television tour of the Governor's mansion and showed off a marvellous array of Christmas trees – cacti and pepper trees – hung with orange, and pink flowers and home-made Christmas cribs that looked as if they had been imported from that first Christian (Coptic) chapel outside Cairo, which has those primitive, comic-strip figures of Adam and Eve and a jolly snake. But here in Austin, Texas, were all the nativity figures: the Wise Men, Joseph and Mary, the shepherds, as marvellous little painted wooden figures which we (the civilized Anglo-European types who couldn't draw a broomstick) call 'primitives'.

Governor Bush, you may have heard, is running for President, and running very hard (the election is only nine months away). And he showed off the delightful Mexican decorations with understandable effusiveness, stopping from time to time to talk in Spanish to a passing child. The public, of course, can visit the Governor's mansion, just as the public makes daily tours of the White House. Incidentally, I ought to throw in that anyone running for public office, for state office anyway, in Florida, Texas, Nevada, Southern California nowadays had better speak Spanish as well as English if he/she holds any hope of being elected.

But whatever variations different immigrant groups may bring in, there is one symbolic expression of Christmas, one that dependably returns every year to appear in theatrical form in city theatres and centres, on national television in half a dozen versions, and is at the moment dazzling nightly audiences in New York City's vast Radio City Music Hall. It is Charles Dickens' *A Christmas Carol*. And the booksellers, including the titans online, indicate that every year the sales of *A Christmas Carol* go smartly up. (Poor Dickens, who lost £200 on the book, sued an outrageous couple who pirated his work and sold it cheaply. He was awarded £1,500 damages, so the couple declared bankruptcy, and Dickens got nothing but had to pay out £700 for his own court fees.)

I suppose that we, for the most of the century, have thought of the *Carol* as the most vivid representation of an old English tradition of Christmas: the feasting and the carolling and Christmas cards and the parties with their particular customs, the tree, the pudding, the kissing and dancing and general merriment. Nothing could be more untrue. For centuries, Christmas was an annual street brawl with a reputation for debauchery and general rowdiness. The Church of England and the Puritans here prohibited it as a religious ceremony (or a celebration of Christ's birth) until well into the eighteenth century. When Dickens published the *Carol* in 1843 nobody had ever seen a Christmas card or a Christmas tree, except at Windsor. The street brawl was still a fact, deplored by respectable people who by then had the custom of taking a half-day off on Christmas Day and holding a special mid-afternoon dinner: the turkey, which had long established himself after his long journey from America, and fowl (I mean game) and pastries, and many, many jellies, and Christmas punch.

When the *Carol* appeared, what delighted everybody was the entertaining, suspenseful plot. But Thackeray said it defied literary criticism. It was a work whose central idea was that Christmas was the paradox of a merry time that entailed duties and obligations, especially to the poor, and added the astonishing new notion that Christmas was a special time of the year for redemption – for everybody to take stock and begin to lead a better life.

It's impossible today to appreciate the shock of this idea disguised as brilliant entertainment. It's at the root of the custom of New Year resolutions. But the wish to make amends for the flaws in one's character is something that some people, a few, become conscious of as they grow old. One was the late, the recently late, actor George C. Scott. Not too long before he died, he gave an engaging, vibrant television interview. He was an engaging, vibrant man. There was much talk about his towering portrayal of General George Patton. When he was asked what his favourite role was, he did not hesitate. George C. Scott was in private life a violent man. It was therefore a surprising and happy thing to hear him say that his favourite role of all was – Ebenezer Scrooge.

2000–2004

The Death of the Old Media

14 January 2000

In America at any rate, the twenty-first century came in with a bang, a sound so loud and so new that I'd guess most people over 60 suddenly felt they were living on a different planet or had, like Rip Van Winkle, been asleep for twenty years and come awake to discover that their world was beyond recognition.

I detect, by extra-sensory perception or a shudder in the radio signal, a slight attack in some listeners of shyness. So, I will cure it at once by going directly to the cause. Does anybody read Washington Irving any more? In blunter words, a question hovering on many lips: Who is Rip Van Winkle? Before oldsters smirk with impatience and roar, 'What nonsense! Of course we read Washington Irving when we were children,' let me remind you of my frequent researches in this matter of assuming that every young person around shares your cultural or folk background, and then adds his or her own. I asked a grandson of mine, in his twenties, very bright, also, better, very intelligent, 'Who was Charlie Chaplin?' 'Er,' he said, 'his name comes up in crossword puzzles.' So do (I learned from other twenty-something-year-olds) the names of Albert Schweitzer, Sigmund Freud and Winston Churchill. Winston Churchill?! A stunning item of disbelief till I recall an early Gallup poll, taken in England in the autumn of 1940. Note the year and the time, when – if the besieged or surrendered free world had a hero – it was Churchill, standing with or for Britain alone against Hitler's armies eighteen miles away on the French shore. Dr Gallup took a poll of the general population of England (not Britain), asking the simple question: 'Who is Winston Churchill?' Dr Gallup, I remember, was scolded at the time for bad taste. But his distinction was to be the first man to want to find out what the people really felt and not what editors or public men told us they felt. His strength was to ask

rude questions that went like a stake through the heart of preconceptions and popular false assumptions.

The result of Dr Gallup's poll was interesting. Of course, 96 per cent
of the English knew all, or much, about him. But 4 per cent had never
heard of him! They were farmers, most, if not all, had no radio, and
they all lived in one county. Its identity was never published. So far as
I know, it remained a secret known only to Dr Gallup, as the identity
of the *Washington Post*'s 'Deep Throat' is locked still in the bosom of
the editor of the *Post* at the time of Watergate.

Well, all this flowed naturally from my rude assumption that quite
a lot of listeners don't know, or have forgotten, the incomparable
tale of Rip Van Winkle and secretly would like to know it. In brief,
here it is.

First, I should say, so nobody will be embarrassed from now on:
Washington Irving was an American essayist and historian, born at
the end of the eighteenth century and lived through the first half of the
nineteenth. He wrote a comic *History of New York from the Beginning
of the World to the End of the Dutch Dynasty*, supposedly written by
one Diedrich Knickerbocker. The book was so popular that the
moniker 'Knickerbocker' became a synonym for a New Yorker. He
was at one time American Minister to Spain, and wrote four volumes
on its history. He retired up in the Hudson Valley and wrote true or
invented folk tales about that part of the state.

The most famous of these was about a middle-aged Dutchman, Rip
Van Winkle. His wife was described as a termagant. He himself was
in no doubt that he was henpecked. (And maybe his popularity – you
never know – was in his appearing as the champion of every henpecked
husband throughout the Republic.) And Rip did what many of them
had longed to do: one day he upped and left home with his dog and
went wandering in the Catskill Mountains. This was just before the
colonies rebelled and started the War of Independence. Rip met a
dwarf carrying a large keg. Rip helped him with it and together they
came into a valley where dwelt a group or tribe of dwarfs. Rip was
invited to celebrate his arrival with these new friends, none of whom
(so far as he could see) had a henpecking wife. He drank a long
sustaining drink and fell asleep. He woke up twenty years later to find
many bewildering changes. He himself was now an old man. He limped

back to his town and found – hallelujah! – his termagant wife dead, his daughter married, and a hanging portrait of King George the Third replaced by a portrait of George Washington. Rip Van Winkle learned that though there had been several moves to make him emperor (one suggestion was 'His Magnificence'), he became of course, plain President Washington. But everything around Rip's house and his town, and all the news and talk, all new, and Greek to poor Rip.

Well, that is the way some of us felt when we read the thundering news last Tuesday: 'The Death Of The Old Media'. It says here, we are seeing the beginning of the end of the bookstore, the auction house, the yard sale, the real-estate agent, the insurance man, the post office, the bulletin board, the newspaper, the radio broadcaster (ouch!), the private club, and I should add, the blessed anchor of our daily life: the retail shop or store, what the young folks who spent Christmas week ordering their presents online call, 'the old bricks and mortar'.

What I'm talking about is the staggering news that a company thought to be wobbling (with, however, a booming share price, but likely any minute to be gobbled up by Mr Gates' Microsoft) bought a huge company whose share price has lagged behind the market all through the bull market. A company riddled with debt, it was suddenly bought by this smallish company which paid 70 per cent more for the debt-ridden giant's shares than the stock market thought them worth. This acquisition of Time-Warner by America Online is being hailed as a brilliant formula, not for rescuing staggering companies but for unimaginable success as an institution that will date and replace all those institutions we've been so cosy with for, say, two hundred years. One financial paper calls it the $164-billion enigma. It is certainly an enigma wrapped in a riddle to most of us who don't spend half our days hanging out on the Internet. The *Wall Street Journal* made the best attempt at defining exactly what this enigma is.

Here is the enlightening passage. Maybe I ought to say before I recite it that much of the language of this piece will be strange to many of the middle-aged and older still. It may sound like jargon, that is to say the vague, pretentious, tortured English used by ignoramuses, highbrows, pompous businessmen, sociologists, art critics, and most politicians. It's something quite different, professional trade talk – as exact as a doctor's professional talk. Now, having said that, what this merger constitutes is all the things it will replace: newspapers, books, television networks, post offices, retail chains, etc., the piece says.

It is all of the above or, if you prefer, none of them. It is, at its core, an architecture, a set of digital protocols, rules and structures, some of them proprietary, some Internet-based, embedded in software running on servers, and linked up to networks. Amazon.com has done it to the bookstore, and hopes to do it to the rest of retailing. e-Bay is doing it to the auction house and the yard sale. AOL is doing it to a broad swathe of messaging, chatter, publishing and broadcasting. And Time-Warner? The parts – its parts – that really matter to this merger represent a grab-bag of old, analog content: CNN/Time Magazine, Warner Brothers, music groups, a television network, all perfectly good businesses well-managed, and generally profitable. But still, very old wine. They'll hang around for another decade or so, but they're history. AOL is the new bottle and for the next decade, at least, the new digital bottlers will be in complete control.

Is that quite clear? No? Well, the good news came next day with a consoling second thought that it won't all change by next Monday morning. Writers as splendid as Tom Wolfe and as humble as yours truly, who bang out their stuff on old manual typewriters, will still compose prose and have it printed between hard covers and hope you'll read it – better still, buy it. But hurry, before they tear down the old neighbouring bricks and mortar.

Running Mates and Carpetbaggers

11 August 2000

I telephoned my son the other day, way up there in the Rockies, just to hear how things were doing in Wyoming, since Mr Dick Cheney, Governor Bush's choice for Vice President, had rushed from his Texas home back to Casper, Wyoming (his birthplace), to register there as a voter, so that, on 7 November, the people who so chose could legitimately vote for Bush and Cheney. (The Constitution specifically forbids the President and Vice President to be residents of the same state.)

There is a comic aspect to the choosing of Mr Cheney that could have come from a chapter in *Pickwick Papers*. Mr Cheney is a man very little known to the public. We saw him and heard him occasionally during the Gulf War, when he was President Bush's Secretary of Defense. He retired from public life after a couple of heart attacks. He came into the news again, just about a month ago, when Governor Bush chose him to head a small team – first, to suggest a name to be Governor Bush's running mate, then to pick several and do thorough background checks on them, a process that is all the more ruthless these days since, about a dozen years ago, the media started digging out small sins (what the victims called 'mistakes' or 'inappropriate behaviour') on the part of the unlikeliest people, including three Senators, and one man who was made Speaker of the House and lasted one day, twenty-four hours being all it took for the media shovellers to dig the dirt.

So, finally, Mr Cheney, head of the team choosing a Republican Vice President, reduced the list to two or three, when somebody – and they say it was Governor Bush himself – had a brain wave. Governor Bush has confessed he is not a great reader, but he's been to the movies often enough to be suddenly struck with recall of one of the oldest plots in the business. Why this far-flung search for the girl of your dreams when she turns out to live next door? In shorter words, why not pick Mr Cheney himself? So, to Mr Cheney's happy embarrassment (oh, Governor, you really shouldn't have), Mr Cheney – in a Pickwickian sense – chose himself. And now it sounds more than ever like the election at Eatanswill: I gather that the Bush team, not only the search-and-destroy team but the campaign advisers, were sitting around thumping each other on the backs, in a manner of speaking, when somebody, a reader of the Constitution perhaps, suddenly remembered that, while the Founding Fathers said nothing about having a President and a Vice President who are both big oil men, it did say that in picking a Presidential candidate and a Vice President (I paraphrase the Twelfth Amendment), 'one of them shall not be an inhabitant of the same state'. I'd love to know who recalled this provision and how Mr Cheney upped and said something like, 'I have it, I was born in Wyoming, and I can whip up there, transfer my Texas vote to my beloved hometown, Casper, and become a legal inhabitant just in time.' Right on! Bully for you, Dick! And off he went. It was a close call. The public, which does not read the Constitution, had not had time to wake up and cry, 'I say there, hold on, old man, I mean', or 'Take it easy, fella'.

So, it was an historic, and a very necessary, moment when Mr Cheney arrived breathless in Casper to embrace his old town, re-establish himself as an inhabitant, and then fly off to meet Governor Bush and begin the long, punishing trail of a campaign tour.

And within the week, the opposition couple did the same, after Vice President Gore broke the last remaining thread of suspense by naming his Vice Presidential partner – running mate. By the way, that's a phrase I'm afraid I take too much for granted. A listener wondered not only what it meant but how it came about. Quite right. Well, it's a horse-racing term and derived from the practice of one owner, one stable, running two horses in a race, the slower one being put in there to pace the star. The pacesetter was known, is known, as its running mate. The phrase is just one century old. But its use to define a Vice President was coined by, of all the non-practitioners of slang, the most scholarly, the most ecclesiastical, of Presidents, Woodrow Wilson. At the Democratic convention in 1912, the Presidential nomination went to Wilson (he got it after a terrific brawl on the forty-sixth ballot) – Governor Woodrow Wilson of New Jersey – and he announced that his Vice Presidential choice would be another Governor: Thomas Marshall. 'And I feel honoured by having him as my running mate.' It brought the house down, the only squeak of humour they'd ever had out of Woodrow Wilson. If Wilson's mother had been alive, she would undoubtedly have scolded him: 'Is it possible that you have been attending one of those vulgar horse-race meetings?'

Thomas Marshall, incidentally, is, like all Vice Presidents, totally forgotten, except today by students of American politics. He is immortal for two slogans he cranked out wherever he appeared in public, which was seldom, during the election campaign. I doubt that either slogan would do him much good today. He was a droll fellow and sophisticated enough to know well the ringing patriotic phrases, the hackneyed rhetoric that would be expected of him. So he parodied even the most obvious phrase, like 'What this country needs . . .' The Marshall version: 'What this country needs is a good five-cent cigar.' The other one, swiped from Kipling, 'A woman is only a woman, but a good cigar is a smoke.'

Mr Gore's choice of a Connecticut Senator, Senator Joseph Lieberman, gives us at last something substantial, even intriguing to talk about. Senator Lieberman is a moderate liberal Democrat, well liked by Democrats and Republicans alike. He was the first Democrat to stand up in the Senate after President Clinton's famous or infamous lie, and say, 'The President's behaviour was not appropriate. It was immoral.' Lieberman is known to be himself without fault or flaw in matters of personal honesty and marital fidelity.

All these were no doubt considered useful qualities to set off against the constant side-swipes at Mr Clinton by Governor Bush and Mr Cheney as they urge the voters to help restore dignity and decency to the Presidency. But the main point about Senator Lieberman is that he is a Jew – the first ever to be put on a Presidential ticket. The Vice Presidency, for much of the past two hundred years, has been a post in which the party wished to honour a nonentity who had done the party some service. It has sometimes been a useful place of exile to shunt off a man whose ideas were too radical or threatening to the party regulars. Theodore Roosevelt did such a job as Police Commissioner of New York City in reforming a corrupt immigration office and, as Governor of the state, of taxing corporations and going after the sweatshop owners, that he violently rocked the boat of the smooth-sailing Republicans. They had the brilliant idea of tossing him into decorative oblivion by getting him appointed as McKinley's Vice President. Till then, the Vice President had been almost a ceremonial post. Well, McKinley was soon assassinated, and Roosevelt became President and the reforming terror of the Republic. And, however much demeaned the office has been, the public today is well aware of the alarming fact that eight Vice Presidents have become 'accidental Presidents' – as we call them – because of the sudden death of the President, five of them after the President's assassination. These are facts which remind every voter that the Vice President is, as they say, one heartbeat away from the Presidency.

It might be possible to have a secular Jew whose race or religion played little part in his public life. But Senator Lieberman is a deeply religious man, a practising Orthodox Jew. He will do nothing forbidden on Saturdays. He has said that, for serious matters affecting the people's welfare, he would go to preside over the Senate (his only official job) but he would walk, not ride, there.

Somebody has said that Jews may not be welcome in many country clubs but they have been received and respected, even venerated, as justices of the Supreme Court. It's been almost a century since the appointment of Brandeis and Cardozo. Today there are two Jews among the nine justices. But the prospect is there of a Vice President – like eight others – suddenly translated to the Presidency.

There is at the moment very lively and knotty discussion about the wisdom or folly of Mr Gore's decision. The leaders of both parties applaud it as an act of courage. Here in the City of New York there is great elation and among some prominent Jews, apprehension. But New Yorkers are probably the worst judges in America of how the rest of the United States thinks and feels about the nomination of Senator Lieberman. For years, I have played a parlour game with visiting Europeans, British men and women who come to this city on business, by saying to them: 'There are 265 million Americans in the United States. How many of them are Jews?' 'Oh, I don't know, they'd say, twenty, thirty, even forty million?' The answer is, six million. Of them, two million live in this city. In other words, one American Jew in three lives here in the City of New York.

A national poll taken two years ago found that about 90 per cent of Americans wouldn't mind having a Jewish President. If true, it is an astonishing figure and shows a heartening decline in what you might call polite, unspoken anti-Semitism that, in my time, has tiptoed throughout the land. Jews settled mostly in New York, Chicago and Los Angeles. How they feel in Omaha, Nebraska, in Salt Lake City, in Cleveland, Ohio, in Michigan, in the other forty-nine states, we shall simply have to wait and see.

The Day of Judgement

3 November 2000

Finally, the day of judgement: Tuesday, 7 November. I have been following American Presidential elections since 1936 – the first time accepting an invitation to join the resident members of the Harvard Club in London, and, thanks to the marvels of modern technology, to listen to a short-wave radio set and hope the signal was steady enough to enable us to follow the results. Most of the time it was. Other times it crackled or whined. Of course, we had to sit up throughout the night because of the five-hour difference in time (an anomaly modern technology could do nothing about), but the officers of the Harvard Club greatly softened this ordeal with copious draughts of the, er, wine of Scotland. It was just as well, for most of the young Harvard men present had learned from their fathers to loathe and fear Franklin D. Roosevelt and his New Deal ('nothing short of galloping socialism', one dutiful son protested), and when the radio gave forth the unmistakable roar of a Roosevelt landslide, they were in urgent need of solace.

They were outraged by the victory (he took forty-six states against the Governor of Kansas' two) because the only poll then extant – a pioneer of polling – was one put out by a magazine called the *Literary Digest*. It had predicted an overwhelming victory for Governor Landon. Soon after the election, a new breed of statisticians examined the *Digest*'s polling method, and found that it had collected its opinions, the numbers, by looking through telephone books and local automobile registration lists. In other words, the *Digest*, and the rest of the country, realized a little late in the day that Governor Landon was going to get the overwhelming vote of the people who had a motor car and a telephone. Sixty-four years ago (in the pit of the Depression), that left out of consideration an awful lot of millions of Americans who didn't own these luxurious conveniences. That infamous poll

435

killed the magazine and opened the way for the beginning of the statistical sample.

Well, today there are at least eight national pollsters, all professing to be objective and for the first time I can remember, they are not only in the dark about what's going to happen – they are not in conflict – they are baffled, bewitched, bothered and bewildered. And even the boldest of them gives either Governor Bush or Vice President Gore no more than a 3 per cent edge, and quickly adds the warning that the prediction is subject to '3 or 4 per cent error.' In other words, for once, everybody has checked out of the prophecy business.

To visitors from abroad, and to foreigners here who follow American politics, a first, even a long second glance reveals no mystery in the relative appeal of the two candidates. This is what they see. On the one hand the Vice President, the Democrats' Mr Gore: twenty-four years in Washington, eight years in the House, seven in the Senate, on the Energy Committee, Science/Conservation, served two years in Vietnam (as a reporter, admittedly, but often close to danger). He's an admitted though self-proclaimed expert on the environment, almost an alarmist on global warming, and deeply concerned about the need to discipline the world's industries. At least half of President Clinton's initiatives in foreign policy were inspired by the Vice President. He broke with his party to vote in favour of the Gulf War, which, you'll recall, was, at the time and ever since, considered President Bush's finest hour. So, for the past eight years as Vice President, Mr Gore has been privy to every public and secret policy of this administration. It has been said of him by many influential politicians, including some Republicans (who dare not of course speak their name), that he is the best trained and qualified man to be President in modern history.

On the other, the Republican hand, Governor Bush, an arrow-straight, handsome chip off the old block – in fact, chipper and handsomer than the old block – Governor of Texas for the past six years, before that an oil man, not doing very well, but well enough to grow affluent during the unprecedented nine-year prosperity to buy and successfully run a major league baseball team. Such a bald summary is cruel, even though it's a favourite Democratic biography of the Governor. It should not be forgotten (remember the Democrats' scorn of Ronald Reagan) that a Governor has to be conversant with every aspect of the political, economic and social life of his state, and for many decades (before Senator Kennedy broke into the White House) a Governorship was thought to be, and in practice *was*, the most favoured stepping stone to the Presidency.

Now, our foreigner, knowing so much and little more of each man's background, has presumably spent the last few weeks listening to the three television debates and to the speeches of the candidates stumping around the country. And the foreign observers agree with the domestic ones, of whatever political prejudice, that if you tap Mr Gore on any issue, he will reel off impressive statistics without taking a breath. I almost said he will give you a detailed answer ad nauseam. And bear that Freudian slip in mind. Governor Bush is not interested in explaining policy and what he calls 'details'. When the Vice President reminds him that an impartial commission found children's health care in Texas to be fiftieth in the roster of the states, the worst in the nation, Governor Bush looks patient and affable and responds quietly: 'We take care of our own.'

But on so many great issues – the long-term protection of pensions (Social Security), the extension of Medicare (the free health system for the old, rich or poor), how much of a tax cut and who should get it – both candidates *have* to go into figures. And they have such different systems of arithmetic, and they're talking about billions and trillions of dollars, that the differences between their policies drown in a boiling ocean of numbers. It's too much for most voters, so the polls report.

But there's one huge assumption that lies behind all this arithmetic which doesn't seem to come up in the campaign rallies. Both the Vice President and Governor Bush assume that the huge moneys for these great reform expenditures will come from the enormous surplus the nation will boast of in 2004, not to mention 2008. Both parties therefore assume that the present economic boom, which is already in its ninth year (a record in the 130-year history of booms and recessions), is going on for ever. This is surely a delusion. It comes up between friends and in families, but it's never brought up to the candidates on the stump for, I believe, the simple, drastic difference between party rallies in Europe and here. In this country, a candidate's rally is a rally of the faithful. You never hear from a heckler. I remember once, in Madison Square Garden, John Kennedy addressing twenty thousand people, Democrats! In between his soaring rhetoric and the punctuating cheers, one time when he paused to take breath, a lone voice cried out 'How about . . .' – the name of a man who'd been falsely arrested in Massachusetts. There was a wave of shocked, responsive, boos. Who was this barbarian? And the cops bore down on the man and carried him out.

However, we have got ahead of ourselves. From the background sketch of both candidates, and the glimpse of the two men's opposing tactics in debate, those foreign observers of mine, say, well, there's no contest, surely. Gore is plainly the man.

But, as we noted at the beginning, to the voters it's not plain at all. And it's agreed, even by the most double-dome commentators, that, probably as never before, appearance, likeability, the manner and the character of the two men seen in public (which today and for evermore means seen in close-up all the time on television), could be the decisive factor. As I talk to you, only days away from the election, more than 10 per cent of the voters, one poll says 15 per cent, are undecided. And the puzzle, the choice, seems to come down not so much to a choice between the looks and manner of the Vice President, and the looks and manner of Governor Bush but between the affability, the likeability of the comparatively ignorant Governor Bush and the knowledge and experience of the unpleasant Mr Gore. For it's also generally admitted – I was going to say universally admitted (except by my passionate Democrats) – that Mr Gore is an unhappy-looking campaigner, like a bad actor running for President, a smart alec, top boy in class, always with his hand up and waving, teacher's pet. And Governor Bush always sounds gentle, composed, authoritative, even when he says we must get our troops out of Haiti (and nobody says, 'wait a minute, all twenty-nine of them?').

So, unable to predict the result, and afraid of falling on their faces, even learned pundits fall back on one of several famous clichés: since no incumbent has ever been thrown out of the White House during an economic boom, they cry, 'You can't beat prosperity.' Then there's 'a new face is always welcome' or 'a new broom sweeps clean', or, as one famous commentator said last night with great gravity: 'I honestly think it'll be either – Bush, or – er, Gore.'

The Origin of the Continental Blow-out

24 November 2000

Last Thursday was Thanksgiving, the first truly American festival and the one that sets more millions of Americans in a turmoil of transit, criss-crossing thousands of miles to join long-separated families at a feast of turkey, cranberry sauce, sweet potatoes and pumpkin, the strange, unknown foods the native Indians introduced to those starving English men, women and children who had landed – three hundred and eighty years ago – on the bleak and unfruitful soil of a Massachusetts cape.

This festival was inspired by a letter from America written by a Yorkshire man, son of a farmer, written as a report on his first transatlantic voyage along with other, mostly humble folk who sought a new land across the ocean in order to practise a religion freed from the corruption – in 1620 – of the Church of England. They had none of our advantages, so William Bradford's writing is bereft also of parliamentary English, Congressional English, business English, advertising English, or the lawyers' English we've been exposed to for the past fortnight in the service of Vice President Gore and Governor Bush.

This company of very mixed types, just over a hundred of them, had been sixty-four days out of England and meaning to settle at the mouth of the Hudson River and start a trading post. However, this is William Bradford's account of what happened. I thought it might be a refreshment.

But after they had sailed that course about half a day, they fell among dangerous shoals and roaring breakers . . . and therewith conceived themselves in great danger. [But] the wind shrinking upon them withal, they resolved to bear up again for the Cape to the north [later to be known as Cape Cod] and thought themselves happy to get out of those dangers before night overtook them, as by God's providence, they did. And the next day, they got into the Cape Harbor, where they rode in safety. Being thus arrived in a good harbor and brought safe to land, they fell upon their knees and blessed the God of Heaven, who had brought them over the vast and furious ocean, and delivered them from all the perils and the series thereof, again to set their feet on the firm and stable earth, their proper element.

But that's not what Thanksgiving is about. Within twenty-four hours, they had good cause to bemoan the place they'd landed on. They had intended, when they left Plymouth two months before, to land in Virginia, 'earth's only paradise', wrote an English poet who'd never been there, 'where nature hath in store fowl, venison, and fish and the fruitfullest soil'. But they missed the southern coast of Virginia; storms sent them up five hundred miles north, kept them from the Hudson channel, blew them another couple of hundred miles and on Cape Cod found – what? 'No friends, no houses, no inns, but [I quote from brave Bradford] a hideous and desolate wilderness full of wild beasts and wild men.'

Well, it was, as I hinted, those wild men who saved most of the Puritans – with their introduction of the (unknown to Europeans) turkey, potatoes, and the red berry they'd never seen either but which was the only fruitful growth of the Cape. The cranberry bogs produced this red berry which, as an accompanying sauce, is considered mandatory at the family Thanksgiving dinner. I had better say at once that cranberry sauce is, to me, one of those things you must be born to, like peanut butter and drum majorettes. Today, cranberry juice has become a mad fashion in this country as a health drink of choice, recommended strongly even by cardiologists since the recent large, and I believe first, long-term clinical trial of vitamin C pills, reported that whatever else vitamin C supplements may do, they are first-rate producers of arteriosclerosis (hardening of the arteries). Consequently, an eminent cardiologist predicts the retreat from orange juice will be as fast as the advance to cranberry juice.

I deduced (I think you'll agree correctly) that, of those four dishes that saved the Puritans' life, the cranberry is the one that would most interest most listeners, since most of them today have known about turkey and potatoes for centuries. Not long ago I ran into an old

English lady who said, 'Turkeys came from America? What nonsense! Why, my grandmother had a turkey every Christmas, and that was in the middle of the nineteenth century!' I hope I made it clear at the start that William Bradford ate his first turkey in 1621, when he was 43. Many of the Puritans died during the first winter, and it was in the early fall of 1621 that they had their first harvest. They had learned, too, about the crop known from the Canadian border to the tip of Chile as corn, but in England (just to be different) as maize. (I often wondered how that early maker of breakfast cereals would have done if he'd tried to popularize maize flakes, which is what they are.) It was some day after the first harvest was in and the Bradford crew knew they were in Massachusetts for keeps that – legend has it – they held a feast. Somebody made up a hymn (the one we sing now is a nineteenth-century invention) and gave up a public prayer of Thanksgiving. That's what we like to say is the origin of the continental blow-out that took place last Thursday.

In dry fact, it wasn't until the middle of the nineteenth century that somebody thought it would be a charming thing to have a national day of Thanksgiving, really to congratulate each other on having settled in America or having been born American. This year, you'll gather, there are in some places some misgivings. Anyway, it wasn't until 243 years after the supposed event that Abraham Lincoln proclaimed a national day of Thanksgiving. Many states paid no attention. But gradually, over about eight years, it dawned on people that it was yet another excuse for another day's holiday. Finally, Franklin Roosevelt not only proclaimed it, but read it over the radio and put in a little sermon of his own about William Bradford and company. And by 1940 it had become an immovable feast, celebrated by Act of Congress on the third Thursday in November.

Forty years ago this weekend, a terrific national panic blew up when, a month or so before Thanksgiving, the Pure Food and Drug Administration, which passes on the safety of all crops and new drugs, put out a general warning. The cranberry crop set aside for Thanksgiving had been found (two shipments anyway) to contain a weedkiller poison, aminotriazole. The Secretary of Health, Education and Welfare was instructed to go through the entire Thanksgiving reserve to see how much threatened the national survival. Two little bags of cranberries were found to be suspect. The rest of the seven million pounds he searched were safe, home free. On the Wednesday evening before Thanksgiving, an enterprising reporter asked if President and Mrs Eisenhower were going to serve cranberry sauce as usual. None of your business, the White House replied. Quite right. A little later, your own enterprising reporter made enquiries. President Eisenhower, the American hero of the Second World War, served apple sauce.

America's Day of Terror

14 September 2001

Last Monday I woke up and, as usual on Monday mornings, I began to ponder what I might talk about this time. I was out of touch, you might say, with what they now call the real world after two weeks' absorption in the fantasy world of the United States Open Tennis championships. But first, as the anchormen say, the weather. (I like to know if it's cool enough for me to venture around the block.) So, first, I turned on the weather channel, and within ten seconds knew all too well what this talk would be about. The man was pointing to a blurry circle just north of Bermuda. The circle had a bull's eye, and it had a name. Its name was Erin, the fifth tropical storm up from the Caribbean this season, and it was said, by the National Hurricane Center in Miami, to be the most lethal in a quarter-century, its winds swirling at a hundred and twenty miles an hour. And, the point that hit me literally where I live, it was headed due northwest and expected to make landfall on Wednesday at Suffolk County, the eastern end of Long Island. Not since 1986 have we had to retire from a hurricane to the underground bunker my wife designed twenty-five years ago.

I had breakfast and thought about when I might take off for the Island to join my wife, and my daughter over from London. Then I went back to the weatherman, who was mysteriously in a very cheery mood. He pointed to the whirling circle and then across the Atlantic water inland to Pennsylvania to show a vertical line of arrows pointing east. They marked a cold front that the experts positively declared would move swiftly east and not merely block the oncoming hurricane but push it rudely due east to expire in mid-Atlantic. For once, the experts were dead right. No more was heard about Erin, and, waking on Tuesday morning, I was free to ponder again.

But not, you'll understand for long. I turned on a twenty-four-hour news station and saw a kind of movie I detest, of the towering inferno type: a roaring image, of a monolith collapsing like a concertina in a vast plume of smoke. Just as I pressed my thumb to switch to 'the real world' I caught the familiar voice of a newsman and was in the appalling real world of Tuesday, 11 September 2001, a date which to Americans will live in infamy along with the memories of Pearl Harbor, 7 December 1941, and 22 November 1963, the grievous day of President Kennedy's assassination.

Before nightfall, an old United States Senator was to call it 'the most tragic day in American history'. And by that time, numb from the apocalyptic images, not even a historian was going to question the Senator's definition by bringing up, say, the Civil War and a million dead. But in our time, in my time certainly, it was the most awful, startling, morning I can remember, not because this was the most awful domestic disaster ever, but because, for the first time in the American experience, an act of war aroused, and television pulverized, our senses in a way we'd never known. Before 11 September, most of the Americans who had seen and felt war on their own shores were nearly a century in the grave. The first word I had from my wife, who was a hundred miles away in that so nearly-fateful Suffolk County, was, 'To think, all these years, I've been saying we were the luckiest people alive, never to have known war in our own country.'

For myself, after the first mere announcement, I thought back to another September, by a fluke of memory of another 11 September. The date is confirmed by the books, but my boyhood memory of the newspapers is sharper. You must bear with me in this. The point will emerge. The first great battle of the First World War was over, the Battle of the Marne, on the 11th, and, in the following days, the newspapers hailed the German retreat as a triumph. The sub-headings printed: 'Heavy Casualties On Both Sides.' I didn't at first know what that meant but soon learned as, during the next four years, it became a standard phrase. We often suggested the German casualties – 60,000 in one day. We didn't print numbers of our own. Later, when the Battle of the Somme was over, Britain had lost a quarter of a million men in that battle alone. We never knew, nor read, that. Many years later, I wrote: 'Is it conceivable that if the British could have been a population of *viewers* – of television viewers instead of newspaper readers – is it conceivable they would have just shaken their heads and gone to the railway stations, as they did, to wave their boys off on the troop trains?'

So, the first thing I felt was, 'This is a war. It's here, it's happening to us.' It is the first thing, I think, for people outside the United States to realize. It is the same feeling of bewilderment and secret fear (what next?) that Londoners felt after the first night of the Blitz, in September 1940.

What next, now? I have reams and reams of notes, made over four days and three nights. But most of them recount heartbreaking scenes and awful facts you yourself will have seen and heard much of. If there is one note, one small note in this whole monstrous story that can be called heartening, it is the act on Wednesday of the NATO ambassadors in Brussels. For the first time in the history of the alliance, the council voted to invoke Article 5 of the original treaty, which says plainly (something that has been quietly and blandly evaded): 'An armed attack against any of the allies in Europe or North America shall be considered an attack against them all.' This was far and away the best news for the White House and the Pentagon in many a year, for it gave strength and credibility to the President's promise of punishment for the perpetrators.

The word 'perpetrators' points at once to the mystery that has maddened everybody, the military especially, since last Tuesday morning. Since the first microphone was pushed in front of an official of any kind, the line I remember best was that of General Schwarzkopf, the commander of the alliance in the Gulf War: 'That's our main problem: how and where to respond to an enemy we can't identify.'

While he was talking, the FBI had organized around its counter-terrorist squad four thousand agents and two thousand others: scientists, forensic lawyers, weathermen, aviation experts, architects, engineers. They have been very busy all around the country, and already from an avalanche of data have learned enough to alert the entire continental American air defence system, and to discover with careful speed the prime suspect to be bin Laden. From now on it would be wise not to believe the welter of rumours that are bound to flood us, and credit only what is confirmed by the American and European intelligence services. Attorney General Ashcroft and his FBI chiefs have been remarkably patient with the media, most conspicuously with the younger television reporters – as with the dense, super-stupid question of the year from a young girl reporter: 'Sir, do you think this attack had been planned?' It gave an FBI terrorist expert the chance to respond dryly. 'I should say it would be brilliant if it had been planned in less than one year.'

Talking of patience before the interminably inquisitive, and often stupid, press, the Mayor of New York City has stood out as a hero, a hero who apparently has to get along without sleep. And as for the unseen heroes, I recall most vividly a doctor who had been in combat in Vietnam. He emerged from this Hieronymus Bosch inferno in a blizzard of ash and rubble and said, 'Never saw anything like this – this is hell.' And there was a young television cameraman, a simple (late twenties I should guess), all-American boy with ropey hair and good looks, wiping the ghostly ash from his face and talking of the nurses, among the hundred-odd doctors there: helping survivors, staunching wounds, day and night on the move, calmly saying, 'Please make way.' The boy said, 'People – are unbelievable.'

What is more unbelievable than the enormous wasteland of downtown New York is the stamina and courage of the firemen rescue workers (over three hundred lost by now), the thousand or more, on their sixteen-hour shifts before they nap for a couple of hours and begin again, slogging through, so far, 100,000 tons of ash and rubble and tangled steel, pointing dogs into dark tunnels of wreckage, on and on, looking for the shape of a life or a corpse.

There is an old song, what we knew as a spiritual, which goes: 'Sometimes, I'm up, sometimes I'm down – sometimes I'm almost to the ground.' Well, today, tonight, America is down. But between the deeds of the rescue men and the words of NATO – if they mean what they say – America is not 'almost to the ground'.

America on Standby

21 September 2001

I make no apology for beginning, yet again, with a memory which has never faded, of the First World War. The late Dr Sigmund Freud said, 'The unconscious has a long memory and a logic all its own', and the senses of a small child between the ages of 6 and 10 are here to prove it. When last week I first saw what so many firemen, doctors and nurses were moving about in, the huge, raw landscape of fog and rubble and twisted steel and what we now call, without a wince, body parts, my memory immediately matched the scene with the newsreel pictures we saw eighty-odd years ago every week in what to me was known as the local picture drome: skeletons of village churches sticking up in a now rotted landscape, no foliage, no leaves, trees shot down to broken matchsticks in a miles-wide tangle of barbed wire decorated with body parts.

In the middle of one thundering battle there appeared in the night sky a glowing figure in a frame of blinding light. All the thousands of soldiers saw was the figure of an angel. It became known as the Angel of Mons. And in time, the sensible wisdom was that it had been seen by either the very religious or the very naive. But hundreds of soldiers who were neither swore they had seen in it an angel of deliverance. Mons was where the British, in the earliest days of the war, first engaged the Germans. And Mons was recaptured on the *last* day of the war, in the eleventh hour of the eleventh day of the eleventh month, 1918. Ever since, there has been an annual memorial service in Mons dedicated to St George, who, you recall, slew the dragon.

While on that dreadful Tuesday morning a week and more ago, we lay, stood or pattered in the first terrified daze of seeing the hellish scene, there arose (to be less poetic but more correct, I think I should say there popped up) a figure, everywhere pointing, taking charge, in a suit, in a sweater, in a helmet, a human figure in the downtown hell, in an uptown church, a well-known figure, not hitherto thought of as an angel – a fallen angel, perhaps, with a rather messy private life – known to most Americans as a very quick-witted public prosecutor and active public servant who had greatly reduced crime and performed other virtuous services in his job as the second most powerful executive in the United States, namely the Mayor of New York City.

More than any Mayor in my lifetime, except Fiorello LaGuardia, Rudolph Giuliani has been loved and loathed. All the truly effective Mayors alienate one group or another: whites, blacks, Hispanics, Jews, the Irish, the Italians, whoever, whatever. The inimitable Ed ('how'm I doin'?') Koch said, with his foxy smile: 'Being well hated in one quarter or another goes with the job.' But before 11 September, if we'd been asked to sum up the mayoralty of Mr Giuliani (his term ends in December), most of us, I think, would have said: a small man, a battery of energy, brainy, ruthless with opponents, and whether likeable or not, immensely competent.

Tuesday morning, within an hour of the shattering of the towers, we saw, deep in the grey-black fog and the writhing steel and the rubble, a man barely recognizable as Rudolph Giuliani, and from then till now, twenty hours a day, everywhere there was trouble, or mourning, or work to be done and ordered, here he was, gentle with widows and old people, enormously instructive at all times, exercising almost saintly patience with the press, never striking a wrong emotional note, never sentimental or platitudinous, never showing a spark of temper. He was what the Greeks called an epiphany, 'a manifestation of a super human being'. And thanks to worldwide television, he was seen for many days as the leader of the nation, an impression that, of course, flashed to us an almost guilty reflection. Where, in a word, was the President?

It took our leading newspaper only two days to write a scolding editorial – I think it is not too harsh a word – complaining that it was not Mr Bush who had so gallantly and quickly stood among the firefighters and the grieving, comforting at a hospital bedside, or praying in a humble church. By a weird coincidence, directly opposite the scolding editorial was a piece written by one of the paper's political columnists. But this was not a matter of opinion, it was hard reporting, and when Mr William Safire turns reporter, he seems to have a direct line to the horse's mouth. It was an account of how Vice President Cheney took command of the whole security emergency, realized in an instant the personal peril the President was in, guessed correctly that the Pentagon bomber was at first intended for the White House, and directed the President to be flown off to secret locations in three other places, one of them, the nuclear control centre deep in the bowels of the prairie in Nebraska. This astonishing story, in effect scolding the scolding editorial, was confirmed in every detail the following Sunday by the Vice President himself in a network television interview.

This journalistic jumping of the gun of judgement should alert us, I think, to the role of the press, the media. Surely a naive question to ask at this time of day. Isn't the media's function what it's always been: to comfort the afflicted and afflict the comfortable? After this catastrophe, the second half of that injunction carries a quite new peril. To afflict the comfortable has always meant in practice to keep an eye on government on behalf of the governed.

But in the past quarter-century there has been a tendency, in this country certainly, to assume that a reporter's job is primarily to smell out corruption and, on bad days, invent it. This drift is due to the remarkable success, in the early 1970s, of the two Washington reporters, Woodward and Bernstein, in unearthing the dirt of the Watergate scandal and pushing Richard Nixon out of the Presidency. Not too long ago I asked a young college graduate what he wanted to be. He said, 'An investigative reporter'. Why not, I suggested, just a reporter?

This ambition flourishes today in reporters who honestly believe that their first job is to find out who's to blame. And already, in the interminable procession of television talk shows and round-table discussions, we discover that the country is absolutely teeming with professors and international affairs gurus, ex-Cabinet officers and journalists who are absolute experts on terrorism.

We're going, I think, to have trouble with this side of the media. I suggest that just now is not the time to stomp around looking for someone to blame. Of course the government must always be open to criticism, but since most living American journalists have never covered a war, there may be lots of ill-feeling ahead if, as happens in all wars, there has to be a form of censorship. Most journalists I've listened to have, I'm sure, no idea that twelve years ago Vice President Cheney, who was then Secretary of Defense, was busy drawing up a study of the care and destruction of counter-terrorism, especially in the Arab world, or *out of* the Arab world *into* America. An old friend, long in government but now on the sidelines of the aged, mentioned how grateful we, President Bush more than any of us, should be that he has on his team Mr Cheney, General (now Secretary of State) Colin Powell, and Donald Rumsfeld, once and present Secretary of Defense, ambassador to NATO, special envoy to the Middle East. These three, and a whole squad of CIA and FBI unknowns, were in the thick of the conduct of the Gulf War and explain, I think, the uncanny job done so far by the FBI in tracking down, without panic or illegal tactics, hot suspects in the most unlikely public places and in obscure suburbs from Maine to California.

For the first week or so, we got mixed signals about the proper military response. The President promised, with thumbs up, that 'we shall smoke them out of their holes and catch them fleeing for the hills'. Next thing, or rather a day earlier, General Schwarzkopf, who spent years in Saudi Arabia, warned us: 'Afghanistan is the size of Texas, desert and rocky mountains, no roads, automobiles, transport by camel and mule, no place to dump missiles and smart bombs. There are a million places and holes and caves in the mountains where people don't hide – they live.' For the great mass of us (the people, I suppose, is a better word), the job ahead is, in the long run, of understanding, along with the government, the nature of this new war.

In the short run, the more difficult task for all of us is the emotional, the psychological one, of knowing this as a new age and knowing how we should act in it. On the first day of the apocalypse, in the midst of the fire and the fog, Mayor Giuliani was asked by a news reporter what we, ordinary people, ought to do. He said, 'Take your kids on a picnic, go out and buy something, pray to God, do your usual job, whatever it is, however humble.' Almost four centuries ago, an Englishman, George Herbert, a poet and later a priest, in a very turbulent

ie in English history, urged the same advice: 'A servant . . . /Makes
'udgery divine, /who sweeps a room, as for thy laws, /makes that and
he action fine.'

The Stars and Stripes

9 November 2001

Something that every first visitor to America notices, and I mean during
my lifetime here, is the constant display of the American flag, in places
both public and private. I couldn't count the hundreds of times that a
visiting European friend, off, say, the morning after arrival on a little
tour of the town or the village, has seen the flag draping from a pole
outside the firehouse or hanging from a humble bedroom window.
And the visitor says: 'Hello! What's the occasion, some famous American date? Independence Day, whatever?' No, you say, nothing special.
Somebody got up in the morning and felt good, and instead of taking
the dog for a trot or cooking up a special batch of pancakes, decided
to hang out the flag. In country places, there are always families who
make a point of hanging out the flag every Sunday morning in summer.

The first flaming public response to 11 September was an outburst
of flags. Overnight, two suddenly famous flag factories were reported
to have gone on a twenty-four-hour working day. And orders came
roaring in for flags to be woven or impressed or embedded into every
sort of item of clothing or decoration. The two teams playing off the
baseball championship appeared, the second night, with a neat Stars
and Stripes planted above or alongside their team's logo. A hundred
flags flew outside Rockefeller Plaza. Flags flapped into the late afternoon fog atop San Francisco's Golden Gate Bridge. Flags were on hats,
sweaters, blouses, trousers, motor cars, bikes, shopping bags, from
windows, roofs, awnings – a continent blanketed by the Stars and
Stripes. I didn't hear or read a squeak of a complaint from anybody

about the wholesale violation (punishable by a fine and a prison sentence) that this coast-to-coast flourish represented, which shows just how old I must be. Some days after the original horror which stirred this vast wave of patriotism, I had a most lively recall of a time when I was begged by the newly arrived British ambassador, no less, to do a broadcast to Britain as soon as possible, and acquaint the people of Britain of the hideous crime that an English manufacturer was perpetrating against the law of the United States.

The time was fifty-nine years ago. The United States had come into the Second World War, and the first shipment of American troops was about to arrive in England. A British clothing manufacturer, in the Midlands I believe, had an idea of heart-warming hospitality, to make and deliver an item of clothing for each and every arriving American soldier which should have knitted into it the American flag. Now whether or not the Foreign Office or the Prime Minister was consulted about this idea, all the evidence suggests that they thought it a splendid, a touching, tribute to the arriving allies. Nobody, it seems, had ever heard of the Code of Etiquette issued by the United States War Department in the early 1920s to dictate once and for all how the flag was to be flown, where and when, and especially certain abuses of the flag which must be for ever prohibited. The code is a pretty elaborate one but the gist of it says that the flag is to be flown only between sunrise and sunset, is to be hoisted *briskly* but lowered ceremoniously, and that it must never touch the ground. It may be displayed at night only on special prescribed occasions, and then it must be lit. Another thousand words prescribe the flag's role, position and function in the United States and its dependencies and at sea, whenever a President or former President dies. The really tough part of the code is the list of prohibitions. The flag must not be dipped to any person or thing; it must not be displayed on a float, motor car or boat except from a staff. It is by no means ever to be used – here's the nub, or the rub – as a receptacle for anything, or for any advertising purpose, not to be embroidered on such articles as cushions, or handkerchiefs, or boxes of any kind. The code did not even reach to what a United States Senator once called 'the obscenity' of the flag's being printed on the cover of a box of chocolates, a very frequent and welcome sight to me as a boy at Christmas time, except, of course, the flag was the Union Jack.

You'll gather at once that no such code had ever been thought of in England, where the royal standard and the Union Jack were, indeed, the most popular emblems for advertisers of everything from biscuits to a mysterious potion, I well remember, called 'a lung tonic'. The implied suggestion, I suppose, was that if it could liven up the royal lungs it certainly could ginger up yours.

So, imagine the moment in Washington, when the British ambassador was told, by some American friend, that a British manufacturer had delivered to this American camp in England a whole year's supply of an object of clothing which violated the official American code in a particularly tasteless way. 'What', asked the embattled ambassador, 'is the code, and what is the offending object?' He was told about the code and, according to his own later testimony, blushed with embarrassment. But the blush was nothing to the groan that followed on his hearing about the item of clothing which the innocent manufacturer, bless his warm intentions, had thought would be especially cute. A pair – a thousand pairs – of, how shall I put this? ladies' short undergarments, the seat being composed of the Stars and Stripes. I was asked to broadcast a report on the War Department's code, and the next we heard was (you can well believe) that the panties were immediately . . . withdrawn, I suppose, is the inevitable word.

The result of this famous clanger or boo-boo was that within months, in June 1942, Congress passed a resolution 'amending into public law all existing rules and customs pertaining to display and use of the flag'. The assumption was that from then on, nobody, not even the British, would dare desecrate the American flag in any of the stated or unstated ways. We had a quarter-century to observe the code and, by now, the law.

We reckoned without Vietnam and the uproar of students on the streets in an outbreak of deliberate burning of the flag, an act so outrageous to many Americans in many states that in 1968 Congress passed a law making it a federal crime to burn or otherwise desecrate the flag, on pain of one year's imprisonment or $1,000 fine. For twenty years that law was on the books but only randomly observed, for in several states the students went on burning the flag. Eventually an appeal against the new law – citing the protection of the First Amendment – was taken to the Supreme Court and the Court ruled, only twelve years ago, that burning the flag was a permissible expression of free speech. The effect of this was to have the flag-desecration laws of all the states declared invalid, unconstitutional. And from now on, plainly, you can do anything you like with the flag: wear it on top or underneath, hang it, burn it, flaunt it or, if the war goes on too long for the already chanting students at Berkeley, you can freely flout it. So, yet another old value bites the dust.

Already, though, the wholesale displaying of the flag, on humans in particular, is fading along the gently falling graph of the President's popularity. Only two weeks ago, eighty-seven Americans in a hundred approved of President Bush and the war in Afghanistan. Today it is down to 69 per cent, and these two parallel falling lines are a graphic reminder of something about the American character, if there is such a thing, which is its impatience with difficult, slow solutions.

This is essentially the nation of the quick fix, the miracle drug. And though so many such promises turn out hasty and false, it's surprising in even the last hundred-year stretch of American history how often the sudden flash of intelligence, rather than interminable research, has produced a blessing to mankind. Think of cheap steel, the dollar watch, the refrigerator, traffic lights, the assembly line, the oil freighter, the electric bulb. The President said a month ago that the new war would be strange and long. He never defined long, but day after day at the White House press briefings, the President – or his press secretary, or Secretary Powell – is unceasingly pressed by the media to say how long. There are people, raving enthusiasts in the week after 11 September, who already suggest the war is not showing results. They can't have thought much about the history of Afghanistan and its guerrilla warriors. They've lived on a battleground for eight centuries. In the nineteenth century, Great Britain fought for eight years to conquer them and failed. In 1979 the Soviet Union moved in and occupied the whole country. After fighting for nearly ten years, with 300,000 men, the Soviets gave up and withdrew.

Our trouble is, I think, that to the older generation of Americans, war recalls the long quagmire and defeat of Vietnam. And to the middle and younger generations, the only war they remember is the

Gulf War, a spectacular display of night missiles flying, minimum casualties, of the enemy surrendering, and all over in a hundred hours. So how long is long?

If Americans are looking for a role model, a man who didn't flaunt his patriotism but acted on it, they couldn't do better than Thomas Edison. He had one brilliant, bright idea: the electric light bulb. Not before he'd failed with six thousand different vegetable fibres did he find, in a Japanese bamboo, a high-resistance filament that would burn permanently in a vacuum. He had inspiration which was god-sent. But he had something better: stamina. And you can sense, I think, that behind President Bush's gung-ho assurances there is a slightly nervous, earnest, appeal that stamina is what more than anything he wants the people to begin to show.

Messiah at Christmas

21 December 2001

I am not myself a great collector of old letters, but from time to time, riffling through the chaos of what I dare to call my files, I come on a note from someone I'd long forgotten. And the other morning I fell on a funny, shrewd letter from a shrewd and funny man who has been lost to us for far too long, a loss I feel now because at a time of pretentious theories in literature, politics and – help! – architecture, this man was the sanest of critics and a splendid slaughterer of sacred cows in England whether of the left or right, the lowbrow or the highbrow, as Tom Wolfe has been in America: Philip Larkin.

I had the privilege of keeping up a correspondence with him in what, alas, turned out to be the last year or two of his life. We exchanged ideas, mostly about poetry, and always about jazz – the word jazz being understood as only and always what *we* agreed to like – namely, jazz from the earliest New Orleans days up to the 1940s – and there an end. The arrival of bebop we both heard as the death knell. Larkin called Thelonius Monk 'the elephant on the keyboard'.

In this – as it turned out – his last letter there was a PS: 'Another thing I note we have in common: you say you play the *Messiah* right through every Christmas. So do I.'

I must not assume, as people of my and indeed the previous genera-tion always do assume, that a permanent item of our culture passes on to the next and the next generation. Nearly fifty years ago, I had the rare, weird pleasure of introducing *Messiah* to – Leonard Bernstein.

Leonard Bernstein came to fame, with a national audience as distinct from the concert audience, everywhere when he appeared first on television. The show was the first ninety-minute show of any kind. It was a collection, collage or mishmash of music, science, drama, poli-tics, history, anything and everything; and Bernstein was one of our earliest stars, when he was already blazing his way from Boston to Vienna in the works of the nineteenth-century romantics, the Russians especially. One day the small core of the staff of our show, a half-dozen of us, were sitting around tossing ideas and we came to sketching out the Christmas show. It was then I threw in what I thought was the very hackneyed but beautiful idea of having Bernstein conduct a short version of *Messiah*. Bernstein, I remember, looked up – 'Handel?' he said with a rising inflection, as if it might just as well have been Gershwin. That's the man. 'You know something,' said Bernstein, 'I don't know it.' Well, need I say he came to know it, and I – as one brought up in the Nonconformist north of England and therefore having known every note of *Messiah* since the age of 5 – had the pride of standing before a television audience of two hundred and ninety stations and introducing George Frederic, a pretty old man (56 was beyond the usual span in 1742), not doing well with his concert music or operas, in bad financial trouble, being invited to go to Dublin for a few weeks and for a price compose an oratorio. He lived alone in two rooms in a small house but, once he had this conception of writing the life of Christ, not as a chronicle but as a series of spiritual musical themes, he scarcely paused from dawn to midnight. He had his meals pushed under the door. At the end of fifteen days only, during the last twilight, he finished the 'Hallelujah Chorus', and wrote in his journal: 'I felt that the Lord God Almighty had come down and did stand before me.' At the end, Bernstein embraced us all. 'What a sublime work,' he said.

One of the oldest musical traditions of New York City is a performance of *Messiah* given with the instruments of the original scoring, first done here in 1770 in a church which stands, miraculously, today only three blocks from the mountainous rubble and ashes of the twin towers. On that 12 September, the minister and the choirmaster padded in gas masks through the horrors underfoot and knew that this 230-year-old tradition was bound to be broken. However, three months have passed, and the ninety pipes of the old organ are still choked, and the burning smell is everywhere, and, though the church has stained glass but no open windows, the ash and the grime and smoke came in through the leading. But last Sunday once more, into an acrid atmosphere, the old tradition stayed unbroken.

It may strike some listeners as odd that of all cities, New York, which houses two million of America's six million Jews, should hold to this by now ancient Christian tradition. But if you knew New York City, as this administration is desperately trying to have it known to the Arab world, you would know this to be most characteristic of the city. Long ago, the most elegant essayist of the twentieth century, E. B. White, wrote: 'the most admirable thing about New York is not the conflict of the races and religions but the truce they keep.'

The word 'Messiah' exists in many languages, though it wasn't until the sixteenth century that translators of the Bible chose to fix its spelling with an aitch – Messia*h* – as sounding more Hebrew. And that's the way it stayed. It meant, as everyone knows, the one who would come and set free the oppressed children of Israel. And ever since, it has been used in general in other languages, to signify the liberator of the oppressed.

When I was watching that appalling tape of bin Laden it struck me that one of the tragedies of this war is the fact of his striking good looks: a sombre and handsome presence, the fine eyes, an expression almost of tenderness. It was hard from the beginning to appreciate that this man is the latest of a dreaded breed we have known to our rage and sorrow in the twentieth century: Stalin, Hitler, Pol Pot, Saddam Hussein, all of them either ordinary or ugly. And here is a totalitarian fanatic whose majestic presence lends itself at least to the role of Robin Hood, which is how he sees himself and – at most – as a Messianic figure who will deliver the impoverished peoples of Arabia from what some see as the superpower bully of the Western world.

Enough of these morbid musings – though I believe they are, unhappily, very relevant to the main American propaganda problem: which is how to define this new, strange war and how to make people recognize the chief personal enemy as an old tyrant in a new guise, let alone to see this war as a bizarre revival of the medieval religious wars: the Middle Ages returned with a bomb and a germ.

But, as I settle for Christmas Eve sipping the twilight wine of Scotland, I shall think of another tape, another television interview, which, in this season of good will it's a pleasure to remark on.

Everyone who has followed a sport for long is frequently caught, I believe, between two emotions in watching the stars of the game: horrified awe at the huge money they earn, and yet relief that they are not paid, as they used to be, at the going rate of plumbers' assistants. We're bound to wonder from time to time what they do with all this loot. And too often the answer is – as one famous golfer put it – 'Well, what d'you think? I used to ride the subway. Now I have six cars, a yacht and a private jet. How *about* that?' The tale I have to tell is quite another story and shines like a good deed in a naughty world. The interview came at the end of the final tournament of the season. It was won by the young man who is without question the best golfer in the world. He had just picked up $2 million from winning this one tournament and was asked if it was true that the money would go to the Tiger Woods Foundation. Yes, it would, he said. His foundation he described simply as a fund with the simple aim of helping poor children of colour make something of themselves. What, asked the breezy interviewer, is your main goal in life? Tiger blinked, as if we'd just had another glimpse of the obvious. 'I said – the Foundation – my aim is to make it global, based in the United States but taking in many, many countries. That's far more important than winning tournaments.'

Here is a young man, just 26, who was urged only four years ago by an old and well-wishing friend, an old man and a ravenous golfer, to stay one more year in college and 'enrich' his life. Tiger decided, on the contrary, to turn pro and sign a first sponsor's contract for $52 million. Since then, new contracts and renewals have poured in like Niagara. And he has grown in maturity as a human being ever since, stayed remarkably modest, and, with his enormous fame, level-headed. From the start, he decided to hand over his fortune to enriching the lives of impoverished coloured children across the globe. At Christmas time, I can't think of a finer role model, young or old.

Ringing the Changes

4 January 2002

We had the warmest fall in recorded – meteorologically recorded – history, a mainly frostless system across the whole state from New York City in the south to the Canadian border (remember, New York State is exactly the area of England).

On Christmas Day there was a now famous photograph of two young women, sunbathing on a bench in the most western city (Buffalo) heretofore famous for having been settled three generations ago mostly by Russians and for having more and earlier big snowfalls than any place in the state. Last week Buffalo paid the price for that very late and continuing warm spell. The usual icy Canadian wind came hurling in from the west, collided with this strange layer of warm air we were basking in, and in four days deposited 7 feet – 83.5 inches to be precise – on good old Buffalo, provoking loud choruses in every pub that had candles to see people with, ribald variations of the famous song urging Buffalo gals: 'Won't you come out tonight?'

So, the winter bore down like a wolf on the fold. Down in the city here, it's been so far too cold for snow, but the days have been as bright as diamonds and I look down to a meadow in Central Park and see tiny muffled moppets frisking around like children in a Dutch painting. It is a very peaceful scene, and only the occasional ripping of the sky by a fighter jet reminds us who keeps it so.

Well, I couldn't keep up this reverie all the short day long. Back to the television, and a review of some of the stories from the past year we'd forgotten, some we're only too happy to have forgotten. Three million animals destroyed in England. That plane mysteriously lost off Long Island. Better forgotten as soon as possible were three topics so shocking at the time that we may never forget them. Mr Clinton's pardoning of the convicted felon and campaign contributor, Marc Rich, and the Clintons' subsequent departure from the White House with a load of furniture – an exit the mildest critic called tacky, and which former President Carter called 'simply disgraceful'. There was, I'm afraid, the indelible memory of those awful weeks during which there was no President-elect. Most memorable of all was the still debatable intrusion of the Supreme Court in a matter the Constitution leaves to the state courts of any state whose tally is disputed. And after that, the twenty-four-hour panic of the United States Supreme Court – so uncertain how to act that they reached the most unsatisfying verdict they ever can: a split 5 to 4 decision, which meant, in a Presidential election, that a President was elected not by the recorded seventy million or so voters, not even by the nine justices of the Supreme Court, but by the one vote that broke a tie of 4 to 4, the swing vote of one person. In a phrase, Justice Sandra Day O'Connor appointed the President of the United States.

There is one man who is not forgotten yet and perhaps never will be forgotten by anyone alive and sentient on 11 September. Time was when *Time* magazine published on its New Year cover its main story with a photograph, the title: Man of the Year. It's now, need I say, Person of the Year. And that person, who is also a man, seems to have met the general national choice of a human being most deserving the title. He is Rudolph Giuliani, who for seven years was known to New Yorkers as the most active, crime-busting, ruthless and best-hated Mayor since the late, great Fiorello LaGuardia. I never met any New Yorker who was in two minds about Giuliani, just as I never met an adult American during the 1930s and 1940s who was in two minds about President Franklin Roosevelt. You either worshipped or loathed him. And that was true till the day he died. The eerie thing about Mr Giuliani is that during his seven and a half year reign as Mayor, even the New Yorkers who decided he had become a good Mayor did so grudgingly. Yes, New York City was orderly again, race relations were at least subdued, and the drop in crime was really dramatic. A final figure appeared on the last day of the year, the last day Mayor Giuliani was in office. The year he came to City Hall, the homicide rate for the year was 2,400. Last year, it was just over 600. All this made Mr Giuliani admirable. His transformation into a man greatly admired but also lovable is the mystery story of 2001.

It induced in a few serious people serious discussion about whether redemption is possible all at once, during a lifetime. Once a year at least, we all enjoy Dickens' happy absurdity of taking a tough, malicious, shrewd businessman and making him over, overnight, into a genial, gregarious, almost saintly old man. No matter how much *A Christmas Carol* may be dismissed as a rollicking good story but a deeply sentimental one, I believe it has stayed alive for a hundred and sixty years because in even the most cynical, rational, irreligious human, there is from time to time a twinge, even an unacknowledged wish, to be a better person.

From 11 September and on till the moment he said farewell to the city, Rudolph Giuliani was no longer merely the impersonation of a successful Mayor. He was acknowledged throughout America to have been a good man who behaved finely through an appalling ordeal. Inhumanly patient and attentive, totally unaffected, open, for twenty-four hours, to any help he could give to every victim in sight. At the very end he was asked if he was not sad to be leaving the Mayoralty. 'Of course,' he said, 'but when, like me, you've seen real sadness all around you day in and day out, you're just grateful to have had the privilege of serving.'

I no sooner had these solemn thoughts than an appropriate sound put an end to them. It was the sound of a tolling bell, very familiar to me. If you were here with me and wondered why it is so loud and clear, you could climb a staircase and go up on our roof and look straight to the north and east – no farther than forty yards away you'd see towering above the adjoining apartment building five onion domes and below them two huge shining gold crosses. You would be looking at the Cathedral of St Nicholas, and might well believe you were in Moscow. But no, you are just off Fifth Avenue. Such are the mind-your-own-business habits of many New Yorkers, there are people who live in the same block as the cathedral and don't know it is the largest, the most prestigious Russian Orthodox church in the United States. It has been there for all and more of the fifty-one years we have lived in this apartment. And in all that time, I never heard its bell or bells ring out merrily. Always at twilight, two melancholy tollings at intervals, bemoaning, it always seemed to me, the enslavement of the Church, of all Churches and church-goers, for seventy years and more, under the tyranny of the Soviet regime, which, you remember, in the very beginning called religion 'the opiate of the masses'.

Well, only a few weeks ago, something most remarkable happened at the cathedral round the corner. The bell tolled continuously. Evidently, something was going on. Across the street from our entrance were two police cars and a cordon closing off 97th Street and the approaches to it. This little ceremony lasted the shortest time. Whoever the big shot was, he prayed briskly and was gone. I was very sad. If I'd known, I would have pattered round the corner and raised my hat to the slim little man who emerged and stepped swiftly from his devotions to a car guarded by two men in dark suits. I can tell you who it was in a short sentence no listener would have believed for sixty years at least. The President of all the Russias had just been to church. Yes, Mr Putin had been to church.

So, on New Year's Eve, though St Nicholas' bell tolled in its usual way, it sounded a new note to me, as I watched one of our television networks tour the festivities in all the capital cities that are well ahead of us in time. We saw a positive blizzard of fireworks from New Zealand to Paris. From Moscow, though, was a note more dazzling than any fireworks display: a national poll in which 78 per cent of all the Russians declared their best friend to be the United States. Bearing in mind our ignorance of Mr Putin's deepest motives, but allowing for his saying in a private interview that he had developed a close and trusting relationship with President Bush, and that not too much should be made of the abrogation of the Anti-Ballistic Missile Treaty – the prospect of, at last, a genuine alliance between Russia and the United States could be the brightest light to shine from the ashes of 11 September.

Arise, Sir Rudolph

22 *February* 2002

Long ago, New York City had a monthly magazine of great elegance. It was published by a man who hired the most famous writers, the best photographers, reproduced the Impressionists (then coming into fashion) in the finest colour reproductions, printed everything on touchably beautiful papers. The whole magazine was maintained with style, and damn the expense: an attitude that, alas, could not be sustained for long after the Great Depression really set in. The magazine folded in the mid-1930s.

One of its renowned features was a monthly full-page colour cartoon by a fine caricaturist, a Mexican named Covarrubias, whose cartoons brought two people together for a social meeting, an interview, two famous people whose appearance in life together anywhere at any time would have been inconceivable, preposterously unlikely. The series was called 'Impossible Interviews'. I won't give you any actual examples because I'm sure the stars of this series are long gone and you would never have heard of them anyway. But if Covarrubias were alive and practising his cunning art today, you might have Tony Blair taking tea with Saddam Hussein, or wilder still – Madonna sharing a cocktail with the Pope.

I thought with affection back to Covarrubias, and not a little yearning, because he drew at a time when there was an abundance of fine cartoonists on both sides of the Atlantic – the *New Yorker* and *Punch*. Each had at least a dozen brilliant cartoonists with a finished individual style recognizable at a hundred feet. Alas, this yearning is sharpened by the recognition that we – both countries – today live in the Dark Age of comic draughtsmanship.

What made me think of Covarrubias and his *Vanity Fair* series was a scene, a shot on television and next day in the papers, which was, indeed, an Impossible Interview. A photograph of one Rudolph Giuliani bowing before the Queen of England. The caption read, 'Sir Rudolph?' And the underlying piece went on to tell us why he might not properly or legally be addressed as Sir Rudolph. Because, the papers said, the Constitution forbids: a delusion which, I am sorry to say, even the good, grey, authoritative *New York Times* appears to share. I have had it explained countless times – once even by the British ambassador to Washington in the act of hanging the cherished silver star around my neck: 'Because, you see, you became an American citizen – the Constitution forbids.' Ah, so! Also, not so!

The Constitution is quite emphatic but also quite precise about who may not accept a foreign title and who, by inference, *may*. During the seventeen-week convention in Philadelphia which eventually produced the written Constitution, the chief authors had, over several days, recited the great range of powers enjoyed by monarchs that would not be allowed to a President. One deprivation was most pungently expressed by the brilliant young Alexander Hamilton: 'this plan [the pending Constitution] gives the express guarantee of a republican form of government . . . and the absolute and universal exclusion of titles of nobility.' The Constitution laid down this guarantee without quite such a burst of emotion. It forbade the granting of titles *by* the United States and forbade federal government officials accepting titles from a foreign state. Here is the crucial clause, in its original eighteenth-century language: 'No title of nobility shall be granted by the United States and no person holding any office of profit or trust under them [these United States] shall accept of any present, emolument, office or titles of any kind whatever from any king, prince or foreign state – without the consent of Congress.'

I don't know of any case in which an American about to be entitled went to Congress and asked, 'please may I use it?' But the point I'm making can be simply stated: no foreign title may be accepted by anyone 'holding any office of trust' in the federal government. So, Secretary of Defense Donald Rumsfeld could not accept a knighthood. But Rudolph Giuliani is not an employee of the federal government. And there is no legal or constitutional reason why he shouldn't be called Sir Rudolph, as P. G. Wodehouse, an American citizen, was dubbed and called Sir Pelham Greville Wodehouse until he died. But there is one very powerful reason that down two centuries has overwhelmed any legal right. It came from Thomas Jefferson, who was in Paris during the early debates on the Constitution. He kept an eagle eye on everything in dispute. He was full of suggestions and recommendations of what should and should not be done. If they'd had e-mail in their day, the delegates wouldn't have been able to keep up a continuous discussion without a blizzard of notes and urgings from Jefferson. First, he was shocked to learn that there was no attached Bill of Rights, and was mainly responsible for its creation. He added all sorts of private fusses. One day after a walk through the centre of Paris, he scribbled down 'No public statues', and rushed the idea off to the next packet. He lost out on that one. But he did have his say about titles of nobility, and it was so sharp and memorable that the delegates quoted it long afterwards. All Jefferson said was: 'Titles of nobility – *a very great vanity*', which, he went on to imply, no proud Republican with any sense of self-esteem would dream of accepting. This sentiment became so firmly planted in the American consciousness that to this day, even distinguished Americans cannot believe in the acceptance of a title by democratic, especially socialist, Englishmen. I remember an American Secretary of State, a powerful intellect and a very sophisticated diplomat. Yet he marvelled when the most famous Labour leader of his day moved to the House of Lords. 'Lord Attlee – sounds absurd does it not? Why would he take it?' The soft answer came from a waspish friend of the Secretary. He said, 'Well, I suppose even an occasional socialist has his quota of human vanity.' Since everyone present had great admiration for Clement Attlee, we moved on to other topics.

However, if Mr Giuliani found himself in London again and wanted to get the feel of what it's like to enjoy his permissible title, I recommend that he drop in for lunch or dinner at any one of London's top hotels. He will be greeted by a tribe of men who scorn the niceties of the uninformed. They are the maîtres d', the head waiters, the commis waiters, doormen, men in the profession of greeting and serving the citizenry. They know what is what and who is who. 'Good evening, Sir Rudolph.' 'Would you care for an aperitif, Sir Rudolph?' 'And after the flutes of sole, Sir Rudolph?' 'Thank you, Sir Rudolph.' 'Goodbye, Sir Rudolph.'

On the other hand, he has cause to be glad, when he gets back home, that he is not a British citizen. I recall the wearisome experience of the actor, the late Cedric Hardwicke; in his day, a very distinguished stage actor indeed, George Bernard Shaw's favourite actor, and the one for whom he wrote a special play, casting him as King Magnus in *The Apple Cart*. Long before Olivier or Richardson, he was knighted – way back, I'm shocked to realize – in 1934. Very soon took his career and his title to Hollywood. And in the beginning there's no doubt that his title was not an obstacle to Sir Cedric's acquisition of agreeable roles. Years later when, towards the end, he was having a rough time, having to do with the high cost of a second divorce, he told me that his title had become 'a very expensive albatross around my neck'. 'Every American', he said, 'who does any kind of service – a bootblack, a waiter, a delivery boy, assumes that a knight is a very wealthy lord with twenty thousand acres – something they hadn't known before. So where I normally gave a quarter tip I had to give a dollar, and at expensive restaurants, where the car parking attendant used to get a dollar, now, unless I give him five, he positively sneers and mutters "cheap skate" to his cronies.'

Which reminds me of a friend who, I discovered fairly recently, shared the universal delusion about knighthoods and American citizens but thought, that 'holding any office of trust under these United States' was a comic invention by a journalist we both admired. No sir, right there, Section 1, Clause 9 of the Constitution. He was thinking of a memorable column by the most famous American journalist of the last century: H. L. Mencken of Baltimore. In the Roaring Twenties, the wonder-boy amateur golfer, Bobby Jones, inspired a new national fad: young and old, the famous, infamous and obscure, took up golf. One day a young reporter walked into the Baltimore *Sun* office wearing plus fours and carrying a golf bag. Mencken was appalled at the costume – 'it makes its wearer look like a stud horse with his hair done up in frizzes'. He sat down and wrote an indignant column which ended: 'If I had my way, any man guilty of golf would be ineligible for any office of trust under these United States.'

The Day the Money Stopped

8 March 2002

The 4th of March is a frightening date in American history, and every time it comes around I am drawn, as by a magnet, back to 4 March 1933. Anyone who was alive and sentient in this country then, most especially in Washington or New York City, will never forget it. I think I ought to try and give you something of the feel of it, so that we may better glimpse what may be ahead of us after the omen, I'll call it, of 4 March 2002, last Monday.

Saturday, 4 March sixty-nine years ago was an almost balmy winter's day, after several roaring blizzards. I was in New Haven, Connecticut, because that is the seat of Yale University, and I was in my second term there, taking no lectures because I was 24, on a fellowship, in the graduate school, and doing my own thing. I was about to take to the train, a ninety-minute stint, to New York City, there to meet on an incoming Cunarder, a young and jolly woman who was the daughter of an old family friend. She was on her first visit to America and I had pledged to spend the weekend showing her, as we used to say, a good time. If this tale is already eliciting a giggle in the expectation of some hanky-panky, I had better disabuse you at once. I was very much in love with an English girl who was, alas, not coming in on any Cunarder. Never was a more high-minded weekend to be spent by a young couple in their early twenties.

In those days, I was blankly non-political, never read a newspaper, except for the theatre page. In America, more than in England, I was a 100-per-cent ignoramus about government and politics. I was aware of the grimness of the Depression from the evidence of my senses, every day seeing the long breadlines of very mixed company: shabby men and elegant men and poor women, people of all classes and ages, and every evening, out with a friend, being solicited half a dozen times by smart middle-aged men who told their wives they were looking for night work. So they were. They were begging for dimes and quarters.

I had enough ready cash to see us through the rest of the day. I checked my theatre tickets, and was on my way. As the Cunarder blew its baritone horn, it little knew it was sounding the trump of doom. But the young lady was in good spirits and in no time I was checking into my usual hotel. I walked over first to the cashier and wrote out a cheque for some, in those days, very lavish amount: could have been $20. He looked at it as at an obvious forgery. 'What is this?' He couldn't possibly cash it. I responded with a line from the then fashionable Noël Coward: 'Do you imagine there's a bank anywhere in the United States that might have the kindness to cash this cheque?' He looked at me with all the zeal of a codfish. 'I don't think so,' he drawled. 'Better go and read the papers, sonny.' (He was, you'll gather, a very old man, couldn't have been a day under 50.) Well, I did. I walked over to the news-stand and saw, across the whole front page of the *New York Times* no less, the blanketing headline: 'Roosevelt To Be Inaugurated At Noon. Declares Moratorium On All Banks.'

All banks. That made no more sense to me than an announcement that the sky would turn to midnight-black for the rest of the day. Still, I was young and sassy and not to be intimidated by a cashier and a word I hadn't a clue to: moratorium. I stopped a passing lift man and enquired. It meant the banks were shut. All the banks, said the lift man, 'of the *You*-nited States'. In other words, he said, 'This is the day the money stopped.' It was a piercing phrase and passed into the language. A later friend of mine wrote a book with that title. But what did it mean, by way of living? And how about a receptive hotel? Mine would have no truck with us, not with a young con man who heard the news and thought to cheat the crisis by cashing a worthless cheque for a king's ransom.

These doubts and questions only came later. At the moment, the young lady and I were looking forward to a lark. How to spend a holiday weekend in New York without money, without even a bed? I had a triumphant idea. I sat the girl down in the lobby of the hotel, told her to eat, read, walk, do anything she chose for two, possibly three hours and I'd be back loaded with lots of lovely money. My ace up the sleeve was a New York to New Haven railway season ticket, or what is called a 'commutation ticket'. It had been provided to me – an advanced student of drama – to help me go to New York whenever I wanted to catch up with the latest plays. (The Commonwealth Fund was nothing if not a thoughtful provider.) So I caught the train and, back at Yale, went the rounds of my friends to borrow what would be my reserve of walking-around money. To my horror, most of them were out, and three of them could cough up only a dollar or two. The last man I called on was my oldest – six-month-old – American friend, a merry-eyed athletic type who had knocked on my door the first night at Yale wondering if I needed help of any sort. He gave me a happy but quizzical look and said a sentence that changed my life.

'Do you know', he said, 'what a due bill is?' I hadn't a clue. But I learned within thirty seconds. Yale's student publication, a very serious, double-dome quarterly was called the *Harkness Hoot*, and its editor was the very man before me. He said that the Hotel St Regis in New York, a positively upper-crust hotel on Fifth Avenue, had an outstanding bill with the *Hoot* for an advertisement at an unpaid cost of $100 (about $1,000 today). 'I think', he said, 'they'll put you up.' No wonder this merry-eyed, quick-thinking lad became Dean of the Yale Law School at the age of 26 and subsequently the President's adviser on atomic energy.

I took the bill and took the train, whipped in and out of my old hotel with a sneer and whisked my girl off to the St Regis. We ran into a small tide of outgoing guests. I guessed, correctly, we were the only new guests. The reservations clerk was suspicious of this young, carefree and probably illegal couple. He summoned the manager, whom I can see now: a dapper, grey-haired man in a cutaway. 'Can I help you?' he asked with the bored tone of a cop turning his flashlight on a burglar. Yes, I said, two separate nice rooms on the top floor. He coughed a high sarcastic cough. I showed him the due bill. He was transformed in a flash. He started clapping his hands like a flamenco dancer, and minions came running. We were swiftly ensconced in a suite with two bedrooms at the outrageous price of, say, $7. We laughed, we lolled, we prepared to see the town. I think there was one other couple in the dining room. We went to the theatre, the stalls were littered with depressed men in crumpled tails and white tie roused by the chorus, which suddenly broke loose from its opening song and changed, to a rhythmic beat: 'We depend on Roosevelt, we depend on him.' Tumult and universal cheers.

We danced some of the night and spent the rest at various Harlem nightclubs, dispensing carefree tips until the ready cash had gone, when I took out my chequebook and faced the taxi driver. He was shocked, insulted, but not for long. He took it, and he was the last cab driver, shopkeeper, waiter, café bartender to demur. A month later, I looked over my bank statement covering that weekend, and saw that my account was sadly depleted: to Helmut Schmidt 45 cents. Antonio Collucci, 65 cents. Connie's Inn, $1.65. And on and on. Next morning, the Governor of Connecticut issued scrip money, and we exchanged that on the promise of repayment in better times.

This experience germinated a lively interest, first in the banking system (what Roosevelt left of it), then in economics, and then in the origins of the Depression.

I learned about Black Thursday, 24 October 1929, the day when blocks of shares went down the river of the New York Stock Exchange, in 20,000 lots. J. P. Morgan and his banker-rescue team plugged the flood with $25 million, and for a month or two things steadied, till the bigwigs said that was nasty but the recession was over. But this was to Congress a band-aid solution. Two Western Senators, one Mr Smoot and one Mr Hawley, proposed a major, curative operation: a radical new tariff bill on imports. A hundred top economists petitioned President Hoover not to abandon his free-trade prejudice. But he signed the bill. The market started to go down, unemployment rose alarmingly, the angry Europeans were less able than ever to pay their huge First World War debt. They retorted in kind. It was depressingly plain, in the spring of 1932, that the Smoot–Hawley tariff had guaranteed the descent into the pit of thirteen million unemployed, and what would be known as the Great Depression.

This past Monday, 4 March, President Bush, over the warning words of the American and European conservative financial papers, and a plea – this time from several hundred American economists – signed a tariff bill, of 20 per cent on imported steel. There was an instant outcry from Japan, Europe, harshest of all from Russia, which sells one-third of its slab steel to the United States and threatened a ban on American poultry. Retaliation has always been the name of the game and the harbinger of recession at best.

An old, wily economist who was there in 1933 said, 'After this, the deluge, remember?' Let us hope, pray, that for once, he's wrong.

Memory of a True Great

15 March 2002

On Sunday, 17 March, St Patrick's Day, in the evening there will take place a continental span of celebration dinners – from New Zealand and Australia, to South Africa to several cities in the United States, and across the ocean, most notably to Scotland – to celebrate the one hundredth birthday of the only American, two hundred years after Benjamin Franklin, to be given the freedom of the city or burgh of St Andrews.

What we might call the shrine dinner was set for Atlanta, Georgia, the birthplace of the man I am talking about: Robert Tyre Jones, lawyer, scholar, engineer and amateur golfer who, in the summer of 1930, performed a feat never accomplished before or since: to win in succession all four of the major golf championships in one year, which, in those days, meant the British Amateur championship, the British Open, the United States Open and the United States Amateur. Like Alexander, having conquered all known worlds, he retired.

But this talk is not to be about the greatest golfer of his day. It is a memoir and personal recollection of, I do believe, the most singular human character I have ever known. The standard reservation to make now is to say of course he was no saint. We always toss in this reminder, forgetting along the way that the early behaviour of some of the saints was not so saintly either.

So, on St Patrick's Day, 1902, in Atlanta, Georgia, was born to a young-middle-aged Southern lawyer and his wife a son. Almost from

babyhood, he was enfeebled by a puzzling disease which later he called
'a digestive system that did everything but digest'. In those days, the
automatic remedy for any affliction, from flat feet to a brain tumour,
was to take a vacation in a balmy climate. But the Joneses were already
in a balmy climate. And Mr and Mrs Jones took up golf and lugged
the 4-year-old along with a sawn-off club. What for? To do him good.
His disease vanished as mysteriously as it had arrived. He took to
hitting a ball the way other boys take to kicking or throwing a ball. He
watched the new Scottish pro. He was a marvellous mimic, and the gift
passed over to driving a ball, and pitching and chipping, and by the time
of his teens he had invented shots nobody else had thought of.

His early prowess was such that he was, at 14, Georgia amateur
champion, at 15 – with the United States in the First World War
– touring the country with the reigning professional golfer, giving
exhibitions for the Red Cross. At 15, too, he had done with school
and went to Georgia's famous Institute of Technology to take the
four-year engineering degree. He won it in three years, so on to
Harvard for an honours degree in English literature, while there picking up the United States Open championship during his summer
vacation.

At 24, he decided to become a lawyer and went back to Atlanta, to
Emory University, to take the four-year course. But towards the end
of his second year, he thought he'd like to see how tough was the bar
exam. He took it, passed easily, so left colleges for ever, became a
lawyer and so remained for life. Quite simply and incredibly, his
summer holidays were spent entering twenty major championships,
winning thirteen, coming second in five, and, at the veteran's age of
28, retiring for ever from competitive golf.

He had, of course, not earned a nickel from the game, so he started
to make some money to keep his wife and three children. He made for
Hollywood (with a string of stars) sixteen fifteen-minute movies about
playing golf, which, amazingly, were a hit in the movie theatres on
three continents. He did a radio talk show, he wrote a weekly column
– the most exact, finest instructional writing we have. During the
Second World War, he was exempted with bad varicose veins from
military service but managed a commission and served in France under
Eisenhower. You'd expect he'd retire and spend the days happily

with his family, playing golf several times a week. But his fame was enormous and during the Depression he had myriad calls for help. He devoted all his spare time to innumerable charities, playing only occasional golf.

After one round, in his mid-forties, he told his partners, 'I don't think I'll be playing with you boys for some time.' He had been struck with an agonizing back pain and had an operation. It didn't help. He began to feel tingling in his fingertips, a leg grew numb. He had a second operation in which bony vertebral spurs were removed to relieve the compression on his spinal nerves. The numbness and muscle atrophy spread to both legs. Finally he was diagnosed with a very rare progressive degenerative disease of the spinal cord, for which there was no cure, and still isn't. Although he was beginning to be paralysed, he determined to appear as a cheerful invalid, kind and genial, without affectation, to friends and strangers and, always, looking out for the shy one in a corner.

The diabolical disease progressed, in the harsh professional language. Soon, all feeling had gone below the waist, his fine hands were reduced to stiff, curled little claws, with which he clutched a cigarette, a tumbler, and always signed his letters with a sprawling three-letter word – B-o-b, done with a pen taped to a tennis ball. He never complained, for twenty-two years retained his matchless courtesy, his ironical amused gaze at life. His last public visit to Scotland was in his mid-fifties, when the provost of St Andrews gave him the freedom of a city Jones said 'has a sensitivity and ability to extend cordiality in ingenious ways'. He hobbled off to his electric cart and began to propel himself slowly down the aisle, as the audience stirred to a single voice and rose to sing 'Will ye no come back again?' The start of the hobble and the fact of the cart were enough to remind us that he never would.

The last two years we were, rightly, not allowed to see him, a tortured wraith of sixty-five pounds. I pray he was well sedated. On the last day, he turned to his wife (to whom he had, as a friend put it, 'in his old-fashioned way kept the faith') and said, 'Is this all there is to it?' and died in his sleep just before his seventieth birthday.

As a boy on his first round at St Andrews, he played badly and withdrew from the championship and threw a little temper tantrum. It was his first and last. He made 'a general apology'. Later he wrote,

'In golf, and maybe in life too, it is not enough to play by the rules, if you don't play by the etiquette, it's not worth a damn.' I suppose what we saw, what we had in him, was something rarer than a great athlete, writer, artist, actor, composer, statesman – a masterpiece of a human life. So, at a time when, across the globe, many nations and two civilizations are busy deploring each other's national character, I thought it might be useful for a change to talk about one human being who, everybody of every nation who met him agreed, was a credit to his race, the human race, that is.

I have written and spoken a good deal about Bob Jones down many years of watching him, covering, being with him – from his last appearance at Augusta way back to his first appearance at Lytham St Annes in 1926. (I was 17 and within hearing distance of the roar that went up for that magical shot to the seventeenth green that sealed the match and his first British championship.) The best I can do to sum up my long view of him is to say again what I wrote in my history of America twenty-eight years ago:

The 1920s were a prosperous, garish, pleasure-bent, often vulgar decade during which New York City started the colorful custom of paying tribute to national gods with what were called ticker-tape parades up Broadway: mainly for generals, admirals, aviators. There was one peculiar choice, but, in him, the 1920s were saluting not so much an athlete but unknowingly an old ideal in the moment of its passing. He was Robert Tyre Jones, Jr., a weekend golfer but the best of his time, amateur or professional. He had a grace and charm on and off the course that, combined with great good looks, made him the idol of two continents, and *that* to people who did not know a putter from a shovel and had only the weekly newsreels in the movie houses to go on. His universal appeal was obviously not as a golfer.

What then? The word that comes to mind is one that is fast becoming an extinct word with no meaning to present generations except as an obsolete class distinction: the word is a gentleman, meaning in Bob Jones' case a combination of goodness, modesty and social ease, unwavering courtesy, self-deprecation, but first and at all times an alert instinctive, consideration for other people.

As for the last dreadful twenty-odd years of his life, even this long decline was heroic. The American golf historian, Herbert Warren

Wind, has said it better than anybody in the fewest words: 'As a young man, he was able to stand up to just about the best that life can offer, and throughout the later years he stood up with equal grace to just about the worst.'

It is in the evening, at around 6 p.m., that I recall Bob Jones best: the moment that E. B. White called 'the time of the most beautiful sound in America: the tinkle of ice at twilight'. I think it is appropriate, on this surely American-Scottish occasion, to tell you that of the whole pharmacopoeia of medications I take every day, far and away the most effective is what I call the twilight wine of Scotland. I had the honour, from time to time, of sharing a teaspoon or two with Bob Jones, and he agreed with me about its power to heal.

The Last of the Old-Time Gangsters

14 June 2002

'John Gotti Is Dead.' To many Americans in the seedier section of cities from New York to Miami to Las Vegas to Los Angeles, that simple sentence was as stunning as, to Frenchmen two centuries ago, the sentence 'Napoleon is dead' must have been.

In random street interviews in New York and New Jersey, you could see and hear that the name John Gotti inspired fear in some, relief in most, and in everybody, awe. Unlike most top officers of the Mafia (who moved swiftly and warily in public in the middle of a wedge of bodyguards, John Gotti, five feet ten inches, two hundred pounds, beautifully garbed in the most opulent Italian suits, his handsome and daily barbered face surmounted by a breaking wave of silver hair (which was also tended once a day), John Gotti made his daily excursion from a barber's chair to his office something of an informal royal procession, bowing to fans known and unknown, scattering smiles and autographs and at regular intervals saluting detectives or FBI men posted on a stake-out. The Dapper Don, they called him. The FBI more testily called him the Teflon Don, because for many years he evaded the law, or defeated it in court, more agilely than anyone since Al Capone.

John Gotti was one of thirteen children born to an under-employed day labourer, son of poor Italian immigrants. A quick-witted, restless boy, he was bored by school, did not pay much attention, and dropped out when he was 16. (Interesting to some Europeans, I think, is that even back then the normal school-leaving age was 18.) The family moved from the comparatively alien borough of the Bronx, downtown among fellow Italians in the Lower East Side, which was in the early 1950s a jungle of petty crime and a recruiting ground for the 'crews' of the Mafia families. At that time, there were five Mafia families: the Bonano, Columbo, Genovese, Luchese, and the one young John Gotti would come to join and eventually dominate so that he could boast, and justly so, that he was *the* Godfather of the United States.

Each of the five mob families worked through crews of about a score of young men, who started as errand boys and moved up, if they were good and ambitious, to be thieves, protection bullies, and odd well-paid hit men. The crews in turn recruited their members from boys' street gangs. John Gotti began his life's work by immediately proving with his fists that he could lead a gang. He recommended himself to the capo (captain) of a crew by his quick mind, and the almost delightful ease with which he could suggest to shopkeepers and restaurants that they badly needed protection from some unseen enemy. In no time, he was himself well in with the Gambino family, and for eight years practised much theft, street assaults and stealing of cars, for which he served six months in jail four or five times. These little stretches were not signs of failure. They were exercises in the normal apprenticeship of a first-class mobster.

Just before he turned 30, he pleaded guilty to holding up and stealing cargoes being delivered to Kennedy Airport. This time, he served three years, and when he got out, at the age of 32, he was ready for the big time. He became the captain of a Gambino crew. A nephew of Gambino himself was murdered, and John Gotti was ordered to per-form the necessary act of revenge, which he managed successfully through a three-man ambush which disposed of the murderer. Gotti was indicted and went to trial. But by now, John Gotti had learned a lesson that the Capone school of criminology had taught long ago: find and clutch to your bosom for life a brilliant and conscienceless lawyer. Mr Gotti's man not only got a life sentence reduced to four years, but did a deal with the county district attorney's office to be allowed out from time to time, to see his family, to dine at a fancy New York restaurant, to visit friends and – in a soft voice – conduct the business of the Gambino family. Only after he was free again was it proved (but not beyond doubt) that some prison guards and bodyguards had been bribed.

Out again and settled for life – like all the top gangsters in a quite modest suburban house – John Gotti very soon moved onwards and upwards from being the capo of a Gambino crew. Through the accident of a series of deaths or jailings in the family, he established himself as the head of the Gambino family itself, and was very busy presiding over big robberies, drug deals, corrupting trade unions, and ordering the 'liquidation' (as Stalin used to say) of rival mobsters, sometimes of ordinary citizens who got in his way, like a motorist who accidentally ran over Gotti's 12-year-old son riding a bicycle. The motorist was never seen again.

It would be excessive to say that all this – Gotti's very active criminal life – went on in the light of day. The only time his innumerable crimes came to light was in the glare of a courthouse. Time and again, Gotti was indicted and tried. And time and again the jury acquitted him. Once, after he'd been acquitted, it was discovered that the foreman of the jury had received a whopping $80,000 bribe. But most of the time the jury lacked the absolutely certain evidence of guilt. Inside a courtroom, Gotti every time defined his profession as that of a plumbing supply dealer with a maximum annual income of $100,000. The investigators, though, had certain evidence that in his life of racketeering he received from his employees something between $10 and $12 million a year.

At long last, the Feds moved in on state and county investigators and examined the extent, the appalling extent, to which the Gambino family and Gotti in particular controlled the pay-cheques and working hours of some of the nation's most vital industries: the labour of the waterfront, the construction industry, the collecting and disposal of everybody's garbage.

Finally, in 1990, with court-approved telephone taps, Gotti was heard by the jury planning hijackings, boasting of murders done. In all, he was successfully charged with thirteen counts of racketeering, five murders, conspiracy, obstruction of justice, and – Al Capone's only punishable sin – tax evasion: fraud.

I go into all this not to indulge a passing bow to the *New York Times*, which had a two-page obituary of him, or because it was time to notice the last of the old-time gangsters, but because from time to time listeners, and friends, say, 'By the way, what ever happened to the gangsters?', such a star feature of American movies in the 1930s and of American crime stories in the 1940s.

The official answer is that in the 1940s, the famous reform Mayor of New York, Fiorello LaGuardia, went after the top mobsters in the biggest way by appointing a special prosecutor of rackets, a city lawyer, one Thomas E. Dewey, who sent to jail the New York leader of the Democratic Party, and a federal judge, and broke Lucky Luciano's prostitution racket, and is also credited with crippling the highly lucrative protection racket. Until the Second World War, every resident of the island of Manhattan paid extra high prices for laundry, fruit and vegetables, in fact most foodstuffs that came on to the island by ferry or tunnel from New Jersey and the South. There were alert gangs on the New Jersey shore very anxious to see that we had clean laundry and edible fruit and vegetables – at a price. Prosecutor Dewey was so successful, he became Governor of New York and twice ran for President.

In the 1970s the federal government appointed a supervising team over the chronically corrupt teamsters union – the truckers – the most influential union in the country since it had come to replace the railroads as the nation's main carrier of goods and foods. In the 1980s–1990s, Rudolph Giuliani, as a federal prosecutor, weakened four of the five families, cleaned corruption out of a big downtown trade show centre, and really broke the grip of the mob on the city's chief fish market.

It is difficult to say today how wide the mob's influence spreads, because down two or three generations, the First Families, so to speak, have transformed their image and, optimists say, their character. The children of the old bosses stayed in school, went to the big universities or to business school, sometimes under new names. Looking, talking and acting like the genuine preppy article, they moved quietly into the more respectable fields of investment banking and related enterprises. So, only a first-rate and daring investigative journalist could say how deep and wide is the Mafia's influence. (A former governor of New York with an Italian name maintained, through the most gruesome days of the mobs, that there was no such thing as the Mafia.)

Today it would be utopian to believe that their hands have been permanently crippled and plucked from the fabulously rewarding industries of construction and garbage removal. Certainly, our garbage everywhere costs a bundle, and the unexplained freakish item of the economy is that, while the stock exchange declines steadily every week, and since half the country owns stocks and people worry about their shrinking income, the cost of building new homes and of rented houses and apartments goes higher than ever.

Farewell to San Francisco

18 October 2002

From time to time, an old acquaintance will call me just before I do my talk and say, 'Well, I think we all know what you're going to talk about this week.' I tend to say, 'That's right', or 'You got it', because I know in my bones, from years of such calls, that they haven't got it. It's always about some appalling natural disaster, a fire, an earthquake, perhaps the assassination of a foreign statesman. In any case, I find no occasion for intelligent comment about the lamentable snipings in the Virginia–Maryland country, or about the nightclub bombing on the once island paradise of Bali. The only reaction must be, 'Isn't it awful?'

There is nothing useful you or I can do about it, except to add that Bali and, possibly, the snipings miserably confirm our discovery that the explosions of the past few years, from Scotland to the South Pacific, are not the spontaneous outbursts *of* fanatical loners but the long-prepared world war of a worldwide network called al-Qa'ida.

But now there is a topic which is not to be guessed at, and was dictated quite simply by my looking at the calendar and reflecting: ah, yes, the third week in October, which has meant for so many years, 'San Francisco time'. Certainly, for the past thirty years or so I have been going four times a year to my favourite city to see how America, its life and affairs, looks from the Pacific Coast.

Visually, the first thing that struck me, from the start, was the Oriental connection. It has been there since the first Chinese labourers were brought in by the Central Pacific Company to work their way east and meet the Irish working west, together to create the first transcontinental railroad. In the middle of the Utah desert in May 1869, two locomotives timidly nosed together, and a lad on a high telegraph pole tapped out for the wonder of the world the message: 'The last rail is laid. The last spike is driven. The Pacific railroad is finished.' That moment has been celebrated in many a sentimental calendar painting with railroad company dignitaries in cutaways banging in a gold spike. A more prosaic, not to say brutal, memory has stayed green in the recollections of the railroad crews and their descendants. Several days before the historic moment, the two grades had run side by side for a stretch, and the Irishmen took such an instant aversion to the little slant-eyed Chinese that they blasted them with dynamite. The Chinese swiftly buried their dead and returned the gesture with pickaxes. The massacre was brief and bloody but the racial feud it brewed simmered throughout the nineteenth century.

By the time I first arrived in San Francisco, just on seventy years ago, Chinatown was the most compact and orderly of all the ethnic settlements. It had a thriving tourist business, and the California–Oriental connection was strong and detectable everywhere, from the old Chinese in the early morning on Nob Hill doing their slow-motion graceful exercises, to the furniture, porcelain, murals and other Chinese decorations in friends' houses and in hotels. Just along the block from the first hotel I ever stayed in was a glittering metallic statue of Sun

Yat Sen, for many decades a cult figure among Californians. He had been a revolutionary who overthrew the last dynasty and was the first President of a Chinese republic.

By the late 1930s, China, overrun by the Japanese in Manchuria, had become California's favourite victim state. However, at that time the ranking villain to Californians as well as to all other Americans was Adolf Hitler. Only experts at the State Department worried about Japan. Only experts, and one Californian, William Randolph Hearst, a national newspaper tycoon, who sat in his castle looking across the Pacific and rang editorial alarm bells warning about the Yellow Peril, about an actual threat of the Japanese to the security, to the shores, of his beloved California.

To visiting Easterners and Europeans, these foaming outbursts were always thought fanciful to the point of absurdity – until 7 December 1941, when out of the blue the Japanese destroyed half the United States Pacific Fleet (and its air arm) at its base in the Pacific, which most Americans, or for that matter ranking members of the British Embassy (and yours truly) had never heard of. It was called Pearl Harbor.

By now, of course, everything has gone into reverse. Japan is, has been, the great modern trading partner, and China, though vilified and warily watched since it went Communist, is being wooed as the second largest Pacific trader. But in San Francisco, the Oriental, or as we must now say the Asian, presence is as triumphant as anywhere in the country. A medical office building I know which twenty, thirty years ago was inhabited by doctors with American-European names now has a third of its tenants Asian. They are refugees from the Communist takeover of Vietnam, or Hong Kong Chinese whose parents came to this country, say twenty-five years ago, without a word of English. Today, they are young medical specialists.

These things I shall miss, but most of all the daily sights and sounds that are San Francisco and nowhere else. First, of course, the nine tumbling hills, and how remarkably the people troop up and down them like one of the great race migrations of the Middle Ages. The white city is seen from across the bay as a vast pyramid of confetti. The genial sun most of the year, the bafflement verging on outrage of the summer tourists shivering atop a hilly street, not having been told that July and August are the coldest months. But summer is memorable also for the arrival from the Pacific in the late afternoon of great plumes of white fog moving in on the city with the motion of a slow freight train. The double moan of the foghorn at night. The deceptively blue waters under the Golden Gate Bridge in whose icy, thrashing currents no Alcatraz escapee has ever been known to survive, only the corpse of one Aaron Burgett.

Over and over again, I recall a short piece of Mark Twain's which says so much about San Francisco in so little. It reports Mark Twain's arrival in San Francisco after he'd been thrown out of the silver-mining town of Virginia City, Nevada, for having written that 'in this noble city, there are two churches and seventy-six saloons – which is just about the right proportion'. This line aroused such fury in the local church matrons that Mark Twain thought it was time 'to get lost – so I absquatulated.'

After the sagebrush and alkali desert of Nevada, San Francisco was heaven on the half shell. I lived at the best hotel. I exhibited my clothes in the most conspicuous places. I infested the opera.

I enjoyed my first earthquake. It was just after noon on a bright Sunday in October and I was coming down Third Street . . . As I turned a corner there came a terrific shock . . . the entire front of a four-story brick building sprung outward like a door and fell sprawling across the street. The ground rolled under me in waves. The streetcars stopped. Their horses were rearing and plunging. Every door of every house was vomiting a stream of human beings . . .

The first shock brought down two or three organ pipes in one of the churches, and the next instant, in the atmosphere where the minister had stood, there was a vacancy. In another church, after the first shock, the minister said: 'Bretheren, keep your seats. There is no better place to die than here.' After the third shock, he waved his flock good-bye and added: 'But outside is good enough for me.'

After a time, I had to cease being an onlooker at the peculiar life of San Francisco and get down to earning a livelihood. My first job was with the *Enquirer*, and my first assignment was accidental: a set-to between a Chinaman and some Irish. Now, the Chinese are a harmless race when white men let them alone or treat them no worse than dogs. Their chief employment is to wash clothes, which they do at low prices with their usual patience and industry. One day, I saw a bunch of Irish toughs descend on an old Chinaman, on his way home after laundering the clothes of his Christian clientele. They sat on him and beat him up. I went back to the office in a state of high indignation and wrote my fill of this miserable incident. But the editor refused to print it. Our paper, he said, was printed for the poor, and in San Francisco the Irish *were* the poor. In time, I cooled off. I was lofty in those days. I have survived.

Most poignantly I recall and miss most a contemporary – long gone – writer, a columnist for the San Francisco morning paper. I often wonder if San Franciscans deserved him, for he never received any special tribute as the best writer ever to come out of that city. His name was Charles McCabe, a funny, beautiful writer of great simplicity, by which I mean he felt deeply and thought clearly. He was never syndicated outside that one paper. 'Why not?' I once asked the editor. 'Well,' he said, 'who's going to buy a man who's more of a meditator than a columnist?' It's true. One day he wrote about the pain of being jilted, next day on Cicero, next a dangerously funny swipe at the women's libbers, next day the life of St Thomas Aquinas.

McCabe looked like a giant, dignified W. C. Fields with a similarly glowing nose. It came at you like a beacon, but before you sighted it your nostrils picked up the unmistakable odour of 'the poteen'. At the end of his life, Charlie McCabe became aware of the one thing that makes any life worth living. 'These days the love I give and the love I get seems spread around rather thin. I am often lonely but seldom bored any more. There's a lot of peace and quiet but I now know it would not be possible without friends. Without friends? I can hardly bear to think about it.' Nor can I.

They are the San Franciscans it will hurt to miss.

Remembering a Dear Friend

13 December 2002

An old journalist colleague was taking his first holiday on a cruise ship. They were sailing along the Mediterranean and the ship stopped at Tangier. It came up on the horizon as what he called 'a featureless strip of sand'. 'Not', he said, 'my notion of Africa.'

I suppose this happens to all of us, though, from not wanting to be thought a bonehead, it's not the sort of thing we mention aloud. My own experience in first sighting America was to the contrary. Sailing into New York, up the bay at twilight on a late September evening; a clear purple sky and thousands of people still at work, which meant that the downtown and midtown skyscrapers were all lit up, a forest of giant firecrackers; nothing could have better fulfilled the imagined scene. New York City, in short, lived up to its billing. 'Not my notion of America' came later. One week later, to be exact, when I took the train fifty miles north to New Haven, Connecticut, where at the Yale School of Drama, I proposed to polish up my directing skills and return to England to revolutionize the English theatre. How that came not to be is another story you'll be relieved to hear some other time, or not at all.

Yale! The only vision I had of an American university had been formed by the musical comedies of the 1920s and the silent movies of Harold Lloyd. The musicals were so rowdy, so facetious, and all turned on the dopey hero winning the football game, and the girl cheerleader on the sidelines, that I knew this couldn't be anything but farce set to music by Hollywood scriptwriters who had never been closer to Yale than the Bronx.

We chuffed into New Haven, and later that day I came on the campus. First thing, I was told to go to the Dean's office and he would tell me where I was going to live. I was made a member of Harkness College (called Hall) and padded off there to find my own cosy room.

It turned out to be a suite – a large study, bedroom, pantry, and, best of all (and new to me in a college) a private bathroom with its own radiator.

It was all splendid, but as an American object it was a shock and a letdown. It was a high, Gothic, gloomy room. At my own college in England, I had looked out on a medieval cloister, dank and melancholy and mouldy with distinction. And I travel three thousand miles to the New World, to the land of Douglas Fairbanks, and George Gershwin, and Bobby Jones, and the lovely white colonial eighteenth-century houses I'd read so much about, and here I was under house arrest in a grey, grim, Gothic room with heavily leaded peekaboo owlish windows. I took a quick walk round the campus and found that everything was Gothic, but strangely new. Later on, I discovered that one architect was put in charge and was given a free hand in 1919 to go berserk with his Gothic mania, and in the next sixteen years he built practically a small city, or large campus, of Gothic, as being most suitable for a historic university. On that first evening, I sat alone in my cloistered prison and silently deplored my fate. A knock came at the door. There stood a middle-sized, athletic-looking young man, black hair with a lick of curl, strikingly black-brown merry eyes and an air of geniality he was never to lose. 'My name,' he said, 'is Rostow, Gene Rostow, and I understand you're a new Fellow.'

'Commonwealth,' I said.

'Commonwealth Fellow,' he said. 'I wondered if you'd care to come over to my place and meet my room-mates.'

Of course, my trajectory to his room was that of Bugs Bunny in pursuit of a carrot. And he had a rather grander suite: a living room, and off it four bedrooms. He had three room-mates, two of whom I knew till the end of their lives. Eugene Victor Rostow, however, was plainly to me the key man and stayed my oldest American friend, with nary a cross word, till the day he died, which was on Monday of last week.

He was the son of a Russian immigrant, a dedicated socialist who christened his son after a famous socialist candidate for the Presidency: Eugene Victor Debs. His younger son (who was to become Lyndon Johnson's national security adviser) was named after the poet Walt Whitman.

The lithe, athletic shape I noticed about Gene Rostow at first sight was well taken. First thing I knew about him was that he was the polo captain. A Jew Polo captain at Yale which had, at the time, an unspoken, unacknowledged quota system. However, Gene was captain of *water* polo, and a powerful thrashing performer he was. But very soon I learned that he was an intellectual whizz, graduating after four years at Yale when he was 19, when most students are in their sophomore (second) year. At the age of 40, he became Dean of the Law School, had several famous pupils (including two later Presidents) and in ten years made Yale Law School quite possibly the finest in the country. His passion for international law and his large knowledge of constitutional law made him destined for politics. And not long after he went to Washington, he drew the attention, and the affection, of Truman's later Secretary of State, Dean Acheson, who looked like a tweedy Spanish grandee with a guardsman's moustache. There was a little private talk that, come the right day, Gene Rostow might make a fine Supreme Court Justice. His intellect, his tolerance of opponents' views, but most of all his genuinely judicial temperament: open-minded, objective, disinterested. It is a rare possession, even among justices of the Supreme Court. However, the talk came to nothing. Gene went on to become an Under-Secretary of State, was put in charge of economic warfare in North Africa, and at the end, of arms control and disarmament.

However, it is not politics but his character I wish to end on. At the height of his fame as Yale's Law School Dean, he was offered a visiting professorship in a famous European university. In a postal muddle, the invitation went to the wrong man, who accepted the post and enjoyed it. There was never a hint or a sigh of complaint from Gene Rostow. He was the first public official of any standing who, in the wake of Pearl Harbor, angrily protested the unconstitutionality of herding practically the entire Japanese-American population of California into detention centres – three generations of them – for the rest of the war. Forty years later, everybody apologized, including the Supreme Court, which made belated restitution to the survivors of the detained.

In a Kennedy year, it was (I'll never forget) 1962, Gene stayed on Long Island with us but at the week's end, he had business in town, and so did I. I drove him back to New York to stay the night. We arrived in the late afternoon, eased off, sat down for a drink. The telephone rang. I took the call. A voice said 'Is Professor Rostow there?' He is. 'This is the White House. The President wishes to speak to him.' After what novelists call a sudden start, I handed over. And this was Gene Rostow's part of the dialogue. 'Yes, sir, Mr President. Well, thank you, and the same. Uh-huh. Uh-huh. Uh-huh. Yes, I know, of course, everybody knew. Uh-huh. Well, I understand, sir. Thank you all the same.' A bright swift chuckle and he hung up. He came back to the sofa, sat down and we went on with our merry conversation. I did not think his business with the President was any business of mine. We sallied off to dinner, came back for a nightcap. At some point, looking both cheerful and mischievous, he said, 'You might wonder what went on with the President, if you can keep it to yourself for a time.' I said something like: 'For a lifetime.'

To understand Kennedy's part in the exchange, I have to draw in a little background. A famous justice, one Felix Frankfurter, had decided to retire from the Court. He was a Jew, and though there is no rule, over the past fifty years or so there is a binding tradition that there must be one Jew, since Thurmond Marshall one black, since Sandra Day O'Connor one woman. Kennedy had offered the coming vacancy to a former Governor of Connecticut, a Jew. Everybody soon knew he'd had the offer. But for personal reasons he told Kennedy he could not take it. Moving swiftly forward in the dark background, Dean Acheson came to Kennedy's aid. Rostow must be the man. Kennedy thought it over. After all, Gene was a Jew, born in New Haven, Connecticut. Kennedy made up his mind and put the call. And this is the brief speech to which Gene Rostow responded with his usual geniality, even with a chuckle: 'Gene, I have a problem. I offered Frankfurter's seat to Abe Ribicoff but the Governor had to turn it down. Yes . . . yes . . . yes, as everybody knew. That's the problem. Well, you were right up there as most qualified. But I'm afraid, I'm sorry, I decided that it's going to Goldberg, of Illinois. Two Jews from Connecticut is one too many. I'm sorry.' 'Well, I understand, sir. Thank you all the same.'

Gene never, to me or anyone I knew, ever breathed a mention of this appalling letdown in his life. But here in the room I speak from, I saw for the first time – and never again, I prayed – a lifetime's ambition shattered in a moment with a chuckle.

Eugene Victor Rostow, a darlin' man, died last Monday week, aged 89.

Meeting the Stars

4 *July* 2003

One of the comical pains of living on and on is something I hope most listeners will not feel for some time to come. It's the pleasurable moment of remembering an anecdote about some famous person you'd once run into, and then suddenly discovering that the famous person is totally unknown to the friend, possibly even grey-haired friend, you're about to amuse.

One time, staying with some friends who lived on a hacienda up in the hills behind Santa Barbara, California, my host remarked, 'Oh, by the way, we're having drinks with the Colmans.' The Colmans? 'Yeah, Ronnie and his wife.' 'Ronnie and his wife!' To me, it was as if a young beginner with the violin had been told by an uncle, 'Oh, by the way, we're dining with Luddy.' Luddy? Ludwig – Beethoven! Ronald Colman, although then in the twilight of his career, had been for three decades just about the most world-famous English movie actor alive. We went to his house, and who should open the door but the man himself. He offered his hand first to *me* and said in his famous velvety voice, 'My dear fellow, do come in. My mother is your greatest fan!' I was moved to say, 'Never mind your mother, how about you?' but was too overwhelmed to say anything by the mere thought of Ronald Colman's mother listening to my talks. This was sometime in the early 1950s.

A year or two ago, I thought this was the sort of anecdote that would appeal to a friend who had stopped by: a pretty, cultivated, on-the-ball woman in her early fifties, who had a professional interest, as a television producer, in actors and acting. I had long ago learned my lesson of never assuming (especially in anybody under 60) a familiarity with *my* heroes and heroines, writers, politicians, movie stars and so forth. So to my woman friend in her early fifties I said, 'Does the name Ronald Colman mean anything to you?' She paused, and looked thoughtful. 'He was, was he not, a United States Senator?' End of Colman story.

So, I begin guardedly this time and introduce the character I'm going to talk about by having you meet her the way I met her. Last Monday morning, her picture, accompanying a huge obituary, took up a page and a half of the *New York Times*. When I saw the photograph, I realized, from the calendar, that it was exactly seventy years ago that, visiting Hollywood for the first time (as a student/tourist), I had the august sensation of being picked up at my humble hotel by a studio limousine – a limousine sent expressly for me, a totally anonymous graduate student driving round the country, the USA, in a second-hand, $45 Ford. It came about this way.

During the previous winter and spring, I had sent to one of the two distinguished English Sunday papers a few theatre reviews of a new O'Neill play (Nobel Prize playwright), and a play by one Noël Coward (then the chicest of English playwrights). Out of what in New York is called chutzpah, I had had the audacity to write to the editor of this Sunday paper, an awesomely famous man, suggesting that, on my summer trip – since I should be stopping by Hollywood – how about my writing a series of six pieces on the movies, beginning with an interview with Charlie Chaplin, then with the celebrated German director Lubitsch, with an English star (how about the monumental C. Aubrey Smith?), an Oscar-winning cameraman, and so forth? Of course, I knew none of these magnificoes. But when, to my astonishment, the awesome editor wrote back and said it just so happened that their film critic, Miss LeJune, was taking off for just six weeks, I might submit the pieces. This made it automatic for me then, swollen with chutzpah, to write to all the stars and say, 'On behalf of the London *Observer* . . . I have been commissioned, etc. . . .' Not one refused to set a date. On the contrary, before they'd even glimpsed this brash 24-year-old, several of them wrote back to be sure a day could be set apart at *my* convenience. I remember an ingratiating letter from Mr Chaplin, the beginning of a beautiful friendship.

When I got out there, I started my grand tour by deciding to write first about a famous director at work. The man I chose, then in the first flush of great success, was one George Cukor. He had just started shooting the immortal Louisa May Alcott's (an immortal woman writer) *Little Women*. Why not come out and spend the day with the cast, in a stretch of what they had turned into a New England landscape, about twenty miles out from Beverly Hills? And so I was driven off and greeted in the warmest way (after all, I represented the *Observer*, owned by the Astors, no less) by Mr Cukor and the cast. I'll call off their names without further definition – you may take my word for it – it was a very starry cast, palpitating in the wake of the veteran actors Paul Lukas and Henry Stephenson and Edna Mae Oliver, Joan Bennett, Jean Parker, Frances Dee *and* Katharine Hepburn. Of course you know her (thanks to television re-runs).

Katharine Hepburn was, indeed, the subject of the *New York Times* obituary. And it was not a lament. She was 96 and long a martyr to an embarrassing trembling of the head and hands, which she swore to the end was not Parkinson's disease.

Back there (seventy years ago in that California valley), what struck me, in watching the shooting of this famous story of four young sisters growing up in New England before the Civil War, was nothing about the play or the shooting of it, but the – how shall I put it? – the social oddity of this girl Hepburn. She stood out, it seemed to me at the time, as a kind of attractive freak. All because of her accent, which was that of a well-schooled, upper-middle-class New England girl just out (she was four years out) of Bryn Mawr (a college of high academic standing but also notable for breeding well-bred, upper-class young women). It had its own distinct variation of an upper-crust New England accent, which is not, by the way, anything like British English of the same class. Miss Hepburn had it, and, in that place and time, it was quite strange.

I don't believe it will be news to older listeners to hear that the majority, maybe a large majority, of American screen actors and actresses in those days – whatever parts they became trained to play – came from humble immigrant South and Eastern European backgrounds. Since the top producers who founded Hollywood had also that background (most of them pedlars who had fled from Jewish pogroms in Europe), one of the notable signs of their feelings of social inferiority, throughout the 1920s into the 1950s, was the alacrity with which they rushed to change the given names of rising stars to English names, since, way back then, those cunning but simple Russian and Lithuanian and German producers thought, wrongly, that the absolutely top social class in the United States was English. Hence, Emmanuel Goldenberg became Edward G. Robinson, Bernard Schwartz – Tony Curtis, Frances Gumm – Judy Garland, Allen Konigsberg – Woody Allen, Issur Danielovich Demsky – Kirk Douglas, Marion Levy – Paulette Goddard, and so on and so on.

Katharine Hepburn was born and stayed Katharine Hepburn, daughter of a distinguished surgeon in Connecticut and a mother who was, as in England, a fervent socialite suffragette. This rationalization of mine, of course, came to me much later, during a period of Hepburn's life, in her late twenties, early thirties, when she made some indifferent movies and was famously dubbed 'box office poison' because, I now think, the movies she was making then were not good enough to overcome the general popular dislike of what was called her fancy accent. In that summertime, all I noticed is that the rest of the cast treated her with particular respect not usually due a young actress. She had, however, won an Oscar the year before. But the three other sisters somehow gave off the feeling that she was not the normal Hollywood product. But she was totally unaffected, she was who she was: an upper-class Yankee of character. They took to her simply because of her character. And what a character. She refused to be bought and sold by a studio, no matter how tyrannical and fearsome a Zukor, a Goldwyn, might be. She had a play written for her by a famous Philadelphia playwright, bought the play, acted in it, and then sold it to a Hollywood studio to be made *her* way on *her* terms. They hated her but the actors (slaves to anything the studio picked for them) cheered her. And for the rest of her screen life she ran things her way, and made tyrants say, 'Yes, Miss Hepburn.' 'Well, Kate. Okay.'

Late in life she said flatly that she had been born of a well-to-do family and felt an obligation to live up to its responsibilities. 'I was not', she wrote, 'a poor little thing. I don't know what I'd have done if I'd come to New York and had to get a job as a waiter or something.' She added she was a success, not because of any great individual talent; 'I had advantages,' she said, 'I had *better* be a success.'

The Pledge of Allegiance
17 October 2003

Every Monday morning, in every public-elementary school in America, the children rise and may recite, if they choose to, otherwise listen to, the chanting by the class of the Pledge of Allegiance to the Flag of the United States. It is a single sentence. This is how it goes: 'I pledge allegiance to the flag of the United States of America and to the republic for which it stands, one nation under God, indivisible, with liberty and justice for all.'

Last week it was announced in Washington that next February or March, the nine justices of the Supreme Court will begin to consider the complaint of an atheist parent who says it's against the Constitution that he should have to make his daughter listen to 'a ritual proclaiming that there is a God'. When it does come up, I imagine that the young atheist parent will have a hard time restraining himself from a cry of 'shame' as he watches the nine justices bow their heads in prayer, as is their custom.

Which clause of the Constitution does he believe is being violated? Why, the very First Amendment – the first item in the Bill of Rights. It is written in the most guileless English. 'Congress shall make no law respecting an Establishment of religion or prohibiting the free exercise thereof.' What could be simpler? Also, what could be vaguer, the moment you reflect what the eighteenth century meant by 'establishment', for instance? So many, many words have changed their meaning drastically since the seventeenth and eighteenth centuries that much of the Bible, much more of Shakespeare, is not understandable without explanatory footnotes. To the Founding Fathers who wrote it, 'establishment' meant a religious sect. What a pity they didn't write the sentence the other way round: 'Congress shall make no law prohibiting the free exercise of religion' – oh! – but, by the way, we are not going, as a nation, to have a preferred sect. Too late for that. It would lead to endless dissension between the Congregationalists of Massachusetts and Connecticut, the Catholics of Maryland, the Quakers of Pennsylvania. So, gentlemen, let's make it plain that we shall not have a national religion like the Church of England. That being so, it should be well understood that no law of Congress can prohibit any man or woman practising his/her own religion freely, everywhere, in church, in the street, in Congress, at home or away – freely.

For a hundred and fifty years, this reading was simply taken for granted by most people. As a learned history of the Supreme Court tells us: 'From the founding era at the end of the eighteenth century well into the twentieth century, religion was thought to be a significant and legitimate component of American public life. By the 1940s, however, American public life had become largely secular.'

One short, offhand sentence covers a tremendous fact: the decline of religious belief in the general population of the Western nations. It has been deeper still in Europe. In France in 1960, one family in three were weekly churchgoers. Today, one in eight. In England today, only six people in a hundred claim to be devoutly religious. In the United States, the comparable devout figure is 65 per cent, but there has been a dramatic increase in the Americans who don't want religion to appear in any shape or form in *public* life. Hence, these continual appeals to the court from keeping religious symbols off any public building, all the way to banning the use of the word God in political speech! To put it more formally, the atheists have gone bananas in the extent to which they misinterpret the First Amendment, as you see from the final appeal of the young father from Oregon who wants 'under God' taken out of the Pledge of Allegiance.

First, let's go back to the pledge and its invention. It was composed by an ex-minister and published in a magazine called the *Youth's Companion*. When? Aye, that's the point. Eighteen ninety-two. The Congress leaped at a happy idea: since 12 October marked the four hundredth anniversary of Columbus' discovery of America, that would be the perfect day to introduce the chanting of the pledge as a daily ritual in the elementary schools. And so it was. But no mention of God. The 'one nation under God' did not appear until 1954. Why 1954, I wondered. I never saw a story explaining why. I thought some digging was necessary. It has turned out that a little digging produced a load of pay dirt.

In early 1954, at a conference of the four allied powers occupying Germany, the United States, Britain and France were all for reunifying Germany under one government. Stalin was absolutely opposed. Stalin had in Europe armies five times the size of the combined other allies. So that was that.

Far away, in French Indochina, the French were collapsing against Vietnamese guerrillas who were fighting to be independent. The French begged President Eisenhower to help with American troops. Eisenhower said 'no troops', but made an impassioned public assertion that the defeat of Communism in Southeast Asia was 'vital' – that if one country went Communist, the neighbours could fall too like a row of dominoes. This was a pressing fear in Washington at that time – fears for Malaysia, for Indochina, for Burma, most of all for India.

Also, 1954 was the heyday of a Midwestern Senator who, after a high State Department official had been convicted of passing papers to the Soviet Union, launched an immensely popular campaign to root Communists out of American government. He gave us alarming numbers but never actually came up with a positive Communist who had not declared himself. Nevertheless, it was the fear of the time that from Moscow to Asia 'godless Communism' might prevail. President Eisenhower and many public men and women used that phrase over and over. And it was by executive order alone that President Eisenhower ordered the pledge now to read: 'I pledge allegiance to the flag of the United States of America, and to the republic for which it stands, one nation *under God*, indivisible, with liberty and justice for all.'

So far as Michael Newdow, the young protesting father, is concerned – the villain of the piece is not, as most people think, the Congress of the United States but the late, great Ike, Supreme Commander of the invading forces in Europe and later President of the United States. If Mr Newdow wins, surely somebody will then mount a crusade to have erased from all dollar bills, of whatever denomination, the sentence

493

printed in brazen capital letters: 'In God We Trust.' And if *he* wins, that will entail destroying every bill and totally reprinting the US currency. It would cost the Treasury (the taxpayer, that is) an estimated $7 or $8 billion. But what's that to the average taxpayer? He's already going to have to find $20 billion for tidying up Iraq.

Towering Glass and Steel

31 October 2003

Forty years ago last Monday morning, a gentle southwest wind carried up through Manhattan what many New Yorkers at first thought was a series of explosions of some kind. Pretty soon there came on television what to most New Yorkers was an incomprehensible sight and sound. The picture showed jackhammers clawing away at the walls of a famous building, and then at slow rhythmic intervals, a huge airborne shining ball swung and crashed against – were they mad? – the long stately Doric colonnade of – were they mad? – the Baths of Caracalla? Well, yes, not of course the original but a superb re-creation of a Roman architectural masterpiece.

Why were they doing this, and who were *they*? What we saw was America's most famous railway station, the Pennsylvania Station. It had been designed at the turn of the twentieth century during the finest hour of the new millionaires, especially the robber barons who had made their fortunes in coke, iron ore and railroads, and when little old Andrew Carnegie was proclaiming the new age of steel. Once such a man became a millionaire, he became eager to advertise the grandeur of his social position by ordering up a new house, a mansion, as like as possible not to the mansions of the new rich of Europe, but to the ancient houses of the old aristocracy, especially the nobles of France and Italy. Just after Goethe had given an encouraging line to the poor or oppressed of Europe who emigrated to America, 'Du hast es besser

im Amerika' (You have things better in America), an American journal-
ist, watching the robber barons fight each other to procure the Old
Master paintings and the models of the old aristocrats' houses, wrote:
'Their motto was they do things better in Europe.'

Such was the temper of the time when the most fashionable architectural firm of the day had an idea beyond the dreams of the culture-
vulture robber barons. McKim, Mead & White proposed to the owners
of the Pennsylvania railroad that they would like to build, not a
mansion for the chairman of the board, but a railroad station for the
city. To do so, they proposed to re-create a jewel of a building of
ancient Rome. Stanford White was a social lion, a dandy, a ladies'
man and a most remarkable architect, possibly unique in his time, as
a master of pastiche. He would, at the shake of a hand or the flourish
of a contract, design an early Georgian house for an Anglophile, a
Venetian mansion for a newspaper tycoon, a monumental arch for the
George Washington centennial, a jewelled Byzantine cross for the
famous actress Eleanora Duse. Why not, he suggested to the railroad
company, rebuild the city's main railroad station by re-creating, if not
improving on, the Baths of Caracalla, the masterpiece of Roman
architecture as the Parthenon was the masterpiece of Greece. Only
Charles McKim or his dashing junior partner, Stanford White, would
have the audacity, and the skill, to attempt such a thing. It was done,
and in 1910 it was opened to the public, who came in awestruck droves
to gaze at the block-long line of stately Doric columns leading to the
vast waiting room which was indeed, with its splendid vaulted ceiling,
a huge image of the Baths of Caracalla. From there you passed into
the great concourse, which Charles McKim had produced as a creation
of steel and glass arches, domes and fan vaulting – a breathtaking
development of the new glass and iron architecture of London's Crystal
Palace. Americans who were not taking any train came to gaze and
marvel at it. So for a time did European tourists.

But fashions in architecture, as in everything else, change. The
European intelligentsia came to chuckle and to sneer. By the mid-
twentieth century, America and American businessmen had been
ordered to admire the revolutionary works of a German, Walter Gropius, a rebel against all classical, all romantic, all Victorian styles of
architecture. He invented what he called an international style. By his

time, certainly, a general reaction had set in against the gaudiness of the Victorian age, the fussiness, the elaborate writhing decoration of furniture, the stuffiness which overtook everything from women's clothes to lampshades. When the Victorian style first came in, the leading Regency architects of the day had called it ugly and barbaric. Just under a hundred years later, by the 1930s, it seems even the ordinary middle classes agreed with them. And then came the führer of the revolution, the new God of modern architecture from Germany, Walter Gropius. He simply, earnestly, dogmatically reacted to everything that had gone before, from the Greeks on. He invented the monolith, the large upright plank of concrete – what an independent American pioneer, one Frank Lloyd Wright, called the new log cabin that misuses steel, faceless, characterless, god-awful rectangles of concrete and steel, leading to its peak in the United Nations buildings which he called 'an ant hill for a thousand ants'. Certainly, the towering planks of glass and steel took over America's cities.

When the Second World War was over, and the building of everything from cottages to skyscrapers could begin again, Gropius, Mies van der Rohe, the so-called Bauhaus school, became almost compulsory for any city contemplating a new airport, a city hall, a big business about to bloom. (The god himself ruled from his pulpit at Harvard.) The tycoons didn't have to like the style. It simply became essential to their social standing. And so, by the 1960s, Tom Wolfe wrote: 'There had never been a place on earth where so many people of wealth and power paid for, put up, and moved into glass-box office buildings they detested.' By then, 'every child went to school in a building that looks like a duplicating machine wholesale distribution warehouse'.

In such an atmosphere, there was only one thing more ridiculous than designing a Victorian or Georgian house, and that was retaining the huge absurdity of a re-created Roman classical building. Such is the hypocrisy of fashion that since the end of the Second World War, I don't recall a visiting friend or tourist ever saying, 'I must go down to 34th Street and look at Pennsylvania Station' as their successors would always obediently pad off to the Museum of Modern Art, the Guggenheim, the Whitney. By that time nobody had heard of the Baths of Caracalla, and nobody cared.

Except the board of directors of the Pennsylvania railroad, who decided in 1960 or thereabouts that their Roman station was an expensive burden and also something of an embarrassment. They decided to destroy it. And so at 9 a.m. on 28 October 1963 the jackhammers clawed and the wrecking ball crashed down on the Doric pillars and would soon demolish what was the last reminder in New York of the grandeur that was Rome.

There had been no pre-emptive campaign of protest that I can remember. It was only when the noisy facts of demolition assailed our eyes and ears that a collector or two, a startled author, then the intelligentsia magazines, woke up. To its credit, it was the *New York Times* that sounded the first protesting trumpet. On its editorial page, it had a leader calling the demolition 'a monumental act of vandalism'. The little spurt of public shame and horror came, of course, too late. It took three years to destroy the station and on its ashes arose what the excellent *Blue Guide* to New York calls 'the utterly graceless and unappealing Madison Square Garden ... a 20,000-seat arena in a pre-cast concrete drum, a movie theatre, a bowling alley and an office building'.

But out of this calamity, out of that ill October wind, there came one great and good thing. In the last year of the demolition, when the long block at 34th Street began to look like a pre-vision of Ground Zero, the small clique of outraged artists, authors, art lovers and citizens, petitioned the Mayor and then the city council and formed a body called the Landmarks Preservation Commission. Since 1965, their agents have snooped around the city with the zeal of the FBI, ticketing period relics of every style to be preserved. There was a big move in the 1970s on the part of the owners of the brilliant and majestic Grand Central Station to have it demolished and replaced by a 54-storey glass-and-steel Gropism. The squabble was fierce and prolonged. Thanks, however, to the tenacity of two members of the Landmarks Commission (one, Brendan Gill, a witty, Irish-American staff writer on the *New Yorker* magazine in its heyday, the other, the Presidential widow Jacqueline Kennedy), the fight was taken all the way to the Supreme Court, which upheld the protest, and in 1978 decreed that Grand Central Station was to be immortal and never to be subjected to the jackhammer and the wrecking ball.

Charlie Addams

23 January 2004

Opening my morning mail (why do I say 'morning' mail? There is no other), I find a letter from a lady in Massachusetts who is about to write a biography of the late, incomparable cartoonist Charles Addams (maybe you remember the Addams Family on television).

As I look up and out, as usual, at the rolling park, I am almost blinded by the ice-blue sky, the blazing sun and the landscape of snow. And I chuckled at this deceptive picture, since the temperature outside was 12 below freezing and no place for yours truly to patter into. The chuckle was a taproot into a famous cartoon by Charlie Addams. First, let me tap your memory of him and his cartoon family: a butler, the spitting image of Boris Karloff as the Frankenstein monster; his boss, a long, thin, weedy young woman with mean, slit eyes, long black hair and a black soul like the two villainous, cross-eyed little kids on the floor cooking up the neighbour's cat for Thanksgiving dinner. The famous cartoon I recalled after glancing at snowbound Central Park was a simple drawing of a slightly surprised skier whizzing downhill and looking backwards after passing a tree. The marks of his track ran parallel coming towards the tree but then curved out around the tree and met again on the downside. He had evidently successfully skied through the tree, and was as surprised as we were.

Charlie Addams was of my generation. He was very tall – I'd guess about six foot three or four, a shambling, rumply faced man with a five o'clock shadow and hair as black as any of his characters. He was also, like many writers of horrid things, extraordinarily gentle. My most vivid memory of him, to which our lady biographer is very welcome, was of one time (there were many times) when my wife and I had driven over to the south shore of Long Island to a party with a magazine editor, who was a friend we had in common. While the party dawdled and chatted out on the hot terrace, Charlie and I moved into the shady indoors. He was at the time much in love with a rather stunning movie actress, not present. It had been going on for some time but, after two failed marriages, he was not about to embark on a stormy third. We sat down with our drinks and I remember saying, 'So, Charlie, how's your love life?' He sipped and paused and slowly shook his head. In his high squeaky voice, he said: 'You know, Alistair, the trouble with women is – they always want a poimanent relationship.' A short story, but a poignant one to many men who are coasting along in a very agreeable relationship but dread any mention of wedding bells.

Charlie Addams was only one of that stable of great cartoonists at the *New Yorker* magazine from the 1930s through the 1970s, each of whom was recognizable at thirty paces, both for a personal style and expert craftsmanship: Addams and Peter Arno and Helen Hokinson and Whitney Darrow and George Price (the artist of the lumpenproletariat) and on and on. Dear me! Looking at the magazine and newspaper cartoonists of today, in both Britain and the United States, I have to lament how far we have fallen into the Dark Age of comic draughtsmanship.

A day or two after the lady biographer's letter, I had an even more touching reminder of Charlie Addams and an unforgettable cartoon, of which I hope to get a laser copy. Must be thirty-odd years ago. Scene: a small bedroom. Present, two middle-aged women, one whispering behind her palm to the other. A bed, containing evidently a husband, bandaged from head to foot; both arms; only his eyes are visible. Clearly, as old American gentlemen used to say, 'not a well man'. On the other side of his bed is an extraordinary figure – a witch doctor, half-naked and tattooed to the waist, face painted like a leopard, hair curled and tied in a high knotted rope. Smoke coming out of his nostrils and ears. He has one knee bent in some sort of ritual dance. The wife across the bed is whispering to her alarmed friend: 'At least he makes house calls.'

The punchline gave a comic twist to – even thirty-odd years ago – a new, sad fact of life. The fact, simply, that not long after the Second World War doctors ceased to make house calls. I'm talking about the cities, and specifically New York. But I'm reliably told that the comfortable habit has spread to small towns. Why, I wonder. It can only be because of the rapid spread, in the past fifty years or so, of specialization. What used to be called in Britain the 'GP' is over. Here is an American dictionary definition of 'general practitioner': 'A physician whose practice covers a wide variety of medical problems in patients of all ages.' A note says '(mainly British)'. When you think of it now, what a marvellously accomplished being he must have been – able, without timidity, to face everything from cancer and diabetes to ingrowing toenails. In this country, even the word 'doctor' is going out. On all printed forms – hospital entrance, health insurance, reimbursement bills – the phrase is 'primary care physician'. And he has always called himself here not a GP but an internist – a practitioner of everything to do with the internal organs that can be treated without surgery. That leaves a lot to other doctors.

I very rarely see my 'primary-care physician' because seven years ago, within half an hour of a diagnosis, he sent me off to a heart specialist, whom I see all the time. You go to the primary man once a year for your annual check-up and call him when you feel ill. He thereupon sets a date for you to call on him. Not, I've just figured, since the 1960s has a doctor called on me. You totter off to him. If your symptoms alarm him, he puts you in the hospital, where about four or five specialists can tend to you. (Cost of ambulance and two splendid paramedics to whisk you five blocks away – $750 – £500! Thank the Lord, as I regularly do, I'm over 65 – when the blessed national (federal) system, Medicare, takes over and pays 90 per cent.)

I said that these medical memories, especially about the disappearance of house calls, were triggered by the request for a tale or two about Charles Addams. But the subsequent recital was due to a telephone call, only two days ago, an astounding, unique call. It was from a doctor, a specialist I had set a date with and then cancelled three times because of the Arctic weather – even a sniff of which the heart man will not allow. Well, this much-pestered doctor asked me if it would be all right for her to come to me, here, at my apartment, to take care of me!! After I'd been revived from the fainting fit, I fell into a Gershwin response. I said it would be 'wonderful, marvellous that you should care for me'. And so she did.

The Democrats' Growing Confidence

20 February 2004

Propped up there against my usual three pillows and having reluctantly just finished a favourite bed book – the collected ribald musings of an old friend, Charles McCabe, I was feeling chipper enough to glance across at two bedside piles and hope for a perfect lullaby before drifting into sleep.

I found it – on one page of a pocket reference book. A very brief history of a short war – so short, so well and briskly fought, the villain so effectively punished, the peace treaty so fair but demanding enough to put an end to any remaining fears about the war-waging villain . . . It was a model of how all United Nations exploits should begin and end.

Listen! It is very short and very satisfying. 'Saddam Hussein, declaring that the Persian Gulf state of Kuwait belonged to him sent his army into that country in August 1990. The United Nations Security Council promptly demanded his withdrawal. He paid no attention. In late November, the Council urged the UN members who were willing, to use "all means" to expel Saddam. Saddam ignored the UN. And 29 countries volunteered to go to war.' (Note that all United Nations use of arms must be voluntary – the great weakness of the UN from its birth has been that it has no forces of its own. It can only ask members if they're interested and would like to come in.) In January 1991, under an American General, American, French, British and Saudi aircraft bombed Saddam's strategic bases. He bombed in kind, firing Scud missiles into Riyadh and the country of the non-belligerent but still the real ancient enemy, Israel.

Enough, said the gallant United States President – one George Bush – we must act, and he directed half a million allied troops to mount a ground offensive and liberate Kuwait. One hundred hours later, the war was over. Saddam's famous Republican Guard was a broken army abandoning hundreds of tanks, battered trucks, wounded aircraft – staggering north on foot in such numbers that General Schwarzkopf ordered all shooting to end. 'It would have been', he said, 'a total massacre.' Within six weeks, Saddam had signed a ceasefire and agreed 'to destroy all his chemical, nuclear and biological weapons'. That is the end of the fairy tale, the lullaby.

The epilogue is sorrowful. Saddam did not give proof of obeying his ceasefire promise. The Security Council passed a resolution ordering him to do so, and threatening 'serious consequences'. Twelve years and sixteen threatening resolutions later, UN inspectors had found much of the condemned material but nobody was sure if he hadn't hidden more. The United Nations Security Council voted to go on and pass more resolutions and offer consequences that never happened.

So what, as Shakespeare asked, is the concernancy? The concernancy is that in February 1991, only a day or two after the fairy tale had come to a happy end, a Gallup poll was taken to gauge the popularity of President Bush (the first). It stood at an unprecedented 89 per cent. I did a talk, I remember, suggesting that even though the next Presidential election was twenty months away, it would save an awful lot of time, sweat and money if some constitutional way might be found to skip or abolish the Presidential election of 1992. I'm sorry to say nobody ever took me up on this. The 1992 election was held and the heroic warrior-king Bush was handsomely defeated by a nationally unknown former Governor of Arkansas, a Southern state which had never before been the cradle of a President.

So, by one of those inscrutable, perhaps cruel turns of fate, the son of the heroic President George Bush came to play over the fairy tale of his father.

All those threatening, non-performing UN resolutions had been going on all throughout the two-term Presidency of Mr Clinton; and don't think he sat back and shared the Security Council's yawn. He went on receiving lots of alarming intelligence about Iraq and Saddam's nuclear and chemical projects, was troubled by the memory of the devastating use of poison gas in Iran and Kurdistan, and must have heard the sentence, attributed to one of Saddam's top advisers but never confirmed: 'Next time, it'll be a chemical fire-storm over Israel.' In all the preliminary twelve-year concern about Saddam's intentions, this fear never failed to haunt the White House: the fear of an overnight Saddam attack and either the outbreak of a whole Middle Eastern war, or the death of the state of Israel. President Clinton fretted over this problem as much as anyone and had plans to go into Iraq (to enact, on his own if must be, 'serious consequences') when Miss Lewinsky became a figure of fate as significant as Napoleon's mistress Madame Walewska. By the time Clinton was ready to mobilize an American or allied force, he didn't possess the moral authority to invade Long Island.

When George W. Bush came in, there came with him a small group of advisers, at least three of them veterans of the Gulf War, who thought that at last the United States should foil the Iraqi intentions it feared, and invade. That is the beginning of the second Bush fairy tale. Under the guidance of Secretary of Defense Rumsfeld, who had proved himself a brilliant wager of the new special-services, precision-bombing kind of war in Afghanistan, President Bush asked him to do the same in Iraq. And it surely was astonishing to see, after only weeks, the vanishing of the fourth largest army in the world, the flight of Saddam and the ever-memorable toppling of his statue on to the streets of Baghdad.

End of second Bush family fairy tale. Shortly after this swift and picturesque victory, the Gallup Poll measured President G.W.'s popularity. It was at 69 per cent.

I do not need to detail or even sketch in bulk the subsequent turmoil and religious conflict, the accursed insurgency that is so woefully successful not only in wounding the Americans and British and Spanish and Poles and Hungarians – in a word, the allies – but seems to do even better decimating the legions of Iraqis who gamely line up to serve as a police force.

Throughout most of the tumult in Iraq, the wholly unexpected weight and range and murderous force of the Iraqis' opposition to the allied occupation, President Bush's public approval has stayed above 60 per cent. But then came the fateful testimony, before the Senate Armed Services Committee, of David Kay, the Central Intelligence Agency's retired chief weapons inspector. 'We got it all wrong,' he said, finally driving a stake in the heart of the administration's main declared reason for going into Iraq. All we found, said David Kay, and are likely to find, are the relics of an abandoned chemical warfare arsenal and of a primitive nuclear programme. Within a week of the Kay testimony, the President's approval rating – for the first time since he arrived in the White House – fell below 50 per cent. A ten-point drop after that simple sentence: 'We got it all wrong.'

If one body, one institution, in the United States was more affected by that sentence than any other it was the Democratic Party. All through the winter and the early primaries, eight Democrats fought each other on domestic issues in the hope of becoming their party's nominee by the spring. Of course, the more they fought each other, the more the White House was delighted. The eight Democrats were often apart on several issues. Only one man, a doctor, former Governor of Vermont, sensed the rising tide of popular feeling against the war, galvanized the young, and in all the public polls was way ahead of the other seven. But, as a campaigner, he was fickle, shooting ideas from the hip, next day reversing his stand, or saying he was sorry he said that. Not the man to have his finger on the button. In the actual primaries, he was time and again a dim, distant third. This week, he joined the other dear departed. But what President Bush's ten-point drop did to the hopeful Democrats was to let them say now without fear that the war was fought for a false reason, and it generated a wholly new conviction, which had little to do with the issues. The three problems which the national polls say are popularly paramount: (1) To recover the two million jobs lost during this administration; (2) reform of the health care system; and, quite a way down, (3) Iraq.

The new, invigorating party conviction is a belief the Democrats had not dreamed of so far. It is the belief that George Bush can be beaten in November. This thought apparently took hold on the primary voters long before it dawned on the Democratic Party as a whole. Hence the fifteen out of seventeen primaries won by the Massachusetts Senator John Kerry, who since the campaign's beginning has sounded an odd and lonely boast: 'George Bush must be driven from the White House, and I'm the man to do it.'